HISTORIC MADISON

HISTORIC MADISON

The Story of Jackson and Madison County Tennessee

From the Prehistoric Moundbuilders to 1917

by

EMMA INMAN WILLIAMS

Southern Historical Press, Inc.
Greenville, South Carolina

This volume was reproduced
from a personal copy located in
the Publishers private library

Please direct all correspondence and book orders to:
SOUTHERN HISTORICAL PRESS, Inc.
1071 Park West Blvd.
Greenville, SC   29611

Copyright 1946 by:
   Madison County Historical Society
ISBN #978-1-63914-616-1
Printed in the United States of America

To
THOSE CITIZENS OF MADISON COUNTY
WHO HAVE MADE THIS HISTORY POSSIBLE
AND
CLARENCE E. PIGFORD
AND
W. A. CALDWELL
WHO ORGANIZED THE MADISON COUNTY HISTORICAL SOCIETY
FOR THE PURPOSE OF PUBLISHING THIS VOLUME.

INTRODUCTION

It is with no little pleasure that the undersigned responds to a request of the Madison County Historical Society to write this Introduction.

In researches for material for the writer's several historical works, he visited the great libraries and archives of the United States; and was surprised to find on the shelves devoted to Tennessee history a marked paucity of printed histories—few indeed as compared with those of our neighboring States. The disparity was most pronounced in respect to county histories.

When the sesquicentennial of Tennessee's statehood was approaching, the writer, as chairman of the Tennessee Historical Commission, recommended that the prime project be the writing and publication of twenty histories of the more historic counties of Tennessee which were without published histories. Madison County was placed high on the list chosen. That county responded with an enthusiasm not equalled in any other of the twenty counties. The enthusiasm did not wane but persisted and along well considered lines: The Madison County Historical Society was organized; a local writer was chosen who had majored in history in a leading university; and others contributed by preparing papers which were read before the Society on subjects with which their life-work rendered them conversant.

The result is that the history of their county is the first of all to be completed and reach the press. Their achievement is worthy of high praise. While many aided, two citizens of the county who have led: William A. Caldwell, president of the Madison County Historical Society and the late lamented

Clarence E. Pigford, a member of the Tennessee Historical Commission. For their intelligent direction and inspiration, the present and future generations of Madison countians are placed under a debt of gratitude.

As an early organized and capital county of West Tennessee, the county's history is rich and eminently deserving of such adequate perpetuation "on the bridge of print."

SAMUEL C. WILLIAMS

"Aquone"
Johnson City, Tennessee

THE AUTHOR'S PREFACE

The difficulties of writing this volume have been many. This story of Jackson and Madison County does not propose to be a biographical or geneological history of the county. It has been the purpose of the writer to try to show how the social, economic, and political forces influenced this inland cotton center, changing it to a commercial center in the midst of a progressive farming area of to-day. Where biographical material has been used, references have been made only to the early leaders who were identified with public events. As the copy goes to press, the writer is fully aware of the fact that many phases of the story of our county have been omitted and it is her sincere desire that some one will finish the history of the county at some later date.

One of the biggest difficulties to overcome was the fact that there were no files of Jackson newspapers prior to 1917 and only isolated copies were available for use. These were found, for the most part, in Cossitt Library in Memphis, in Carnegie Library, Tennessee State Library, and Tennessee Archives at Nashville. Some of the missing links of the story were supplied by the use of papers in the neighboring towns. The diary of Robert H. Cartmell used through the courtesy of his great-grandson, Cartmell Townes, furnished invaluable information. The writer is greatly indebted to each member of the Madison County Historical Society for his or her interest and support; to those who have prepared papers to be read before the Society and made this information accessible to the writer; to each of those who have aided financially in the publication of this book; to each person who has placed material in the hands of the writer, and especially to Judge Samuel Cole

Williams, Chairman of the Tennessee State Historical Commission and Prof. Thomas C. Clark of the University of Kentucky for the use of copious personal notes; to the late Clarence E. Pigford, J. H. Meriwether, W. A. Caldwell, Guy Hall, Miss Guy Leeper, Neely Key, C. R. Bray, Roy Black, Fonville Neville, and Mrs. W. W. Tucker for placing their private collection of books and papers at her disposal.

This study was begun at the University of Chicago and submitted in 1941 as a partial fulfillment of the requirement of the degree of master of arts. Others became interested in the subject and Madison County was chosen by the Historical Commission as one of the counties to publish a history as a part of the Sesquicentennial Celebration in June, 1946. If a complete list of acknowledgments were included, it would weary the reader, therefore, the writer wishes to express her appreciaiton to each one who has helped make this publication possible. The writer is particularly indebted to Prof. Avery Craven of the University of Chicago for introducing her to Southern history; to Mrs. John Trotwood Moore of the Tennessee State Library and Robert Quareles of the Tennessee State Archives for their encouragement and assistance; to Prof. Daniel M. Robison of Vanderbilt, who has read the entire manuscript; to Harris Brown, editor of the Jackson *Sun;* Seale Johnson, member of the State Historical Commission, and several other friends who prefer to remain anonymous, for reading the manuscript, making invaluable suggestions, and above all listening patiently to my innumerable problems.

EMMA INMAN WILLIAMS

April 8, 1946

CONTENTS

CHAPTER		PAGE
	INTRODUCTION	vii
	AUTHOR'S PREFACE	ix
	HISTORIC MADISON IN PICTURES	
I	PROLOGUE	1
II	THE RED MAN'S COUNTRY	11
III	THOSE EARLY YEARS	29
IV	NOTABLE MEN OF THE EARLY NINETEENTH CENTURY	48
V	FRONTIER POLITICS	70
VI	OUR EARLY CONGRESSMEN	86
VII	THE MILITIA AND THE SEMINOLE WAR	100
VIII	THE SANTA FE EXPEDITION	105
IX	THE COUNTY AND TEXAS INDEPENDENCE	107
X	THE MEXICAN WAR	111
XI	EARLY TRANSPORTATION	120
XII	THE RAILROADS	136
XIII	THE COUNTY AND THE SECTIONAL CONFLICT	156
XIV	THE DAYS OF RECONSTRUCTION	190
XV	THE PLANTER AND THE FARMER	198
XVI	THE COURTS	227
XVII	JOHN A. MURRELL, THE OUTLAW	237
XVIII	CRIME IN MADISON	245
XIX	MEDICINE IN MADISON	248
XX	THE PRESS	263
XXI	EDUCATION	275
XXII	RELIGION IN MADISON	292
XXIII	BANKS AND BANKING	323
XXIV	TOWNS AND COMMUNITIES	333
XXV	AN INDUSTRIAL CENTER OF WEST TENNESSEE	355
XXVI	RISE OF THE CITY	366
XXVII	POST CIVIL WAR POLITICS	382
XXVIII	"PURSUIT OF HAPPINESS"	388
XXIX	EPILOGUE	399

LATER PICTURES

APPENDICES 403-532
Andrew Jackson Letters 403
David Crockett Letters 420
A Tennessean in Texas in 1843 429
Poe-Tomlin Correspondence 432
Mexican War Letters of Wiley Hale 444
Excerpts From Diary of Juliana Conner in 1827 . . . 456
John Rogers in West Tennessee, 1836-1840 479
Calvin Jones Correspondence 486
Ladies' Soldiers' Aid Society of '61 489
Revolutionary War Veterans 491
Mexican War Veterans 491
Civil War Veterans 492
Spanish-American War Veterans 505
World War I Veterans 506
County Officers 524
Members of General Assembly 527
Congressmen 528
Mayors of Jackson 530
Jackson Postmasters 531
INDEX 533

MAPS

	PAGE
Map of West Tennessee in 1824 . . . . *Historic Madison Pictures*	
Fortification and Mounds near Pinson, Tennessee . .	12
Plan of the Town of Alexandria	36
Plan of the Town of Jackson, 1822	40
Plan of Jackson, 1871	376-377
Modern Road and Community Map of Madison County	520

TABLES

No. 1	Farm Lands in Madison	220
No. 2	Produce For Market	221
No. 3	Fruit Bearing Trees	222
No. 4	Live Stocks	223
No. 5	Dairy Produce	224
No. 6	Manufacturing	363
No. 7	Population	532

Madison County Historical Society

HARRIS BROWN, *President*
GRACE EVERETT, *Vice-President*
CARTMELL TOWNES, *Treasurer*
BERNICE BARRY, *Secretary*

EXECUTIVE COMMITTEE:

WM. A. CALDWELL, *Chairman of the Board, First National Bank,*
HU C. ANDERSON, *Presiding Justice Tennessee Court of Appeals*
CARTMELL TOWNES, *Circuit Court Clerk, Madison County,*
SEALE JOHNSON, *President, McCowat-Mercer Press,*
C. B. IJAMS, *Superintendent of City Schools.*

Historic Madison
in
Pictures

(From an old print in J. G. Cisco's Historic Sumner County)

A FLATBOAT

One of the most popular means of transportation into the Western District

A drawing of Jackson during the early years when it was considered a rivertown

The Pioneer

Published in Jackson, was the first newspaper in West Tennessee

(From a photostat of an issue at University of North Carolina)

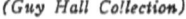

JACKSON, TENNESSEE, IN 1834.

(Guy Hall Collection)

By James M Hardin
George th[e] Chehaw P.O.

PIONEER

Volume—I.   JACKSON, TENNESSEE, TUESDAY, January 28th, 1823.   Number—9.

"OUR ARE THE PLANS OF FAIR DELIGHTFUL PEACE—UNWARP'D BY PARTY RAGE, TO LIVE LIKE BROTHERS."

THE PIONEER published once a week, at three Dollars a year, and is sent to subscribers. Price, $3 50cts. in advance, paid at the expiration of six months, or $4 if not at the end of the year.

No paper will be discontinued—but at the option of the Editors—until arrearages have been paid.

Advertisements to the Editors, post paid, will be attended to.

TERMS OF ADVERTISING.

Seventeen lines or less—First insertion $1—each continuance 37½ cents—persons will mark on the margin the number of insertions.

INTERESTING CORRESPONDENCE.

From the Boston Christian Register.

The following letters have been obtained by solicitation; and are sent to the press by the permission of their venerable authors. The character, standing, and age of the writers, the one in his eightieth, the other in his eighty-seventh year give them a peculiar interest, and they cannot fail to be read with great pleasure. It is delightful to witness this kind of correspondence between these two distinguished men, the separately of party by which they were at one time separated, worn down, and nothing remaining but the kindness and respect. It is charming to see an old age like this, retaining

as good that I dread it still. The rapid decline of my strength during the last winter has made me hope sometimes that I see land. During summer months, it is my employment, and it is my delight, to saunter in my garden and wonder if the approach of winter, and wish I could sleep through it with the door mouse, and only wake with the swallow in spring or so. They say that Starke could walk about his room. I am told you walk well and firmly. I can only reach my garden and that with some fatigue. I ride, however, daily; but reading is my delight. I should wish never to patter on to paper; and the more because of the treacherous practice some people have of publishing one's letters without leave. Lord Mansfield declared it a breach of trust and punishable at law. I think it should be a penitentiary felony; yet you will have seen that they have drawn me out into the arena of the newspapers. Although I know it is too late for me to buckle on the armor of youth, yet my indignation would not permit me pass silently to receive the lurk of an ass.

To turn to the news of the day, it seems that the cannibals of Europe are going to eating one another again. A war between Russia and Turkey is like

people to fight, and the anticipations in your last letter, I believe, are a quarrelsome tendency. This is Jacobins, as the Greeks, Scythians, Bridges, or French cannibals, eating Maestheird cannibals, reminds me of the fragment of Lear;

"Tigers, not daughters, what have you perform'd?——
Humanity must perforce prey upon herself.
Like monsters of the deep."

But I have not seen battles; and heaven keep us, if we believe Hindoos, Jews, Christians, and Mahometans, has not always been at peace. We need no trouble ourselves about these things perfect ourselves because of evil doers, at safely trust the "Ruler with it Stars." Nor need we dread the approach of dotage; let it come, if it must it seems still delights in history and of that his Bennington, and excited in the tears; and Starke reminded of the former glory; the worst of the evil is, that our friends will suffer more by our imbecility than we ourselves.

I wishing for your health and happiness, I am, very selfish; for I love for more letters—this is worth a thousand five hundred dollars to me, for it has already given me, and will continue to give more pleasure than a thousand M\$s, who is about your age. I am told experiences more decay than you do.

I am your old friend.

Imprisonment for Debt.

Extract of Mr. B. M. Johnson, of Ky. in the Senate, Dec. 16th, on introducing a bill against imprisonment for debt.

Mr. Johnson, of Kentucky, said, in pursuance of notice given him a former day, he would now ask leave to introduce a bill to abolish imprisonment for debt. He was prepared to contend it yesterday; he did not wish to interrupt (there were no so) that others had noted now, to make many remarks upon this motion; reserving to himself the privilege of introducing the subject more fully, when its merits should be more properly before the Senate. He was happy to learn, he said, that he should have assistance in his exertions from some honorable members, who he expected opposition from others. The subject had been before Congress two or three sessions previous, and that a form would have been a favorable reports from select committees, to whom it had been referred, without any final decision, for want of time. He hoped at the present ses-

State of Tennessee, Madison County.

To any lawful officer to execute and return:

Summon David Crocket

to appear before me, or some other Justice of the Peace for said county, to answer Armour & Lake in a plea of debt under one hundred dollars. Herein fail not. Given under my hand, this 20th day of _____ 1827.

M. Debery J.P.

Doll: 11 38/100

Jackson 19th February 1825

One day after date I promise to pay Armour & Lake eleven dollars and thirty eight cents, value received, witness my hand and Seal

David Crockett {Seal}

Although David Crockett did not call Madison County home, he was a familiar figure here as he came to buy produce, to campaign against Dr. Butler for the General Assembly, and against Adam Alexander and Adam Huntsman for the U. S. House of Representatives. Numerous letters and legal papers can be found with his signature attached.

(From an oil painting in the possession of Thomas Henderson Butler)

DR. WILLIAM EDWARD BUTLER
"The Father of Jackson, Tennessee"

(Original in the possession of Karl K. Wilkes)

Plat of Homestead of Samuel Jackson Hays, lying east of Royal and north of Deaderick Avenues, showing the "mansion house" and grounds of 32 acres. The whole plot included one thousand one hundred acres. The Dominican Sisters purchased the Homestead and used it for a school in the 1870's

(From a miniature in possession of Henry Hays)

STOKLEY DONELSON HAYS
One of the Founders of Jackson

COURTHOUSE IN JACKSON ABOUT 1870

JUDGE MILTON BROWN
Lawyer, Congressman and Railroad President

WEST TENNESSEE 1824
(Finlay)

(Roy Black Collection)

(From a painting owned by Tennessee State Historical Society)

WILLIAM T. HASKELL
Mexican War General, Congressman, poet, and orator

SHIPPED IN GOOD ORDER AND WELL CONDITION-
ED, BY John W. Campbell
For account and risk of whom it may concern, on board the good ___Flat___ Boat called the ___Turk___ whereof ___John Lacy___ is Master for the present voyage, now lying in the ___Sth. Fork Deer River___ and bound for the Port of ___New Orleans___ the following articles described below, which are to be delivered without delay, in the like good order and condition at the Port of ___New Orleans___ (the dangers of the River and Fire excepted,) unto ___Siddall Greene & Co___ or to ___their___ assigns, he or they paying freight for the same at the rate of ___Three Dollars per Bale___
___Twenty Bales of Cotton___

In Witness Whereof, the Master or Clerk of said Boat, hath affirmed to ___three___ Bills of Lading all of this tenor and date, one of which being accomplished, the others to be void. Dated at ___Jackson Tenn___ this ___2d___ day of ___March___ 1854

PRODUCE.	QUANTITY	MARK.	NUMBERED FROM / TO	FOR ACCOUNT OF.	CHARGES
Cotton	Eighteen Bales	J. W. Campbell	No. 20. 18. 19 / 21. 22. 23 / 24. 25. 26 / 27. 28. 29 / 30. 31. 32 / 33. 34. 35	John W. Campbell of Jackson Tenn	Three dollars per Bale
Also	Two Bales	A.W.C.	41 & 42		

Test James Hoppers

John + Lacy
his mark

(Seale Johnson Collection)

Cotton went to market by the Forked Deer until the railroads came in the late 1850's

COURT-HOUSE SQUARE, JACKSON, TENN.

A RAIL-ROAD BATTERY.

EARTHWORK TO PROTECT THE R.R.

COLTON FORT AT JACKSON, TENN.

THE WAR IN THE SOUTHWEST.—SKETCHED BY MR. A. SIMPLOT.—[SEE PAGE 617.]

(Used through the courtesy of May Harris)
SOUTHWESTERN BAPTIST UNIVERSITY ABOUT 1885
Later Union University

(Used through the courtesy of Charles Hanebuth)
ADAMS HALL, SOUTHWESTERN BAPTIST UNIVERSITY, 1897

(Used through the courtesy of Merle Curtis)
MEMPHIS CONFERENCE FEMALE INSTITUTE, 1886

MEMPHIS CONFERENCE FEMALE INSTITUTE, 1904
Located on Chester Street, extending from Royal to Institute Streets, the present site of the National Guard Armory

MADISON COLLEGE AT SPRING CREEK, 1872

ST. LUKE'S EPISCOPAL
CHURCH, 1853

Northeast corner of Church and
Baltimore Streets

CHURCHES IN JACKSON IN 1904

Reading from left to right: St. Luke's Episcopal, First Presbyterian, St. Mary's Catholic, Cumberland Presbyterian, Campbell Street Methodist, First Christian, First Methodist, First Baptist, Middle Avenue Methodist, Hays Avenue Methodist

"ROSE HILL FARM," in the East Union neighborhood. This home of Mathias Deberry was built about 1825.

"EDGEWOOD," the ante-bellum home of J. W. Campbell and his son, Alexander W. Campbell, is located on South Fairgrounds Street, but originally the lawn extended to Poplar Street

Home of Judge Henry W. McCorry, built in the 1840's, located at the intersection of Main and Bolivar Streets

Ben Barr Home, the birthplace of Judge Ben Lindsey, on the present site of the Independent Oil Mills on Bolivar Street

GENERAL ALEXANDER W. CAMPBELL
of the Armies of the Confederacy

COLONEL WILLIAM H. STEPHENS
of the Sixth Tennessee C. S. A.

COLONEL ROBERT I. CHESTER
Early settler, postmaster, and prominent citizen

ROBERT H. CARTMELL
Farmer and author of the Cartmell Diary

General U. S. Grant's Headquarters during Federal occupation of Jackson during Civil War. The house was built by James S. Lyon in 1837 and was located on Main Street, two doors east of Royal Street

ROBERT GATES
Private in the Confederate Army, later well known newspaper man, and public-spirited citizen

GENERAL WILLIAM H. JACKSON
of the Confederate Armies

GOOD ROADS IN MADISON COUNTY, 1904
Cotton wagons on the Campbell Levee at the intersection of the Bemis Road

NORTHEAST CORNER OF MAIN AND MARKET STREETS ABOUT 1900
The present site of the First National Bank Building

JOHN A. GREER
President of First National Bank, 1890-1903

JUDGE HOWELL E. JACKSON
Associate Justice of the United States Supreme Court

SOME MEMBERS OF THE JACKSON BAR, 1900
First Row: B. J. Howard, S. D. Hays, Clarence E. Pigford. *Second Row:* E. L. Bullock, B. A. Enlow, Phillip Holland

HIGHLAND PARK, 1900
Now a residential area bounded by Prospect, Campbell, Crescent, and Walnut Streets

BAPTIST FEMALE SEMINARY, 1872
Located on southwest corner of Baltimore and Market Streets

(Curtis Bay Collection)

JAMES W. ANDERSON
Founder and President of the First National
Bank, 1873-1879

JOHN L. WISDOM
President of First National Bank, 1881-1890;
1903-1909; Vice-President of Second National
Bank

THOMAS POLK
President of Second National Bank, 1907-1928

ROBERT S. FLETCHER
President of National Bank of Commerce,
1905-1931

MADISON COUNTY COURTHOUSE, 1910
Showing east and north entrances

POSTOFFICE AND FEDERAL BUILDING, 1885-1933
Northeast corner of Baltimore and Market Streets

CLARENCE E. PIGFORD
Lawyer, publisher, financier, and public-spirited citizen

SCHOOL BOARD ABOUT 1895
G. R. McGee, J. H. Hirsch, Jesse Thompson, W. F. Alexander, Luther Mathis, Hu. C. Anderson, Sr.

Hu C. Anderson, Sr.
Lawyer, Banker, Mayor of Jackson (1894-1908), and Speaker of the State Senate 1915

Mrs. Camile Bright Bell
Beloved teacher in the City Schools for over forty years

TOM GASTON
Chief of Jackson Police at the turn of the century

HAM KING,
Mayor and proprietor of King's Palace Saloon, noted meeting place of Tennessee politicians

"CASEY" JONES
The railroad engineer of song and story

ANNEX BAR, 1897
During those days before prohibition

COURTHOUSE, PYTHIAN CASTLE, AND OPERA HOUSE
The latter being located on the southeast corner of Main and Liberty Streets.
The Opera House burned in 1902.

SOUTHERN HOTEL, 1904
On the southwest corner of Baltimore and Liberty Streets, a hotel that was made famous by the late Mrs. J. A. Day

COURTHOUSE, 1912

WILLIAM HOLLAND, SR.
Confederate Soldier, prominent merchant, and churchman of the Post Civil War Era

JUDGE HENRY W. McCORRY
Lawyer and political leader of the late Nineteenth Century

COURTHOUSE GROUP IN THE EARLY 1880's

1, Judge Levi Woods. 2, Jim Porterfield. 3, Ben Howard. 4, Frank Malone. 5, R. A. Sneed. 7, J. W. Woolard. 8, Att Thomas. 12, Bob Clayton. 15, Jeff Newton. 17, —— Rushing. 18, Chas. Brown. 19, Liberty Weir. 20, Jim Marks. 21, Fred Adamson. 22, A. B. McGeehee. 23, Alex Person. 24, E. S. Mallory. 26, —— Campbell. 28, Chas. Gates. 30, Miles Hammond. 31, Major Clark.

A GROUP OF THE JACKSON BAR AND COUNTY OFFICIALS, 1887

1, W. F. Porterfield. 2, Judge Levi Wood. 3, John L. Brown. 4, B. A. Person. 5, A. B. McGeehee. 6, Frank Young. 7, R. A. Hurt. 8, Stoddert Caruthers. 9, Joel L. Rushing. 10, Col. R. A. Sneed. 11, J. N. Trout. 12, John Tomlin. 13, Stokley D. Hays. 14, W. F. May. 15, J. W. Wallace. 16, Fred Adamson. 17, B. F. McLemore. 18, Richard Hays. 19, Ben J. Howard. 20, John A. Pitts. 21, E. A. Clark. 22, B. F. Howard, Sr. 23, E. S. Mallory. 24, T. C. Muse. 25, Henry Mc-Corry. 26, W. H. Meeks.

BISHOP ISAAC LANE

Lane College, 1946, a four year liberal arts college, began in 1882 as the colored Methodist High School. Much of the success of the school is due to the leadership of Bishop Isaac Lane, an ex-slave, who was the founder of the college.

LANE COLLEGE IN 1912 DURING BUILDING PROGRAM

HISTORIC MADISON

CHAPTER I

THE PROLOGUE

Those early Tennesseans who came to the Western District were proud to bestow upon their county and the county seat the names of two distinguished Americans—James Madison and Andrew Jackson. The members of the Tennessee General Assembly of 1821 created a new county almost in the geographical center of the Western District and gave it the name of their beloved James Madison and hoped that the people who settled here would build a county that would be worthy of his name, for "What constitutes a State? ... Men who their duties know, but know their right and knowing dare maintain. ... These constitute a State!" At the time of James Madison's death Andrew Jackson spoke of the "respect which is due to the memory of one whose life contributed so essentially to the happiness and glory of his country and to the good of mankind."[1] Upon this same occasion a Nashville paper mentioned the fact that the nation realized that "their beloved Madison gradually sank to the grave, wrapped in the halo of his fame and embalmed in a gratitude that his virtues had enkindled."[2]

James Madison is remembered as a fiery advocate of separation from Great Britain, as a member of the Second Continental Congress, as an invaluable legislator from Virginia, as one of the writers of the "Federalist Papers" and thus an important factor in the ratification of the Constitution, as Secretary of State under Jefferson, as President of the United States from 1808 to 1816, but probably above all for his work in the great Constitutional Convention of 1787. Considering the fact James Madison's influence was so great at this convention that he has been called the "Father of the Constitution," and so good was the work of these Constitutional

---

[1] *National Portrait Gallery of Distinguished Persons* (Philadelphia, 1936), 11.
[2] Nashville *Republican*, July 12, 1836.

fathers that the Constitution, the rock upon which the whole American government rests, has been made to fit an expanding and growing nation for over one hundred and fifty years. The citizens of Madison County may, therefore, be justly proud that their county bears the name of this illustrious American.

It is almost a tragedy to the writer that a copy of a Jackson, Tennessee, paper at the time of Madison's death cannot be located but a few words from the Randolph *Recorder,* a contemporary of the Jackson *Truth Teller,* probably express the sentiment of most of the papers of the Western District: "Madison was the principal architect in its [our government] construction, if he did not lay its corner stone. He lived to see it endure many trials, survive great dangers, promise endurance for ages!"[3] Madison Countians are proud that the name of James Madison was bestowed upon their county at its birth.

Andrew Jackson, that great American hero and statesman for whom the seat of justice of Madison County was named, was to the early citizens of the town a typical frontier lawyer, an unexcelled Indian fighter, the hero of the War of 1812, a Tennessean. Moreover, he was the uncle of several of those founding fathers. More weight should be given to the last three qualifications than the first and it should be remembered that the name was bestowed upon the small frontier town years before "Old Hickory" became the popular president. Mrs. William E. Butler, Mrs. Robert J. Chester, Stokley D. Hays, Samuel Jackson Hays, and Miss Narcissus Hays were all the children of Jane Donelson Hays, a sister of Rachel Donelson Jackson.[4]

---

[3]Randolph *Recorder,* July 22, 1836.

[4]That Jackson was very close to and fond of his nieces and nephews in Jackson is shown by his frequent letters to them. On February 26, 1824, Jackson endorsed a draft for Dr. Butler; in 1842, he wrote to Frances P. Blair: "Dr. Wm. E. Butler belonged to the Hospital staff of Tennessee Militia, a man whose veracity will not be doubted by anyone." J. S. Bassett, *Correspondence of Andrew Jackson* (Washington, 1933), VI, 166. In a letter to R. J. Chester in 1833, Jackson expressed his happiness at hearing that Dr. Butler's family was in good health continuing: "With all our connections, to whom present my kind salutations, say to all that nothing could afford me more pleasure than to see them all." Bassett, *Correspondence,* V, 150. Letters from Mrs. Jackson in 1814 show that Dr. Butler must have been the postman between the General and his Lady. *Ibid.,* III, 232.

James Caruthers, one of the early surveyors and settlers, Dr. W. E. Butler, the "Father of Jackson," Robert J. Chester, Stokley D. Hays, and Colonel Thomas Williamson, a senator from this district, had all served under Jackson in the recent war against Britain. What could be more appropriate than the selection of the name Jackson for Andrew was a Tennessean who had been made a national hero and he was their own General and their own uncle to whom they were devoted and of whom they were very proud.

The sandy-haired freckled faced lad of the frontier became the tall, erect, graceful man with bright eyes, abundant reddish hair, and a fiery temper. This fearless fighter with Indians or the British was equally fearless in dueling or in politics. As a roaming, rollicking, horse-loving, struggling young lawyer, Andrew Jackson became a frontiersman by crossing the mountains and coming to Nashville in 1788 as prosecuting attorney of the Western District of North Carolina. Here he became famous for helping to maintain law and order in this wild region of the new west. He had his faults, to be sure, but what person doesn't? Jackson's faults were so overshadowed by his nobler qualities—patriotism, fearlessness, and integrity—that friends forgot his faults very quickly and enemies forgot them in due time. In Jackson was bundled up almost every characteristic that appealed to those early men of the Western Waters, so if Andrew Jackson had not been a close relative of those early settlers, they probably would still have named their town Jackson.[5]

In the summer of 1825, a committee composed of Judge Hook, Adam R. Alexander, and Joseph Talbot invited General Jackson to visit the Western District before he departed for Washington. A committee was appointed to make prepara-

---

[5]The town came very near losing its name, for in 1820 a bill was introduced in the Legislature to name a town in Bedford County *Jackson*, but the name was struck out and Royalport was inserted. It was rumored at the time by the Richmond *Enquirer* that this was a reflection upon General Jackson but the *Niles Register* placed a different light upon the subject, saying that this was a "token of respect for the General, that a place of more probable importance might be called after him." S. C. Williams, *Beginnings of West Tennessee: In the Land of the Chickasaws*, 1541-1841 (Johnson City, Tennessee, 1930), 137, quoting *Niles Register*, August 26, September 16, 1820. Hereinafter cited as *West Tennessee*.

tions,⁶ Jackson accepted, and the General with his Lady arrived on Sunday, September 18, 1825, accompanied by his colleague in the Senate, Major J. H. Eaton, and Judge John Overton. The visiting celebrity was escorted into town by a delegation headed by C. D. McClean and given a special welcome by the Masons, for the charter of the Jackson Lodge No. 45 was obtained while Jackson was Grand Master of Tennessee. In an address of welcome at the courthouse, Wm. Stoddert, Esq., referred to the debt of gratitude that the people of the Western District owed to Jackson concerning his part in the negotiations of the Chickasaw Treaty of 1818:

> When it is recalled that out of the lands thus acquired the war-worn soldiers of the Revolution and their descendents were anxiously looking forward for the satisfaction of their claims for services and that by this treaty justice though before so tardy was quickened into life and a new spring given to the hopes and fortitude of these long neglected persons; what a debt of gratitude do we owe you!⁷

Then Andrew Jackson arose, accepted the tribute and replied as follows:

> It is true that I was fortunate enough to conclude that treaty of 1818 which gave to our South the fertile and prosperous country which you occupy. The execution of this important trust had been assigned to me in connection with an esteemed man, Gov. Shelby of Kentucky. We spared no pains and left no effort proper to be used untried to effect the purpose of our mission. To me an inestimable satisfaction is derived from the evidence now offered that the haunts of the Savage man have been exchanged for the cultivated farm. You are yet young in years but press on; practice industry, and economy and soon you will claim in the State that prosperity to which the fruit of your soil and your already refined population abundantly entitles you.⁸

At a public dinner given by the people of the town and neighborhood, Colonel R. H. Dyer, assisted by Colonel Thos.

---

⁶A committee of welcome included: William E. Butler, Duncan McIver, H. Haralson, Adam Huntsman, Colonel Robert H. Dyer, Thomas Loftin, Stephen Lacy, Major Jason Wilson, Alexander B. Bradford, Captain Alfred Murray. Jackson *Gazette*, July 9, 1825. The Jackson Lodge No. 45 prizes very highly an apron presented to the lodge by Captain James Brittle, which in turn was presented to his uncle, P. S. McMurray who became a Mason in 1822 while Andrew Jackson was Grand Master of the Masons of Tennessee.

⁷Jackson *Gazette*, September 24, 1825.
⁸*Ibid.*

Henderson, presided. All survivors of the Revolution were invited as special guests. The General's toast was: "The town of Jackson where but lately roamed wild beasts and savages; behold now the abode of civilization, refinement, and hospitality."[9] Here, as always, Jackson never lost a chance to try to instill into the people a real love of their country and homeland. The following excerpt from his address is just another illustration of his patriotism and his appeal to the people:

If in my march through life it had been my good fortune to be an actor in scenes which eventuated beneficially, my greatest satisfaction is in knowing that at this day, they are considered as they were intended, for the benefit and advancement of our common country. The last spot on the globe where liberty has found a resting place, will not, I hope want defenders, and sincere ones, whenever an assault may come. The world can not remain at peace. Human nature is restless and man as he ever has been, ambitious. Because our government is formed upon new principles, we must not trust alone to that but mark with care and caution the secret and silent inroads which intrigue, ambition, and cunning from time to time may originate. In selecting, at any time, any agent to discharge those important functions which under our form of government must necessarily be confided to him who represents us, let mind be our great consideration; but above all, let it be ascertained that virtue and purity have with him, taken up their abode, dwelling with him, and he with them. By this means and only this can our government, go down unimpaired to posterity. Mere form and ceremony in the guidance of our affairs can avail but little. We must be careful and vigilant to adhere to those principles which characterize and mark the government we possess.[10]

The *Jackson Gazette* reported that in the evening "a concourse of the beauty and fashion of the district paid their respects to Mrs. Jackson." The reader's imagination will have to be depended upon to expand this brief statement, for there must have been an elegant party given by the nieces, nephews, and friends of the beloved General and his Lady. Another conclusion concerning how the hours of this visit were spent must be made from only a few scattered facts. In the 1820's Dr. Butler had a race track on the lot later occupied by the

---

[9]*Niles' Weekly Register*, October 22, 1825, XXIX, 113. "General Jackson with his lady on a visit to some relatives to Jackson, West Tennessee, was invited to and partook of a public dinner, given by the people of that town and its neighborhood."

[10]Jackson *Gazette*, September 17, 1825.

Memphis Conference Female Institute and now by the National Guard Armory. Andrew Jackson is said to have run his horses on this track. In several letters of Jackson to Dr. Butler there are references to Butler's looking over some horse for "the Western District," or the sale of a certain horse. It is more than probable that the General saw his own horses run on the Butler tract while he was here in 1825. The visit came to an end on the first of October when the guests, who were on their way to attend a dinner in Paris, Tennessee, were escorted to the corporation limits by a special delegation.

As the years passed Jackson kept in close touch with his relatives in the Western District, wrote to them often, and did what he could for them. It was through his influence that Robert J. Chester was appointed postmaster of Jackson in 1825. As other lands of this new west were opened up, Jackson secured or tried to secure posts for those experienced men of the west, S. D. Hays and R. J. Chester. Stokley D. Hays was register of a land office in Mississippi at the time of his death in 1831. A letter to R. J. Chester from Jackson (November 2, 1830) shows that Jackson was trying to get an appointment for Hays:

> I do wish you to say to Col. S. D. Hays that he must get and send on here, as early as he can, testimonials of his sobriety and capacity as a surveyor. This will be necessary for so sure as an opportunity offers, if one should, to give him a surveyors District, that in order to mortify me his appointment will be opposed in the Senate and Crockett and Deshea will represent him as intemperate. Let the recommendations be strong and go to his capability and ability to give the necessary security, if required.[11]

---

[11]Bassett, *Correspondence*, IV, 199. Stokley D. Hays passed away soon after this, at which time the following appeared in the *Southern Statesmen*, September 10, 1831: "Mr. Hays death of bilious fever has spread an unusual gloom around us—possessed of hospitable, kind, and generous feelings, even to a fault, no man had fewer enemies . . . Hays was by profession a lawyer—endued with a strong mind, and possessing advantages of liberal education. Fame and fortune were within his grasp, but such were his social habits that neither ambition or parsimony could find a resting place within his bosom. For the purpose of removing his family, he had just returned apparently in good health from Clinton, Mississippi, where he had been for some time attending his official duties as Register of the Land Office. He has left a widow, two children, and numerous train of relatives. Masonic honors."

Three years later Jackson appointed Robert J. Chester as surveyor of the Chickasaw Territory, but the appointment was rejected because Chester was not a resident of Mississippi. Jackson regretted this event but committed himself to continue to look out after the interests of those he loved in the Western District. "I am mortified at your defeat," he wrote, "but remembering for the present the old adage, that what cannot be cured must be endured, still you may rest well assured that no opportunity will be omitted that can be embraced with propriety to promote your interest."[12]

Fifteen years elapsed from the time of the first visit of "Old Hickory" to Jackson until he came again. Time had brought many changes into his life. Rachel Jackson had passed away, he had served as President of the United States for eight years, had advised his Martin Van Buren as President for four years, the Whig party had been formed and had become so strong that there was danger of the Western District, which once was Jackson's stronghold, voting a Whig ticket. "Whiggery" was raging in Madison.[13] Andrew Jackson was an old man and ill, having just injured a rib in his left side and he did not feel that he was able to go to the big political meeting in Jackson that was a part of that rollicking campaign of 1840, but he determined to do so for his friends thought it would ensure a majority. "I must make the effort," he wrote to Andrew Hutchings, "least, if we were to lose a majority in the Western District, it might be said, that it was owing to my not going to this great meeting at Jackson."[14] A few weeks later Jackson again wrote of the importance of this meeting: "My friends have invited me to a free barbecue to be given on the 8th proximo at Jackson in the Western District—my friends say that will insure there a majority."[15]

The people of the Western District made great preparations for this glorious meeting of the Democrats on the eighth of October, 1840, a day treasured in the memory of Democracy as hallowed by the presence of the man "who had saved the

---

[12] Bassett, *Correspondence*, IV., 198.
[13] Madison County voted 1312 for Harrison and 537 for Van Buren in the 1840 election, Nashville *Union*, November 19, 1840.
[14] Jackson to Andrew Hutchings, September 7, 1840, Bassett, *Correspondence*, VI, 74.
[15] Jackson to Frances P. Blair, September 26, 1840, *Ibid.*, 78.

sovereignty of the people." Ten thousand were expected and more than ten thousand assembled (some accounts said seven). Revolutionary soldiers, invited guests, and citizens of the county formed in front of the court house and proceeded to Dr. Butler's where General Jackson, Governor Polk, and Felix Grundy joined the procession, which made its way to the grove which had been selected for the festivities of the day.[16] Arriving at the speaking grounds, General Jackson was received as a guest of West Tennessee by Samuel McClanahan, Esq., in an address which was "highly honorable to the heart and intellect of the orator." McClanahan called his fellow citizens to renew their pledges to "the first benefactor of the beloved State," for that vast assemblage of countenances beaming with delight was proof of the fact that the "venerable tenant of the Hermitage is dear to the hearts of the people."[17] Jackson's reply was characteristic of that venerable sage of the Hermitage:

> It affords me unspeakable pleasure to be able to meet you on this occasion. It is probably the last time that I shall have it in my power to exchange salutations with you—the last opportunity that I shall have to thank you personally for the many proofs you have given me of your respect for my character and services. The infirmation of age admonishes me, that I can not much longer be a partner with you in the vicissitudes of this life; and I can therefore have no other feeling when honored with the cordial welcome you have accorded me, but that which belongs to a heart full of gratitude and sincerely anxious for your happiness and prosperity individually and collectively. . . . My health is too feeble to sustain me in an attempt to express fully the reflections which are excited in my mind, by the view you have taken of our public affairs at this time. I cannot forbear however a brief response to some of the topics you have touched . . . This my fellow citizens is a great and momentous crisis in our national affairs in which our dearest rights as freeman are concerned. The Presidential Election is near at hand, which will decide the fate of our Republican system;

---

[16]There was a beautiful grove of trees just opposite the present Water Works where the Colonial Bakery stands. It was here that the guest from the Hermitage was entertained. Uncle King Anderson, the man of three wars, the perfect picture of a frontiersman, kindhearted and true to his friends, baked a huge ash cake which weighed 120 pounds (some say he used a bushel of meal). Jackson asked to shake the hands of Uncle King, Vick and Reavis who helped barbecue the meat and make the squirrel stew. T. M. Gates' Scrap Book.

[17]Nashville *Union*, October 12, 20, 1840.

whether it will be perpetrated on the great general principle laid down in our written Constitution or changed to a great consolidation trodden under foot, our glorious Union burst assunder and your constitutional liberty lost forever.[18]

After Jackson finished Governor Polk addressed the people for two and one half hours in his "most powerful manner" and then Judge Grundy spoke for about the same length of time on "currency, public expenditures, and extravagances of the 'palace' ". His speech was received with thrilling interest and deafening applause. About 4 o'clock when the addresses were concluded the ladies (and there were about one thousand present) and gentlemen went to the tables and partook of the most sumptuous barbecue. It was a glorious day for everyone and " 'tis true and pity 'tis occasionally a 'palpable bit' would cause the BOYS to raise a shout for 'Tip and Ty', done doubtless to show their mothers present, they had cut their apron strings."[19]

All foregoing reference to Jackson's visit came from his correspondence or Democratic papers. The Whig papers in Nashville spoke of Jackson's "electioneering expedition to the Western District," adding that they knew the people of the Western District too well to think that they would bow to the dictations of any man, for these people were an "intelligent, high-spirited independent population." The Whigs bragged that they had really gained from the visit, for they thought the old chief had proven that he would stoop to party politics. The same paper ridiculed the welcoming orator for speaking very badly a portion of Webster's address to LaFayette and Governor Polk for reading Jackson's prepared manuscript. [A frontier gathering did not like to have a speech read to

---

[18]Nashville *Union*, October 20, 1840.

[19]Nashville *Union*, October 20, 1840. Jackson wrote to Andrew Donelson on October 8, 1840: "We had a large meeting today. Polk and Grundy both spoke, to an attentive audience and all things look well in this District. I have no fear of the results, the abolition question begins to draw attention, I may say the serious attention of the people here. You will see in the Union soon the address delivered to me and my reply with the addition I found necessary to make to it, which I think you will approve. I set out in the morning on my return home, Col. Polk returns with me and has engagements to address the people at two points on the way." Bassett, *Correspondence*, VI. 79.

them.] In fact, the Whigs considered the "whole affair an example of political officiousness."[20]

That Jackson had some of his strongest friends and bitterest enemies in the county is shown by the overwhelming majority that old "Tippacanoe and Tyler, too," rolled up on that election day in November 1840.[21] This was the beginning of that stronghold of "whiggery" in the county that lasted until the Sectional Conflict.

---

[20] Nashville *Republican Banner*, October 26, 1840.

[21] Men of Madison were joining in the fun and helping to make the Harrison-Tyler campaign one of those gay, rolicking ones in the history of American politics.

CHAPTER II

THE RED MAN'S COUNTRY

That section of Tennessee between the Tennessee and the Mississippi rivers was the last portion of the state that the red man surrendered to the white man. This trackless wilderness had been occupied for unnumbered centuries by a prehistoric people—an ancient race which built mounds and extensive fortifications. These silent monuments of a forgotten people only furnish proof that an early race lived here. No man knows who they were, whence they came, or whither they went. Merely a few speculations can be made from material remains, such as the various mounds in the country to-day.

Numerous mounds may be found within the present bounds of Madison County. In the 1880's, J. G. Cisco found a stone pipe of curious workmanship and a number of arrow heads in a small mound at the south end of Market Street west of the Illinois Central Railroad. He excavated a few mounds on the farm of J. W. Campbell about one or one and a half miles west of Jackson and found a pit filled with ashes, charred human bones and partly burned wood.[1]

---

[1] J. G. Cisco, "Madison County," *American Historical Magazine*, VII (1902), 329. J. G. Cisco, who made printing and editing a newspaper his vocation, made local history and archaeology his avocation and did much to interest the people in the community in Indian relics by having a minature museum at the office of the *Forked Deer Blade* and writing a history of the county which was published in the *Blade* and later republished in the *American Historical Magazine*.

According to Dr. Charles W. Davis, there are eleven mound sites in Madison County. The following ones have been surveyed by Mr. Davis: 1. The great Pinson Group—thirty mounds or more; 2. Group of the Johnson Farm, Hart's Bridge Road—three large mounds, small mounds and cemetery site; 3. Denmark Group—three mounds; 4. Spring Creek vicinity—three mounds; 5. Old Medina Road—Small mound on the Spann farm and one on the Newton farm; 6. Southeast of Medon—two mounds of medium size; 7. Haynes mound on

From William E. Meyers "Art and Archaeology," September, 1922.

About ten miles southeast of the present city of Jackson near the town of Pinson are some of the most interesting remains left by the stone-age man in the United States.[2] An adventurous party in 1820, surveying old grants for Colonel Thomas Henderson, emerged from the Forked Deer bottom, discovered a large bold spring of water and a mound some six or seven feet high and extensive enough for houses and a small yard. Joel Pinson, one of the members, was so pleased that one of the surveying party proposed to call it Mount Pinson.

---

the old Medon Road, one mile north of Medon; 8. Mound on Brotie Wilson's farm near Poplar Heights; 9. One mound opposite the Yarbrough orchard; 10. Small mounds on the Bells Highway on Will Hall's farm; 11. Three mounds on property of the West Tennessee Expermient Station.

[2]David, the brother of Chief Justice James W. Deadrick, came with Rev. David Nelson to the Western District in 1826, visited these ancient fortifications and considered them "the largest perhaps in any part of the West"; J. G. Cisco in the 1880's considered them the most interesting in the Southern States; W. Myers in 1922 enlarged the field to that of the United States. Cisco, "Madison County," 329; William E. Myers, "Recent Archaeological Discoveries in Tennessee," *Art and Archaeology*, September, 1922, p. 141.

Sketch of Great Central Mound. Height 72 feet. Base 370 ft. x 300 ft. Top 60 ft. x 50 ft

From William E. Meyers "Art and Archaeology," September, 1922.

This party did not know of the larger mounds two miles further south until months later, but other people seeing the large mound supposed this was the one that the party named—thus Mount Pinson was the name adopted for the larger mound.[3]

J. G. Cisco had created so much interest in these mounds in the 1880's among the local people that when William E. Myers visited this site in 1916, he gave the name of the "City of Cisco" to this great ancient walled city, with outer defenses measuring fully six miles in length, with elaborate outer and inner citadels, including in all thirty-five mounds of various sizes. These range in height from three or four feet to the great Saul Mound, which towers to the height of seventy-two feet.[4] Some of the earthen embankments have been destroyed in recent years by cultivation, but a few older citizens can still remember their exact location. The great "City of Cisco" extends along the bluffs of the Forked Deer for a distance of two and one half miles where there was probably a continuous line of wooden palisades.[5] The largest mound is pentagonal in form, the base being made up of five crescents, all curving inward. Where these crescents join, the mound has the appearance of steep ramps which extend all the way to the summit. The base is 300 feet by 370 feet; and its flat summit, 38

---

[3]"Recollections of Memucan Hunt Howard," *American Historical Magazine*, IX, (1925-26), 15.

[4]Myers, "Archaeological Discoveries," 141. In 1826 Judge A. D. Murphy took the measurements of the highest mound and found it to be seventy-eight feet; the difference is probably the result of the passage of a century. This mound is higher than the Miamisburg Mound, the tallest in Ohio, which is sixty-eight feet, and taller than the Graves's Creek Mound in West Virginia, which is seventy feet. From a paper read by C. W. Davis at the June meeting (1944) of the Madison County Historical Society. A few material remains have been found in this vicinity. Bits of flint and stone axes have been found. In the early years the English introduced a tomahawk pipe for trade purposes. This was a metal hatchet with the butt of the blade hollowed out into a bow which connected with a bore running through the handle—one end of the handle served to chop, the other to smoke. Thus, the Indian had a weapon of war and a symbol of peace. These copper pipes were made in England for Indian trade. Such a pipe was found at the Pinson mounds some years ago.

[5]*Ibid.*

feet by 60 feet. It contains 92,300 cubic yards of earth.[6] Mr. Myers considered this large mound about the sixth in size in the United States. It was probably once used as the location of the great house of the king.

The "twin mounds" in this group at Pinson are very unusual. They have the appearance of two elliptical mounds built end-to-end with the ends coalescing. These are each ninety feet long, seventy-five feet wide and sixteen feet high.[7] The "temple mound," high on the river bank, was probably devoted to sacred ceremonial purposes and supported some sacred building. It appears to resemble a bird with outstretched wings and this is highly possible for the thunder bird and other sacred birds played an important role in the religious rites of the stone-age man in the South. Mr. Myers concluded his story of the "City of Cisco" as follows:

> There is abundant evidence showing this city was the central city and capital of a large region; that it had a population of several thousand, and was built by some conqueror-king. This great fortified city was occupied only for a short time after it was completed. Then the conqueror king was overthrown. His stronghold was taken and destroyed. It was left desolate and never occupied.[8]

In 1875, E. H. Randle of McKenzie visited these mounds and made some very sensible speculations based upon what he found. Chips of flint of every variety furnished evidence that the flint was brought there from elsewhere and here manufactured into the implements of husbandry and of warfare. Therefore, this must have been a manufacturing city. There was no flint indiguous to West Tennessee; therefore, they must have brought it from a great distance. They were then a commercial people, which is further evidenced by the remains of an old road which must have been large and well beaten, leading out from the city southwest. The extensive and costly preparation for living shows that they must have been a well settled and also a nomadic people. Considering the immense labor with nothing but stone implements with which to erect the fortifications, they must have had a well-

---

[6]Gail Buck, Madison County engineer, told C. W. Davis that he made the survey of this whole group for Mr. Myers.
[7]C. W. Davis.
[8]Myers, "Archaeological Discoveries," 142.

organized government over obedient people. Old Mount Pinson must have been the capitol city of a powerful tribe. From such a vantage point, the bold chieftan could look over endless country as he surveyed the laboring of his people and the marching of his troops and watched for possible assaults of an enemy.[9]

Since these early denizens of the wilderness [many scholars insist that these mound builders should not be confused with the Indians] were in all probability commercial people, their highways should be mentioned. Where nature provided water ways they, like the Indians and the white men of later days, found it convenient to use them, but overland trails had to be made also. One ancient trail led from the "City of Cisco" to the Bolivar town which was also fortified. Here one prong led to Memphis, Arkansas, and Southwest; the other to the ancient Indian town of Pontotoc, near Pontotoc, Mississippi, and on to the towns of Mobile Bay. Another trail left the "City of Cisco" towards the east crossing the Tennessee near Johnsonville and on to Nashville, after leading to the two great groups of mounds on the Harpeth River.[10]

Indian trails probably followed the same paths of the ancient trails. The West Tennessee Chickasaw Trail reached from Jackson south to Bolivar into Mississippi and Alabama and was used by the Chickasaw and Choctaws in going from Mississippi and Alabama to West Tennessee and beyond. The old fortified town and populous region around Cisco seemed to be the crossing of the Indian highways for one trail left here for the north, went to Jackson and Denmark; a Savannah-Cisco Trail led from here to populous settlements of the Tennessee River in the region of Savannah.[11] Park Marshall suggested that Natchez Trace followed the old Chickasaw Trail, but a wagon road could not closely follow a foot path in a wild hilly country through which many streams cut their way. S. C. Williams states that an ancient trail of the Chickasaws passed through Madison County. He says that this was

---

[9]The *Jackson Sun*, August 27, 1875.
[10]Myers, "Archeological Discoveries," 142.
[11]William E. Myers, "Indian Trails of the Southwest," *Forty-Second Annual Report of the Bureau of Enthnology, 1924-25*, (Washington, 1925), 815, 853-854.

called Natchez or Massac Trace, that College Street of Jackson was laid out along the course.[12]

A history of West Tennessee or any county of West Tennessee would be incomplete without some brief statements about the people who owned this territory for years and years, who loved it, who defended it from all intruders, and who literally made it "the land of the free and the home of the brave," until Andrew Jackson and Isaac Shelby "out generaled them" in 1818 and left the white man to carry on the traditions that the Indians had begun. For years the interior of the Chickasaw country was a trackless wilderness, a closed country to all but the Chickasaws who had their villages near Pontotoc, Mississippi, but used this section of the west as a hunting ground. Early travelers, French, Spanish, and English, called at the Chickasaw Bluffs, but none penetrated into the interior during those early years.

The Chickasaws, the most intrepid warriors of the South, were known as a nation of Indians that were the irreconcilable enemies of the French and the ancient allies of the English. They were famed for their bravery and ferocious bearing in war. They were patriotic—ever ready to lay down their lives in defense of their homes and their lands. In intelligence they probably excelled all other tribes except the Cherokees. They were always neatly dressed and clean in their habits and person in comparison to other tribes. They were a proud and independent people. In fact they were called: "the bravest of the brave," admirably proportioned, athletic, active, and graceful in their movements, and possessed of open and manly countenances.[13] It is said from the best sources available that this small nation was outnumbered seven to one by the Choctaws, six to one by the Creeks, three to one by the Cherokees, but that the Chickasaws always emerged victorious in any conflict not only with their warlike neighbors, but also with the French and the Spanish. Numbers are not so important to people who are deeply religious, to people who go to war with that religious fervor and zeal that means so much in winning a war. Then one secret of their success against

---

[12]*Ibid.* 815; S. C. Williams, *West Tennessee*, 49, quoting Jackson *Gazette*, September 4, 1824.
[13]Williams, *West Tennessee*, 97.

their enemies may be attributed to their prowess upon the waters as they fared forth in their cypress bark canoes upon the Mississippi. These Indians were as much the rulers of the inland waters as the English were rulers of the seas.[14]

A few bits here and there from the records left to us by the early travelers who went through the Mississippi Valley give us a glimpse of these Chickasaws—those early land-owners of Madison County. Their intelligence and common sense is illustrated by a description in Father Marquette's narrative of 1673:

> Let me tell you how the Indians of these parts (Chickasaws) do defend themselves against them (mosquitoes). They raise a scaffolding, the floor of which is made of simple poles, and consequently a mere grate-work to give passage to the smoke of a fire which they build beneath. This drives off the little animals, as they cannot bear it. The Indians sleep on the poles, having pieces of bark (and skins) stretched so as to keep off the rain. This scaffolding shelters them from the excessive and unsupportable heat of the country; for they lie in the shade of the lower story and thus sheltered from the rays of the sun enjoy the cool air which passes freely through the scaffold.[15]

La Salle's party about 1680 reported two thousand warriors of the Chickasaws. Father Douay on the return expedition of La Salle in 1687 spoke of the nation of Sicacha (Chickasaws) as a very numerous nation: "they count at least four thousand warriors, have an abundance of every kind of peltry."[16] Could part of this abundance of peltry have been the result of those happy hunting grounds in West Tennessee?

In 1796 Francis Baily, an Englishman, traveled down the Mississippi by boat and returned overland through the countries of the Choctaws and the Chickasaws to Nashville. At the Chickasaw Bluffs he noted them as a warlike race as follows:

---

[14] James Malone, *The Chickasaw Nation*, (Louisville, Kentucky, 1922), 242, 284. Historians may differ upon some points of history but not upon their opinion of the Chickasaws for "truly history nowhere upon its pages, ancient or modern, records a nobler or braver little nation of people than the Chickasaws of North America." C. H. Cushman, *History of the Choctaws, Chickasaws, and Natchez Nations*, (Greenville, Texas, 1899), 468.

[15] Samuel Cole Williams, *Early Travels in the Tennessee Country 1540-1800* (Johnson City, Tennessee, 1928), 43. Hereinafter cited as *Early Travels*.

[16] *Ibid.*, 55, 62.

One that preserves a good understanding with America which the latter is obliged to keep up by presents sent annually to them. . . . These Indians were a well-made, handsome race of men. . . . They receive us with every mark of friendship and attention. The chief part of them were dressed in printed calico shirts, which (together with what they call a breech-clout) form the whole of their dress, except a pair of mockasins, which serve them for shoes. Those mockasins are made of deer skins, which are smoked instead of tanned and are thereby rendered very soft and pleasant to the feet; they are sewd together at the top with the sinews of deer, and are finished oftentimes in a very curious manner with wampum and porcupine quills. They soon offered us the pipe of peace, of which each of us having smoked a whiff or two, our introductions to them were completed and they began to trade with us, and show us everything worthy of observation in the place.[17]

As this party made its way overland, friendly Chickasaws and Cherokees saved them from rapid waters when their raft was out of control, gave them directions to the next river that was "three sleeps" away, offered them all the venison they could eat and what they wanted to take with them when they encountered a hunting party. Two Indians, going on an express, left the Indian villages in northern Mississippi at the same time the white man did and made the same speed that the white man made, although the Indians were on foot and the Englishmen were on horseback. This was simply an instance of their perseverance and activity.[18]

Among the stories that James Adair relates, illustrating the fact that these Chickasaws were as brave as ever trod the ground and faithful under the greatest dangers even to death, was that of forty Chickasaw braves who escorted two English traders and their cargo through the woods—all the time knowin that eighty French Choctaws were near by but dared not attack them. Another tale was that of a hunting party of seventeen Chickasaws accompanied by their wives and children being

---

[17]*Ibid.*, 390.

[18]*Ibid.*, 401-408. When the Indians went on an express, they had no guns, only blankets and a few strings of jerk which they hung round their necks. On this and this only will they travel for hundreds and hundreds of miles through the woods, partaking of no other liquor but the clear streams they met on the way. One young Chickasaw ran 300 miles in 42 hours—a trip that would have taken an experienced traveler 140 hours to make, riding a very superior horse. Malone, *The Chickasaw Nation*, 60.

attacked by sixty Chocktaws. The seventeen drove off the sixty shamefully. Adair added:

> It is usual for the women to sing the enlivening war songs in the time of attack; it inflames the men's spirits so highly, that they become as fierce as lions. I never knew an instance of the Indians running off, though from a numerous enemy, and leaving their women and children to their barbarous hands.[19]

During the eighteenth century the Chickasaws had an unending, bitter warfare against the French. In fact it was mainly through their efforts that the territory east of the Mississippi was saved from the French for the English. The English trader, James Adair, recognized this fact and highly recommended that Indians should be rewarded accordingly:

> As the Checkkarah fought the French and their red allies with utmost firmness, in defence of their liberties, and lands to the very last, without regarding their decay; . . . equity and gratitude ought to induce us to be kind to our steady friends and only purchase so much of their lands as they would dispose of for value.[20]

During these French and Indian warfare days, the Chickasaws asked for aid from Georgia who sent munitions by a trader, John Brown. They asked aid of the "King of Carolina" to help them keep their land for they had not had the liberty of hunting for three years. "We have enough to do to defend our lands and prevent our women and children from being slaves of the French."[21] Then in 1763, the Chickasaws were of great service to the English in taking over the forts of the territory. Major Robert Farmer reported in 1765 that the Chickasaws were well-behaved and that other Indians stood in awe of them.[22]

Again during the Revolution it was the Chickasaws who saved this section of West Tennessee from passing into foreign hands—this time into those of Spain. The Chickasaws because of age-old alliances were loyal to the British, had resented the erection of forts by George Rogers Clark near Columbus,

---

[19] S. C. Williams, *Adair's History of the American Indians*, (Johnson City, Tennessee, 1930), 342-3. Hereinafter cited as *Adair's Indians*.
[20] *Ibid.*, 384.
[21] Williams, *West Tennessee*, 28-29.
[22] Williams, *Early Travels*, 216.

Kentucky. Spain in all probability would have built a fort at the lower Chickasaw Bluff if it had not been for fear of the Chickasaws. Finally in 1782 General James Robertson established a depot at the bluff and sent supplies to the Indian nation.[23]

Although the white man did not come into West Tennessee to build homes until after the treaty with the Chickasaws in 1818, he had been planning and thinking of coming here for two hundred years. The land that we call West Tennessee—that fertile land lying between the Mississippi and the Tennessee rivers—has had several names during these years and several others have been suggested that have not been used. West Tennessee was first included in the early charter (1606) of Virginia, then in 1629 the King granted the province of "Carana" to Sir Robert Heath who failed to plant colonies. "Carolina," which extended "to the west as far as the South Seas" was then granted to eight of the king's favorites. Thus the region became a part of the future state of North Carolina. Then in the early part of the eighteenth century colonization schemes were launched to establish a Swiss colony, a Welsh colony, which was to be named "Annarea" in honor of Queen Anne, an English colony to direct fur trade to Charles Town.[24]

Virginia and North Carolina both considered this section a part of their state, but Virginia, in the early days, was more interested than North Carolina. About the middle of the eighteenth century, Virginia sent two men "to go upon discoveries on the River Mississippi." John Sally, one of the men, wrote of this country: "It is a large, spacious country, endowed with all the natural advantages; that is a moderate climate, sweet water, rich Soil, and a pure, fresh air, which contribute to the Benefit of mankind."[25] In the middle of the eighteenth century, Samuel Hazard formulated detailed plans for planting a "separate government" in the West as a buffer state against the French and Indians. He secured the "Subscriptions of between four and five thousand persons, able to bear arms, some of whom were worth thousands" to follow him to the West.[26]

---

[23]Williams, *West Tennessee*, 37.
[24]*Ibid.*, 12; S. C. Williams, *Dawn of Tennessee Valley and Tennessee History*, 66-67, hereinafter cited as *Tennessee Valley*.
[25]Williams, *West Tennessee*, 13.
[26]*Ibid.*, 14.

In 1763, some influential citizens of Virginia and Maryland, the Lees, the Washingtons, the Fitzhughs and others, organized the Mississippi Company for the purpose of obtaining a royal grant of two million five hundred thousand acres of land on the Mississippi River for colony planting. In the same year plans were laid to send four thousand persons from Philadelphia to establish a colony of New Wales in the West. Three years later General Phinias Lyman of Connecticut tried to revive the Hazard scheme and Jonathan Carver visited the West and drew a map locating eleven colonies, and wrote of his travels, evidently visioning this section as the seat of a future empire: "At some future period mighty kingdoms will emerge from these wildernesses, and stately palaces and solemn temples supplant the Indian huts." These men proposed to incorporate North Mississippi, West Tennessee, and Western Kentucky into a separate colony to be called "Georgiana." The contemporary historian, James Adair wrote:

This fair country, Georgiana, invites Great Britain to smile upon it and in return to receive its grateful tribute of tobacco, hemp, silk, flax, cotton, indigo, wine, and tea in plenty, besides other valuable products.[27]

Just previous to the Revolution, plans were made by Richard Caswell of North Carolina to negotiate with the Indians for the purchase of lands lying to the westward of the territory

---

[27]*Ibid.*, 18. Through the years, it is interesting to note the development of sectionalism in Tennessee—the contrast between East and West. In 1802, a French traveler said that "East and West Tennessee" would ultimately form into two distinct states. These differences, the result of geographical peculiarities, have existed from the days of the Cumberland settlement when the people failed to join in the movement for a State of Franklin. In 1841, there was a resolution, introduced by Andrew Johnson, in the Senate for the secession of East Tennessee to be called "the State of Franklin" and to counter balance this John A. Gardner introduced a resolution for the creation of a new "State of Jacksoniana" out of the territory of the Chickasaws. *The Huntingdon Advertiser* supported this idea of the formation of a state made up of the original domain of the Chickasaws, Northern Mississippi, Western Tennessee, and that part of Kentucky which lies west of the Tennessee River. This movement to establish "Jacksoniana" was defeated in the Senate by a vote of 9 to 14. If it had passed, Memphis or Jackson would have been the capital. S. C. Williams, *Lost State of Franklin*, (New York, 1933), 284-286.

of Richard Henderson and Company. The Governor of North Carolina was merely expressing the idea of numerous far-sighted men when he wrote: "I have no doubt that if some effectual stop is not put to this daring usurpation [The frontier had been closed by British authority] that such adventurers will possess themselves soon of all the Indian country."[28]

North Carolina was one of the last states to cede her western lands to the federal government. In the spring of 1783 by an act of the Legislature, provisions were made for the opening of a land office where entries could be made by any citizen of North Carolina for not more than five thousand acres of land for ten pounds in specie or paper money at depreciated value for every one hundred acres. Two and one half million acres of the Chickasaw country was entered, mostly by the politicians of North Carolina who had opened the office in the beginning and now closed it six months later. Literally a "land office business" was done for six weeks. Men were so clamorous and disorderly in the newly opened office that no business was transacted for the first three days that the office was opened, at which time it was decided to cast lots to see the order in which the entries were made.[29]

All this haste should have been in vain, for these lands were still in the possession of the Chickasaws who loved every acre and they were not going to sell them for nothing or be swapped out of them for another thirty-five years. It is no wonder that when the lands were really opened up for settlement, this section was called "The Promised Land," the "Land of Canaan," and the "Garden of Eden."

Nevertheless, the following year (1784), the Legislature of North Carolina sent surveyors into the new country to locate and survey the entries that were recorded during that six weeks of big business. William Tyrell Lewis was elected surveyor of the "Western District"—the name first applied here in 1784 and used to some extent to-day (1946). James Robertson, Henry Rutherford, and Edward Harris were selected to go to the District and survey the lands. They left Nashville in June 1785 and descended the rivers in canoes to the mouth of a small

---

[28]Williams, *Tennessee Valley*, 423.

[29]John Haywood, *Civil and Political History of Tennessee*, (Knoxville, 1823), 107-109. Williams, *West Tennessee*, 42.

river of the District which emptied into the Mississippi River from the east. Rutherford said the Indians called this stream the OKEENA, but the party soon changed its name. A buck deer with horns of a peculiar shape was killed here and the stream became known as the "Forked Deer." Rutherford spent three months of the year in the District, establishing on the first bluff of the Forked Deer "Key Corner," from which he began his surveying. When provisions ran out the party lived upon deer, elk, bear, and wild turkey, which they found in great numbers. The unusually rank growth of pea vines were a great inconvenience, for they were so dense that the dragging of the surveying chains left a trail and they were afraid that the Indians would resent this excursion into their territory, so the party always camped a half mile away each night. When they returned to the East though, they reported that they had not even seen an Indian.[30] These reports of the surveyors were destined to arouse the men of the East—those land speculators who would soon be looking for good cotton lands. A description of the region of West Tennessee published in 1793 predicted the Chickasaw Treaty and the great migration which followed it:

> The progress of population in this western country is no more to be prevented or restrained than the flowing of the rivers. It cannot be retarded by the laws, nor by treaties, nor by a stronger curb—the fear of death.[31]

From 1783 on North Carolina continued to grant lands but all the grantees could do was to call this land their own as long as there was that Chickasaw title. In 1807, William Sharpe inquired of General Robertson what were the prospects

---

[30] *Ibid.*, 42-44.

[31] *Ibid.*, 116. The desire for lands completely blotted out any scruples that most of the men might have had about taking lands which the Chickasaws still owned. William Tatum was almost alone when he raised objections to further indulenge "to our speculators to encroach upon the Chickasaw Indians who had so gloriously boasted their friendship for the white people, and who instead of deserving the ungratitude we have shown by trespassing on their rights and taking their lands away without their consent, without cause or provocation, have ever shown us an example worthy of our imitation; and a specimen of maganimity far above our reach." *Ibid.*, 47-48.

of extinguishing the Chickasaw claims.[32] In 1814, Benjamin Williams was desirous of knowing whether it was safe to view the lands. In 1811 and 1816, Henry Rutherford visited the district to refresh his memory for a future day. In 1818, Calvin Jones visited the district prospecting and wrote extensively of the country that he saw. According to his story that was written for the Raleigh *Register* and republished in the Nashville *Whig and Tennessee Advertiser,* this "Land of the Chickasaws" had never been inhabited by the Indians, it had only been used as a hunting ground and that very rarely. He reported that there was not a white family or a trading house in the district except possibly at Fort Pickering. When he told of this land of excellent soil and numerous rivers he predicted that "the spirit of emigration is such, the number of emigrants is so considerable, and the degrees of wealth and taste so variant that every rock, swamp, and sand hill, if it but lie beyond the mountains, has value. These men (Rutherford, Harris, and Roberts) surveyed one million four hundred thousand acres of which nine hundred and ninety-three thousand acres were patented by the University of North Carolina."[33] Thirty-four years had passed since the surveying; names of the rivers on new maps were different; so there would be, according to Calvin Jones, great difficulty in locating old lands, but many an individual was made rich by the fact that lands that sold at $12\frac{1}{2}$ to 25c an acre in 1813 were selling for $50 an acre in 1818.[34]

Considering the fact that the Chickasaw Country between the Mississippi and the Tennessee rivers contained some of the most desirable land in the new west, it is remarkable that this territory remained in the hands of the Indians for twenty-two years after the State of Tennessee was admitted into the Union. Kentucky had repeatedly memorialized Congress to get the Indian title removed from what she considered her portion of the Chickasaw Country, but nothing was done. Finally in 1818, after the death of General James Robertson, a memorial went to Congress from the Legislature of Tennessee and commissioners were appointed to negotiate the treaty. General Andrew Jackson of Tennessee and Isaac Shelby of Kentucky began

---

[32]*Ibid.,* 71.
[33]Nashville *Whig and Tennessee Advertiser,* December 12, 1818.
[34]*Ibid.*

negotiations. When the Chickasaws reported to Jackson that they had "no lands either to exchange or sell," he sent them back word that the "Citizens had been kept out of possession of those lands for thirty-odd years and individuals who had bought and paid for it demanded possession of this land, and their father the President will be compelled to give it to them . . . to take the land allowing the Indians such compensation for their *right of occupying their land as hunting grounds.*"[35] This treaty at Old Town of the Chickasaw, near Tuscumbia, Alabama, was an important one in the history of the Southwest —that land of opportunity in the first half of the nineteenth century. After twenty days of negotiations and even arguments between the leaders themselves, the treaty was signed on October 19, 1818. By this treaty, the Indians were to receive $300,000 in fifteen installments and personal gifts to sundry chiefs who kept the details of the negotiations secret, for they personally had profited at the hands of their tribesmen.[36]

The completion of the Jackson-Shelby treaty with the Chickasaws was the green light for speculators from North Carolina, East and Middle Tennessee, and South Carolina, some of whom were on the treaty grounds and were considered "the men concerned" from whom Jackson and Shelby borrowed the money to make a payment and thus seal the treaty, leaving no way for the Senate to reject it and thus shut the door of opportunity to these men of the West. Some of those on the treaty grounds returned home through the Western District and spoke "in raptures" of the country, adding that "the tide of emigration was set in that direction."[37] Surveyors like James Vaulx, Richard Hightower, and Henry Rutherford advertised

---

[35] Williams, *West Tennessee*, 86.

[36] *Ibid.*, 92-93. Some of the treaties with the Indians are spoken of as "heart-breaking treaties." Those land-hungry Americans wanted the land so badly that they found various excuses for trespassing upon lands and breaking treaties with the red man. James Malone was of this opinion for he thought that the chiefs and leaders understood the terms but that the average Indian was at the mercy of the white man. For example, the leaders knew what interest meant, but it was with the greatest difficulty that this could be explained to the rank and file of the Chickasaws in 1832. Finally the interpretor illustrated it as a hen laying eggs, explaining that one hundred dollars would lay six dollars each twelve months. Malone, *The Chickasaw Nation*, 325.

[37] *Ibid.*, 98.

that they had procured transcripts of old entries or already had them plotted and desired to locate grants for certain percentages of acreage, such as 600 out of each five thousand acres that Rutherford said he was charging.[38]

Rutherford addressed his communications "to the owners of the granted land warrants on the waters of the Wolfe, Forked Deer, Obion, Big Hatchie, Loosahatchie, Reel Foot, and Long Rivers." He had refreshed his memory by visits in 1811 and 1816, and therefore believed that his knowledge of "granted and vacant lands" superior to anyone living. He identified old surveys and prepared new entries on the shares, locating a 5,000 acre tract for 600 acres, a 1,000 acre tract for 125 acres. The report that much of the land in the district was well adapted to cotton set the speculators on fire.[39] By 1820, there were one hundred surveyors in the land and "Western District fever" was almost as bad as the California fever of the mid-century.

Surveyors, land speculators, adventurers, and home seekers rushed to this new land. A Nashville paper of 1820 carried a long article which furnished information to those persons desiring to explore the Western District. All the roads into the District went through Reynoldsburg. One went to the south connecting with the Natchez Trace and then the Chickasaw Trace. Houses of accommodation were found every five or ten miles along this one. Another route went to Colonel Dyer's on the North Forked Deer to Harris Bluff. Few settlements were along this route. Soon another route was to be opened up from Colonel Dyer's to the South Forked Deer. Only Rutherford's settlement was on this trace. The report upon the conditions in the West continued:

> The quality of the lands improve as you go from south to north. The Tennessee hills are miserably poor, afford some streams of pure water. From their base to the high hills that bound the margin of the Mississippi bottom, the soil is loose and fertile and the timber thin. The Mississippi hills rise high, have a rich soil, are heavily timbered and afford an abundance of pure water. The Obion and the Forked Deer are unequaled for navigation. Steam boats of the largest size can go

---

[38]*Ibid.*, 101.

[39]Nashville *Whig*, November 21, 1818, reprinted in Nashville *Banner*, February 29, 1939.

to their respective forks and boats carrying one hundred fifty barrels to their very sources at all seasons of the year. The Hatchie is navigable for seventy or eighty miles with keel boats. The Wolf is wide, shallow, and rapid, and affords only a winter and spring navigation. There are at present several modes of crossing these rivers—swimming, fording, log-rafts, and canoes—all these modes are adopted as convenience requires, for surveyors and speculators are stopped by no difficulties. Early in the spring there will be at all the places named, flats and ferries.[40]

The sturdy men of the day read such descriptions as this, made their plans, and went west when spring did come.

[40]Nashville *Gazette*, November 18, 1820.

CHAPTER III

THOSE EARLY YEARS

When spring came after the Chickasaw Treaty of late 1818, prospectors, surveyors, and settlers from North Carolina, South Carolina, Virginia, Middle and East Tennessee became a part of the westward march of civilization of the nineteenth century as they pushed into this land known as the "Jackson Purchase" or the "Western District." Countless letters to friends back East and stories of the cheap but rich lands in this newly opened-up country aroused the interest of the already land-hungry, adventurous Americans of that era and sent them scurrying into this "land of Canaan." Just a few of these glowing reports would convince a reader of to-day that it was time to leave the worn-out soil of the east and go west. Newspapers retold reports which certified that few sections of the west were as inviting as the Western District. In January 1819, Henry Rutherford, that surveyor of 1784, contradicted Calvin Jones's report that the lands were "indifferently timbered," adding that they were "beautifully clothed with great variety of beautiful timber, such as different kinds of oak, poplar, hickory, ash, elm, mulberry, walnut, beach, sugar, dogwood, papaw, and spice trees."[1] In the summer 1822, Archibald D. Murphey, jurist and historian of North Carolina, visited the Western District and sent back the following report:

> I have never seen such a beautiful country before, nor one where industry can be so well rewarded. There is a fertility in its poorest soil

---

[1] Nashville *Whig and Tennessee Advertiser*, January 16, 1819; Jackson *Gazette*, February 19, 1825. John Haywood, the early historian of Tennessee, wrote of these lands of the Western District: "In going from Jackson in the Western District of Tennessee and thence to Florence, near the Tennessee line, the alluvial land of the western district cannot fail to attract the attention of the traveler." John Haywood, *Natural and Aboriginal History of Tennessee up to the first Settlements there in by the White People in the Year 1768* (Nashville, 1823), (in commentaries).

that I have seen nowhere else. Except the swamps there is really no poor land, if we are to judge from its production; for on its poorest ridges I have seen six or eight barrels of corn or one thousand pounds of cotton in the ordinary crop. What is there called good land brings an average ten barrels of corn and thirteen hundred pounds of cotton to the acre. . . . I have traveled from the Kentucky line across the country to the South Forked Deer, and everywhere have seen beautiful lands, and fine crops. The soil is rich, black land, varying in depth from four to ten inches; then comes a good clay.[2]

Land! Land! Land! Those words are repeated so often in the newspapers and correspondence of those early days that it is almost like a chant from morning till night. Most of these would-be citizens of the new west came to the land to improve their living conditions by obtaining land at small prices and "growing up with the country." This territory near the geographical center of the Western District was a fair land, a favored land—a gradually sloped plateau through which wended the Hatchie and the Forked Deer rivers. It was literally a forest primeval, untouched by the woodman's axe, inhabited by beasts of the forest, fowls of the air, and fish of the stream. Innumerable springs, rich sandy soil, long summers and short winters, an abundance of timber and game, and streams that were navigable for small flat-boats and keel-boats—all this free from the fear of the Indians—were points of attraction to these new lands. It was a land of promise and adventure. The disadvantages such as the frightful howl of the wolf, the sharp startling screams of the panthers, the unmistakable track of the bear were regular experiences of this man of the new west, a courageous, expert rifleman whose wants were simple and whose loyalty to his friends was undying. In 1820, Herndon Haralson wrote that "thousands of people will move to the District this fall and winter. There are as yet no counties laid out, neither will there be until after the next session of the Legislature in September 1821."[3]

Part of the incoming population spread out like a wave on ruffled waters approaching from the east and the rest came down the Ohio and Mississippi rivers and up the Forked Deer

---

[2] Archibald Murphy to Thomas Ruffin, *Murphy Papers*, I, 245.
[3] Williams, *West Tennessee*, 135, quoting Haralson to Judge Murphy. Evidently Haralson overlooked old Hardin County which was erected by an act of November 13, 1819.

or Hatchie. James Caruthers and William E. Butler, with several other men, came on a keel-boat on a prospecting tour in 1819. Caruthers was commissioned to locate some land warrants for the University of North Carolina, a job which he was most capable of performing.[4] Samuel Dickens, Sugars McLemore, John McLemore, and Memucan Hunt Howard formed a partnership (1822) to locate land warrants and they located something over 330,000 acres and received pay by taking a percentage of those located, usually one-sixth. John McLemore and James Vaulx, both surveyors, were on their way to this district when negotiations with the Chickasaws were then in progress and they did not know that they had been completed until they reached a point near the Bluff City.[5] Colonel Thomas Henderson had been authorized to procure proof of the University of North Carolina's claims to lands escheated to the University—warrants that had been issued to Revolutionary soldiers who died leaving no heirs to claim the lands. Hunt and Dickens located 300,000 or 400,000 acres and Henderson paid Hunt $400 a year and a per cent of the land,[6] in fact he agreed to look after the escheated lands and for his services he was to receive one half the land. All these men had dreams of riches; some realized the dreams. Judge Archibald Murphy, attorney for the University of North Carolina, saw prospects of individual wealth adding "that Col. William Polk, Col. Thomas Henderson, Samuel Dickens, John McLemore and

---

[4] James Caruthers, an outstanding civic-minded person, is associated with the growth of the young community. At the time of his death in 1863, R. H. Cartmell wrote a beautiful tribute to him in his diary: "When I say he was one of the purest men living I do not say too much. No man possessed a more delicate feeling of honor, liberal in his own views, kind, benevolent, possessing all those qualities ennobling man universally beloved and respected. We feel sad that such men leave earth when their example only promotes the cause of virtue and religion. Many times have I been at his house in my school days." Robert H. Cartmell Diary, MS.

[5] "Recollections of Memucan Hunt Howard," *American Historical Magazine*, VII (1902), 60; "Reminiscences of Memphis" in *Old Folks Recollections*, 403. Samuel Dickens advertised land for sale "on all rivers of the Western District," Jackson *The Pioneer*, September 9, 1823.

[6] "Recollections of Memucan Hunt Howard," *American Historical Magazine* (1902), VII, 58-60; Williams, *West Tennessee*, 110-111.

Gen. Bryan owned about as much as either of them could desire."[7]

In the early part of the nineteenth century, land was the most attractive place to invest a surplus capital. When a new section of the country was opened up people from the older sections bought lands. Some migrated to the new lands, some resold at a profit, and many seemingly had so much or so lost interest that the land was sold for taxes. It is difficult for us to realize to-day the large quantities of land that these men were dealing with without considering many of the entries in the deed books, the lists of unpaid taxes in the county records and the newspapers. Samuel Dickens, a former member of the North Carolina Legislature and Congressman from that state, was a most astute, vigilant and dependable agent for the University of North Carolina. His name was connected with innumerable transfers of land in large parcels. The following names and acreage from unpaid tax lists illustrate the interest in land sales by men from other parts of the state and the size of the purchases:

Martin Armstrong	1,860 acres	A. D. Murphy	4,350 acres
William Blount	1,500 acres	Benjamin Smith	47,000 acres
Hugh Dunlap	10,000 acres	John Rutherford	1,100 acres
Jesse Benton	5,000 acres	Jetton Summer	1,800 acres
A. D. Murphy	6,000 acres	William Pillow	3,400 acres
James Robertson	1,500 acres	Jacob Harris	5,000 acres
James Robertson	1,000 acres	Martin Armstrong	25,000 acres[8]
Calvin Jones	3,580 acres		

In 1819, the first settlement in what was to be Madison County was made in the Cotton Gin Grove community about eight miles from Jackson by John Hargrove, Roderick and Duncan McIver and their families.[9] Later in the same year John

---

[7] Williams, *West Tennessee*, 111. Colonel Thomas Henderson, former editor and publisher of the *Raleigh Star*, as a representative of the University of North Carolina removed to Madison County in the early 1820's and made his home near Pinson. The University of North Carolina received 147,853 acres of land surveyed by Henderson and his sub-agents, who also received the same number of acres.

[8] Madison County Minute Book 1821-1825: Deed Book 1821-1825: Jackson *Gazette*, July 31, 1824.

[9] J. G. Cisco, "Madison County," *American Historical Magazine*, VII (1902), 334.

Bradberry settled near Spring Creek and Seth O. Waddell settled in the old sixteenth district. The following year Adam R. Alexander, James Porter, James Brown, and William Doak (later moving to Spring Creek) made a third settlement on the Forked Deer about two miles west of Jackson. A fine spring and an abundance of timber had attracted these settlers. The home of Adam Alexander, a surveyor of the United States range survey and registrar of the Land Office of this section, became known with the surrounding settlement as Alexandria.[10] Thomas Shannon, Herndon Haralson and others came to the county before its organization.

Good cheap lands that could be had almost for the asking upon payment of 50c an acre and a surveyor's and registration fee, low taxes (12½c for every 100 acres in 1821), 25c poll tax which could be paid in squirrel or crow scalps as these were pests, all lured the people to the west so rapidly that the counties of Hardin, Humphreys and Shelby were created by the Assembly of 1819 and Carroll, Henderson, and Madison were created by that of 1821.

For purposes legal, the Western District had been under the control of Montgomery County from November 14, 1801, until November 1, 1803, when it became a part of the new county of Stewart.[11] On November 7, 1821, by an act of the Assembly, the counties of Carroll, Henderson, and Madison were formed. The act, so far as it affected Madison County, provided for the administration of justice in the court of Pleas and Quarter Sessions which was to be held in the home of Adam Alexander, field officers of the militia should be elected, and the bounds of the county defined as follows:

> Be it enacted, that all the territory included in the lines hereafter mentioned shall constitute a country to be called and known by the name of Madison county; Beginning two miles and a half south of N.E. corner of range 2 section 11 in the 9th district, running thence west

---

[10]"There were five surveyor's districts and offices opened: one where Lexington, Henderson County stands; one a mile or two below Jackson; one on the bluff; one at McLemoresville, Carroll County; one at Col. Dyer's eight or ten miles north of Jackson." "Recollections of Memucan Hunt Howard," *American Historical Magazine*, VII (1902), 59.

[11]Henry D. Whitney, *Land Laws of Tennessee* (Cincinnati, 1893), 695, quoting *Acts of Tennessee*, 1803.

parallel with the sectional line to the 3rd range line to a point two miles and a half south of the sixth sectional line in said district; thence east parallel with said section line to the second range line in the 9th district; thence north on said range line to the beginning.[12]

The county above described was in the form of a perfect square with each side twenty-five miles in length, giving an area of six hundred twenty-five square miles; and was located in both the Ninth and Tenth Surveyor's Districts of the State. The territorial bounds were subsequently changed by the creation of Crockett County in 1871 and Chester County in 1879. The same legislative enactment that created Madison County, also established the territorial bounds of several counties to be organized and named subsequently; and, over the territory so laid off for two counties (later organized and named Haywood County and Hardeman County) it was provided that such territory was to remain a part of Madison County, and the inhabitants of this attached territory were to enjoy all the privileges and be subject to all the duties as citizens of Madison County, with this exception, that no tax should be laid or collected within the attached territory for the purpose of erecting public buildings in Madison County. In the territory laid off for a new county (later organized and named Dyer County) which by legislative act of 1821 was attached to Carroll County, was in 1822 attached to Madison County for jurisdictional purposes; it being enacted by the Legislature of Tennessee, that all process theretofore or thereafter issued by the County Court or Circuit Court of Carroll County should become returnable to the County Court or Circuit Court of Madison County as the case might be.[13] Failing to distinguish between the territorial bounds of Madison County, and the jurisdiction given to the court functioning within that county, an early mapmaker showed the Mississippi River as being the western boundary of Madison County, which was not the fact. The Mississippi State line was the southern boundary for the time between the organization of Madison and the organization of Hardeman, but at no time was the Mississippi River the boundary of the county. That the county court of Madison dealt with affairs in this at-

---

[12] *Acts of Tennessee*, Chapter 32, Sec. 5, 1821.
[13] *Ibid.; Acts of Tennessee*, Chapters 108, 145, 1823, *Acts of Tennessee*, Chapter 199, 1822.

tached territory is shown by the fact that election places were placed at Henry Rutherford's Key corner (Lauderdale County) and Thomas McNeal's a mile north of the present town of Bolivar; that rights were granted to Thomas Hardeman to build a water mill on Pleasant Run (three miles west of Bolivar); that rights were granted in 1822 to Colonel John Murray to establish a ferry on Hatchie River near Bolivar.[14] Madison County courts conducted this business.

According to that act of the Legislature of 1821 establishing the county, a court of Pleas and Quarter Sessions was organized by the justices of the peace appointed by Governor William Carroll for that purpose.[15] These men elected Herndon Haralson, chairman;[16] Thomas Shannon, sheriff; Roderick McIver, clerk; John T. Porter, registrar; James Brown, ranger; William Atchinson, trustee; William Griffith, coroner. This first meeting was held at Alexander's land office, the home of Adam Alexander, a two room log house, well-daubed with mud and two dirt and stick chimneys on east and west ends. Court records indicate that business was conducted at Alexandria until September 17, 1822, at which time the new log court house at Jackson was ready for use. The business of this early court included the selection of voting places; the granting of mill rights which would not interfere with the navigation of the river; the granting of ferry rights and the setting of toll rates; the opening of roads, such as the one from the court house by way of the Forked Deer post office to Frances Taylor's mill; the appointing of hands to work the roads; the allowing of money for bridges; the granting of right to operate an ordinary as the saloons were then called;[17] the allowing of from $2 to $3 for the killing of a wolf; the recording of "stock marks"; and the making of plans for the permanent location of the seat of justice for the county.

---

[14]Madison County Minute Book 1821-1825.

[15]Members of this court were: Bartholemew G. Stewart, David Jarrett, William Atchison, Robert H. Dyer, John Thomas, Adam R. Alexander, Duncan McIver, Joseph Lynn, James Trousdale, H. Haralson, William Braden, Samuel Taylor, William W. Woodfork.

[16]An autobiography of the colorful character, Herndon Haralson, may be found published in a later chapter in this volume.

[17]Thomas Shannon, Robert Dyer, and John Reden received such a license on June 17, 1822. Minute Book 1821-1825.

N.B. the 16 Lots that front the Square are 105 feet 9 inch in length and 51 feet 10½ inch wide the whole of the other Lots are 103 feet 9 inch Square Except the 10 Lots that form the South boundary of the Town which is 127 feet 9 inch by 103 feet 9 inch the Streets are 90 feet wide and the Allys 20 feet Except the back ally which is 22½ feet on 3 sides and the ally on the South boundary is 33 feet broad. Lott No 54 is Reserved for the Prepaid—

Plan of Town of Alexandria found in Madison County Court Records.

By an act of the Legislature of November 16, 1821, Sterling Brewer, Speaker of the Senate, James Fentress, Speaker of the House, and Adam Murray were appointed to "fix on a place" for the county seat, procure the land by purchase or otherwise and appoint five commissioners to "cause to be laid off in their respective counties with necessary streets at least 90 feet wide, reserving at least four acres for a public square on which shall be built a court house and stocks, also reserving a public lot sufficient to contain a jail."[18] They were to sell lots at public sale on one year's credit—the money being used to purchase land, build the court house, prison and stocks. Deeds dated April 9, 1822, show that John McNairy, Joseph Phillips, and William E. Butler conveyed 30 acres and 18 poles to Sterling Brewer and James Fentress and that Thomas Shannon conveyed three lots containing an aggregate of 24 acres and 111 poles to the same officials. These two tracts of land adjoined and were platted together and land sales began on August 1 and 2, 1822, and continued for about a week.[19] According to tradition Joseph Lynn was allowed $20 for whiskey to encourage the bidding. Prices ranged from $31 to $503 for each lot. An aggregate sum of $19,202 was realized from the sale of one hundred and four lots.

By an act of the Legislature of August 17, 1822, the name of the seat of justice was changed from Alexandria to Jackson, commissioners were appointed to pass necessary laws and use any money left to erect a church and purchase a grave yard.[20]

---

[18]*Acts of Tennessee,* 1821, p. 194.

[19]Butler and his associates donated this land but reserved a lot for each in the sale of town lots. The commissioners purchased the Shannon land at $10 per acre and Shannon reserved a choice lot. Goodspeed, *History of Tennessee* (Madison County edition, 1887), 808. The report by Brewer and Fentress to Legislature read: "Your Commissioners then repaired to Madison County and fixed the site of the County Seat on the land of Shannon and Butler who made a donation of fifty acres and your Commissioners purchased —— acres." MSS, Legislative Petitions, Box 129, Tennessee State Archives, Nashville, Tennessee.

[20]"That the town heretofore laid off for the seat of justice in the county of Madison, by the name of Alexandria, shall be known and distinguished by the name of Jackson and that Stokley D. Hays, Wm. E. Butler, Herndon Haralson, Vincent Haralson, William Stoddert, David Harton, William Arnold, Adam Huntsman are hereby appointed commissioners for the town of Jackson in addition to the commissioners

According to tradition, as well as to an account by Captain Thomas M. Gates (who came here with his father about 1840), there were three sites considered for the seat of justice—one the community that had grown up about the land office of Adam Alexander, the second Golden Station which was a couple miles south of the land office, and the Butler farm. The present location on the lands of Butler and Shannon was thought to have been chosen because of the fact that it was nearer the Cotton Grove Community, which was of considerable size for this section at that time.[21] Tradition says that Alexandria was on the Forked Deer, southwest of Jackson on the property of the present University of Tennessee Experiment Station of the Department of Agriculture; the act of the Legislature and a "Plan of the town of Alexandria," just recently located, show that it was where the city now stands. Street names have been changed, such as Butler to Main, Huntsman to Lafayette, Haralson to Baltimore, Hays to Liberty, Cumberland and College streets were listed as alleys.

Within two years the log court house, built on the northeast corner of the square with a dirt floor, judges bench and door of hewn puncheon, and a chimney of sticks and mud (total cost $135) was replaced by a brick one two stories high.[22] Here was a thriving community which could boast of a newspaper, *The Pioneer,* founded just a few months after the town was laid out and followed by the *Gazette;* of a $95 jail erected by Thomas Shannon in 1822; of a Jackson Male and Jackson Female Academy; of ordinaries and "houses of entertainment" such as the Bell Tavern and the Jackson Inn; of a postmaster Samuel Taylor who was operating a post office from his own home and promised regular eastward weekly mail; of a board of Commissioners with Herndon Haralson, chairman, who had drawn up an excellent code of laws for the community which was trying to preserve good order in the new town; of a Methodist (1826) and a Presbyterian (1823) church; of a

---

appointed by the County Court of Madison." *Acts of Tennessee,* 1822, chapter 99.

[21] T. M. Gates's Scrap Book used through the courtesy of his grandson, Charles McMillan.

[22] This was replaced by a still larger one in 1839, which cost $25,000. Goodspeed, *Tennessee,* 807-808; J. G. Cisco, "Madison County," *American Historical Magazine,* VII, 342; VIII, 26.

Masonic Lodge; of a court of Law and Equity for the Eighth District presided over by Judge Joshua Haskell; of Dr. Bedford and Dr. Childress's shops that could furnish medicines suitable to the climate; of the Perkins and Deaderick book and drug store; of Moses Priest, the cabinet maker who had all kinds of material on hand; of Robert Davis, the saddle, harness, and trunk maker; of Robert Murray and Armour and Lake, the commission merchants who were ready to ship cotton to the markets in New Orleans in their two keel-boats; of the twenty-two lawyers who had started practicing here within the first five years of the town's existence.[23] Those first laws of the frontier town give a very real picture of the problems of such a community. On the second day of January, 1823, the Board of Commissioners passed the following laws:

1. Any person or persons found guilty of disorderly or riotous conduct within the limits of the Corporation shall forfeit and pay $5.

2. Any person or persons, putting, or attempting to put any stud horse or Jack to a Mare or exhibiting the same to public square or streets or alleys of the Town shall for each offence forfeit and pay $5.

3. All Pedlars and Showmen shall before they proceed to sell or exhibit, as the case may be, pay $10 license to do so which shall be good for the month, at the expiration of which time said license must be renewed at the rates of $10 pr. month so long as they may continue to sell, exhibit, in the Town of Jackson—and an failure to procure said license as aforesaid, they and each of them shall forfeit and pay $50, for each offence.

4. Any person or persons who shall run a horse race or run a horse at full speed within the incorporated limits of said town, shall forfeit and pay the sum of $20 for each offence.

5. Any person or persons who shall shoot a Gun or Pistol within the said Town, shall forfeit and pay the sum of $20 for each offence.

6. Any person or persons who shall be found guilty of the mischievious and dangerous practice of fastening matches or other combustible sustances to dogs or other animals, within said Town—shall forfeit and pay $5 for each offence.

7. It shall hereafter be the duty of Merchants and every other person who may wish to retail Goods, Wares, or Merchandise within said Town, to procure a license first; which shall be good and sufficient for the term of one year from and after the date thereof. Provided

---

[23]Madison County Minute Books 1821-1825; Jackson *Pioneer*, January 28, 1823; Jackson *Gazette*, July 24, December 12, 1824; May 29, June 19, 1824.

PLAN OF TOWN OF JACKSON

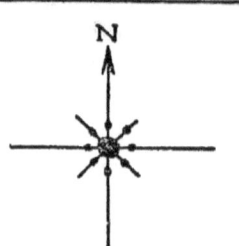

By deed dated April 9, 1822, John McNairy, Joseph Phillips, and William E. Butler conveyed 30 acres and 18 poles by deed to Sterling Brewer and James Fentress, Commissioners by Act of General Assembly, to establish permanent seat of justice, and on the same day Thomas Shannon conveyed three lots containing 19 acres 22 poles, 2 acres 2 poles, 3 acres 89 poles, to the same commissioners. These lands were platted together and 104 lots were sold August 1 and 2 and a few days following, for $19,202.

#100 S. H. Shannon $190.00	#101 L. Shannon $120.00		#102 C. C. Collins $160.00	#103 G. H. Gibson $60.00
#99 J. D. Shannon $201.00	#65 Thos. Jones $170.00		#66 W. Arnold $200.00	#67 D. Fields $251.00
#98 A. Wilson $142.00	#64 Wilson McEemore $200.00		#38 W. F. Dillon $201.00	#39 M. Fisher $300.00
#97 W. Williams $218.00	#63 L. B. Anderson $200.00		#37 A. F. Gray $207.00	#17 Thos. Shannon (Reserve)
#96 W. Muden $200.00	#62 Jos. Davis $206.00	STREET	#36 V. & H. Henderson $307.00	#16 V. & H. Henderson $503.00 / #15 W. J. Hess $375.00
#95 C. Harber $108.00	#61 Jas. Cloud $195.00	LIBERTY	#35 Benj. Gohlston $276.00	#14 A. Greer $358.00 / #13 B. Gohlston $400.00
#94 J. Ridings $80.00	#60 Rob Sevier $157.00		#34 D. McIver $200.00	#12 D. McIver $402.00
#93 J. Riding $54.00	#59 W. Espey $69.00		#33 A. Greer $117.00	#32 Alex Greer $250.00
#92 J. Welch $41.00	#58 Jno. Harrison $40.00		#57 David Thomas $53.00	#56 Lounder Smith $75.00
#91 A. Hays $35.00	#90 J. G. Caruthers $35.00		#89 O. B. Hays $40.00	#88 L. B. Anderson $31.00

[GE] STREET / [COLLEGE STREET]

| #104 W. Williamson $307⁰⁰ | #69 Thos. Shannon $330⁰⁰ | | #70 Jno. McLemore $303⁰⁰ | #76 A. Wynn $277⁰⁰ | | #72 Taylor $250⁰⁰ | #73 Saml Shelon $250⁰⁰ |
| #68 R. H. Dyer $304⁰⁰ | #41 Jno. McLemore $304⁰⁰ | | #42 D. Thomas $354⁰⁰ | #43 J. Riding $300⁰⁰ | | #44 Stoddert & McIver $200⁰⁰ | #74 Stoddert & McIver $200⁰⁰ |

[ETTE] STREET

| #40 J. Greer $304⁰⁰ | #21 J. Hutchinson $406⁰⁰ | | #22 W. H. Prewitt $330⁰⁰ | #23 J. F. Cloud $130⁰⁰ | | #45 W. R. Hess $162⁰⁰ | #75 J. Hicks $141⁰⁰ |
| #18 W. C. Butler $450⁰⁰ / #19 D. Marton $400⁰⁰ | #20 M. H. Prewitt $400⁰⁰ / J. Hutchinson $500⁰⁰ | | #2 W. E. Butler (Reserve) | #24 J. C. Butler $310⁰⁰ | | #46 A. Greer $160⁰⁰ | #76 R. Wilson |

STREET

PUBLIC SQUARE			#3 B. L. Coob $412⁰⁰	#25 B. L. Coob $250⁰⁰		#47 W. R. Hess $100⁰⁰	#77 S. J. Hays $75⁰⁰
			#4 B. L. Coob $280⁰⁰				
			#5 Jas. Cook $210⁰⁰	#26 Jas. Moore $176⁰⁰		#48 J. McKnight $85⁰⁰	#78 J. S. Collins $65⁰⁰
			#6 J. Cary $300⁰⁰				

[RY] STREET / [LIBERTY STREET]

| #11 Al. Fry $250⁰⁰ / #10 J. Greer $201⁰⁰ | #9 J. Greer $195⁰⁰ / #8 J. Greer $211⁰⁰ | | #7 Jas. K. Polk & J. Brown $325⁰⁰ | #27 Jas. K. Polk & J. Brown $100⁰⁰ | | #49 Jno. Harrison $106⁰⁰ | #79 A. Greer $54⁰⁰ |
| #31 Jas. Greer $166⁰⁰ | #30 Jas. Greer $139⁰⁰ | | #29 Jas. K. Polk & J. Brown $157⁰⁰ | #28 W. Espy $77⁰⁰ | | #50 W. R. Hess $60⁰⁰ | #80 S. F. Crofton $51⁰⁰ |

[TER] STREET

| #55 J. P. Thomas $56⁰⁰ | #54 Jail Lot | | #53 J. Riding $41⁰⁰ | #52 J. Wilson $50⁰⁰ | | #51 S. H. Thomas $44⁰⁰ | #81 J. Shannon $41⁰⁰ |
| #87 O. B. Hays $40⁰⁰ | #86 L. B. Anderson $31⁰⁰ | | #85 L. B. Anderson $33⁰⁰ | #84 L. B. Anderson $41⁰⁰ | | #83 W. Brown $41⁰⁰ | #82 A. F. Gray $57ᵈᵈ |

nevertheless, that no Merchant or other person shall be entitled to receive such license without previously paying into the hands of the proper officer the sum of $12.50 and every Merchant or other person who shall violate this law shall forfeit and pay the sum of $25.

8. No person or persons shall retail Spirituous Liquors within said Town without first procuring a license from the proper authority which said license shall be good and sufficient authority to such persons or persons for the term of one year. Provided nevertheless, that no person shall be entitled to receive said license without first paying twelve dollars and fifty cents. And any person selling or retailing spirituous Liquors without a license shall forfeit and pay $25.

9. Each lot in the Town of Jackson is hereby subjected to an annual tax of one half per centum ad valorem, agreebly to the original price given for said Lot—to be collected by the Town Constable for the present year so soon as practicable.

10. Any person or persons who shall be found guilty of playing cards, Dice, or any other game of Hazard or address within the incorporated limit of said town shall forfeit and pay $10 for each offence.

11. Any Inn or Tavern Keeper or Keepers of any Ordinary who shall suffer any game of Hazard or Address to be played in their house or houses shall forfeit and pay $25 for each offence.

12. It shall be the duty of the Town Constable from time to time to cause to be removed all nuisances from said Town. The expense of which shall be charged to the person or persons who may have caused or erected the same, for which services the Board of Commissioners shall make the said Constable a reasonable allowance.

13. It shall be the duty of the Town Constable to preserve good order during Public Worship in said town. And to take notice of any person or persons who may disturb those so worshipping.

14. It shall be the duty of the secretary of said Board of Commissioners to issue license to any person applying for the same. Provided said person may be entitled to the same by the authority of the foregoing BY-LAWS and for every license so issued the said Secretary shall be entitled to receive the sum of Fifty cents, from the person applying for the same.

H. HARALSON
Chairman of the Board

W. Arnold
Sec. Pro. Tem.[24]

These early settlers clad in homespun with seats and knees padded with buck-skins blazed the way into a trackless wilderness. They brought with them a year's supply of those things

---

[24]Jackson *Pioneer*, January 28, 1823.

which made living semi-comfortable—coffee, tea, rice, sugar, flour, medicines, cards, cotton, spinning wheels, seeds, farm implements, powder, lead, milk cows, and hogs.[25] The Indians had explained when questioned by the white man that they had not made permanent homes in West Tennessee because "it leaked too much." This fact, however, did not seriously deter that early frontiersman, for after the first settlement, a real boom was on according to accounts in the local papers, the papers of Middle and East Tennessee, and those of North Carolina. A Knoxville paper of 1825 mentioned the fact that four or five thousand carts, wagons, and carriages were passing to the West. "It is not uncommon to see eight, ten, and fifteen wagons passing in a single day . . . wending their way to the more highly favored climes of the West," stated the *Carolinian* in 1821, while the Jackson *Gazette* spoke of their arrival. "We learn that a vast number of families are preparing to emigrate from North Carolina to the Western District. We hail them welcome." In 1825, Judge A. D. Murphy wrote that "there are nearly one hundred families in Orange, Chatham, Davidson, and Rowan Counties who are moving to the Chickasaw Purchase this fall. The emigration is astonishing." His son added two years later: "The Western District begins to assume the appearance of a civilized and thickly settled country. There are several considerable towns in it. The crops are excellent."[26]

The editor of the Jackson *Gazette* noted the tide of immigration in 1824 thus: "Immigration to the Western District is rapid beyond expectation, of the most sanguineous and of a character highly respectable and valuable." In 1825 he wrote: "Few sections invite emigrants equal to the Western District. In many instances of from twelve to fifteen hundred weight of fine quality cotton can be grown. Lands can be bought for less than their value because of the scarcity of money."[27] When James Deaderick was visiting this country in 1826, he was most favorably impressed with what he saw:

---

[25] Joseph S. Williams, *Old Times in West Tennessee* (Memphis, 1873), 8-9, hereinafter cites as *Old Times*.

[26] Jackson *Gazette*, September 7, 1828; Murphy Papers, North Carolina Archives; Williams, *West Tennessee*, 117. Inscriptions on tomb stones in the Riverside Cemetery in Jackson show that many of the early inhabitants came from states mentioned.

[27] Jackson *Gazette*, December 4, 1824, February 19, 1825.

The appearance of the western district is in the summer season very beautiful. Almost the whole country is covered with luxuriant grass, on which the cattle of the country subsist without food. No undergrowth except the grass is seen in many parts, which gives the appearance of rich and beautiful meadows. The grass soon disappears when the country is much tramped and grazed; about Bolivar it has already been eaten out. This district has a soil very congenial to cotton, but contains so much sand that I fear the soil will soon be exhausted under the management which is common in that counrty. Corn and cotton usually succeed each other, and I doubt whether any crop will be in general use which will be ameliorating and enriching to the soil.[28]

The *Southern Statesman* reported considerable growth of the community during the year 1832; both in population and in wealth:

We have no given data by which we can, with any degree of accuracy, ascertain the number of souls which have been added to our population, by emigration within the above named period, but we think Madison County has augmented upwards one thousand.[29]

There is a question as to whether the people wrote glowing reports to attract other people or whether this was really a land of unexcelled opportunity and the people came in large numbers. By and large, it was good propaganda, for the population increased from 675 in 1830 to nearly 900 in 1833[30] In all the papers there was located only one unfavorable tale of this section and this one was told by a visitor who came from the other side of the mountains. The hardships of Tennessee were too much for Sarah Henrietta Fitzhugh when she came to visit her brother in Bolivar in 1830, but her view should be considered

---

[28] A typed copy of the Deaderick manuscript used through the courtesy of Roy Black of Bolivar, Tennessee.

[29] Jackson *Southern Statesman,* March 17, 1832.

[30] In 1833 and 1835 John Holden, a school teacher, wrote of his school of 35 pupils north of the city. He was paid $225 a year, boarded for $4 a month. He described the town as a place of business and resort: "The buildings are mostly of brick constructed with taste and neatly arranged and is a very handsome and pleasant town." He boarded with William E. Long, a wealthy farmer and highly respectable citizen, who lived six miles west of Jackson. Long had an orchard, vegetables, many acres of cotton and corn. "Land is perhaps higher in this county than any other in the district. . . . Cotton sells for 2 and 2½ cents per pound." The original letters could not be located, but copies came from an old scrap book.

in order that a reader may draw his own conclusions. This visitor to West Tennessee had been used to better accommodations on the other side of the mountains. Her trip "through the country" was a difficult one. The coarse fare of the taverns, the "indifferent," crude open house, the high prices of taverns, the difficult fords of the streams that became swollen with the least rain were all very irritating to the traveler who kept a daily account of this long journey. She thought that this was a "money-making" country, where the people cared little for the comforts of life. "You seldom meet with a close home unless it is owned by a Dutchman. They say a tight house is not considered healthy," wrote Mrs. Fitzhugh. Twice during

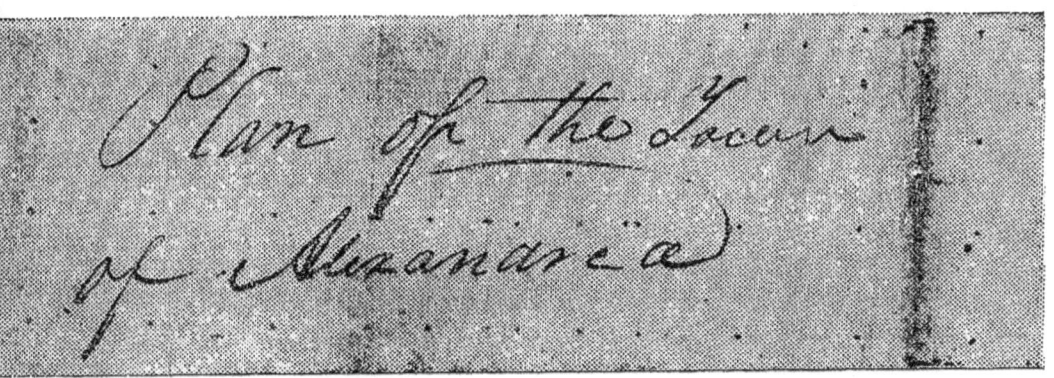

Memorandum on back of map of Alexandria, page 36.

the journey, her crinolines in the bags in the back of the gig got wet when the ford was very difficult and the rest of the day was spent trying to dry them out. The travelers were averaging twenty miles per day on this trip.

Henrietta Fitzhugh painted a fascinating word picture of the people, the country, and the towns in 1830. Two excerpts from her diary are more real than any rewritten account:

Oh woeful! woeful! It has been raining all night and all the morning, and to be confined to one of those Tennessee taverns where there is no resource whatever against *ennue* is more dreadful than any of you can imagine. There are good tempered kind people enough, but extremely ignorant and not a book in the house; they are quite rich although no one would suppose it from the appearances around, for with us they would not pass for comfortably fixed, and they live exceedingly coarse and dirty. A miserable bed, but I have written so many Phillippics against the lodging in that it was a *Tennessee bed*.

They seem to think of nothing in the world but accumulating wealth, and it really seems to avail them little. This man is living on extremely rich land with scarcely a comfort around him, his house an open half-finished log barn, he is a lazy opiniated red-faced fellow, who twists his legs around the porch bench, barbecues the King's English and sets up to entertain his customers with a dish of politics and leaves all the work for his wife to do. I am this long-winded in my description of all the Tennessee Tavern Keepers because it answers the description of all the Tennessee Tavern keepers I have seen. I could not help smiling at a remark made by the Hostess, a fat good humored Dame. She observed to me: "You had better persuade your husband not to move to this country." "Why?" "Because all the men become lazy, they set down all day long and talk of accumulating wealth and leave all the work for the women to do. They will promise to fix so wonderfully well, but never get beyond the 'halfbuilt log house'."

After the party crossed the Tennessee River the writer of the diary continued in her journal:

It will be scarcely believed when I say I have never seen so poor a country in my life; it cannot support a population and the inhabitants on the road live by fleecing poor travelers. But they tell us the road passes over the worst part of the country. That may be, but Providence has been very good to make this poor ridge so very straight to suit travelers. Arrived at night at a very decent house kept by Williamson on the North Fork of the Forked Deer, about sixteen miles from Jackson. I omitted mentioning the different counties we have passed through since we crossed the Tennessee River because they are remarkable for nothing, but sterility, bad accommodations, high hills and sickly mean looking people. We did not pass through any of the towns. We came through Humphreys, Carroll, and I am now in Madison; our most direct road would be by Lexington, the county town of Henderson, but the road is bad and indifferent and difficult to find and we prefer making an angle by Jackson. . . . The clouds look rather threatening after a very cold night and a hard frost; the road very fine, and the country much more interesting than any we have come through; more thickly settled. And as Charles (one of the black boys) says: "Gentle-folks houses." Some of very large cotton and corn fields. Passed through Jackson, the county town of Madison. We were very disappointed in the appearance of the town, as we expected to see a very flourishing place, from the accounts we have heard of it back home. We ate our dinner on the Forked Deer, after crossing it on a bridge about a mile south of Jackson.[31]

---

[31]Unpublished Diary of Henrietta Fitzhugh 1830, used through the courtesy of Roy Black.

Frequent references in the Nashville papers of the splendid quality of cotton and corn that was raised in large quantities in the new west explained why a veritable cavalcade of emigrants was being attracted to the District. The older sections in the east were actually distressed over the depopulation of the country by the best citizens and implored them to stay at home and improve the soil with manure rather than be lured to the west.[32] The editor of the *National Banner and Nashville Whig* told of fine cotton lands which were cheap, of a place to invest money, of a community blessed with navigable rivers upon which fruits and flour from Ohio and Pennsylvania were arriving daily. Another story of 1833 told of the good transportation facilities, of the roads which were considered excellent, of the healthy country in which the doctors would testify that if a person had ague or fever he had caught it in Middle Tennessee, of the people who were wealthy, intelligent, respectable, polite, and hospitable. Still another story enlarged upon the idea of the good cheap lands that could be bought for two to three dollars an acre, as fertile as the most highly favored spots in the old country and all this in a refined community with excellent opportunities for education and unlimited facilities for the exportation of the staple crop, adding that "those who may be disposed to charge us with extravagance in our remarks are invited to come and judge for themselves."[33] And many did come who judged for themselves and found things attractive enough to stay. By and large, the people were so enthusiastic about this "far west," a real land of Canaan, that they believed the "Star of the Empire had taken its course westward and already the great valley of the Mississippi, the Egypt of America, had become the heart of the United States."[34]

---

[32]*Southern Statesman*, April 28, 1832, quoting a Raleigh, North Carolina, paper; Williams, *West Tennessee*, 117, citing Raleigh *Register*, January 29, 1819.

[33]*National Banner and Nashville Whig*, September 30, 1826; Nashville *Republican and State Gazette*, September 3, 1833.

[34]Horace Polk to Dr. Richard Haywood, Bolivar, Tennessee, June 12, 1846, "Personal Letters," *Tennessee Historical Magazine*, IX (1925-1926), 79.

CHAPTER IV

NOTABLE MEN OF THE EARLY NINETEENTH
CENTURY

Many leaders of the community are mentioned in the story of the business and professional life of the community in other places in this volume, but the writer felt that the narrative should be interrupted long enough to mention a few colorful characters of those early years. An account of the beginning of the town of Jackson would be most inadequate without a short biography of the man who donated part of the land upon which the town was located and who was closely identified with all the public and private enterprises of Jackson—Dr. William Edward Butler, the man who has been justly styled the "father of Jackson."[1]

William Edward Butler (1789-1882), the son of a Revolutionary soldier, was born in Carlyle, Pennsylvania, graduated in medicine at the University of Pennsylvania before he removed to Murfreesboro, Tennessee. Here in 1813 he married Martha (Patsy) Thompson Hays, a niece of Mrs. Andrew Jackson. During the War of 1812, Dr. Butler enlisted on the staff of Colonel Thomas Hart Benton of the Second Regiment of Infantry under General Andrew Jackson, and accompanied the units to the scene of the great battle of New Orleans on keelboats which floated down the Mississippi. Dr. Butler went with Jackson to quiet the Indians after the massacre at Ft. Mimms and accompanied him again to the First Seminole War in 1818.

With Butler's brother Robert as secretary for the Commission signing the Chickasaw Treaty of 1818 and Andrew Jackson

---

[1]Most of the material for this sketch was taken from a paper read by Seale Johnson before the Madison County Historical Society on September, 1943. His material had been gathered from Cisco's *History of Madison County, The Life of David Crockett* by Himself, interviews with older citizens in the county, Madison County Court records, and Goodspeed's *History of Tennessee*.

one of the chief diplomats, Butler had a good chance to get in on the ground floor in the land grants of the District. Although the Indians had two years to evacuate, many prospectors such as Butler, Dickens, Henderson, Alexander, Caruthers, and the Shannons came "prospecting." William E. Butler came in 1819, returned to Middle Tennessee, became interested in the land sales of Memphis in 1820, serving as one of the agents for the sale of land at that place, but he decided that the land in the center of the Western District was more to his liking. Thus, in 1821, Dr. Butler loaded his family and furniture on a flat-boat, floated down the Cumberland, the Ohio, the Mississippi, and by shoving with sticks and poles the party made its way to the head waters of the Forked Deer, located a fine spring near the old tannery in South Jackson, built a double log house here on land that was included in that 640 acres which was entered in his name and called this his home.

Dr. Butler set to work to develop his land and help build the young town. In 1821, he planted his first crop of cotton and erected a cotton gin that was brought all the way from Davidson County.[2] He donated over 30 acres of the land on which Jackson was located, served as agent for the old State bank, was a devout member of the early Presbyterian Church serving on the first building committee in the early 1830's, donated the land for the building of the Memphis Conference Female Institute,[3] also gave the land for the old M. and O. Shops on Chester Street, signed the articles of Association of St. Luke's Parish in 1832, served on the board of trustees of the Jackson Male Academy in 1825, and was a member of the county court which conducted the business of the day in this frontier community.

In an old Jackson *Tribune and Sun* of 1881, there appeared a very interesting account of an interview with Dr. Butler concerning the debated question as to whether or not cotton bales were used as part of the breastworks at New Orleans. Many people resent the destruction of the pleasing myths of history, many of which if destroyed will weaken people's belief in all history. Dr. Butler said he saw the cotton bags or bales in the breastworks, that he stood on them, walked on them, but

---

[2]Williams, *West Tennessee*, 202.

[3]This was the land that he had used in the first decade of the life of the community as his own race track.

that dirt was thrown against the cotton bags. Possibly some of those who questioned the tale never dug under the outer dirt. When Butler was questioned about this in 1881 he stormed, "Hell, I was there behind the damn bales and I ought to know."

This might have been a day of gun-toting, or even "cussing" citizens, but it was also a day of deep religious beliefs. One story in the family about the old Doctor was that after he had called his grandsons to family devotions with no results, he cried, "You know damn well it's time for family prayers!"

In the 1880's Dr. Butler built a fine large brick home on Royal Street in Jackson. The spacious banquet table was made to seat thirty guests. Beautiful furniture and rugs were in the house and oil paintings of the Doctor and his wife and steel engravings were on the wall. But it was not this stately mansion that David Crockett visited, it was the double log cabin north east of the present water works. One of the most colorful chapters in the life of this early Jacksonian was that of the time that he ran against David Crockett, the famous old Indian fighter, backwoodsman, and later hero of the Alamo. According to tradition, Crockett visited in Dr. Butler's home during the campaign, accepting an invitation because he knew he would get a good dinner and an excellent glass of whiskey. In the parlor Crockett was bewildered over the beautiful carpet on the floor, for he was accustomed to a very rough frontier home. Much to the surprise of the host, the bear-hunter leaped over the rug to a chair which was not on the rug, and left the room in the same manner never touching the rug. Crockett used the story of Butler's luxurious home as he mounted the stumps in the new country and spoke to the brawney people of the day, trying to persuade them to elect *him* to the Legislature. Imagine the appeal of this fellow who wore the coon-skin cap when he cried, "Why my fellow citizens, my wealthy competitor walks every day on 'store goods' finer than any your wives and daughters ever wore!"[4] This settled the matter with those brave but

---

[4]Cisco, "Madison County," *American Historical Magazine*, VIII, (1903), 30; Jackson *Tribune and Sun*, July 9, 1882. A different version of the story was that the old hunter hopped from one place to the other on Dr. Butler's carpet trying to keep from stepping on the flowers. Anyway, the Butlers were from this on accused of living like

rough old pioneers who could not tolerate "airs" and luxury and the vain pomp and pride of carpets.

Stories of this famous campaign are numerous. Butler had a beautiful, well-written, dignified speech which he delivered several times. In those days opposing candidates spoke to the same crowd on the same afternoon. Dr. Butler usually spoke first, but one day Davy persuaded the Doctor to let him speak first, to which the Doctor consented. Davy mounted the stump and with a twinkle of mischief in his eye began: "My fellow citizens" and proceeded to give Dr. Butler's speech word for word. Alas! when the time came for Dr. Butler's speech, he was speechless, for Davy had already delivered his.

Crockett's own story of this famous campaign may have been painted to suit his own taste, but parts of it are too colorful not to repeat. Crockett said that he set out for a little town called Jackson (about forty miles away) to sell his skins, and buy some coffee, sugar, powder, lead and salt. Here he talked with the candidates for the legislature and returned home only to have a man come after him a few days later and say that he, Davy, was to be a candidate for the Legislature. Crockett considered this a joke at first. Finally, two of the other three candidates withdrew and it became a political duel between Butler and Crockett. Crockett admired and probably feared the Doctor for he said, "Doctor Butler was a clever fellow, and I have often said he was the most talented man I ever run against for any office. His being related to General Jackson, also helped him on very much; but I was in for it and I determined to push ahead and go through or stick."[5] Election day was preceded by a jolly campaign. Crockett knew his people and knew how to make them laugh with him and at Dr. Butler. When a politician has done this, he has won his election.

At any rate the people couldn't vote for the man who was said to live in luxury and turn a cold shoulder to one of their

---

"royalty" because they had carpets on their floors—hence the name of "Royal Street" of today.

[5]*Life of David Crockett* by Himself (New York), 134-136. According to traditions, poverty, manners in the rough, open handed but rude hospitality and a generous capacity to dram-drink on all occasions were the chief recommendations to office. The temperance man in store-bought clothes and manners had little chance of the suffrage of these pioneers of the Western District.

own walk of life such as Davy was. Probably Dr. Butler was too aristocratic to succeed in politics, but he had his revenge in later years when he helped place the whole Jackson machine behind Adam Huntsman to defeat Crockett. This time Crockett was through with Western District politics, so bidding all his friends and enemies good-bye he told them that they could go to hell but he was going to Texas.[6]

Little has been written about Captain Herndon Haralson, an officer of the Revolution, the first chairman of the Madison County Court, and chairman of the commissioner of the village of Jackson. The training that he received serving as deputy surveyor for Colonel Archibald Murphy in the land office for Caswell County, North Carolina, as a member of the House of Commons from 1793-1800, and as clerk of Caswell County, qualified him to serve Madison County well. He was very active in the affairs of Madison County until his removal to Haywood County in 1825, where he lived until his death in 1847. Five years before his death, the gallant captain wrote an autobiography, so it is well to allow him to tell his story in his own language:

My grandfather, Peter Haralson, immigrated from Holland to North America in the year 1715, and landed in Virginia.

Soon after he married a young lady by the name of Chambers in Hanover County. They had four sons and one daughter. About the year 1760, these four sons (after their father's death) moved and settled on Hyco, a small river of the Dan in Orange County, North Carolina.

Paul, the third son and who was my father, married Nancy Lea in 1754. She was the daughter of James Lea, then of Orange County and of the ancient family of Leas now living in the County of Caswell in the said state. They had eight sons and five daughters. I, being the first was born October 12th, 1757.

I had a limited English education as was customary in those days. When nineteen years of age and at the opening of the land office of North Carolina, I was appointed deputy surveyor for Caswell County and continued in office until 1789, at which time Colonel Archibald Murphy, the Clerk of Court, employed me as a deputy in his office, with whom I continued until Lord Cornwallis entered the State and passed through to the State of Virginia. On his march through Carolina he passed immediately (with his army) by the office of Col. Mur-

---

[6]*Ibid.*, 252.

phy, he being then in the army. I collected the records (to prevent their falling into enemy hands) and deposited them safely.

I then applied for a Commission to raise a volunteer company—it was immediately granted me and in a few days I raised a Company—well equipped and I joined the army under General Greene.

At this juncture the Tories embodied the neighborhood of Hillsborough under the command of Col. Piles (a Dutch doctor). We marched immediately, surprised and cut them to pieces killing 180.

On February 21st, a few days afterwards to wit: the 2nd day of March, 1781, we fought the battle of Whitsell's Mill on the Ready Fork of the Haw river, a severe skirmish on their the enemy's allowance. Afterwards to wit: on the 15th day of March, 1781, we fought the battle of Guilford Court House and from thence we marched with the army of Gen. Green and fought the fierce battle of Eutaw Springs in South Carolina. This was a bloody battle. Here I had a major's command of three companies of mounted infantry, called the martial Corps.

After this battle I returned to Hillsborough, North Carolina, with 500 prisoners in charge, and was then discharged.

I again took charge of the Clerk's Office in Caswell County until the year 1784. An offer was then made me by Robert Donald and Company, importing merchants of Petersburg, Virginia, as clerk of that house. I accepted it and continued in their employ for three years. I then returned to Caswell County, and took charge of the Clerk's Office until 1791, at which time and on the 4th day of October, I was married to Mary Murphy—daughter of said Archibald Murphy and settled in that county; by her I had eight sons and three daughters—viz: Archibald, born July 5th, 1792; Jonathan, born February 12th, 1794; Herndon, born Jan. 20th, 1796; Paul, born June 20th, 1798; Green Lee, born July 27th, 1800; Betsy Murphy, born August 15th, 1802; William Henry, born September 2nd, 1803; James Madison, born April 3rd, 1807; Jane Ann, born Nov. 6th, 1809; Mary Herndon, born July 6th, 1813; John Haywood, born June 24th, 1817.

I was then employed by one Robert Payne (who was elected County Clerk) to take charge of his office. While engaged in the business and in the year 1793 I was elected representative in the House of Commons for this County and continued as such by annual elections until 1800, after which time I declined and was appointed by the Judge of the Superior Court, a clerk of that County and continued to act until 1816. I then resigned the office and moved to the town of Danville in Pittsylvania County, Virginia; from thence in the year 1818 I moved to the town of Haywood, Chatham County, North Carolina, then in 1820 I moved to the State of Tennessee and settled in the wilderness on the Forked Deer River. Two years afterwards the Western District being organized, laying out counties and establishing courts. My residence fell in the County of Madison near the town of Jackson.

I was commissioned for years and continued till the year 1825. I then sold my land and moved to Haywood County, where I now live. In the year 1826 I was appointed agent for Bank of the State and continued until the funds were directed to be paid over to the school commissioners. In the year 1832, Congress passed a law for the payment of pensions to Revolutionary officers and soldiers who had served six months in the war, commencing on the 4th day of March, 1831, payable semi-annually during life. Being one of that description I made my declaration for a pension as a captain and was allowed at the War Office $180.00 per annum.

The History contained in this declaration as to myself is truly interesting. It was made out and prepared from the recollection of my services written by my own hand and it was passed without hesitation.

Having thus in a short and explicit manner given part of the history of my past life, being on this 84 years and 8 months of age, this July 12th, 1842.

HERNDON HARALSON[7]

Three counties of West Tennessee were named in honor of men from Madison—Dyer in honor of Colonel Robert H. Dyer, Gibson in honor of Colonel John H. Gibson, and Chester in honor of Robert I. Chester. Another county, Wisdom, in honor of John Wisdom, was laid out but never organized and Chester was organized including most of the territory included in the proposed Wisdom County. Robert H. Dyer was a North Carolinian by birth who was reared on the Holston River in East Tennessee. As a youth he was commissioned lieutenant of the Regiment of Cavalry, 5th Tennessee Brigade, and later as lieutenant-colonel served in the Natchez Expedition of General Jackson, in the Creek War, at New Orleans, and in the Seminole campaign of 1818. Dyer's name appears in the list of those men who made up the first county court of Madison; he was the defeated candidate for major-generalship of the militia in 1824 (Colonel William Arnold being elected); he was one of the commissioners for improvement of the navigation in the Western District in 1824.[8] His prominence in the Western District is also shown by the fact that his house was the location

---

[7]Unpublished diary of Herndon Haralson still in the possession of the family in Brownsville, Tennessee.

[8]Jackson *Gazette*, November 13, October 30, 1824; Williams, *West Tennessee*, 142.

of one of the five land offices when the District was first surveyed and opened for sale. Further prominence is shown by a Nashville paper's description of the roads into the District in 1820—one road went to Colonel Dyer's house and another was to be built south from the Colonel's house.[9] An excerpt from the eulogy of Colonel Dyer published in the Jackson *Gazette* and copied in full in the Knoxville *Enquirer* shows the chivalrous part of Dyer in the battle of Talledega during the Creek War:

> In the crisis of that battle, he was ordered to take command of 200 chosen men, which were placed in the rear as a *corps de reserve*. Owing to some misunderstanding, the volunteer regiment gave way; Gen. Jackson ordered Dyer to dismount and charge. The enemy at that time were pressing hard on our troops, which were in the act of retreating before them. Never was there a command more promptly obeyed. Dyer, like a mighty Hercules, ordered a charge which spread dismay and death throughout the enemies' ranks, and immediately checked their progress.[10]

Colonel John H. Gibson, the man for whom Gibson County was named, was a major of the Cavalry Regiment of Colonel John Coffee under Jackson in the Natchez campaign in 1812-13; served under Brigadier General Coffee in the Creek War of 1813; was requested to join General Coffee and Colonel Dyer to help Jackson prevent the British from landing in the South in 1814. One of Coffee's main reliances in the Battle of New Orleans was Gibson. Thus, the name of another hero of long ago is preserved in the name of a county of West Tennessee.[11]

Colonel Robert I. Chester, the man for whom Chester County was named, was known to all as a man scrupulously exact and upright in business relations, a life-long Democrat, a Southern man in everything that the term implied, courteous, gallant, always cheerful and public-spirited. As quarter-master of the Third Tennessee Regiment in the War of 1812, Colonel Robert I. Chester (1793-1892)[12] served under his friend An-

---

[9] "Recollections of Memucan Hunt Howard," *American Historical Magazine*, VII (1902), 59; Nashville *Gazette*, November 18, 1820.

[10] Knoxville *Enquirer*, June 23, 1828, quoting the Jackson *Gazette*.

[11] Williams, *West Tennessee*, 144.

[12] Colonel Chester explained the shift in the initial in his name as follows: "My grandfather was Robert Johnson Chester, after whom I

drew Jackson. In 1817, as a frontier merchant at Carthage, Tennessee, he rode horseback to Philadelphia to purchase goods, which were hauled on wagons to Pittsburg. Here the horse and goods were loaded on keel-boats and brought to Louisville, Kentucky, at which point the goods were again loaded on wagons and thus the last lap of the journey to Carthage was completed. In the same year Chester made a trip to New Orleans with a fleet of flat-boats loaded with tobacco. During the panic of 1819, the price of tobacco and produce fell so sharply that Chester lost $30,000 on his tobacco. This fact was probably the real reason why he determined to leave Carthage and go west. While prospecting, he bought lands in the county and came here in 1825 with his young wife, Elizabeth Hays, a niece of Rachel Jackson.

In this new town of the Western District, he was a merchant, the postmaster (1825-1833), the United States Marshall for the Western District under President Taylor and President Pierce, a partner in a lumber business and steam mill on Reelfoot Lake, a land speculator, and a contractor.[13] In 1835, Colonel Chester went to Texas, bought lands on Brazos River and planted a crop of cotton, but he and his two brothers-in-law, Butler and Samuel J. Hays, feared that the Mexican government would really free their slaves and this would mean that they were ruined financially (they had 40 men with them), so they decided to return to to Tennessee. In the meantime, Chester was commissioned by General Houston to raise an army to fight with the Republic. Chester returned and was recruiting when General Houston's victory at San Jacinto removed the necessity of having an army. In 1884, Chester was the messenger from Tennessee to carry the electorial vote of the State to Washington. His tall, straight figure, courtly bearing, and white hair attracted wide attention at the nation's capital.

---

was named, but in olden times in writing we made the letter "I" and the letter "J" so much alike that I came to be known and called Robert I. Chester. This change was fixed upon me in so many ways that I finally accepted it." Recollections of Robert I. Chester in Nashville *Banner*, November 18, 1891.

[13]William S. Speer, *Prominent Tennesseans* (Nashville, 1888), 20. He owned several negroes who were good carpenters, brick masons, and plasterers, thus he had the contract to build the Presbyterian Church and the Memphis Conference Female Institute.

Colonel Robert I. Chester was an outstanding figure in the community in the highest sense that phrase can be used.[14]

Colonel Chester admired his brother-in-law and was very fond of his friend, Andrew Jackson. "The General" was entertained in the Chester home when he visited Jackson in 1840. Chester and his wife both wanted their daughter, Mary Jane, who was in school in Columbia, Tennessee, to see the General and become acquainted with him when he returned to Nashville via Columbia. Chester wrote to Mary Jane: "This will introduce you to your dear and venerated relation, Genl. Jackson. See him, kiss him, stay with him. I know you will love him."[15]

In later years when questioned about Jackson's greatness and temper, he answered that Jackson was equally able in great and small things. "He was a man of force and used his temper to gain his ends, but was not of bad or ungovernable temper. His manners were courtly, and the expression used about him at the time was that he was as able in the cock-pit as in the battlefield, as capable in small as in great things. He was a believer in predestination, and trusted and believed in special Providence, considering the battle of New Orleans as an evidence of Divine favor vouchsafed him. I served under Jackson at New Orleans and he once said to me that the battle was won by Coffee's repulse of the night attack of the British. When I lived in Carthage, Gen. Jackson passed through the town, on the way home from the Burr trial. The tavern was crowded. Jackson ordered the customary treat all around. A man sneered out something about 'Your friend Burr.' Jackson's glass was at his lips but he threw the whiskey into the speaker's eye."[16]

If it is true that history lives in the men who make it, then the history of our community should live in the accounts of the individuals who lived here. One influential citizen in the county was John Williamson Campbell, the county's first banker, an influential planter, owner and operator of a large saw-mill and thus an early lumberman, and a devout member of the First

---

[14]Most of the material for this sketch was taken from an account of an interview with Colonel Chester just a few months before his death. Nashville *Banner*, November 18, 1891.

[15]R. I. Chester to Mary Jane Chester, October 9, 1840. Original letter used through the courtesy of Mrs. Harold Bond.

[16]*Magazine of American History*, May, 1892 (XXVII), 386.

Presbyterian Church. J. W. Campbell (1799-1874) was born in Lexington, Kentucky, educated in Dickinson College, in Pennsylvania, moved with his family to Nashville, where he read law in the office of Felix Grundy. Before he was well established in the legal field, the Union Bank was chartered and as few had had banking experience (J. W. had experience with his father in Greenfield, Kentucky), Campbell with his college education, his legal background, was well qualified for the position of cashier of the branch of the Union Bank that was to be established at Jackson. Early in July, 1833, this branch of the Union Bank was opened with James Caruthers as President and J. W. Campbell as cashier. In 1844, J. W. Campbell opened the Jackson branch of the Nashville Insurance and Trust Company, insuring the log and brick buildings about the "Public Square," the dwellings, smoke houses and chicken coops, and bills of goods, which in one case was a carriage valued at $500, which were shipped up the Mississippi to Obion Point and then up the Forked Deer to Jackson.[17]

After living in the town for a number of years, J. W. Campbell purchased 1,300 acres of land west of Jackson from John B. Hogg and in 1856 the new home, which was called "Edgewood," was begun with slave labor. The work on this beautiful and stately home, located to-day at the head of South Fairground Street, consumed two years of time. When the house was first built, there was a circular driveway leading up to it through a grove of virgin forest trees. Six well-lighted, large rooms, with folding doors occupied the lower floor of this stately old home. The flower gardens, the family portraits, and the elaborately decorated high ceilings were a delight to the many guests who were entertained here.[18]

---

[17] Original letter book kept by J. W. Campbell. Material for this sketch was taken from William Speer, *Prominent Tennesseans*, 27-30; an old Presbyterian Session Book; and material furnished by Miss Mary Timberlake, who in turn had information from Miss Mary Campbell.

[18] An old Session Book of the First Presbyterian Church, of which Campbell was a ruling elder reveals how faithfully he had served the church: "He maintained in every walk of life an unblemished character and has left behind him the record of a life of unsullied principle. In this he hath bequeathed to the church and the world the richest of all legacies as a gentleman and friend, he was at all times reliable; as a citizen he was frank and unselfish; as a Christian and a ruler in God's house, he was meek and unpretending. He loved principle for its own

Among the first settlers in the Western District were two brothers, Stokely Donelson Hays and Samuel Jackson Hays, grandsons of Colonel John Donelson, who is famous in the annals of Middle Tennessee for his voyage in the "Adventure."[19] Surveyor and treaty-maker in negotiations with the Indians, Colonel John Donelson well deserves the numerous tributes which have been paid him, chief among these being tributes by S. G. Heiskell and Theodore Roosevelt. Perhaps next to James Robertson, he deserves credit for establishing the Cumberland settlement.

Inheritance of famous ancestors does not necessarily betoken achievement; yet it often occasions that quality of pride which is essentially human. From their great-grandmother, Stokely D. and Samuel J. inherited a bent toward religion or business affairs. She was Catherine Davis Donelson, daughter of the Reverend Samuel Davis, first minister of the (Presbyterian) Makemie Memorial Church, at Snow Hill, Maryland. The wife of Colonel Donelson was Rachel Stockley, of Accomack County, Virginia.

The Donelson home was at first in Halifax County, Virginia. Later, when a new county, Pittsylvania, was made from the western portion of Halifax County, Donelson was chosen to represent his county in the House of Burgesses. Numbered among his friends were Patrick Henry and Thomas Jefferson.

The father of the two boys, Stokely D. and Samuel J., was Colonel Robert Hays, a native of Scotland. He was active in the Revolutionary War. Ensign of the Fourth North Carolina Continental Infantry, and later First Lieutenant, he was not without honor in the First Regiment, to which he was transferred. He was taken prisoner of war, May, 1780, at Charleston, North Carolina. At the conclusion of the war, he became a member of the Society of the Cincinnati, an organization of the officers of the Revolutionary Army.

---

sake and through a long and eventful life was never known to sever or deviate from what he believed to be right. After an illness of only three days he gently fell asleep in Jesus on the 30th of June 1874, greatly lamented by the entire community who mourn the death of our oldest and most distinguished citizen."

[19]This sketch was prepared by Miss Grace Everett from a paper which she read before the Madison County Historical Society in November, 1943.

On January 27, 1786, Robert Hays was married to Jane Donelson, at Haysboro, on the Cumberland. Mrs. Hays's sister, Rachel, later became Mrs. Andrew Jackson, and the fortunes of the Hays family were thus inextricably linked with the history of this hero of the West. Colonel Hays became one of the outstanding citizens of the Cumberland settlement, and was, at one time, a large land-owner.[20]

Others have pictured for us the beginnings of Jackson, when deer roamed its environing forests and wild beasts came to drink from its abundant springs. They have told us of the Forked Deer River, which the Indians called the *Okeena,* on which flat-boats floated to their destination. To this region, overgrown with matted pea-vines, there came, in the year 1822, young Stokely D. Hays and his wife and only son, aged six months. When he came to Jackson, he was thirty-four years of age.

He had had his youthful adventure. When Aaron Burr had made his last visit to the Cumberland, in 1806, young Hays had gone with Burr, for Andrew Jackson, Stokely's uncle, had urged him to do so. Both Jackson and Hays were mistaken as to Burr's intention. A letter written by young Hays has been preserved, in which he stated that he had been instructed that if anything inimical to the United States were intended, he was to return or place himself under the care of Governor Claiborne. Fortunately, by order of President Jefferson, Burr was arrested when his flotilla reached the Natchez country, and he was taken to Richmond for trial. Thus ended an episode which might have had tragic consequences.

Of his education little is known, except that he had a knowledge of surveying and that he studied law. Together with six other lawyers, Stokely D. Hays took the oaths prescribed by law as "attorney-at-law in this court" in the home of Adam R. Alexander, at a Court of Quarter Sessions, June 17, 1822. Accounts in old minute-books of Madison County reveal the fact that Hays, in his capacity of surveyor, gave considerable aid in opening up new roads leading from Jackson.

A member of the first board of commissioners of Jackson,

---

[20]The children of Colonel Robert and Jane Hays were published in the account in the Jackson *Sun* November, 1943.

Hays was later chairman of the board. He was active in village enterprises and deeply interested in the cause of education. When the Jackson Male Academy was incorporated by act of the legislature in 1825, Hays was among those chosen as the "body politic and corporate."

In the year 1830 Andrew Jackson was deeply interested in helping Stokely D. obtain the position of surveyor of a land office in Mississippi, but the desired office was never obtained. Within another year Hays, son of Middle Tennessee pioneers, had died.[21] He was survived by his wife and an only son, Richard, aged nine.

That he received the affectionate regard bestowed by Andrew Jackson on all the nieces and nephews of Rachel Donelson Jackson, can scarcely be doubted. Reference is made to him in the account of the life of Emily Donelson. A miniature faithfully preserves his likeness, and shows him to have been a strikingly handsome man, wearing a broadcloth suit, the coat of which is adorned with brass buttons. Like others of his family, he is said to have possessed much personal magnetism. In this miniature, there can easily be seen a noticeable resemblance to the other members of the Donelson family, whose portraits have been painted by the artist, Earl.

Prior to his coming to the Western District from his home on the Cumberland, he had taken part in the Creek War of 1813, had probably lain in the swamps at the battle of New Orleans, had ridden with Coffee, that trusted officer and friend of Andrew Jackson. On one occasion he had helped save the life of Andrew Jackson, in the famous Benton affray.

General Samuel Jackson Hays, younger brother of Stokely D. Hays, is reputed to have owned one thousand slaves, three hundred of whom had been a marriage dower from John Middleton to his daughter, Frances Pinckney Middleton. Born at Haysboro in the year 1800, while the infant nation struggled to maintain itself, he lived during the War of 1812, the Mexican and Civil War periods, dying in 1866, at the homestead in the town which he had helped to fashion.

It cannot be stated with certainty just when Samuel Jackson Hays came to this community. In a letter dated November 7, 1830, written to R. I. Chester, Andrew Jackson mentioned

---

[21]See "Prologue" for other references to Stokely D. Hays.

"Sam'l J. Hays and his sweet little wife." This letter must have been written shortly after the family moved to Jackson. Mrs. Jane Hays made her home with her son, Samuel. The property was known as "Hays Hill," the original home being a double log-house.

Samuel Jackson Hays became a planter on a large scale, ginning the cotton which his host of slaves picked. To the region of the river which the early settlers had named Forked Deer, he brought something of the "pith and moment" of the great world. At West Point he had been a classmate of Jefferson Davis, whose friendship he valued all his life.

At Jackson's Inaugural Ball, in 1829, Samuel J. Hays met pretty Frances Pinckney Middleton, daughter of John Middleton, of Charleston, South Carolina, and niece of Arthur Middleton, one of the signers of the Declaration of Independence. According to a member of the family, President Jackson took a lively interest in the two.

When President Polk ordered troops into Mexico and shortly thereafter declared that a state of war existed, Hays as Major General of one of the divisions of the State Militia, was actively engaged in patriotic duties. The Memphis *Daily Eagle,* under date of June 1, 1846, recounts the fact that General Hays had accepted Captain Cook's company. The same paper, dated June 2, 1846, refers to Major General Hays, of the volunteer companies of the 4th Division, Second Army of Tennessee. The issue of the *Eagle,* dated January 12, 1847, tells of the election of W. T. Haskell as Major General, to assume the duties of General Hays, who had resigned.

For many years the family lived in a home purchased from Colonel Robert I. Chester, on "Miller Hill." About 1847 Hays and his family moved from this home, having built a house which was long remembered as one of the most magnificent of the homes of Jackson, with its lawn adorned with statuary imported from Italy, its furnishings of rosewood and mahogany, its liveried Guinea slaves. The house was built on what is now Preston street, the gate to the long driveway opening on what is now Hays Avenue. Visitors in the home were impressed by the General's gracious manners.[22]

---

[22]Further details concerning the history of this family were published in the Jackson *Sun,* November, 1943.

The almost paternal devotion of Andrew Jackson toward this nephew of his "beloved Rachel" is evident in the letters which passed back and forth between Hays and Jackson. A visit of Jackson to the Hays family was a memorable occasion.

Toward the close of his life, when the South's "peculiar institution" brought echoes of strife to Madison County, Jefferson Davis visited the General, offering him at this time, it is said, a commission as General in the Army of the Confederacy. But Hays replied: "I am sending four sons and two sons-in-law. I cannot go myself, but I will equip a company." He is said to have done so, at his own expense.

Feeling the weight of burdens and responsibilities, and knowing that his life was drawing to a close, Hays went to Memphis to purchase a metallic coffin. He had it brought home and placed in the attic, where it is said to have remained until his death.[23]

The will of Samuel J. Hays was recorded in 1866. He had bequeathed his property to his four surviving children. Besides real estate in this county and in Shelby County, and in Arkansas, he mentioned his library, the furnishings and silverware of the homestead. Nor did he neglect to mention his faithful old servant, Abraham, and his servant, Amy.

Thus it is clear that Stokely Donelson and Samuel Jackson Hays had reason to be proud of the Donelson and Hays families. In the words of Judge Samuel C. Williams: "The spirit of independence was their birthright."[24]

Quite a number of Madison's early citizens were notable residents of the counties from which they came. They did not wait until they came to the Western District to make themselves famous. Pleasant M. Miller was a famous son of Knox County before he removed to this section. Miller, one of the ablest

---

[23]Captain "Mid" Hays, a descendant of General Hays, took part in the Battle of Shiloh, receiving severe shoulder wounds. He was active in the organization of the Ku Klux Klan in this county.

[24]Sources of information for the sketches of Stokley D. and Samuel J. Hays include: Thomas Perkins Abernathy, *American Lands and the American Revolution; From Frontier to Plantation;* Zella Armstrong, *Notable Southern Families,* Vol. II; Octavia Z. Bond, *Old Tales Retold;* Pauline Wilcox Burke, *Emily Donelson of Tennessee;* James Parton, *Andrew Jackson;* A. W. Putnam, *History of Middle Tennessee;* Theodore Roosevelt, *Winning of the West;* Samuel C. Williams, *Beginnings of West Tennessee;* scrap books.

men of the early bar of Tennessee, was born in Lynchburg, Virginia, in 1773. He came to Rogersville, Tennessee, in 1796. On April 11, 1801, he was married to Mary Louisa Blount, daughter of William Blount, governor of the Southwest Territory. Before he left Knox County, he served one term, 1809-1811 in Congress and was a member of the lower house from that county in 1819-1822 (State Legislature). In 1812, he was a member of a company which marched under John Williams, also of the Knoxville Bar, to aid American residents of Florida against Spaniards and the Seminoles.[25]

No doubt Miller moved to Western Tennessee to look after the interest of his father-in-law's estate. In the Western District, Governor Blount and his two brothers, Thomas and James Gray held immense holdings of lands granted by the State of North Carolina in the 1780's. Miller gave much attention to land litigations and, able lawyer that he was, he amassed a large estate. The Jackson *Gazette* of July 31, 1824, announced the intentions of Miller to move to the Western District that fall. He did come that fall from Knoxville down the Tennessee and started to practice here the following spring.

Pleasant M. Miller was a very successful lawyer here practicing in the regular courts for a decade and then served as the Chancellor in the new Chancery Court. The first Legislature after the Constitutional Convention of 1834 had created a new division of the Chancery Court covering West Tennessee and Pleasant M. Miller served as the first resident Chancellor, resigning from this position in March, 1837. (He served from 1836-1837.)

When Pleasant Miller came to the county in 1824, he settled upon his farm eight miles north of Jackson, which place became known as Holly Hill. Here, he lived until 1847, when he sold it to Henry McCorry and removed to a farm which he owned six miles north-east of Trenton. His wife died in 1847 and was buried in Jackson. Miller died in 1849 and was buried in Trenton.

Miller was an able man, himself, but he was also connected by marriage with prominent and influential families in Tennessee. His wife was a Blount, a daughter married Charles

---

[25]Samuel C. Williams, "A Forgotten Campaign," *Tennessee Historical Magazine*, VIII (1924), 271.

McClung of Knoxville, another daughter married General Alexander Bradford of Jackson, another daughter married Joel Dyer of Trenton, and another daughter married Colonel William H. Stephens of Jackson.

Jackson's first Chancellor was a man of limited education, but by the power of intellect, by industry stimulated by necessities and by perseverence he gained highest honors in his profession. During his early years, as a legislator, he proved to be a skilled antagonist of Felix Grundy in the respect of measures introduced to meet the near panic and depression of 1819-1822 in Tennessee. Grundy opposed squatters' rights, but Miller, a man of the true West, successfully opposed Grundy's view with "great ingenuity." It was really an accomplishment to hold his own with the great Felix, famed as one of the trio: "Thomas Walker, Felix Grundy, and the Devil."

Although Miller lived in a time when he had distinguished men for contemporaries, men with advantages of superior education, his fellow members of the bar admitted him to be their equal. He was original and independent in the formation of his opinions, and bold in their avowal. A. W. O. Totten, Esq., concluded the resolutions adopted by the Bar of West Tennessee at the time of Miller's death with this tribute:

> As a member of Congress and of the State Legislature, and as chancellor of the Western Division, his name stands intimately connected with the legislative, judicial, and political history of Tennessee, demonstrating the confidence his fellow-citizens had in his capacity, ability, and personal honor, proving that he served faithfully his day and generation, and leaving a monument to his memory of which his friends may well be proud. During his long life his capacity was always admitted, and his integrity never doubted. He reared a numerous and highly respectable family, a few of whom and many descendants remain to mourn the loss and cherish the memory of their ancestor.[26]

One of the leading Democrats of the county in the early years was Samuel McClanahan. Before he came to the county, he worked on a farm, then served a four year apprenticeship under a tailor in South Carolina at the same table with Andrew Johnson, then read law under Judge Elmore of Columbia. Coming to Jackson in 1828 when lawyers were plentiful (there were

---

[26] 29 Tennessee, 369-370.

ten here in 1830), Samuel McClanahan found it more profitable to teach school than to practice law for a few years. Notices in the papers of 1831 and 1832 tell of the opening of a school for boys and girls by Samuel McClanahan, who offered special preparations for college entrance, an excellent course in geography with the use of a recently acquired set of globes, and board in the teacher's home if desired. The public was invited to the examinations of his young ladies and young men which were held at the courthouse. In 1851, the two year law course at West Tennessee College was under the direction of Samuel McClanahan.[27]

In 1834, he formed a partnership with Andrew L. Martin. About six years later he built a home at the north end of Liberty Street (where the telephone exchange now stands) and it was here that his friend, Andrew Johnson, visited soon after the Civil War, speaking to the crowd from the upstairs front porch. In 1843, McClanahan purchased and re-chartered the levee across the Forked Deer south of Jackson which still bears his name.[28] He was a loyal Democrat in politics, remaining true to the cause and Andrew Jackson during the days when the Whigs were the strongest party in this section. In 1840, when Andrew Jackson came to the Western District to rally the Democrats to the cause, Samuel McClanahan was chosen to welcome the beloved hero of New Orleans.[29] Records in the Session Book of the Presbyterian Church at the time of his death in 1873 and contemporary papers of the same year, tell of this leader in the community who was a faithful elder in the Church, a man of energy and commanding talents, a man of warm impulses, but one who never suffered those impulses to do injustice to fellow lawers or opponents in politics in the heat of debate.

Of Samuel McClanahan's brothers, James was a skilled and popular teacher, David was a farmer, John was a journalist and editor and an efficient captain of a company of volunteer in the Mexican War. Nelson also served in the Mexican War. Both Nelson and John returned from the theatre of war and went to Memphis where John was part owner of the Memphis *Appeal*.

---

[27]Jackson *Southern Statesman*, December 17, 1831, September 3, 1832; Jackson *West Tennessee Whig*, March 6, 1851.
[28]Jackson *Blade*, March 20, 1895.
[29]See "Prologue" for the details of this event.

One of the leading citizens and most popular judges in the early days of Jackson was Judge Joshua Haskell, the father of Tennessee's famous orator and poet, General William T. Haskell. In 1821, when Judge Haskell was appointed judge of the newly created Eighth Circuit, he moved to Madison County. These were pioneer days in the Western District in every walk of life and the legal profession was no exception. These early lawyers were often learned but always resourceful. These were the days of circuit riding both for ministers and lawyers, of few books and few precedents, of lasting friendships made in rude taverns, and of dramatic pleading of cases before large audiences who came to enjoy themselves.

Judge Haskell was a very popular man in the community, but he failed to abide by the rules of the bench. He was known to be a judge "Who got things done." At one time he tried forty cases in seven days and then called a half day off for refreshments and a well-earned rest. An early Jackson paper recorded the fact that much business was dispatched in a manner reflecting the highest degree of credit to "his honor, Judge Haskell, for the promptitude and ability with which he discharged the duties of the bench."[30]

In 1829, both the friends of the Judge in the legal circles and other walks of life were astonished at the impeachment of Judge Joshua Haskell by the lower house of the Legislature. The State Senate formed a court before which he was tried for "negligently and illegally omitting, failing and refusing in courts holden by him, to hear, attend to and superintend the testimony of witnesses and the argument of counsel; that he negligently and illegally absented himself from the court house, and the jury, counsel, and witnesses proceeded without his presence; that he signed records without knowing whether they were true or false."[31]

Judge Haskell was very able defended by Pleasant M. Miller. Some of the star witnesses were prominent men from the Judge's very own home town—Andrew L. Martin, Adam Huntsman, William Armour, Joseph Talbot, and Alexander Bradford.

It was not a question of the honor and character of the

---

[30] Jackson *Southern Statesman*, December 10, 1831.
[31] *Senate Journal of State of Tennessee*, 406.

Judge, it was a question of whether the Judge had a right to hold the office to which he had been appointed for a term of "good behavior" when he was known to leave the court room for various reasons during the session of court. Charles McLean, Madison's representative in the Legislature, reported that there would not be much trouble for the "Ermine" should be unspotted and the confidence of the people in the integrity of the Judiciary should be unimpaired and unshaken. A numerous train of witnesses of the most respectable men of the state concurred in representing Haskell as being in private life, in all social relations, humane, kind, generous, hospitable, and in the language of one witness (Gov. Carroll) "possessing some of the finest feelings of the human heart"—that his character for honesty and integrity has always been unsuspected and unblemished; that in the late war he had distinguished himself for his intrepidity and gallantry as a soldier; that as a lawyer he had been attentive to the business entrusted to his care, and had been successful in his profession; that as a judge he was extremely popular with a great body of the citizens of his circuit who were well pleased with his administration of the law among them; that in all his official acts, they believed him to have been governed by the strictest impartiality and integrity; and that the citizens of his circuit were generally most warmly opposed to his removal from office.[32]

The testimony of some of the witnesses does not necessarily reflect discredit upon the character of the Judge, but it does give a picture of this section of the Western District as a true part of the growing "west" in 1830. One of the witnesses testified that when the Judge first came to the district, when he left the court room, business was suspended but that he soon directed them to continue, and the people had gotten used to it. Most of the witnesses agreed that the judge left the bench when he probably should not have, but they couldn't agree upon how long he was gone, how far away he was, or what he was doing. One testified that he had gone eighty yards from the court house to look at a horse; several testified that he had left to engage in conversation; another (when the court had lasted till mid-night) testified that he had seen the Judge "at a stall where cakes and cider were sold"; another that he had left

---

[32] *Ibid.*, 409-410.

the court room and ate a water melon with him in the yard; another (at a trial in the Hardin circuit) testified that the Judge was absent from the bench during most of the trial, but was seen in the back of the room at times but, he added, the house in which the court was held was very uncomfortable—it was occupied by hogs during the recess of the court and infested with fleas; others testified he was not prompt in attending to business when his attention was called to difficulties (in one case a fight), settling questions of law, or charging the jury.[33]

The judge was acquitted, but as some of his friend reported—it was a narrow escape, for the vote on three specifications was 9 to 9. Nevertheless the Judge was embarrassed and after this paid more attention to the proprieties and dignity of his office. That he appreciated his "second chance" and served the people efficiently in later years is shown by the warm expression of great respect and good feeling of the people that was shown to the judge upon his retirement from the bench in 1835. His friends considered that he had through his ability, philanthropy, hospitality, and other admirable qualities rendered himself worthy of their highest confidence and warmest affections.[34]

---

[33]*Ibid*, 434-436.
[34]Nashville *Union*, April 29, 1835, quoting from the Jackson *Truth Teller* of April 24th.

CHAPTER V

FRONTIER POLITICS

The Western District in general and Madison County in particular was the scene of a political battle from 1825 to 1836 that was important in the field of national politics and the echoes of the battle were heard until the Sectional Conflict of 1861-1865. At first it was the writer's intention to write only a sketch of "Adam Huntsman and David Crockett" but as the story grew it became one of "Crockett and Huntsman" or rather "Crockett and Andrew Jackson" for Adam Huntsman was the able, clever politician who was selected as the only man who could beat Davy, and the Jacksonian Democrats were compelled to eliminate David and his influence. Crockett has never been given credit for his part in the ground-work of the Whig party and the opposition to Andrew Jackson that was started right here in Madison County where Jackson's relatives were the leading citizens.

The scene of this political battle between Crockett and Huntsman, the Andrew Jackson man in the Western District, was the real frontier, a frontier where stump speaking was the chief means of winning votes, where on election day candidates could be seen actively engaged in wooing the people for their votes while the cake women, cider sellers and melon people plied their trade; where many a resolution, deliberately formed to vote one way, was hastily changed for another, the argument irresistible eloquence and a drink of grog.[1] The following

---

[1]Nashville *Whig,* July 30, 1825. Major Charles Sevier, a leading Democrat in Madison County and a perfect Hercules in strength, was so loyal that according to tradition when a voting precinct was set up in his home, he rolled up his sleeves and let it be known that he was ready to purge the polls of any man who would not vote for "Andy Jackson." In 1844, he was such an enthusiastic supporter of James K. Polk that on election day he rode in to Jackson upon a white bull stripped with polk berry juice from head to tail.

description of this battle of ballots that was so bitterly fought cannot be improved upon:

> War waxeth warm as the election approaches. Our paper has been the arena of combatants. . . . We have observed the commanders of different divisions and their field officers marching and countermarching their forces, occupying various ports and assuming different positions. We have seen them actively engaged in the field, encouraging their troops and inviting recruits to their standards. We have seen considerable skirmishing. . . . Every preparation is made which skill and tactic can suggest for the general engagement on the first Thursday in August next and the ensuing day. Couriers with dispatches are rapidly moving through the District in every direction—all is bustle, excitement, electioneering.[2]

Democratic and Whig mass meetings and speakings were held in Jackson, Medon, Spring Creek, and Pinson; log-rollings were held in Crockett's neighborhood where straw votes were taken; free barbecues were given at which time the people listened to numerous addresses. All were truly electioneering![3]

David Crockett,[4] a member of the State Legislature from Middle Tennessee counties in 1821, entered West Tennessee politics soon after he came to live on the Obion River (1823) by defeating Dr. Butler of Madison County for the State Legislature.[5] In 1826, the bear-hunter stumped the District and rolled up a majority of 2784 against Adam Alexander of Madison County and went to Washington as a member of the House of Representatives. During his second term there, after he was returned by a large majority, he began to press his "Occupant Bill," which gave the then occupants priority claims to the unappropriated lands in the Western District. This bill was defeated, but his vast majority gave him enough assurance

---

[2] Jackson *Southern Statesman*, July 23, 1831.

[3] *Ibid.*, January 4, 1831; Jackson *Republican*, September 13, 1844.

[4] David Crockett (1760-1836) was well born, having a father who was a Revolutionary soldier and a mother who was a sister-in-law of Governor John Sevier. He had a fine record in the Creek War. His shrewdness, eccentric manners and peculiar wit made him a conspicious figure in national politics. Records in the Madison County courts and quoted letters from the originals in this volume are ample evidence to prove that contrary to some early writers, David Crockett could write.

[5] See the account of this campaign in the sketch of Dr. William E. Butler.

to come out against Andrew Jackson—a desire that he had kept suppressed since the days when he and Jackson were both engaged in the Creek War and earlier disputes in State politics, though he had told his followers that he broke with the Jacksonian Democrats over the bank and Georgia-Cherokee question.

DAVID CROCKETT ELECTIONEERING
From an early edition of David Crockett's Autobiography.

Adam Huntsman, who had fun writing in the papers just to make his opponents mad, told of this member of Congress who rode a brokendown horse named OCCUPANT, who was lost, strayed, or stolen from the Jackson ranks. Andrew Jackson was afraid of Crockett's influence. In 1830, he heard that Crockett would try to represent S. D. Hays as intemperate just to mortify him [Jackson] and that is just what Crockett proceeded to do, much to the delight of Jackson's enemies in the District.[6] Whereupon Jackson called upon his relatives and other Democrats in the District to band together to beat Crockett. He wrote thus to Samuel Jackson Hays:

> I trust your congressional District will not disgrace themselves longer by sending that profligate man, Crockett, back to Congress.[7]

When Crockett came out in the open against Jackson, Crockett claimed that he was "hunted down like a wild varment" by every little newspaper and pin-hook lawyer, that the leaders made appointments to speak over the district telling that Crockett would be there but these "small-fry" lawyers who didn't tell Crockett about the engagements would appear at the appointed time and tell the people that Crockett was afraid to come.[8] In 1831, Crockett wrote to Calvin Jones about his break with Jackson, demonstrating his independence and honesty:

> I would rather be beaten and be a man than to be elected and be a little puppy dog. I have always supported measures and principles, not men. I would rather be politically buried than to be hypocritically immortalized.[9]

A legislative gerrymander of the congressional District, favoring Fitzgerald of Weakley County (Crockett's opponent in 1831 and 1833) was a disgrace to the nation, but when the election day came the people of the District, according to Crockett's version of the story, came to polls and voted for

---

[6]Bassett, *Correspondence*, IV, 199; Jackson *Southern Statesman*, June 18, 1831.

[7]Jackson to Hays, April 23, 1831. Quoted in full in the Appendix.

[8]*A Narrative of Life of David Crockett* (Philadelphia, 1835), 207-209.

[9]David Crockett to Calvin Jones, August 22, 1831. Quoted in full in the Appendix.

Crockett proving that they could not be "transferred like hogs and horses, cattle to the market. . . . I had Mr. Fitzgerald for my open competitor, but he was helped along by all his little lawyers again, headed by old Black Hawk, as he is sometimes called (alias) Adam Huntsman, with all his talents for writing 'Chronicles' and such like foolish stuff. . . . The contest was a warm one, and the battle well fought, but Crockett was proud to add that he would not find upon his collar engraved: 'MY DOG, Andrew Jackson.' "[10]

In 1821, the rough and tumble lawyer, the very able criminal lawyer, the artful politician, the distinguished wit and humorist and practical joker, Adam Huntsman, came to Madison County to live. A Virginian by birth, he first settled in Tennessee in Overton County, serving in the state senate from that region from 1815 to 1821. This peg-legged lawyer who had lost his leg in the Creek campaign was one of the very early settlers of the new county of Madison on the old Cotton Grove road (where the Collier place is now located) and took an active part in the legal, political, and business life of the young town of Jackson. He was a member of the first board of Commissioners for the government of Jackson, was on the Board of Trustees for the navigation of waters of the Western District in 1824, and was practicing law with his partner, William Stoddert, in the circuit courts of the Western District in the same year.

Huntsman was a member of the state senate from Madison in 1827 and 1829, the first member from the district that was strictly western. He represented his district at the Constitutional Convention of 1834, serving on important committees. He advocated a tax upon white polls for the support of public schools and signed a committee report which favored slavery, but sympathized with the conditions under which the free Negro of that day had to live.[11]

This frontier lawyer, who was more devoted to politics than to his legal profession, was such a good stump speaker, such a forceful campaigner, such a unique and colorful figure that he was picked by some of the Jackson politicians as the only man who could defeat the people's choice for Congress—

---

[10] *A Narrative of the Life of David Crockett*, 209-211.
[11] Williams, *West Tennessee*, 197, 212; *Biographical Dictionary of American Congress*, 1134.

§] Adam Huntsman's Fight with a Panther.

Early one morning, my neighbor Adam Huntsman, who run igin me for Congress the last election, was going through the woods where he knowed there was a smart chance of bears, with three dogs which he knowed was a match for their weight in bears any day. Their names was Black Hawk, Jackson, and Growler. Jackson was ahead as usual, and tother two dogs was running along behind their master as usual. Presently he heard Jackson making a tarnal strange noise. Twant as if he had got hold on a bear, for he made a bigger fuss than ever he did for any bear that ever he seed. So Black Hawk and Growler looked up and listened a minute, and then they were off in no time. Adam thought it was about time for him to be off too, as there was no knowing what tarnal critter they had got a scent of. Well, he went ahead as much as half a mile, and didn't see nothing till he come to a bit of a clearing, where was a big tree wit' vo big branches growing out of the trunk, and right in the crotch was the biggest painter that you ever seed, and the dogs was howling and barking most beautiful. Adam hadn't got no kind of weppun with him only a pistol, so he saw he must come alongside the varmint right off. He goes up and gets hold on the painter's tail with one hand, and with the other he got a blizzard with his pistol, and hit him in the neck. That made the varmint as mad as a skinned eel, and he looped right down in the midst of the dogs. Growler caught him by the nose, but he up with his fore paws and knocked him a rod. Jackson and Black Hawk dove at his throat, but he grabbed Jackson by one ear and took it clear off. Adam never felt so in his life, for the pesky varmint rolled up his eyes like a duck in a thunder squall. And what was worse, the dogs began to look astonished. Adam told them to go ahead once more, and he loaded his pistol again at the same time, but no sooner had the dogs jumped at the painter than they were rolling belly up amongst the leaves, and yelling like seven tornadoes. He then made a spring right at Adam, and Adam looked round for a fair shake to run, when Jackson caught the critter by the tail. When the varmint felt him hanging to his tail, he darted right up a tree, and Adam right arter him and caught him by the tail and give him the whole charge in his tarnal profile, which brought him to the ground as dead as a sign post.

If the Partridge had but the Woodcocks thigh,
It would be the best bird that ever did fly.

David Crockett and Adam Huntsman were well met in the art of telling tall tales. The above facsimile of Crockett's tale about Huntsman comes from "Davy Crockett's Almanack or Wild Sports in the West and Life in the Backwoods." (Published for "The Author" in Nashville.)

Adam Huntsman's Fight with a Panther.

A political cartoon of 1836 from Crockett's Almanack. Note the cartoonist neglected to show Huntsman's wooden leg. Used through the courtesy of Stanley Horn.

David Crockett. In 1828, Huntsman felt that his chances of success were slight and consequently did not oppose Crockett, but he did express his disapproval of the use of "white-faced whiskey" in elections and Crockett's methods of "going up creeks, down valleys, over hills, and into dales for the purpose of collecting votes, as tax gatherer would his tax, is so far beneath the dignity of man or of a correct politician, that I would not descend to such acts of degredation."[12]

"Old Black Hawk," as Crockett called Huntsman, opposed Crockett on the stump and in the press. In 1831, he cleverly ridiculed Crockett for supporting the occupant law and opposing Jackson. This political feud was talked about at home and abroad. Huntsman's comments upon the occupant law were published in the *Southern Statesman* and copied in many papers of the day. Over a hundred years later it is rich enough to quote:

Going! Going! Gone! Strayed or stolen from the Jackson ranks a certain member of Congress from the Western District named David Crockett. Davy is upward of six feet high, erect in his posture, and has a nose extremely red after taking some spirits. He possesses vast bodily powers, great activity and can leap the Ohio, wade the Mississippi, and carry one steam and two flat boats on his back. He can vault across a streak of lightning, ride it down a honey-locust; grease his heels, skate down the rain bow, and whip his weight in wild cats and panthers. Davy took the country in the Western District, enlisted in the Jackson ranks, performed prodigies of valor in divers engagements between the Jacksonites and the Adams boys. He defeated and put to flight the celebrated John Wright by comparing him to a monkey with spectacles on; he demolished the little Prince by telling him that the people of the Western District danced all their toe nails off at Saturday night frolics and grinned a panther to death at Washington City. The last that has been heard of him, he was riding towards Yankee land upon a broken down pony which he called OCCUPANT. Occupant is a noble little fellow. He has made some daring plunges and would (if he had been well kept) perform succeeding journies to Congress, but this darling animal has been fed upon hopes and promises until he is getting lean and gaunt for want of more substantial food, for it seems he can't get nothing out of Uncle Sam's crib.[13]

---

[12] Jackson *Gazette*, June 28, 1828.
[13] *Southern Statesman*, March 12, 1831. This was copied from the Raleigh *Star*, April 21, 1831.

An election in those days was indeed a battle and often the engagements were well fought by the most picturesque characters. No prank was too mean to play if one could get by with it; no story was unfit to tell under the same conditions. These frontier politicians loved to out-smart their opponents. Some of the tricks they played on each other go to prove that it is not what is actually true that makes history, but what people think is true. A tale was told about the time when Huntsman was serving in the State Legislature. A colored boy who waited on the gentleman at the boarding house came running down stairs after going up to get Huntsman's boots. The poor boy was frightened to death and said that he could not stay in the room where that man was, because he took all the hair off his head and laid it under the table, and took his teeth out and then took off one of his legs. The boy said, "Laws, I can't go where that man is; he's taking himself to pieces!"[14] Huntsman was once charged with the paternity of an illegitimate child. He replied that he would own it if it had a wooden leg but not otherwise.

In one campaign Huntsman opposed Crockett unsuccessfully. It is said that the following incidents had much to do with Huntsman's defeat. The two politicians had stopped one night on their rounds at a well-to-do farmer's, who was a great Jackson man and of course for Huntsman, though he did not admire his rakish propensities. Crockett and "Peg-leg," as Huntsman was called, were put in the same room to sleep. The house was of the ordinary country kind of that day, two log cabins, with a passage between, and a porch extending the whole length in the rear, with shed-rooms at each end, in one of which the two candidates were placed, while the farmer's daughter occupied the other. After all had retired Huntsman went to sleep and Crockett went to planning. An idea occurred to him which he carried out perfectly. Getting up quietly, Crockett opened the door, taking a chair, and walking stealthily across to the young lady's room, made an apparent effort to force her door, which noise awoke the girl. She uttered a scream, so Crockett hastily caught the chair by the back, and placed his foot on the lower round using it as a leg hurried back to his room, dropped the chair, hopped into bed, and went

---

[14] Jane Thomas, *Old Days in Nashville* (Nashville, 1897), 73.

to hard snoring. The next moment the farmer rushed in, and was about to kill Huntsman, whose protestations of innocence he paid no attention to. "Oh, you can't fool me!" he exclaimed, "I know you too well, and heard that darned old peg-leg of yourn too plain."[15] The consequences were that the farmer, with many others changed their votes and Crockett was triumphantly elected. Huntsman would never have entered another campaign had not Crockett considered the joke too good to keep.

The scene of another famous anecdote of Crockett's campaign is supposed to have been in Madison County. A band of voters had assembled and were much interested in Crockett's opponent's "speechifying and treating." They were willing to listen to Crockett but not upon the dry subject such as the welfare of the nation unless they had something to drink. The bar-tender at a shack near by would trust no one and Davy did not have the price of a quart, so he saw that the crowd was melting away and that unless he got some whiskey very quickly his election was gone. So shouldering his gun, he went to the woods and returned within fifteen minutes with a coon skin which he flipped on the counter and called for a quart. Then with the crowd in a good humor, Davy had an appreciative audience when he mounted the stump. When the speech was half finished, the constituents demanded another drink and so they adjourned to the shantee-bar and Crockett began to think that his fate as a successful politician depended upon his shooting another coon, when he spied his previous skin between the logs that supported the bar. He gave it a jerk and flung it on top, demanding a quart. During the day he got ten quarts in the same manner with the same skin. The constituents saw the fun and concluded that Davy was very clever, for they considered the bar-tender as sharp as a steel trap and if Davy could out-wit him, he could out-wit old Nick himself. Davy's cleverness with the bar-tender won him that election and Davy retold

---

[15]James D. Davis, *History of Memphis* (Memphis, 1873), 151-2. Colonel Robert Chester remembered Crockett as a keen-eyed, observant, backwoods-man who told anecdotes on the stump that pleased the people but was without influence in Congress. Chester spent the night at Crockett's house, slept on a bear-skin, ate bear meat with a bowie knife and a cane fork. *Magazine of American History,* May, 1892, XXVII (New York), 386.

the tale as an illustration of his political ability and reminded Adam Huntsman that such would be his fate if there was a "fair fight and no gouging."[16]

The people and the candidates both enjoyed an approaching election in those early days, for each man literally stumped the district, but in 1835, it was said that when Crockett and Huntsman were considered, in a matter of "stump eloquence or finesses, a matter of twee-deidum and tweedle dee."[17] Huntsman, his friends and those of Andrew Jackson were strong enough to defeat Crockett. At the close of the campaign, Crockett, in accordance with the statement that he had made during the campaign, left for Texas and Huntsman concluded that if "the two opponents could weigh their grievances they would come out about even but that the reason Crockett lost the election was that he did not get enough votes."[18] It took a good politician with some strong politicians behind him to defeat Crockett—a man of the people whose popularity was the result of his strong common sense, his sterling honesty, and his fine vein of fun.

No material could be collected that would more clearly illustrate Adam Huntsman's fine vein of fun and loyalty to the Democratic party than a few references from his own letters

---

[16]*Life of David Crockett; the Original Humorist and Irrepressible Backwoodsman* (New York), 241-245. The bar-tender, according to tradition, was a very "smart" fellow who had made money from his business of turning mahogany saw-dust into cayenne pepper. He had inherited his ability from his father who had invented wooden nutmeg but failed to take out a patent and thus he let the business get out of his hands. *Ibid.*, 244.

[17]Randolph *Recorder*, April 17, 1835.

[18]Nashville *Union*, December 1, 1835. One account told that Crockett was not defeated this time on merit, but by a party trick of his opponent, resorted to on the eve of the election, too late to be exposed. Marcus Wright, "Col. David Crockett of Tennessee," *Southern History Magazine*, January, 1897. Another tale of this campaign concerned the last time both opponents spoke. Both opponents had spoken together for what they agreed was the last time. They started home, but both remembered that a large crowd would be gathered in Dresden, so each went by. Crockett arrived first and was up speaking when Huntsman arrived. Huntsman hitched his horse and pushed his way into the crowd, right in front of Crockett. When Crockett's eyes fell upon his opponent he stopped a moment and then exclaimed: "Adam Huntsman, I believe if I were to go to hell, that you would follow me there." From Scrap Book of T. M. Gates.

to President James K. Polk. This frontier politician loved the game of politics and a game it was to him. In 1838, Huntsman wrote to Polk that the Democrats were gaining in the District, that "there has been genuine fun here [Jackson]. The Nullers and Martins have quarreled. Their friends are taking part. I stand off and hiss. . . . The game is for Carroll to offer, for Gov. Cannon has become very unpopular this season. Grundy should offer against Bell by the next election, he can either beat him or cripple him so bad he will be broken down and I would offer him a sufficient employment in his own district to prevent his mischief getting out of it. . . . I am ripe for a polick and have been and intend to be engaged occasionally in writing little pieces in the papers for the sole purpose of setting mischief afloat in the ranks and making quarrels among themselves. I could have been elected, I believe but if I had it would have been like Pyrrus' victory. The party had so arrayed their slanders, purchased Presses, told lies, and nobody here to contradict them that in two more years they would have lied my friends and myself into the Pacific ocean. I therefore concluded to stay at home and attend to them for a while. I have got them in a glorious way. They are quarreling amongst themselves very bitterly while I am drinking apple toddy and eating mutton."[19]

In the national campaign of 1840, Huntsman assumed the leadership in the District for the Democrats. Although he was ill he planned to scour the counties in the name of democracy. He planned an extensive speaking tour at which time both Democrats and Whigs would speak. "I propose that we will make appointments through all the counties and confine our lies to two or three hours speeches each. I never did nor could make a longer one and talk sense, nor can he. If he (Foster) chooses to take the whole day then I will make my own appointments and attend them."[20]

---

[19] Adam Huntsman to James K. Polk, January 1, 1838. MS. Photostats of Huntsman Correspondence in Tennessee State Library.

[20] Huntsman to Polk, May 25, 1840. That Andrew Jackson regarded Huntsman as an able politician is shown by his letter to Robert I. Chester, April 9, 1840: "It gives me great pleasure to hear that Huntsman has taken the field and that you will give the Whigs a sure defeat this fall. S. G. Heiskell, *Andrew Jackson and Early Tennessee History* (Nashville, 1920), I, 620.

Come what may Adam Huntsman was "ready to do battle for the cause of Democracy where the party may think it advisable for me to fight, attend the lead of a division or in the private ranks." It was in that campaign of 1840 that he planned "a bitter dose" for Ephriam Foster by planning democratic speakers on his "right flank and on the left flank" as he progressed through the district.[21]

But an election day did not finish the job for Huntsman, when this one was over, he accepted the returns and continued the fight for Democracy. On March 9, 1841, he was whipping up Democracy in general to defeat Milton Brown of Madison County, the Whig candidate for Congress. In October, 1842, he reported a political meeting of five or six hundred Whigs and three hundred Democrats in Jackson. "Things passed off heavenly," wrote Huntsman about the Whig meeting, "no enthusiasm nor could any excitement be got up, not one single convert, I think. I passed through the outskirts of the congregation, partook of their dinner, and converted a few to democracy while the Whig speakers were defending the Bankrupt law."[22]

Huntsman was very pleased with James K. Polk's nomination for the presidency in 1844 and wrote as follows:

I suppose miracles will not cease to exist in the land. To have supposed it possible that such a Possum looking fellow as you were twenty-five years ago would ever have been nominated for the President of the U.S. But so it is and we must make the best we can out of you. ... The Texas question is a powerful lever in our hands and will give us many Whig votes and we have set every engine to work already to put our forces in motion. Mr. Ewell will take the trail immediately.[23]

It was Huntsman who arranged to make speeches himself and for Polk to speak when the county and circuit courts were sitting. It was Huntsman who was "chucking full of fight" for the Democrats, even to numbering the stumps in the District. It was Huntsman who wrote for the Democratic papers under the name "A Subscriber" and reported in 1838 that ten out of fifteen Madison lawyers would go for Van Buren against Clay and Webster. It was Huntsman who recommended Henry Mc-

---

[21]*Ibid.*, July 20, 1840.
[22]*Ibid.*, October 21, 1842.
[23]Huntsman to Polk, June 11, 1844.

Corry, a worthy, qualified, and loyal Democrat for the position of Attorney-General (1838), who recommended that they fight the northern tariff laws by refusing to wear anything but "our Western home-made stuff," who recommended that they renew the combat for Texas, who collected the Democrats and "ate dinner upon a large scale" as they spoke at Denmark, Brownsville, Huntingdon. Here Huntsman added that he would not take $500 for his share of the fun. This was the one-legged political boss of the Western District of the Jacksonian Democrats.[24]

The year 1848 found Huntsman still interested in fighting those hot headed Southerners who were refusing to vote for any one who would not come out broadly against the Wilmot Proviso, but he added, "I have not applied to the state or general government heretofore for any sort of an appointment and confidently ask now for one at your hands, President Polk —to wit—that you will send me a commission under the great seal of the United States to stay at home."[25] Our politician must have been getting weary of "stumping the District!"

Too much emphasis cannot be placed upon the fact that Andrew Jackson and his Democrats were determined to get Crockett out of their way, that Jackson's relatives who normally would have been Whigs, put their shoulders behind a man like Huntsman and defeated Crockett so badly that he retired from the Western District and United States politics, bidding his friends and enemies good-bye very briefly but positively: "You can go to hell, but I am going to Texas!" This was a stupendous victory for the Jacksonian Democrats, for the frontier politician Crockett could be a dangerous enemy for anyone, and his unique personality had brought him and his district into nation-wide notice.[26] David's arrival in Texas in time to become a national hero at the Alamo, caused his political friends in Tennessee to renew the fight against the Jacksonian Democrats. Now the West Tennessean had become a national figure and people were ready to overlook his faults:

---

[24]*Ibid.*, January 1, 1838, May 26, 1838, June 30, 1838, November 17, 1838, December 16, 1838, January 20, 1840.

[25]*Ibid.*, April 23, 1848.

[26]See Appendix for several Crockett letters concerning the political affairs of the day.

Whatever may have been the imputed eccentricities of the frank Tennessean's political career, we believe he left no enemies on earth and that many a noble heart will heave a sigh at the recollection of his manly virtues, his uncalculating honesty of purpose and independence of character, his simplicity and kindness of heart and the generous gallantry which impelled him to such an untimely but glorious death beneath the swords of the Mexican enslavers. May the flowers of the far prairie cluster thickly and brightly above his moundering ashes![27]

West Tennessee rapidly became a stronghold of "Whiggery" and although Jackson himself spoke at the great Democratic rally in Jackson in October, 1840, the county went Whig, sending Whig representatives to Congress, Milton Brown (1841-1847) and William T. Haskell (1847-1849).[28] Two thousand five hundred attended the Whig convention in Jackson in October 1842 when speeches were delivered by Milton Brown, C. H. Williams, John W. Crockett, son of David, and Governor James K. Polk, when "fat pigs, sheep, turkeys and good old hard cider was enjoyed by the crowd."[29] Several hundred Whigs met at the courthouse in Jackson in 1849 to urge members of the party to unite, while in August, 1852, there was a spirited little affair in the way of a political tournament between young Whiggery and old Foggism represented in the persons of W. H. Stephens and Samuel McClanahan. Stephens made a two hour speech, McClanahan an hour speech, in which he showed that he [McClanahan] was a man of ability, a favorite of his party and an authority upon party questions. The warriors returned to the battle field after supper when Stephens again spoke three hours to the entire satisfaction of his warmest admirers. As the "Knights Clad in Armor" advanced upon the field, the contemporary reporter related the story thus:

His [Stephens] calm and composed manner, his impurturbable good humor and his chivalrous bearing, won all hearts and rallied to his standard the manly and the brave. He showed that the democracy of the South was against the Compromise [1850] . . . that Democracy had taken the stand that Congress could pass no law to punish any crime not specifically enumerated in the Constitution, as Negro stealing was not so defined the Fugitive Slave Law could be null and void.[30]

---

[27]Nashville *Republican*, May 12, 1836.
[28]The Whigs carried West Tennessee until 1856.
[29]Memphis *American Eagle*, October 21, 1842.
[30]Jackson *West Tennessee Whig*, August 5, 1852.

In 1855, when Andrew Johnson, the Democratic candidate, and Meredith P. Gentry, the Whig candidate, were running for governor, the two came campaigning in Jackson. The court house was filled to its capacity to hear the two candidates. It was Gentry's time to open the discussion, so he arose, dressed in a tailor-made suit; and as he walked to the speaker's stand, he laid a fine gold watch and chain on the table near the stand. He was an orator of rare ability who thrilled every person in the audience. After Mr. Gentry's first speech was over, Andrew Johnson arose amid loud applause. When he reached the speaker's stand, he laid on the table a large silver bull's-eye watch with a steel chain attached. James S. Lyon, an influential Whig of the county, remarked to all those around him; "Look at that demogogue! That bull's-eye watch will make him 500 votes in Madison County!" The bull's-eye watch exhibited throughout the state helped to roll up the votes, so that when election day came Johnson won by a few thousand votes.[31]

The Whig party in Tennessee was a powerful part of the party nationally. One portion of the Tennessee Whig party was born in Madison County. Not only Madison County became Whig, but also Henderson, Gibson, and Carroll were more so and the town of Jackson was the focal point of the Whig strength in the Western District. The bear-hunter, David Crockett, gave Andrew Jackson and his Democrat, Adam Huntsman, plenty of reason to worry, for these were men who were powerful enough to split the Democratic party. The Democrats called it a "motly party" made up of Black cockades and Blue Light Federalists, Nullifiers, Tariffites, and United States Bankites," those political heritics who have left the true political church and all others who have been enlisted by the Whig recruiting officers from the Republican ranks,"[32] but they had reason to be afraid of the strength the Whigs had gathered within a few short years. This was indeed a "whiggish community!"

---

[31]Charles McMillan, "Tales of Other Days in Madison," *Jackson Sun*, February 7, 1944.
[32]Nashville *Union*, April 22, 1835.

CHAPTER VI

OUR EARLY CONGRESSMEN

During the years from the organization of the county until 1917,[1] six natives of Madison have represented the people of this section in the Congress of the United States—five in the House of Representatives and one in the Senate. Adam R. Alexander, Adam Huntsman, Milton Brown, William T. Haskell, and B. A. Enloe served in the House, while Howell E. Jackson was the member of the Senate and later became a Justice of the Supreme Court of the United States.

Adam R. Alexander, the surveyor general of the Tenth District in the "Jackson Purchase," official of the land office in this district, born in Rockbridge County, Virginia, came to Tennessee in 1801 and located in Blount County; served as a member of the state senate from Maury County in 1817; moved to the Western District about 1819; was a member of the first County Court in 1821 which court was held in his home. In 1823-1827 he represented this district in the Eighteenth and Nineteenth Congresses, although Crockett came within an ace of being elected in 1825. One commentator said that for once the people showed good sense and elected Colonel Alexander by a large majority.

After he was defeated for re-election in 1828, he moved to Shelby County and was the representative from this county to the State Constitutional Convention in 1834. He returned to the Legislature in Nashville in 1841-1843.[2]

Chronologically the story of Adam Huntsman's career should appear here, but his career is so closely associated with that bear hunter and unique politician, David Crockett, who in

---

[1]The year 1917 has been used as the closing year included in this volume. A complete list of those men who have represented Madison in Congress may be found in the Appendix.

[2]*Biographical Dictionary of American Congress:* 1774-1927, (Washington, 1928), 630; Madison County Court Records.

turn was an important figure in the formation of the Whig party in Tennesse, that the writer has chosen to lift Huntsman from this chapter and place him in the story of Jackson, the political capital of West Tennessee.

As civilization moved westward, the adventurous leaders of the movement had little time to keep records, for they were making history, they were breaking the trail for future generations to follow. Milton Brown (1804-1883) was a typical leader of this era. Judge Brown was not only a politician who had the progress of this section at heart, an able and convincing speaker, a successful leader in the movement to build railroads to the new west, but he was an outstanding lawyer and a man of fame in both state and national politics.[3] Milton Brown, whose forefathers served in the Revolution, was born in Lebanon, Ohio; moved to Nashville at the age of nineteen at which place he read law in the office of Felix Grundy; traveled on horseback over a mere trail through dense timber and thick undergrowth to Paris, Tennessee, where he stayed a short while before his removal to Jackson in 1832;[4] served as judge of the Chancery Court of West Tennessee, 1835 to 1841; was president of the Mississippi and Tennessee Central Railroad from 1854 to 1856; was president of the Mobile and Ohio Railroad from 1856 to 1871.

In 1834, Milton Brown, a promising young lawyer of this new west, defended the noted outlaw, John A. Murrell.[5] So intense was the feeling against Murrell that many friends of the young lawyer advised him not to take the case as it would ruin his prospects. Other lawyers in this section are said to have refused, but Brown took the case regardless of the circumstances. When Murrell was caught, it was thought that he would surely hang for murder, but he was indicted for slave stealing. Brown told his associates that he had evidence that

---

[3]The writer gratefully acknowledges the use of a paper prepared by Mrs. Randall Vann, a granddaughter of Judge Brown, and read before the Madison County Historical Society in 1944.

[4]Milton Brown and William Stoddert announced the partnership and law office in Jackson. Jackson *Southern Statesman*, June 31, 1832.

[5]A more detailed account of this famous trial may be found in a later chapter, "John A. Murrell."

Murrell was a thief and not a murderer. Murrell was convicted of stealing slaves but not of murder.[6]

Milton Brown was the favorite orator of the day in this section of the Western District. It was he who was selected to give the "spread eagle" speech on the Fourth of July occasions before a very large and attentive crowd.[7] It was he who crusaded in the name of the "iron horse," attending public meetings in the county seats of the west, and partaking of barbecues such as the one at Jack's Creek in 1852. Here he made a convincing speech, showing that the railroad was much safer, quicker, and cheaper conveyance than the steam-boat.[8]

Every community must have a man with vision. Milton Brown was just such a man, for in the 1830's Milton Brown and William Armour were planning to build a railroad through West Tennessee. This dream of the "iron horse" did not die when the plans of the early thirties did not materialize. It was Judge Brown and General R. P. Neely of Bolivar who were the leaders in the movement to build the first railroad into Jackson, The Mississippi and Tennessee Central.[9] There were three obstacles in the building of railroads a century ago—finances, engineering, and antagonistic public opinion. Brown was an ideal person to be a leader in such a movement, for he believed in securing the services of good engineers, he had connections in Washington and in England with people who had money themselves and had confidence in him, and last, but very important, Judge Brown was a convincing speaker and thus the very one to present the problems to various gatherings and sell stock in the road. According to tradition his popularity with the stockholders and the people was shown by the fact that the first engine that came over the Mississippi and Tennessee Central into Jackson had the words "Judge Milton Brown" in gilt on the engine.[10] As president of the Mobile and Ohio from 1856 to 1871, he rendered invaluable service, keeping

---

[6]T. M. Gates's Scrap Book; Recollections of Mrs. Sarah T. Dancy in papers of Mrs. Randall Vann.
[7]*Southern Statesman*, July 13, 1833.
[8]*Tennessee Historical Magazine*, IX, 202.
[9]This road was built from Grand Junction to Jackson, a distance of 47.7 miles.
[10]T. M. Gates's Scrap Book. Contrary stories say "Gen. Rufus Neely" was on the first engine.

harmony among the officials, stilling the fears of those who doubted whether the road would ever be finished or not, and obtaining loans in the East and in England for the completion of the road bed. Then, after the Civil War when the road was almost a total wreck (Forrest and his men had done an excellent job while West Tennessee was occupied by the Federals), Judge Brown turned a deaf ear to the yelping crew and complaining customers and went to work to secure materials for the restoration of the road. When he was re-elected to the presidency of the road in 1866, the editor of the Mobile paper wrote: "Few men, if there is a single man in the south that could have accomplished as much as Judge Brown did. . . . Judge Brown is better fitted to continue as president than any other man."[11]

This famous lawyer and progressive citizen was elected as a Whig to the Twenty-Seventh, Twenty-Eighth, and Twenty-Ninth Congresses of the United States (1841-1847). Here, although he was a Whig, he frequently had the approval of many Democrats. On January 2, 1843, he delivered a forceful speech against the repeal of the bankrupt law. But it was the bill for the annexation of Texas that he is remembered more often than for anything else. Various bills had been defeated and it looked for a while as if the fate of Texas was extremely doubtful. In January, 1845, a resolution was brought before the Senate by Mr. Foster of Tennessee and before the House by Milton Brown of Tennessee. This resolution was finally passed and Texas was annexed. Democrats accused the Whigs of shifting positions, saying that the House Resolution moved by Milton Brown was "as an arrow from a friendly quiver,"[12] but when the whole question was considered the same editor concluded that Milton Brown had the peace and the welfare of the country at heart, not party politics. He then added:

> In this movement of the Whigs members from Tennessee, they have acted under the most solemn convictions of duty and patriotism. I know not in what light our friends at home may view the matter, but I feel sure they would agree with us if they had been here seeing things as we have seen them.[13]

---

[11]*West Tennessee Whig,* April 28, 1866.
[12]*Nashville Whig,* February 11, 1845.
[13]*Ibid.,* February 27, 1845.

During his entire life, Milton Brown showed a keen interest in education. In 1834 he was listed as one of the Trustees of the Madison Male Academy (later West Tennessee College and Union University). He gave his moral support to the Memphis Conference Female Institute and contributed liberally from his personal funds for the construction of the west wing of that building. Bishops and interested friends met at his home to discuss the organization of the Colored Methodist Church South. He was greatly instrumental in influencing his wife's friends, Mrs. Vanderbilt and Commodore Vanderbilt to donate money for what later became Vanderbilt University.[14] Brown was one of the trustees of Vanderbilt until his death.

Fortunately Milton Brown was a man who was appreciated during his lifetime. The Memphis *Avalanch* of 1874 spoke of him as "one of the first men, intellectually in Tennessee and in dignity and purity of character, he had few peers."[15] Another tribute to the Judge is found in a paper of 1855, at which time his name was suggested to fill the vacancy in the Supreme Court of Tennessee. The recommendations for this judge of West Tennessee read:

> In looking over the names of the leading members of the Bar of West Tennessee, I think the Hon. Milton Brown the most prominent. He has devoted more than twenty years to the study and laborious practice of the law. There are not many better real men in Tennessee and there are not many who could bring to the Supreme Bench as much legal ability. Added to this, he is a political man. He is a man of excellent common sense. His habits of laborious research, his intimate knowledge of the details of practice as well as of the great principles of science of jurisprudence; his age and standing all point to him as a person upon whom the State might safely rely, as a member of its Supreme Judiciary.[16]

That William T. Haskell, the lawyer, congressman, military hero, poet, and orator was one of the most brilliant men in the history of Tennessee and the most eloquent speaker the State has ever produced is an undisputed fact. In his *The Bench and Bar of Tennessee,* Joshua W. Caldwell said that it was a universal opinion that Haskell was one of the most elo-

---

[14]Recollections of Mrs. Sarah T. Dancy.
[15]Papers of Mrs. Randall Vann. *Avalanche*, March 12, 1874.
[16]Jackson *West Tennessee Whig,* August 31, 1855.

quent speakers in the state. John Trotwood Moore in *Tennessee: The Volunteer State* spoke of him as "an orator of wit, sarcasm, fiery invictus, flowery peoration, moreover one of the greatest intellectuals of the time." Oliver P. Temple in his *East Tennessee in the Civil War* very succinctly placed him on the pinnacle of the intellectuals, thus: "William T. Haskell surpassed all his contemporaries either in or out of Tennessee in dazzling brilliancy."[17]

William T. Haskell, the tall, black-eyed, imperial looking idol of Tennessee, was born in Murfreesboro, Tennessee, in 1818. He was the son of Joshua Haskell, the first judge to hold courts in West Tennessee and nephew of Honorable Charles Ready, a member of Congress from Murfreesboro District. Private tutors prepared him for entrance to the University of Nashville in 1835, at which school he was a most negligent student. His love of excitement caused him to leave school without his degree and to become a soldier in the Second Seminole War in Florida in 1836. After his return from Florida, he resumed his study of law, was admitted to the bar in 1836 and practiced law in Jackson. He served in the lower house as representative from Madison County in 1840.

Soon the drums of war could be heard again. As colonel of the Second Regiment of Tennessee Volunteers, he bravely led his men off to the Mexican War to defend the flag whose honor had been questioned. One hundred and eighteen men and boys from Madison County followed their leader on the three days' march to Memphis. He was a gallant soldier, a capable leader, very popular with the troops under his command. A typical comment from one in his command came from John W. McClanahan: "We are much rejoiced here and I know our friends will be at home at Haskell's election. He is very active and energetic."[18]

It was doubtless upon his ability as an orator that most of his fame rested among the Tennesseans and those outside of the state. Before the Civil War, Tennessee was known as

---

[17] John Trotwood Moore, *Tennessee: the Volunteer State: 1789-1923*, (Chicago, 1923), I, 423; Joshua Caldwell, *The Bench and Bar of Tennessee* (Knoxville, Tennessee, 1898), 238-240. Hereinafter cited as *Bar in Tennessee*.

[18] John W. McClanahan to Mrs. Sarah Taylor, August 15, 1846. MS. Guy Hall collection.

the "stump speaking state" of the Union. Haskell did his part to help give it this name, for in 1844 he stumped the state for Henry Clay and was considered one of the most brilliant speakers, notwithstanding the fact that John Bell, Gustavus A. Henry, "the Eagle Orator," Neil S. Brown, Meredith P. Gentry, Cave Johnson, Aaron Brown, and Andrew Johnson were his contemporaries and noted orators all. Newspapers of 1844 speak of "glorious Whig meetings." At such a meeting of ten thousand Whigs in Memphis, Haskell was cheered enthusiastically.[19]

One of his most dramatic and best orations was delivered in 1856 on the summit of Methodist Hill in Knoxville before a crowd of twenty thousand. He spoke for four hours and it is said that not one person in the audience withdrew. As his enthusiasm grew and the day became warmer, he cast aside his coat, tie, and vest. His wonderful voice could be heard by every person present. His enthusiasm and patriotism seemed to set fire to his heart and free the unlimited flow of purest and strongest words, the richest imagination. At one time during the oration he summoned the spirits of the mighty leaders of the Whig party who had gone to the Great Beyond. Calling first the shades of Webster and Clay, he turned towards the home of Hugh Lawson White, "the American Cato," and explained that the spirit of White was before him. He painted his word picture so vividly that men's faces paled, women shrieked and fainted from terror. Then he very calmly waved the spirit away and continued the speech. Tradition doubtless is correct when it declares that his was one of the grandest orations heard on Tennessee soil.[20]

---

[19]Memphis *American Eagle,* May 31, 1844. The true and powerful Whig orator was still bearing himself gallantly in 1852 according to an account from a Nashville paper: "We have rarely ever listened to a more brilliant and powerful argument than that of Gen. Haskell on Broad Street Tuesday evening. . . . The audience was very large; and we never saw one more chained in attention to the speaker. The many Whigs present were greatly strengthened in their confidence and determination to carry the State. Our friends from a distance may rest perfectly assured that Gen. Haskell is a powerful debater and greatly an over-match for Col. Guild with whom he will canvass the State. We have heard the opinion expressed by a clear-headed sensible man that this speech was in better taste and in every way the ablest speech ever delivered within the corporation of Nashville." *West Tennessee Whig,* August 5, 1852.

[20]Caldwell, *Bar in Tennessee,* 238-240.

One account reprinted in the Franklin, Tennessee, *Review and Journal* in 1881 tells of a three hour speech delivered in a grove near Colonel H. S. Ewing's by this "erratic genius, the most powerful orator that has ever appeared upon the hustings of this State. It is remembered to this day as an oration of tremendous power, beauty, and eloquence. It swayed the vast audience like the tempest does the eagle when its black wings are spread to its utmost tension. In one of his bursts of oratory he used a figure which likened the old Whig party to a vast sea, in which sported such leviathians as Webster, Clay, Prentiss, Bell, and others. The crowd from its very verge inclined bodily towards the inspired speaker, and was as splendid an exhibition of the power of eloquence over the hearts of men as was ever seen."[21]

This gifted orator was elected to Congress in 1847 but he did not like the life connected with the position, so he refused re-election.[22] His sensitive nature, his highly strung nerves, and the irregularities of his life did not fit him to deal with practical affairs. The people of Tennessee mourned over the fact that the last days of this genius were spent in a hospital for the insane at Hopkinsville, Kentucky. That his friends and the public in general were very happy over the news of his improvement, shortly before his death, is shown by a Nashville paper which reported that soon they would have an intellectual treat, for General Haskell was planning to entertain his friends with some lectures and recitations.[23] He died on March 12, 1859, and was buried in Riverside Cemetery in Jackson.

When Nature bestows her blessings upon individuals, she often allots many talents to one person. William T. Haskell had a gift for song. One of his poems, "The Ransomed," has been compared in style and beauty with the work of Edgar Allan Poe. It is known to Tennesseans by the first line, "I'm adrift on life's ocean," rather than the title under which it was printed in contemporary papers. This poem is said to have been written during one of his lucid periods while he was at the asylum in Kentucky. If the first part is as wild as a cry of

---

[21] Franklin *Review and Journal*, 1881.
[22] A MS of the Whig vote in one of the precincts in Madison County showed the popularity of Haskell. The vote was 566 to 106 in 1844.
[23] Nashville *Daily Gazette*, June 7, 1858.

a lost spirit, the second is as peaceful and beautiful as the dream of the blest:

THE RANSOMED

Part I

I'm adrift on life's ocean, and wildly I sweep,
Aimless and helmless, its fathomless deep;
The wild winds assail me, it threateningly storms,
The clouds roll around me in hideous forms;
I drift to a lee shore! I strike! am aground!
The mad waters whelm me! I drown! Oh, I drown!
Mercy! Oh, mercy! Oh, Lord set me free,
And take me, Oh, take me, to Heaven and Thee.

I wander life's desert—lone, desolate, sad!
Faint, reeling, and weary; I'm mad! Oh, I'm mad!
No glad waters greet me, no streams flowing free;
I perish, I perish! Oh, God, set me free.
Ah! hopeless I pray Thee; 'tis idle and vain!
I perish! I perish! Rain, rain! give me rain!
Let the stress of deliverance flow gently to me,
And drift me, Oh, drift me, to Heaven and Thee.

'Mid the wranglings of men and their conflicts so fierce
Half mad and despairing, my lips spit a curse,
Instead of imploring a refuge and peace
From life's maddening battle, for hope and release,
I bear on defiantly, proud, reckless, unblanched
At the dangers that hem me—the curses I launched
At earth and at Heaven, Lord Mercy for me!
Receive me! Receive me! to Heaven and Thee!

Part II

But the storm howls no longer, the desert is gone—
The battle's fierce strife no more hurries me on;
The tempest no more last the ocean's calm breast,
And the clouds float in beauty afar to the west.
I more through life's bowers full of bliss and love.
Looking fondly to earth and with transport above—
And an angel soft whispers: "The Lord sets thee free,
To come to me! come to me! dwell here with me!"

I thank Thee, Oh, Lord that roving career
Was checked by the hand of Omnipotence here;
That struck from its jarred equilibrium the mind

Whose balance my madness and folly combined
Had periled fore'er in my earthly career,
While night's thick'ning darkness encompassed me here;
And my soul is ransomed, unprisoned and free
I am coming, Oh, Lord! I bow before Thee.

Joy! Joy! Oh, anguish and sorrow no more
Shall lend me its victim on Life's crumbling shore,
The winds waft me gently, I perish no more;
I thirst not the war of Life's struggle is o'er
Hope beckons me on with the sweet whispering tale,
To walk through, all hopefully, Life's pleasant vale;
And I come to Thee, Lord! unprisoned and free,
And I bless Thee! ah! bless Thee! for mercy to me![24]

Among the most distinguished sons of Madison County appears the name of Howell E. Jackson, who rose like a meteor from lawyer to state senator, United States Senator, Judge of the Federal Court, and justice of the United States Supreme Court. The county has sent numerous state officials to Nashville, five to Congress but only one to the Supreme Court of the land.

Howell E. Jackson was the son of Dr. Alexander Jackson, a cultured, refined gentleman, an early member of the medical profession in Tennessee. Howell E. Jackson was born in Paris, Tennessee, April 8, 1832; came with his parents to Jackson, in 1840; graduated from West Tennessee College in Jackson in 1848; studied at the University of Virginia in 1851-1852; read law with Judge A. W. O. Totten and Judge Milton Brown, and graduated in law at Lebanon, Tennessee, in 1856. After practicing law in Jackson for two years, he went to Memphis where he practiced until the outbreak of the Civil War. As a strong Whig he opposed secession, but when Tennessee seceded he proved that he was loyal to his state and her fate in the Confederacy, serving as receiver of sequestered property for West Tennessee during the war.[25]

Following the Sectional Conflict, Jackson returned to Memphis, but came on to Jackson in 1874 where he formed a partnership with General A. W. Campbell, again meeting with

---

[24]William T. Haskell as a General in the Mexican War is discussed more fully in the story of the Mexican War.

[25]*Biographical Dictionary of American Congress,* 1142.

success in his chosen profession. He was described by his friends as a man of rather small statue, quiet, and reserved in manner, but genial and companionable with his intimates and withal a man of accurate learning, sound judgment and strict integrity.[26]

In 1880, Jackson was elected to the legislature, only to be chosen the following year for the United States Senate, when it seemed that not one of the Democratic Candidates had a chance of being chosen. (Jackson not only was not a candidate but did not want the office.) Here, in the Senate, he soon distinguished himself among his colleagues as a very able lawyer. Towards the end of the term he was appointed by President Cleveland as Circuit Judge of the United States Sixth Judicial District. Although he was reluctant to accept the position, his friends persuaded him that it was his duty to do so and he accepted. His services in this capacity were distinguished with "learning, common sense, fidelity to the entire satisfaction of the bar and the public."[27] A beautiful tribute to Jackson appears in the records of the United States Circuit Court of Appeals for the Sixth District. Here Jackson's characteristics are spoken of as follows:

"He was a man of quick and clear perception, ripe in learning and experience and ready and almost unerring in the application of both to the points presented. He was at the same time considerate, patient, careful, and thorough, sparing neither labor nor pains in investigating the facts and the law, and testing his own cool, deliberate judgment before finally adopting them. No judge knew better how to hear cautiously, to answer wisely, to consider soberly, and to decide impartially; four things that Socrates tells us belong to a Judge."[28]

In 1891, when the Circuit Court of Appeals was established in Cincinnati, he became the first presiding judge. The duties of the bench appealed to Jackson more than the storm and stress of politics. In 1893, he was appointed by President Benjamin Harrison to the United States Supreme Court, Harrison opposed Jackson in political views, but knew that his Democratic Senate would probably not affirm a Republican appointment and he

---

[26]Sketch by Douglas Anderson in Nashville *Banner*, 1925; Speer, *Prominent Tennesseans*, 424-425.

[27]*In Memorium;* United States Circuit Court of Appeals for Sixth District (Cincinnati, 1895), 4.

[28]*Ibid.*

also recognized Jackson's ability as a judge. Harrison wrote to Jackson at the time of the appointment that he was certain that he would "exercise the duties of this very high and responsible office with industry, fidelity, and patriotism. . . . I know you to be a conscientious and industrious judge and a God fearing man."[29]

Jackson distinguished himself during the short time that he served as a Justice of the Supreme Court, but he soon became ill and growing weakness kept him from his official duties most of the term of October 1894, when the eight justices were equally divided in their opinions on an Income Tax case, and Jackson summoned all his strength to take his place on the bench, expecting to cast the vote which would decide the validity of the income tax. One of the other judges changed his opinion and Jackson's dissenting opinion was read in May 1895. A few months later he died at his home in Nashville. (1895)

Strange things seemed to have happened in Jackson's life. If he had followed his own ideas rather than those of his father, he would have been a farmer—not a fancy farmer, but just a dirt farmer. He was a state credit Democrat, but he was elected to the Legislature when his opinions were offensive to the majority of his party; a Democrat he was elected to the Senate by Republican vote; he was appointed to the bench when he did not seek the place; and finally being still a Democrat and having been a supporter of the Confederacy, he was nominated to the supreme bench of the United States by a Republican president and confirmed by a Democratic Senate.[30]

The name of B. A. Enloe appears upon the list of famous sons of Madison County. This intensively active man represented the Eighth District in Congress from 1887 to 1895, gaining while there a reputation as a Democratic leader and fighter against Republican misrule. It was here that he worked untiringly to purge the padded pension rolls of unworthy graft upon the federal treasury. W. H. Carroll wrote of this in 1894: "The defeat of Enloe would be a great delight to Pension sharks who have been living on money fraudulently appropriated by the Government . . . his election will be a continuation of honesty and economy."[31]

---

[29]*In Memorium by United States Supreme Court* (1895), 5.
[30]Caldwell, *Bench and Bar*, 360-362.
[31]W. H. Carroll to Henry McCorry, October 19, 1894.

Enloe seemed to know how to sympathize with the masses and their hardships and proved himself to be their friend. In 1894, John E. Givens of McKenzie, although he was a Populist, threw his support to Enloe, stating that he was a "true and honest man—a man of principles. He [Enloe] has never violated pledges he made to the people or disobeyed their instructions. He voted for the free and unlimited coinage of silver in every Congress and he fought for it on the floor of Congress. He made a square fight for it in the late race for re-nomination. He risked his seat in Congress before his own party on the issue. We demand selection of United States Senators by the people (which he voted for), the passage of the anti-option law (which he introduced in the house), the low tariff (which he and the people's party voted for.)"[32]

Writing in 1916, the editor of the Jackson *Sun* spoke of Enloe as an extraordinarily busy man, a man unexcelled in Tennessee in his fight for what he deemed to be the best interests of the state and its people. Gus Enloe was considered by many people the most level-headed, capable man in the game of politics of Tennessee, one that was capable of gracing any office. During the years of Enloe's life in which he was engaged in the newspaper business, he always had some special purpose in view, some reform to establish, or some abuse to abolish. He and Colonel Robert Gates founded the Jackson *Sun* in 1875. Enloe was editor of this paper for fourteen years.

After his eight years as a representative of this district in Congress, he turned his energy towards establishing a Nashville *Daily Sun*, and later the Louisville *Daily Dispatch*. In 1904, he was elected to the Tennessee Railroad Commission and was soon made its chairman. In 1911 and 1913, he came within a few votes of being elected to the United States Senate.[33]

The *Biographical Dictionary of American Congress; 1774-1927* gives the following summary of the important events in the life of B. A. Enloe:

---

[32]Hand Bill, October 27, 1894. "Enloe was known to his associates as a man of unquestioned integrity, as an effective speaker, as one who mixed well with the great, near great, and the populace." Philip Holland to the writer, May 19, 1945.

[33]Morgan Blake and Stewart Towe, *Lawmakers and Public Men of Tennessee* (Nashville, 1915), 177.

Born near Clarksburg, in Carroll County, Tennessee, January 18, 1848; attended the public schools, Bethel College, McKenzie, Tennessee, and Cumberland University at Lebanon, Tennessee; while a student at the latter institution in 1869 was elected a member of the State House of Representatives; re-elected under the new Constitution in 1870; was graduated from the law department of Cumberland University in 1872; was admitted to the bar in 1873 and commenced to practice in Jackson; delegate to the Democratic National Convention at Baltimore in 1872; presidential elector on the Democratic ticket of Tilden and Hendricks in 1876; appointed a commissioner by the Governor in 1878 to negotiate a settlement of the State debt; served on the State executive committee 1878-1880; delegate to the Democratic National Convention in Cincinnati in 1880; edited the *Jackson Tribune and Sun* 1874-1886; elected as a Democrat to 50th, 51st, 52nd, and 53rd Congresses (1887-1895); unsuccessful candidate for reelection 1894; edited the *Daily Sun* in Nashville for two years; secretary of State Fair Commission and director of exhibits from Tennessee at World's Fair in St. Louis in 1903; railroad commissioner of Tennessee from 1904 to death in 1922 in Nashville; interment in Mount Olivet Cemetery.[34]

Enloe lived in those days when Madison County was playing a leading role in state politics, when men took their religion and politics seriously, when Henry McCorry, Ernest Bullock and Enloe were important figures in the affairs of the state. Correspondence between Enloe and McCorry show the closest friendship between the two and Enloe's unlimited confidence in McCorry's ability as a political leader.[35] That Enloe was a good orator and loyal Democrat is shown by the following account of a Democatic rally at Trenton in 1880:

Mr. Enloe's speech was full of good Democratic food and fuel and the grace and ease of his towering form added force in what he said. A man could look at him and see that he was a Democrat.[36]

---

[34]*Biographical Dictionary of American Congress: 1774-1927*, 946-7.
[35]Enloe to McCorry, September 17, 1888, August 27, 1888. Curtis Bray collection.
[36]Jackson *Tribune and Sun*, July 23, 1880.

CHAPTER VII

THE MILITIA AND THE SEMINOLE WAR

It is difficult for us to-day to understand the position that the organization of the State Militia played in the social and civic life of the people in the early days of this county. As soon as a few people moved into a community, voting precincts were formed, certain houses were selected as voting places, and militia organizations were made. The same legislature of 1821 that created the county of Madison made provision for the militia set up in the county thus: "The militia of Madison shall compose of the 75th regiment and shall hold their regimental muster at the place of holding court in the said county on the third Friday in October." All persons between the ages of eighteen and forty-five (with the exception of court officers, ministers, public ferry men, mail carriers, and keepers of grist mills) were required to serve in the militia. Officers, a captain, two lieutenants, and an ensign, were elected by the men in each company which consisted of at least forty and not more than ninety men. On July 21, 1822, Robert H. Dyer of Madison County reported that Andrew Hays was elected captain, James Tidwell, lieutenant, and Granberry Chambers, ensign of the 75th Regiment. Tax lists were made out from the muster rolls and by persons from each company. Taxes were paid on "Muster Days."[1]

Positions higher in rank in the Tennessee militia were strongly contended for by the military leaders of the State. There was a battle-royal in 1825 over the major-general-ship of the Old Third Division. Two men from Madison County were most desirous of the position—Robert H. Dyer and William Arnold, both with the rank of colonel at that time. Arnold was elected the first major-general of the District by

---

[1] Minute Book Madison County 1821-1825; letter of William Braden to Daniel Graham, July 31, 1822, MS.

a vote of twenty-five to sixteen.² In 1831, General A. B. Bradford of Jackson was elected Brigadier-General of the 14th Brigade Tennessee Militia by a vote of sixteen to eleven. Two years later General Bradford was elected Marjor-General to fill the place vacated by the resignation of General William Arnold who had held that position since 1825. Frequent references to these elections in the contemporary papers show the great interest that these contests aroused in the community.³

No day with the exception of court day when the people came to laugh at anything droll which came up, was as exciting as "muster day." There was a penalty by law for not appearing on muster day, but this was useless, for these days— the battalion muster in the spring and the regimental muster in the fall—were the greatest days of the year, veritable "field days." The old who were past muster, the young, the under age, the women, the children, and Negroes all came, for there were parades by the crack company of light infantry, the "Hickory Guards" (attached to the 75th by the Act of 1832) in front of LaFayette's Inn. Dances on the green usually followed the noon meal at which time "the body of the county" had gathered to visit with each other; to admire the plummed warriors in their gayest trappings as they drilled in the morning with the tallest men always leading the company; to cast straw votes upon various political topics of the day;⁴ to witness and participate in "shooting matches" and running races; and last but not least to settle or witness the settlement of some difficulty that had arisen on road working day or upon some other occasion in the neighborhood. This last event was usually done not with pistols and knives, but with brawny fists that were hardened with endless days of toil. One important feature of the day was the music of the drum and fife and no company was allowed to be mustered in without the drum and fife major. This "divine" music to the tune of "Yankee Doodle" and the "Jay Bird Died with the Whooping Cough" brought out the most thrilling patriotic demonstrations, arousing the "spread eagle" feeling in everyone's bosom.⁵

---
²Jackson *Gazette*, July 2, August 6, 1824.
³Jackson *Southern Statesman*, August 24, 1833.
⁴Jackson *Southern Statesman*, July 9, 1831.
⁵J. S. Williams, *Old Times in West Tennessee* (Memphis, 1873), 131.

Jackson was the depot for the arms and munitions of the western division. Frequent notices in the papers announced that "stands of muskets" had been packed in Nashville and would be delivered on the appointed days. Notices in June, 1832, told of the new company of "Jackson Guards," commanded by Captain Miller, which made such a fine appearance that they would do honor to the town and themselves. Great plans were made for the Fourth of July celebration of 1832. The cavalry attached to the 75th Regiment was to parade in the town of Jackson equipped with "horses sufficient strong and active to leap a pole at least five feet high, to perform sword exercises and the cavalry manoeuvers at large."[6] The Declaration of Independence was read, an oration delivered and a barbecue eaten by all those "who saw fit to partake." Milton Brown presented the colors to the company in behalf of the ladies of the community, inspiring all with these ringing words:

In this country the science of war is too much neglected. In the enjoyment of peace and prosperous in everything that can make us happy as a nation, we are losing that spirit of patriotism and chivalry which constitutes the safety of a republic. Our arms are growing rusty by disuse. The military science is becoming more and more neglected and it is to be feared will fall into entire disrepute, unless it should be revived by the patriotism of volunteer companies. It is upon them that we are to depend in the future for a knowledge of tactics. They are to be the schools in which will be taught the science of war. Your fellow-citizens, therefore look to you with pride, with honor and success. But what will be most gratifying to you is that the ladies of Jackson and its vicinity, your female friends, who know you personally have been witnesses of your zeal and patriotism. May you never forsake or dishonor this standard of color. Should days of peril and war again return to our country and you be called on to defend her rights, the moment dangers gather thick around you raise your eyes to that Eagle and remember that none is worthy to look upon it who has not in his bosom the heart of a soldier. Let it go before you and lead you to victory. Let it be the first and the last to retreat from it, and when it shall have waved in triumph on the field of victory, witnessed the laurels you have gathered under its wings, bring it back with you to your homes, present it to those who gave it to you and say to them that you have not dishonored it.[7]

---

[6]Jackson *Southern Statesman*, May 5, 1832.
[7]*Ibid.*, July 7, 1832.

THE SEMINOLE WAR

Madison countians played their roles in the Seminole War of 1836. Richard Henderson met a tragic death in the wilds of Florida on December 28, 1835 in Dade's desperate battle with the Seminole Indians. He had graduated from the United States Military Academy in 1835 and had planned to resign his commision and go into the field of medicine. While he was in Pensacola he heard of disturbances among the Seminole Indians, the result of attempts to move them to the West, and so he went as a volunteer with the column which Major Francis L. Dade was leading into Florida. Six miles north of Withoacoochee, the column was ambushed by Indians led by the chief Osceola of the Seminoles. Henderson was wounded in the first general fire but kept on fighting. There were 800 Seminoles and at least 100 savage Negroes who completely destroyed Dade's column of 108 men, leaving only one survivor.[8] A beautiful monument of white marble was erected at West Point to commemorate "Dade and his command."

Men of Madison could not resist a call for volunteers to fight the Indians that came in the spring of 1836:

CALL FOR VOLUNTEERS: The call presents an opportunity to show to the world, that here, at least the days of chivalry are not gone, and that when their country calls, it will be answered by our going with an alarcity worthy of the high character of Tennessee. Now is the day, and now is the hour, ye chivalrous spirits of Madison County. There is no mistake this time, your favorite, General Gaines calls upon you—it is the services you prefer the theatre of operations has the eyes of the world upon it—honor, distinction; immortal fame are to be won on this field. Let it not be said, that Madison County failed to answer to a call when there was no mistake about going.[9]

Fifteen hundred volunteers from West Tennessee including Company B, "the Madison Grays," proceeded to Fayetteville, the place of rendezvous. Officers of this company included J. H. McMahon, captain; Wise Cook, 1st Lieutenant; W. O. Butler, 2nd Lieutenant. Among the field officers was A. B. Bradford of Jackson who was elected colonel. These well mounted, handsomely equipped men presented a martial appearance as they responded to President Jackson's call, showing that the men from Madison were merely some of those typical

---

[8]Nashville *Banner*, December 28, 1935, quoting a paper of 1835.
[9]Randolph *Recorder*, July 22, 1836, quoting the *Truth Teller*.

Tennesseans who were ready for the field of battle when the call came and they were always inspired by a seemingly limitless amount of American patriotism.[10]

The Tennessee brigade arrived at Tallahasse in the late summer of 1836 and started through the Indian country, suffering from want of food for themselves and their horses. In the fall and winter they fought a successful campaign in which Colonel Bradford and Captain J. H. McMahon were favorably mentioned in the reports.[11] Although the campaign was not a brilliant one because of the unfavorable territory, in which they had to operate, yet the contemporary historian was confident that there was never a more "patriotic, courageous brigade" that left the State of Tennessee. "The soldierly bearing of the men was conspicuous both on the march and in battle. By their courage, their bold and fearless charges, they drove the Indians into the Everglades."[12]

Madison Countians were writing their names in the military annals of the State during the early days.

---

[10] Jo Guild, *Old Times in Tennessee* (Nashville, 1878), 122.
[11] *Ibid.*, 133-134.
[12] *Ibid.*, 138.

CHAPTER VIII

THE SANTE FE ADVENTURE

Adventurers as well as home-seekers came to the Western District in the early days. No story of those early days has more of a western flavor as that which appeared in the March, 1825 issue of the Jackson *Gazette*. It was announced that the organization had been formed, known as the "Santa Fe Company," a trading company headed by Lieut. Jesse Embrey. These men from Madison were joined by other men of adventurous spirits from Winchester, Tennessee, Davidson County, and Memphis. A band of forty, "each having one pack-horse, besides the one he strides and some two," set out on an expedition to the far-away Santa Fe Country.[1] Current issues of the Jackson *Gazette* contain several references to the plans for the departure. The company partook of a farewell dinner at the Bell Tavern, and then set out for Memphis, Little Rock, and the far west.

Months passed and nothing was heard of the fate of the company until the following November when several of the party returned in good health. They brought with them 630 fine looking mules, though in bad order, $138 in gold, and $13,000 in silver.[2] The company had the misfortune of losing 130 of the animals on their return trip, which was caused by the sudden erruption and howling of a gang of wolves late in the night. The sentry awakened and was so terrified that he came running and screaming into camp, exclaiming: "Indians! Indians!" This alarmed the mules and 130 broke from the gang and were irretrievably lost.[3] (Mr. Gholson, alone, lost thirty.)

---

[1]Jackson *Gazette*, March 5, 1825; Samuel C. Williams, *West Tennessee*, 244.

[2]Jackson *Gazette*, November 26, 1825; S. C. Williams, *West Tennessee*, 244.

[3]Nashville *Whig*, December 12, 1825, quoting the Jackson *Gazette*.

The adventurers described the country they had seen in the West as very poor, mostly prairie; the people as indolent and ignorant who cultivated no farms of consequence but lived in villages and raised large stocks of mules and sheep. These Sante Fe mules were so used to grazing that they had to be taught to eat corn by cramming the corn in their mouths. The natives of this far West used knives, rather than shears, to sheer their sheep and they were so expert in the use of this knife that they could "divest ten sheep of their coats whilst one is sheared in the usual way of this country."[4]

As the days passed, other members of the company drifted in. Among these were Dr. Royal, who proposed to publish a "Journal of the Tennessee Caravan which left Jackson April 1, 1825 for Sante Fe, New Mexico"; Abram and B. Smith of Madison County and Samuel Winchester of Memphis who sold their goods at the Pass and turned their faces homeward, but were robbed within six days by a party of Indians who took seventy-five mules from them; Miller, Botts, Voorheer, Massie, Nesbitt, and Smith who returned by Texas, and Louisiana; Joseph Nicholson, who offered nine "first rate Santa Fe Mules for sale."[5]

Thus began the trek of the West Tennessean to Texas! Where land was cheap, these adventurous men of the Western District could not resist the temptation to go and invest. A great migration took place as the years passed—the Santa Fe Adventure was only the beginning!

---

[4]*Ibid.*
[5]Jackson *Gazette,* December 17, 1825; January 28, 1826; S. C. Williams, *West Tennessee,* 245.

CHAPTER IX

THE COUNTY AND TEXAS INDEPENDENCE

Tennesseans went to Texas during the years 1821 to 1835 in considerable numbers. This fact coupled with the fact that Sam Houston and David Crockett were among those Tennesseans who went to this new country in search of cheap lands and a new home made everyone in Tennessee interested in the fate of Texas. Contemporary newspapers furnished enough news about this "new country" which was attracting Tennesseans to show that Texas was just a part of the story of American expansion and that Tennesseans, among whom were many Madison Countians, were a part of that westward migration. Those aggressive Americans of the 1820's and 1830's were accused of going to Texas with the Constitution in their pockets. If the following quotation from the Jackson *Truth Teller* of 1835 is considered, it is more than probable that some West Tennesseans were among those who were guilty of having that Constitution with them:

Nothing short of cessation of wheels of nature could check emigration, which would soon be so great that it would be sufficient (if necessary) to maintain their independence against the Mexican Government via arma. . . . If you want to make property faster than you are making it, if you wish to see a prettier country than you have ever seen, if you want to find that place where a family can live with less labor, and yet where labor is more profitable than any where else, go to Texas![1]

Authorities in Washington were careful to observe the obligations of neutrality, but local officials and communities did not recognize any such formalities. A Randolph *Recorder* reporter visited Jackson in November, 1835, and found that the young men were discussing Texas and organizing a corps to fight her wars. This western reporter concluded: "We be-

---

[1]Nashville *Union*, July 22, 1835.

live them [the young men] not only fine but gallant and chivalrous. With Colonel McMahon at their head, they would form a corps as invincible as Gibraltar. There is not a braver and more chivalrous band of spirits in the world than the young men of Tennessee."[2] After the fall of the Alamo, March 5, 1836, interest increased until mass meetings at which resolutions were adopted, funds were donated, and volunteers raised were held all over the state.[3] Money, sympathy, bayonets, bullets, and hearts were offered with a spirit that patriotism and liberty alone have the power to inspire.

A meeting of a "large and respectable" character was held in Jackson when public sympathy was expressed towards oppressed Texas. Honorable Joshua Haskell presided over this meeting, while Joseph H. Talbot acted as secretary. Judge Read made an eloquent plea for the defense of his "brothers and sisters." A general expression of patriotism and philanthropy was manifested throughout the multitude that was present and funds and volunteers were raised and enrolled with much nobleness of spirit. The subscription list mounted to $750 at this meeting.[4] The spirit of Liberty had kindled from heart to heart over the whole country, for Texas, bleeding, and struggling, had fired the hearts of all American patriots. These citizens of Madison County were just some of the patriotic Americans who were aroused to the point of drafting resolutions and appointing a committee to "solicit and receive contributions of money for the purpose of arming and equipping such persons as may volunteer in the service of Texas." This committee was composed of General A. B. Bradford, J. S. Lyon, William Taylor, John Freeman, Colonel J. H. McMahon. The Memphis paper recorded further details of this stirring meeting as follows:

Judge Read explained the subject to the meeting in a speech characteristic of the philanthropy of that distinguished gentleman, and

---

[2]Randolph *Recorder*, November 13, 1835.

[3]The first accounts of the Alamo told that Charles Haskell, the son of Judge Haskell, and Major Autry of Jackson were among the victims. Later, Haskell was reported safe, but was killed at Goliad. In 1836, the editor of the Memphis *Enquirer* predicted that 500 Tennessee riflemen could conquer Mexico, that Colonel R. I. Chester had returned to raise these 500. Memphis *Enquirer*, April 12, 1836.

[4]Memphis *Enquirer*, May 4, April 27, 1836.

proved to the satisfaction of all present, that the cause of Texas was a struggle between liberty and despotism—between our kindred and a military despot, who had violated every principle of the constitution of Mexico, adopted and promulgated in 1824 under which, and the allurments held out by the Mexican government our friends and relatives had been induced to settle in a wilderness country and endure all the privations incident thereto. He was followed by Milton Brown, Esq., who, with his usual and happy eloquence, exhorted the young and enterprising to engage in the cause of Texas—that their cause was literally our own—the cause of free principles.

The meeting was then addressed by Major Joseph Chalmers, who read the Declaration of Independence lately promulgated at the town of Washington, the seat of Texas in solemn convention assembled. There was a degree of fervor and zeal displayed by the speaker, and a solemn breathless attenion given by the listeners that spoke well for the cause of Texas. The meeting was addressed by Col. Robert Chester, lately returned from Texas, explaining the situation of affairs there, and giving notice that he was authorized to advance funds to all who wished to join the army of Texas, to bear their expenses on their journey.[5]

These young men of the West, who knew how to handle a rifle and a knife and who were inspired by stories of their Revolutionary forefathers and of Andrew Jackson, were ready to march by the thousands to secure for themselves immortal honor and glory out of the wilderness and wars of Texas.[6] Two companies of volunteers were raised in the county of Madison The "Madison Grays," sixty-five in number, was officered by Captain A. B. Bradford; First Lieutenant, J. H. McMahon; Second Lieutenant, W. O. Butler; and ensign, W. K. Cooke. The "Jackson Blues," sixty-eight in number, were officered by Captain Samuel J. Hays; First Lieutenant, Henry W. McCorry; Second Lieutenant, M. B. Stewart; and ensign, William Willis. The signal victory of General Sam Houston at San Jacinto on April 26, 1836, brought an end to the movement for the time being, only to be revived again ten years later.

Those who had volunteered were actually disappointed when the Governor's call for troops was countermanded. The papers spoke of it as a "sad defeat to the martial spirits" of the people. Part of the editor's comment in the Randolph

---

[5]Memphis *Enquirer*, May 4, 1836.
[6]Randolph *Recorder*, May 27, 1836.

Recorder might have been tinged with green-eyed jealousy, but there was some truth to it, also:

The countermand of Gov. Cannon's and the glorious termination of the war in Texas has been a sad defeat to these martial spirits, particularly to the Governor's aid, Col. McMahon of the Jackson *Truth Teller* whose editorial noodle has been completely unset for the past four weeks in preparation to show the border Indians the Mexicans what sort of stuff he's made of. Never mind Colonel another opportunity and not impossible a half dozen of them may yet offer, where ye may wreathe from blood a garland of military glory to encircle your brow. Our enemies at home are yet in the field. Throw down your broad sword and firelock and let your goose quill again bristle away with its accustomed spirit.[7]

The war-fever of 1836 served its purpose, for a multitude answered the call in 1846, in fact so many volunteered that the services of a number of regiments had to be declined!

---

[7]Randolph *Recorder*, June 10, 1836.

CHAPTER X

THE MEXICAN WAR

The war message of President Polk infused an increased military ardor throughout the west, north, and south and nothing was heard on the streets in 1846 but the tap of the rolling drums. Volunteer companies paraded, drilled, and "beat up" additional volunteers. The story of Madison County's sons in this war shows that she did her part towards earning for Tennessee that title of the "Volunteer State." Early in May, 1846, the papers were filled with such challenges as this: "Tennesseans! American blood has been shed by an enemy of our country and BLOODY WAR has been proclaimed against her glorious Flag! A call for 2,400 soldiers from Tennessee . . . Tennesseans! once more to the defense of your country's standard and honor!"[1] Volunteer companies from the 4th Division (Western District) were ordered to report to General Samuel J. Hays at Jackson, from which point they were to march to Memphis for rendezvous. Six companies from the Western District were accepted. Company F of the 2nd Tennessee Volunteers were enrolled on 26 of May, 1846, in Jackson by Captain Timothy Jones.[2] Tennesseans answered the country's call to war with unlimited enthusiasm. Twenty companies reported to Governor Brown, desiring to be sent immediately to the theatre of war, in fact they were disappointed because the Governor had not given the order to proceed to New Orleans; and they were perfectly furious when they saw a convoy of 660 Missourians pass Memphis on their way to the Rio Grande.[3]

Jackson and Madison County were just typical counties of Tennessee these days when the people were excited over the

---

[1] Memphis *Daily Eagle*, May 18, 1846.

[2] This company was mustered in June 4, 1846, in Memphis and mustered out May 25, 1847, at New Orleans.

[3] Memphis *Daily Eagle*, May 25, 1846.

war. A hundred and eighteen men from Madison rallied around the brave and fearless young lawyer, William T. Haskell. No training period was planned. These men just went to war. Some were not men, but boys such as George Wiley who was still in his teens and looked so youthful that Haskell would not accept him when he volunteered. However Wiley hid under a wagon when the caravan left Jackson and was not found until they reached Brownsville. Colonel Haskell let him go along, for he concluded that any one who wanted to go to war that badly would certainly make a good soldier. Only a few days elapsed between the time the men signed up and the day of departure. On the evening of June 2, 1846, a large crowd assembled at the courthouse to witness the presentation of the flag to the Company by the ladies of the town. Miss Caroline Haskell, the colonel's daughter, addressed the Company and Lieutenant Hale accepted it in the name of the Company. Their addresses are typical of the day and show how the people were fired with patriotic zeal. Miss Haskell brought this message from the ladies of Jackson:

Avengers! I am delegated by the Ladies of Jackson to deliver unto your keeping this Banner of your Country. You are to bear it hence to-morrow, to place it in a land, over which, until recently that lordly eagle, the majestic emblem of your country's glory emblazoned on its fold, had never hovered save in peace and where its Stars and Stripes had never streamed amid the storms of war. It is confided to you with unshaken trust that the same Banner which fluttered in triumph above your fathers upon so many gory battle-fields will not be tarnished by their sons in the new theatre to which they bear it.

Avengers! Look upon that Banner! There is no stain upon its silken folds—no spot to dim the brightness of its sheen. If when you return with it, no stain of dishonor shall attach to it, though it be all tattered and torn, its stripe obliterated, its stars all faded; and its eagle grim and blackened with smoke of war, still it will be purer and more beautiful in our eyes than now. If it should be your fortune ever to rally beneath it as it flutters above the shock of armed men, one glance upon its folds may serve to cheer you by reminding you, that far away around the fireside you leave to-morrow, up from the lips of those who wove that Banner for you—daily and nightly will ascend the fervent prayer to HIM, who is the God of Battle to be with you always and in that hour. One glance at the inscription upon its folds, will strengthen your arms and serve your hearts; for they will tell you that there is blood upon the walls of the Alamo still crying up to heaven, and scat-

tered ashes on the plains of Goliad, uncoffined and unrevenged! Avengers! take this Banner!
To you 'tis given
To guard this Banner of the Free,
To shield it 'mid the sulphur smoke,
To ward away the battle stroke,
And bid its blending shine afar,
Like rainbows o'er the clouds of War, The Harbingers of Victory!
As you bear it hence, followed by the prayers and blessings of the young and old, while beauty weeps for you her fond farewell, so it you bring back not dishonored, but with the shouts of Welcome, and the Beauty greet you with her sweetest smile.[4]

Lieutenant Hale, in the name of the Company, accepted the flag, pledging their word that they would always remember the sacred trust that had been placed in them. No recruiting officer was needed in a community where one, whose brother had fallen at Goliad and whose father was leading them into battle, made such a speech of farewell as Caroline Haskell made.

After the dinner given to those who were departing for "the Rio Grande" by J. H. Day of the Hotel and A. L. Patterson of the Inn, the company departed amid the waving of handkerchiefs and the tossing of hats, keeping step with Uncle King Anderson's drum and Aaron Day's fife, joyfully following the leader that they adored—Colonel William T. Haskell. On the first day they marched twenty miles, reaching the Hatchie, and camped about eight miles below Denmark. Other companies joined them in Memphis. Some had come down the Cumberland into the Mississippi; others, such as the ones from Giles County had marched overland.[5] At Memphis, the troops were transferred to steam-boats, such as the *Brownsville* on which the "Avengers" went to New Orleans, and thence by ship to points adjacent to the seat of war.[6]

Those men who answered the call of their country in 1846 did not expect to repose upon a bed of roses, they intended to encounter hardships, dangers, troubles that they might show

---

[4]Jackson *West Tennessee Whig*, June 5, 1846.

[5]The company from Giles County was met by many of the citizens of Jackson with a brass band two or three miles out of Huntingdon. They were welcomed in Jackson by speeches and refreshments on the public square. Memphis *Daily Eagle*, June 30, 1846.

[6]*Ibid.*, June 11, 1846.

their own fortitude and courage. They longed for an opportunity to show "the lion-hearted fortitude and indomitable courage of our ancestors had not degenerated in their sons."[7] They had expected bloodshed in battle but they did not expect the diseases of the Mexican climate to kill or render unfit for military service more men than the regular duties of a soldier did. Numerous letters from the war zone show the great number of sick. In October, 1846, a report from Camargo told of a powerful American Army in number but dreadfully crippled and cut down by sickness. In the Second Tennessee 317 were ill out of an aggregate of 588.[8] Before the Second Tennessee started on the campaign in the south, all the sick were sent home. This seemed to be the only thing to be done, but many deaths occurred anyway.

No attempt will be made to describe the general military operations of the war in which United States forces were always outnumbered, but one in which they enjoyed such a superiority of both *morale* and *material* that they gained glorious victories, but often at the expense of bloody fighting and a great loss of men. Letters and newspaper accounts show how pitifully outnumbered they were, but that morale was always high. These troops took great pride in the election of their own officers. General satisfaction was abroad when William T. Haskell was elected commanding Colonel of the Second Regiment of Tennessee Volunteers. Other officers included: David Cummings, Lieutenant Colonel; David McKnight, surgeon; Enoch P. Hale, assistant surgeon; Lieutenant Wiley P. Hale, adjutant; Lieutenant William B. Davis, quartermaster; Legrand Jones, sergeant major; Isaac Nichols, quartermaster's sergeant.[9]

When the news of the Battle of Monterey of September,

---

[7]Correspondence of John R. McClanahan from Camargo, Mexico, October 25, 1846. These letters and other Mexican War papers were used through the courtesy of Guy Hall, Jackson, Tennessee.

[8]Memphis *Daily Eagle*, September 20, 1846.

[9]Correspondence of Wiley P. Hale to his mother, August 17, 1846. A list of the names included on one muster roll of Company F will be found in the Appendix; also, the text of a group of letters written by Wiley P. Hale to his mother. The "Avengers" were outstanding. McClanahan stated August 15, 1846, that with the exception of the other company from Nashville, "the Avengers" had taken the shine off all other companys in the state." Correspondence of John McClanahan, August 15, 1846.

1846, came to the ears of the Second Tennessee Volunteers, they beamed with pride over the stories of the "gallant Tennesseans, the heroes of Monterey," but they fretted and were quit bitter over the fact that the Second Tennessee was denied the opportunity of sharing the danger and participating in the glory of their friends and brothers of the First Tennessee. Many of these battle thirsty Americans were like Lieutenant Hale who had just one desire and that was to get into one good battle so that he could have an opportunity to do something for which he could be mentioned in the reports back home.[10]

The Second Tennessee left camp at Camargo on December 8, 1846, and occupied Victoria on December 29. Then the regiment became part of the army which undertook the campaign in the south—that march to Mexico City along the route that Cortez had followed three centuries before. A successful landing was made about two miles south of Vera Cruz. The march to the city was begun and the heights about the city were occupied. Some opposition was encountered here when the Second Tennessee was ordered to occupy a high sand hill some 1,500 feet above the level of the sea which had that morning been occupied by 1,000 Mexican cavalry. Skirmishing lasted five minutes and then the charge. A contemporary account of this action must be quoted at this point:

Gen. Pillow who was in our midst, ordered a charge up the hill which was so steep that he had to dismount to get up. We gave one "Yell" and up we went, while the balls, fired at random from the escapet guns of the cavalry on the hill whizzed over our heads. Col. Haskell dashed up, calling on the men to follow or rather to climb, for we had to pull up by the bushes. On we went and at last perfectly exhausted, reached the top of the hill where we saw that our foes were "vamossing" almost a quarter of a mile in the distance. We gave them a parting salute, which they had not however the politeness to return. We had not a single man struck. So impetuous had been the charge, and so loud the cheers, that it seemed as if they were so frightened that they could not shout. The whole regiment and all the officers from Col. Haskell down to the privates, behaved in the most daring manner.

---

[10]Memphis *Daily Eagle,* November 11, 1846; Correspondence of John R. McClanahan from Camargo, Mexico, October 25, 1846; Lieutenant Hale reported 123 killed or wounded out of 350 in the 1st Tennessee. Correspondence of Lieutenant Hale from Camargo, Mexico, October 3, 1846.

Col. Haskell and his adjutant Wiley Hale (former associate editor of the Jackson *Whig*) were among the foremost [to reach the top of the height] and cheered on the men. No regiment can boast of two more gallant or daring field officers. Col. Haskell is the same chivalrous man in the midst of danger and that voice which in the days of '44 thrilled by its eloquence so many desponding hearts, rung like a clarion as his regiment with him in their midst stormed the heights. We held these heights all evening and until morning, the artillery playing upon us until dark. Each man with his bayonet scratched himself a little ditch and slept secure while the balls whizzed over our heads.[11]

Lieutenant Hale got his "chance" at Vera Cruz. His own account of this charge is thrilling to read a hundred years later:

The General then ordered the glorious 2nd Regt. (Col. Haskell's) to charge the heights and drive in the force which was firing upon us. We gave a shout and commenced the charge amidst a shower of bullets which fell around us like hail. You should have seen our boys as they rushed up that hill with one continual shout of defiance—though the hill side was covered with an almost impenetrable "chapparel" (thicket of bushes) we gained the summit of the height in less than 15 minutes. The Mexicans who had been firing upon us from this height, fled precipitously upon our approach. We gave them a parting fire as they ran down the hill towards the city which was in full view—planted our flags—and *gave three cheers for Tennessee and Col. Haskell!* Our shouts must have been distinctly heard from the walls of the city—for as the echo died away, a heavy discharge of cannon was pound into us from several forts, which we did not by any means take as a compliment but gave three more shouts as a token of our defiance.[12]

At Vera Cruz Colonel Haskell distinguished himself for his heroic intrepedity. Reports were filled with accounts of the bravery and energy of all the officers, including Haskell who was first to leap the parapet of the bridge. But the first real resistance on this march to Mexico City was encountered at Cerro Gordo — a high hill which Santa Anna had fortified so well that it looked as if it were as impregnable as Gibraltar. Here Santa Anna threw 13,000 troops against General Scott's 9,000. It was in the action at Cerro Gordo that Colonel Haskell won immortal honor by his lion-courage and bravery. An Extra

---

[11] Memphis *Daily Eagle*, April 7, 1847.

[12] Correspondence of Lieutenant Wiley Hale, February 18, 1847.

[13] Cadmus M. Wilcox, *History of the Mexican War* (Washington, 1892), 257; Jackson *Republican Extra*, May 7, 1847.

of the Jackson *Republican* of May 7, 1847, told of the heavy losses on both sides, the rough and rocky road through the dense Mexican brush which was lined with American dead and wounded.[13] Seventeen pieces of artillery and the fire of two thousand musketry played upon Colonel Haskell's force during the whole engagement, during which they moved forward under one of the most terrible fires ever pounded upon the hearts of gallant soldiery. Another report continued:

> They [the men on the field of battle] beheld three of their field officers shot down, three company commanders fall dead before them and one third of the entire force laid low by death or disabled by wounds; yet there was no faltering—they marched almost to the mouth of the deathdealing cannons and never retired until a voice cried out "Retreat! Retreat!" and taking it as the command of their officer, they fell back as good soldiers under the cover of the hill. There was no panic, no fear—in a few moments the remnant of the gallant band were again in order for battle with vengeance written on every brow.[14]

All the field officers of Colonel Haskell's command were wounded except the Colonel himself. Lieutenant Thomas Ewell of the Rifles was very seriously wounded (later died); Lieutenant Wiley Hale was seriously wounded (later died).[15] General Pillow had given the order for the Second Tennessee to charge. A veritable hurricane of grape, cannister, musketry cut down one third of the men in three minutes. The Colonel assembled the scattered remnants and reformed for a second charge. General Pillow coming up cast his eye over the gallant band and asked: "Where is your command, Colonel? There are not half of them here!" "There they are, Sir!" replied the intrepid Haskell, pointing toward the enemy's batteries. "There they are, Sir, dead and dying on the field to which they were ordered!"[16] The list of the killed and wounded and the blood they spilt upon the battlefield proclaim a eulogy to the heroism of these men of '46 and '47 beyond anything else a writer can say. Two of the heroes who made the supreme sacrifice,

---

[14]Memphis *Daily Eagle*, May 20, 1847.

[15]Haskell received his injury after battle in superintending the blowing up of a fort. While setting fire to a train of parcels of cartridges, powder lying near exploded which caused him to burn his hand severely. Memphis *Daily Eagle*, May 18, 1847.

[16]*Ibid.*, June 11, 1847. Of the 118 men who went from the county only twenty-eight returned.

Lieutenant Hale and Lieutenant Ewell, were brought back to Jackson in sealed coffins and laid to rest at Riverside Cemetery. Lieutenant Ewell, in June, 1846, was recruiting for five years service in the "Rifles." In later months he proved that he could fight as well as he could write, but few with a spirit of adventure who had not already set out for the Rio Grande could resist Ewell's picture of real adventure in the new West:

> If you will go with me we will cross the most beautiful and fertile country in the world, where vast provinces are awaiting our coming to shake off the Mexican yoke, where we will be the pioneer of civilization and of freedom, and whence we will bring our banner radiant with new stars. . . . Come, then brave sons of Tennessee, rally beneath the stripes and star. . . . Straws will stop the timid unenterprising man, but adventurous spirits stop to listen to no doubts or objections but throw aside all obstacles, and press on in the paths of fortune. I present you an opportunity of going where you can carve your way to fortune and to glory. . . . I might have recruited elsewhere, but I preferred giving the daring and adventurous sons of Tennessee whom I knew the opportunity. . . . Come to my Headquarters at Jackson and give yourselves to glory and your country.
>
> Thos. Ewell.

June 23, 1846.[17]

Just a short year afterwards it was the privilege of the beloved leader, brilliant orator, and talented genius, William T. Haskell to pay tribute to this brave Lieutenant. He told of Ewell's reconnoitering on the night before the Battle of Cerro Gordo and his discovering then of the salient of attack, of his throwing himself heroically far in advance of the charging column, thus he was the first to encounter the enemy alone. Haskell's tribute continued:

> When Gen. Scott ascended the height, he threw himself from his charger; kneeling by his side, lifted his head upon his knee—his face bathed in tears and his voice, trembling with manly emotion exclaimed: "My brave boy, you will not die, you must not die, you shall not die! Live! Live! Live! History shall record you were the hero of Cerro Gordo!"

Lieutenant Ewell was born in Fauquier County, Virginia, and was appointed to the army from Jackson in Madison County, Tennessee. He was a grandson of Benjamin Stoddert, Secretary of Treasury

---

[17]Memphis *Daily Eagle*, June 30, 1846.

(Navy). He fell at the early age of 23. He was my intimate, personal friend, and school boy companion.

Will not Tennessee erect a mausoleum to his memory and consecrate him to immortal glory?

>Sweet sleep the dead, who sink to rest
>By all their country's wishes blest!

His comrade in arms
WILLIAM T. HASKELL
of Tennessee[18]

The "Avengers" had signed up for twelve months, so they were mustered out at New Orleans May 25, 1847. After the resignation of General Hays, Colonel Haskell's name had been recommended by his friends for the major-generalship to which position he was elected early in 1847. Colonel Haskell, eleven officers, and one hundred and seventy sick and wounded of the Second Tennessee Regiment arrived in Memphis on June 2, 1847. A hasty reception was held at the Gayoso Hotel before the Colonel and his men from Madison departed for the final lap of the journey homeward. At this reception Haskell paid beautiful tribute to Lieutenant Ewell and displayed a few trophies of war, such as some "real live" Mexican boys and a brass six pounder which had been captured at Cerro Gordo.[19] These gallant citizen-soldiers who had borne the Stars and Stripes triumphantly amid the shot and shell of Vera Cruz, Cerro Gordo, and Chapaultepec appreciated the joyous receptions tendered them by the citizens of Memphis, but what they wanted most of all was to go HOME. It matters not where the theatre of war is or in what century a war is fought—this is the desire in common with all men of war when the excitement is over.

---

[18]Nashville *Banner*, July 9, 1942. From an article written by William E. Beard. Ewell was killed as he leaped the breastworks at Cerro Gordo. Stoddert served as Secretary of Navy under John Adams and Jefferson, 1798-1801.

[19]Memphis *Daily Eagle*, June 3, 1847.

CHAPTER XI

EARLY TRANSPORTATION

Rivers are the highways of commerce, but in the early part of the nineteenth century, they were the only highways of commence. Thus it meant the very life of the Western District when Dame Nature was generous with her streams and gave so many to this section. These unbridged rivers hampered wagon transportation, but they became the roads into the interior. Two of these rivers, the Hatchie and the Forked Deer served as the first highways of Madison County. They played a double role in the life of the county, for the frequent rains caused the streams to overflow the generally level land, adding fertility to the soil each year and making it stand the drought unusually well, therefore the rivers enriched the land and brought in the new population. Many a prospector or an early settler made his way to the newly laid out town of Jackson, in 1822, on flat-boats, down the Cumberland to the Ohio, to the Mississippi, to the Forked Deer and up that small stream to his destination.[1] These flat-boats were the cheapest, the easiest, and the safest means of transportation into this former hunting grounds of the Chickasaws; which were still inhabited by enough wild game to furnish food and enough bears and wolves to keep the white man on the alert. A familiar sight in the 1830's and 1850's was the "emigrant ark"—a huge flat-boat one hundred feet or more in length with a long oar at either end and a pair on either side provided only for assisting the ark in negotiating bends in the river and remaining in the current. Aboard was all the family, fowls, a pair of goats, horses, cattle, hay, and a canvas tent. A wood fire burned upon an improvised hearth above which swung a steaming pot pre-

---

[1]Goodspeed, *Tennessee,* 797-798; J. G. Cisco, "History of Madison County," *American Historical Magazine,* VIII (1903), 20, 93-95. Hereinafter cited as "Madison County."

sided over by a resolute matron. Standing off to himself, leaning on a long barreled rifle, was the head of the emigrant family, a man clad in rough jeans, his figure erect and athletic. This was civilization moving westward!

Jackson was once a "river town!" This is an established historical fact. Keel-boats, flat-boats, and small steam boats came up the river from Memphis and were built at the boat yards in Jackson to carry cargoes to Memphis and New Orleans. Seventeen were counted at the dock at one time. There were boat-yards, such as the one owned by Armour and Lake, where many an old timer was engaged in the building of these river crafts. One of the boat yards was located several hundred feet south of the Riverside Cemetery. It was a thrilling sight to see even these small crafts fashioned for the shallow Forked Deer glide into the water and not a boy in town was absent

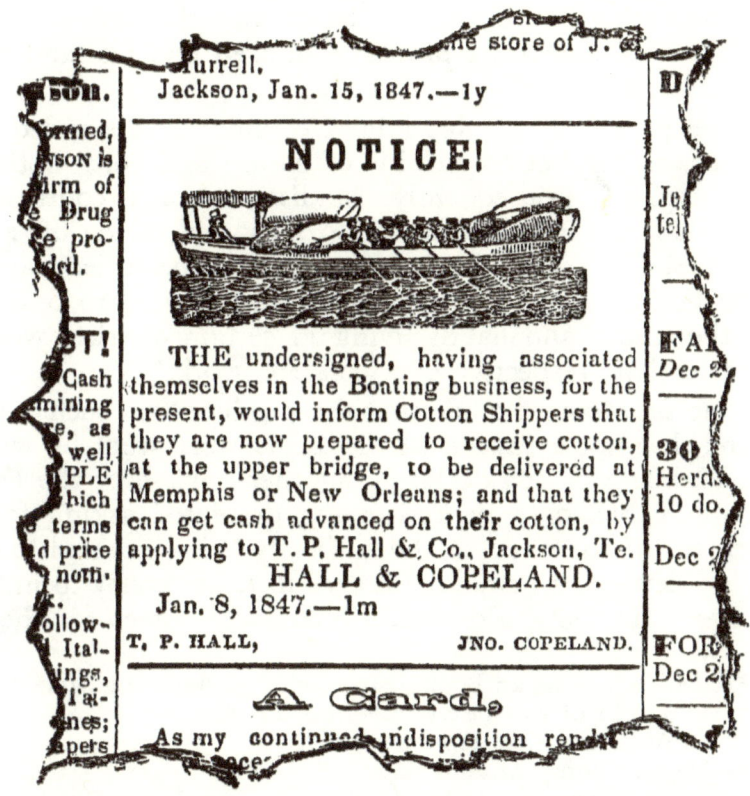

West Tennessee *Whig*, February 2, 1847. Guy Hall Collection.

at a launching if he could help it.[2] Often a flat-boat loaded with cotton was taken to New Orleans; the boat, upon arrival, was broken up for lumber, and the crew made the trip home overland. There were usually four, besides the captain, in a crew, the cook, two pilots and one pilot to substitute. The captain upon such a boat had to be a man of integrity to leave New Orleans, which was a heaven for carousing, with any money at all, and he had to be a man of bravery to return through the wilderness, usually up the famous Natchez Trace, which was often infested with robbers, with his "hard cash" in his saddle bags. These boatmen were a jovial set of fellows, generous, noble-hearted, adventurous, men who loved to face the dangers of the winding swollen streams or the highwayman or the wild beasts of the trip home overland. William Coward, while on a return trip for the firm of Armour and Lake of Jackson in 1824, had only a hickory stick to defend himself, so he swung by a limb to an oak and then holding on with one hand, he swung himself down "larapping" the wolves with his stick. In this manner he protected himself and his saddle bags until daylight came.[3]

The prosperity of this inland community depended upon its ability to market its surplus of cotton and corn, both very bulky staples. Consequently, Madison County courts, from 1821 to 1828, appointed juries "to view and to leg off a road of the first class" from Jackson to the most convenient landings on the Forked Deer. Overseers were appointed to build and keep the roads, and hands living in certain districts were assigned to their respective overseers for work.[4]

The problem of marketing the produce was such a pressing one that not a session of the Legislature went by without some act being passed declaring another portion of the Forked Deer navigable, or a petition being presented asking for improvement of the river, or the authority being granted to some men to "devise a scheme of lottery" to raise money to improve the river.[5] In 1824, although a board of trustees for the nav-

---

[2] T. M. Gates's Scrap Book. Mrs. Sarah Taylor, who came to Jackson in 1826, told of this heavy travel on the river.
[3] J. S. Williams, *Old Times*, 151-182.
[4] Madison County Minute Book, 1821-1826.
[5] *Acts of Tennessee*, 1823, 1826-1838; Legislative Petitions, Box 66, 75, Tennessee State Archives, Nashville.

igation of the rivers of the Western District was created with Moses Woodfin, Robert Dyer, and Adam Huntsman from the Forked Deer, the grand jury called attention to the fact that not a single effort had been made to improve the navigation of this river, though the preceding year it had been declared navigable by an act of the Legislature.[6] These men of the West were determined to make use of the river if possible. Memorials which were sent to the legislature to have the rivers of the Western District "dredged by taxation" fell upon fruitful soil, for an act was passed (1824) allowing the county court to levy a tax of $12\frac{1}{2}$ cents per one hundred acres upon the land in Madison County for opening and improving the navigation of the river. The tax was levied and Adam Huntsman called a meeting of the Commissioners for Navigation for the following year in Jackson.[7]

Spring rains kept the Forked Deer in good boating order, but its channel in 1834 was from thirty to forty-five feet wide and from three to twelve feet deep, so occasionally an account in the paper told of the channel which was literally obstructed by keel-boats in sinking condition.[8] As early as 1821, Herndon Haralson wrote of these boats in Madison County:

> When I left the Forked Deer there were three Keel-boats at Alexander's landing one and one-half miles below Doak's, freighted with corn, bacon, whisky, etc. Many boats had stopped at Key Corner and cribbed their corn. These boats came down the Tennessee, Cumberland, and Ohio.[9]

---

[6]Jackson *Gazette*, June 5, November 13, 1824; *Acts of Tennessee*, 1823. It did not take the citizens long to realize that it took more than a legislative act to really get the river in a navigable condition. An editor noted in 1840: "If a legislature, by a bill or otherwise declare a river navigable, is that river navigable? That's the question." Nashville *Union*, January 28, 1840.

[7]Madison County Minute Book, 1821-1825; *Acts of Tennessee*, 1826; Jackson *Gazette*, September 4, October 30, November 13, 1824, March 5, 1825. Commissioners for lottery included: James Vaulx, W. E. Butler, Henry Lake, James Caruthers, Joseph L. Talbot, Alexander Neilson.

[8]Jackson *Gazette*, September 4, 1830; Eastin Morris, *Gazetteer* (Nashville, 1834), 55.

[9]Williams, *West Tennessee*, 165, quoting Murphy MSS., North Carolina Archives.

In 1824, Armour and Lake received two keel-boats within a week laden with dry goods and groceries, while two years later the keel, MESSENGER, 110 feet long arrived from Louisville loaded with flour and whiskey. It, with several other boats loaded with cotton, set out for New Orleans. When Elijah Bigelow ordered goods from Massachusetts in the 1820's, he insisted that the heavy ones be sent during winter months so that they could come all the way by water, rather than be hauled from "Frog Jump" on the Forked Deer—forty miles away.[10]

The two decades before the building of the railroads through the district probably saw the heaviest shipping on the Forked Deer. Scattered records tell of the keels, NERO and NUMROD, loaded with sugar, coffee, and sundries arriving at the Jackson landing and departing for New Orleans loaded with cotton, chickens, and geese; of the good flat-boat TURK with John Lacy as master which left from J. W. Campbell's landing with thirty bales of cotton for New Orleans (at the rate of $3 per bale); of the good boat MARY which left from the same landing with cotton for Memphis at $1.50 per bale; of boats owned by J. W. Campbell which could carry 6000 bales during the season; of the machinery shipped to Campbell and Alexander from New York to New Orleans, then to Obion Point, and up the Forked Deer to Jackson.[11] The wording of an old insurance policy of J. W. Campbell's agency traces such a route:

> I desire to have insured a carriage of the value of Five Hundred Dollars, ten per cent additional, shipped from New Orleans, insurance to New Orleans; thence to Obion Pt., Tennessee, Thence to Jackson by Keel Boat.
>
> Jas. L. Talbot[12]
>
> Dec. 26, 1845.

The high, the low, the politician, and the merchant were all interested in improving the navigation of the Forked Deer. David Crockett had an amendment to offer to the Harbor Bill

---

[10] Jackson *Gazette*, April 1, 1826; Correspondence of Elijah Bigelow, May 18, 1828, February 3, 1829. Used through the courtesy of Seale Johnson.

[11] T. M. Gates's Scrap Book; Bills of lading of J. W. Campbell; Letter Book of J. W. Campbell; *West Tennessee Whig*, January 18, 1850.

[12] Letter Book of J. W. Campbell.

for the benefit of his district which was to call for the removal of obstructions in the Hatchie, the Forked Deer, and the Obion, but he went out to dinner and the bill was laid on the table.[13] Samuel Lancaster, Commissioner for Internal Improvements for Madison County, hired hands to work on the river. These hands were well paid and were relieved of militia duty while working. In 1843, Lancaster was secretary of the board of Commissioners to have logs, trees, high sand bars, timber, brush, and all leaning trees within five feet of the river, and stumps that might interfere with the navigation removed from the Forked Deer so that the planters could get their surplus produce to market; for petitions were still being received daily from the planters who wanted obstructions removed so that they would not have to "waggon their produce to the Tennessee."[14] It seems that legal records and statistics insisted that the river was navigable, such as DeBow's *Review* of 1850, which reported 195 miles of the Forked Deer navigable, but in reality, there were plenty of sand bars, and leaning trees which were the death of the small river crafts.[15]

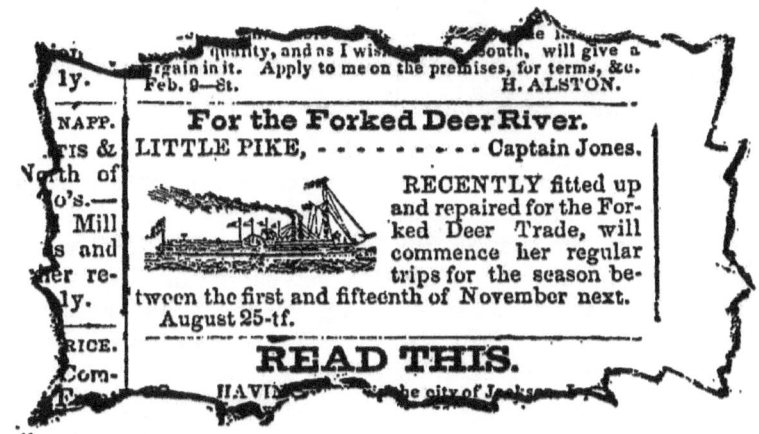

West Tennessee *Whig*, March 9, 1854. Mrs. W. W. Tucker Collection.

These ambitious westerners tried steamboats on the tiny Forked Deer. Samuel Lancaster built the "Eliza Ann" at Jackson in the early 1830's, while the "Gray Eagle" arrived at

---

[13]Randolph *Recorder*, July 25, 1834.
[14]Jackson *Republican*, February 23, 1843; Jackson *West Tennessee Whig*, January 27, 1843; Madison County Minute Book, 1848-1850.
[15]DeBow's *Review*, VII (1850), 283.

the landing at Jackson in 1836. Men, women, children, and slaves scattered helter-skelter when the boat let off steam, for they had heard or read descriptions of the horrible "blowing up" and the destruction of life caused by these monsters. A steam boat often hit a snag or had to stop while the crew chopped away the fallen timber or removed the driftwood from the stream.[16] In 1847, a substantial steamboat, the "Davy Nunn," was built expressly for the Memphis and Forked Deer travel, to run as high as Jackson, to carry 600 bales of cotton. Plans were made for it to make regular trips back and forth, the trip itself requiring eight days. In 1854, the "Little Pike" was fitted especially for Forked Deer commerce.[17] Thus, steamboats did come up the Forked Deer, it matters not how small they were. Citizens of to-day remember riding on them, and many remember the hull in the old channel of the river that served as a fading and decaying monument to this river navigation. It was soon realized that these numerous small streams were inadequate for the needs of the growing district, for they were seldom navigable during the summer and early autumn months. These men must have been the worst kind of "diehards" though, for the editor of the *Forked Deer Blade* in 1884 was trying to attract new enterprises to the community and still insisted that water transportation was profitable:

West Tennessee and especially the Forked Deer valley, is abundantly supplied with timber which, for excellence of quality and variety is not surpassed by any section in the South west. We have the different varieties of oak suitable for hubs, spokes, and other wagon material while the poplar and cypress is accessible for furniture, doors, sash and blinds. There is also an almost inexhaustible supply of hard wood, such as the beech, ash, and hickory for awl, chisel, and auger handles. With the river open to navigation, there is no reason why these timbers should not be obtained at a comparatively small cost, and thus make it profitable for manufacturers of such articles at Jackson. We know of one or two such establishments in the north that have made fortunes for their owners where the timber is bought and rafted or shipped more than a hundred miles; and why could it not be done with the material at hand?[18]

---

[16] Jackson *West Tennessee Whig*, November 23, 1849; J. S. Williams, *Old Times*, 257-258; S. C. Williams, *West Tennessee*, 167.

[17] Memphis *Daily Eagle*, January 20, 1847; *West Tennessee Whig*, January 19, 1854.

[18] Jackson *Forked Deer Blade*, January 19, 1884.

Suggestions for more internal improvements soon began to appear, such as a canal to be built from the Forked Deer to the Mississippi in 1825, and another from Savannah on the Tennessee to Big Hatchie near Bolivar in 1835.[19] Congress, to the astonishment of at least one reader of the *Gazette*, in 1826, ordered an immense sum of money for a road to be cut at public expense from the village of Memphis to Little Rock. "The minds of the people have become heated and intoxicated upon the subject of *internal improvements*," said this astonished gentleman. "This mania, I fear will never rest until it has caused the United States Treasury to be disgorged of her last shilling."[20] It is quite possible that this gentleman from Jackson might have approved of the road if there had been a chance of its being built to Jackson!

These enterprising westerners were not satisfied with the slow and rather uncertain river transportation, and they were not getting the canals built. Other measures had to be resorted to. Turnpike companies, after 1800, had been given the authority by the general assembly to build short roads, charging toll according to rates usually fixed by five men. These companies "cut and cleared, measured and marked" the roads, erected bridges, and causeways, and received their pay in toll.[21] By a legislative act of 1826, Philip Alston, Allen Deberry, William E. Butler, Mathias Deberry, and James Greer were commissioned to "devise a plan for a toll bridge across the Forked Deer" for which the following toll was to be charged:

Each horse and rider	.12½ cents
Each wagon and team	1.00
Each led or loose horse	.06¼
Each cart and driver	.37½
Each two wheel pleasure carriage	1.00

---

[19] S. C. Williams, *West Tennessee*, 167; *Acts of Tennessee*, 1825; James Phelan, *History of Tennessee; The Making of a State* (New York, 1889), 284. Hereinafter cited as *Tennessee*. An appropriation of $1,500 was made for the survey of the canal from Savannah to the Big Hatchie, Stanley F. Folmsbee, *Sectionalism and Internal Improvements in Tennessee* (Knoxville, 1939), 153. Hereinafter cited as *Sectionalism in Tennessee*.

[20] J. S. Williams, *Od Times*, 196.

[21] Albert C. Holt, "The Economic and Social Beginnings of Tennessee," (Nashville, unpublished Ph.D. Thesis, George Peabody College, 1923), 72.

Each carry all... .25
Each head of cattle, hogs, sheep, goats................................. .01
Each foot passenger... .06¼
Each led mule or jack... .06½[22]

In many cases the acts provided that the navigation of the river should not be obstructed by the bridge, that no toll should be charged going to or returning from preaching, muster drill, court, or an election, and a fine of five dollars was charged for passing the gate without paying the toll. With some of the toll keepers business was done on the credit basis, with some by cash, and others by yearly contracts.[23] An Act of the Legislature of 1824 appropriated money to build a twenty-five foot road, one foot above the high water mark, through the swamp ground of the Forked Deer, crossing the river at a bridge at Shannon's Landing.[24] In 1831, the Kirkman ferry announced a new boat house across the Tennessee, good roads that connected with the ferry, and a bridged causeway over the swampy places of the bottom, making it passable during the "highest freshes."[25]

By 1837, commissioners of internal improvements were ordered to examine a "portage below Dyer's warehouse," as it was impassable during high waters. Turnpike companies, individual concessions, state aid, and lottery were each tried by these energetic westerners in their efforts to get their produce to market. William Armour, of Jackson, was so enthusiastic that he wanted to borrow a million dollars from Europe for a road from East to West. He and Milton Brown both opposed private companies for the "only thing that they can look to is the toll at the gates." Adam Alexander and other delegates from the Western District urged the Secretary of War in 1826 to have engineers survey the route for the National Road through the Western District.[26] By 1843, sixty miles of the

---

[22]*Acts of Tennessee*, 1826.
[23]*Acts of Tennessee*, 1832, 1847; J. W. Campbell Account Book.
[24]In June 1824, Josiah Pullen was allowed $650 for the building of this bridge. Thomas Lacy, Adam Huntsman, and David Jarrett were the commissioners for this road. *Acts of Tennessee*, 1824; Madison County Minute Book 1821-1826.
[25]Jackson *Southern Statesman*, February 5, 1831.
[26]Addie Lou Brooks, "Early Plans for Railroads in West Tennessee 1830-1845," *Tennessee Historical Magazine*, Ser. 2, III (1932), 31. Hereinafter cited as "Plans for Railroads."

Ashport Turnpike had been completed, extending in a westerly direction from Jackson to the highlands beyond the Forked Deer; and the citizens were petitioning to have a graded road like this turnpike built from the town of Jackson to the Mississippi. Four of these turnpike companies qualified for state aid in West Tennessee; the Big Hatchie Turnpike and Bridge Company, together with the Ashport, the Fulton and the Forked Deer Companies. In the year 1838, only $43,000 in state aid was allotted West Tennessee, while millions of dollars was granted to the Middle Tennessee companies. Then, gravel was far away and the managers thought it was no harm to cheat the state if it were done according to law.[27]

Roads and mail service are inseparable. The early roads were not more than wide blazed trails. The editor of the *Pioneer* in 1823 suggested that Samuel Taylor, the postmaster, would have to offer a better contract to the carrier of the weekly east-bound mail, for the previous man had not kept his contract and there was no communications to the east. By 1825, there was a weekly mail westward to Memphis, and other routes were developing and improving rapidly, considering the wilderness through which these mails had to be carried. By the 1830's the horse mail, with two to four horses depending upon the depth of the mud and the time allotted for the trip were running on regular schedule. A coach was scheduled to leave Nashville at 6 A. M. on each Tuesday and Friday and to "arrive in Jackson every Thursday and Sunday by 6 P. M." The Western post left Jackson every Friday at 6 A. M., arrived in Bolivar in the evening of the same day and in Memphis on Sunday evening in time to make connections with the mail boat for Mississippi travel. Post offices in the county were along these routes at Annsville, Clover Creek, Mount Pinson, Point Center, Spring Creek, Whiting, and Cotton Grove.[28] Many of the small streams were not bridged and the winter and spring rains caused the mails to have to "swim across." The result

---

[27]Folmsbee, *Sectionalism in Tennessee*, 185; S. F. Folmsbee, "The Turnpike Phase of Tennessee Internal Improvement System of 1836-1838," *Journal of Southern History*, III (1937), 463-468.

[28]Jackson *Gazette*, September 5, 1829; Jackson *Southern Statesman*, February 5, March 26, 1831, March 16, 1833; Map of Kentucky and Tennessee, Post Offices and Post Roads (David Barr, 1839).

West Tennessee *Whig*, June 23, 1853. Mrs. W. W. Tucker Collection.

was that notices appeared in the papers such as these from the Randolph *Recorder*:

Wet Mail again. Our eastern mail came to us as usual dripping from its baptismal fount. Our Tuesday's mail arrived at Jackson after having suffered the penitence of immersion . . . part of our papers were drowned between Jackson and this place. The mail contractor deserves some extra allowances of fines for his trouble in watering the mails. . . . Wednesday's mail came as usual, dripping wet, soaked and slobbering from its watering place, about 6 hours after due. Truly the mails come on swimmingly.[29]

As the years passed, service became better. In the 1850's

---

[29]Randolph *Recorder*, December 19, 1834, January 23, 1835.

EARLY TRANSPORTATION 131

there were three mails a week to Nashville, which trip was made in twenty-four hours. At this time the line was stocked with a superior type of Troy coaches, pulled by four horses that were driven by sober, careful, and accommodating drivers. The round trip cost $16. This road in 1852 was described as "an excellent high ridge road."[30]

The arrival of the stage coach in the little town of Jackson was a thrilling and magnificent sight. When the stage driver reached the top of the hill coming into town, he sounded his stately horn. Down the street at full speed came the stage drawn by four or six horses with the driver perched high on the front seat holding fast to the reins. Every other vehicle gave way to the approaching coach, for this was the passenger express which made full speed from town to town, with relay stations every twelve or fifteen miles to change horses for fast travel. These coaches which accommodated eight to ten persons were the only means of travel in the early years, except by water. There were wagon stages, a two or three wagon train with each wagon pulled by six strong horses, which brought merchandise here from the Tennessee River, from Estanuala, or all the way from Memphis. These "land ships," which usually went in pairs or more so that in case of trouble each one could help the other, hauled many a dollar's worth of merchandise into this section.[31]

The stage roads that the frontiersmen proudly called "good roads" were in reality quite crude, according to the description in *TransAtlantic Sketches* by J. E. Alexander of the 42d Royal Highlanders, who, in 1831, traveled from Memphis to Nashville in a wagon drawn by four horses:

> The driver showed great dexterity in turning the horses round the stumps and the blackjacks, or burnt trunks, but we were awfully shaken for he went over fallen trees without the least compunction or mercy shown to his wagon or the bones of his passengers. These abominable roads are easily accounted for, the population being so widely scattered. . . . Sometimes the jolting was so continued and dreadful that it seemed as if the tilt would fly off the wagon every moment and our heads after

---

[30]Jackson, *West Tennessee Whig*, February 12, 1852, August 31, 1855; June 23, 1853. For postmasters, see Appendix.
[31]Recollections of Mrs. Sarah T. Dancy; T. M. Gates's Scrap Book; Ledger of Hearn and Rogers, 1859.
[32]S. C. Williams, *West Tennessee*, 260.

it. Corduroy causeways, broken bridges, and stumps all impeded our progress. I got out and walked whenever I could do so without sinking in the mud to the ankles.[32]

When a wagon jolted along through the swamps and the mud and bumped over the trees and stumps, it is no wonder that these roads soon came to be called "break-neck" roads, not from the speed, which was only four miles per hour, but from what happened to the bones of the traveler. By 1830, according to the *Gazette*, these "four horse wagons" had become a line of elegant coaches, frequently carrying twelve or thirteen passengers and seldom less than nine. A spirit of progress was really in the air when the same paper could add: "The facilities of intercourse are increasing daily by the construction of bridges, turnpikes, the running of stages and steamboats."[33]

This mania for internal improvements in the Western District not only endured but increased, as railroads came to play an important part in the development of the area. As early as 1827, the *West Tennessean* was urging "ye patriots and honest farmers" to lend their aid to the building of twenty miles of railroad from Columbia to Paris, so that the businessmen and the "pleasurers" could "delight in skimming the fertile soil of the West, for a railroad would encourage the development of the resources of your infant country."[34] In 1833, when there was precious little railroad mileage in the entire United States, these ambitious men of Madison County managed to get the Western Railroad Company chartered, for the purpose of building a railroad from the town of Jackson on the most practicable route to the Mississippi. The state appropriated $500 for the survey of this road. In October 1837, Albert Miller Lea, the Chief Engineer of the State of Tennessee, made a report to the governor, recommending that the road run from Ashport to Fulton on the Mississippi to Perryville on the Tennessee, seemingly assuming that the line would run through Jackson. In this report, he reviewed the conditions of transportation of this interior section, which had no navigation during a greater part of the year, no material to make paved roads, and yet there were excessively bulky exports and a great demand for imports. His suggestions, if followed, would have opened up the entire Forked Deer Valley, and were as follows:

[33]*Ibid.*, 170.
[34]Paris *West Tennessean*, March 10, 1827.

Having reached the Forked Deer Bottom, the suited route turns a little south of east and runs in nearly a straight direction along the south side of the river on almost level ground, subject to little overflow.... Crossing the Cherryville and the Jackson turnpikes, near their southern extremities, it keeps up the south side of the Forked Deer to the mouth of Little Middle Fork, where it crosses the main river and pursues up the south side of Little Middle Fork and up South's Fork to the dividing ridge and passes the ridge near Nathan Green's and the Lexington and Mifflin road.... Very few facts will be cited to show the very great local convenience of such a road. It is only during about three months in the year that the Forked Deer River is navigable as far as Jackson; their exports and imports to or from the Mississippi River at an enormous expense, but when chance does favor them with water it never costs less than two dollars per bale to get their cotton from Jackson to the Mississippi. But by the railroad it may be taken for 50 cents.... A traveler wishing to go to the Mississippi River takes a stage for Memphis travels continuously for thirty hours and pays $10.00 for the trip. By the railroad he could do so at an expense of one twelfth the time and one third the money.[35]

Meetings were held in the courthouse at Bolivar, Jackson, and Nashville "to agitate the subject." William Armour and Milton Brown were outstanding leaders at each of these meetings. At the convention held in Jackson in August, 1836, William Armour made the report and all candid persons were called upon to admit that the Forked Deer was wholly inadequate to carry to market with safety, dispatch, and in proper season, the future abundant productions of the country. A contemporary editor continued on this subject:

We cannot depend upon it [the Forked Deer] until Christmas and when our floods do come, they continue but a few days and we lose the benefit of them unless we are ready at the moment with our boats to float with the first tide. Then our cotton arrives late and we do not get first price. Some will say 'remove the logs from the bed of the river,' but this won't work for the river doesn't carry enough water and this has to be done over every two or three years.[36]

---

[35]*Report of Chief Engineer of State of Tennessee on Surveys and Examinations for the Central Railroad and Central Turnpike* (Nashville, Tennessee, 1837), 27-29. The Tennessee and Jackson R. R. was chartered to build railroad, macadamized or wooden turnpike from Jackson to Perryville. The Western Railroad Company was changed to Jackson and Mississippi Central R. R. in 1837. *Acts of Tennessee*, 1837.

[36]Jackson *Southern Statesman*, August 21, 1833.

Enthusiastic planters pleaded for this dreamed of road thus:

> What a glorious thing it would be in this backwoods' country to breakfast in Jackson, drive to the Mississippi, transact business, and return home all in the same day! ... Rather than be without a railroad it would be a wise policy for the planter to sell one half of his land and negroes and appropriate the proceeds towards the construction of one, in as much as the remaining half, independent of the stock taken, would be worth more than the whole as the matter now stands.[37]

At the Nashville convention, citizens of Madison County advocated the borrowing of ten million dollars at six per cent interest by the state, the appropriating of the surplus United States fund to internal improvements, and the building of a central railroad at state expense. The planters failed to subscribe to the $50,000 worth of stock. This fact and the opposition of leaders in Nashville and Memphis brought an end to the movement, so that in the January, 1837, *Truth Teller* appeared the announcement of the failure of the road: "Its enemies in the bitterness of their jealousy called it the 'road to ruin,' but in defiance of their 'wise saws and modern instances' it became a road to nothing." Some of the editors had approved of internal improvements for it was glorious to imagine a smooth beautiful railway running by one's door at the rate of 25 miles per hour, rather than the "present inconveniences of traveling on horseback, taking our cotton to market by brute force at the rate of about two miles per hour and upon such intollerable roads that it was almost enough to make the people cry: 'Railroads! Railroads!,' but railroads were not built for a ballad or whistled into existence and they doubted whether it was the proper time and place to build."[38]

Although this enthusiasm did not bear fruit until the early 1850's, many of the citizens, like Judge Brown and William Armour, realized that railroads were necessary to the prosperity of this inland agricultural section. Judge Austin Miller of Bolivar wrote of these railroad enthusists of Jackson:

> The people of Jackson have gotten the notion of a railroad through that place in their heads. The expending of millions of dollars among them to build it, the enhancement of value of their property are considerations too alluring for inaction, and they cannot rest until they find

---
[37]*Ibid.*, September 4, 14, 1833.
[38]Randolph *Recorder*, July 14, 1834.

a candidate [for governor] who will go for the borrowing of millions upon the faith of the State.[39]

Not only West Tennessee but also East and Middle Tennessee wanted internal improvements. The sections, however, could not agree upon where to build, what to build, and how to pay the bill. Middle Tennessee wanted macadamized roads and the money deposited in the Nashville banks, East Tennessee wanted railroads and river improvements, and most of West Tennessee wanted a central railroad paid for by the state, though there was great rivalry between the towns as to where the roads were to be built. The following from a Knoxville paper is really typical of most of Tennessee of that day when it possessed a railroad "mania":

> Give us an outlet to market and there is nothing to prevent a great increase of business. Show the capitalist a cheap route to market and he will speedily avail himself of the water power for manufacturing. Tennessee with a noble and fertile country has nothing wanting but the hands of art to complete what nature so liberally placed within our reach.[40]

---

[39]S. C. Williams, *West Tennessee*, 172-173.
[40]Quoted in the Nashville *Standard*, June 18, 1845.

CHAPTER XII

THE RAILROADS

People who conceive new ideas and walk upon untrodden paths are considered insane by the majority of their fellowmen. A queer prophecy was published in 1813 telling of the time when people would travel in stages moved by steam-engines from one city to another, about as fast as birds can fly, fifteen or twenty miles per hour. "To accomplish this two sets of railways will be laid, made of wood or iron or smooth paths of broken stone or gravel with a rail to guide the carriages so that they may pass each other in different directions and travel by night as well as by day; and the passengers will sleep in these stages as comfortable as they now do in steam boats . . . but the body of the carriages will be shaped like a swift swimming fish to pass easily through the air. . . . The United States will be the first nation to make this discovery and adapt the system and her wealth and power will rise to unparalled height."[1] A prophecy made over a decade before the county was settled, began to be realized in the mid-nineteenth century but it was not until 1934, when "The Rebel" began its trips south, did the county see "carriages swimming like a swift fish" in order to pass easily through the air. Those men of early Madison were literally pioneers in the railroad industry and these of to-day are still carrying the torch of progress.

It is hardly conceivable in this modern day how difficult was the task of the railroad builders of a century ago in comparison to what it is to-day. A century ago, the value of the railroad was not realized; competent engineers were few; capital was scarce; labor supply was uncertain and expensive; legislatures were unfriendly; the pioneer companies could not profit by the experience of others; plans, conventions, and dreams did not produce completed roads. Some of the plans had to

---

[1]Reprinted in *Harper's Magazine*, June, 1857.

materialize before the produce could go to market and the stockholders could be satisfied with dividends. A few phases in the story of the building of the Mobile and Ohio Railroad are reviewed not because they all happened in Madison County —far from that—but because the coming of this pioneer road and the Mississippi and Tennessee Central meant the change of the town from an inland cotton center to a city that was to become a manufacturing center, a city located in the midst of a country that was facing a new agricultural era. And last but not least, this was a road whose completion should be credited to Judge Milton Brown of Jackson, Tennessee—no man contributed more greatly to its completion and its rebuilding after the Civil War.

Early plans of the 1830's for railroads in Madison having failed, the plans to build a road from Mobile to the Ohio began to spring up in scattered places throughout the Ohio and Tennessee valleys. Madison County might profit by this scheme to construct a road which would drain a part of the produce of the Ohio and Tennessee valleys to Mobile rather than to New Orleans. Thus, the rivalry between two Gulf cities was to bring the railroad through the county. In the beginning, this new project was considered a crazy scheme in the hands of crazy promoters. Mobile, a town of only 20,000, had never helped finance such a thing! J. C. Baldwyn, the chief promoter, had never built a railroad, but at length he interested the people in his maps, a temporary organization was made, a preliminary survey was made which proposed a route well adapted to railroad purposes across the State of Mississippi to the Tennessee River at Savannah, thence across Tennessee to the Mississippi at Columbus, Kentucky, making 500 miles. Charters were applied for in each state through which the road was to pass and these were granted in 1848.[2] A contemporary magazine

---

[2]The original act of 1848 granted the charter "for the purpose of constructing a railroad from Mobile to Tennessee River and from thence to some suitable point near the mouth of the Ohio River." An act of 1860 contained a rider which proposed that Mobile and Ohio need not go to Tennessee River if the company would build a branch from crossing at Misssissippi Central at Corinth to Tennessee River. This was never done. Fairfax Harrison, *Legal History of the Lines of the Southern Railway Company* (Washington, 1901), 1422. Hereinafter cited as *Legal History*.

favoring the new project told of the favorable conditions of the route, the savings of river insurance, the lowering of rates, the great military importance, the shortening of the route from 1,012 miles by water to 470 miles by rail, and of cutting of the time from six days to twenty-five to thirty hours.[3]

Strange as it may seem, the promoters of the road had more trouble convincing the population along the proposed route that this was a worth while project than they did selecting the proper route. Proceedings of the Moble and Ohio R. R. Company of 1848 tell of the suggested route via Savannah, Tennessee, through West Tennessee, there tapping the fertile cotton, corn, and grain section—a section occupied by a growing population where connections could be made with the Memphis and Charleston and the Tennessee Central. The old report summarized the advantages of the Mobile and Ohio transportation over the Mississippi River as follows:

Unlike the Mississippi River it will afford a transportation combining the three requisites of well regulated commerce, *safety, certainty,* and *dispatch*. The Railroad brings with it no overflows, no destruction of property and no sickness. Its course is never shifting but permanent and direct from point to point and it is unimpeded by ice, by low water, snags, and sand bars.[4]

Books were opened, stocks sold in Mobile and vicinity, and ground was broken in October, 1849, for the new road. For the next three years all the energies of the company were centered upon building the first thirty-three miles of road from Mobile to Citronelle.[5] As the years passed further surveys

---

[3]Frances Clark, "Mobile and Ohio R. R.," *Merchant's Magazine*, December, 1848.

[4]"Proceedings of the Stockholders Meeting of the Mobile and Ohio Railroad Company," (Mobile, 1848), 5.

[5]It took the pioneer Southerners a long time to build their road, but they enjoyed the building. Mr. Baldwyn started the work at Mobile in 1849 and drove the golden spike near the Mississippi line on April 22, 1861, completing the road from Columbus, Kentucky, to Mobile, Alabama. The iron rails proceeded north with ceremony. A Fourth of July Excursion in 1854 from Mobile to Winchester, Mississippi, was typical of the day. The party received salutes of artillery all along the way. Mouths were agape at the spectacle of the iron horse. The guests were entertained by a drill by the Mobile Rifle Company, with several speeches and dinner. Mobile *Daily Advertiser*, July 6, 1854. The

were made, road bed prepared, usually by letting the contracts to local contractors such as Samuel Jackson Hays of Jackson who used slave labor in the work, and track was laid. Annual reports show the track creeping northward, but all the while the company was confronted with obstacles—financial ones principally but at times enemies of the enterprise burned bridges, such as the one over the Chickasaw River in 1851, or greased the tracks to stop the trains.[6]

Public land grants in Mississippi and Alabama were obtained in 1850, which put the road on a firmer footing in that section and Tennessee, by an act of 1852, allowed the company $1,180,000 with which to purchase rails for the 118 miles of road in Tennessee with something additional for bridges. Further financial aid was necessary, so Sidney Smith and W. R. Hallett of Mobile went to London to secure loans for the purchase of the rails (1854).[7] Part of the financial troubles were solved by cities and counties levying special taxes to purchase stock such as the $250,000 purchased by Madison County in 1852, after the matter was presented to the Court by Judge Milton Brown and the issue was voted upon by the people. This type of support was brought about in each section by influential railroad men who sold the idea to the community that the road could be built and would be profitable. Honorable Milton Brown and William H. Stephens, real railroad enthusiasts, went from place to place speaking in behalf of the Mobile and Ohio. These men spoke at Huntersville and Jack's Creek in 1852, at Denmark in 1853, while a large meeting was held at the court house in Jackson in April of the same year, and the editors of the papers made a noble effort to convince the readers that the railroads should come:

> The late rains we understand have had no perceptible effects upon the Forked Deer and Hatchie Rivers. Navigation is entirely suspended

---

writer is indebted to Prof. Thomas Clark of the University of Kentucky for the use of innumerable notes concerning Southern Railroads.

[6]Mobile *Advertiser*, July 8, 1851. Not long after the road was finished between Corinth and Jackson, a cow belonging to a Mrs. Walsh who lived just south of Henderson was killed by one of these new "iron horses." When the road did not pay damages promptly, she took the tallow from the said cow and put it on the track each day, so that the train had to stop, the track had to be sanded in order to pull a grade just south of Henderson.

[7]*Railroad Journal of 1854*, p. 591.

(Used through the courtesy of Mrs. O. L. Spencer)

with no prospect of a rise. When will ALL MEN become advocates of RAILROADS?[8]

Every kind of obstacle seemed to get in the way of the builders of the road. After Madison County purchased $250,000 worth of stock and individuals invested, it looked for a while as if the road would run a mile and one half east of town rather than "brushing its margin." This and the location of the depot was settled after considerable municipal squabble and the entire work through Madison County was taken by local contractors.[9]

By 1855, the work on the road was almost forced to a halt because of the laggardness of stockholders to pay. There were also rumors of bad faith and bad management. Governor Winston of Alabama vetoed the state aid bill saying that the railroad enriched the favored few, but Milton Brown made a long and "encouraging speech" to the stockholders and tried to show them that there was no reason to be discouraged.[10]

---

[8]Jackson *West Tennessee Whig*, April 8, April 29, February 12, 1852, June 23, 1853; Madison County Court Records 1849-1853.

[9]"Proceedings of Seventh Annual Meeting of the Stockholders of Mobile and Ohio Railroad Company, 1855"; Mobile *Advertiser*, March 23, 1855; *Alabama State Sentinel*, May 10, 1855.

[10]"Proceedings of the Seventh Annual Meeting of the Stockholders of the Mobile and Ohio R. R. Co." (Mobile, 1855).

These were the times that tried men's souls, particularly railroad men's souls. A large mass meeting was held in the courthouse in Jackson to consider the railroad crisis. Only 197 miles of the road north of Mobile was completed, bridges were burned, and engines were not delivered. Thirty miles of the road north had to be ready to be ironed by February, 1856, or the state aid would be lost. Tennessee bonds could only be spent for iron, chains, equipment for the portion of the road in Tennessee and could not be loaned to Mississippi.

Just at such a critical time as this (1857) Judge Milton Brown of Jackson was elected president of the company without a dissenting vote. It was the current opinion at this time that Brown's election gave bright hopes for the early completion of the road, for he would quiet the dissention and bring harmony to the organization.[11] Material evidence of real progress was also seen, for construction engines and rails were sent to Columbus, Kentucky, from New Orleans and plans were made to start laying immediately for all the Kentucky mileage was ready and 109¾ miles of the Tennessee mileage were ready. Although the track laying on the upper Kentucky end was begun in 1857, a year later the track had reached the state line. At that time only 800 feet of the iron had been laid north of Jackson, but on November 19, 1858, track laying parties met near Trenton. The first passenger train now (1858) came from Columbus to Jackson. This event had been predicted for months, men had talked and dreamed of the railroad for years. Plans had centered around the coming of the whistles of the locomotive—even an iron fence had been built around the courthouse to be in keeping with the spirit of progress. The *Whig* editor concluded:

> It was an occasion for much rejoicing to us to hear the snort of the iron horse, as with headlong fury, he came dashing on his way over forest and valley dragging behind him his golden train.[12]

In the late 1850's, Judge Brown succeeded in obtaining some advantageous loans while he was in London. For this he was entitled to the gratitude of the stockholders and all

---

[11] Jackson *West Tennessee Whig*, March 13, 1857.
[12] Mobile *Register*, November 27, 1858; Jackson *West Tennessee Whig*, March 13, 1857; "Proceedings of the Eleventh Annual Meeting of the Stockholders of the Mobile and Ohio Railroad," (Mobile, 1859).

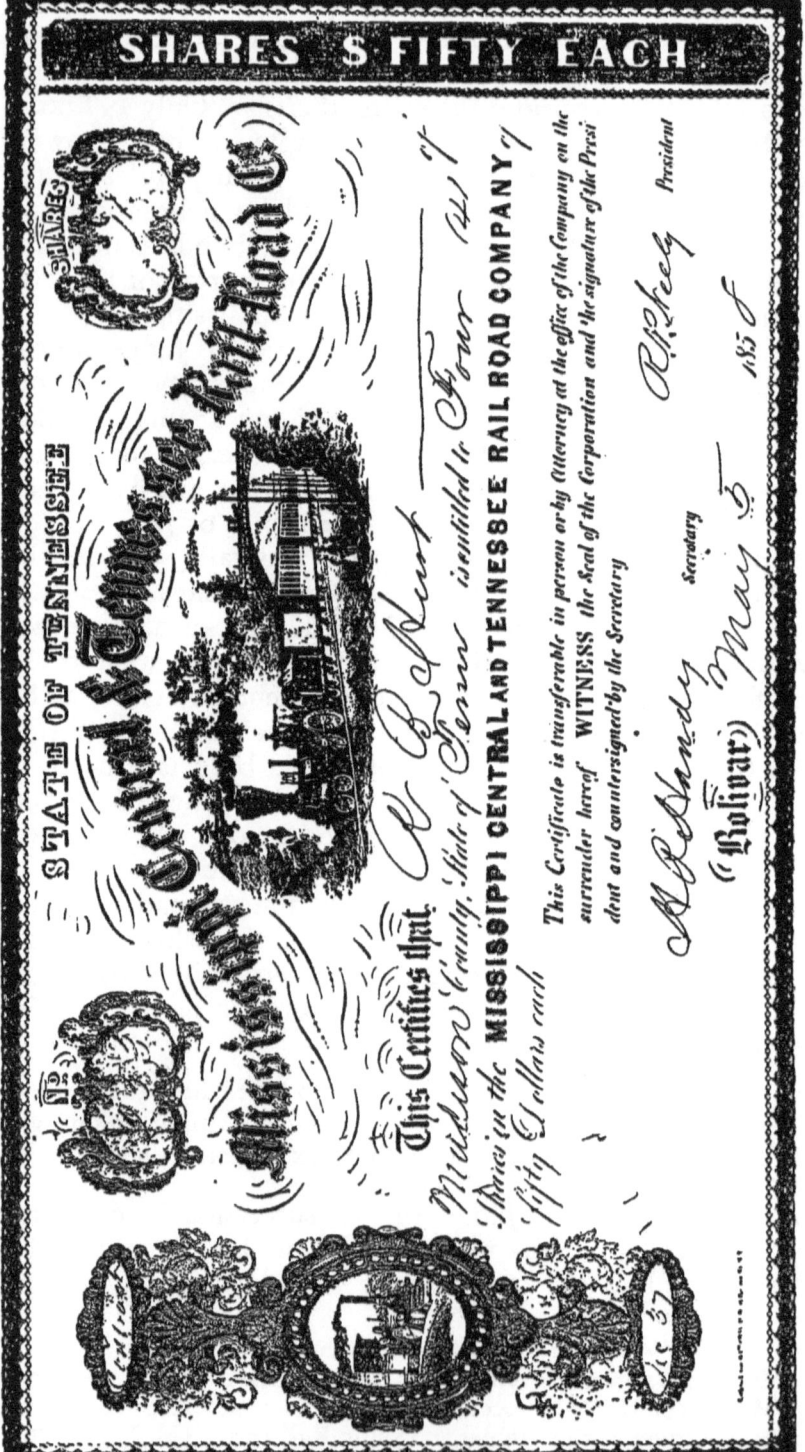

Stock certificate of Mississippi Central and Tennessee Railroad Company, upon whose rails the first "cars" came to Jackson in 1857. This later became a part of the Illinois Central System. (Used through the courtesy of Miss Guy Leeper)

interested persons, for it opened up an era of confidence and hope for the future.[13] Fate was good to the road this time and on April 22, 1861, J. D. Baldwyn drove the last spike amidst a large group of spectators near the Tennessee-Mississippi state line just in time for the road to be of great value to Confederate and Federal forces during the succeeding Civil War.

After the Sectional Conflict of 1861-65 the road was a "splendid wreck," physically and financially. The Company lost $5,228,562.23 in Alabama State bonds, fifty negroes which had cost $119,691, and over four million dollars in cost of transporting Confederate troops and supplies. All bridges were burned, trestle-work, warehouses and station buildings between Union City, Tennessee, and Okolona, Mississippi, were destroyed. The rolling stock was reduced to one fourth of what was necessary, the repair shop at Jackson was broken up.[14] Few men could have, in such a short time accomplished what Judge Brown did in bringing order out of chaos. Within a few months after the war was over, the company had freight and passenger trains moving.[15] Judge Brown remained president of the road until 1871.

The mid-nineteenth century witnessed the entrance of a second road into Jackson—the Mississippi Central and Tennessee. The previous decade in this section might be called an age of experiment, for roads were dreamed of, chartered, but never built. No promoter had the slightest idea of the problems to be met or how much traffic was necessary to make the enterprise profitable. Thus, many of the roads did not progress beyond the paper stage, but the little Mississippi and Tennessee Central was different. Trains were running, after surprisingly little difficulty, within four years after it was chartered.

The account of the building of the Mississippi Central and Tennessee from Grand Junction to Jackson, Tennessee, was just a part of the story of the efforts of the promoters to drain the trade of the Mississippi valley to New Orleans rather than eastward as it was seemingly drifting. This road, only 47.7 miles long, was a small link of the road which was finally absorbed

---

[13]Debow *Review* XXVI, 1859, p. 341.

[14]Harrison, *Legal History*, 1433.

[15]Jackson *West Tennessee Whig*, April 28, 1866.

in the great Illinois Central System. In the beginning this road like the Mobile and Ohio gradually crept northward. The New Orleans, Jackson, and Great Northern from New Orleans to Jackson, the Canton and Jackson Railroad, the Mississippi Central, the Mississippi Central and Tennessee, and the Cairo extension ultimately became a part of the Illinois Central.

To discover that the Mississippi Central and Tennessee was just a short line is susprising until it is learned that under the laws of Tennessee a special charter had to be obtained in order to secure State aid, so on November 30, 1853, the charter was granted for the specific purpose of extending the Mississippi Central from Grand Junction to Jackson, Tennessee. Commissioners were: Milton Brown, John W. Campbell, Thomas Read, Jacob Hill, William E. Butler, A. W. O. Totten, S. J. Hays, Edwin Polk, Citizen S. Woods, W. W. Herron, David Green.

Three thousand persons attended a big celebration in Bolivar, Tennessee, on September 21, 1854. Several speeches were delivered by Judge Milton Brown, Dr. A. Jackson, John V. Wright, Mr. McCoy, a picnic dinner was served, and ground was broken for the new road.[16] The first terminal was established at Bolivar with turn table and machine shop. Contracts were small, often being let to farmers and citizens along the way who would cut a few hundred yards of the embankment with shovel and wheel barrow.[17] At the August meeting of the directors the site for the depot and the right of way to the connections with the Mobile and Ohio was accepted from the citizens of Jackson, Tennessee. This bit of track crept north reaching Medon, where the engine was "switched back up to the end of the track" slowly and cautiously on May 15, 1856. "The iron-horse" entered Jackson in 1857. This event was recorded by R. H. Cartmell as follows:

> Went down to Mississippi railroad—the track is finished and the cars come up for the first time tonight. [August 29, 1857]. There was a large crowd from town and country to witness first arrival in daylight of a train of cars. I saw nothing or heard nothing on account of my old fool horse. He jumped and pitched and tried to run—a

---

[16] *Railroad Journal,* September 30, 1854.

[17] J. C. Robinson in his "Personal Recollections of the Mississippi Central" told of the first rails that were shipped from Europe up the Mississippi to Memphis and thence to Grand Junction, of the small early engines with cylinders 12 inches in diameter, drivers 5 feet, but

perfect fool and only real fool horse that was there—remained in town had a mock celebration of the occasion—a burlesque on Memphis and Charleston—an oration by Tom Gamerville and a mingling of the waters of Pegues pond with the Forked Deer. . . . September 16, 1857. Today devoted to celebrating the arrival of the cars on the Mississippi Central and Tennessee Railroad. A barbecue was prepared, speeches made, cannons fired at night, fire works, balloon raising and a party—the whole passed off finely without any accident. A large number of strangers from adjoining counties and Mississippi were present. There were perhaps 4000 persons present, some said eight or ten thousand.[18]

Before the "Iron-Horse" was within "whistling distance" of Jackson the people were planning a grand jubilee to celebrate the rule of the "Iron-Majesty."

The following years of the life of the road may be told by consolidations, destruction during the Sectional Conflict, reconstruction, growth and more consolidations. On March 12, 1859, the Mississippi Central and Tennessee and Mississippi Central were consolidated under the name of Mississippi Central Railroad.[19] Then, on April 13, 1874, the Mississippi Central and the New Orleans, Jackson, and Great Northern were consolidated under the name of New Orleans, St. Louis, and Chicago Railroad. Three years later the Central Mississippi and the New Orleans, Jackson and Great Northern Rail-

---

each engine had a name such as the *General R. P. Neely* and the *Judge Milton Brown,* of the brass and paintings of the engines, of the celebrations with champagne and whiskey when the line was completed, of instances of washouts when the local people would take teams and help cut timber and assist the railroad force in raising trestles, cribbing up tracks and making it ready for the passing of the trains without one dollar charge against the company. C. R. Calvert, "Brief History of the Illinois Central Railroad," MS, Crossitt Library, Memphis, Tennessee.

[18]R. H. Cartmell's Diary, August 25, September 16, 1857. Two of the famous engines with the names in gilt were the *Gen. Neely* and *Judge Brown.* The *Judge Brown* was a 16 ton engine built in Patterson, New Jersey. Thomas Clark, *Pioneer Southern Railroads* (Chapel Hill, 1936), p. 156. The people of Medon celebrated the coming of the "cars" with a public barbecue. *West Tennessee Whig,* April 10, 1857; *Jackson Madisonian,* June 20, 1857.

[19]Mississippi Central and Tennessee originally cost $872,503, not including the rolling stock. $26,835.31 was spent to purchase 54 negroes and 2,860 acres of land. In 1860, there were 10 locomotives, 120 freight cars and passenger cars, and six mail cars. *Railroad Journal,* August 4, 1860.

road Company were consolidated under the name of Chicago, St. Louis and New Orleans. On December 1, 1912, all of the property owned by the Chicago, St. Louis and New Orleans Railroad Company was leased to the Illinois Central System.[20]

At the close of the Sectional Conflict, the Mississippi Central was left a complete wreck, nothing but rusty streaks of disrupted tracks, disabled locomotives, washed out bridges, and the famous "Sherman's hairpins"—rails wrapped about tree. Four years of raids one right after the other by both armies had destroyed a decade of building. Connections were made to Jackson, Tennessee, by May 18, 1866, the Cairo extension was completed so that the first train ran to Cairo from Jackson on December 24, 1874. President West's report of the conditions of the road in 1865 gives very succinctly the story of the destruction:

> At the time I took charge of your road, in October 1864, it was in operation only from Oxford to Canton. . . . The superintendent was a prisoner of war; the road was nearly run down; there were but four contractors getting our wood on the whole road; but one getting our bridge timber; and all with small working forces wholly inadequate to our requirements; and not enough money in the treasury to pay debts then overdue for operating the road and paying the Confederate Tax. The Road and its rolling stock were greaty damaged and much of it destroyed by the numerous raids of the United States and Confederate troops. From Oxford to Jackson, Tennessee, it was a wreck. Notwithstanding these raids, we had in October last a respectable amount of rolling stock and a limited amount of machinery, but, between that time and the first of January, raids of the most damaging character followed each other in such rapid succession as to leave the road without a single engine in working order north of the Yalabusha River. The bridge over that river having been destroyed, the engine on the south side was not available. . . . The line was rebuilt [that is, completed] to Jackson, Tennessee on May 18, 1866.[21]

The machine shops and transfer shops at Jackson, which in 1876 employed thirty hands, were entirely inadequate, so new shops were opened with a big celebration on January 1, 1880. The Mobile and Ohio and the Chicago, St. Louis, and New Orleans ran trains every few minutes and every carriage in the

---

[20] Information furnished by Attorney Lucius Burch of the Illinois Central System, Memphis, Tennessee.

[21] C. R. Calvert, "History of the Illinois Central," MS, 39.

city was employed to carry the multitudes to the vast new building where the banquet and ball was held. A contemporary paper described the event as the most brilliant entertainment of Jackson. Magnolias, palms, and green bay trees made the halls look like tropic lands; mammoth pyramid cakes adorned the tables; General A. Campbell gave a brief history of Jackson.[22]

The time of another field day for railroad promoters came again from 1870 to 1890, and the place again was Madison County. Great rivalry was on between the neighboring towns and there were so many roads, planned, surveyed, and chartered that they could be arranged alphabetically. Thomas Blain and Gilbert Anderson were appointed by Mayor King to attend the great Southern Railroad Convention in Memphis in 1875.[23] There was the proposed Memphis, Jackson, and Knoxville Railroad, which was to run through Denmark, Cedar Chapel, Somerville, and Mason. The petition of incorporation in the Chancery Court at Jackson was signed by J. C. Theus, W. P. Robertson, W. W. Gates, R. B. Hurt, W. D. Robinson, A. R. Reid, James Neely, Thomas Newberg, W. A. Morgan, and S. P. Caldwell. In September, 1871, the editor of the *Whig and Tribune* tried to arouse the citizens out of their stupid languor by reminding them that the iron horse was girding the earth, that Bolivar, which was not lacking in public spirit wanted the road, too, and that if Bolivar did get it, Jackson had lost it forever. The road was chartered and two months later, R. B. Snipes, Colonel Sneed, Dr. Campbell, R. B. Hurt were appointed commissioners, and paper reported that the new road should be running in time to carry off the next cotton crop.[24] A battle-royal was on between Jackson and Bolivar. Hardeman County called her citizens together to listen to speeches and eat barbecue. The editors copied the enthusiastic editorials from the Jackson papers and followed them by local propaganda. The Bolivar *Bulletin* carried this quotation from the Jackson paper:

Memphis favors the road through Jackson for she wants no more branch roads. . . . If Fayette County is caught by the Bolivar bait, she

---

[22] Jackson *Tribune and Sun*, January 1, 1880.
[23] Jackson *Whig and Tribune*, November 20, 1875.
[24] Jackson *Whig and Tribune*, September 16, 1871; Bolivar *Bulletin*, November 3, 1871.

will repeat the folly of years ago when she refused to extend her little branch road to Jackson. . . . The country beyond Bolivar is the poorest in the State and the most rugged. The people have but little money. The people, poor as they are, cannot nor will not incur a debt or contribute sufficiently to build one fourth of the road. But come to Jackson and you have connections with the North and South.[25]

There were enough "anti-railroad men" to keep the road from being built. The argument of one of the "anti's" is rich enough to quote:

The people is gone wild on this ere railroad machine. Horses that is worth forty-dollars won't be worth five dollar a hed. Wagin makers will starve to death. Otes won't be worth nothin' and we'll have to quit raisin them Coon skins won't be worth a d—n; bank stock'll go clear down and the billering steam wagon'll skerr all the game outen the kuntry. I'll sell my forty and gin for Arkensaw if you don't stop this durn ralerode.[26]

The 1880's brought surveyors for the Jackson and Nashville R. R.[27] and the Brownsville and Jackson Railroad, which was chartered in 1882 to connect Brownsville and Jackson. Four years later the Ohio Valley Railroad was chartered by J. W. Allison, J. L. Wisdom, W. P. Robertson, E. S. Mallory, and J. H. Head, to connect some point of the Tennessee-Kentucky line with Hardeman County. These were all "dreamed-of" roads, but in 1886 enterprising citizens of Virginia and Tennessee obtained a charter to construct a line of railway through Tennessee from Memphis to Knoxville via Jackson and Nashville to be known as the Tennessee Midland Railway Company. The early estimates disclosed that an easy alignment was possible, with a maximum grade of not over one per cent and at a cost of not exceeding $17,000 per mile. Sponsors of the new enterprise met in July, 1887, and sub-

---

[25] Bolivar *Bulletin*, October 20, 1871.
[26] *Ibid.*, September 1, 1871.
[27] Jackson *Tribune and Sun*, April 20, 1880. In 1872, the citizens of Denmark subscribed $25,000 to the Denmark, Brownsville, and Durhamville R. R. and only a few hundred feet of the embankment was built. Therefore in the 1880's when they were asked for subscriptions of $3,000 to Tennessee Midland they refused. They thought the road would be forced to come through Big Black Creek bottom anyway. The road was built a mile south, Mercer grew overnight, and the knell of Denmark was sounded.

scribed $1,250,000. Contracts were let, work began with the result that eighty-five miles of the road from Memphis to Jackson was soon put into operation.

Contemporary newspapers contain scattered items about the progress of this dreamed-of railroad from east to west—in October, 1887, iron for the Midland road arrived; in December General A. W. Campbell was at work getting right of way east of the city and the first engine was put on the Midland's track [the Jackson citizens thought it should be named the "City of Jackson," for Jackson was the first city voting its subscripton to the road]; in January, 1888, news items told of the railroad which was nearing completion; by March work was progressing nicely from both ends of the line and cars were running to three miles west of the Hatchie River; by April Colonel Robert Gates, right of way agent for the Midland Road, was at work on the line in Perry County; on June 1, 1888, the first train ran from Memphis to Jackson; in July work on the Midland depot was begun and John L. Wisdom, contractor, announced the completion of one mile of Midland's east of Mobile and Ohio R. R., showing that the promoters intended to push on to Nashville.[28]

That first day of June, 1888, was a real day of celebration in Jackson, for the first train from Memphis arrived in Jackson. This special train of six coaches bearing officials of the road, pressmen, and one hundred and fifty other prominent citizens arrived at the Illinois Central freight depot at 2 o'clock. Here the guests were met by a special committee and conducted to the Supreme Court Room. Here E. L. Bullock, in his usual happy manner, delivered the address of the day and then the guests were escorted to the Circuit Court Room where the Woman's Exchange served a splendid dinner upon tables that were so beautifully decorated that they gave a fairy-like appearance to the dingy old court room. A tour was then made of

---

[28]Jackson *Forked Deer Blade,* October 15, December 10, 24, 1887, January 9, March 3, 24, April 7, June 2, July 14, 1888. Upon one day during the period of construction, the materials did not arrive, so John L. Wisdom, Sr., took the negroes and in the one day's time built the lake north of the old power plant. Now, the workmen did not have to go so far away to fish. The construction camps moved along as the road was built. Many of the present citizens of Jackson remember visiting the camps when they were small boys.

the city in carriages furnished by the livery stables of the city, and thus ended a memorable day for the visitors of Memphis who had been favorably impressed by the view of their new neighbor.[29]

The construction and operation of the Midland east of Jackson was held up due to the crossing or undercrossing of the Illinois Central at Jackson, so that it was not until 1890 that the road was extended to Lexington and to Midland City (now Perryville).[30] With the building of the Midland road, there came a suggestion by a syndicate of eastern capitalists to make Midland City on the Tennessee River, a real "Pittsburg of the South." Thus, paper plans were made to build a city that would be a rival to Jackson as the business center of West Tennessee, but none of the plans progressed further than the papers or the minds of the promoters.

The first Midland Time Table in 1888 called for a freight schedule between Jackson and Memphis of eight hours and thirty minutes, with four hours for the trip of the daily passenger train. In April, 1895, a new passenger train "The Jackson Belle" left Jackson at 6:30 and returned at 8:30 making the trip in three hours fifteen minutes and also making it possible to spend the day in Memphis.[31]

In 1895, the Louisville and Nashville purchased the Tennessee Midland and Paducah, Tennessee and Alabama railroads and promptly leased the two roads to the Nashville, Chattanooga and St. Louis for ninety-nine years. Thus, Madison County was linked with Memphis on the west, Paducah on the north, and Nashville on the east. By 1928, the company realized the increasing potentialities of the Jackson territory, so the freight office was moved from Paducah to Jackson. The Nashville, Chattanooga and St. Louis Railroad has not only furnished an invaluable outlet to the eastern markets for produce from the county, but has encouraged scientific agriculture in this section, has promoted new industries in the county such

---

[29] Jackson *Forked Deer Blade*, June 2, 1888.

[30] The writer is indebted to R. H. West of the Traffic Department of the Nashville, Chattanooga and St. Louis R. R. for his manuscript "History of the N. C. and St. L. Railway." Much of the general information concerning the Midland is taken from this.

[31] Jackson *Forked Deer Blade*, April 12, 1895. The same trip in 1945 is made in two hours and twenty-four minutes.

THE RAILROADS 151

as the Jackson Creosote Company, has selected such men for its agents who would promote good will and good business,[32] has encouraged its employees to be good citizens, and has been a good citizen itself. The Midland of old and the Nashville, Chattanooga and St. Louis of the last half century have been a substantial part of the physical and economic life of the community.[33]

The twentieth century witnessed more railroad building into Jackson and further consolidations until by 1945 new roads had come, old roads had merged into others, and the three old roads had become a part of the growing Gulf, Mobile and Ohio System. On August 16, 1910, the Birmingham and Northwestern Company secured a perpetual charter from the State of Tennessee for the construction of a road from Jackson to Dyersburg—a distance of 49 miles. The first officers included R. H. Hall, president; I. B. Tigrett, vice-president and treasurer; R. F. Spragins, secretary and general council; C. F. Morgan, manager; C. H. Morris, auditor. The capital stock of $300,000 was held by citizens of Jackson, Bells, and Dyersburg. By 1912 I. B. Tigrett, a man with big ideas, became president of the struggling road. The road was completed on June 9, 1913. Forty-nine miles of two streaks of rusty steel tracks wound its way on a crooked path through West Tennessee, an area of acres of standing timber and fertile soil. Current stories of that day record the conditions of the road during those first years such as the two wheezy second-hand locomotives, the wooden day coaches, the road bed upon which the trains were often forced to slow down to six miles an hour, the circus that was moved from Dyersburg to Jackson in twenty-one hours.[34]

For years officials of the Gulf, Mobile and Northern Railroad dreamed of an outlet to the northern markets. This dream began to take form in 1917, when the decision was made to

---

[32]The first agent, C. F. Morgan, who was appointed in 1888, was followed by D. T. Patrick (1905), A. W. Jones (1906), and Will Luckman (1906).

[33]December 11, 1945, marked the completion of a century of service by the N. C. & St. L.; the charter under which this company is operating is dated December 11, 1845. The Jackson branch of this road is not a hundred years old but it is proud to be a part of the system that boasts of such an old charter and so many years of service.

[34]Memphis *Commercial Appeal*, June 17, 1945.

build the road from Middleton to Jackson. The citizens of Jackson voted $100,000 worth of bonds to the project provided that the work be completed within three years. Unforeseen and insurmountable obstacles made the progress slow, difficult, and expensive. An extension of time had to be granted, but on September 9, 1919, the new road was open for traffic, although entry into Jackson was temporarily made on the Nashville, Chattanooga and St. Louis tracks.[35]

As the years passed connecting links were added and mergers took place, such as the Gulf, Mobile and Northern and the Birmingham and Northwestern in 1927, the Gulf, Mobile and Northern and the Mobile and Ohio forming the Gulf, Mobile and Ohio in 1940, and finally the Gulf, Mobile and Ohio and the Alton in 1945. I. B. Tigrett, of Jackson, the president of the forty-nine mile Birmingham and Northwestern in 1912, had become the president of the Gulf, Mobile and Ohio and Alton in 1945 with 2908.55 miles of track. Thus, another connecting link was made from the Great Lakes to the Gulf.

The railroads have been the life line of the community; they have meant the growth of the community. As the citizens began to realize that transportation of the Forked Deer was very uncertain and in fact impossible at times, railroads began to assume their place in the life of the community and Jackson was transformed from a river town to an inland railroad center. Wherever the railroad has touched, it has become a shuttle, weaving vital transportation service back and forth through the warp of the community life to produce a tapestry of economic and physical growth whose colors are rich, strong, and enduring. During those early days, there was many a time when the shuttle moved in uncertain directions, often in starts, jerks, and even to a stand-still, nevertheless the records remain that wherever it touches the community, the effect of the railroad has been one of definite value and sustained growth.

---

[35]The writer is indebted to I. B. Tigrett and his staff for the material concerning the Birmingham and Northwestern and the growth and consolidation of the Gulf, Mobile and Ohio. Most of the real growth of the system came in the recent years which were not intended to be included in this volume. For this reason a bare mention of this period is made.

CASEY JONES IN SONG AND STORY

Jackson has not only been the home of railroad presidents but the home of many faithful and competent employees of the roads which enter the city. Probably the most famous of these men was Casey Jones, the engineer who died at his post of duty back at the turn of the century. Casey's tragic death was the cause of the singing of what may be called a folk ballad by one of his colored admirers. The story of Casey Jones and the song have become a part of American life. The song of the brave engineer from Jackson, Tennessee, who rode to death and to fame on his "heavy six-wheeler" has been sung in many variations wherever railroaders have gone—all over the United States, in France, Germany, and even among the natives of South Africa. It was accorded due recognition in B. A. Botkins, *Treasury of American Folklore* (1944).[36]

Casey (so-called from his home town Cayce, Kentucky) Jones known among his friends as a "fast-roller" and the engineer with a mournful but musical whistle. These were the days when a whistle was personal property, not standard equipment. An engineer in St. Louis had given "Casey" his peculiar whistle and he, according to the colored wipers and oilers at the shops could "just natchell get mo' music outta dat whistle dan ennybody else on de ole I. C." Residents along the line of the Illinois Central learned to recognize Casey's whistle, a long, drawn-out, soft note which rose and then died away in a whisper. All the switchmen knew by the engine's moans "that the man at the throttle was Casey Jones" when Casey was the throttle puller of the I. C. "Cannon Ball" on the Memphis-Canton run.

On Sunday night, April 29, 1900, Casey and his fireman, Sim Webb, had just brought their train in when they learned that Engineer Lewis was ill, so Casey immediately volunteered to take No. 638 on her run. At four o'clock on the 30th of April, the train, having already made up her lost time, approached Vaughn, Mississippi, where a side track began at the end of a curve. Casey and Sim Webb both saw the freight on the siding but neither knew that there were two sections

---

[36]The song and the story belongs to Jackson, Tennessee, and to Mrs. Janie Brady Jones, the widow of the engineer, who has lived in the community for over a half century. The writer is indebted to Mrs. Jones for the details of this account.

of the freight, that the rear of section two was on the main line, hat the freight engineer intended "to saw by."

A rocket was placed up the track to slow Casey down but plans went astray, Casey rounded the curve, heard the rocket, saw the cars ahead, set the air brakes, and yelled to Sim Webb, the fireman; "Jump, Sim!" Then, Casey rode the roaring 638 into a holocaust of crashing wood that splintered like a match box. When Casey's body was taken from the wreckage, it was said that one hand was found on the whistle cord and the other on the air-brake lever. Sim Webb remembered that as he jumped Casey held down on the whistle in a long piercing scream. He must have been trying to warn the freight conductor in the caboose. The engine and the baggage cars were the only ones that left the track. No one else was killed.

Days passed and Wallace Saunders, a negro wiper at the round house who was continually making up songs about his favorite engines and engineers, began humming a tune and singing a few lines about "an engineer Casey Jones." The song remained a true uncopyrighted folk ballad until 1909 when it was popularized locally by a vaudeville team known as the Leighton Brothers and some song-writers, Newton and Seibert, changed the words and published it. Though the words were changed, they retained the lilting refrain and the name of Casey Jones.

It matters not whether the words are true to the facts of the story or not, there is a fascination about them, so the following version is quoted:

> Come all you rounders for I want you to hear,
> The story told of a brave engineer;
> Casey Jones was a rounder's name
> On a heavy six-eight-wheeler he rode to fame.
>
> Caller called Jones about half-past four,
> Jones kissed his wife at the station door,
> Climbed into the cab with the orders in his hand,
> Says, "This is my trip to the promised land."
>
> Through South Memphis yards on the fly,
> He heard the fireman say, "You've got a white-eye,"
> All the switchmen knew by the engine's moans
> That the man at the throttle was Casey Jones.

It had been raining for more than a week
The railroad track was like the bed of a creek.
They rated him down to a thirty mile gait,
Threw the south-bound mail about eight hours late.

Fireman says, "Casey, you're runnin' too fast,
You run the block signal the last station you passed,"
Jones says, "Yes, I think we can make it through,
For she steams much better than I ever know."

Jones says, "Fireman, don't you fret.
Keep knockin' at the firedoor, don't give up yet;
I'm goin' to run her till she leaves the rail
Or make it on time with the south-bound mail."

Around the curve and a-down the dump
Two locomotives were abound to bump.
Fireman hollered, "Jones, it's just ahead,
We might jump and make it but we'll all be dead."

'Twas around this curve he saw a passenger train;
Something happened in Casey's brain;
Fireman jumped off, but Casey stayed on,
He's a good engineer but he's dead and gone—

Poor Casey was always all right,
He stuck to his post both day and night;
They loved to hear the whistle of old Number Three
As he came into Memphis on the old K.C.

Headaches and heartaches and all kinds of pain
Are not apart from a railroad train;
Tales that are earnest, noble and gran'
Belong to the life of a railroad man.

THE COUNTY AND THE SECTIONAL CONFLICT

CHAPTER XIII

"The people of Tennessee are conservative, love the Union, and will bear much and long before going to extremes," wrote Robert H. Cartmell in February 1861. Thus, a typical citizen of the community summarized the feeling of a majority of the people in the county, for they were here just as they were in other sections of the State, particularly in West Tennessee—torn between two desires, the desire to stay in the Union where their rights would be protected and the desire to aid their sister states to the South who were tied very closely to them because their way of life was similar. West Tennessee, in particular, had "Southern Sentiments," for she had many more things in common with Mississippi and Alabama than with East Tennessee. The election of Lincoln in 1860 was a signal for the radicals of Tennessee to follow South Carolina's example and go out of the Union, but the majority of the people of Tennessee refused to act hurriedly and were unwilling to withdraw from the Union until the new administration did something which forced them to take action.

That there were men of opposite views on the question in Madison County is shown by the fact that some of the radicals suspected a man of holding "abolitionists sentiments," whereupon they seized him, put him upon a rail, and rode him out of town.[1] The majority of people were more conservative. They wanted to protect the rights of the South in the Union if possible. Some considered all this talk of secession "mad-man's folly"; many approved of Mr. Crittenden's compromise movement in the Senate and condemned the people who called those seeking compromise "submissionists":

> This term is not applied by those who favor immediate secession to those who do not. There is no propriety to truthfulness in the ap-

---

[1]Jackson *West Tennessee Whig,* December 14, 1860.

plication of the term. We believe it to be indisputably true, that a large majority of people of Tennessee are unalterably opposed to being dragged out of the present Union until after all the remedies under the Constitution, for the existing evils have been tried and failed. *Then* we believe the people of Tennessee, without a dissent, will be willing to try those remedies which the fire eaters now propose; but not before. To apply the term to any respectable citizen of Tennessee, as it is now indiscriminately applied by some is simply to utter a great lie, upon very small grounds.²

W. H. Stephens of Jackson was one of the twelve delegates from Tennessee who went to Washington to that peace conference in February, 1861, and was astonished to find the feeling so bitter.

The firing upon Fort Sumter in April, 1861, and Lincoln's call for troops tipped the balance of the scales and the people had to decide whether to defend the Confederacy or to help crush it. Secessionists and thousands of former Unionists joined hands to take Tennessee out of the Union. Feeling ran high as meetings took place at the courthouse where fire-eating orators stirred up the people, as delegates were elected for the proposed convention in Nashville, as A. W. O. Totten of Madison was appointed as one of the commissioners to enter into a military league with the Confederate States, as men, such as Robert H. Cartmell, contributed money to buy uniforms for companies such as the "Southern Guards," and as the people in general became convinced that they were ready for any emergency. Contemporary papers assumed a very belligerent attitude, as illustrated by the following quotation from the *West Tennessee Whig:*

NO SCARCITY! The Northern people miserably deceive themselves if they believe the South is not prepared with an ample amount of provisions for any war which may be made upon them. They take it for granted that because the Southern States have heretofore drawn large amounts of provisions from the Northwest that if this source of supply is cut off, we would of necessity starve. We assure them that in this matter they are mistaken. Besides having enough for all ordinary purposes, there are now at this place and along the line of the Mobile and Ohio Railroad south of here, at least a hundred car loads of bacon, to say nothing of the corn and flour of which articles the supply is ample till our glorious wheat crop, the largest ever known

---

²*Ibid.*, January 18, 1861.

in the South, shall be harvested and ready for market. Talk about starving people thus bountifully supplied as the world has ever seen before. The idea is preposterous—the South can stand the blockade of all provisions for a century if the North can. Do your worst, gentlemen.[3]

On the eighth of June, 1861, when the people went to the polls, the western two-thirds of the state cast an overwhelming vote for separation or their "Declaration of Independence." In Shelby County, where there had been a threat of a secession of Memphis, there were only five votes cast for the Union; only seven in Lauderdale County and only twenty in Madison. Drums beat and fifes shrilled in the streets. Thirty thousand volunteers were organized and equipped within two months and town after town became storehouses of the essentials of war. The citizens of Jackson, which was a storehouse for provisions, gallantly defied the "Black Republicans" in Washington to starve them out:

There is at the present time more than a million and a half pounds of bacon in the town of Jackson, and yet our late friends of the North pretend to believe they can starve us into subjection to the domination of the black Republican rule at Washington. Gentlemen, you are mightily mistaken, if you think we can't live without you or your support. If we can't we have made up our minds to die in the attempt.[4]

Nothing could make this period, when the clouds of war were gathering, more real than to review a few entries in the diary of Robert H. Cartmell, a man who sincerely wanted to preserve the Union but predicted that if Lincoln were elected, Civil War or Revolution was sure to follow. The following entries bring life to the story of old:

October, 1860—So certain as he [Lincoln] undertakes to carry into effect the principles of the leading men of his party or attempts to meet the expectations of his party, so certain will this Union be dissolved and Civil War uncertain in its direction, certain in its consequence be the result. We are hovering over a volcano ready to burst at any moment. What a pity! to sever, tear up and destroy the best Government ever devised by the ingenuity of man or revealed by heaven, except for the slavery question. THE UNION OUGHT TO

---

[3]*Ibid.*, May 17, 1861.
[4]*Ibid.*, June 8, 1861.

BE PRESERVED. . . . These times are critical. The historian would be baffled in the attempt to paint a picture in colors sufficiently black.

November 9—Mourning over Lincoln's election, for the South would not put up with the "Higher Law" doctrine and yet the Union ought to stand.

December 25—There is an unsettled state of the public mind, of uneasiness and dissatisfaction which will in all probability terminate in a dissolution of the Union. The South has no disposition to submit to his election the Black Republican, Abe Lincoln. . . . The clouds grow larger and blacker.

March 7, 1861—Civil War is inevitable!

April 13—The North have by a systematic course of intermeddling and agitation, abuse, slander driven the South into Revolution! The end we cannot see.

April 16—Went to town where a large crowd at the courthouse was listening to speeches.

May 15—A big crowd in Jackson of seven companies of volunteers mustered into service as a part of 55,000 volunteers that Lincoln's army will have to cut through. Lincoln's troops will have to work to make it through the country with his hirelings. They can stay at Cairo and feast on chills and fever and enjoy mosquitoes but if they leave there 'twould be better for them to go North.

May 25—Madison County troops leave tomorrow.

May 26—Eight companies from Madison, one from Haywood, one from Fayette left at noon on the cars. All men, women, children were there. Many tears shed, an occasion of melancholy interest, the very flower of our citizens going forth to mingle in a civil war.[5]

The voters of Tennessee defeated the idea of a convention in February, 1861, "to ascertain the attitude of the State towards the Federal Government," but the legislature passed an act to reorganize the militia. "Bureaus of Military Supplies" were established in the cities, one of which was in Jackson, where contributions of money, blankets, and supplies were received. By May 4, 1861, over a month before Tennessee formally became independent of the Union, there were stationed in West Tennessee, mainly in Memphis and Jackson, thirty-nine companies of infantry, two of cavalry, two artillery. The "Jackson Gays" and "Southern Guards" had drilled for several months before they became a part of that Regiment which has been designated as the Madison County Regiment—The Sixth Tennessee, it being composed of eleven companies from Madison, one from

---

[5]Diary of Robert H. Cartmell, 1860-61. MS.

Fayette, and one from Haywood counties. Its organization occurred at the old fairgrounds, soon to be called Camp Beauregard, in Jackson on May 15, 1861, when men were sworn in by Lieutenant-Colonel Alexander W. Campbell and field and staff officers were elected and appointed.[6]

Companies gathered at various places in the country and were ordered to Camp Beauregard in Jackson. John Johnston of Denmark related the story of the first few weeks of the Denmark company. The scene he described was probably typical of other places in the county:

> Colonel John Love, a veteran of the Mexican War, was the first drill master. The citizens furnished the cloth and the ladies soon had gray flannel shirts, coats and trousers with a dark strip down each leg made for them. Orders came to report to Jackson. All met at the Presbyterian Church to hear a sermon by Dr. Cochran. In the church yard the company was presented with a beautiful silk flag with the name of the company painted on it, by Miss Emma Cobb, with a speech prepared for the occasion. Capt. Ingram accepted with a speech. The company was transported to Jackson in farm wagons to the camp out at the fairgrounds on the western edge of the city.[7]

On May 26, 1861, as the Sixth Tennessee started to the front, over twelve hundred strong, in the highest hopes, little did they know that many of them would never return and that those who did return would come to a community that was wrecked by four years of war. People from all parts of the county assembled to bid farewell to their loved ones. The line of march from the camp to the Mobile and Ohio depot was thronged with people. Contemporary writers were reluctant

---

[6] Lists of Confederate veterans may be found in the Appendix.

[7] "Reminiscences of John Johnston" MS., used through the courtesy of his son, Addison Johnston. When the news of the firing upon Fort Sumter and Lincoln's call for troops came, the people of the South "let up a howl and other states seceded." Young Johnny Johnston, a true Southern patriot, lost no time before he purchased some red, white, and blue cloth and got his sister to make him a Confederate flag, which he placed on a fishing pole and mounted his pony the morning after the exciting news had arrived, he rode through the village of Denmark on his way to school. When he arrived at the seat of learning, his comrades assisted in placing the banner in the top of a tree and whipping one of the boys who made an unwelcome remark about the new flag. Here in Denmark, the first flag was raised in the community and "fighting" began.

to try to describe that scene of grief, despair, and speechless horror as the troops left by the cars for Union City, but one writer told of the "sea of humanity which surged about the train" and the "acres of weeping women, shouting men, frantic girls."[8] At Union City under Colonel William H. Stephens, the Sixth Tennessee became a part of General Cheatham's first brigade and it was to Colonel Stephens that much of the credit must be given for infusing into this regiment a spirit of discipline and pride which was responsible for its eminent degree of efficiency in later months and years.[9]

As late as the closing months of the year 1861, it was the opinion of many that peace would still be made, and that if there were fighting, there would be very little.[10] But the invader who was threatening the firesides of the Confederate States materialized in February, 1862, when Grant proceeded from Cairo, Illinois, up the Ohio and Tennessee rivers and took Fort Donelson and Fort Henry. The Sixth Tennessee was a part of that Confederate army which retired to the South and met the enemy in battle for the first time at Shiloh. On the first day of battle the Sixth Tennessee was ordered to charge a battery on its right front. The regiment had advanced in gallant style through an open field to within one hundred yards of the battery when a withering fire was opened up from an ambuscade of infantry concealed in the woods upon both sides. Here the immortal Sixth lost 250 men as it marched into the mouth of hell. On the second day many more of the best men fell near a pond which was in front of one of their positions.[11]

---

[8]John B. Lindsley, *Military Annals of Tennessee* (Nashville, 1886), 205-6. Hereinafter cited as *Military Annals*.

[9]During the first few months at Union City the troops lived high. The colored cooks were organized under "Colonel Matt Dyer," a slave of Milton Brown. This "boss cook" was in authority among the negroes for he had cooked for the famous Colonel Dyer in the War of 1812.

[10]Letter of J. J. Neely, December 21, 1861. MS.

[11]At the end of the second day of fighting at Shiloh, there were 500 out of 1,200 of the Sixth Tennessee that were either killed, wounded or missing. Among the first injured was J. M. Cartmell. Captain Jo Freeman was mortally wounded on the first day, but he refused to quit his command for hours after he was injured. Captain Mid Hays was seriously wounded, but was brought off the field by friends. Others who were killed in this battle were Lieutenant Isaac Jackson, John W. Campbell, August Eppinger, Thomas McCorry,

This Battle of Shiloh was merely the beginning of a glorious record for the Sixth Tennessee fighting heroically in the battles of Perryville, of Chickamauga, of Missionary Ridge, of Murfreesboro, the siege of Atlanta, the Battle of Franklin where a chronicler states: "It stood and conquered . . . a matchless division of the Western Army. There it stood amid the wrecks of battle, its dead that outnumbered the living, without a general officer left, with but one field officer able for duty."[12] This Sixth Tennessee was one of those regiments in which the privates deserved to be immortalized as well as the officers for they never waited to be led into battle by dashing officers, they went where they were ordered with promptness and resolution. Though many lives were lost as the Six Tennessee met the shock of notable battles fought on Tennessee soil, it made a record for gallantry on the field of battle that is a source of pride to-day and is a sacred heritage to the succeeding generations.

If Tennessee had not already been known as the "mother of volunteers and the birth place of soldiers," she would have earned the title during the years 1861-1865. So many men from Madison went to war that the Confederate Monument on court square bears the inscription: "Madison County furnished more soldiers than she had voters." Besides those companies of the Sixth Tennessee Madison County furnished Company C of the 38th Infantry; one company of 33rd Regiment commanded by General A. W. Campbell; men from the four companies from Madison and Henderson Counties of the 51st Tennessee; four companies of the 14th Tennessee cavalry. Company C of the 38th Infanary fought at Shiloh (losing ninety men), at Murfreesboro, at Chickamauga, at Missionary Ridge, at Franklin, Nashville, and surrendered in North Carolina in 1865. Company B of the 33d Tennessee Infantry went into training at Union City, fought at Shiloh, at Perryville, at Murfreesboro, at Chickamauga, at Missionary Ridge, at Atlanta, and surrendered in North Carolina in 1865. The 14th Tennes-

---

James Haddaway, J. W. Temple, G. W. Black, J. T. Emmerson, E. H. Morgan, J. B. Sims, Edward Barton, J. A. Nelson, C. W. Humphries, R. R. McCutchen, T. J. Neilson, J. McAdams, W. M. Thompson, J. E. Spain, E. H. Davis, William Davis, B. H. Smith, W. G. Caldwell. Lindsley, *Military Annals*, 225-6.

[12]*Ibid.*, 223.

see Cavalry enlisted behind the Federal lines in West Tennessee. The men from Madison forming Companies C, G, I, K equipped themselves. No conscripting was done, in fact many were too young to have been conscripted.[13] Part of the Regiment guarded the Hatchie River near Estanuala while Forrest was recruiting in Jackson and then engaged Colonel Prince while Forrest put 2,900 unarmed men and supplies across the river; prevented Federals from reenforcing Fort Pillow while Forrest captured it.[14]

The departure of the men in the Sixth Tennessee was only the beginning of the war for the people of Jackson and the surrounding territory. By June, 1861, minute men who met once a week for drill in each civil district were appointed by the county court; "county script" was issued in denominations of five cents to three dollars for aid to families of Madison County soldiers; orders were issued by the court for allowances to certain families of soldiers; the bell in the courthouse was offered to General Beauregard to be recast into weapons of war; the Beauregard Hospital in charge of Dr. R. R. Dashiell was opened for wounded Confederate soldiers; citizens of the community helped furnish food for soldiers who were being trained at Camp Beauregard; Negroes of the community were sent to the college [West Tennessee Collge] to help wait upon the sick, mostly afflicted with typhoid fever.[15] The war became more and more real as Gilliam and Burrus advertised to buy 200,000 pounds of meat for the Confederate army; as O'Connor Brothers took such large orders for army shoes that they could not make them for civilians; as R. B. Hurt, Milton Brown, Benjamin Barr, J. L. Moore bought up horses for the Confederate army; as the Young Ladies' Knitting Society with Miss Annie Bullock, president, and Miss Mary Campbell, secretary, was organized for the purpose of furnishing Colonel

---

[13]Chester G. Bond, the father of Colonel Harold Bond, was one of those who were so young that they were called "Bell's Babies." Judge Bond, dean of the local bar and active churchman, was a man who was in sympathy with the rich and poor, the young and old, a man who was respected for his ability and beloved by his friends. *Ibid,* 899.

[14]*Ibid.,* 900-901.

[15]Diary of R. H. Cartmell; Madison County Court Records; "Civil War Diary of Willie Micajah Barrow," edited by W. H. Stephenson. Reprinted from *Louisiana Historical Quarterly.*

Stephen's regiment with plenty of warm socks, for they were determined that "in the second great war for independence, the hardest battles will be fought, the greatest victories will be achieved by the women of the South"; as the following call came for blankets and clothes for the coming winter: "Let every family in Madison MAKE enough thick warm woolen cloth to furnish at least one or two additional suits of clothing for one man or more if possible and have it sent to this place to be forwarded to our brave volunteers."[16] Then war was at hand when General Beauregard arrived from Corinth on his way to Columbus (February 16, 1862); as Captain J. B. Long called for 150 four-horse wagons with harness, 600 mules, and 50,000 bushels of wheat; as the order came in March, 1862, to remove the Confederate hospital further south; as the order came to burn all the cotton before the "Yankees" came. Sarah Johnston of Denmark related the story of these cotton "burners" as follows:

> Beauregard ordered all cotton burned and cavalry commenced two days ago. Our cotton is piled for the torch. Everyone who wanted spinning cotton was told to come get it. . . . Two cotton burners stayed with us last night. It was reported that the Yankees were at Jackson, Somerville, and all around.[17]

Most of the citizens of the county wasted no love upon Grant, Sherman, or any other Federal officer, but they realized the stern truth in Sherman's definition of war. Most of the people considered that the less said the better about the hardships of that year of formal occupation—from June 6, 1862, to June 6, 1863—and the rest of the years of the war when the country was subjected to raids that were worse than actual occupation, but a few scattered bits serve as samples of hardships of those days. On June 6, 1862, General Sullivan with a large force marched down the streets of Jackson which by this time was occupied by mostly women and children, those men too old to fight and those too young. General Sullivan selected the James Lyon place on Main Street (where the Butler school recently stood) as the place for his headquarters. Other homes were ordered to be vacated for uses of different depart-

---

[16] Jackson *West Tennessee Whig*, August 30, September 6, 1861.

[17] Diary of Sarah Johnston, entries of May 31 and June 1, 1862. Used through the courtesy of Addison Johnston.

ments of the army such as the Isham Boyce place on Chester, the G. N. Harris home on Main, Mrs. A. W. Campbell's place, the Ben Long place upon the site of P. J. Murray's home on Royal Street, which was used by General Logan when he assumed command in Jackson;[18] the William Marshall home on College Street, General Oglesby's headquarters in the Peguese home in the rear of the Tomlin home on Main Street. Federal troops were quartered over a large part of Jackson. There were no houses south of Madison and east of Royal streets, so this plot of ground extending to Irish town was lined with tents. On Haskell Hill (Main near Hays) was a battery of artillery camped, in the valley below here a regiment of infantry occupied most of the land south of the McCree place (and it was here that General and Mrs. Grant are said to have stayed); Still's Hill now known as West Jackson was covered with tents; back of the McCorry home west to the Campbell house two negro regiments camped; in front of the Robert Cartmell place on Chester Street was another regiment of cavalry; other troops camped upon the farm of General Samuel J. Hays in the northern part of east Jackson. For years the remains of earthen breastworks could be seen in the northwestern and northeastern parts of the city on the west side of old Talbot Hill and at the top of the hill on Fairmont Street. The Federals, searching Mr. Harper's gun shop on Church Street, found many guns hidden in air vents and under the floor.[19]

Stories of the burning of cotton, houses, corn, the taking of wagons, mules, horses, cattle, corn, wheat, bacon, bed clothes, pistols, and slaves are found in various old papers. Robert Hurt had $45,892 worth of articles burned or confiscated and slaves

---

[18]General Logan was in the Mexican War and at one time was thrown with the Tennessee troops commanded by General Haskell. In some engagement Uncle King Anderson saved his life. During the Federal occupancy of Jackson, Uncle King came to town with a dozen or more squirrels tied to his belt. After he disposed of his game, he imbibed too freely of corn juice and standing in front of the courthouse, he cried, "Hurrah for Jeff Davis!" The guards stationed on the square rushed to him and carried him before the general. When General Logan saw Uncle King he recognized him and ordered the guards to let him come and go at will, explaining that Uncle King had once saved his life. Reminiscences of T. M. Gates.

[19]*Ibid.*

stolen or freed.[20] The people were suffering in many ways. Lazy negroes were strutting about the streets, soldiers were drinking all the water out of the cisterns and things would have been a thousand times worse, in the opinion of Robert Cartmell, if it had not been for the Federal officers, in fact, he believed that the privates if left alone would have hanged the citizens.[21] Much credit was given to men like Colonel Bob Ingersoll and Lieutenant-Colonel Meeks for demanding some discipline among the Federal troops. A Federal Mason advised Robert H. Anderson of a search that was to be made the following day, so Anderson and his wife removed the flooring in one room and hid most of the food supplies, leaving only enough to convince the searching party that they had found all he had.[22] One hundred and fifty citizens, "secessionists or secessionists sympathizers," were assessed from $3 to $60 each for the support of Union refugees. These amounts could be paid in provisions or money, but orders were issued to penalize those who did not pay within twenty-one days. The officers were to collect an extra twenty per cent or seize the property.[23]

Fully understanding that a good historical fact must be substantiated by two or more eye witnesses, or that both sides of a question must be presented, the writer has only one source of information for the story of the days of occupation of Jackson by the Federal troops—the diary of a rebel, Robert H. Cartmell. Unfortunately his plantation was wrecked—his house burned, his horses stolen, his milch cow killed, his timber cut, his corn and bacon confiscated, his potatoes dug, and even the last roots of his "pie-plants" reserved for the Federals as they threatened to arrest "Aunt Em" if she dug up any more of it from his own garden. This was enough to make anyone become a "rebel." It is amazing to the writer that the account is not more bitter than it is.

Cartmell told of a small fight at the grave yard near Salem camp ground (December 20, 1862), of the negroes going into a panic, of negroes cutting wood without permission of the

---

[20]Diary of Robert Hurt. MS. Used through the courtesy of Miss Guy Leeper.
[21]R. H. Cartmell Diary.
[22]Correspondence of Mrs. Cora B. Anderson Holland to the writer.
[23]Special Orders, Number 25, 30, 35. MS.

owner for "city purposes," of the business houses in town closing, of three thousand troops in Jackson inside the fortifications, of the foraging wagons, of negroes quartered and cooking in the office of James Caruthers right on the square. A few entries from Cartmell's diary are quoted:

December 28, 1862—Supplies low as communications from the North still cut. Gen. Sullivan allowed citizens two weeks rations and ordered men to take the balance. Saw several loads of fresh killed meat along the street and saw Federals carrying Mrs. Milton Brown out of her smoke house. An order also issued to get all spare cooking utensils and wood.

December 24—Citizens not allowed out. Forrest has broke up the railway north, taking 800 prisoners at Trenton, 50 waggons and teams without firing a gun.

December 30—Heard cannonading in direction of Lexington nearly all day.

January 3, 1863—A Federal cavalry regiment of 1200 camped in yard and took possession of our kitchen.

January 8—I got an order to the adjutant of 3rd Michigan cavalry to remove waggons, mules out of my yard. When I handed it to him, he swore he would not comply, would see the commandant in hell and I could tell him so. I told him I did not wish to be the bearer of his communications. [Cartmell was furious over the distorted story of the skirmish at Red Mounds or Parker's Cross Roads of December 31 as told in the northern papers. This reporter said that Forrest approached within two miles of Jackson and commenced throwing shells within— to which Cartmell added that he was there all day and not a shell came.]

February 13—Talked with Capt. Brown who had returned from Alton prison where conditions were terrible.[24]

Rumors began to float about that the Federals were to leave Jackson, thus leaving the country open for guerilla warfare—a thing to be greatly feared. Robert Cartmell could not see how anything could possibly be worse than what they had had for the previous twelve month. But as the days passed he learned, just as the others in the community did, that the days of evacuation of the town and the raids which followed were worse than the formal occupation. As the Federals moved out, they set fire to Mr. Peguese's stables, James Taylor's shop, Dr. Chester's stables, the frame building on Huntingdon road where the negro corral had been, and to many other houses in

---

[24]Robert H. Cartmell Diary.

the community. This burning was a part of the work of Fielding Hurst's men—they seemed to be very careless about fire! After General Oglesby left the Peguese house which he had used for headquarters, an orderly and a negro returned, broke glass, chairs, abused, "cussed," and did everything that words could do to insult. They also took the keys to the house so that they could not lock up. The negroes, thousands of them, gathered together with their plunder at the railroad station to leave as the Federals left, for they had been told that they would be killed when the "Sessesh" came into power. When the year of occupation was over Cartmell concluded: "The country and especially the town is a shell, gutted, resembles a cinnamon tree—the bark stripped off. The history of this war in detail confined only to West Tennessee would make volumes. How

West Tennessee *Whig*, May 17, 1861. Mrs. W. W. Tucker Collection.

would it be if the whole particulars would be recorded."[25] Then by the 8th of June when the Federals were all gone, the town "looked lonely and still about like a grave yard," but it was not to remain this way for long. This was only a quiet before a storm.

On June 18, 1863, one hundred Federal cavalry came to town "jayhawked" men of their watches, money, horses, buggies and wagons, emptied Goodell's livery stables (George Harris' carriage and horses, Sam McClanahan's horse and buggy, Billy Alexander's money, Dr. Butler's pistols were all taken), burned Chester's mill. The raiders informed the inhabitants that they were ordered to destroy everything for the North would have to starve the Southern people into subjection. On June 21 most disorderly troops of the 15th Illinois, 10th Missouri, and 7th Kansas entered the city and acted very badly. They burned, stole and plundered. "In one instant," wrote Cartmell, "taking the horse out of the vehicle which contained a corpse and leaving it in the road—cursing and calling ladies damned liars, threatening to knock old gray headed men's brains out." The Federals had been told that a Confederate Flag was flying in Jackson and that the jail was full of hanging negroes but added Cartmell: "A few individuals or squads of rebels had passed through here. A Capt. Hicks and a few men I understood by some means got hold of a Yankee negro and for his impudence hung him between this and Denmark but the citizens have conducted themselves in a very prudent manner." The duration of the war was uncertain but the consequences *certain*—ruin to both sections.

Scarcely a month had passed since the Federals departed when Colonel Biffle's cavalry entered Jackson and camped near the Memphis Conference Female Institute. This town became a very important recruiting center. Then on the thirteenth of July, Jackson was the scene of a battle between three hundred of Forrest's men, two companies of Biffle's Regiment, and Newsom's Company, in all about 450 Confederates and eleven hundred and 2000 Federals which included the 3d Michigan, the 9th Illinois, 2nd Iowa, and Fielding Hurst's 1st Tennessee or "Home made Yankees" as they were called. The Federals approached by way of Denmark, there being some

---

[25]*Ibid.*, June 7, 1863.

HEAD-QUARTERS, 1ST DIVISION,
Reserve of the Army of the Tennessee,
JACKSON, Tenn., June 22d, 1862.

GENERAL ORDERS,⎫
   No. 19.   ⎬
                ⎭

General Order No. 4, issued from Head-Quarters U. S. Forces, Jackson, Tenn., under date of June 11th, is hereby revoked; and hereafter all notes and scrip of any denomination, purporting to have been issued by the Confederate States, will cease to be a circulating medium. Also, all notes of individuals, of any denomination whatever, and also all notes of any Bank of any denomination less than one dollar.

All citizens and soldiers are forbidden to circulate or offer the above-mentioned notes, or either of them, under penalty of arrest and punishment at the discretion of the commanding officer.

BY COMMAND OF BRIG. GEN. JNO. A. LOGAN:

                              R. R. TOWNES,
                              Assistant Adjutant General.

(*Courtesy of Miss Guy Leeper*)

cannonading about Campbell's bridge, in fact there was skirmishing at each bridge. Then a portion of men in gray, many of whom had never been under fire and some of whom were unarmed, passed up Main Street in a *hurry* as though something might be coming behind and very soon the Blues came firing away. The women, children, and older men stood at the gates and watched the enemy pass.[26] The story should be continued in Robert Cartmell's own words:

Soon heavy firing began north of town, a short distance from and south of the Episcopal parsonage [the present location of Jackson High School] here was the heaviest severest fighting. The fight north of town lasted some half hour when the Rebels retreated. The Fed-

---

[26] An official record of Colonel Hatch reported that the women of Jackson "carried ammunition for the enemy in a very gallant manner." Miss Pet McCorry is said to have made many trips with bullets in her apron from her home to beyond where O'Neal Commission Company is today. A high brick wall gave some protection. *Rebellion Records*, Ser. I, Vol. 24, 673.

OATH OF ALLEGIANCE.

I ...*D. C. Johns*... do solemnly swear that I do hereby abjure and renounce all allegiance to the so called Confederate States of America—that I will not voluntarily bear arms against the United States—that I will not give aid, countenance, counsel or encouragement to persons, engaged in armed hostility thereto—that I will not yield support to any pretended government, authority, power or constitution, within the United States, hostile or inimical thereto. And I do further swear that, to the best of my knowledge and ability, I will support the Constitution of the United States against all enemies foreign and domestic—that I will bear true and faithful allegiance to the same—that I take this oath freely without any mental reservation or purpose of evasion, and that I will well and faithfully discharge the duties of a citizen of the United States, So HELP ME GOD.

. . . .

Sworn to and subscribed before me, at my office in *Medem Zem,* this *23d* day of *Jany* A. D. 1862*3*

W. W. Pussulyn
Lieut
Provost-Marshal

(Curtis Bray Collection)

erals had 4 or 6 six pounders. The loss so far as I could ascertain was about the same—one Confederate was killed near Mrs. Hale's, one was at the city Hotel, one at the Methodist parsonage died since the fight. . . . The stores in Jackson were broken open and such destruction I never saw. At John Miller's a fire was built in the middle of the street and thousands of dollars worth of fine bolting cloth, at least a thousand dollars worth of Indian rubber builting and large quantity of jeans and goods thrown all over the floors, tramped upon, torn, bent, etc., his safe was bursted into atoms, money taken, books, accounts, same things done at Murrell's and others. I understand Mrs. Newman, a lady, a widow lady, kept a millinery store, was literally ruined. Uncle Iho had a large quantity of tobacco, some domestics, shoes—all destroyed. 'Twas sickening to look at such wholesale and wanton destruction.

June 14—Hurst regiment is gone but the citizens were burying the dead. Before Hurst left he went to the hospital to parole the wounded, took some exceptions to a remark made by a young lady made to a Dr. Still, saying that it was directed to him, Hurst, he became furious, called the lady a d—d s— and told her if she did not get out he would kick her out as quick as he would kick any damned s—. There were other ladies present; and several physicians. I heard those present repeat his language and worse than I have written. This is truly a war upon private citizens and private property. They pass through the country, burn and rob.[27]

The Federals pursued the retreating "Rebels" until they were five miles north of town and then fearing an ambush, they turned back. A part of this skirmish had taken place on Talbot Hill.[28]

It was upon one of these Federal cavalry raids into Jackson that James S. Lyon, one of Jackson's prominent citizens, was approached by a squad of robbers and cut-throats flying the colors of the United States Army. They demanded to know where his gold was hidden, and although Lyon was a man advanced in age, he had the nerve of a Spartan so the band of enemy soldiers with fixed bayonets did not intimidate him. When he refused to tell them the secret of the hiding place, a rope was brought and he was drawn up two or three times, once being allowed to remain in the air until life was almost extinct. At length when he still refused to tell where the gold was, the bandits struck him over the head and left him in the house more dead than alive.[29]

---

[27]R. H. Cartmell Diary, July 13, 14, 1863: Colonel Hatch wrote of this event in his report: "Our men found 30 barrels of whiskey. It gave me as much trouble to save the town from fire during the fight as it did to whip the enemy. . . . I saved the town from burning, protected private property. The stores I regret to say were plundered by negroes and stragglers during the fight. *Rebellion Records*, Ser. I, Vol. 24, 673.

[28]Jackson *Forked Deer Blade*, May 15, 1895.

[29]Reminiscences of T. M. Gates.

Headquarters Post of Jackson,

District of Jackson, 16th Army Corps.

Jackson, Tenn., April 6, 1863.

Special Orders,
No. 25.

I......A Commission consisting of
    Lieut. Col. JED. LAKE, 27th Reg. Iowa Inftry. Vols. ;
    Major JOHN W. TRUE, 54th Ill. Inftry. Vols.;
    Capt. JOSEPH McLAIN, 62d Ill. Inftry. Vols.,
appointed by Special Order No. 22, par. V, from these Headquarters, to assess upon the property of secessionists, and secession sympathizers, at this Post, an amount sufficient to defray the cost of supporting the Union Refugees arriving at this Post, having assessed upon the property, of persons, whose names are subjoined, the amount set opposite each. Captain CHANNING RICHARDS, Post Provost Marshal, will at once proceed to collect from the said persons, the said amounts, set opposite their names respectively, as follows, to wit:

NO.	NAMES.	AM'T TAX'D	NO.	NAMES.	AM'T TAX'D
1.	Milton Brown,	$60 00	19.	D. W. Robinson,	$ 9 00
2.	W. H. Long,	30 00	20.	A. J. Cross,	15 00
3.	Sam'l I. Hayes,	60 00	21.	J. W. Campbell,	15 00
4.	James Lyon,	45 00	22.	Isam Bogs,	22 00
5.	Wm. E. Butler,	60 00	23.	Wm. P. Butler,	15 00
6.	Benj. Pearsons,	15 00	24.	C. N. Still,	9 00
7.	A. T. Pegues,	22 50	25.	J. A. Toliver,	15 00
8.	Robert Hurt,	45 00	26.	Robt. Chester,	7 50
9.	D. Wormack,	15 00	27.	Alex. De Berry,	30 00
10.	Alex. Jackson,	15 00	28.	John Alston,	30 00
11.	Sam'l Lucky,	15 00	29.	Lorenzo Lee,	15 00
12.	James Glass,	7 50	30.	S. McClannigham,	7 50
13.	Benj. Long,	15 00	31.	W. H. Hunt,	30 00
14.	G. N. Harris,	15 00	32.	James Vaun,	15 00
15.	Benjamin Barr,	22 50	33.	T. D. Theis,	22 50
16.	W. H. Stevens,	15 00	34.	T. P. Scurlock,	6 00
17.	J. H. Talbot,	15 00	35.	Amos Jones,	6 00
18.	James Miller,	15 00	36.	Dr. R. R. Dashiel,	6 00

The foregoing tax may be paid in provisions at Government contract prices, or the amount may be commuted and paid in money, at the option of the person taxed. The Provost Marshal will deposit the money, or the provisions, when collected, with the Commissary of Subsistence, to the credit of Major T. P. ROBB, U. S. S. C., in charge of Refugees, taking duplicate receipts from the C. S. therefor, one copy of which receipt will be returned to these Headquarters, and the other retained by him.

BY ORDER OF

Col. James M. True,

E. R. WILEY, Jr.,
Post Adjutant.

(*Courtesy of Miss Guy Leeper*)

The Battle of Britton Lane on August 31, 1862, was a mere skirmish as military history goes, but it was *the* battle as far as the town of Denmark was concerned.[30] The battle was a culmination of a raid led by General Armstrong who had been sent by Forrest from Holly Springs up the Mississippi and Tennessee Central Railroad to destroy as much of the track as possible. The 20th and 30th Illinois Regiments had been stationed at Estanuala and were on their way to reenforce the fort at Medon where 140 men were on guard duty. Since the Federals were in Jackson and had been in Denmark, there had been many exciting escapades when young Confederates came home on leave for a new uniform, a fresh horse, or a new saddle. Two members of the Seventh Tennessee had been caught at church and had escaped capture by hiding between the pews under the voluminous hoop skirts of the patriotic ladies. These events helped to throw the good people of Denmark into a fever of wild excitement and anxiety when they began to hear first spasmodical firing and then cannons booming steadily. The tramp, tramp of feet through the night previous had created more excitement than there had been in the quiet village since the days of the infamous Murrell. According to a Federal account published in Jackson, 8,000 men under General Armstrong attacked 5,000 Federals in Britton Lane, the attack lasting four hours and the Federals being left masters of the field.[31] William Witherspoon, a member of the 7th Tennessee, claimed that the Federals were completely routed. All accounts agree that it was a bloody battle, none agree on the number killed and wounded. Many of the wounded were taken to the homes of the people of Denmark, particularly to Jack Bryant's where they were cared for by Mrs. Bryant. After the battle the Confederate cavalry marched to and across the Jackson Road a mile or two through the woods and then westward passing through the Johnston farm, as it went towards

---

[30]This account of the battle is based upon R. H. Cartmell's Diary; Reminiscences of John Johnston, and an account by Fonville Neville of Denmark.

[31]Official report of Britton Lane read: "The forces of the enemy numbered 6,000. The engagement resulted in a victory to our arms, the most brilliant of the men. The enemy left on the field 179 dead; wounded not known. Our loss is 5 killed and 51 wounded." *Rebellion Records,* Ser. I, Vol. 17, 49-50.

the Hatchie which it crossed at Estanuala. The Battle of Briton Lane was indeed a famous episode in the history of Denmark.

That "Wizzard of the Saddle," Nathan B. Forrest, who according to Robert Cartmell "fought Yankees better or whipped them more effectively" than any other officer in the Confederate army was in and out of Jackson several times during the Civil War, foraging, destroying communications, capturing equipment, and recruiting men. Many a son of Madison County, clad in a uniform made by his wife, sister, or mother, brought his own horse and rifle and went to war under Forrest's command. The General was just the kind of an officer that they liked—a past master at the game of bluff, surprise attack—a man who recruited his men from under the very nose of the enemy and then captured enough equipment to fit them out in the best style of the United States Army.

On the thirteenth and fourteenth of December, 1862, General Forrest with 2,100 poorly equipped men and only four guns, crossed the Tennessee River at Clifton on two small flat boats. Lieutenant-General John Pemberton, Confederate commander in Mississippi, had asked for relief from Grant's forces, so Forrest was sent to dismantle the supply lines, the Mobile and Ohio and Mississippi and Tennessee Central Railroads. Thus, Jackson was the principal town that he must visit. West Tennessee at this time was swarming with well-equipped Federal forces under Brigadier General Jere Sullivan, commander in Jackson. As soon as the "Rebels" were dried out from the crossing of the river, they started west and successfully engaged the Federals about five miles from Lexington, capturing one hundred and fifty officers and men, arms, munitions, two hundred horses, some wagons and Colonel Robert Ingersoll himself.[32]

General Forrest and his men now pressed on towards Jackson, though the town was occupied by superior Federal forces (reported to be 1,500 well-equipped troops and thirty pieces of artillery). The Confederates put up such a game of bluff that they soon drove the Federals "to take shelter behind their works which consisted of a heavy line of infantry epaulements con-

---

[32] John A. Wyeth, *Life of General N. B. Forrest* (New York, 1899), 104-44. The accounts of Forrest's activities are based chiefly upon Wyeth and Jordan and Pryor.

necting some five or six open-gorge works for field-pieces that commanded all the approaches to the position."[33]

As rumors were about that Federal re-enforcements were arriving rapidly from both north and south of Jackson, Forrest set out to capture or have captured stations on the railroad in both directions. He then scattered his forces in such a manner that he deceived his enemy as to the real strength of his forces. He dispatched Colonel Dibrell to destroy the Mobile and Ohio bridge over Spring Creek, Colonel Stornes to capture Humboldt, Forrest, himself, captured Trenton, although it was strongly fortified by a breastwork of cotton-bales and hogsheads of tobacco. He then pressed on to Union City and again forced the surrender of a large force and captured quantities of provisions and munitions. As the General paroled over a thousand prisoners he was careful that they were impressed with the magnitude of his forces. During this campaign, which lasted only a fortnight, numerous skirmishes and three battles were fought, about fifty bridges and trestles on the Mobile and Ohio completely destroyed, a half dozen stockades were burned, 2,500 troops were killed or captured, ten pieces of field artillery were taken, 10,000 stands of excellent small arms, 1,000,000 rounds of ammunition, and fifty wagons were captured. All this was accomplished during most horrible mid-winter weather when troops and wagon trains had to make their way over roads that were considered impassable. Mud holes were filled with logs and even sacks of flour; wagons and guns were drawn across rickety bridges over the Obion bottom by man power. General Sullivan thought that he had Forrest in a tight place, but he did not know Forrest's ability. When Forrest recrossed the Tennessee River at Clifton on the same flat boats that had been sunk and raised again when they were needed, he had a surplus of five hundred Enfield rifles, 1,800 blankets and knapsacks.[34]

The purpose of the expedition had been accomplished. The severing of the lines of communications changed the whole picture for Grant. He decided to abandon his campaign into

---

[33]Thomas Jordan and J. P. Pryor, *The Campaigns of Lieutenant General N. B. Forrest and of Forrest's Cavalry* (New York, 1868), 196. Hereinafter cited as *Campaigns of Forrest*.

[34]*Ibid.*, 221.

the interior, to repair the road to Memphis, and to make the Mississippi River his principal route of supplies.

In the winter of 1863 after repeated appeals from the prominent people of West Tennessee, General Forrest pushed through into West Tennessee to assemble the scattered forces for defense and offense. Depending upon his personal influence and prestige, he pushed across the "frontier" into Tennessee about fifty miles east of Memphis with only 450 men, two guns and five ordnance wagons. When he reached Bolivar on the fifth of December, he was enthusiastically received and entertained in the home of Colonel J. J. Neely. On the following afternoon he arrived in Jackson where he was welcomed by the whole population with deep feeling and where, as at Bolivar, an abundance of forage and subsistence had been provided. Robert Cartmell did not think that any man was more dreaded by the "Yankees" than Forrest, for with a force of six or eight thousand men, and he was sure that Forrest would have that many by the time he finished recruiting in West Tennessee, he and his men would give an enemy no little trouble. Forrest, himself, was highly pleased with the healthy spirit manifested by the people in the community.

Colonel Tyree Bell, General R. V. Richardson, Colonels A. N. Wilson, R. M. Russell, and Lieutenant-Colonel D. M. Wisdom, men favorably known in West Tennessee, were busy assembling absentees, and recruiting as many new forces as possible to join Forrest at Jackson. Within a short time about twenty thousand Federal troops surrounded Forrest at Jackson. They thought they had the fox trapped at last, but they didn't know the General. Hurlbut from Memphis, A. J. Smith from Columbus, William Sooy Smith from Middle Tennessee, and Crook from Huntsville, Alabama—15,000 men after 3,500 with barely a third armed—all turned their attention to General Forrest and his recruiting station in Jackson. Forrest sent out men to hold the crossing of the Hatchie at Estanuala, he sent Colonel D. M. Wisdom to engage forces coming from Corinth. Wisdom's forces met the Federals in an all day battle at Jack's Creek and after a forced march during the night, Colonel Wisdom brought his men to the Hatchie crossing on December 25, 1863.[85]

---

[85]*Ibid.*, 366-368.

On Christmas Eve, 1863, with three thousand unarmed, raw men, a large wagon train, artillery and cattle under convoy of six hundred men, Forrest withdrew to the southwest. Scouts learned of a bridge at Lafayette which had not been destroyed in the Federal effort to catch the fox. The boards of the flooring had been removed, the planks hidden on the south bank, but the "Rebels" soon had the floor relaid and over they went into more friendly territory. This strategy was accomplished right under General Hurlbut's nose whose headquarters were in Memphis. Forrest had again out-witted his enemies. During this short campaign Forrest's troops had fought five successful battles, at Jack's Creek, Somerville, Lafayette, Estanaula, and Collierville, losing less than fifty men during the campaign. At the close of the campaign on December the twenty-seventh, at Lafayette Station he had 3,500 men, well-mounted, forty wagon teams loaded with subsistence, 200 heads of beef cattle, 300 hogs, and his artillery intact.[36]

Jackson had not seen the last of that infamous Fielding Hurst. There was probably no man who was feared in West Tennessee any more than this "homemade Yankee." There was the story of his company's capturing six Confederate soldiers, Captain Wharton's men, all from McNairy County and all men that he knew. On the road from Purdy to Pocahontas, he killed one every mile and buried them as mile posts.[37] This same band captured seven of Colonel John Newsome's command, killed them, and pinned their bodies to a tree near the road. It was Hurst who played the role of Nero in Purdy, even singing songs and praying while the church was burning. It was Hurst's men who helped set fire to stores in Jackson when the Federals left in 1863. On this trip there was one store, Mrs. Newsome's, a British subject who owned a millinery shop on the southeast corner of the present post office lawn, was the center of attraction for the Federals. Hurst's men took her hats and adorned the heads of their horses with them as left town. But, Mrs. Newsome complained in Washington and an order came to stop the pay of the "bandits" until damage was repaid. Then, it was that Hurst and his men rushed into town and asked a ransom of five thousand dollars or he would burn

---

[36]*Ibid*, 375-376.
[37]Report of a letter of D. M. Wisdom. *Rebellion Records*, Ser. II, Vol. 6, 202.

the town. Robert Cartmell gives the following details of the disaster:

> Col. Fielding Hurst with about one hundred men came in *full tilt* taking one to all as much by surprise as ever a people was surprised. I had been out at home to feed my hogs, had come in, turned my horse in the lot, come in and set down when by they went. One caught a glimpse of my horse and before I knew it, he went as a good many others have gone—*stolen*. I had been keeping them for a year or so in town (another horse) slipped them in the back yard and had them as well as I could get behind the cedars. 'Twas near night. They left town after dark to camp at Mr. Bond's 3 miles out of town. I got out next morning and took the 2 horses to the river bottom and tied them in the cane, before they got back to town during the day. Sunday these fellows went down in to the bottom and brought out some mules and one good mare but did not succeed in finding mine. Col. Hurst called for some of the most prominent citizens and announced to them that five thousand dollars had to be raised or the town would be burned. They concluded it would be better to raise the money than to have the town sacked, no doubt but Hurst would have turned his soldiers loose upon the town, if he had not burned it. Some burning would have occurred any how. These men are capable of the most brutal conduct and were ripe for the word. The money could not be raised on that day. Twenty of the citizens obligated to raise the amount in 5 days. On Friday following Hurst came in with an escort, his regiment camped at Bob Chester's 2 miles south of town.[38]

On the day after the demand for the money, a negro of Jesse Caruthers was seen talking for two or three hours with Hurst's men. Some of the citizens were convinced that he was reporting to the "Yankees," so he was marched down to the Forked Deer, shot, and thrown in. But it was on the night of February the twenty-fifth that although the bandit had received his ransom money, the town was set fire and burned. The fire started in the building on the southeast corner of Lafayette and Market streets and when the fire was put out there was nothing but burnt walls from Lafayette to Baltimore and from Shannon to Market. Robert Cartmell said that it was the biggest fire that he ever saw—fourteen buildings. Mrs. Hawkins, another citizen of Jackson in those days, told that the fire could have probably been checked but the well ropes had been cut and

---

[38] Robert H. Cartmell Diary.

before water could be brought it was beyond control.[39] Considering all this destruction, it is a wonder that more than one dead "Yankee," thought to be one of Hurst's band, was not found in the river near McClanahan's levee the following day.[40]

In March, 1864, Forrest set out for West Tennessee and Kentucky to harrass the Federal armies in the West and get those 3,000 men and supplies that he had not been able to get out during the previous Christmas campaign. When he arrived in Jackson he found the people in great distress over the wanton destruction by Fielding Hurst some weeks before. Numerous complaints had also been registered concerning the behavior of the Federal forces at Fort Pillow. It was while he was in Jackson that Forrest decided to take this fort about which so much propaganda has already been written. It might be added here that although these were both Confederate accounts, neither John Johnston nor Robert Cartmell described the taking of the fort as a "massacre." Entries from the Cartmell diary concerning this event are as follows:

April 15—Men thought Forrest was going to Memphis but it turned out he was after Ft. Pillow. . . . Pillow which was taken with 250 prisoners, some negroes . . . burned commissary and quartermaster stores.

April 18—There were some 100 negro soldiers and two or three hundred white ones. The Rebels killed all except some 30 or 40 negroes and most of whites. Forrest lost 15 killed and double wounded. There was no firing after the Rebels got inside the fortifications. Negroes and Yankees broke for the river, jumped in, hid about, some were drowned and some shot in attempting to swim away. . . . Ft. Pillow and Paducah have been the "cities of refuge" for traitors. Forrest has pretty well broken up the nest, at least for the present. Forrest had one horse killed under him, one so badly wounded as to be unable to get away and 4 bullet holes through his clothes, one ball inflicting a slight wound. I wonder that he was not killed. He leads his men, charges among Yankees, cutting and slashing with his sabre. He might be picked out among hundreds by one who had never seen him as General Forrest. He is a terrible man in a fight and one of the best cavalry officers the war has produced.[41]

---

[39]Mrs. Jobe Hawkins to W. K. Jobe, March 1864. Used through the courtesy of Dr. Herman Hawkins.
[40]Robert H. Cartmell Diary.
[41]*Ibid.*

Historians have transmitted to posterity in lasting form the thrilling story of the Immortal Rear Guard of Hood's army, fighting the retreat after the Battle of Nashville. As Forrest directed the army inflicting blow after blow upon the enemy, he showed that he was capable of handling an army of any size. When the army was safely out of Tennessee a rest camp was set up and Forrest, the diplomat, the orator and leader of men, expressed his appreciation to his men. The following address to those men of Jackson, Tennessee, is an illustration of the secret of his ability as a leader of men. Those in his command were always strengthened and invigorated by such words of their leader:

SOLDIERS,—The old campaign is ended, and your commanding general deems this an appropriate occasion to speak of the steadiness, self-denial, and patriotism with which you have borne the hardships of the past year. The marches and labors you have performed during that period will find no parallel in the history of this war.

On the 24th day of December [1863] there were three thousand of you, unorganized and undisciplined, at Jackson, Tennessee, only four hundred of whom were armed. You were surrounded by fifteen thousand of the enemy, who were congratulating themselves on your certain capture. You started out with your artillery, wagon-trains, and a large number of cattle, which you succeeded in bringing through, since which time you have fought and won the following battles—battles which will enshrine your names in the hearts of your countrymen and live in history an imperishable monument to your prowess: Jack's Creek, Estenaula, Somerville, Okalona, Union City, Paducah, Fort Pillow, Bolivar, Tishomingo Creek, Harrisburg, Hurricane Creek, Memphis, Athens, Sulphur Springs, Pulaski, Carter's Creek, Columbia, and Johnsonville—fields upon which you have won fadeless immortality. In the recent campaign in Middle Tennessee, you sustained the reputation so nobly won. For twenty-six days, from the time you left Florence, on the 21st of November, to the 26th of December, you were constantly engaged with the enemy, and endured the hunger, cold, and labor incident to that arduous campaign without murmur. To sum up, in brief, your triumphs during the past year, you have fought fifty battles, killed and captured two thousand horses and mules, sixty-seven pieces of artillery, four gunboats, fourteen transports, twenty barges, three hundred wagons, fifty ambulances, ten thousand stands of small arms, forty block-houses, destroyed thirty-six railroad bridges, two hundred miles of railroad, six engines, one hundred cars, and $15,000,000 worth of property.

In the accomplishment of this great work you were occasionally sustained by other troops, who joined you in the fight, but your regular number never exceeded five thousand, two thousand of whom have been killed or wounded, while in prisoners you have lost about two hundred.

If your course has been marked by the graves of patriotic heroes who have fallen by your side, it has, at the same time, been more plainly marked by the blood of the invader. While you sympathize with the friends of the fallen, your sorrows should be appeased by the knowledge that they fell as brave men battling for all that makes life worth living for.

Soldiers, you now rest for a short time from your labors. During the respite prepare for future action. Your commanding general is ready to lead you again to the defence of the common cause, and he appeals to you, by a remembrance of the glories of your past career, your desolated homes, and, above all, by the memory of your dead comrades, to yield a ready obedience to discipline, and to buckle on your armour anew for the fight. Bring with you the soldier's safest armor—a determination to fight; to fight until independence shall have been achieved; to fight for home, children, liberty, and all you hold dear. Show to the world the superhuman and sublime spirit with which a people may be inspired when fighting for the inestimable boon of liberty. Be not allured by the siren song of peace, for there can be no peace save upon your separate, independent nationality. Be patient, obedient, and earnest, and the day is not far distant when you can return to your homes and live in the full fruition of freeman and around the family altar.[42]

Contemporary records of the last months of the Civil War are filled with stories of robbery and disorderly conduct. In March, 1864, four men (two from Kentucky and one from New York) were court marshalled, condemned to hang and were hanged. A well-dressed man came to town in 1864, boasted of killing 20 Yankees, left flourishing a pistol, shooting a man as he rode down Lexington Street. The bandit was captured by a squad of Confederates and was placed before a firing squad and shot. Colonel J. F. Newman was sent into West Tennessee "to break up the bands of lawless men who infest the country,"[43] for as Robert Cartmell said "you cannot go any distance without running a great danger of being robbed . . .

---

[42]From a copy of the speech that was distributed to the men at the time it was delivered. Used through the courtesy of Curtis Bray, Jackson, Tennessee.

[43]*Rebellion Records*, Vol. 49, Ser. I, Part II, 712.

Stealing, robbing and murder is the general order of the day."⁴⁴ Officially, the war was over, the southern states were conquered territory, but peace was not there. The people in The South in general and Madison County in particular had learned the horrors of war and they had spent many an hour praying for peace. Little did they know that the days of reconstruction were the real days which were to try their souls, but many did realize that there was darkness ahead and could silently pray with Robert Cartmell as he wrote:

> God grant these times may soon pass, no more never to return, may posterity be wise and avoid war especially CIVIL WAR where unarmed citizens, women and children suffer, cruel indeed in civil strife and this perhaps the most cruel war ever waged against any people. History will not record and future generations will not be able to form an adequate idea of its inhumanity, its cruelty, its utter violations of every principle of civilized usage, law and custom.⁴⁵

* * * * *

At least three officers from Madison County should receive special mention for the part each played in the War for Southern Independence—Alexander W. Campbell, William H. Jackson, and William H. Stephens.

Willim H. Jackson, son of Dr. Alexander Jackson and brother of Justice Howell E. Jackson, graduated from the United States Military Academy at West Point in 1856, was known for his gallantry, tact, and good judgment in Indian fighting while he served in the Southwest with such men as Kit Carson, Larue, and others as his guides. When war came in 1861, his loyalty to his state caused him to resign his commission in the United States army and to report to the Confederate government for an assignment, serving as a staff officer under General Gideon Pillow.⁴⁶ In the Battle of Belmont, he was unable to land his battery, but he went ashore himself and while leading three regiments of infantry in the rear of Grant's army, his horse was shot from under him and he himself severely wounded. For his gallantry at Belmont, Jackson was promoted to colonelcy and placed in command of all cavalry in West Tennessee, capturing trains on the Memphis and

---

⁴⁴Robert H. Cartmell Diary, November 24, 1863.
⁴⁵*Ibid.*
⁴⁶William S. Speer, *Prominent Tennesseans* (Nashville, 1888), 446-450.

Charleston Railroad, opposing the Federals at Holly Springs where he captured and parolled 1800 Federals, captured large quantities of supplies and private papers of Grant. This campaign caused Grant to change his plans concerning the taking of Vicksburg.

General "Billy" Jackson, as he was affectionately known to his men, was next under General Bragg in command of a division at Spring Hill, Tennessee (1862). Here he lost 265 men in twenty minutes, but he captured 1600 of the Federal infantry. Next, serving under General Joseph E. Johnston in the entire memorial Georgia campaign, and then under General Hood, Jackson again distinguished himself. General Hood selected Jackson to accompany him in his move around Sherman into Tennessee where under Forrest, Jackson's column led the advance into Tennessee; held Schofield's army at bay at Spring Hill, particpated in the bloody battle of Franklin, led Confederates to within three miles of the strongly fortified city of Nashville, moved to the Columbia and Franklin turnpike and sat in front of the victorious Federals under General George H. Thomas until the Confederates could start their retreat, then his command "bore the brunt of the retreat from there to within twenty miles of the Tennessee and did more than any other command in preventing the capture of Hood's entire army."[47]

After the war, General Jackson returned to his plantations near Jackson. In 1868, he married Miss Selene Harding of Belle Meade near Nashville, and joined General Harding and after his father-in-law's death, his brother Howell E. Jackson in the development of Belle Meade, bringing it to first rank in the South. Jackson's interest and leadership in Agricultural affairs is demonstrated by his presidency of such organizations as the Bureau of Agriculture of the State under Governor John Brown and the National Agricultural Congress. The Jackson brothers seemingly inherited a love of the land and a capacity for leadership, especially from their father Dr. Alexander Jackson.

William H. Jackson died at Belle Meade on March 30, 1903.

Another illustrious son of Madison County was General

---

[47]*Ibid.*, 448.

Alexander W. Campbell, the son of Jackson's first banker, John W. Campbell. General Campbell was born in Nashville, June 4, 1828 and came to Jackson with his family in 1833, at which place he attended the Jackson Male Academy and West Tennessee College.[48] After reading law for over a year under Judge A. W. O. Totten, he entered the department of law of Cumberland University from which institution he graduated in 1852. He practiced law in Jackson until the outbreak of the Civil War. From 1854-1860 he served as United States District Attorney from the Western District of Tennessee. He was a Democrat of the Jeffersonian school, so he did not hesitate as to which side he should taken when hostilities began. When the call came for volunteers to repel the invason of the South, he enrolled himself as a private in the "Independent Guards," which became a part of the Sixth Tennessee, but he was soon appointed Assistant Inspector General in the provisional army. After serving five months on General Cheatham's staff, he was elected colonel of the Thirty-Third Tennessee and distinguished himself leading his regiment at Shiloh on the 6th and 7th of April, 1862. During the battle he was shot in the arm, injured in the foot, and had his horse shot from under him, but he did not leave the field until his gallant regiment left and then he was among the last to leave.

General Campbell fought in the battle of Perryville and of Murfreesboro. In 1863, he was sent to West Tennessee by General Bragg to recruit cavalrymen but while he was here he was captured and taken as a prisoner of war to Johnson's Island where he remained for a year before he was exchanged. General Campbell served the remainder of the war as commander of one of Forrest's brigades.

After the Civil War, General Campbell resumed his practice of law in Jackson in partnership with Judge Totten, H. W. McCorry, Howell E. Jackson, John L. Brown, respectively. He had a large and lucrative practice but he spent his money freely. His motto being: Be honest, do your duty, and let the consequences care of themselves.

The people of the community had great confidence in General Campbell. He was elected mayor in 1856; was president of the Bank of Madison from 1866-1881; was a director

---

[48]*Ibid.*, 29-30.

of the Mobile and Ohio Railroad from 1868-1872; was a delegate from Tennessee to the National Democratic Convention in 1868 and 1876; was a delegate from Madison County to the State Constitutional Convention in 1870, serving on the judiciary committee. On several occasions he served as special judge of the bench of the state.

Thus, as a lawyer, a banker, a planter, a Democrat, a mayor, a general, and a far-sighted citizen, Alexander Campbell occupied the place of one of the outstanding leaders of the community during the last half of the nineteenth century.

William H. Stephens (1816-1887), an early lawyer of Madison County, was clerk of the Supreme Court of Tennessee at Jackson from 1840 to 1857, at which time he resigned to make a canvass for Congress as the nominee of the Whig party against William P. Avery. During the years spent in the county he was trustee of the Jackson Male Academy and West Tennessee College, a director and president of the Union Bank at Jackson. In 1861, he was one of the twelve delegates elected by the Legislature of Tennessee to the Peace Conference in Washington. He was unanimously elected colonel of the "Sixth Tennessee" before the regiment left Camp Beauregard in Jackson for the field of battle. It was during the presidential campaign of 1856 that W. H. Stephens, then living at his country seat, Willow Banks,[49] that he wrote a letter calling James Buchanan a "trickster, a weathercock, a trimmer, a moral coward" and continued to say everything unkind that a fearless Whig might say about a Democratic nominee during those stormy days just preceding America's tragedy—that Sectional Conflict of 1861-1865.[50] This letter is said to have been widely

---

[49] The present site of the Pigford home. The original brick home on this site is still standing, being used as a servant's house. The old brick house has "1824" inscribed upon the rafters in the attic. The home was built by William Knight in 1824 for William Espy who had been granted 640 acres on November 4, 1824, by the State of Tennessee.

[50] That William H. Stephens was an ardent and able supporter of the Southern cause is shown by a story which told that he was invited to speak in Lexington, Tennessee, in behalf of the South, but that he was hissed down and the crowd would not let him speak. The editor of the *West Tennessee Whig* denied this story by saying that the whole story was a lie, that Stephens did visit Lexington, did speak, did some good, but he had been speaking for twenty years and had never been hissed down. *West Tennessee Whig*, May 17, 1861.

quoted in Northern papers as an illustration of Southern whiggery. The celebrated "Willow Banks epistle" quoted below was quoted in the Jackson *Madisonian* of June 20, 1857, which was copied from the Memphis *Appeal,* which paper had in turn copied it from Brownlow's Knoxville *Whig:*

Willow Banks, Aug. 14, 1856.

MY DEAR SIR: Your letter of the 6th inst., was received today, and I hasten to show my appreciation of your kindness by writing at once.

You write as though a contingency might possibly occur which would induce you to vote for Buchanan. No such event can occur to me. I have surveyed the field, and even if Fillmore should be beat a thousand times over and over, I could not so humiliate myself as to vote for any democrat, much less such a hoary hypocrite and juggler as Buchanan. He has been nearly forty years in public life, what has he ever said or done that was magnanimous or wise: What is he but a trickster, a weathercock, a trimmer, a moral coward, a parasite, the flatterer of Jackson and the slanderer of Clay, without the courage to deal like a man with either of them?

What is the Cincinnati platform but a swindle? It endorses the Kansas bill to catch the poor silly South and then its candidate puts on it his squatter sovereignty construction to save the North. The platform is a dose to be swallowed by all the Democrats; but in the language of old Benton *"to be puked up again"* by those who don't like it. They have already puked up the internal improvement ingredient by over-riding poor Pierce's two vetoes. And the Senate has just puked up the pro-foreign ingredient, by adopting Adam's amendment to the Kansas bill. They are death on the tariff and yet they nominate a high protectionist who voted for the tariff of 1824, 1828, and 1842. They have the hydrophobia of Federalism, and yet nominate the man that denounced Jefferson, Madison, and the whole Democracy in more bitter terms than any man now living. They profess great love for the poor people, the dear people, and nominate an aristocrat who wanted to reduce wages to the European standard.

The rascals make great professions of respect for the old line Whigs. I understand their tactics, and they can't fool me. They reviled and slandered and cheated us for twenty years, and hunted old Clay to his grave like a wild beast; and if we had a candidate now—if Gen. Washington was alive now and was our candidate—the wicked wretches would paint him blacker than Satan. They are a pretty set to call on us to help them out of danger. Who arrayed the North and South against each other and dug the gulf that now separates us? Who furnished the abolition candidates for the Presidency from 1844 down? What are Birney and Van Buren, and Hale, and Fremont, but

Democrats? Who invited and encouraged the tide of immigration which is about to overwhelm the land? Who pandered to the unholy passions, the wild "isms", the lawless, cupidity of the rabble? Who stimulated and created the lust of conquest and annexation, regardless of our prophetic warnings against the dangers of expansion and annexation? Who now covets and is ready to STEAL the Island of Cuba? Who is ever reply to bully foreign powers to get the credit of bravery at home? Who "Thunders in the index" and rails in the performance? Who pledges to put down "all slavery discussion," and forthwith begins its agitation from the Aroostook to the Golden Horn? Who promises economy in the government and spends seventy-five millions per annum one-half of it is rewarding and corrupting its parasites? Who denounces, as midnight conspirators those who love their own countrymen better than the Lazaroni and Felons of Europe? Who preached up liberality and toleration to all, and yet ostracises and crushes down every man, Whig, American or Democrat that dares to think for himself?

What rights have you or I got under the Federal Government? Are we not more under the ban than every poor heritic was under the anathema of Holy Roman Church? Is not the lowest Irish laborer on your railroad fitter to fill any office in East Tennessee than Ebenezer Alexander; and in a contest between them would not the Foreigner beat the Native?

Down with the monster, say I. Down with this foul, false mockery! this veiled prophet of Khorassan! Down with this stupendous Imposture!

I could fill a quire at this rate. I go for Fillmore if no other man in the Union goes with me; and such powers as God has given me shall be devoted to his cause. Your aunts are as ardent as I am on this subject. We will have a hot contest here. I have to take some part in it, and will make my first speech on the 16th, at Mason's Grove.[51]

William H. Stephens's term of service in the Confederate army expired May 15, 1862, so he returned to Jackson to hold the Courts of the Judicial Circuit of which he had been elected judge during his absence. His brother, Daniel M. and his son William D. were both in the Battle of Shiloh under his command and the latter was severely wounded. When the Federals approached Jackson in June, 1862, he went South and stayed there until the Federal occupation was ended.

---

[51]Jackson *Madisonian*, June 20, 1857. Mrs. W. W. Tucker collection.

Resuming his practice at the close of the war, he moved to Memphis in 1867, was elected delegate to the Constitutional Convention of 1870 from Shelby County. He moved to Los Angeles in 1875 and to a farm in San Gabriel in 1877, where he died, March 8, 1887.[52]

---

[52]Notes belonging to Mrs. Albert Stone, compiled by Mary Louise Stephens.

CHAPTER XIV

THE DAYS OF RECONSTRUCTION

As those "men in gray," clad in tattered uniforms of their defeated country, turned their faces homeward, they realized that the future was very dark. They found their homes destroyed, their fields neglected, their system of labor supply turned upside down, their money worthless, the transportation facilities destroyed, the business at a complete standstill, the social system swept away, and the government in the hands of the Brownlow men. These men, who had been politically disabled by the Fourteenth Amendment, had been reasonably or even well off financially at the beginning of the war. Now they found it a bitter pill to see where and to what they were tending, but they managed by hard work to barely clothe and feed the family. For example, Maria Womack Campbell and her husband, who had between $30,000 and $40,000 at the beginning of the war, had only $2 in 1866, but they had some land and they were going to try to plant some cotton with "the Freedmen" and trust God for the future.[1] The only hope for any of the people of the South was to go to work so that by industry, and economy, the homes, the city, and the county could be rebuilt. Many a Confederate assumed the attitude that *he* had killed as many of the "Yankees" as they did of the Confederates, so *he* was going to work, and although he was faced with the prejudice and passions of war, there was an indescribable yearning for national peace.

Jackson and Madison County were in a sad condition at the close of the war: from Lafayette to Baltimore and from Shannon to Market had been burned by Hurst's men; the block east of the courthouse was in blackened ruins; the block north of the courthouse was only delapidated brick houses mostly

---

[1]Diary of Maria Womack Campbell used through the courtesy of Mrs. Elizabeth Symonds, the daughter of Mrs. Campbell.

THE DAYS OF RECONSTRUCTION 191

vacant; the Baptist and Methodist churches were in bad state of repair; tumbled down one-story frame shanties and blackened or charred walls were all around; hogs and goats were the chief occupants of the streets; few stores were open for business and these had little goods in stock. A tall wooden fence enclosed the courtyard over which four stiles led to the courthouse. Dogfennel and jimson weeds covered the square. Hitching racks outside the fence accommodated the country people when they came to town. Add mules, horses, and wagons of all kinds to streets sticking in mud from one to two feet deep, hog wallows about the square, crowds of negroes in their "clover of freedom," and numerous members of Brownlow's militia walking about and you have a view of court square in Jackson during the first few years after the Civil War.[2]

---

[2] Jackson *Whig and Tribune*, January 1, 1880. There is a story that the courthouse, delapidated to the last degree, was the dwelling place of a flock of goats. This fact proved to be the source of a very embarrassing event in Judge Micajah Bullock's life. He had his office in the upper rooms of the courthouse. One night in the Judge's absence the goats had managed to get in and the door closed. Late at

ate of Tennessee, ss.
County of Madison.

All who shall see these Presents, Greeting:

Be it Remembered, That *W. E. Hutchings* being a male inhabitant of the State of Tennessee, of the age of twenty-one years, a citizen of the United States, and a resident of said county for six months now last past, and having proved before me, by two competent witnesses who are known to me to have been at all times unconditional Union men, who are personally acquainted with the said *W. E. Hutchings*, that they verily believe that he has never been guilty of any of the disqualifications specified in the Act of February, 1867, is duly registered as a voter of said County, and entitled to exercise the privilege of the Elective Franchise.

Given under my hand, this ___8___ day of ___July___ 1869.

___J. M. McRee___
Comm'r of Registration for Madison County

(*Curtis Bray Collection*)

On June 24, 1865, Robert Cartmell reported that no courts were yet organized, although a month before there had been heard the ringing of the bell in the courthouse for the first time in many a day to call a meeting of the citizens "to take into consideration the new order of things and organize civil government."[3] The organization of the county court took place on July 17, 1865, when Governor Brownlow vested in George Perkins the power to reorganize the court. The names of twenty-eight men were submitted who had commissions from the Governor. A. S. Rogers was elected chairman of the court; Philip C. McCowatt, trustee. The new court proceeded immediately with such business as letting contract for the clearing out and repairing of the well on the east side of the courthouse, repairing the windows and roof of the courthouse, and making plans for the construction of a new jail.

During ordinary times, this organization of the court would be considered irregular but those days of reconstruction were not ordinary times. Governor Brownlow's legislature had given him the power to do this, though some of the justices in the court, such as Justice William Alexander, claimed that the court had been illegally organized but he refused to vacate his position. Robert Cartmell did not mind saying that he did not like the Brownlow government and the things they did. Concerning this he wrote:

> Heard courthouse bell ring this morning at 8 o'clock, election for members to Congress and in this senatorial district for state senator. I believe Governor Brownlow and his legislature resolve themselves the Government for the next two years. This county is represented by a man named Waters, a black leg—I think the meanest looking man I ever saw about Jackson a good deal 4 or 5 years ago traveled around with Hurst's regiment. The whole thing is a burlesque on Republican Government. I did not go to town would not have been

---

night the Judge went to his office for papers, absorbed in meditation, he opened the door only to be greeted by "Bahs" and pattering feet. One goat struck his right leg, another the left, others went between his legs, keeping him dancing a highland fling. One big goat knocked the Judge down and he would no sooner get off his all-fours than he would be knocked down again by the rushing flock. When the last goat departed, the Judge arose and assumed his usual dignified carriage, but woe be unto the person who mentioned the goat story to the dignified Judge! *Ibid.*

[3]Robert Cartmell Diary.

allowed to vote if so disposed. Any person engaged in a rebellion is disenfranchised.[4]

R. A. Hurt and a few of his companions took an oath of allegiance to the United States. With so many disenfranchised there were only a few left to vote, only a small number of whites and the negroes.

The first few years after the war brought lawlessness beyond words. Numerous stories of disorder appeared, such as the one of pistols being fired into the room where votes for sheriff were being counted, as the one about Henry McCorry's Negro being stabbed to death, as the one about Mr. Boyd's being killed for helping a Yankee squad go after a horse thief, the story of the malicious shooting by J. B. Long and John G. Mann, and numerous stories of robbery and plundering, and riot and bloodshed at elections.[5] Negroes came to town in flocks and did not want to work. In fact there was such general disorder that the mayor had to close all saloons and keep them closed and order all Negroes to remain out of town until further order.[6] Into a setting like this came Brownlow's militia and the South's answer to it—the Ku Klux Klan.

The presence of the militia simply made life not worth living to the citizens. These peacetime soldiers made life so miserable to the people that when the soldiers were gone the people simply did not want to talk about it. Thus, to-day it is difficult to get even a glimpse of the conditions of the times. The city Council addressed the Governor praying that they have some relief from this militia. The Council ordered that the drinking places be closed, that business houses on election day be closed, and appointed thirty-three leading citizens to serve as policemen under A. W. Campbell to try to preserve peace and quiet on election day. Many citizens dared to defy the militia. Five or six tragedies in a week were not rare. The local "boys" finally cowered the militia and got them so they were afraid to leave their fortified camps after night. All men who had seen service in the recent war went day and night with

---

[4]*Ibid.*

[5]Robert Cartmell told of numerous instances of robbery and plundering and added: "There will have to be some more hangings."

[6]Minutes of the City of Jackson, December 5, 1865.

their six-shooters buckled around them. Whiskey and six-shooters were the principal currency of the day.[7]

In 1867, during the days of militia troubles, Major Thomas H. Hartmus was shot by a squad of Brownlow's band, who, according to one citizen of the day, were the worst outlaws that ever afflicted the community, terrorizing and intimidating those who were loyal to the South.[8] A few days after the arrival of the militia, the commander issued an order to disarm every citizen of Jackson, which order created indignation but nevertheless, it was in force under a penalty of arrest and imprisonment. A party of the militia, under the influence of liquor, ordered Captain J. T. McCutchen home from town. He joined some other Confederate soldiers and they were discussing the situation as to whether they, the Confederates, should arrest the militia, kill them, or take them to camp. At this moment a shot was heard and Captain March excitedly exclaimed, "They've shot someone!" The militia had taken Hartmus's pistol away from him and headed east on Lafayette and made a slight stand at the corner of Liberty and Lafayette. A battle lasting a few minutes occurred and then they fled. This all happened between ten and eleven o'clock at night but the news spread like wildfire and the streets were soon filled with crowds of wildly excited and indignant people clamoring for revenge. One popular proposal was to attack the camp and wipe the whole company of militia from the face of the earth. Fortunately the level-headed were in the majority but the next morning every citizen of Jackson was on the street. All business was suspended and every man and boy that was old enough was armed or had a weapon that he could obtain. A delegation of the prominent citizens visited the militia camp and demanded that the would-be assassin be turned over to them to be dealt with by the civil authorities. The militia officers reported that the disturbers of the peace had left the camp. When the citizens heard this, hundreds volunteered to pursue the bandit and several squads were organized. Captain McCutchen, Middleton Hays, and H. W. McCorry led the Spring Creek squad. B. A. Person and Captain Hart led the Mifflin Road men. Both squads made forced marches until they reached the Tennessee River but the guilty men had vanished.

[7]Jackson *Whig and Tribune,* January 1, 1880.
[8]Reminiscences of T. M. Gates.

Such conduct could not continue in a community where there was such a stronghold of Confederate men who had nerve and pride. The political, social, and economic life of the community was turned up-side down. When nearly fifty per cent of the population was suddenly freed, when all those who had taken part in the rebellion were deprived of a voice in the government, and this county had furnished more soldiers than she had voters, when an incompetent military government was set up, the right-thinking men of the community sought any means to protect themselves and their property. The Ku Klux Klan or the Citizens' Committee was the answer. Few facts about the organization of the Ku Klux Klan are obtainable because of the nature of the organization. Members did not tell their families or mention their activities in a diary. They dared not, for Governor Brownlow had called a special session of the legislature to deal with this Ku Klux Klan, which according to the Governor was a secret organization of ex-rebel soldiers who were "hatching plots to scatter anarchy and permanent disorder." In fact the Governor considered the conduct of these bands in Middle and West Tennessee "murderous and violent." If a person were found connected with the organization that was disturbing the peace, he was subject to a $500 fine and five years in prison and, furthermore, an informer was given half of the fine. It is no wonder that there are no records of who were members of the organization.[9] Only the barest facts have come down from preceding generations. According to tradition, it was General Forrest himself who approached Middleton Hays and Henry McCorry in Memphis one day about coming back to Jackson and organizing a unit of the Ku Klux Klan. These men had served under Forrest during the war, they were young, fearless leaders of the community. Therefore they were well-fitted for the task before them. They returned and in the dead of night held a meeting on the east side of the court square. Patriotic ladies who included Misses Ellen, Musidora, and "Pet" McCorry made the robes that were to become so famous. Most of the time the Madison organization operated in other counties and the organizations of those counties operated here, so that no voice would be recognized.

During the conflict, General J. J. Neely of Bolivar had

---

[9] *Acts of Tennessee,* 1868.

met a band of "home-made yankees" under Fielding Hurst and routed them at Little Clear Run Creek near Bolivar. After the war, the same band returned and continued to give trouble. The situation had become very bad on the streets of Medon. One Saturday night, three of them who had been appointed United States Marshalls (Wilson, and two Lowery men from "up on Piney") came to the home of a Miss Murchison and threatened her; but when she pulled a gun to defend herself, they mounted, rode on, but promised her that they would be back after they had "cleaned up Medon." Fortunately her brother came home about this time and, upon hearing what had happened, he grabbed a gun, rode hard and by taking short cuts, he was able to warn the people of Medon. When the "Hurstites" came in, began drinking and became rowdy, the Citizens' Committee began marching them off to the calaboose to let them "sleep off their liquor." Suddenly, a shot rang out from an upper window, and one Lowery fell with his backbone broken just above the waist line—then another shot, and the other Lowery was wounded in the same part of the body. Wilson ran, but he was also shot as he was trying to get through the fence of the Methodist Church. Murchison, the brother of the young lady, was a noted sharpshooter. This scene was the last one of its kind in this neighborhood. Hurst's men gave no more trouble here.[10]

News came one day that a white man was to speak at a negro meeting in a school house north of town. Robed figures appeared at the windows as the crowd gathered. When these appeared, the crowd disappeared into thin air and there was no more speaking. A negro, Arch Wharton, was elected as a member of the county court from the Huntersville district. The Ku Klux Klan came to see him one night and left their card at his front door—a beautiful new coffin! Arch Wharton never served as magistrate! The famous secret organization would also take care of such matters as a secret organization among the Negroes against the whites to resist the system of hiring to the whites, the system of cropping on shares and the attempt to force the whites to sell them lands. Logan, a negro preacher, was having meetings exciting the negroes. The editor

---

[10]Mrs. Lena Lacy Murdock, "Early Days in Medon, Tennessee," paper read before the Madison County Historical Society, June, 1945.

of the Jackson *Dispatch* thought that he must have been a rascal, but the leader of the Klan probably acted first and thought later.[11]

Years later Colonel R. A. Sneed, one of the leading citizens of Jackson during the days of reconstruction, recalled those days of 1867 and 1868 when he had seen "Yankee" bayonets crossed before the door of the courthouse to prevent a Confederate soldier or the son of a soldier from casting his ballot. The Colonel's summary of these days that really tried men's souls should in conclusion be quoted:

> I remember when Madison and other counties of this section were dominated by the carpetbaggers who placed negroes in authority. Those were the troublesome days for the South. We who had survived the four years of war saw our civilization crumbling into the discord, lawlessness and gang rule supplanting the law and order of which the South had boasted.
>
> That situation was a challenge to the men and women of the South and they met it. I joined the old Ku Klux Klan in Jackson on the second floor of a building where the First National Bank now stands. We Ku Kluxers did not harm the hair of a negro's head, but we did serve notice that we were still masters of our civilization. We drove out the carpetbaggers and we silenced that element of the negroes who had been under the political domination of the scalawags that came from the North after the war to seek the spoils. By 1870 we had restored Democratic rule in this section of the state.[12]

---

[11] Jackson *Dispatch*, 1873.

[12] Jackson *Sun*, August 1, 1933. Colonel Richard Alexander Sneed, who was rightly called "The Grand Old Man," was closely identified with Madison County politics, rendering conspicuous service here in restoring order out of chaos and wresting the government from "carpet-bag rule," before he went to Oklahoma and became one of the leading men of that state. Serving as a member of the convention which wrote the State Constitution, he was offered the governorship but he declined feeling that a younger man should be chosen. He served as State Treasurer and Secretary of State of Oklahoma. Colonel Sneed felt that his crowning achievement came in 1929 when he was elected Commander-in-Chief of the United Confederate Veterans. The Colonel died in 1936 at the age of ninety-one. He was revered by Oklahomans and others who knew him because he personified the fighting spirit of that undefeated South that arose from the dust and the blood of Appomattox.

CHAPTER XV

THE PLANTER AND THE FARMER

The story of agriculture during the one hundred and twenty-five years of the life of Madison County is the story of the transition from the one crop system, the transition from the raising of cotton upon large land holdings with slave labor and slow transportation to the production of most of the essential crops upon small land holdings with free labor and an excellent net work of railroads and highways. Those men of the soil—the planter or the large land owner of the nineteenth century and the farmer or the smaller land owner of the twentieth century—had much to do with the growth and development of Madison County.

Soon after the Western District was opened up for settlement, cotton and corn became the staple crops of this section. West Tennessee of which Madison County was a part became a part of the "cotton kingdom" and Jackson on the Forked Deer became an important cotton depot. The demand for cotton and cotton goods throughout the world in the early nineteenth century created a desire for new cotton lands which in turn caused pioneers to rush into the Western District giving it life and moulding its life into a distinct type of society. By 1860, Madison County had become a part of that "cotton kingdom" for West Tennessee produced six per cent of all the cotton produced in Tennessee, Alabama, Georgia, Louisiana, and Mississippi.

During the shipping season at Jackson on the Forked Deer, the tiny stream was usually reported in "fine boating order," but travel was slow and dangerous. Delay, however, did not harm the cotton, and these "well-known and experienced navigators of the Forked Deer" loved danger and adventure. Settlers who came in such numbers that one editor said "the land was swimming with land hunters," who had been lured to this section by stories of land which was "congenial to cotton," of land which could be bought for from $2 to $5 per acre that produced a thousand pounds of seed cotton per acre.[1] Even a traveler's guide of 1834 told of the abundance and fine quality of cotton in the Western District.[2] By 1824, the life of the community was beginning to be firmly shaped around the staple, cotton. Men bought land and settled to raise cotton to pay off their debts, though they realized that they should raise other crops. Armour and Lake had a Carver's gin in complete operation and were ready to receive and ship cotton. The *Gazette* announced two commission merchants who were desirous of business in December, 1824:

They [Armour and Lake] have two large Keel-boats, which they design sending to New Orleans as early in the season as possible and will receive cotton on freight. As they have used every means in their power to be able to accommodate the planters of the Western District, they hope to receive a liberal share of their patronage.

JUST RECEIVED—a large quantity of SWEDE'S IRON and have in the store SALT, WHISKEY, which they will sell on reasonable terms for CASH OR COTTON.[3]

Robert Murray's commission house had 2,000 weight of bacon and a "large quantity of PRIME OLD WHISKEY" to sell to the planters if they could be persuaded to trade with it.[4]

The cotton business increased over night when the planters realized that the Forked Deer and Western District cotton brought from one to two cents more per pound in New Orleans than that from the other districts. The life of the community became more and more centered around the staple, and new fields were planted just as soon as the land could be cleared. This was the cash crop. The *Truth Teller* of 1835 reported the flattering prospects of the planter, for both cotton and corn were in a flourishing condition.[5]

Estates consisted of land, Negroes, cotton, and corn with a few horses, hogs, and sheep added. Each was so necessary to the other that when the planter had the land, he acquired

---

[1] Jackson *Gazette,* April 17, 1830; Randolph *Recorder,* October 23, 1836.
[2] *View of the Mississippi of the Emigrant's and Traveler's* (Philadelphia, 1834), 205.
[3] Jackson *Gazette,* December 13, 1824.
[4] *Ibid.*

the Negroes as he could and the other products were not so difficult to produce of the new soil. All business seemed to revolve around cotton. Gins that "pick well" were ready to receive it, commission houses of Jackson, Memphis, and New Orleans were ready to handle and insure it, and warehouses were ready to store it. Men were sent to New Orleans early in the season to "devote their entire time and attention to the receiving and selling the produce, filling of orders, receiving and forwarding goods." The most trusted merchant was the one who promised that he would not risk one dollar on speculation. A real boom was here and cotton was everywhere. It was sold in the fields, at the warehouses, at regular markets, and was used in the stores for exchange—cotton was as good as cash.[6]

By 1831, the whole quantity of cotton raised in West Tennessee was from thirty to forty thousand bales per year, which was valued at about a million dollars. Five thousand bales of this was shipped from the landings of Madison County.[7] A failure of the cotton crop or an early killing frost would cast a gloom over the faces of the planters who met on the streets on Saturday or gathered at the Jackson Reading Room "to devise means of meeting the calamity."[8] As the business increased merchants prepared themselves to take care of it. In November 1849, J. W. Campbell and R. H. May were ready to store cotton and, at the first rise of the river, to ship it in covered boats each week, to pick up cotton at landings below Jackson, and to handle six thousand bales during the season. These merchants were expecting such a big crop that they were ready for any emergency, for they had a good "barge boat with a first-rate tarpaulin ready to run the river should the freight warrant it."[9]

---

[5] Jackson *Southern Statesman*, March 19, 1831; Nashville *Union*, June 10, 1835, quoting the Jackson *Truth Teller*.

[6] Jackson *Gazette*, December 13, 1824; Paris *West Tennessean*, November 13, 1827; Jackson *Southern Statesman*, May 21, April 30, 1831; Jackson *District Telegraph*, March 30, 1838; Jackson *Republican*, February 24, 1843; Jackson *West Tennessee Whig*, November 23, 1849.

[7] Jackson *Southern Statesman*, May 21, 1831. See accompanying table for census reports of produce for market.

[8] Jackson *Southern Statesman*, December 3, 1831.

[9] Jackson *West Tennessee Whig*, November 23, 1849.

The emigrants from the older states acquired plenty of virgin land, in quantities ranging from several hundred thousand acres down to two and three hundred and even to fifty acres, but they came with few Negroes. Citizens of Madison County to-day speak of their grandparents coming to this section in the 1820's and 1830's with only one or two Negroes. Many of the planters either went back for the slaves, bought them from the slave traders at the slave marts, such as those of Gardner and Barham, Hargrove, Witherspoon, or had them brought out from the older sections, especially from North Carolina. Good hands under constant supervision were necessary for a profit in cotton at the end of the year.[10]

In those early days many men had no Negroes, while the average planter had one or two, and few had as many as nine, eleven, seventeen, and twenty-five slaves. In 1853, Robert H. Cartmell made forty-three bales of cotton with nine hands, showing a profit at the end of the year of $421.35.[11] During the first few years of the life of the community the average slave brought from three to four hundred dollars, but when the value of cotton increased the price of Negroes very quickly rose to five and six hundred dollars in 1850 and to thirteen hundred dollars in 1860. In 1857, a woman and five children sold for $3,415, a girl of fifteen years sold for $1,250, and a boy seventeen sold for $1,725.[12] The slave population of all West Tennessee increased from 25,161 in 1830 to 41,456 in 1840. Madison County had a greater number than any other county of this section. There were 4,167 slaves in the county in 1830, 6,073 in 1840, 8,552 in 1850, and 10,012 in 1860, while the whole white population in 1860 was only 11,440.[13] Negro house-servants, blacksmiths, carpenters, women, boys, and girls were advertised for sale in lots of twenty, twenty-five, and fifty. The Negroes and the master's house were some-

---

[10]Madison County Will Book, 1821-1835; Jackson *Gazette*, December 12, 1824; Jackson *Southern Statesman*, February 19, 1831; Minutes of the City of Jackson, 1858-1861.

[11]Madison County Will Book, 1821-1835; Robert H. Cartmell Diary.

[12]Will Book of Madison County, 1821-35; Bill of Sale of Slaves; Robert H. Cartmell Diary.

[13]*Fifth Census of the United States*, 1830; *Sixth Census of the United States*, 1840; *Seventh Census of the United States*, 1850; *Eighth Census of the United States*, 1860.

times mentioned in the same sentence of the advertisement. Men thought of the Negroes as "personal property," and the most valuable portion of all property besides the land, consisted of slaves. Two slaves of an estate, which included a wagon, a sugar chest, "raisor and strop," three cows and calves, brought $1,035, while the whole estate brought only $1,490. The entire estate of Richard Tomlinson was valued at less than

State of Tennessee, Madison County. Received of Samuel L. Anderson thirty five hundred Dollars in full payment for a certain lot of negroes (to wit) namely as follows: Willis age about twenty two years of age, Easter age about twenty seven years of age, Eliza age about Eighteen years of age, Mary age about Eighteen years of age, Luranee age about Seventeen years of age, Ritter age about Sixteen years of age, Phil age about thirteen years of age. I warrant the title of said negroes to the said Anderson free from all lawful claims whatsoever & I also warrant said negroes to be sound healthy sensible and slaves for life this 16th day of Nov. A.D. 1847.

James Fussell

J. J. Hay

V. L. Camp

(Curtis Bray Collection)

John Camp, of Obion County, entered into a partnership with R. I. Chester in 1846 for the purpose of "buying and selling slaves for profit." Chester furnished the money; Camp came to Jackson and conducted the business, buying a house, building a "negro yard" with a picket fence around the house where he kept his negroes ready for sale at all times. From original manuscript in the Curtis Bray Collection.

$5,000; and this included five hundred acres of land at $2,197, a cotton gin at $150, and thirty-three Negroes at $2,000.[14]

The Negroes of this section were quite like those of any other similar section of the South of this time. There were the sickly ones who were not worth much of anything; there were the young field hands who were worth $500. In one case a carpenter and his tools brought $910, and a child of four years was sold for $250.[15] The ones who ran away, usually on Saturday nights and Sundays, "took" extra clothing and a horse or two before they headed for the free states. They wore wool hats, fur hats, roundabout jackets, blue cashmere pantaloons, which were usually "tollerably well-worn." Some of the Negroes were knock-kneed, scarred on the face or hands; some had down cast looks; some stuttered when spoken to if alarmed; some were fond of chewing tobacco, singing, and drinking. In some instances the Negroes were allowed to buy

---

[14]Jackson *Southern Statesman*, February 19, 1831; Madison County Will Book, 1821-1835.
[15]Madison County Will Book, 1821-35.

Bill of sale of a slave, 1860. Courtesy of Mrs. Robert Emmerson.

at the country store and charge the articles which included tobacco, cigars, calico, looking glasses, "ribbons," knives, hats, shoes, hoop skirts, cologne, ear screws, and fringe. A reward of one hundred dollars was offered for Lewis (age 19) who was "raised in the house as a body servant," and had absconded without any cause or provocation whatever when he was entrusted with an important errand. Another reward of one hundred dollars was offered by the master of Granderson (age 18) who was handy with all kinds of plantation tools.[16]

Even if the Negro were property, he seems to have been well cared for property. Records show that they were allowed clothes and shoes that were frequently as costly as those bought for the white children. Almost every planter had a domestic medicine chest that he and his wife made use of, but doctors were also paid for attending Negroes who were ill. Numerous entries in Robert Cartmell's diary tell of having Dr. Snider or Dr. Dashiell with the Negroes. James Freeman paid twenty dollars for doctoring, and six dollars for boarding the Negro, Lucinda, when she was sick. The same physician that cared for the master cared for the slaves. It mattered not whether cotton was three or fifteen cents a pound, the slaves were cared for. They looked to the planter for care and protection with the same confidence that a child looks to his parents for support. Those slaves who were not strong or were recovering from an illness were put to light work, such as making baskets or spinning. In one case the slaves of an estate were hired out by the year, but Boy Bob, who was afflicted, was kept at home.[17]

Life on a plantation was just one day's work after the other for both planter and slave. Days were filled with knocking down cotton stalks, plowing, planting, chopping, picking cotton, planting corn and caring for it, planting vegetables, fixing roofs, splitting and hauling rails, hauling wood to town or cotton "to the river," setting out apple trees, killing hogs, threshing wheat, cleaning stables, fixing chimneys, chinking houses, making wagons and often tools. There were days when

---

[16]Jackson *Gazette*, December 13, 1824; Jackson *Southern Statesman*, February 19, April 9, 30, June 19, 1831; Account Book of Rogers and Hearn store, 1858-59. Used through the courtesy of Mrs. W. C. Blackmon.

[17]Madison County Minute Book, 1821-28; 1848-50; Robert H. Cartmell Diary.

the Negroes did not have to work, such as those that the master spent serving on the jury, or just when he went to town, Saturdays, or days when it rained, for plowing, chopping, picking or other work had to stop when the weather took things in hand. When the planter was ill and had to remain in the house all day he found that the hands did almost nothing, but Robert Cartmell did not believe that whipping did any good, for "the young ones will not work unless there be some one to see them and make them do."

The relationship between master and slave depended upon the personality of each, just as that of the employer and employee to-day. There are good and bad in both classes. During a period of seven years on the plantation of Robert Cartmell, there were only a few references to the slaves being punished and then the planter seemed to regret having to chastise "my boys." Upon one occasion he had them putting dirt around the house to keep the water from running in the cellar when he had to strike one of the boys "for trifling." Three of them ran away, some six or seven miles on the Lexington road, supposedly for a free state in the North, but they got frightened and came back. The planter recorded that he whipped them, thinking that it might prevent trouble when they became older. Negroes were a problem. The planter couldn't do without them and yet he had a struggle doing anything with them. "Negoes," wrote Robert Cartmell, "were not inclined to do much when not hurried up.... They require constant watching. They feel an interest in nothing *only punctual* in coming *regularly* when their meat is given out."[18] Upon another occasion the diarist had a "frolic" with a Negro who lied to him, at which time he gave the Negro "plenty of peach tree." One negro Dave had a bad habit of running away. After Robert Cartmell had paid the costs of his capture several times, he decided that he had better sell Dave "South."

Many of the small planters were their own overseers, in fact this was the best method, but the labor required such constant attention that if a man could get a good overseer he usually did so. But, securing an overseer who would work the slaves hard enough to keep the work done on the plantation and at the same time be kind to the negroes was a real problem.

---

[18]Robert Cartmell Diary.

NEGRO MAN FOR SALE.

IN MADISON COUNTY COURT.

William H. Stone, administrator of Sarah Stone, dec'd.,
PETITION TO SELL SLAVE.

Pursuant to an interlocutory decree, made in the above cause, at the January Term, 1856, of the county court of Madison county, Tennessee, I will sell to the highest bidder, in the

TOWN OF JACKSON,

before the court house door, on Monday the 4th day of February next, a very valuable negro man named SAM, belonging to the estate of said Sarah Stone, deceased.

Terms of Sale.

Said negro man will be sold on a credit of 12 months. Bond and approved security will be required of the purchaser, and a lien retained for the purchase money.

THOS. W. GAMEWELL, C. & M.,
Commissioner.

M. Bullock, Attorney.

January 11, 1856.

Seale Johnson Collection.

Furthermore the overseer was paid such a small sum, that one could not expect to get very efficient help. For a while Robert Cartmell's father worked more hands under an overseer than Robert did under his own supervision, and yet the son produced as large a crop as the father. Nevertheless, in 1854, Cartmell hired an overseer for $12½ a month for he could not be with the Negroes all the time and they cut up too much cotton and would not work unless they were made. Four years later, the same planter dismissed an overseer because he beat a negro and bruised him. J. F. Clark recommended a Mr. Johnson to J. W. Campbell, but suggested that Johnson might not be a good overseer. J. F. Clark wrote:

> I think he will suit you for that business [overseer] as he is attentive enough, but you will have to bind him not to beat up your negroes with unnecessary whip such as a stick or a cudgell. He will govern your hands but he is very excitable and by cautioning him I judge he would do right.[19]

A very interesting view of the Negro in the late 1850's is revealed in an old ledger of the Hearn and Rogers store in the Pinson community. At least half of the accounts were those of the Negroes. Some of the accounts were settled when the Negro brought fruit, hides, or furs to the store, Rogers' Tom brought $43.36 worth of furs at one time, but most of the accounts were settled by the master in November and December when the crops were sold. Accounts of the slaves were listed as Rogers' Margaret, who bought one bottle of cologne at 15c and six yards of muslin; Rogers' Tom who was charged with a looking glass, ribbon, snuff, tobacco, a cloth coat for $5 and a pair of ear drops for 70c; Rogers' Chloe who was charged with lawn, calico, a hoop skirt at $1.25 and a palm fan at 25c. Most of the accounts were from $5 to $30, but Rogers' Tom had a bill of $84.08. Other accounts were in the names of Lancaster's Ben, Hearn's Bod, Davis' Coll, Weaver's Methilda, Temple's Ephriam. Upon the account of E. L. Lancaster there were four pairs of negro boots at $14.40, three negro blankets at $8.50, ten wool hats at $6.50. Osnaberg and inexpensive coats were the usual items on the accounts of the slave owners. The Negro always bought tobacco and "sundries."[20]

---

[19] J. F. Clark to J. W. Campbell, MS. Curtis Bray Collection.
[20] Ledger of Rogers and Hearn Store, 1858-1859.

Enough interest in the welfare of the Negro was created by 1830 for a branch of the American Colonization Society to be organized, with William Armour, president, and John Read, secretary; but the people of this section did not give their wholehearted support to this enterprise. At this time there were 2,570 free persons of color in West Tennessee, who according to the editor of the *Southern Statesman*, could be useful individuals, but under the circumstances, jealousy and hostility blended together to make the free blacks a "degraded and troublesome class."[21]

Although free persons of color were forbidden to immigrate to Tennessee after 1831, court records show that free persons brought their freedom papers, presented them in court and were allowed to stay in the county as long as they did not disturb the peace. A few slaves were freed by their masters, who usually signed the bond for their former slaves' good behavior. Some slaves bought their freedom or had it given to them by their master's will. Allen DeBerry freed his man Donalson, gave him $500. In the same DeBerry will there were provisions made for each of his slaves to be settled upon his land with some money set aside for their use. Free negroes appeared in court and satisfied the court that they were good moral character and "industrious habits" making a bond that was signed by prominent citizens that they would "keep peace and be of good character." The state laws, augmented by local regulations, and enforced by the citizens of the county, kept the number of free persons of color at a minimum, for there were only thirty-six in Madison County in 1840, only thirteen in Jackson and sixty-one in the whole county in 1850, and eighty-three in 1860.[22]

Slaves in some parts of Madison County were taught to read and write, but the public in general was a little afraid of this because it generated discontent. Margaret Givens left Negroes to each of her children with the instructions that they "be taught to read, write, and know the Scriptures."[23] In the

---

[21]Jackson *Southern Statesman*, September 3, 1831; S. C. Williams, *West Tennessee*, 213.

[22]Madison County Minute Book, 1848-50; Will of Allen DeBerry, MS; *Sixth Census of the United States*, 1840; *Seventh Census of the United States*, 1850; *Eighth Census of the United States*, 1860.

[23]Jackson *Southern Statesman*, October 22, 1831; Madison County Will Book, 1821-1835.

winter of 1831 there were rumors of insurrection drifting about the country, to the effect that the slaves planned to rise on Christmas Eve and massacre as they went. Although the planters wouldn't believe the rumor, they watched every movement. The *Southern Statesman* recorded the unrest thus:

> We noticed the rumors were so wide spread . . . we believe that there was never a slave population better satisfied with their condition than that of the Western District . . . at present well-clothed, well-fed, unannoyed by constables, regardless of who is President and in no wise distracted with the nullifying doctrines of some of our southern politicians, nor the tariff, nor anti-masonry, nor the Georgia question. They appear comparatively happy in this humble station of life.[24]

Again at Christmas time 1856, there were rumors of a general uprising. Therefore the slaves were watched closely and deprived of much of their usual holiday fun.[25]

Jackson had its own code of laws regulating the conduct of the slaves "in order to prevent the evil consequences to be apprehended from large collections of slaves." No gathering except for the purpose of public worship was allowed within the corporation. Slaves, who did not live within the corporation or who came within the limits unless on business of the master, were not allowed to remain there after 10 o'clock at night without a pass. This pass was a protection of the slave during his good behavior.[26] Many of the troubles with the slaves resulted in their congregating for the purpose of dancing or other pasttimes, so the masters did everything that they could to prevent the gatherings in large bodies. By 1847, the numbers had increased and laws in turn became more stringent. A slave who caused a disturbance was subject to punishment of thirty lashes and two days imprisonment. If slaves engaged in disorderly conduct and did not dispurse immediately when ordered, they should be given from two to thirty lashes. No sale of liquor to slaves could be made without a permit from the master. No slave could hire himself out within the cor-

---

[24] Jackson *Southern Statesman*, January 23, 1832.
[25] Robert H. Cartmell Diary.
[26] Jackson *Southern Statesman*, March 30, 1832. During the decade preceeding the Civil War, the old bell in the courthouse tower rang at nine at night which was a signal for the slaves to leave the streets or be subject to being whipped if caught.

West Tennessee *Whig*, March 6, 1851.   Courtesy Mrs. W. W. Tucker.

poration. No assemblies could be held at night under the pretext of prayer meetings unless at regular churches of the whites."[27] A Mr. Butler, who enjoyed a lucrative trade as a "slave catcher," owned a pack of vicious dogs. Many a runaway was caught not at home but up a tree. The free negroes in the community were always blamed for any trouble that occurred.

Many of the slaves, by the time they lived their whole life in the community with some one family, became a valuable part of the life both of the family and of the community. Robert Cartmell was genuinely grieved over the illness and death of his slave, Dick, for he had been the main stay among the Negroes, a settled, well-disposed, peaceable, and attentive man. "Dick was a great help to me," wrote Robert Cartmell, "but I hope he is better off and in a better world."[28] The fact that few death notices at all appeared in the papers makes this one more significant:

Died—In this town on Saturday last, Isaac, a coloured man, aged about 70 years, for many years an honest and industrious resident of this town. He was familiarly known as "Uncle Isaac" and was much respected by all who knew him—fully verifying the assertion that many a noble heart beats under a dusky form.[29]

[27]Jackson *West Tennessee Whig*, February 10, 1847.
[28]Diary of Robert H. Cartmell.
[29]Jackson *Southern Statesman*, March 19, 1831.

THE PLANTER AND THE FARMER   211

Negroes had the usual characteristics of human beings. They were neither all good nor all bad, neither all lazy nor all industrious. All types make up any race and the colored race is no exception to the rule. When spring came and there was extra work to be done, the advertisements for runaways appeared in greater numbers than during the winter months, but this desire to escape work, after all, is a most natural one. Robert Cartmell, just as many an overseer or planter of old or an employer of to-day, became exasperated with his Negroes at times and said that if he had it to do over again that he would never engage in any business that would throw him in contact with Negroes, for they "were mean, unprincipled, rogish, lazy, fit only to fret a man's life out of him," for it required the patience of Job to work with them and to be severe as a tyrant. Such an entry in the diary must have been written on a day when things all went wrong, for the following day the diarist admitted that he was out of temper the preceeding day.[30] But after all the problems of the planter were just the labor problems of the nineteenth century.

The Sectional Conflict of 1861-1865 interrupted a courageous attempt on the part of Southern planters to devise some plan by which they could improve the agricultural conditions of the land. Tennessee's lands were being exhausted and by 1850 many of the wide-awake, far-sighted citizens realized that the future prosperity of the state depended upon improvements of methods in agriculture. An act of Legislature of 1854 created an Agricultural Bureau and provided for the organization of state and county agricultural societies. Robert Cartmell went to R. A. Hurt's in 1854 to a meeting of the Madison County Agricultural Society. Both of these men might be called progressive farmers. Cartmell considered farming as honorable a profession as medicine or law, for it furnished just as much room for the exercise of the intellectual faculties. That he was a part of that progressive movement in the county is shown by the following entry from his diary in 1853:

> Heretofore, in this country, land being very cheap; a man could afford to cut down, wear out and move to fresh land, hence a new country presents the appearance of an old and exhausted one, but a different course is now beginning and for the future must be pursued.

---

[30]Diary of Robert H. Cartmell.

Land has risen in this country within the last four years from 4 to 6 dollars to 12 to 15 and impossible to be got or nearly so. From this time on through out this century at least a systematic rotation of crops, deep plowing, manuring and clovering must be attended to. Old and fields now turned out must be reclaimed cotton bales must not take the foremost place in the farming world, in other words a systematic improvement of the soil must be followed. Everything raised on the farm that can conveniently be raised or made without too much cost must be raised and then a bale of cotton as a surplus, then and not until then will men cease to complain. . . . Good negro cabins will then become common, well fed and well clothed negroes will be

West Tennessee *Whig*, January 18, 1850. Courtesy of Mrs. W. W. Tucker.

THE PLANTER AND THE FARMER 213

seen everywhere, good shelter for everything, good hay, good pasture and no more stock than can be attended to.[31]

In 1858, according to entries in the same diary, the planter was more convinced that ever that diversified farming was the answer to the farmer's problems. This planter was trying to ditch and terrace to prevent washing for "it is an absolute necessity to use every precaution or soon we will have to be satisfied with a bare subsistance or emigrate to a new country. In the course of time this county will become a farming county or a provision county. Cotton is an uncertain impoverisher of land, exposes lands, now of necessity we must raise it."[32]

Dr. Alexander Jackson, a prosperous farmer of Madison, was a delegate from the county to the meeting of the State Bureau and was chosen as one of the three delegates to attend the United States Agricultural Society in Washington. At the meeting of the State Agricultural Society in 1855, plans were made to encourage home production of products that had once been brought in, to improve the soil that was wearing out each year while the population was increasing.[33]

The principal means of arousing the people was the staging of State and divisional fairs, the first of which in West Tennessee was held in Jackson October 23-26, 1855. The farmers planned to exhibit their produce of the year and to see what their neighbor had produced and to learn how it had been produced. Six or eight thousand people attended this first agricultural and mechanical fair in the Western District, the first fair ever to be held in this section except the one held in the preceding September in Fayette County. The people who came from all over the county to the small town of Jackson in 1855, came to enjoy the exhibits, visit with friends, and to listen to six lengthy speeches delivered by Rev. James C. Coggesshall, Lewis Williamson, Charles Dod, James C. Jones, Colonel John Pope and Governor A. V. Brown, who addressed an immense audience at the courthouse one night during the fair. Dr. Alexander Jackson served as president of the fair during the first year; James S. Lyon was vice-president; Alexander Campbell, secretary, and John W. Campbell, the director from this county. Charles D. McLean was elected crier, but

---
[31]*Ibid.*
[32]*Ibid.*
[33]*Report of the Tennessee Agricultural Bureau, 1855-1856.*

did not attend, so R. J. Hays served to the satisfaction of the entire community. Seven hundred and ninety-seven dollars were distributed in premiums. William O. Butler won the prize for the best bale of cotton, although James S. Lyon and A. S. Rogers exhibited fine bales; H. W. McCorry won the prize for the best acres of mixed hay; James Lyon won several prizes on his horses. Besides the expected prizes to the ladies for canned fruit, embroidery, flower displays, there were awards to the makers of the best shoes and carriages. Although the State Bureau lent much aid to this undertaking financially and John W. Campbell donated nine acres of wooded timber for building and fences when the affair was over, there was a deficit of $601, but the directors were confident that many people had not realized the value of this new project and that they could make a better showing next year.[34]

In a prize winning essay of Dr. Jackson, the whole subject of scientific farming, rotation of crops and the improvement of stock was ably discussed. He felt that the lack of improved roads had compelled the farmers to stick to the bulky crops, for these could be delayed in getting to market and there was no real harm done. "This reliance upon river transportation has for a great number of years, seriously disturbed the financial and commercial operations of the county and embarrassed the agriculturists, the products of whose labor are often detained on the bank of a sluggish stream awaiting the replenishing aid of uncertain clouds while his credit and interests suffered for want of ability to meet a well considered promise to pay." Dr. Jackson was confident that the Mobile and Ohio Railroad, which was then under construction, would completely change this situation, changing this from a "planting district" where cotton was the monopolizing crop, to a "farming district" with numerous crops for distant new markets.[35] Dr. Jackson was indeed a man with vision!

The third meeting of the Western Division fair was held in Jackson in October, 1857. As Jackson had been selected as the permanent meeting place thirty acres were purchased in the surburbs of the town (the triangle from North Fairgrounds Street and Poplar Corner Road). An exhibition hall 40 by 80

---

[34]*Ibid.*
[35]*Ibid.*

feet, about 900 feet of stabling, 325 feet of seats covered by a substantial shed around the show ring were erected. In all twelve acres were enclosed with a fence seven feet high. Too much emphasis cannot be placed upon the influence that these fairs had in this section for they were very popular. These fairs were a new mode of entertainment and they were stimulating intellectually to the planter who was trying to improve conditions. An item from a Nashville paper of 1858 told of improvement in stock:

> There is abroad in the Western District among the farmers the proper spirit with regard to the improvement of stock. . . . Among those in West Tennessee who are taking no little notice in the stock improvement are Robert Hurt, Esq., and Col. R. I. Chester of Madison County. Col. Chester, during the past Spring imported a large string of horses from Virginia. Among them are several fine-blooded mares, a beautiful Morgan stallion. Col. Chester deserves great praise for his liberal efforts to improve the horse stock in the county.[36]

The Civil War caused a paralysis of agriculture, but when wars are over the farmer returns to his field and plough and the artisan to his trade, but this time the negro did not return to his vocation. When the Southern soldiers returned to their lands, they found their stock gone, their sheds and barns destroyed, their wagons and harness confiscated, their labor vanished. When the farmer acquired a few animals and tried to obtain labor he found that he had to make labor contracts through the Freedman's Bureau, which organization was obnoxious to the former Confederate soldiers. These contracts called for the employer to furnish food, clothing, shelter, and fuel and pay a share of the crop when it was gathered. Robert Fenner made a contract with Nelson Holbrook, his wife and six children to furnish the above mentioned quarters and agreed to pay him $33 per month. Henry McCorry agreed to furnish food and quarters, half of the crop and $40 for Hiram McCorry's services for the year.[37] Each laborer promised to be "respectful, obedient, and industrious." In 1867 William H. Jackson entered into an agreement with the State of Tennessee

---

[36]Nashville *Daily Gazette*, August 1, 1858.

[37]Labor Contracts dated 1866 and signed by Henry McCorry and Robert Fenner. MS. Used through the courtesy of Mrs. Tom McCorry, Sr., and Hill Burnett.

for the importing of sixty-nine laborers from South Carolina. Entire families were brought to the Western District. The ages ranged from ten years to sixty, while wages ranged from $40 for a thirteen year old to $200 for a man fifty. Most men received from $130 to $150. The workers agreed to do all kinds of work common to the farms. In return for this labor Jackson agreed to furnish comfortable quarters, sufficient rations, treat them kindly and encourage the establishment of schools and pay them when the crop was gathered.[38]

An account book of A. W. Campbell of the years 1875 and 1876 revealed a story of the unstable condition of labor. One after the other came to the farm and worked three or four days at 75c and $1 per day; some hired for $12 a month plus 12 pounds of meat and a bushel of meal; others hired for $285 a year or five days work a month for rent on a house; others hired for $50 in cash, $10 worth of clothing, $20 in flour, meat and wood. Many a laborer left after only a few days or were discharged for worthlessness. The farmer was faced with the problem of rebuilding his farm and making it pay and he had to do this with the freedmen who were not sure where they wanted to work, for whom they wanted to work or whether they wanted to work at all. The following plea to the freedmen of Madison County shows the unstable conditions of the day:

To the Freedman of Madison County—Make your contracts for the year, so that the planter will know what to depend upon and you will find homes and employment.

You must abandon the idea that the Government will make a division of this Southern Country and give each of you a farm, stock, farming implements. . . . Anyone who told you this, told you a falsehood, for the Government will do no such thing. It cannot do it, and it is unreasonable to think of such a thing. If you ever own land, you will have to work for it, as white men have to do.

To work is the law of God! and is the only protection against pauperism and crime. . . . There is an inclination on the part of many of you to gather about towns and cities in order to loaf and idle away your time. There is no employment for half the number who congregate in these places. The result is you must resort to dishonorable means for support, such as stealing, begging and the like.[39]

---

[38]Labor contract of William H. Jackson, MS. Bray Collection.
[39]Jackson *West Tennessee Whig*, February 7, 1879.

Much credit should be given to those ex-Confederate soldier-planters who returned home and began to stage the brave attempt towards an agricultural revival. Through the Agricultural Societies, the State Fairs, and the newspapers, they scattered wonderful propaganda about the possibilities of diversified farming, improvement in stock, sheep raising, improvements in grasses which would thereby make the expansion of the dairying industry possible. In 1886 A. J. McWherter wrote:

> She [West Tennessee] enjoys the distinction of having originated in her borders several of those schemes for agricultural reforms of immigration and capital and general progress which are today being developed and pursued with encouraging success all over the state and in other states of the South. . . . West Tennessee is on the march forward and nowhere in the South does the light of the new morning shine with more encouraging promise.[40]

Literature was even published giving plans for wholesale immigration, *A West Tennessee Directory of 1872*, and J. B. Killebrew's *West Tennessee: Its Resources and Advantages* (Nashville, 1879), and numerous newspaper articles in the contemporary papers all painted a wonderful picture of the advantages of this section. In the late 1870's J. B. Killebrew published and distributed widely a pamphlet "Come to Tennessee" but the yellow fever of 1878 destroyed the effect of this. Frantic efforts were being made by the leaders of the county to attract immigrants and to persuade people to let cotton alone and turn to diversified agriculture and manufacturing, for cotton at ten cents a pound was not a profitable crop and besides it impoverished the soil more than any crop that could be grown. Innumerable articles described the soil of Madison County as that which was suitable to diversified agriculture. A paper of 1884 told of bodies of people, such as one Quaker group, who were corresponding with Gates and Fairchilds, real estate agents, and Caruthers and Mallory, attorneys, about obtaining two to three thousand acres for their settlement and the West Tennessee Directory of 1872 gave detailed plans for a colony of settlers to follow.[41] No modern chamber of com-

---

[40] A. J. McWherter, *Revised Hand Book of Tennessee* (Nashville, 1885), 182.

[41] Jackson *Tribune and Sun*, January 25, 1884. Used through the courtesy of Mrs. Grace Arrington Kenzie.

merce can produce articles which would compare favorably with those published in these old papers. The theme of each article was that the South had an abundance of rich land, a good climate, and plenty of natural resources, but that she had lagged behind and her citizens were trying to do something about it, and they thought that diversified farming and manufacturing were the answers to their problems. In the years gone by, they felt that there had been "too much land and too little cultivation; too much initiation and too little real tillage; too much devotion to cotton alone, to the exclusion and neglect of diversified agriculture; too much 'hog and hominy' imported and too little materials manufactured and exported."[42]

The West Tennessee Agricultural and Mechanical Association was organized in 1871 and the first fair was held that fall. Reports to the state department of agriculture show great interest in these exhibits and many farmers felt that they derived untold benefits from them. The progress made in the 1870's and 1880's was merely an outgrowth of that agricultural revival that was started before the war and renewed as soon as possible after the soldiers returned. A farsighted editor of 1867 was trying to relight the torch when he wrote:

The wealth of the state does not consist of full treasury, flourishing trade, enlarged commerce. It consists of moral and intellectual worth and strength of its people permanently secured by wise laws by cultivation of soil, development of resources. . . . Man was never more in his natural sphere and never more obedient to the laws of his nature than when bending all his best, noblest, most cultivated energies to the scientific and successful cultivation of his mother earth.[43]

Other reports during this period stuck to the same theme—that there was a wonderful opportunity in Madison County where there was good land for sale, where farmers had already demonstrated that clover could be grown successfully, where profits in fruits and vegetables are very good, where the railroads offered facilities for a first class market, where there was a county seat noted for intellectuality and refinement.[44]

---

[42] *West Tennessee Directory of 1872*, p. 16.

[43] Jackson *West Tennessee* Whig, May, 1867. Used through the courtesy of Fonville Neville.

[44] J. B. Killebrew, *West Tennessee: Its Resources and Advantages*, 49. In the same publication J. B. Killebrew quoted a letter from J. R. Neely of Denmark which gave both the dark picture and the bright

Special conventions created much excitement in the town in the 1880's and with the coming of the railroads Madison Countians, as other Americans became great believers and lovers of conventions. The Northern and Southern Dairy Convention of 1884 was an outstanding event in Jackson. Hand bills were circulated in the North, trying to entice the people to this convention that was to be held in "this wide-awake town of 8,000," for this was the future location of a new dairying industry together with the new creameries that were to be built in Tennessee. The meetings of the Convention were held at King's Opera House and Tomlin Hall, where the visitors were entertained by addresses by A. J. McWherter on "Immigration to Tennessee," Robert Gates on "Fruits and Market Gardening," B. A. Enloe on "Farming." Robert Gates realized the value of such a gathering when he wrote:

> The value of such an exhibition to Tennessee is obvious. It will show those of the North seeking farming lands what our soil is capable of producing; and those desirous of investing in manufacturing the variety and character of our timber resources. There will be a large number of home seekers and many looking out sites for manufacturing among the attendants from the North on the convention and through the exhibition suggested they will be soonest and most fruitfully reached and impressed. We know that this is an off time for such a display, but we also know that many articles can be shown that will fairly and profitably advertise our section.[45]

On February 24, 25, and 26, 1887, there gathered in Jackson a large number of delegates for a meeting of the Interstate Agricultural and Industrial Convention at the invitation of associate commissioner of agriculture, Robert Gates. Sixteen lengthy and learned speeches were delivered during the convention by such distinguished persons as A. J. McWherter, Commissioner of Agriculture, A. A. Cawdrey of Illinois, F. C. Curtis of Wisconsin, Edward Hays of Iowa, and I. B. Nall of Louisville, Kentucky. Special excursion rates were arranged for on the Illinois Central and the M. and O. The visitors

---

one. He mentioned the labor system as one of the difficulties in the way of success, the one crop system that was followed from necessity, but that it was a healthful county and that if the farmers would leave the old paths gradually and grow bread and meat at home, there might be a future in fruits and vegetables, and dairying. *Ibid.*, 88.

[45] Jackson *Tribune and Sun*, January 25, 1884.

TABLE No. 1—FARM LANDS IN MADISON

	Acres of Land in Farm		Size of Farms—Acres Per Farm						
	Improved	Unimproved	3–10	10–20	20–50	50–100	100–500	500–1000	Over 1000
1860	160,401	206,772	7	125	461	398	437	44	7
1870	94,169	148,225	1	40	908	383	211	5	......
1880	129,946	167,838	21	234	503	538	955	70	10
1890	145,828	143,594	26	166	646	525	1013	50	5
1900	157,657	140,706	82	333	1363	841	1015	26	3
1910	168,232	140,425	68	428	1586	889	995	29	4
1920	179,052	88,350	152	460	1824	1081	918	26	4
1930	166,354	94,157	219	710	1926	1068	717	10	......
1940	178,661	117,232	312	1853	1120	877	929	32	4

were shown all the advantages of the rich agricultural section and the small but progressive town of Jackson.[46] Further plans to attract northern interests were made in 1888 when citizens arranged to send free cars furnished by the Illinois Central through the Northwest, stopping at the county fairs, carrying agricultural exhibits and printing matter on the climate and soil of West Tennessee.[47]

Years passed, progressive farmers pled for diversification, promoters exhausted themselves and their vocabularies describing the advantages of the country. J. G. Cisco in his *Forked Deer Blade* had his hand in trying to attract capital and to encourage scientific farming. At last in a report of the Commissioner of Agriculture of 1885 there appeared an item about lands congenial to strawberries in Gibson, Madison and Crockett that a few years ago sold for $5 per acre but could not be bought for $30 an acre then for the farmer was frequently netting $100 per acre.[48] In less than a decade Madison County reported an acreage eight per cent greater than it was the preceeding year in strawberries. This was the small beginning of one of the

[46] *Biennial Report of the Commissioner of Agriculture of the State of Tennessee*, 1885-1886.

[47] Jackson *Forked Deer Blade*, March 24, 1888.

[48] *Biennial Report of Commissioner of Agriculture, Statistics, and Mines of State of Tennessee* (A. J. McWherter, 1885-1886), 27.

best cash crops that Madison farmers can produce to-day. The phenomenal increase of production is shown by the fact that census reports of 1910 show 413 acres and 520,391 quarts of strawberries, while by 1940 there were 986 acres in production with 1,712,068 quarts produced.[49]

Another revival in the interest in scientific farming at the turn of the century culminated in the establishment in 1907 of the West Tennessee Agricultural Experiment Station, which is a branch of the University of Tennessee. This was the fulfillment of a part of that old idea to establish agricultural colleges in each section of the state. According to a soil survey of Madison County in 1906 by the Department of Agriculture of the United States, there were great possibilities of reclaiming much of the poorly drained lands and raise crops that were better adapted to the types of soil. This survey had been made at the request of the Mayor Hu C. Anderson and Aldermen of Jackson. Exceedingly encouraging were the parts of the report

TABLE No. 2—PRODUCE FOR MARKET IN MADISON

	Bales of Cotton	Tobacco in Pounds	Corn in Bushels	Wheat in Bushels	Potatoes Irish	Potatoes Sweet	Market Garden Produce	Strawberries
1830								
1840	5,582	136,632	793,215	65,178				
1850	15,823	134,340	1,045,424	34,707	38,626	67,245		
1860	24,187	97,950	941,645	64,599	9,366	82,144	$ 250	
1870	9,255		692,910	44,599	2,961	9,724	3,613	
1880	19,257	32,419	906,255	50,918	11,506	38,175	1,426	
1890	11,146	4,020	756,012	14,334	13,599	23,608	6,320	
1900	12,488	3,800	985,050	39,940	7,867	17,427	44,354	
1910	11,895	924	869,740	24,111	23,200	38,307	142,244	413 Acres 570,391 qts
1920	16,568	424	804,955	13,781	24,956	90,264	115,220	529 Acres 734,413 qts
1930	30,189	1,241	851,270	8,712	23,113	90,449	211,519	1066 Acres 1,027,413
1940	19,570	None Reported	755,557	999	24,371	52,790	65,841	986 Acres 1,712,068 qts.

[49]*Thirteenth Census of the United States*, 1910; *Sixteenth Census of the United States*, 1940.

TABLE No. 3—FRUIT BEARING TREES AND GRAPES IN MADISON

Year	Apples	Peaches	Pears	Plums	Cherries	Grape Vines
1880*	....	....	....	....	....	....
1890	22,231	28,231	1021	15,064	848	*
1900	54,882	40,342	4283	31,930	7524	7934
1910	42,679	32,762	5589	4942	3185	2081
1920	30,302	17,712	1744	589	641	2638
1930	18,515	17,625	2022	705	632	3056
1940	15,705	17,272	1586	914	725	2143

*Data Not Available

which told of the $300,000 that had been recently spent for macadamized roads in the country, the interest in truck crops for northern markets which included tomatoes and strawberries.[50] This United States survey simply set the stage for the fight to locate the Experiment Station in Jackson, for Jackson was the geographical center of West Tennessee. It had superior railroad facilities, superior roads (65 miles of paved roads to a distance of six miles), the county contained all types of soil of West Tennessee. Jackson was the business, educational and legal center of West Tennessee. If the farms were located near Jackson, all the visitors could see workings of Experiment Station. The most forceful argument in favor of its location here was that sixteen counties in West Tennessee had endorsed this as the proper location and the County Court had offered to donate the land for the site.[51]

It was natural that other towns of West Tennessee should enter the fight to secure the new Experiment Station for their town. Milan and Union City were big rivals of Jackson but the Experiment Farm was located in Madison County because of all the various types of soil that were found in West Tennessee, these types could be found upon the location selected and because it was near Jackson, which offered such excellent trans-

---

[50]W. S. Lyman, Frank Bennett, W. C. McLendon, *Soil Survey of Madison County* (Washington, 1907), 6.

[51]*Pamphlet on Location of West Tennessee Agricultural Station and Model Farm.* Brief in behalf of Madison County.

portation facilities. Judge Senter of Humboldt introduced the bill to establish this branch of the University of Tennessee and it was understood that the station was to be in Gibson County, but after much excitement in the papers, public meetings, such as the one at the courthouse in Jackson attended by Governor Patterson when Senator Senter spoke in behalf of Gibson County and R. F. Spragins spoke in behalf of Madison County. Finally the Shelby County delegation got behind the Madison County politicians and the site approved by the commission appointed by the legislature was considered, and the decision was made in favor of Madison.

About one hundred and eighty acres of land "admirably suited for experimental and demonstrational work" with "soils sufficiently divertified to be representative of this part of the State" was donated by the County of Madison in 1908, the buildings were started, and the experimental work with both crops and livestock were begun that year.[52] As the soil was

TABLE No. 4—LIVE STOCKS IN MADISON

	Cattle	Sheep	Swine
1830	......	......	......
1840	......	17,563	64,503
1850	3,696	14,564	56,981
1860	15,313	11,055	48,645
1870	10,672	3,558	31,906
1880	12,392	4,439	28,645
1890	13,206	10,028	24,611
1900	13,868	2,613	26,700
1910	13,468	2,509	16,234
1920	16,524	1,079	21,487
1930	12,885	376	9,837
1940	15,421	500	2,770

[52]This land was bought from John H. Pearson, W. J. Ross, and A. M. Alexander. The writer is indebted to H. A. Morgan of the Tennessee Valley Authority, C. A. Mooers of the University of Tennessee Agricultural Experiment Station, Shelby Robert, former director

TABLE No. 5—DAIRY PRODUCTS IN MADISON

	Whole Milk Sale (Pounds)	Cream Sale (Pounds)	Milk Product (Pounds)
1899*	....	....	....
1909*	....	....	....
1919	1,913,018	28,505	14,125,818
1929	3,753,315	93,784	22,434,486
1939	4,576,069	176,309	24,009,652

*Data Not Available.

depleted in the county, the experts at the Station worked out methods of restoration, answering the needs of the farmer as the problems arose from day to day. In the effort to show the usefulness of such an experimental farm to the farmers of West Tennessee, railroads ran free excursions at intervals to bring those interested to see this new work. So much interest has been created that to-day there are from ten to fifteen thousand that visit the farm annually.

During those early years when the Station was facing so much opposition, it could not have existed had it not been for the cordial support of such men as Hu C. Anderson, Sr., trustee of the University from 1909 until 1913, and I. B. Tigrett, local trustee of the University from 1913 to the present, Robert Hurt, Sterling Anderson, and J. D. Johnson. Neither could it have succeeded if it had not been for such farsighted farmers as Charlie Key, J. S. Matthews, Sr., Tom Long, M. V. B. Exum, Albert Johnson, W. R. Hawk, Marmon Pope, Bert Neely who accepted the findings of the station and made use of them. These and others like them began to treat "white" soil with potash, to plant alfalfa and crimson clover, to rotate crops under various lime and fertilizer conditions, to develop good strains of cattle, plant orchards, vegetable crops, and grow strawberries according to the suggested methods.

One of the most outstanding of the Station's discoveries was the utilization of early sown crimson clover either alone

---

of the West Tennessee Experiment Station, and Ben Hazelwood, the present director of the West Tennessee Agricultural Experiment Station, for the information about this project.

or better in a mixture with rye grass to furnish fall, winter, and early spring grazing. By this means and with spring and summer pastures of bluegrass, bermuda grass, white clover, and lespedeza, supplemented by small acreage of Sudan Grass, very nearly full year-round pasturage can be obtained, thus reducing greatly the need of both concentrates and hay for cattle.[53]

The accompanying statistics are a partial picture of the results of good methods in farming in the county. Cotton, after a century, is still a good cash crop but to-day the same amount of cotton is produced on a much smaller acreage than that upon which it was produced seventy-five years ago; corn production has remained constant (with the exception of years of drought such as 1870 and 1930); cattle produced in 1940 was almost the same amount produced in 1860 but there is a remarkable increase in the amount of milk, butter, and cream produced; sweet and irish potatoes are still produced in great quantities; tobacco has disappeared from the reports, although there were 138,632 pounds reported in 1831; market garden produce has increased from $250 in 1850, $211,519 in 1930, $65,841 in 1940; strawberries have increased within forty years until there are 1,712,068 quarts produced on 896 acres in the county. A beautiful agricultural section it is to-day and much of the credit for this is due to the expert direction of the Experiment Station under F. C. Quereau, Shelby Robert, and Ben Hazelwood, who assumed responsibility here in 1929 and has served competently since that time.

In May 1941, at the suggestion of I. B. Tigrett, the Agricultural Committee of the University of Tennessee Trustees met at the West Tennessee Agricultural Experiment Station. I. B. Tigrett, aided by Frank Caldwell, was able to convince those visitors that the station here was doing a wonderful work but that they needed more land. The result of this meeting was the purchase of additional acreage, so that there are 670 acres now upon

---

[53]Report of Director C. A. Mooers of University of Tennessee Agricultural Experiment Station. Prof. Mooers, who is responsible for the genius that went into the basic plans of the station in West Tennessee to meet the needs of West Tennessee, has been greatly aided by Prof. S. M. Bain and S. H. Essary, who have contributed to the organization of the station and its scientific research. H. A. Morgan to Hu C. Anderson, January 9, 1946.

which are located a house for the superintendent, silos, commodious barns, greenhouses, assembly hall, and other needed buildings for this model farm. From the very outset keen interest was shown in the work of the West Tennessee Agricultural Experiment Station and those people who looked upon "text-book farming" as theoretical rather than practical soon came to realize the value of the advanced procedures recommended by this institution. The whole hearted support given by the citizenry of West Tennessee served as a stimulus to spur those in charge on to accomplish much that was worthwhile and to the public generally goes a good part of the credit for the success of the West Tennessee Agricultural Experiment Station.

CHAPTER XVI

THE COURTS

A history of the courts of Madison County is merely the story of the progress of the county. The yellow pages of the court records that are filled with the old fashioned handwriting of over a century ago draw a partial picture of a group of surveyors, land speculators, lawyers, doctors, carpenters, merchants, and planters who came to the new west in 1821 to seek their fortune. These were the days when questions of law were simple, when the purpose of the court was to see that men got justice, not that they might escape it, when there were plenty of new problems confronting these builders of the West each session, but when everyone was willing to assume his share of the responsibility, and records show that they laid a sturdy foundation for their county of Madison.

The County Court is in a peculiar sense very close to the people.[1] It is the people themselves acting in a formal way through representatives elected by the voters of each district of the county. It is both legislative, or law making, and judicial or law determining in its character. The County Court in the early years of the county had a broader jurisdiction than that of today. Having jurisdiction over both civil and criminal cases, it had its own juries, grand and petit, and was a court of both original and appellate jurisdiction, cases appealed from justices of the peace being heard by the County Court from which court an appeal lay to the Circuit Court. The County Court granted licenses for the exercise of certain privileges, such as keeping ordinaries, fixed rates to be charged for food, drink, and shelter for man and beast and the rates of ferries and toll gates. Records of large business transactions are fre-

---

[1] J. T. Rothrock, Jr., "A History of the County Court of Madison County," the Jackson *Sun*, May 21, 1916. The following sketch of the County Court has been revised from the Rothrock sketch.

quently found on the pages of the minutes of the court. Credit seems to have been good, the people progressive, land cheap, taxes low, and Negroes valuable. During the early 1820's, land could be had for the asking upon the payment of fifty cents per acre, and a small incidental expense for surveys and registration. Taxes were only $12\frac{1}{2}$ cents upon every one hundred acres. Poll tax was fixed at twenty-five cents and this could be paid in squirrel skins or crow scalps.

That act of November 7, 1821, which established the County of Madison also provided for the establishment of a court of pleas and quarter sessions for the county, and pursuant to said act, the following men, having been commissioned as justices of the peace by William Carroll, the governor of the State, met at the house of Adam Alexander, about two miles west of Jackson, on December 17, 1821, and organized the court of common pleas and quarter sessions which was the first court ever held in the county: Bartholemew G. Stewart, David Jarrett, William Atchison, Robert H. Dyer, John Thomas, Adam R. Alexander, Duncan McIver, Joseph Lynn, James Trousdale, Herndon Haralson, William Braden, Samuel Taylor, William Woolfork. Herndon Haralson was elected chairman; Thomas Shannon, sheriff; Roderick McIver, clerk; John T. Porter, registrar; James Brown, ranger; William Atchison, trustee; William Griffith, coroner.

There were no fixed bounds of district with magistrates from each district in those days. All white males between the ages of 18 and 45 constituted the state militia, and were divided into Captain's companies of not less than forty and not more than ninety members. Each Captain's Company was entitled to two justices of the peace. Thus, the number of justices was dependent upon the population of the county and was not determined by fixed bounds of districts.

The problems of the early court were many. After selecting a site for the county seat, making plans for the selling of lots and the building of a court house and a jail, the greatest problem that remained was that of providing means of transportation for the community. Innumerable juries were appointed at one dollar each member per day to view and leg off a road of the first class (a stage road twenty feet wide if practicable from the situations of the ground), of the second class (twelve feet wide) to Mount Pinson or the Shannon landing on the Forked Deer, where a bridge was to be built "that would not materially obstruct the navigation of the said river." The names of Butler, Haralson, Greer, Dyer, Doak, appear on one jury right after the other to mark off the roads. In this new country in 1821, not a court session passed without at least two or three citizens appearing and either producing the wolf scalps or the witness to prove that they had killed one or more wolves in order to collect the bounty of $3 or $5 allowed for each by the laws of Tennessee. Thomas Lacy either lived in a neighborhood where the wolves were entirely too plentiful or he was an unusually good shot, for no one seems to have collected quite as much bounty money as he did.

The members of the court spent the rest of the hours that the court was in session recording stock marks, hearing cases of assault and battery, of which there were many, where the fines varied from one cent to $5, and collecting debts. The early Madison County court house might have been a log one in the wilds of the new west, but dignity and order were maintained at each court session. In June, 1822, Patrick Duffey and William Bolding were fined $2 each for contempt of court. Sheriff Thomas Shannon was fined $10 for "absenting himself from court." On September 27, 1824, John Fussell had a fight in the court yard with "one certain John Montgomery." The following day he was fined $10 for contempt of court—the excitement had disturbed the court which was in session.

As the years passed, the court sessions reflect the progress of the city, such as the subscription for 25,000 shares of stock in the Mobile and Ohio Railroad in 1853, the issuance of $12,000 eight per cent bonds in 1861 for the purpose of equipping the Home Guards of Minute Men of Madison County, and the appropriation of $4,500 for the relief of indigent families of volunteers in the Confederate Army.

There was no meeting of the court from June 4, 1862, until July 17, 1865, at which time Governor Brownlow appointed George Perkins, sheriff; P. C. McCowatt, clerk of the court; an order was given to register the voters of Madison County under the "Franchise Act" and plans were made for an election in August.[2] From 1865 to the present the history of the court has been uneventful. Probate and administrative

---

[2]Madison County Minute Book 1860-1865, entry of July 17, 1865.

matters, questions of purchase, improvement of roads, assistance to railroads and other public matters appear on the pages of the records. The county court no longer has its own juries nor does it have extensive jurisdiction. It concerns itself with the establishment and maintenance of the schools, the roads, the care of the poor, and the financial interests of the county. During its career of over a hundred years it has been the pulse of the people. When the people are agitated, the court is agitated. It reflects the progress and intelligence of the county, and its record is one of which the county may well be proud.

Good roads is one of the subjects upon which the court is uniformly agreed, and the people have always been vitally interested in this movement. Wide interest in gravel roads was aroused in 1901 when a small portion of Neely street just outside the corporation limits of Jackson was graveled. In 1903, the county court, having been empowered by an act of the legislature of 1903, mostly through the efforts of Stoddert Caruthers, issued 4 per cent bonds for $300,000, payable forty years after date for the purpose of graveling and grading county roads. In 1907 an election was held in the county at which the voters of the county voted that additional bonds of $200,000 be issued for the building and maintenance of good roads. With the expenditure of $500,000 on good roads, carrying out J. J. Williams's plan of building each road out five miles, Madison County took rank as the foremost builder of good roads in West Tennessee and even attracted national attention, for this was a new project in the country. At one time there was an experiment in the county, under national supervision in general and Sam Lancaster in particular, of macadamizing five miles of the roads leading from the city.

In 1905, the county judge supplanted the county chairman. He acts as probate judge and as presiding officer of the quarterly courts. Judge Thomas McCorry, Sr., was the first county judge and served from 1905 until his resignation in December, 1913, with faithfulness and ability. Judge A. W. Stovall served as judge from 1913 to 1918; Judge J. T. Rothrock, Jr., from 1918 to 1923; Judge Karl Wilkes, from 1923 to 1932; Judge Frank Johnson, from 1932 to 1934; Judge August Wilde, from 1934 to the present.

The Circuit Court of Madison County was established by an act of the legislature passed November 4, 1821, and was called the "Court of Law and Equity for the Eighth Circuit."[3] A commission was issued by General Carroll, governor, to Judge Joshua Haskell, November 14, 1821, and the oath of office was administered to him by John Smith, the presiding justice of the Court of Pleas and Quarter Sessions of Rutherford County. The first session was held in the home of Adam Alexander. The officers of the court besides Judge Haskell were Thomas Shannon, sheriff, and Beverly Randolph, clerk. Upon the organization of the court the following attorneys were admitted to the bar: J. W. Clark, Alex B. Bradford, James Jones, Robert Hughes, and Arch B. Hall. Alex Bradford was named as the first attorney-general or district attorney, at that time called solicitor-general. He was succeeded by H. W. McCorry who held the place for several years.

The minutes of the Circuit Court reveal many interesting stories of the people and the customs of the day, such as the first case of the state against Squire Dawson who was convicted of petty larceny and sentenced to be taken "to the common whipping post on this day between the hours of three and five in the evening and to receive twenty lashes well laid on his bare back, that he be rendered infamous and then be imprisoned one hour";[4] such as the first divorce cases filed by Patsy Dunn against Joseph Dunn and James Ricketts against Jenny Ricketts in 1822; such as fines for betting on cards, roulette, "basoon" and the wheel of fortune; such as the case of Adam Lowery in 1824, who was convicted of stealing a horse and sentenced to be taken to the public whipping post and there receive thirty-nine lashes, that he be branded upon the brawn of the thumb with "H. T.", that he be sent to jail for thirty days and that he be made to stand in the pillory two hours of every three days out of seven, that he be rendered infamous and made to pay the cost of his prosecution; such as the case of Thomas Jamison who killed his intended father-in-law and with his accomplice was convicted of murder, so he and the accomplice were taken to "a convenient place near the town of Jackson" and hanged; such as the case of James Wright in 1826 who when convicted

---

[3]H. C. Pearson, "Circuit and Chancery Courts," Jackson *Sun,* May 21, 1916. This sketch has furnished invaluable information to the writer.

[4]Madison County Minute Book 1821-1828.

of manslaughter was fined $25 and branded on the thumb with the letter "M."[5]

The Circuit Court records of 1861-1865 show that John Read signed the minutes of May 16, 1861, at which time the court adjourned "to court in course." When the time for the September meeting arrived, the clerk opened the court, but no judge appeared from day to day, therefore the clerk adjourned "to court in course." The same procedure took place at the January and March terms. Conditions were too chaotic for courts to function normally. No more meetings of the court took place until George Perkins produced an order from Governor Brownlow to open court in 1865.

In the intervening years Madison was in the 12th judicial circuit. The 16th judicial circuit was created by the Acts of 1905, Chapter 57, and the jurisdiction of the judge of that circuit was given general common law and statutory jurisdiction in all civil cases arising in Madison County, leaving jurisdiction of cases of a criminal character to the jurisdiction of the judge of the 12th judicial circuit to which Madison had theretofore belonged. Judge S. J. Everett was the first judge of the new Court, serving until 1918, when he was succeeded by Judge R. B. Baptist of Covington, who was succeeded in turn by Judge Lamar Spragins. Thus, there is a split jurisdiction in Madison County which is very unusual.

The jurisdiction of the "Court of Law and Equity" for the Eighth Circuit was of a legal and equitable nature from 1821 to 1846.[6] On January 21, 1846, the legislature passed an act creating the chancery court for Madison County and provided that sessions were to be held in Jackson twice each year. The first session of the court was accordingly held in Jackson in May, 1846, with Honorable Andrew McCampbell sitting as chancellor. Upon the organization of the court, General Gibbs, R. J. Hays, and George W. Bond were enrolled as attorneys. During the Civil War litigation in the chancery was at a minimum and for several years no session was held,

---

[5]*Ibid.*

[6]*Acts of Tennessee,* 1845, Chapter 82. According to an account in the Jackson *Gazette,* September 4, 1824, Herndon Haralson asked for Chancery and Supreme Court in the Western District, for some of the memorialists had to travel 200 miles to these courts for they were all in Middle Tennessee.

in fact none of the courts functioned during the war. Judge John Read signed the minutes of February 18, 1861. No chancellor appeared at the August term (1861), so the clerk opened court for three consecutive days and kept it open until 4 o'clock in the afternoon but no chancellor appeared, so he adjourned "to court in course" and no meeting was held until August, 1865, when the court was reorganized by Hon. J. W. Harris. At this time attorneys who entered their names were Samuel McClanahan, Henry Brown, W. H. Stephens, J. L. H. Tomlin, and J. R. Stephens. In 1875 Madison was detached from the regular chancery divisions and there was created the Common Law and Chancery Court for Madison County alone. This court existed until 1886, during which time Judges Henry McCorry and T. C. Muse were judges.

Tennessee has been divided and redivided by the legislature in chancery division and the sessions of the various courts in the various counties have changed so often that the list of divisions and dates becomes a maze of figures.[7] In 1931 the Fourteenth Chancery Division of Tennessee was created and Judge N. R. Barham was appointed Chancellor, serving until September 1932 when he was succeeded by Judge DeWitt Henderson.[8]

Records of the Supreme Court during the early years of the life of the county carry little detail.[9] The first meeting of the Supreme Court of Tennessee in Jackson was in 1830, at which time Judge Whyte, Haywood, Emmerson, Peck and Catron were present. Records of 1832 show that the court was composed of John Catron, Robert Whyte, Jacob Peck, and Nathan Green. In 1835, Nathan Green was presiding, with John Catron and Jacob Peck sitting with him. An attempt was made at the Constitutional Convention of 1834 to move the location of this court. It was proposed to strike out "Jack-

---

[7] As the years passed Madison was in the 6th Chancery Division in 1858; the Common Law and Chancery Court from 1876 to 1886; in the 9th Chancery Division in 1886; in the 8th Chancery Division in 1896; in the 10th Chancery Division in 1905; in the 14th Chancery Division in 1931.

[8] A list of the Chancellors may be found in the Appendix.

[9] *Acts of Tennessee,* 1829, Chapter 104, provided for a Supreme Court of Errors and Appeals at specified places. Jackson was one of the named places. This said court was not to possess original jurisdiction.

son" and substitute "Purdy" as the seat of the Supreme Court in West Tennessee, but the motion failed. As the pre-Civil War days passed and death and resignations took men off the bench, other names appeared such as W. B. Reese, W. B. Turley, Robert J. McKinney, A. W. O. Totten, R. J. Caruthers, W. B. Harris, Archibald Wright.

No session of the court was held during the Civil War but on the termination of the war Governor Brownlow appointed the following judges: Samuel Milligan of Greeneville, J. O. Shackleford of Clarksville, Alvin Hawkins of Huntingdon. In 1868 by legislative enactment, the court, together with all records, books, furnishings, et cetera, were removed from Jackson to Brownsville, for Jackson was too great a stronghold of Confederate sentiment for a reconstruction government to leave any important business to be conducted here. When the new Constitution of 1870 went into effect, the place of holding was returned to Jackson, the place selected for the court of West Tennessee to sit. Through the years of the last half of the nineteenth century and the twentieth century the other members of the court were: W. O. P. Nicolson, Peter Turney, T. A. Nelson, James W. Deaderick, Thomas Freeman, J. L. T. Sneed, Robert McFarland, W. C. Caldwell, D. L. Snodgrass, Horace H. Lurton, William C. Folks, William McAlister, W. D. Beard, M. M. Neil, John Wilkes, John K. Shields, A. S. Buchanan, Grafton Green, C. L. Lansden, Samuel C. Williams, A. R. Gholson, Francis Frentress, Frank P. Hall, Colin P. McKinney, Alex Chambliss, William L. Cook, D. W. DeHaven, M. L. Bachman, William Swiggart, Alan M. Prewitt, Frank H. Gailor.

Early in its history Jackson became known as "the temple of law" as there were so many courts that met in the town. As the years passed, the population and business of the county and West Tennessee increased which caused more cases to be brought into the courts, so other courts were organzied to meet the problems of a growing state. Jackson was again and again chosen as the meeting place for these newly created courts. By an Act of the Legislature of 1895, Chapter 76, the court of Chancery Appeals was established. Jackson was the meeting place in West Tennessee for this appellate court which had jurisdiction over all appeals in equity cases from the lower courts in West Tennessee except those involving state revenue.

This court was followed by the Court of Civil Appeals created by an Act of the Legislature of 1907, Chapter 82. This court which had five judges had limited appellate jurisdiction over civil cases and met on the first Monday in January in Jackson. The Court of Civil Appeals was succeeded by the present Court of Appeals composed of nine judges authorized to sit *en banc* or sections of three in Jackson, Nashville, and Knoxville. Created by an Act of Legislature of 1925, Chapter 100, the jurisdiction of the Court of Appeals was broadened greatly.

The fact that Jackson has been the meeting place of the Federal Courts of West Tennessee has also contributed to the making of Jackson into a "temple of law."[10] In 1801, Tennessee was divided into two judicial districts known as East Tennessee and West Tennessee and the Sixth Judicial District was established of Kentucky, Ohio, and Tennessee. By an Act of Congress of June 1838, Tennessee was divided into three districts to be known as the Eastern, Middle, and Western Districts of Tennessee. During the same year an Act of Congress was passed requiring a session of the District Court to be held at Jackson in September of each year. The first term of the Federal Court in West Tennessee was in the Presbyterian Church at Jackson.

Originally there was created a District and Circuit Court and Judge for each with the District Court having jurisdiction principally over criminal offenses and the Circuit Court principally over law and equity. Separate dockets were kept for each court. The District Judge however, under designation of the Circuit Judge, would generally try both dockets so Congress passed an Act imposing the duty on the District Judge to try both Criminal and Law and Equity cases.

The first terms of the District and Circuit Courts for the Western District of Tennessee held after the Civil War were held at Jackson, Tennessee on the 28th of April, 1879 with Judges E. S. Hammond and John Baxter presiding. As the United States government had no place to hold court here, the terms were held in the Supreme Court room of the Madison County court house. On November 23, 1883, the Federal

---

[10]The writer is indebted to Mrs. Elizabeth J. Trice for the preparation of a sketch of the Federal Courts of the Eastern Division of the Western District of Tennessee.

government bought of H. W. McCorry and others the lot west of the Madison County courthouse, upon which was constructed the post office that was completed in 1885. During the tenure in office of Judge Harry B. Anderson additional land was condemned adjacent to the old post office and court building and the present building erected in 1933.

In 1921, soon after Judge Ross's appointment the records of the Eastern Division were moved from the Memphis office to Jackson and the clerk's offices in the old post office building were permanently established.[11] Judges of the Circuit and District Courts who have presided over court in the Federal Court at Jackson include: Judges John McNairy, Morgan W. Brown, West H. Humphreys, Conally F. Trigg, H. H. Emmons, John Baxter, Howell E. Jackson, E. S. Hammond, John E. McCall, J. W. Ross, Harry B. Anderson, John D. Martin, and Marion S. Boyd.

The Eastern Division of the Western District of Tennessee of the Federal Court has had an important role to fill since the office was established in Jackson. The volume of these cases in shown by the fact that approximately five hundred War Risk Insurance cases were brought into this office after World War I; one hundred fifty tracts of land were condemned for the Milan Ordnance Defense Plant and Storage Depot and Camp Tyson at Paris; land for an auxiliary landing field near Ridgely was also condemned; condemnations of the Tennessee Valley Authority for land to be used for flooding, seasonal flooding, malaria control connected with the Kentucky Dam.

The meetings of the Federal Courts, the Appellate Courts together with the other courts of original jurisdiction made many a day in the history of Jackson "Court Day."

---

[11]D. E. Mitchell of Henderson, was deputy in charge of the offices in Jackson in 1921 under Sam Johnson who was then clerk. Other clerks included: A. O. Matthews, Alex Y. Scott, Finis E. Wilson, Sam Gordon, Holice Powell, and William L. Johnson. Resident deputies included: D. E. Mitchell, John H. Trice, Mrs. Elizabeth J. Trice (who had served as clerical assistant without pay since 1930), and Mrs. Anne Henry Sawyer.

CHAPTER XVII

JOHN A. MURRELL, THE OUTLAW

Strange as it may seem, the American people are attracted to books, papers, and movies which relate the exploits of an outlaw or a desperado. One of the most fascinating figures of a century ago operated in eight states of the old Southwest, but he called Madison County his home. John A. Murrell, the "Western Land Pirate" of the nineteenth century, came to this county from Middle Tennessee, but he lived here for years. Phelan, historian of early Tennessee, says that "it is beyond the power of historic research to separate the false from the true in all that has come down to us"[1] about Murrell, but fact or fiction, the stories of his exploits are more popular reading a century later than those of some statesmen of the same years.

A few brief court records, two or three newspaper items, and the narratives written by the captor, Virgil A. Stewart, are the only written records of this "Land Pirate" of the Western District. The rest is tradition or "facts" which when traced to their origin are all based upon story after story that in the beginning came from the Virgil A. Stewart story.

John A. Murrell was born in Middle Tennessee in 1804. His father was a Methodist preacher of good moral character; his mother, according to Stewart's facts about Murrell, "learnt" him and all her children to steal as soon as they could walk, so that by the time he became of age he was a "confirmed evildoer and formally adopted robbery as a profession."[2] Murrell's name first appears in the court records of Williamson County in 1823 when he was fined fifty dollars for "riot," at which time three Murrells, one of which was the infamous John A., were bound in a sum of $200 to keep peace. Two years later he was in court for gaming. Soon he was indicted for stealing

---

[1] Phelan, *History of Tennessee*, 347.
[2] *Ibid.*

a black mare from a widow in Williamson County. The case was taken to Davidson County on change of venue where he was convicted, flogged until he bled, branded on the thumbs, H T, and sentenced to twelve months in prison.[3] In later years a small boy who witnessed the branding recalled the scene in the crowded court room, the judge seated on a high seat surrounded by a hand railing, and the prisoner's box near by. John Murrell, handsomely dressed but quite unconcerned, was conducted to the prisoner's box, instructed to lay his hand on the railing while the sheriff "took from his pocket a piece of new hemp and bound Murrell's hand securely to the railing." The eye witness continued:

> In a short while a big negro named Jeffry came in bringing a tinner's stove that looked like a lantern and placed it on the floor. Being anxious to see all that was going on, I climbed upon the railing close to Murrell. Mr. Horton, the sheriff, took from the little stove the branding iron, a long instrument, which looked very much like the soldering irons now used by tinners. He looked at the iron which was red hot and then put it on Murrell's hand. The skin fried like meat. Mr. Horton held it there until the smoke rose probably two feet when he removed the iron. Mr. Horton then untied Murrell's hand. Murrell, who had up to this time never moved, produced a white handkerchief and wiped his hand several times. It was all over, and the sheriff took Murrell back to jail where he was yet to suffer punishment by being whipped and placed in the pillory.[4]

Murrell, who is said to have read criminal law in order to avoid its dangers and had learned to preach revival sermons while his confederates stole the horses, now began to realize more than ever the value of "friends" in his "business" of horse stealing and slave stealing.[5] According to Virgil Stewart's story, he also might have been classified as a professional murderer, but this part of the tale may be merely tradition.

---

[3] Williams, *Beginnings of West Tennessee*, 246.

[4] Nashville *Banner*, March 20, 1921. A story of Douglas Anderson, who was quoting C. W. Nance, the boy who had witnessed the branding.

[5] According to tradition, Murrell once occupied the pulpit of the Presbyterian Church at Denmark and held the attention of an audience while his gang stole the worshippers' horses. Neither church records nor tradition tells whether he used the Eighth Commandment for a text.

Although the outlaw was supposed to have operated in seven or eight neighboring states, Murrell made Madison County in the Western District his home. He kept the corral near Hickman County, Kentucky, but sent his horses to Jackson and the surrounding country to be sold. He made big money stealing slaves, telling each one of his plan to resell them three or four times, and then divide the money with them and let them escape to the free North. When the slave became too well known, that is, after he had been restolen and resold several times and too many advertisements appeared in the newspapers for him, then Murrell would select some quiet spot in a lonely road, kill the slave, "debowel him," fill the cavity with rocks, and dump him into some convenient stream. It seemed that the secret of the desperado's success was his "thoroughness" with which he destroyed condemning evidence.

By 1834 Murrell had either become so bold in his crimes or the citizens of the District were desperate, for the planters could not sit quietly by and have their most valuable possessions, horses and slaves, cleverly stolen by this Dr. Jeckel of the Western District—this handsome 5 feet 10½ inch, dark haired, blue eyed "princely fellow," this "noble leader," this "wonderous man" who was unrivalled in mental powers, this "man great from force of his own mental powers" rather than from his station in the world, this man who was universally beloved by his friends.[6] Murrell now made the mistake of stealing two slaves from Rev. John Henning. Virgil A. Stewart, a former resident of the county and a friend of the Hennings', entered into the hunt for the slaves, fell in with Murrell on his way to a rendezvous with the "speculators," wormed his way into Murrell's confidence and went with him to his Council House on as island in a lake in the swamps across the Mississippi Here he met the lordly band of "speculators," took the oath of allegiance to the clan, obtained a list of this Mystic Clan from Murrel himself, and then managed the arrest of the great "Land Pirate."[7]

---

[6]Virgil Stewart, in the *History of Virgil Stewart* by H. R. Howard (N.Y., 1836), succeeds in making Murrell an attractive person.

[7]This was part of the story told by Stewart in his testimony in court. Many people in the community thought that Murrell would surely hang. Milton Brown said that his client was guilty of slave stealing and not murder.

Murrell was arrested in Florence, Alabama, confined in prison in Brownsville, and placed on trial in Jackson in July and August, 1834. An item from the Jackson *Truth Teller* copied in the Randolph *Recorder* gives the best contemporary account of the exciting trial of that day:

The trial of this far-famed personage closed last week in the circuit court of this county, and resulted in his conviction and a sentence to confinement and labor in the penitentiary for ten years. The crime charged against him was Negro stealing. The high reputation he had acquired as one of the talented leaders of a lawless band who infest the banks of the Mississippi and the incident connected with the crime charged imparted an interest to the trial seldom if ever before witnessed in this community. His name was associated with all that was bold and desperate in villany. He had been regarded as a master spirit in an organized system which had repeatedly deprived our citizens of their property, and evaded every effort made for the detection of the felony. He had been taken, broke out of jail and was again retaken in a neighboring state, engaged as was supposed in

From an old print in Coates's *Outlaw Years*.

directing the operations of his accustomed employment. Everything associated with his character was calculated in the highest degree to inflame the public mind.

When he was brought to the bar for the trial the courthouse was thronged to overflowing by the deeply anxious spectators who were brought together by the occasion. The prisoner informed the court that by reason of his poverty he was unable to employ counsel and his honour, Judge (Joshua) Haskell, who was presiding under the humane provision of our law, assigned Col. Read, Mr. Hodge, and Mr. Brown (Milton) of the Jackson bar and Mr. Harris of Brownsville, to appear in his defence. Gen. (Alex) Bradford and Maj. Martin appeared as prosecuting counsel on behalf of the state. The evidence on part of the state chiefly depended on an individual witness. This witness gave at length the incidents of a most romantic adventure, by which he had wormed himself into the confidence of Murrell, and obtained from him a confession of his guilt. He occupied five or six hours in giving his testimony and whatever difference of opinion may exist as to the merit of the witness, all will admit that his story, if well written out and properly embellished, would form a legend in real life unsurpassed by anything produced by fiction. The witness made too much effort at display, otherwise the story would have been finely told.

The principal scene of the adventure was near the Mississippi River. The witness started in search of the Negroes, which had been stolen and before he had traveled far, accident threw him in company with Murrell who was ignorant of his name and his business. He represented himself as residing when at home in the State of Mississippi and soon made the impression on the mind of Murrell that he was seeking employment under the auspices of that predatory band for which the western bank of the Mississippi had become so famous. Under this artifice he gained the confidence of Murrell, who seemed to feel secure in his plans, and believed they were too deep and well arranged for detection. He had his whole mind and heart engaged in his employment, and dwelt with much satisfaction on the prospect of future wealth and the high distinction to which his powers would elevate him among his fellows. He thought Negro stealing when properly directed entirely safe, and the sure road to fortune. And as proof of this he gave many examples of splendid success, and among others disclosed the means by which he had decoyed off the Negroes which the witness was then in search of.

The witness returned to this county, disclosed the adventures and Murrell's confession, and upon this Murrell was arrested and convicted.

The argument of counsel both for the state and the prisoner were able and interesting. The ladies of our town were present during the argument and partook of the rich intellectual feast which the occasion presented. Everything seemed calculated to impart importance to the trial, and make all feel the majesty of the law exerting itself to bring a hardened offender to justice.[8]

A notice of the trial that appeared in the *National Banner* and *Nashville Whig* shows how wide-spread the interest was in this desperado of Madison County:

> This notorious public offender John A. Murrell has been lately tried before Judge Haskell at Jackson, and convicted of Negro stealing and sentenced to confinement in the penitentiary at hard labor for ten years. He belonged to the organized band of Mississippi robbers and thieves, who have lately infested the coast between Memphis and Randolph, principally the Arkansas side.[9]

Murrell was convicted of Negro stealing, but not of murder of which the star witness, Stewart, was accusing him. The Madison County Court record of July 29, 1834 read:

> "After due trial, the court passed the sentence according to the verdict of the jury and the law of the land—that the said defendant John A. Murrell convicted as aforesaid do undergo confinement at hard labor in the Penitentiary house of the state for a term of ten years."[10]

The Sheriff was ordered by the court to take the defendant to jail and to the Penitentiary as soon as possible. He was received August 17, 1834. In April 1837, his case was appealed to the Supreme Court and Murrell was brought to Jackson for trial on appeal by J. S. Lyon, the Sheriff of Madison County. William Yerger and J. W. Chambers defended him but the conviction was affirmed and he was returned to the penitentiary where he remained until he was discharged from the Nashville Penitentiary April 3, 1844.[11] He then went to Pikesville, in Bledsoe County, and followed the

---

[8]Randolph *Recorder*, September 5, 1834. According to the Stewart story, Brown's defense was based upon the argument that Stewart took the oath of the Clan and had then betrayed the leader; therefore Stewart's word in court was not worth anything. Brown's attack upon the character of Stewart caused Stewart to write his *own* defense.

[9]*National Banner and Nashville Whig*, August 12, 1834.

[10]Madison County Minute Book 1834. The records of this trial were mysteriously cut from this book while the books were in storage when the present court house was being built, but this record was copied before the deletion.

[11]Williams, *Beginnings of West Tennessee*, 249; *Journal of the House of Representatives of the State of Tennessee* (October, 1845-46).

blacksmith trade until his death a short while later. To some of the friends that he made there, he admitted his thieving career, but he continually denied that he was guilty of murder.[12]

After following every clue wherein it was possible, the writer is reminded of the fact that good historical fact is only an incident that is told by two eye-witnesses soon after the event occurred without collaboration. Writing in 1920, Park Marshall, after years of extensive investigation, including interviews by himself and J. G. Cisco with old citizens in the vicinity of this "Land Pirate's" operations, was convinced that Murrell and his gang were merely common thieves, secretly stealing horses and Negroes, that he was not a wholesale murderer. All the stories of murder and the plans for the Negro insurrection eminate from Virgil Stewart's story by which he received more fame than he could have ever attained merely as the adventurer who captured a Negro thief or a horse thief.[13] Could it have been possible that Stewart received great pleasure out of telling such a thrilling tale of his own exploits? This was the "New West" in 1834 and the people loved an exciting story! Some people believed that Stewart was once a member of Murrell's gang in his peculiar line of business and for some unknown reason lost favor in the sight of the leader, so he wrote his story to get revenge upon Murrell.

A few sentences from a contemporary newspaper give evidence of the fact that many people at that time did not believe Virgil Stewart's story, although it had created a feverish excitement:

> We have now before us a letter from a gentleman in Denmark which states that 'Stewart and Murrell lived two years in that vicinity within 2½ miles of each other, before and at the time of the great trip taken, and that they were both strangers at Estanaula.'[14]

The Randolph *Recorder* of November 21, 1835, reviewed the story as Stewart told it but concluded:

> We wish he had been convicted under different circumstances. For although the law may recognize as right, the abuse and betrayal of confidence pledged as inviolate, in order to bring an offender to justice

---

[12]W. E. McElwee, March 26, 1921, to Douglas Anderson.
[13]Park Marshall, "John A. Murrell and Daniel Crenshaw," *Tennessee Historical Magazine*, VI (1920), 6.
[14]Randolph *Recorder*, January 8, 1836.

yet there are many who look upon the betrayer with coldness and distrust. . . . We think the whole affair should be read with many grains of allowance, for although the whole of it may be true, *we* are disinclined to believe a word of it.[15]

The Randolph editor thought it a pity that Stewart did not pocket his "silver penny" that he made out of his book, instead of stalking about the country hunting certificates of his own character and destroying the character of others. Upon a recent visit to Jackson, when he rashly declared that there was not a half dozen honest men in Madison County, he was called to account by bystanders and ordered to leave town. The editor admitted that some good had come from the Murrell book, but doubted seriously that it had been published with any good intentions. The editors of the Paris paper and the Nashville *Banner* thought that there was undue excitement in relation to Virgil A. Stewart and an attempt on his life near Paris as Stewart told the story in his book. The editor concluded: "No unprejudiced man, it seems to us, could read the story without feeling satisfied of its utter want of truth and it is so considered throughout the whole neighborhood where this 'Eleven men in Buckran' transaction is alleged to have taken place."[16]

How true was the prediction that if the story were well written and embellished upon, it would form a legend in real life unsurpassed by fiction!

---

[15]Randolph *Recorder*, December 25, 1835.
[16]*Ibid.*, December 4, 25, 1835.

CHAPTER XVIII

CRIME IN MADISON

A shortage of time and space prevents a lengthy discussion of crime and criminals in Madison County, but the volume would be incomplete without a few references to one unsolved murder and a few famous hangings.

On the night of February 3, 1859, the usual quiet of the supposedly well-behaved city of Jackson was upset between the hours of six and nine, in the evening, for one of the most cold-blooded murders that ever occurred in this community was committed. George E. Miller, clerk in the Jackson Branch of the Union Bank, was murdered and the bank was robbed of $20,860 in notes on out of town banks and $4,545 in gold, mostly twenty-dollar pieces. A mass meeting was held at the court house on the following Wednesday at which time the citizens attempted to adopt efficient measures to extend and continue the investigation of all facts and circumstances connected with the murder and robbery.

George Miller, the young banker whose deportment and integrity was unquestionable, had a lodging place in one of the rooms of the bank (then located where the New Southern Hotel now stands). Evidently, Mr. Miller had been persuaded to go into the bank and make out a check, when the murderer came up from behind and struck him with a heavy hammer from which blow his head was crushed. The vault was then looted, the check which had probably just been written was torn out of the book, the key to the door between the bank and Miller's room hidden under the pillow of the bed, and the intruder escaped. Excitement ran high in town. The papers of the day and diaries of the day were filled with stories of the rumor, but no one then or now knows who killed George Miller.[1]

---

[1] Memphis *Daily Appeal*, February 6, 9, 1859.

During the past century an interesting change has taken place in the method of punishment of crime.[2] To-day when an electrocution takes place, it is well nigh impossible to obtain entrance into the rooms. For this reason it is hard for us to realize that a century ago everyone came from miles around to witness a hanging and that there was such a place near Jackson as a "hanging grounds." One of the most interesting hangings here was that of Reilly about 1838. The criminal had been convicted of murder after confessing to the crime while intoxicated and denying it when he became sober. The crowd gathered on the outskirts of the town, just west of the Gulf, Mobile, and Ohio Railroad station on Highway 70. Although the victim had been convicted of the crime, he still maintained that he was innocent and prayed that the Lord save him by some sign from heaven. The gallows was prepared and the rope was about to be placed about his neck when a horrible storm arose, such a bad one that the crowd dispersed, but the victim remained on the spot until the storm abated when the officers and crowd returned and proceeded with the ceremony—the hanging. Years later a man on his death bed in Obion County confessed that he had committed the murder for which Reilly had been hanged.

In 1875, Milton McLean was convicted of the murder of Thaddeus Pope, and sentenced to be hanged on January 7, 1876.[3] Such an immense crowd gathered to witness this event that the original purpose of laws and courts—trying to prove to a community that crime does not pay—was almost forgotten on this day, for the crowd was fascinated with the pomp and ceremony of the occasion and the dignity and bravery that was displayed by the prisoner. On the banks of those "sleepless waters" of the Forked Deer one half mile south of the court house on Liberty, gallows were erected at the "hanging grounds." A contemporary paper reported that friends called to see the victim, that various ministers tried to get him to profess religion, that he remained cool and indifferent to the course of events. When the hour came, the prisoner dressed in a neat black suit, left the jail, mounted the waiting wagon, and seated

---

[2] Mrs. Otis Trentham, "Some Notes on Crime and Punishment in Madison," a paper read before the Madison County Historical Society at the February meeting, 1946.

[3] The Jackson *Sun*, January 7, 1876. C. R. Bray Collection.

himself between the two ministers on the coffin. A melancholy cortege this was indeed as a company of guards composed of Mayor King, the sheriff riding a gray horse, and the entire police force took positions to form a circle about the wagon.

Arriving at the hanging grounds, the prisoner ascended the scaffold and said to Sam Brown who had erected the scaffold, "I hope, Sam that you have made a good job of it." To which the carpenter answered, "I have done my best." Rev. McNair read the scripture, the crowd joined in the singing of "There is a fountain filled with blood," Dr. Slater prayer, the sheriff read the legal sentence of the courts and asked the prisoner again if he had anything to say, to which he answered as he had done many times before, "Nothing." Ten minutes remained until the hour of the execution—one o'clock, so each person present waited in silence as these last precious minutes were marked off by the watches and the clocks. At the appointed time, the prisoner stepped forward and aided the sheriff in adjusting the rope about his own neck. The black veil was thrown over the face and the fatal drop fell. Death by strangulation did not occur until twenty-five minutes later. At intervals during these minutes, the doctor examined the pulse, finding life until twenty-five minutes after one o'clock, when Dr. Collins and Dr. Lanier pronounced him dead. The body was cut down at 1:20 and the remains turned over to the wife and friends who took it to Hardeman county for buriel.[4]

In 1877, a negro, Min Wilson was hanged for killing Capt. Perkins, the brother of Sheriff George Perkins. In 1904, Ben Springfield was hanged for shooting his wife. Two lynchings occurred in the courthouse yard, Eliza Woods, in the 1880's and John Brown in 1891.

The pioneer people who came to this wilderness were impatient towards such crimes as horse stealing, slave stealing, and murder. The people came from far and wide to see a human being pay the supreme penalty for a crime. The very fact that there were public whipping posts, a pillory, public hangings here a century ago makes the story of such crimes and punishments of interest to citizens today, for the purposes of courts and laws have not changed, but their methods have changed completely.

---

[4]*Ibid.*

CHAPTER XIX

MEDICINE IN MADISON

Early travelers and prospectors of the Western District paid particular notice to the locations of springs, the rich lands, and healthful sites for future homes. They showed that they had good business sense when they chose lands rich enough upon which they could make a living and common sense when they chose sites where they could live. One of the first bits of advice to those who came west to settle, even those who came to Jamestown in 1607, was to select a healthful site. In 1826, James Deaderick considered Jackson "too low and too near the Forked Deer to be healthy until the swamps, which extend a mile or more in width, should be cleared." At such a point as this though, business advantages had to enter, produce had to be taken to market, the Forked Deer was the best way that was then available, so settle they did on the Forked Deer and hoped to clear the swamps later.

The planter and his wife had a "Domestic Medicine Chest" that they used when occasions demanded. This chest, filled with medicines made from native herbs, castor oil, and "painkillers," in the hands of people with a level head and common sense, was invaluable to the family unit. People acquired practical knowledge of home remedies, passed them down from one generation to the next or copied them into a diary, as R. H. Cartmell did, from agricultural magazines. The few doctors (five were listed here in 1824 and 1834) and the home remedies must have been adequate for the climate, or at least sufficient to meet the emergencies, for in the summer of 1824, a small epidemic of billious fever broke out in Jackson and the vicinity, and although the five doctors were very busy, a paper of August twenty-four reported that the conditions were improving. Doctors T. H. Wynne and James Pullen were practicing here then.[1] In 1831, the *Southern Statesman* reported that the health of the community was excellent, and though there was a population of seven hundred there had not been a single death among the adults; that the cases of fever were few, seldom fatal.[2]

A cheerful report upon the health of the community seemed to have been a powerful argument by which people from the older sections were convinced that this was the place to settle. In 1832, the editor of the *Southern Statesman* reported that the Western District continued healthy, that the cases of disease were few, that these were attended with as little fatality as could be expected.[3] One account of a camp meeting read: "It is a source of pleasure and congratulation to the citizens of the Western District that our population is healthy beyond any former period since its settlement. We attended the camp meeting near Denmark this week, whence there were between two and three thousand persons and during the meeting we heard of but one case of fever, a slight attack on a delicate lady who has since recovered."[4]

Because of the fact that the medical schools were few in number in the early part of the nineteenth century, many of the doctors gained their professional knowledge and skill through apprenticeship, which was supervised by medical societies. Harvard and the University of Pennsylvania were the outstanding schools in this country, but many an ambitious young man did not get to attend these good schools, although even they had very low standards in the early part of the 18th century. In 1827, the Paris *West Tennessean* was pleading that the State Legislature establish a Medical Board so that those who entered the profession could be examined like the lawyers were. "If a lawyer loses his suit, he can appeal to a higher tribunal; but in the other case [the doctor's] there is NO APPEAL."[5] Action was taken upon this and other similar pleas, for the Legislature of 1830 organized the Medical Society of Tennessee and Board of Censors. By 1831 the local paper announced a meeting of the Medical Board in Jackson and invited all the gentlemen who wished to become "Licen-

---

[1] Jackson *Gazette*, August 24, 1824.
[2] *Southern Statesman*, September 17, 1831.
[3] *Ibid.*, September 8, 1832.
[4] Jackson *Gazette*, September 5, 1829.
[5] Paris *West Tennessean*, November 15, 1827.

see" in Medicine to present themselves for examinations.⁶ That the professional men of this county took an active part in the aims of the State Medical Society is shown by the fact that Doctors James Young, Robert Fenner and Loring were charter members of the organization. Dr. Young must have been a promising man in his profession, one with energy and ability, for he was on the committee to adopt the code of by-laws for the organization and was also dean of the board of censors of the Western District.⁷ He was also a progressive physician. In 1831, one case of small pox appeared in the county. Dr. Young vaccinated the other members of the family with "kind pock" matter and not a single member of the family of those so treated took the disease. The whole community felt that it owed its thanks to Dr. Young. That his ability was recognized abroad is shown by the fact that in the same month, Dr. Young was appointed surgeon for the staff of the 14th Brigade of the Tennessee Militia.⁸

Very little is known about the doctors and dentists of those early days in the Western District. Court records show that bills of $20, $30, and $40 were paid when estates were settled, diaries contain entries of the visits of the doctors to members of the family and the slaves, and newspapers carry advertisements of the opening of new offices. In the newspapers of 1824 can be found the name of Dr. Childress, whose shop was above Wilson and Stewart'ts store. He informed the youthful community that he would practice "medicine suitable to the diseases of this climate."⁹ The papers of 1831 published notices of Dr. Gillespie who, having permanently located in Jackson to practice medicine, offered his services to the public;¹⁰ Dr. E. B. Church who, having practiced in New York and Philadelphia, was offering his services "to insert artificial sets, fill, plug, and extract" teeth. Dr. Church, who boasted of having the most complete and splendid set of instruments in the Western country, was willing to visit the ladies at their residences if requested and to make country calls when "the

---

⁶*Southern Statesman*, March 5, 1831.
⁷*Transactions of Medical Society of State of Tennessee for 1830* (Nashville, 1830), 8.
⁸*Southern Statesman*, April 9, 1831.
⁹Jackson *Gazette*, December 13, 1824.
¹⁰*Southern Statesman*, April 9, June 19, 1831.

horse was provided."[11] In December, 1854, David Meriwether paid $28 to Doctors Newbern and Murchison for bleeding, blistering, and prescribing quinine and cough syrup for a Negro, George. Not long afterwards the family records show that a coffin was bought for George.[12]

The name of Dr. Alexander Campbell is associated with the beginning of this county, both in the field of medicine and the field of religion. The First Presbyterian Church began as a mere preaching unit under his leadership. Then too, he was an able physician who became an outstanding minister, thus spending his life preaching as a missionary and ministering to the sick.

One of the early members of the medical profession of the Western District was Dr. Alexander Jackson, the father of General W. H. Jackson and Mr. Justice Howell E. Jackson. He was one of the charter members of the State Medical Society, though he was living in Paris, Tennessee, at the time. In 1833 he read a paper on the "Medical Topography of West Tennesssee" before the state society.[13]

Copies of contemporary papers reveal the names of many of the early physicians, but tell little about those brave men who served the community so faithfully in the capacity of the "family doctor," the vanishing American of to-day. There may be found the names of Dr. Thomas Harris, T. C. Reavis, sur-

---

[11]*Ibid.*

[12]MS.

[13]Dr. Jackson was a very influential man in the community in professional, business, and social circles. Born in Halifax County, Virginia, about 1802, left an orphan, graduated from the University of Pennsylvania in 1823, removed to Paris in 1827, and Jackson in 1840, where he practiced until he retired in 1847. He was very active in agricultural exhibits of the first fair in West Tennessee. He wrote the sketch of Jackson in the *West Tennessee Directory of 1872.* The tribute in the local paper at the time of his death in 1879 shows he was one of the beloved characters of the community: "Dr. Jackson was a man of good cultivation of mind and memory that embraced everything brought to his attention. The elegant sayings of distinguished table-talkers and humorists were familiar to him and he would illustrate his narrative by some apt quotations and weave in his jokes which made him the most companionabe of men. His quaint and humorous style of conversation, his personal peculiarities, his wise maxims beautifully expressed will live vividly in the memory of all with whom he ever associated." *Tribune and Sun,* January 24, 1879.

geon dentist; Dr. Fenner and Dr. Harris, both surgeons and owners of a "drug and medicine store" (one having regularly graduated from the Philadelphia College of Pharmacy); O. V. Ward, the surgeon dentist who was prepared to perform all operations in his profession as he regularly visited Denmark, Trenton, Bolivar, and Lexington.[14] Among the other early doctors were Dr. John F. Brown who came to Jackson in 1823, Dr. Wynne, Dr. Bedford, Dr. Erasmus Fenner, Dr. Godwin, Dr. S. W. Vaughn, Dr. George Snider, who arrived on horseback in 1822 after a one thousand mile journey, Dr. Thomas Wilson who had studied at Transylvania University, Dr. N. I. Hess, who came in 1824, and Dr. J. W. Anthony.[15] Thomas McCowat's name should be associated with the medical field, for he ground all the surgical instruments that were used by the physicians in this district.[16]

Dr. Dashiell came to Jackson in 1847 as a physician and a farmer. The *West Tennessee Whig* of 1849 announced that he would continue to practice his profession in Jackson. During the Civil War, he was appointed by Governor Isham G. Harris as surgeon of the Sixth Tennessee Confederate regiment (Colonel William H. Stephens) and served in this capacity through the war. He was one of the earliest members of the Medical Society of the State of Tennessee. He occasionally contributed articles to medical journals, chiefly on diseases peculiar to the Forked Deer Valley.[17]

Two epidemics in the later part of the nineteenth century can never be forgotten by those who were living here at that time—the small pox in 1877 and the yellow fever in 1878. During both years the people of the county did everything that they knew to do to stamp out the dreaded diseases. The newspapers and city records during the months of May, June, July, and August of 1877 tell a tragic story of the brave fight against this intruder in the homes—small pox. Twenty-one cases at

---

[14] *West Tennessee Whig*, November 23, 29, 1844.

[15] *Transactions of Medical Society of State of Tennessee* for 1830; Jackson *Gazette*, August 24, 1824, March 19, 1825, September 15, 1829; *Southern Statesman*, September 3, 1831.

[16] *West Tennessee Whig*, November 23, 1844.

[17] William S. Speer, *Prominent Tennesseans*, (Nashville, 1888), 233. Dr. Dashiell was postmaster during Cleveland's first administration and a trustee of the Memphis Conference Female Institute.

one time were reported—eight deaths resulted from these. After much delay the Mayor took it upon himself to see that houses were isolated and guarded by fifteen special police. Dr. W. J. Arnold was employed to treat cases, a public meeting was held to take steps to compel all persons to be vaccinated. Although some of the people thought that the disease had been allowed to spread because the aldermen were too niggardly about hiring special guards, city records contain many entries of money expended for cleaning pest houses, for supplies for pest houses, for removing patients to pest houses, and for Dr. Sam Chester for vaccinating patients. Robert Dillon was allowed $56.65 for guarding small pox for one month; George Reid, $10 for cleaning up pest house; John Dodd, $66.35 for guarding pest house for 33 days. News of one new case spread like a prairie fire and grew as it passed from person to person. The editors of the papers tried to keep the public informed but calm. One reported: "A blarsted fool negro who believed small pox to be black measles slipped into an affected house the other day before the guard saw him and there he is yet and there he will remain until all danger is passed. So much for being and unmitigated ass!"[18]

A story is told to-day of one very unusual treatment of small pox which in this one case was seemingly successful. A wagon load of Negroes was being taken to the pest house east of the city, when the mules became frightened while they were crossing a stream west of the pest house. The wagon, the mules, and the five patients were dumped into the stream which was swollen by a recent rain. The thorough soaking that the negroes got cured them of small pox—at any rate they recovered.

This small pox epidemic took as part of its toll the life of one of Jackson's beloved physicians, Dr. John Chester. According to an account in a contemporary paper which carried the headlines: "Great Hearts of Jackson Pour out grief at the Loss of Its Noblest Citizen," the news spread like a chant over the city, "Dr. John Chester is dead!" Dr. Chester visited a negro child and had pronounced the disease small pox. About two weeks later although he was ill, he continued to make his

---

[18]Minute Book of City of Jackson, 1877; Jackson *Sun*, May 11, 1877. There were many cases of smallpox off and on through the years. In the winter of 1918 there were over sixty cases at one time.

calls. Finally the disease overtook him and small hope for his recovery was held from the very beginning. In the "darkness and stillness" of night, a funeral cortege of only a brother, two brothers-in-law, the Sisters from the Catholic school, a colored servant, lighted only by a couple of dim candles made its way through the streets of the city. Without pagentry and ceremony this man who had friends by the thousands was laid away to sleep. Under other circumstances his last rites would have been attended by one of the largest assemblages ever assembled in Jackson. A meeting was held at King's Opera House to draft resolutions concerning this martyr to his profession, who was beloved by the whole community, for he had the reputation of being a kind, charitable, brave, Christian man. Many citizens were too grief-stricken to attend the meeting, but the house was still overflowing.[19]

During the late summer and fall months of the year 1878 the "yellow jack" had gotten a fair start and was spreading death and destruction in the Mississippi Valley, particularly in Memphis, New Orleans, and the surrounding territories. The citizens of Jackson were terrified over the reports of twenty to forty deaths within twenty-four hours in Memphis and New Orleans. On August 12, 1878, the Mayor and Aldermen of this city organized the Board of Health composed of Dr. F. B. Hamilton, president, Dr. W. J. Arnold, secretary, Dr. John S. Fenner, Dr. R. R. Dashiell and Mayor W. D. Robinson. This board immediately established a quarantine against New Orleans, Memphis, Grenada, Mississippi, appropriated $200 for sanitary purposes, and called for a public mass meeting at

---

[19] General A. W. Campbell was chosen chairman of the meeting. While the committee on resolutions was out at work twenty citizens delivered eulogies. Among these were Dr. A. W. Jackson, Colonel John Brown, Rev. J. E. Bright, Dr. T. W. Harris, Judge H. W McCorry, R. H. Anderson, Captain J. T. Beveridge, Robert and B. F. Gates, E. H. Bullock, W. A. Caldwell, E. S. Mallory, J. H. Tomlin, Dr. Hamilton. Dr. Chester was born on May 18, 1824, the son of Colonel Robert J. Chester and Elizabeth Hays. He attended West Tennessee College from which he graduated with highest honors in 1846. During the Mexican War, he was among the first to plant the Stars and Stripes on the walls of Montezuma. After he completed his medical training in Philadelphia in 1850, he returned home to practice. Again, the clouds of war gathered and he joined the Confederate Army, rising to a full colonel commanding the Regiment of the Tennessee Volunteers. Jackson *Tribune and Sun*, June 8, 1877.

the court house to "devise means to enable the city to keep yellow fever out of the city." A request was made to the officials of the railroads for the use of baggage cars to use as quarantine stations. The request was granted.[20]

Various means were devised to keep yellow fever away from the city. An extra 25 cent per $100 tax was levied to provide the money to cleanse and disinfect the city, but $500 was borrowed for immediate use. The city records show that $95 of this was spent for one hundred barrels of lime, $84 for carbolic acid. Mayor Robinson objected to the high priced carbolic acid, but the need was great and the other men of the board seemed to have wanted the acid badly enough to pay the price. Special police were paid by the city for certain guard duties. The Chicago, St. Louis and New Orleans R. R. donated 300 barrels of lime, a baggage car, and all freight charges of disinfectants which the city ordered.[21]

Stories of the disease from adjoining counties and towns really caused more fear than the actual cases at home. Trains were stopped at Carroll and Malesus to get the mail and fumigate it. Papers and letters were put in an oven, for the people thought that the heat would destroy the germ. Then, the idea was spread abroad that the yellow jack could be driven from the city by smoke which came from a fire built in a mound of mud-covered pine cones. These volcano-like mounds were built eight or ten feet in diameter and twenty to thirty feet high at various places in the city. There was one at Liberty and Baltimore, another at Shannon and Baltimore, another on Royal near Madison, and another on Royal near Preston. Strange as it may seem, the smoke did some good, for the mosquitoes were driven away—but the mound-builders were not aware of the fact that the mosquitoes were the carriers of the yellow fever germ.

When the stories of the spread of the disease were repeated and added to, the people were panic stricken and rushed to the country like an exodus from the land. People in the adjoining towns where the epidemic was more acute than it was in this county tried to slip in here, often at night. Hence at the sound

---

[20]Minute Book of the City of Jackson, 1878. Several other times through the years, 1888 for instance, there were yellow fever scares and quarantines set up, but no real epidemic.

[21]Minute Book of the City of Jackson, 1878.

of the courthouse bell late in the afternoon, the young men of Jackson assembled, divided themselves into ten squads to guard the ten roads leading out of town. At the guard stations these six to ten patriotic young men, each one armed, built a bon fire, got some benches, and spent the night swapping yarns and guarding the roads. By and large, the strict enforcement of the quarantine regulations and the use of disinfectants were responsible for this city's not having a bad epidemic, although there were twenty-two cases in the county, all of which were fatal.

By October 16, 1878, an old copy of the Jackson *Dispatch* could truthfully try to still the fears of the citizens of the community, even if there were exciting stories of the disease in other nearby towns. There were no cases of the fever in Jackson, so there was no reason why the people should not feel safe to come here to trade. A story had been circulating that L. Murrell had purchased goods in Memphis. Mr. Murrell's denial of the story shows how careful everyone had tried to be to prevent the spread of the fever:

> The people of Jackson and Madison County know that I would not be so inhumane as to imperil the community to the ravages of yellow fever. Besides no goods are allowtd to be brought from Memphis or any other place which has the fever, according to the rules of the quarantine. Every bill of goods which we have received this fall has been accompanied with certificates to certify that the goods were not from the infected regions. I can assure you that the people can come and buy their goods without any fear of YELLOW JACK, as we have received no goods from any city infected with it.[22]

The medical profession as well as other professions went through a period of reconstruction after 1865. Some of the doctors did not return to Jackson and other new names and faces appeared. Dr. B. R. Harris came here from Purdy, McNairy County, in 1865. He had an extensive practice, was a good financier, a successful grocerman and a real estate man.[23] Dr. James G. Womack, a graduate of the famous Chapel Hill

---

[22]Jackson *Dispatch*, October 18, 1878.

[23]Dr. Harris at the time of his death in 1891 was considered a Mason of highest esteem. His son W. T., was active in book business, one of the organizers of the Jackson Public Library, assisted in organizing the Southern Engine Boiler Works. J. T. Moore, *Tenn. Volunteer State*, III, 122; Jackson *Sun and Tribune*, November 12, 1891.

College, came to Denmark about 1841 and to Jackson in 1859 where he practiced until 1874.[24] Doctors William and Charlie Still had advanced ideas, for they believed in giving medicine rather than bleeding. They also believed in advertising their "Botanic Practice" while they were devoting their undivided attention to medicine and surgery. The following announcement appeared in the contemporary paper:

> All we ask is "fair field and an open fight" with disease; without any sly and unfair interference or misrepresentation, by anyone, when cases are under our treatment. We are prepared to treat all persons afflicted with chronic and supposed incurable forms of disease, who may apply at our residence. We will also pay reasonable price for negroes afflicted with chronic diseases when not too old and not too far destroyed by mercury. Send them in![25]

During the latter part of the nineteenth century and the early part of the twentieth century, we find many names of those faithful servants of the people—each one dearer to the hearts of the family in which he served than the famous sons and daughters of the community who as politicians, lawyers, and as business men, had sat in the halls of Congress, on the bench of the highest court of the land or served as president of the railroads. Dr. W. F. Rochelle began practice here in 1880 as a health officer. With his red hair and full beard he presented an unusual figure as he rode horseback. He was a pioneer in the movement to establish hospital facilities for the community. Dr. Orlando Bartholemew, who volunteered his services during the yellow fever epidemic in Memphis, was of the opinion that it could be cured with quinine. In the end he was a victim of the disease himself. Dr. Frank B. Hamilton, who came here from Medon, built up a wide practice, but in later years on account of rheumatism his patients had to come to him as he sat in front of Nance's Drug Store. Here he spent his time chatting with friends and patients. It was said that Dr. Hamilton carried sunshine into every home he entered. His great bodily affliction merely added true sympathy to his nature and only served to sharpen his intellect.[26]

---

[24]Jackson *Sun*, May 21, 1903.

[25]*West Tennessee Whig*, March 16, 1849.

[26]Jackson *Sun*, May 22, 1923. The writer is indebted to Dr. Herman Hawkins and Dr. Jere L. Crook for the information concerning the

Dr. John Fenner was a man of high reputation. He often went by to see a patient at 2 o'clock in the morning whether he was called or not. He led all in his day in the size of his practice. By his quiet confident, sympathetic bearing, he brought instant relief of mind to the suffering and was unusually successful in his treatments.[27] Dr. J. T. Jones won the confidence of all who knew him. "Dr. Jimmy," as he was affectionately known, was more interested in keeping his patients in good health than in ministering to them during illness. A monument to his memory was built in the hearts of Jackson people, for none knew him but to love him, none named him but to praise him.[28]

Other names are suggested by medical directories of various years. In that of 1867 were the names of W. B. Spencer and J. A. Arrington, who were popular dentists in Jackson. Dr. Arrington's splendid bearing, his love of children and horses, his kind and cordial treatment of all classes made the people proud of him as a friend and fellow citizen.[29] Doctors J. T. Herron and G. C. Savage were associated together as eye, ear, nose and throat specialists. Dr. Savage also served as a lecturer on anatomy and hygiene at Southwestern Baptist University. He and Dr. Herron were considered excellent church officials, superior citizens, and successful physicians. Dr. Murchison, a native of North Carolina, came to Denmark before the Civil War and spent his life here practicing and farming. Dr. Sam Chester (1840-1898) fought under the Confederate flag in the Sixth Tennessee, acquired his medical education after the war, and returned to Jackson to practice. The presence of a competent physician with a genial disposition such as Dr. Chester added a ray of hope to the somber hue of each sickroom that he visited. Dr. L. L. Webb (1855-1925) of Carroll

---

physicians of the late 19th and 20th century and for the accounts of the early hospitals.

[27] *Ibid.*

[28] Captain Gates's Scrap Book, May, 1923. Dr. Fenner served in the Confederate Army during the entire period of the war. No peril or exposure even for one moment deterred him from the discharge of his duty. Once when a steady diet of too much salt meat caused the scurvy to break out, he ordered the boys to the woods to chew certain green things as fresh meats and vegetables could *not* be obtained. Lindsley, *Military Annals*, 215.

[29] *West Tennessee Whig*, May 11, 1867; Jackson *Sun*, May, 1923.

was a physician and farmer who was particularly successful in the treatment of pneumonia patients.³⁰ Dr. Webb was one of the ablest physicians in West Tennessee, a man who could have enjoyed a lucrative practice in a city, but he chose to live on the farm his father had bought in 1845 and serve the people who knew and loved him.

Dr. Ambrose McCoy, the son of Dr. N. A. McCoy of Pinson, was recognized as a man of exceptional ability, not only in the medical circles of Tennessee but in the whole South. In addition to his large private practice, he was president of the Tennessee board of medical examiners for fourteen years, secretary of the Southern States Association of Railroad Surgeons for five years, and local surgeon for Mobile and Ohio Railroad for twenty-seven years. He was beloved in the community because of his professional ability, his sympathy for both rich and poor, his strong convictions which he expressed freely, if often bluntly, his whole-hearted love for humanity. Associated with Dr. McCoy as chief surgeon of the Mobile and Ohio Railroad and in one of the early hospitals of Jackson was Dr. John W. Gresham (1873-1915). Dr. Gresham began his practice in Jackson in 1898, after graduating from Kentucky Medical College in Louisville and continuing his post graduate work in New York City, he continued to practice here until his death in 1915. Another associate of Dr. McCoy was Dr. Robert H. Cartmell (1858-1923), who graduated from Bellview Medical College in New York City before he returned to Jackson where he also served as surgeon for Mobile and Ohio Railroad.

Dr. David Hardie Parker (1832-1901) was brought to Madison County when he was scarcely a month old. He graduated from Botanical Medical College in Memphis in 1853 and returned to Medon where he spent the remainder of his life as an active member of the Methodist church, as a progressive citizen of the county having interests in such projects as the coming of the Bemis Mills, as a successful physician and farmer. Dr. George Lacy (1848-1931), a son-in-low of Dr. Parker, practiced in Medon for fifty-eight years, his professional career

---

³⁰Countless other names might be added to these lists, such as Dr. Gale of Spring Creek, Dr. Critenden and Dr. Snipes of Denmark, and Dr. Rush Jones, but space does not permit the writer to continue, though each name was a beloved one in the home in which he practiced.

being interrupted during the Civil War while he served under Forrest.

In the State Medical Society, there were many of the county's physicians. Nine members from West Tennessee were at that first meeting of the State Medical Society, three of these were from Jackson—Doctors Young, Fenner, and Loving.[31] Four from the community have served as officers: two presidents —Dr. Joseph Alexander Crook (1901-1902) and Dr. Jere L. Crook (1909-1910), and two vice-presidents from West Tennessee—Dr. A. B. Dancy (1921-1922) and Dr. J. W. McClaran (1927-1929). Dr. Joseph Alexander Crook (1847-1922), a graduate of Madison College at Spring Creek and then the Jefferson College in 1870, started his practice in Henderson where he was associated with his brother, Dr. Jere Crook. He came to Jackson in the late 1880's where he was associated with his son Dr. Jere L. Crook, the two having built and operated the Crook Sanitorium. He was particularly successful in the treatment of typhoid fever and for thirty-five years was division surgeon for the N. C. and St. L. Railroad. He was one of the organizers and later president of the West Tennessee Medical Society.[32] Dr. J. A. Crook will be remembered as the friend and physician who was a good doctors, a useful citizen and a Christian gentleman.

Dr. A. B. Dancy (1877-1933) was probably one of the most eminent specialists of the county, for he was recognized in all West Tennessee. He was educated at Southwestern Baptist University, Vanderbilt, Harvard, New York Polyclinic, Ophthalmic and Aural Institute, and the London Ophthalmic Hospital. He was a public spirited citizen and a physician who was loved by all who knew him.

Dr. George Leon Williamson (1881-1941), the co-founder with Dr. C. F. Webb of Webb-Williamson Hospital, was a graduate of Vanderbilt University Medical School in 1904. He

---

[31] Among the very early physicians of the county who were members of the State Medical Society were Doctors John F. Brown, Wynne Bedford, Erasmus Fenner, Godwin, S. W. Vaughn, George Snider, James Young, Loving, M. B. Cook. *Centennial History of Tennessee State Medical Society, 1830-1930*, (Nashville, 1930), 520.

[32] The West Tennessee Medical Association, organized at Humboldt in 1892, for ten years held its annual meetings in Jackson. In recent years it meets here every other year.

was the typical "family physician," the loyal friend to his patients who had "healing in his hands and humanity in his heart as he ministered to the ills of the people of the community. He was the very essence of gentility, kindliness, forbearance, and understanding."

Dr. James Walsh McClaran (1888-1945) will long be remembered as one of the leading surgeons of the city who worked untiringly to enlarge the Memorial Hospital. He was a graduate of Vanderbilt and did graduate work at the University of Nancy and Edinburg. Serving with the French Army in 1915-1916, he was decorated for his service there before he entered the U. S. Army in which he served as a Captain.

For many years the physicians of this county dreamed and talked of a hospital. There was no money and the physicians were loath to take on the responsibility. In reality the city owes a debt of gratitude to Dr. Mark C. Matthews, a Presbyterian minister in the closing years of the nineteenth century, for it was he who was the moving spirit in the establishment of the first hospital in Jackson. "The Presbyterian Hospital" was located in the old jail building (the one used before the Civil War and now used as a colored clinic) on Liberty Street. It was planned that the Presbyterian Church should support the new institution, but the plans did not materialize and it was opened mainly by individual contributions. It was operated under this name for a few months by Dr. Jere L. Crook; from 1897 until 1899 by Dr. A. McCoy and Dr. Joe MacDonald. In 1900, Dr. MacDonald died and Dr. McCoy assumed entire charge, using the name McCoy Sanitarium.

About the turn of the century, Dr. W. F. Rochelle and Dr. Warford built a hospital on East Main Street. This building was later used as the high school, then as the Walden Hotel, and then as dormitory of Union University.

In 1908, Dr. Crook and his father, the late Dr. J. A. Crook, built a ten-bed hospital on the lot on Baltimore just opposite the post office which was originally occupied by the office of Dr. Snider. Within a few years this was enlarged into a twenty-five bed hospital.[33]

---

[33]The Crook and Civic League Hospitals were adequate for the community for a number of years, but in 1923 a new wing and new equipment were added to the Crook Sanitorium and in 1929 a private hospital was built by Doctors Charles F. Webb and G. L. Williamson.

An agitation was begun about 1906 to build a community hospital. It was a group of ladies who formed the Civic League Society who were behind this movement. On this first board were: Mrs. Love Jones Drake, president; Mrs. J. C. Felsenthal, secretary; Miss Mamie Caldwell, treasurer, which officers could never have accomplished what they did without the untiring efforts of the other efficient members: Mrs. Carrie Felsenthal, Mrs. P. J. Murray, Mrs. M. A. Long, Mrs. Jennie Murdock, Mrs. I. B. Tigrett, Mrs. J. W. Buford, and Mrs. J. W. Vanden. Some money for the project was raised by the endowment of beds. After one thousand dollars was appropriated by the County Court when Mrs. Felsenthal and C. E. Pigford presented the matter to them, locations began to be considered. Robert Hicks offered to donate a site on Fairmont, but this was entirely too far from town. The old Duke place on Highland was considered, but this, too, was too far out. The lot on Royal was purchased for $6,000. In 1909, a modern twenty-bed hospital was opened. It was planned in the beginning for the Catholic Sisters to run the hospital, but they refused to take charge unless the owners would sign over the property to them, so the Civic League opened it literally on a "shoestring." An open-house was held, showers of linens and furnishings were held, gifts of supplies, food, even chickens, vegetables and eggs were accepted. At first the city paid $75 a month for all charity patients, but this unfair practice has been changed and now they pay on a proportional basis.

As the community developed its professional men advanced with it. Those doctors of the frontier days were typical of the doctors of their day with most of their knowledge acquired through work with another physician in his office or at schools which were far below the standards of to-day. It was actually considered impossible to have a written examination at Harvard in 1870 for a majority of the students could not write well enough. Frequent advertisements of patent medicine and testimonies of the "cured" patients encouraged the people to take a deep interest in their interiors. Years have brought great changes in the story of the preservation of life, so to-day competent, well-educated physicians are ready to administer to patients in their homes or in the well-equipped modern hospitals that can be found in the community.

CHAPTER XX

THE PRESS

In treating of the history of the press of Madison County, there are five outstanding characters—Charles D. McLean who published the Jackson *Gazette* from 1824 to 1830; Colonel W. W. Gates, who entered the publishing business in Jackson in 1842, and continued in it for over thirty years; J. G. Cisco, who established the *Forked Deer Blade* in 1883 and was known for his brilliant writing and his independent editorial policy; Honorable B. A. Enloe, who established the *Sun* in 1875 and remained in the newspaper business for a period of some 25 years and who served in Congress and on the State Railroad Commission; Attorney Clarence E. Pigford, who became publisher of the Jackson *Sun* in 1914 and has not only published a newspaper worthy of the best traditions of its predecessors, but has also contributed immeasurably to the development of Jackson, Madison County, and West Tennessee in a period in which this section has enjoyed its most substantial growth.[1] Newspapers present a living and moving picture of the times, giving authentic materials for history or rather they are history itself— a history of the thoughts, words, and actions of men, a history of the natural intercourse of the state of society, of government, of the rise and fall of nations. Thus, the men who were editors and publishers of the papers in this community are the men who not only made the history of the County themselves but recorded the actions of their fellow-citizens.

The story of the press in this section might be said to contain a veritable forest of newspapers, but the first tree of this forest was the *Pioneer,* the earliest newspaper in the Western District. What an appropriate name for a four page sheet that

---

[1]This chapter is based upon a paper prepared by Harris Brown, editor of the *Jackson Sun,* and read by him before the Madison County Historical Society October, 1944.

was literally published in the heart of a wilderness! Scarcely three months had passed after the laying off of the town and the sale of the lots until two enterprising men, A. C. and D. A. C. Hays, saw the need of a newspaper. In November, 1822, these publishers presented the first issue of the *Pioneer* to the people of the Western District.[2] On May 20, 1824, Charles McLean, publisher, and Elijah Bigelow, editor, presented the first issue of the Jackson *Gazette,* which had for its motto: "Friendly to the best pursuits of man, friendly to thought, to Freedom and to Peace," and was ready to support Andrew Jackson in everything that he did.[3] This paper had a wide circulation and great influence. Its columns were frequently copied in the Randolph, Memphis, Nashville, and North Carolina papers.

Charles D. McLean, a native of Virginia, was born in 1795, of Scotch-Irish descent. Before he came to Madison County, he had published the Clarksville *Recorder* from 1815 to 1820 and had also been a former proprietor of the Nashville *Whig*. In 1825, when he had sold the *Gazette* to Richardson and Read, he issued a proposal to publish the *Western Sentinel*. The prospectus of this which appeared in the Nashville *Whig* in 1826 shows that McLean thought another paper could flourish here in the midst of such an intelligent body of citizens:

> It argues well of the intelligence of the people, to see newspapers abound and flourish and from a large portion of those who have settled the Western District, we would expect more than ordinary intelligence. They are not the fragments of population detached from other states, but on the contrary, composed of the most respectable, intelligent and worthy citizens of our own and several neighbor states.[4]

The *Sentinel* was never published and McLean again got control of the *Gazette* and continued its publication until the plant was bought by Judge John Read and Timothy Spurlock and the name of the paper was changed to the *Southern Statesman*. McLean seems not to have sought public office, but in the legislature of 1831, he sat in the lower house of representative

---

[2] *The Pioneer,* January 28, 1823, (Vol. I, No. 9). There are only two issues of this paper that are known to exist, one in the Library of Congress and the other at the University of North Carolina.

[3] Williams, *West Tennessee,* 223.

[4] Nashville *Whig,* March 16, 1826.

of the Counties of Madison, Henderson, and Haywood. In 1833, he left Jackson, removing to Shelby County and lived there on his farm. He took a lively interest in matters historical and was a member of the first Shelby County Historical Society. As president of this society for seven years, he was a moving spirit in it. He was about ninety at the time of his death.[5]

The *Southern Statesman,* a Jacksonian organ, published from 1831 until 1833, was a well edited and much quoted paper. This was merged into the *Truth Teller* in 1833, which paper was edited by the military-minded James H. McMahon until he left for the Seminole War. In the mid-thirties, B. H. Shepherd established the *District Telegraph.* His newspaper venture was a failure, even though he proposed that "facts are the element of knowledge and the right use of knowledge wisdom." This seemed to be a period of failures, for the next two papers, the *Democrat* was published by a Virginian, Ed Street, another paper by Henry Swan, the *Jacksonian* published by J. H. Youngblood.[6]

This period of failures came to an end when that leading figure of Madison County journalism, Colonel W. W. Gates, came to Jackson in 1842 from Paris and established the *West Tennessee Whig.* As editor of this paper, he devoted all his energies and talents to the building up of the community. He advocated the location and building of the two railroads, the establishment of West Tennessee College, the location of the West Tennessee Fair, the distribution of stories of the glorious prospects of our town in the papers of the north. In fact most of the editorials in the northern newspapers about Jackson came from his pen and for its size Jackson became one of the best known towns of the South. Colonel Gates never stooped to personal abuse. At the threshhold of his career, he seemed to have learned that in order to have one's opinion respected, a proper respect should be shown to the others. If he did not always know what was best to put in his paper, he certainly knew what was best to keep out of it. In this way he was al-

---

[5]McLean preserved the files of the Jackson *Gazette* and it is thought that the files that are in the library at the University of Wisconsin are the ones that he preserved.

[6]Goodspeed, *History of Tennessee* (Madison County) (Nashville, 1887), 815.

ways the editor of a good paper. As a political writer he was beloved by his party and respected by his opponents.[7]

No editor in the state knew better how to manage a political campaign than W. W. Gates. His rallying cry reached every nook and corner of the district. Just before an election the thousands of readers of the *West Tennessee Whig* were encouraged and animated by such expressions as: "Once more to the breach, dear friends, once more! Now by St. Paul the work goes bravely on!" Gates's paper did much in shaping the policy of the Whig party in this section. He wrote with fire of enthusiasm, with the vigor of truth, with the strength of conviction. Standing firmly on the principles of his party he never wavered. In all his long career as a journalist, he always wrote what he thought to be the truth and to the best interest of the people, regardless of public opinion and popular clamor. "I would rather be right than edit a paper against my convictions," was his conclusion at the time he descended from the editorial tripod and retired. Such a man with unwavering convictions was a powerful force in the development of politics in this growing community. Gates was identified with the Anti-Jackson Party known as the National Republicans. C. H. Williams, of West Tennessee, and Thomas D. Arnold of East Tennessee were elected to Congress by that party. Early in January, 1836, the great split took place in the Jackson-Van Buren Party and the Whig party was revised. A conference was held in Nashville, at the old City Hotel, for the purpose of organizing the movement in Tennessee. There were present at that famous meeting: John Bell, Hugh L. White, Ephriam Foster, Dr. Boyd McNairy, Allen A. Hall, Dr. John Shelby, Thomas A. R. Nelson, and C. H. Williams and W. W. Gates from West Tennessee. Thus the Jackson editor was present at baptismal vows of the Whig Party in Tennessee.[8]

---

[7]From a Scrap Book in the Gates Family; *Forked Deer Blade*, January 7, 1888. In 1838, Colonel Gates was secretary of the convention of the Press in Nashville, at which time a code of ethics for newspapermen was prepared. They resolved to observe gentlemanly courtesy in debate and not indulge in personalities, to use nothing of personal nature except as advertising matter. "Tennesseans on the March," Nashville *Banner,* August 15, 1938, used with the permission of the author, W. E. Beard.

[8]All the material concerning the Gates dynasty of newspapers came

This Nestor and pioneer editor of the *West Tennessee Whig* possessed the respect of his political foes and the admiration of his friends. Of personal enemies he had fewer, perhaps, than any other man who took such an active part in the political struggles during half a century. When the clouds of war gathered in 1861, Colonel Gates doubted the wisdom of secession. Although he was finally won over to the cause and his sons served in the Confederate Army, he deeply regretted that circumstances had so shaped themselves that an armed conflict should ever take place between the two sections of the country. Colonel Gates continued the publication of the *Whig* until the occupation of the city by the Federal forces June 8, 1862. During the remaining years of hostilities, the editor remained in the town, subjected to the many regulations and hardships that were imposed upon the citizens by the Federal forces, and the community had to depend upon papers from outside for their news. Most of the time these "rebel readers" were incensed over the way the "Yankee papers" distorted the truth, especially when a paper carried a story of some skirmishing in the county and the local citizens knew this to be an untrue account.[9]

When the war was over, Colonel Gates revived the *Whig* and took in as partners John M. Parker and Harvey Brown. In 1866, John T. Hicks bought Parker's interest and Don Cameron bought Brown's in 1869. The following year, the *Whig* was consolidated with the *Tribune* which had been established in 1868 by the Milligan brothers, but owned at the time of consolidation by D. M. Wisdom. When the *Whig and Tribune* was consolidated with the *Sun* in 1877, the "Whig" name was dropped, which act did not please Colonel Gates, who had retired from his job in 1872, so he proceeded to revive the *Whig*, which after a year passed into the hands of his son, John W. Gates, who later sold to W. H. Bruton and he was succeeded as publisher by L. J. Brooks.

At the time of his retirement in 1872, the editors of Tennessee paid many beautiful tributes to W. W. Gates. The Nashville *American* wrote:

---

from the *Forked Deer Blade*, January 7, 1888, and the scrap books of Charlie McMillan and Miss Anna Butler.

[9]R. H. Cartmell's Diary.

Col. Gates has not the honors of public office, nor has he the riches of the public spoilman; and perhaps he has never had the flatterers which like a shadow disappear whenever a cloud comes over the head; but in his old age he has the respect of all that class of people who speak words of praise from the heart; and better than that, he possesses a conscious truth that makes him respect himself, for having been all his life what God made him—a man with a mind and a will which were not the subject of barter and a courage to declare the right as he saw it, waiting, bravely and patiently for public approval.[10]

Another journalist wrote of this pioneer journalist of the mid-nineteenth century: "He was kind sympathetic and never failed to make friends and the public generally had the highest confidence in him as an honorable man—one with whom his principles were a never-failing guide. . . . He was a typical American of the old school, loved his whole country, was proud of his birthright of liberty and rejoiced at the great and rapid strides that the Republic had made in reaching its greatness."[11] What a heritage this editor left to those who were to follow in his footsteps!

W. H. Bruton was a publisher of firm convictions, editing a paper of strength and prestige. His son, Pink D. worked with his father on his paper, later with McCowat Brothers and still later in his own business. L. J. Brooks published the *Whig* here for a number of years, before he sold out in the 1890's to Jeff D. Newton and J. M. Simmons. Brooks went to St. Louis where he became engaged in the real estate business.[12] John W. Gates left law school in 1861 to join the Confederate Army, in which he fought for the duration of the war. He served as mayor of Jackson for a number of years, during which time Jackson built the first sanitary sewage and street pavements. John W. Gates was considered one of the finest orators of his day.

---

[10]*Forked Deer Blade,* January 7, 1888.

[11]Gates's Scrap Book.

[12]L. J. Brooks was perhaps the most active and enterprising newspaper man of his day in West Tennessee. He was constantly hammering away at some new enterprise and he was able to get the people interested in them. His influence helped bring several factories to Jackson. Another project was the building of a canal that would connect the Tombigbee River in Alabama and the Mississippi with the Tennessee. Efforts to secure appropriations in Congress failed, but other efforts are being made to secure this appropriation.

The Jackson *Dispatch,* which was established in 1873 by J. J. Worrell, was the only Jackson weekly paper which was not turned into a daily. As the years rolled along this was published by J. W. N. Burkett, Colonel R. S. Fletcher, and Charles R. Collins. Industrial expansion and agricultural development were the chief interests of J. W. N. Burkett. During his tenure as a publisher, he did much to encourage the farmers in the development of the West Tennessee Fair. Charles Collins, the son of a Confederate Army officer, did much toward getting the Confederate monument erected in Court Square, and also contributed to preserving the history of the Civil War while he was publishing a newsy and constructive newspaper. Colonel Fletcher, a merchant, newspaperman, and banker, was also interested in the commercial and agricultural development of this section, for he frequently referred to the desirability of some new project for Jackson and Madison County in the columns of the *Dispatch.* Colonel Fletcher was named a colonel on Governor Bob Taylor's staff, for they were warm friends throughout the years. The Colonel made the race against Mayor Hu Anderson about the turn of the century, but Anderson was reelected. One highlight of the race was a joint debate between the two candidates in the old courthouse here. Even after he helped organize the Bank of Commerce and served as president of that institution, he did not lose his zest for newspaper work and represented the Nashville *Banner* here for many years as correspondent of that paper.

The *Forked Deer Blade* was established in 1883 by Jay Guy Cisco. During the decade of its life, this excellent paper was devoted to the interests of Jackson and Madison County. Cisco had a vigorous editorial policy and frequently got at odds with some of his fellow townsmen. The editor never failed to express his personal conviction, though that conviction might not be the popular one. After he left Jackson, he was a public relations man for the L. and N. Railroad, and still later served as United States Consul to Mexico during Cleveland's administration. He did a great deal to preserve the history of Madison County, by creating an interest in the Indian remains and writing a short history of the county which he published in the *Blade.* Cisco was remembered by many as a brilliant, fearless, mysterious, erratic, pugnatious man: During the years of his editorship of his "One horse Forked Deer Blade," as he called it himself, Cisco was a picturesque figure in the life of the community. At times when dollars were a bit scarce with him, his friends noticed that his clothes were neatly pressed though darned and his shoes polished though badly worn.

Cisco was a fearless man. When he thought he was right he stuck to his principles to the end even though things became so warm at times that he "packed" his gun, for both he and his friends knew that his life was in danger. That was the day when men took their religion and politics seriously.

An article that the editor wrote about himself in the *Blade* is said to describe himself very fittingly. The editor recalled a story that he heard in his youth about a young man who, when his heart was full of love for mankind, had started a newspaper. This youthful editor wanted the paper to be one of the people and for the people and so he determined that not one word that was obnoxious and offensive to any patron should appear in any of the columns. The result was that no view of the editor appeared, subscriptions fell off, the paper sold to the sheriff, and the editor became a tramp. The *Blade* editor had vowed that if he ever got the job of editing a paper that he would please himself alone. "I started a paper called 'The Forked Deer Blade'," wrote Cisco, "It should please its editor. It would express just sentiments as he thought right regardless of who objected. My own convictions should find expression, even if every reader and subscriber said 'Stop my paper.'" A few subscribers did stop their paper when a political campaign came along, more stopped their paper when the editor discovered what he termed an "infamous scoundrel—a wolf in sheep's clothing," but for every one that cut the subscription, others took the place.

Editor Cisco lost a journalistic battle in the late eighties. He was strongly supporting state-wide prohibition, but, fight as he did, he could not muster the support he had contemplated and the fight was lost.

Other men who were lured by the work of the newspaper should be mentioned. Robert, nephew of W. W. Gates, was associated with D. M. Wisdom in the publication of the *Sun* from 1875 until 1884 at which time he became Assistant Commissioner of Agriculture of Tennessee and later an industrial agent of the L. and N. Colonel Wisdom moved to Oklahoma in the late 1870's. Colonel Robert Moore Gates, son of Robert

Gates, began work on the Jackson *Blade* in 1894 and later worked on the *Whig,* the Nashville *American,* and still later with newspapers in Memphis and Louisville, before going to Washington as special correspondent of the *Commercial Appeal.*[19] Rev. Frederick Howard, the pastor of the First Baptist Church, established the *True Baptist* in 1885, but its life was very short. In 1888, John B. Balch and Charles B. Herron established the Jackson *Times* and published it until the plant was sold to the Bolivar *Bulletin.* Herron retired to his farm, and Balch became foreman of the *Sun.*

"Cy" Balch, as he became known to the two generations of printers who served under him, was not only a good printer but he had the happy faculty of being able to teach others the printing art. His neat designing of advertisements became a model for others. Two generations of printers owed much to him for his instructions. Very kindly disposed he exercised much patience in teaching apprentice boys and was never harsh when errors were made. When confronted by his superiors with errors made by those under his direction he assumed responsibility and made amends, walked back into the composing room, mentioned to the one who had made the error, the nature of it, lighted his pipe and chuckled: "Oh, well, there is a heap of fun in America." John Balch inherited the talent and learned the trade of a printer from his father, David Balch, who had come to the town from Franklin, Tennessee, in the 1860's to work for Colonel Gates on the *Whig.* The elder Balch was also an excellent printer, both when he had a printing press of his own and when he was foreman of the *Whig* composing room.

Some local publications had such short lives that the names are almost completely forgotten and either single copies or no copies can be located. In 1857, the *Jackson Madisonian* appeared. In 1871, two papers appeared—the *Daily and Weekly Plain Dealer,* established by Harry Cozine, and the Jackson *Weekly Telegraph.* About the close of the century, there appeared a very spicy, popular paper called the *Gab-Fest,* which was published by John Balch and edited by Lelia Morgan

---

[19]For the past three years (1944) he has been with the Federal-State Relations Bureau, War Division, Department of Justice. He is regarded today as one of the most brilliant newspaper men produced by Tennessee.

Murrell. The *Farmer's Advocate,* in the 1870's, was a sixteen page farm journal of but a few issues. This was published by the *Whig and Tribune*.[14] Another paper that had but a few issues was *Fact and Fiction* (May 15, 1894). This was edited by Iverson C. Wells and carried stories by John Spencer, later of the Macon *Telegraph,* Macon, Georgia.

Many of the editors previously mentioned had hand and later steam printing presses where they did job work. One of the earliest books known to be published in Jackson was Obadiah Dodson's *Moral Instructor and Guide to Youth: A Book Containing Answers to Eleven Biblical Questions and Also Seventeen Propositions Upon the Training of Children.* This was published in 1844 by Gates and Parker. In the late 1880's McCowat Brothers established a job printing place. Later Ed Mercer became a partner and the firm took the name of McCowat-Mercer Printing Company.

The Jackson *Sun* was established in 1875 by B. A. Enloe and Colonel Robert Gates.[15] Two years later, it was consolidated with the *Whig and Tribune* and became known as the *Tribune and Sun.* By 1898 the *Sun* had passed into the hands of J. B. Gaines who sold to E. S. Trussell in 1905. Trussell certainly believed in freedom of the press, for he, a dyed-in-the-wool Yankee, permitted Miss Pet McCorry, who was one of the organizers of the United Daughters of the Confederacy, to write some very pungent editorials on Grant, Sherman, and Lincoln. In 1910, I. B. Tigrett bought the *Sun,* at which time Jesse Long became manager and Harris Brown became managing editor. In 1909, John W. Buford established the Jackson *Democrat,* but this was a political venture and soon ceased publication. In 1912, there was established the *Morning Jacksonian.* Head of the new enterprise was C. E. Pigford. Inability to get competent men to staff the new enterprise was a handicap. Sam Stockard, the editor, wrote some caustic editorials about the *Sun,* charging among other things that the *Sun* had borrowed a scuttle of coal from the *Jacksonian* and had never paid it back. The *Sun* came back and charged that the *Jacksonian* had borrowed everything from that paper except its

---

[14] No copies of the *Farmer's Advocate* have been located.

[15] A sketch of B. A. Enloe appears in a preceeding chapter, "Our Congressmen."

editorial policy. Stockard of the *Jacksonian* came back with the assertion that the *Sun* had no editorial policy which could be borrowed. Soon the *Jacksonian* was consolidated with the *Sun* when C. E. Pigford, Harris Robertson, Dr. J. L. Crook, Thomas Hughes, and J. W. Vanden bought the *Sun* from I. B. Tigrett, although the latter retained some stock, but Pigford was owner of the majority of the shares and so he became president and publisher. Albert Stone became general manager and vice-president, while Harris Brown kept his position as managing editor and was elected vice-president. Editor Brown wrote of his years with the *Sun:*

> As I look back over the 38 years in which I have been connected with the *Sun*, including the four years in which I did daily work while at college, I can see in our newspaper my ideal of journalism. For the publisher has not only given the people of this community a first class newspaper, the equal in dissemination of news to Memphis, Nashville dailies, but it has likewise maintained a strong editorial policy, looking always to the service of the community and striving at all times to make Jackson and Madison County bigger and better.[16]

The Sun's editorial policy and influence generally have contributed greatly to the growth and development of the city and county. It was vitally interested and fought for the locating of the M. and O. shops here, a million dollar investment, the locating of Lambuth College here, in helping Union University weather a financial crisis some years ago, in getting general aid for the new courthouse, and getting appropriations for the new Federal Building—two hard fought battles, in locating the Army Air Training school at McKellar Field, the shell loading plant near here, and other enterprises which have been the life of this growing community.

Through all these years the community has been blessed with men who had vision, ability, and dared to do what they thought was best for the good of the people. The press in the hands of such men is an engine of might and not of evil. An old *Whig and Tribune* of 1871 probably set the standards for those who were to follow with these words:

> Whenever an editor loses sight of the noble dignity of his calling and becomes a partisan—a blackguard, the tool of aspiring demogogues,

---

[16]Harris Brown before the Madison County Historical Society.

it would be good for the rising generation if his press could be blotted from society. . . . An editor that can not defend truth and justice and expose error and tyrany, in at least decent language had better throw up his profession and go to something else. If the people would have good order in society and good government, let them preserve the dignity of the press![17]

These publishers and editors of Madison have carried out the ideal that one of the most cherished American ideals is freedom of the press, and the community to-day is much larger and better because each one of them lived here.

[17] Jackson *Whig and Tribune*, September 16, 1871.

CHAPTER XXI

EDUCATION

Adequate funds for early common schools were nonexistent in the Western District. Practically no funds could be acquired from public land sales because all the best lands were already taken up by the settlers or included in the North Carolina land grants. Surveyors placed no value on the swampy lands which frequently overflowed and these were left largely unclaimed at from fifty cents per acre down to one cent an acre. A report of E. C. Chrisp, principal surveyor of the 10th district of Tennessee in 1828, contained the sad news that there was not one tenth of the vacant lands in this district that was worth twelve and one half cents per acre, that all of the valuable lands had been appropriated by military land warrants from North Carolina. In the same year Adam R. Huntsman made a report on the lands in the district that were unappropriated, to the effect that not more than half of these lands could be sold for $12\frac{1}{2}$ cents per acre.[1] The result of these financial difficulties was that during the pre-Civil War days, education was a private matter. Ministers, lawyers, and even newspaper editors frequently added to their income by serving as pedagogues, teaching the boys how to think by using the switch "decently and in order."

It was the natural course of events for these pioneers who came of the best families in North Carolina, South Carolina and Virginia to open some schools for their children very soon after they provided food and shelter for them. According to tradition, a log school house was built northwest of Jackson in 1822 and was taught by a Mr. Tyner. The Jackson Male Academy was opened in February, 1823, by R. C. Green. The Jackson *Gazette* of 1824 advertised the Jackson Female Academy under the direction of Miss Cameron and the Jackson

---

[1]Randolph *Recorder*, February 18, 1836.

Male Academy, of which Joshua Haskell was president. The following year the Academy of Jackson was opened in a building situated in a grove of beautiful oaks on the east side of the public square, and the Mt. Pinson Academy was opened by Thomas Henderson and his neighbors under the supervision of Rev. Andrew Caldwell and Rev. Stark Deeping.[2] During the same year the Jackson Male Academy was incorporated by an act of the legislature with William E. Butler, S. D. Hays, J. F. Brown, John Read, and Joshua Haskell appointed as the "body politic and corporate." By 1831, James Caruthers, president of this academy, was advertising for teachers and offering to pay them seven or eight hundred dollars annually for their services. William Stockwell must have answered this advertisement, for when school opened in the fall of 1831, it was he who with Samuel McClanahan was ready to instruct the gentlemen in algebra, geometry, trigonometry, and natural philosophy, charging the pupils from $8 to $16 tuition and $50 for board, washing, lodging, firewood and candles with a room to study for a session of five months.[3] In some of the announcements, a note was made that if each student would furnish a load of firewood, fifty cents would be deducted from the total cost. William Stockwell came to the academy well recommended and he was not easily forgotten, for he never permitted his rules to be wantonly violated without inflicting prompt punishment regardless of age or size of the pupil. He and Samuel McClanahan, who had a private school of his own in which he also taught the girls in an exclusive room to themselves, pledged themselves to prepare their students for college as well as any school in the state.[4]

Other instructors during those early years who thoroughly taught and scientifically flogged were Dr. McNutt; John Harton; Mr. Sloan; Mr. Gist, as zealous a devotee of the dictionary as he was skilled in the use of the rod; Mrs. Stark, who taught a school for girls; Mrs. Johnson, who had a music school; Mrs. Sarah Brown, who also had a school for girls; John Holden and the Bigelows. By 1826, a girl's academy (back of the Waddill place on Royal street) was opened by

---

[2]Jackson *Pioneer*, January 28, 1823; Jackson *Gazette*, May 24, June 11, 1824; June 4, 11, 1825.
[3]Jackson *Southern Statesman*, August 13, September 3, 1831.
[4]*Ibid.*

George Bigelow and his wife, a lady of rare culture.[5] Forty pupils attended this school this session. It must have been only for a short period, but the Bigelows also conducted the "Forked Deer Academy" for a time. John Holden came to Jackson from North Carolina in 1833, clerked in a store and taught a school nine miles north of Jackson. His was a subscription school, charging the pupils $3.50 per quarter. If he could get 35 pupils the school would be worth $225 a year, but he was boarding with James Fussell at $4 a month, so possibly he did not live in poverty.[6]

The general interest in education in the community is shown by the fact that in one single issue of the *District Telegraph* in 1839, there were five advertisements or announcements about the schools. James Vaulx, one of the trustees of the Jackson Female Academy demanded that the stockholder pay $3 per share; M. T. Purcell of the Denmark Female Academy was trying to secure a classical teacher immediately; Mrs. Bigelow was advertising her girls' school; James McClanahan, his school; Mrs. McIver was resuming her school duties; Mary B. Ganaway was opening an infants' school. There seemed to be more interest here in education than in some of the other sections, for these numerous institutions of learning attracted the attention of neighboring editors who commented upon the situation, thus:

The editor of the *Truth Teller* says there are in Jackson three schools devoted to female education—two to male and female, an academy to the instruction of boys and young men in the higher branches, and an INFANT SCHOOL. The citizens of Jackson must be rich in the poor man's blessings, and still richer in an enviable spirit of enlightened patriotism. The editor closes with the following patriotic sentiment: "Keep, if ye will, your boys at home, and learn them, but to dig and toil and gather together the 'filthy lucre' of the earth; but ye be patriotic and philanthropic, and love your country and your kind, neglect not the education of your daughter."[7]

---

[5]Jackson *Gazette*, March 25, 1826. This Bigelow school continued to exist until 1857. Mrs. Bigelow's granddaughter, Miss Cassie Mason, left Jackson after the Civil War and established "The Castle," a select girls' school at Tarrytown-on-the-Hudson, N. Y.

[6]Letter of John Holden from Jackson, Tennessee, August, 1833.

[7]Randolph *Recorder*, April 8, 1836; Jackson *District Telegraph*, January 8, 1839.

Denmark, too, was an early educational center blessed with both a male and a female academy. The male academy, established in the 1840's, was conducted by a Mr. Black, but it was the Female Academy that attracted students from West Tennessee and North Mississippi. By 1831, there were thirty-five pupils who were "variously examined in science, English grammar, geography, rhetoric, philosophy, chemistry, history, and painting." Two years later the trustees of the academy, headed by E. Mabry, placed the institution under the supervision of Lemuel Evans. By 1838, French, drawing, useful and ornamental arts and needle work was added to the curriculum under the supervision of Rev. Peyton and his Lady who had come here from Virginia. "If sufficient number of scholars can be obtained," the trustees advertised, "to justify the expense of the instruments, music on the piano will be taught." Board at very low rates was offered in Rev. Peyton's or other respectable homes.[8] As late as 1858 announcements of examinations and commencement exercises of the Denmark school can be found in the papers. At the close of this year a cantata, "Florus Festival," was presented by the pupils for the pleasure of the public in general.[9]

The name of "S.W.B.U." of old and "Union" of to-day is dear to the hearts of many a professional or business man in Madison County. Southwestern Baptist University had its origin in the old Madison Male Academy which was chartered by the Legislature of the State of Tennessee in 1834 with the following appointed as the first trustees: James Caruthers, Milton Brown, William Armour, John W. Campbell, Joshua Haskell, Andrew L. Martin, J. H. Creighton, C. A. Street, and W. H. Stephens. In 1843-44 the institution was reorganized under the name of "West Tennessee College" with James Caruthers, John W. Campbell, W. H. Stephens, Milton Brown, Robert Fenner, M. Cartmell, Alexander Jackson, J. L. Talbot, Samuel Lancaster, A. W. Campbell, Samuel McClanahan, George Snider, A. W. O. Totten, and James Vaulx as trustees. In 1846, the United States released to the State of Tennessee its title to certain lands in Tennessee on the establishment of a college at Jackson, so the treasurer of the State was directed

---

[8]*Southern Statesman,* June 19, 1831; March 23, 1833; Jackson *District Telegraph,* March 30, 1838.
[9]*West Tennessee Whig,* June 18, 1858.

to issue to this college in Jackson a warrant for $40,000 worth of Tennessee five per cent bonds. With this aid from the Federal government, supplemented by private subscription, the college became very prosperous. When the institution took its new name, James Caruthers exchanged the old academy property plus the payment of $3,000 for the ground upon which the institution now stands. The original plot contained forty-six acres and was a part of land owned by Andrew L. Martin.[10] An old insurance policy describes the buildings that were erected on this new location:

> The President and Trustees of West Tennessee College wish to insure in your office [J. W. Campbell's] the college building. It is a frame building, the one now occupied by the College House. There are no other buildings within forty feet of the house and these are small log houses. It is wished to insure $2,000 on the college house which is thought to be worth $3,000.
> Very respectfully yours,
> JAMES CARUTHERS,
> President of Trustees.[11]

Gleanings from the newspapers of the 1840's and 1850's show that the faculty and trustees worked unceasingly to make this a real college of West Tennessee and far more solicitude was felt for the quality of the work than in regard to the number of students. A full course of college studies was offered by efficient teachers who kept a watchful eye on the students, for no trifling or inefficient students were retained.[12]

West Tennessee College came out of the Civil War with very little injury. At times the campus was used by the Federal Army for camping grounds, the buildings for headquarters and as a hospital. The college was re-opened in 1865 with Rev. William Shelton, D.D., as president and was more largely attended than it had been before the war.

In 1873, after a cholera epidemic in Murfreesboro, Tennessee, it was considered advisable to change the location of Union University, maintained by the Baptist of Tennessee, North Alabama, and Mississippi. Jackson was selected as the location

---

[10]Goodspeed, *History of Tennessee*, 828.
[11]J. W. Campbell Letter Book, MS.
[12]*West Tennessee Whig*, August 31, 1855; April 27, 1860. The faculty in 1855 included: Charles Dod, president; James Holmes, Lorenzo Lea, M. R. Gabrielle, George D. Holmes.

and Union University of Murfreesboro and West Tennessee College were merged and the name changed to Southwestern Baptist University. The town and county of Madison subscribed $50,000 worth of stock, on the condition that $300,000 be raised by the church within ten years. As the drive got under way on the part of the Baptist to raise their part and the citizens of Jackson to support the institution, a very able faculty was assembled which included W. D. Shelton, president from 1875 to 1877, who was followed by Professor George Jarman, chairman of the faculty, and Dr. G. M. Savage who was president from 1890 until his retirement in 1935.

During that first year of the Southwestern Baptist University the trustees were simply bursting with pride over the faculty that they had secured for the law department. Three very able lawyers, Howell E. Jackson, Alexander Campbell, and Thomas Freeman, were on this faculty. Howell E. Jackson, was described as one of the ablest lawyers and most refined gentleman of which Tennessee could boast. Alexander Campbell, the famous general of the Civil War, who had earned an honorable reputation in his profession, and Thomas J. Freeman, an "ornament alike to the bar and bench," added much to the prestige of the institution.[13] Professor H. C. Irby came to the University in 1883. No one has left a more lasting impression on the students who sat under him than did Dr. Irby. He loved his students and they loved him. He was a Christian scholar and gentleman, who knew his Bible so well that he would arise in chapel, fold his hands, announce his chapters and verses and repeat his readings for the morning without opening the Bible. He was spoken of as a model man and an admirable scholar.[14] Other members of the faculty and students who are often recalled are Dr. George Jarman, the man of great force of character; Dr. G. M. Savage, the Godly man with culture; Ben Lindsay who was responsible for the establishing of the Juvenile Court and the Court of Domestic Relations; Walter Holmes, editor of *Matida Zeigler*, the first magazine published in the U. S. for the blind; Sam Lancaster, Jackson's engineer, who left here and built the Columbian Highway. The name of South-

---

[13]Jackson *Sun*, July 30, 1875.
[14]*Forked Deer Blade*, January 19, 1884. It was said that Dr. Irby was such a fine teacher for he inspired his students with his nobility of character, was gentle but demanded good work.

western Baptist University was changed to "Union" September 17, 1907 and has continued to be a center of educational and cultural life in the community.

In the mid-nineteenth century, when most of the educational program of the day was under the guidance of the church, the Memphis Conference, realizing the need of a girls' school in West Tennessee, undertook to place such an institution in Jackson. The Memphis Conference Female Institute was organized in 1840, located on five acres of land donated by William E. Butler (the former location of his race track), and buildings, brick ones with a wooden roof were erected.[15] Rules were strict, so strict that by 1849 the school had enjoyed the liberal patronage of the most respectable families of North Mississippi and the Western District. A contemporary editor added: "No southern Gentleman need look beyond our institution to find for his daughter an education at once thorough and refined under the best security which judicious arrangements, parental discipline and unremitting attention can furnish."[16] Much credit for the standing of the school is due to the presidents, Dr. Lorenzo Lea, Rev. Benjamin Hubbard, Dr. Amos W. Jones (1853-1878), and Dr. A. B. Jones who succeeded his father and served as president for twenty-five years. These leaders with such instructors as Mrs. Dick Hays, Miss Cassie Mason, Miss Ida Duncan, Miss Duval, Miss Mary Sue Mooney trained hundreds of Christian women who have done a noble part in the moulding of the next generation.[17]

In 1924, the Memphis Conference Female Institute was expanded into the present Lambuth College, which is located

---

[15] The Trustees of this institution also insured the property with J. W. Campbell, whose records tell of a brick building, with a smoke house and a kitchen 60 feet away from the main building, of the mahogany sofa, mahogany bedsteads, chairs, pianos, and one thousand ninety pounds of feathers. No boarding school could be well recommended without plenty of good feather beds and bolsters.

[16] *West Tennessee Whig*, March 16, 1849.

[17] A list of the trustees in 1878 give a splendid idea of some of the people of the community who were interested in Christian education. Those included were: Rev. A. W. Jones, Milton Brown, Dr. Alexander Jackson, Rev. J. H. Evans, Dr. J. W. Collins, D. E. Palmer, Dr. John Chester, Rev. Lorenzo Lea, Rev. John Moss, Rev. R. V. Taylor, J. E. Heard, Rev. J. H. Brooks, Rev. B. A. Hays, Rev. W. T. Harris, Robert Haynes, Dr. R. R. Dashiell. *Catalogue of the Memphis Conference Female Institute*, 1878.

in Jackson. This four-year institution is endeavoring to preserve and carry out the best traditions of its mother institution and yet fit its students for life in a modern world.

Madison College at Spring Creek was also a denominational school of the pre-Civil War days. Jerry Haughton, the outstanding educational leader in the community, was very interested in the school. A three story brick building occupied a commanding position in the shady grove in the thriving village of Spring Creek. The school, operated under the patronage of the West Tennessee Baptists, had a faculty made up of Rev. Joseph Hamilton, president, and four teachers, Lysander Houk, Giddings Buck, Isaac Day, and Alexander Askew. The standards were high and its discipline was strict. Of the forty students who were enrolled for the session of 1859-60, thirteen were expelled during the year. The institution boasted that it would not tolerate idleness, intemperance, or any vice by which injury is committed upon all who are in any way connected with the institution, that "no student will be retained in the institution who is guilty of intemperance, profanity, or any species of immorality or any conduct which renders him an unfit associate for young gentlemen of correct habits."[18]

Although we may smile when we read accounts of the early schools and the masters who frequently "taught and scientifically flogged," who were zealous devotees of Mauray's grammar and the dictionary, and who were quite skilled in the use of the rod, we cannot help from admiring them for making the attempt to improve the minds of the youth of the day and promote education in general even if this was a frontier community. Book and drug stores combined were opened in the community in 1824, men like Elijah Bigelow made special orders of dictionaries, slates, arithmetics and Bibles, but the libraries of the planters were small. Many had no books at all, some had one, a few had 15 or 25, and one John Weatt, a lawyer, had 94 volumes which included four volumes of Shakespeare, the life of Washington, Tom Paine, six volumes of Scott, three volumes of Milton, and a volume of Burns. James Cockrill, a typical planter of 1826 had 600 acres of land, 17 negroes, $445 in cash, hogs, cattle, and plantation tools, but only three books—the *Bible*, the *Constitution of the United States,* and James' *On*

---

[18]Catalogue of Madison College, 1859-1860.

Domestic Medicine. Robert Fenner felt that education meant so much that he provided in his will for the education of his younger children before the estate was divided and also provided that each orphan grandchild "receive from the General Stock or the Estate, Board and such other allowance as may be deemed necessary for defraying the expenses of a Good English Education."[19]

The smoke of battle of that Sectional Conflict had not blown away before the people of the South began to rebuild. One of the important phases of the reconstruction was the opening of adequate schools. At least seven schools were opened within the first few years after the war in Jackson—one by the Presbyterians, one by the Catholics, one by the Baptists, one by the Colored Methodists, and the others by individuals.

The Presbyterian High School, which offered an extensive curriculum under the able direction of Rev. Johnson Eaton Bright and his corps of teachers, which included Mrs. Sarah B. Bright, Misses Camile Bright, Lilla May Bright, and Carrie Drew, was located in the old Caruthers place on East Baltimore.[20] J. W. Campbell was president of the board of trustees and Colonel Robert I. Chester was vice-president.[21]

The Baptist Female Academy, established in 1871, was located on the site of the present Jackson *Sun* building. Ninety-three students were enrolled here in 1872, where the lady teachers extended close supervision over their charges, "frequently accompanying them in walks for recreation and *occasionally to the stores."* Rev. G. W Johnson was assisted by four teachers in conducting the work of the institution.[22]

The Academy of Immaculate Conception was chartered by an act of the Legislature of the State of Tennessee in 1869 with the names of Vincencia Fitzpatrick, Mary Pius Fitzpatrick, Dominica Fitzpatrick, and Josephine Whelon on the charter. These Dominican Sisters, led by Sister Mary Pius, the brilliant and lovable "Mother Superior," purchased the palatial homestead of General Samuel J. Hays located on the gentle rise northeast of the Mobile and Ohio Railroad station on Hays

---

[19]Madison County Will Book 1821-1835. As the community advanced in years it also advanced in wisdom—the size of the libraries.
[20]This place is called the Bray place today.
[21]*West Tennessee Directory of 1872.*
[22]*Catalogue of the Baptist Female Institute 1872.*

Avenue near Preston, and opened a school under the system of education used by St. Agnes in Memphis. The building was destroyed by fire in 1873, so the school was moved to the homestead of Judge Milton Brown on Baltimore street. The Dominican Sisters of the St. Agnes Community had charge of the school, which had been moved to the present location on Main street, from 1891 until 1900, but the St. Cecilia Congregation of Nashville assumed responsibility of the school in 1900 and are still in charge of the school, which has played an important part in the educational and religious life of the community.[23]

The Harper Academy existed before the Sectional Conflict, for on September 6, 1860, the mayor and aldermen of Jackson rented the Temperance Hall to "Major" Harper for $50 for the rest of the year, but the rent should be appropriated to payment of tuition of indigent children. During the war Harper conducted a gun shop in connection with his school. In 1868, the J. H. Harper Male and Female Institute was chartered for thirty-three years.[24] Professor Harper, an independent and efficient teacher, was assisted in 1876 by Kate M. Harper and Fannie B. Harper. A handbill of the school and an advertisement in a contemporary paper are an illustration of the great zeal that Professor Harper had for popular education:

> True education is the only guide to happiness. We believe that education is the common birthright of every child of men, and that the legislator who refuses his influence to perfect the title to this greatest of all human rights, is simply a disgrace to the position he occupies, and a robber of the rising generation of its brightest jewel, which is liberty to know the truth. Send the children to the Jackson Male and Female Institute, and they will be received and properly educated; and to the poor and needy and to those who have no money, we say, "Come."[25]

---

[23]*Acts of Tennessee 1869-70; West Tennessee Directory of 1872; Forked Deer Blade,* January 7, 1888.

[24]*Acts of Tennessee of 1868.* Besides teaching a regular "army" of children through the years, Mr. Harper served as city recorder, alderman, as mayor in 1860, and as postmaster in 1866-1868.

[25]Goodspeed, *History of Tennessee,* 868; *Whig and Tribune,* August 5, 1876. This academy was located on College Street near Royal. In 1857, the editor of the Jackson *Madisonian* said that Professor Harper should "be lauded for his indomitable energy and determined zeal" in establishing the high-grade school. Jackson *Madisonian,* June 20, 1857.

This was a bold stand for an educator to take at this time, for these were the days when the public school system was being advocated and there was much opposition to the whole idea by the wealthy and influential men of the community.

As early as 1878, plans were being made by the Colored Methodist for a school. The epidemic of 1878 hindered plans but at the meeting of the Conference in 1879, it was decided to purchase a lot in Jackson. On January 15, 1880, four acres of land was purchased for $40 and thus began the work that has been a powerful factor in the uplifting of the colored people of the South. Much credit is due to these early workers for they were scarcely a dozen years from slavery, inexperienced and untaught.

A building was erected in 1882, and school opened under the name of the Colored Methodist High School with Miss Jennie Lane as teacher. In 1884, the institution received a charter under the title of Lane Institute, while eleven years later a new charter was granted to Lane College. The Methodist Episcopal Church, South, saw the need for Negro education, so Rev. T. F. Saunders was appointed by the Conference to come to Lane about 1886. There were not more than a dozen pupils there at this time. Rev. Saunders was the first president of the college, serving until 1903 and rendering a great service to the colored people in the field of Christian education when such work was frowned upon by many. But Rev. Saunders was well chosen for his task, for he was a former teacher, an energetic minister in the Methodist Church and a former Confederate soldier.

Much of the success of Lane College is due to the untiring efforts, leadership, and self-sacrifice of Bishop Lane, the founder of the college. He grew to manhood on a plantation just five miles east of Jackson. As one of twenty-seven slaves on the plantation of Cullen Lane, he was not harmed by the whites during the war. His master was ruined financially by the war and died in poverty. Isaac Lane purchased his master's library in order that the money might be used to give his former master a nice funeral. When Isaac Lane became free, he established the habit of regular hours for reading and studying the Bible. The Bishop's son, Professor J. F. Lane, became president in 1907 and served until 1944. Jackson owes these two early presidents a debt of gratitude for their efforts to educate and Christianize a large part of the population in the community.

Bishop Lane gave much credit to the financial aid and advice that was given to him by many of his white friends, especially Wyatt T. Taylor. In fact the Bishop doubted whether his venture would have proven a success or not without this aid. W. A. Caldwell, Chairman of the Board of Directors of the First National Bank, wrote about the Bishop and the importance of Lane College in this community:

> I have often heard my good friend, the late Bishop Isaac Lane, an outstanding citizen of this community whose long useful life of 104 years was possibly the most potent influence in promoting the cordial relationship which exists between the races in this section, state that the advice and financial aid of his loyal white friends here enabled him to make an humble beginning in the founding of Lane College, which was afterward through the years generously augmented by gifts from many other sections. It is a monument to him and to his unselfish lifework, and promises to continue as an abiding influence for good, to all time. Born in slavery, by his own initiative and force of character, he laboriously acquired an education, and through his unselfish efforts enabled thousands of the youth of his race to secure this blessing.[26]

This saintly old man was beloved by the community. He was a welcome visitor in the white churches in the city, always sitting in the rear of the balcony, often praying most beautiful prayers at the close of such services.

Another private school in the 1870's was the Medon Academy. This was taught by F. H. Williams and Mrs. L. W. Cradle. The school occupied the lower floor of the Masonic building.[27]

Leaders in the southeast corner of Madison County, such as Dr. John D. Smith, Dr. S. A. Smith, Dr. John Sherill, Rev. D. J. Franklin, P. B. Farrow, John West, J. B. Crook, G. L. Ross, C. M. Mason, I. J. Gailbraith secured a charter for the Henderson Male and Female Institute in 1870. By 1876 this was operating under the name of Henderson Masonic Male and Female Institute with one hundred sixty-six students under

---

[26] W. A. Caldwell, *Wise Sayings of Wise Men*, (McCowat-Mercer Press, Jackson, Tennessee, 1945), 35; Jackson *Sun*, May 21, 1916; May 22, 1923.

[27] *Whig and Tribune*, May 15, 1875.

the direction of G. M. Savage, president, and eight faculty members: N. P. Hackett, J. B. Inman, J. D. Futrell, Dr. W. J. Crook, Misses Annie Owen, S. E. Kendall, Dora Brooks.[28]

An act of the Legislature of Tennessee of 1873 provided for the establishment and maintenance of a uniform system of public schools out of a fund derived from state and county taxes and also provided for the creation of a board of three directors.[29] W. P. Robertson, the chairman of this board, was assisted by James O'Connor and John E. Glass. These early board members secured the brick building south of the present Madison County Health Unit and opened a five months' school under Miss Kate Stark, her sister, and Miss Sophie Read.

During this time there was much opposition to the free school, as the more wealthy citizens were still saturated with the ideas of the old academy of former days—they did not like the idea of the "new fangled free schools, for they would take scholars away from the University and the Institute. One academy lover wrote: "Let the people pay for the fancy education, not the public. Some citizens think it is as much the job of the community to educate a man's children as it is to vote a tax to clothe them. Why spend this money this way and leave the beautiful city of Jackson at the mercy of a match! No engine, no water, and yet without providing for it, men insanely vote away one tenth of all her tax receipts to educate white and black scholars to speak Latin and Greek and to build three story brick school houses with mansard roofs."[30] An advocate of the public schools answered the above saying that it was not the intention to teach scholars:

> To speak Greek
> Like pigs squeak
> But to teach them, black and white
> To know their duty and the right
> That ever one may learn in youth
> A love for justice and the truth.[31]

---

[28]*Acts of Tennessee,* 1870; *Catalogue of the Henderson Masonic Male and Female Institute 1876.*

[29]C. B. Ijams, "City Schools of Jackson," Jackson *Sun,* May 21, 1916. The sketch of the city schools is based upon this sketch by C. B. Ijams.

[30]Jackson *Dispatch,* 1880, from a clipping in scrap book belonging to Ernest Edenton.

[31]*Ibid.*

Eight citizens formed a committee and purchased the W. H. Long residence, which was situated on the lot where College Street building now stands, that they might establish a Presbyterian Academy. But, Dr. Bright, who was chosen to open the school, declined to become its president and the effort was a failure.

The short term school that was established in 1873 was not adequate, so in 1879 an ordinance was passed creating the Jackson City Graded Schools, levying one mill per dollar on real estate and personal property. This first school had only seven grades, but one year was added in 1882, others in 1901, 1903, 1908, 1912, and finally the twelfth in 1914. Three presidents of the board of education, W. P. Robertson (1879-1898), W. F. Alexander (1898-1912), and J. A. Thompson (1912-1915), were assisted in the educational work by other board members: E. S. Mallory, James O'Connor, J. H. Hirsch, J. H. Duke, John W. Gates, Hu C. Anderson, W. T. Nelson, J. W. McDonald, R. S. Fletcher, L. E. Mathis, S. P. Anderson, W. T. Blackard, J. H. Price, M. H. Taylor, L. O. Sweatman, S. B. Enochs, Dr. J. M. Glenn, R. F. Spragins. These early board members worked unceasingly and without financial remuneration. They knew that their only reward was the manhood and womanhood of the next generation.

The Long property was purchased from the "Committee of Eight" and the board erected on this lot a frame building where College Street School was erected. The "Fourth Ward School," later known as West Jackson, was erected in 1893, the present College Street building in 1897, Alexander in 1909, High School on Deaderick in 1912 (the Rochelle sanatorium had been used as a high school for two years and then the third floor at College Street), the Junior High Annex in 1915, the High School on Allen Avenue in 1929, the present Whitehall building in 1920, Merry High (Colored) in 1938.

There have been eight superintendents connected with the city system: J. C. Brooks, 1879-1882; T. J. Porter, 1882-1883; Frank M. Smith, 1883-1887; Thomas H. Paine, 1887-1899; S. A. Mynders, 1899-1903; G. R. McGee, 1903-1912; R. L. Bynum, 1912-1916; C. B. Ijams, 1916-1946. Three of these have served as state superintendents of schools—Thomas Paine, 1883-1887; Frank M. Smith, 1887-1891; S. A. Mynders, 1903-

1907. C. B. Ijams served on the State Board of Education for twenty years.

J. C. Brooks stood for discipline, thoroughness, punctuality, making pupils feel that they must earn their way to advancement; Thomas H. Paine was a most beloved and respected superintendent; S. A. Mynders was an efficient organizer and later president of West Tennessee State Teachers College; G. R. McGee, a cultured gentleman and author who stood for high ideals; R. L. Bynum, the pioneer in the Junior High system in Tennessee and the United States; Miss Fannie Fenner, "a woman of culture who had great love in her heart for children"; Miss Kate Stark, "a lovely lady and a good teacher"; Mrs. W. F. Barry, a gracious lady and a brilliant teacher; Mrs. Camile Bright Bell, a "woman whom words could not describe." One would have to know her to appreciate her. She left her impress upon the schools of Jackson. The late Monroe Anderson said of her: 'There was never a dull moment in her school room.' "[32]

By an amendment to the city charter in 1915, the aldermanic government became a commission form. The board of education was abolished and all its functions and perogatives were assumed by the commissioner of education, who acts with the other two commissioners on all matters pertaining to the schools.[33] These commissioners included Z. K. Griffin, Joe Pope, T. H. Campbell, J. D. Johnson, J. L. Harris, and Perry Callahan.

As early as 1873, the influential planters of the Pinson community, with A. S. Rogers, chairman of the Board of Trustees, had built up a high school with an enrollment of one hundred. The commencement in 1876 was a gala occasion. Over a thousand people attended the concert, the commencement exercises, partook of the bounteous dinner, and listened

---

[32]Miss Alice Shapard, "History of Education in Madison County," paper read before the Madison County Historical Society, April 1944, and published in the Jackson *Sun*, April, 1944.

[33]When the educational bill was passed in 1909 which provided for a normal school in each grand division, Jackson put in her bid for this institution and a survey of the county was made which showed ten very strong points for its being located here. "Brief in Behalf of the County of Madison and City of Jackson in the Matter of Locating the State Normal School for the Western Division."

to the orator of the day, E. L. Bullock, a most forceful speaker, one of the most eloquent in the state.[34]

In 1838, the General Assembly of the State of Tennessee passed an act to have elected five commissioners from each civil district in the several counties to "establish common schools," and immediately following the first school census in Madison County was taken.[35] There were 3,493 white children with $2,176.66 in public school funds. In the 1840 report there were 19 schools listed, 19 teachers with an average salary of $15.71, and a term of five and one half months. District No. 1 reported the building of a new school house at a cost of $15. No records were kept from 1846 until 1907. When the new Public School Law was passed in 1873, the "poor schools" were abolished and "schools were declared free to all persons between 6 and 21 years of age." District boards governed the schools until 1907 when a County Board was created by an Act of the Legislature. The first board included W. S. Pope, Charlie Key, Benjamin Tyson, J. T. Raines.[36] The school census of 1907 showed 17,035 children in the county including Jackson. Fifty-five teachers taught the sixty-eight schools for eight months in the white schools at an average salary of $42 per month. There were 36 colored schools where the average teacher's salary was from $20 to $30.[37] Some time after the County Board was established, a High School board was created which existed until it was consolidated with the County Board in 1921. As the years passed the county schools grew, new buildings were erected, consolidations were made, transportation facilities were improved, and conditions in general improved, until though the period covered in this volume only extends to 1917, it must be added that the County and its

---

[34]*Whig and Tribune*, June 19, 1876.

[35]*Madison County Education System, Bulletin* I (1941).

[36]*Ibid.* Members of the County Board of Education who have served since its creation in 1907 not including those already mentioned are: J. C. Pearson, R. C. Mayo, A. S. Johnson, M. V. B. Exum, Esq. Gunter, J. D. Hopper, R. E. L. Henderson, J. B. Young, J. T. McCutchen, T. E. Mercer, J. E. Watson, A. R. Matthews, Charles Key, J. A. Futrell, H. T. Crittendon, E. T. Blackmon, A. B. Foust, J. E. Spencer, J. P. Outland, J. N. Robinson, J. L. Mays, L. T. Greer, L. F. Ware, John H. Meriwether, George Swink, Hugh Harvey, J. S. Matthews, Jr., Fred Harris, Tom Patton.

[37]*Ibid.*

board members have a right to be proud of the present school system.[38]

The foregoing long train of schools should be ample evidence to prove that the people who came to the Western District carried with them a desire to be well educated and to see that their children had an opportunity to learn. It is no wonder that Jackson soon became known as "the seat of learning and the temple of law." It might be said that a Western District paper of 1839 set the pattern and the following generations followed the pattern, the result of which are schools that any community can well be proud. This editor of 1839 wrote:

EDUCATION—History bears incontestable evidence that ignorance and superstition have caused the downfall of every previous Republic. Intelligence then is the very vital spark from which the sacred flame of all civil and religious Liberty was kindled—it cannot be cherished too dearly or prized too highly.[39]

---

[38]County Superintendents: Benjamin R. Campbell, 1873-1875; Dr. J. D. Mason, 1875-1877; Alfred Oliver, 1877-1878; M. C. Meriwether, 1878-1881; W. G. Cockrill, 1881-1887; T. H. Drake, 1887-1895; C. P. Lowe, 1895-1897; W. M. Wharton, 1897-1905; L. C. Holt, 1905-1907; R. E. L. Bynum, 1907-1913; W. A. Malone, 1913-1925; J. L. Harris, 1925-1932; Kit Parker, 1932-1944; Bruce Bailey, 1944——.

[39]Paris *West Tennessean,* July 26, 1839.

CHAPTER XXII

RELIGION IN THE COUNTY

With a rifle in one hand and the Bible in the other, many an emigrant set forth for the Western District to make his future home. Small churches arose in this section just as soon as a few people could get together for religious conversation and worship. These people were not mere transients, they were old settlers from the eastern districts who had denominational preferences and had been accustomed to church organizations. The first meetings were in the crude log houses of the day. Then the chancel of the court house, occupied by the lawyer at intervals for six days in the week, was occupied by the man of God on the seventh—often by ministers of different denominations at different hours on that seventh day. Methodist, Baptist, and Presbyterians appeared in this new section very soon after the district opened up. As to which appeared first, a correct answer has not been found. The Methodists appointed two ministers to go to the Jackson Purchase in 1820 "to labor and report in the ensuing spring the true situation on the country"; records of the Western Presbytery, September 25, 1823, tell of a congregation being organized at Jackson since the last meeting;[1] the Western District Baptist Association was formed in 1822 and a call for a meeting of the Baptist "at a meeting house southeast of Jackson" for the purpose of forming the Forked Deer Association appeared in the Jackson *Gazette* of 1825.[2] It is no wonder that one of the early Methodist minsters reported that he had three enemies to fight —the wilderness, the devil, and the Scotch-Presbyterians.

Every frontier, and this section was no exception, was in a pressing need of moral restraint and guidance and the guardian

---

[1] S. C. Williams, *West Tennessee*, 186; Records of the Western Tennessee Presbytery, 193, Presbyterian Archives, Montreat, N. C.
[2] Jackson *Gazette*, June 25, 1825.

of the morals of the little communities was the frontier churches. The church frequently assumed the responsibility of regulating business dealings, the amusements of the community, and the relationship between master and slaves. Some of the causes of the discipline of the early Baptist church serve as an illustration of the place of the church in the life of the community. Lieing, fighting, dancing, gambling, intoxication, immoral conduct, selling an unsound mare, stealing and playing cards were against the rules of the church. With liquor twenty-five to fifty cents a gallon, drunkenness was really the cause of most of the trouble in the church and the community. Plenty of liquor meant many hand to hand fights, when "they tasted often, drank deep, and would let fly the fists and smack several noses." Seldom was there a public day without "sundry fights, without somebody's nose smashed, eyes gouged or head bruised."[3] One Presbyterian minister of the Shiloh Presbytery was charge with being drunk himself, at a corn husking, at a school entertainment, and at a social gathering at his own home. A witness testified that on one occasion when the minister was asked to serve the chicken, he missed the chicken and stuck the fork in the table.[4] Resolutions in the Methodist Conference in 1833 urged the ministers to refrain from the common mode of "electioneering," as it had an evil influence upon society. The Methodist historian, McFerrin, contended that strong drink "had blasted the character, destroyed the intellect, and undermined the estates and carried to premature graves tens of thousands of citizens of the country."[5]

Two short years after the Western District was obtained from the Chickasaws, the Tennessee Annual Conference of 1820 appointed Rev. Hezekiah Holland and Lewis Garrett, Jr. to come to the region. At the end of the first year, the two reported a membership in the district of 146 whites and 13 colored, all of which were thought to be former Methodists

---

[3] William T. Sweet, *The Church as Moral Courts of the Frontier* (Reprint from *Church History* March, 1933), 10-13; J. S. Williams, *Old Times*, 134-135.

[4] W. T. Sweet, *Church as Moral Courts of the Frontier*, 20.

[5] John McFerrin, *Methodist in Tennessee* (Nashville, 1895), II, 424, 438. "Electioneering" was the frontier term for the politicians furnishing plenty of liquor—in fact enough to get sufficient votes to win an election.

who had come to the district to live.[6] These two men and Andrew Crawford, who was appointed to ride the circuit of the Forked Deer District in 1822, were better known as "circuit riders." These knights of the saddle and messengers of God in the wilderness, the pioneers of religion in West Tennessee, hewed civilization and the church a way through a forest primeval. What the Catholic priest was to Mexico, the circuit rider was to Tennessee. On his raw-boned horse, across which was flung a pair of saddle-bags, this simple and sincere man of God with his hard, austere, almost terrible view of life came into the new country to save souls. His path was beset by death. He would ride for days at a time through inclement weather to keep an appointment to preach the Word to those who hungered for it. Scarcity of food, long hours of work, a bridge swept away by heavy rains, heavy snow fall that obscured the trail might have caused others to turn back, but not this man whose yearly stipend was rarely more than eighty dollars but whose religion was a real thing. His manners were unpolished but he managed to open up a world of eternal happiness to those who listened to him "preach the Gospel to every creature."[7]

In 1822, when the Forked Deer presiding elder's district was formed with Lewis Garrett, Jr., presiding elder, there were sixteen ministers under him and a membership of 687. He was followed in 1823 by the "much beloved and eminently useful" Robert Paine, Joshua Boucher (1824-1826) and Thomas Smith (1827-1830). Although G. W. D. Harris, an early presiding elder, was the brother of Governor Isham G. Harris, and the Supreme Court Judge William R. Harris, he was ranked by many as the greatest of the three. He left this description of the early church in the West: "The country was but sparsely settled and the appointments far between. We preached generally in private homes. Some church buildings began to spring up; rude indeed, most of them of rough hewed log-houses. Soon camp meeting grounds began to dot our country. Our beloved Methodism soon spread over the land and in an emi-

---

[6]Embree Blackard, "Planting Methodism in West Tennessee" (Unpublished Thesis, Emory University, Atlanta, Ga.), 37; S. C. Williams, *West Tennessee,* 186.

[7]James Phelan, *Tennessee,* 227-232.

RELIGION IN THE COUNTY

nent sense became the religion of this country."[8]

In 1826, the Methodist Episcopal Church, (later known as First) was organized in Jackson under the leadership of Rev. Thomas Neely with eight members, among whom were Wyatt Epps and wife, Joseph Douglas and wife and Robert Brown. The organization took place in the log courthouse on the northeast corner of court square. "At early candle light," services were held here and in privates homes until 1831, when a house of worship was built on the lot just across the street from the present location of the church. In 1833, there were forty-two white and thirteen colored members in the church. In 1851, the trustees, Amos W. Jones, Joseph C. Sharp, and Milton Brown, sold this property to the Jackson Sons of Temperance for $900 and purchased the south half of block number 50 for $250, on which was built a two story brick building by the contractors, Brown Brothers and Newell.[9]

The Methodist in the Medon community began meeting in the home of Mauldin Reeves in 1826 and met here for ten years before a log church was constructed on the land furnished by William R. Reeves. This house of worship became known as "Reeves Chapel." In 1850, a half-acre of land was bought from the Masonic Lodge in Medon and a frame church was built, being dedicated by Dr. A. W. Jones with Robert Gregory, preacher in charge. This was a typical frontier Methodist church with a glorious revival held by Rev. John Vincent, and others held each year, with a strict observance of the Sabbath, with no unholy music but much hymn singing with the minister lining the hymns, with camp meetings that were prepared for a year in advance—wonderful spiritual occasions—with many homes of the members, such as the Reeves, Swinks, Harrisons, the Manleys, always open to the preachers.[10]

---

[8] S. C. Williams, *West Tennessee*, 188.

[9] During the Civil War, the church building was used as a hospital and as a stable. In later years (the 1880's) the Federal Government paid for damages done by Federal troops. The church building of 1851 was remodeled in 1886 at a cost of $10,000. This building was destroyed by fire in 1912. The present building was opened September 6, 1914, with services conducted by Bishop Murrel. The part the church played in Christian education will be discussed in the chapter on "Education."

[10] Mrs. Lena Lacy Murdock, "Early Days in Medon," Jackson *Sun*, June 17, 1945.

Among the early settlers of Madison County were Adam and Aquilla Brown who purchased land seven and one half miles northeast of Jackson on December 8, 1824 from Isaac Ruthland and built a home on a site on the above mentioned land. Soon they built a larger home in which there was a parlor twenty-four by twenty-four feet and it was here that religious meetings of the good Methodists of the community were held until a church could be built. On April 2, 1835, Adam Brown conveyed one acre of land to the following trustees: D. D. Bennett, Jas. L. M. Donald, Thomas Rawlings, Fordham Blackmon, Mathew Jackson, and J. G. Thornton "to erect and build thereon a place of worship for the Methodist Episcopal Church in the United States of America." This was the beginning of the church that is known today as "Brown's Church." This building of 1835 was a large white frame building. On May 17, 1859, the same Adam Brown conveyed another lot, adjoining the first, of about one and one-half acres to Fordam Blackmon, Thomas Rollins, Sr., William D. Brigance, John T. Thomas, and James Blackmon as trustees of the church.[11]

Among the Methodist churches in the county, Bascom Chapel in the old tenth district should be mentioned. The congregation lives only in the memories of the sons and daughters of those faithful members of the mid-nineteenth century. Among those were Dr. Wood who gave the ground for the house of worship, Dr. John Stovall, Giles White, David and Hal Yarbrough, Benjamin Brooks, Sam Matthews, Willis Small, James McClelland.

The Presbyterians in the county organized a congregation in the late 1822 or early 1823,[12] but evidently the organization was not complete for a *Gazette* of June 26, 1824 announced that Rev. Mr. John Gillespie "will attend at the academy this day for the purpose of establishing a Presbyterian church."[13] J. W.

---

[11] Other members of this early church known as Brown's Church included the following families: The Adam Brown, the Seward Anderson, Rev. James Blackmon, William Henderson, William Hutchison, Jordan Boone, William Watson, Cullen Lane, Mrs. Catherine Nobles, Henry Kirby, Tip Thompson, Kem Parrish, Samuel Hopper, Mrs. Emily Persons, John Bumpus, Fogg, James Rollins, Doak, Carpenter. This list was furnished by Mrs. J. C. Page of Nashville, who is the granddaughter of Adam Brown.

[12] Records of the Western Tennessee Presbytery, Montreat, N. C.

[13] Jackson *Gazette*, June 26, 1824.

Hall served as the minister for Jackson, New Providence, and Mt. Pleasant for several years. By 1832, the growing congregation realized the need of a house of God for their own and a regular minister. Dr. Alexander A. Campbell, who accepted the call to be the first minister, donated the lot on the northeast corner of Main and Church streets for the church building. A building committee composed of William E. Butler, John W. Campbell, J. H. Mahon, Phillip Warlick, N. F. Warlick and James Greer was appointed and the contract was let to David Warlick. James Greer laid the corner stone of this large brick building, painted grey, with two entrances into a vestibule. The simple but elegant pulpit, a gift of John W. Campbell, was in front of a straight aisle. The colonial type of pews had doors at each end. A bell hung in the tower of the church.[14]

Many of those early Presbyterians were the "blue-stocking" kind and observed Sunday like most of the devout members of the church thought it ought to be observed. James Greer, an early citizen of Jackson, came to this section as a government surveyor. He lived in a large brick house seven miles out on the Christmasville road. Every Sunday morning the family barouche drawn by two or four horses brought all the family to church. If the roads were too bad, the men of the family came on horseback. This was a family where Sunday was observed as the Lord's day—only breakfast was cooked on this day, the other meals being eaten cold after being prepared the day before; where negroes were not allowed to chop wood on the seventh day; where the children were entertained on Sunday afternoons with pioneer and Bible stories and no visiting was allowed.

Records in a Presbyterian Session Book about the mid-nineteenth century show why it has been said many times that this was a time when men took their relgon seriously. These church members took turns accompanying the preacher in visiting the congregation; called upon former members who had absented themselves from services; tried to encourage singing by the congregation for it was a real part of worship; came before

---

[14]This building was remodeled in 1881. The present building of Indiana limestone was built in 1912 at a cost of $65,000. The building committee of this structure was L. L. Curtis, J. W. Vanden, J. W. Dickinson, and C. E. Pigford. Mrs. Bertie Owen, "History of the First Presbyterian Church," unpublished.

the session and confessed intemperance and asked for forgiveness; and called others before the Session to answer charges of intemperance, dishonest dealing, gambling which conduct was "unbecoming a Christian and inconsistent with the vows he, a member of the church, had taken."[15]

The silence of the ancient forest had never been broken by the praises to God, for the Indian war-hoop had scarcely died out amid the mighty oaks, when some study and devout Scotch-Presbyterian came to the region of what is now Denmark. John T. Bryant settled on the Estanuala road, James, David, and Frank Meriwether of Georgia and Robert Johnston of Virginia settled on "Johnston's Creek." In 1827, John Wharton and David Weir of North Carolina settled on "Cub Creek." These familes had already congregated for religious conversation, so when Rev. Weir arrived in 1827, the "Hopewell" church was soon organized with not more than twelve members, but David Weir was the minister, Robert Johnston and John Wharton were the ruling elders. A crude log house served as a meeting place for six years until this small congregation was merged with that at Denmark and the church became the "Presbyterian Church of Denmark." Here they used the school house as a meeting place, but one Sunday another denomination took their hour of meeting for the following Sabbath. Whereupon the Presbyterians became so incensed that before the next Sabbath they built a church of their own and services were held at the appointed hour. This building that they called "Jonah's Gourd" was especially sacred to the members because the building like the heaven and earth had taken place in the space of six days.[16]

Although the First Baptist Church in Jackson was not established until 1837, there were many Baptist and numerous "meeting-houses" in this section for at least fifteen years previous to this, for the Western District Association of Baptist was formed in 1822 and there was a call for a meeting at the meeting-house southwest of Jackson near Major Arnold's in 1825 to form the Forked Deer Association, which became the

---

[15] Session Book of the First Presbyterian Church, Jackson, Tennessee.

[16] Sketches of the Denmark community written for the *Presbyterian Herald* by a Mr. Caldwell and published during the months of July, August, and September, 1882.

mother of other important Baptist organizations in West Tennessee. This first meeting took place at Liberty Meeting House, Madison County, October 2 and 3, 1825, at which time Obadiah Dodson, the minister at Liberty, reported $1.00 contribution from Liberty, fifteen churches in the association, with four to five hundred members contributing $12.62.[17]

The following year (1826) the second session of the Forked Deer Association was held at Union Meeting House, Madison County, with Elder David Gordon preaching the opening sermon. Nineteen members were reported from the Union Church, three sermons were had on Sunday at which time the minsters preached "to a numerous audience and visible signs of the out-pouring of the spirit of God were seen in the congregation." The third session of the Forked Deer Association was also held in Madison County, this time at Big Black Creek Meeting House fourteen miles southwest of Jackson, at which time it was decided to make a sub-division of the churches and many of the Forked Deer Churches went into the Big Hatchie Association, composed of 13 churches, and organized at the Big Black Church near Denmark in 1828."[18]

The Baptist were spreading their gospel over the District and they were growing rapidly in number. Seeds of discord were sowed. The Forked Deer Association had been Anti-Masons and now they found Anti-Missions and "Two Seeds" among them. The "Two Seeds" doctrine (or Parkerism, named for the man who started it) was a belief which stated that a portion of the human race were the literal descendants of Adam and for them Christ died and they will be saved, but the great mass of human race are the children of the devil, for these Christ never died and they are eternally reprobated.[19] At the meeting of the Forked Deer Association in 1834, two "Two Seeds" ministers preached and a discussion arose which developed into a resolution to dissolve the association. Soon eight

---

[17]David Benedict, *A General History of the Baptist Denomination in America and the Other Parts of the World* (New York, 1846), 805; Smith Hanesborough, *A History of the Forked Deer Baptist Association* (Memphis, 1845), 5, 6. Hereinafter cited as *Forked Deer Baptist*.

[18]Hanesborough, *Forked Deer Baptist*, 15. The Big Black Creek Church had been organized in 1823 with J. Maudlin, J. W. Fort, J. Anderson, and W. Waddell as charter members.

[19]H. C. Irby, *Central Baptist Association* (Jackson, Tennessee, 1912), 34.

churches which opposed "Two Seeds" and Missions and Bible Society organized what they called Forked Deer Association, Revised, but this soon passed out of existence. The Pleasant Plains Missionary Baptist (organized in 1832 with six members) was one of the five strong churches which organized the Central Baptist Association at Eldad Church in 1836. Early members here included J. R. Vann, Rufus Gooch, W. A. Perry, Rane Hicks, Radford Withers, and Edward White. Other early churches in the county which were a member of this association were the Ararat, organized in 1850 with 52 members and located on Cypress Creek near the colored Bethlehem Baptist Church; the Cotton Grove Church, organized in 1837 by Elder Elisha Collins, James Senter and George Williams with six members.[20] The Spring Creek Church, organized in 1851 with Jeremiah Haughton, Enoch Gaskins, James Hearmore, Steven Johnson, Martha Haughton and Sarah Gaskins, all of whom had letters of dismission from the Cotton Grove Church; the Cane Creek Church, organized in 1822 with Rev. Allan Hill the first pastor and Jacob Hill, William Robertson, and Thomas Campbell the first deacons. That too much emphasis cannot be placed upon the importance of these frontier churches is shown by the trials of the deacons and elders in all the churches. One member of the old Cane Creek Church was charged with having a barrel of whiskey on hand. He claimed that he had it for medical purposes. When the trial came off, the church authorities agreed to a compromise to the effect that he was to get rid of all except a reasonable amount for medical purposes and then and only then would he be allowed to remain in the church. The old records did not reveal who was to be the judge of what amount was termed "medical purposes!"

It was on January 29, 1837 that the Baptist Church in Jackson was organized with twelve members.[21] Dr. John Fin-

---

[20]During the pastorate of Elder Reuben Day, 1846-1856, the church enjoyed a wonderful revival, for a hundred converts were added. H. C. Irby, *Central Baptist Association*, 66.

[21]These early members included: Elder John Finlay, Mrs. Finlay, Mrs. Mary Armour, Thomas Evans, Moses H. Prewitt, Miss Mary Ganaway, Richard Rawlings, Mrs. Lucinda Jobe, Miss Elizabeth Lake, Miss Elizabeth Meachum, Mrs. Hawkins, and —— Lake. It was not until December 1, 1875, that the church was incorporated under

lay, the first pastor, was also a teacher at West Tennessee College. He was considered a teacher without peer and a Christian without fault. In fact those who remembered him felt that the church was lovely because of Dr. Finlay's noble spirit: "Like priest; like people." Records of the Baptist bear out very strongly the theory that the churches played a major role in regulating the conduct of the community. Mingled through the records of whites and blacks being baptised and expenses of the church are records of members being expelled on charges of evil speaking of the church and non-attendance of worship (1842); of members enduring suspension of all rights and privileges for six months (1843); of objecting to disorderly "walking members"; of opposing intemperance, dealing in lottery tickets and dancing (1850).

In 1844, a building committee composed of J. R. Taylor, Dr. Snider, John Norvel and Dr. Steel was appointed and soon the records show that work on a "worship house" was begun. This early house of worship on the west corner of Market and College was described as follows by Mrs. S. M. Hawkins:

> My earliest recollection of the churches centers around the old Market House Baptist Church, which occupied the corner of College Street and Highland. The original structure was built for a market house, but for some reason its use for that purpose was discontinued and it was converted into a place of worship for the Baptist denomination. The open sides were boarded up in the temporary manner. A pulpit was placed at the north end, benches supplied and other necessary changes made. The brick floor was not changed. Candle holders hung on the walls, and the announcement for the evening services was: "Preaching tonight at early candle light." The benches were without backs, and chairs were supplied for elderly people. The men and the boys sat on one side and women and girls on the other. There was but little chance for flirting among the young people in those days. The pulpit was of the kind that someone has called "jack-in-the-box"—a tall square frame of wood hung around with curtains of dark green worsted.... Some of the ministers who pounded the old green cushion would have won laurels as pugulists had they lived until this day of enlightened ideas and had turned their attention to the prize ring.[22]

the title of "First Baptist Church," at which time J. R. Chappell, W. H. Brown, W. D. Dupree, and Abner Lawler were named trustees. H. C. Irby, *History of the First Church*, Jackson, Tennessee (Jackson, Tennessee, 1911), 10, 38.

[22] Mrs. S. M. Hawkins to J. G. Cisco, 1893. MS.

During the Sectional Conflict, the congregation met in private homes and just after the war, they met in the Masonic Hall until the services could be held in the new building in 1876.[23]

One of the most picturesque characters of the early Baptist in the county—one who made a living farming but preached to the good Baptists of the county trying to get them to rear their children properly and let liquor alone was Brother Obadiah Dodson. He was described as a very affable courteous man, one who always wore a bandana handkerchief of the conventional size and spots; one who rode a sorrel horse and wore a white fur hat. When the hat was new, it gave the appearance of preeminence, but when it became weather beaten and illshaped it gave him the appearance of a grist miller. But, appearance was nothing with Brother Dodson; he was always, everywhere and in all circumstances, God's nobleman. He was not scholastic, but well read, and encouraged the people to educate the children, even publishing, probably the first book in the county, *Moral Instructor and Guide to Youth; a Book containing Answers to Eleven Biblical Questions; and also Seventeen Propositions Upon the Training of Children.* During the winter and spring months, when steamboats ran the river from Memphis to Bolivar, the pleasure boats carried large crowds on Sundays and Brother Dodson conceived the idea that he could keep "monthly appointments" on one of these boats. This was not only a success from Brother Dodson's viewpoint but also from that of the captain of the ship, for this boat soon became one of the most popular ones on the river.[24] Another writer told of this unique preacher whose face was set in solemn lines that never relaxed into a smile. On one occasion he sat back of the minister who was finishing his sermon with his red handkerchief thrown over his face and head, peeping out in a very comical manner. The gravest had to smile and of

---

[23]The auditorium was not completed until 1885. In 1909, during the pastorate of Dr. H. W. Virgin, plans were made to take down the old building and a building committee composed of J. C. Edenton, I. L. Grady, Henry White, W. R. Fite, W. D. Sanders, and Dr. Virgin was appointed. Services were held in the new church on April 2, 1911. In 1938, the building was remodeled and enlarged under the direction of J. S. Gest, A. V. Patton, H. H. Waldrop, and Spencer Truex.

[24]Irby, *History of the First Baptist Church*, 24.

course the children giggled, but this didn't bother Brother Dodson one bit. He was the typical unconventional preacher of the frontier who reached the people with the style of the day; "I tell you my brethren All! Sinners All, the judgment day is coming!"

The Clover Baptist Church, now in Medon, was once near the Hardeman County line, but the Baptist of Medon held their membership there. This church was organized "On Saturday before the third Lord's Day, in March 1826, but the "Abstract of principles" was not signed until 1845. A strong effort was made in 1850 to move the church to Medon, but it failed and a church was organized in Medon. In June, 1851, the Clover Baptist Church excluded from its membership B. Starkey, N. S. Johnson, D. Lacy, Sarah Lacy, Catherine Lacy and the James Emersons and the William Butler families for "disorderly conduct" in joining the Medon church, which the Clover church said was illegally constituted. Members in this early church were excluded for non-attendance, profanity, drunkenness, fighting, possessing liquor, "playing marbles and other un-Christian conduct." The first mention of the preacher's salary was made in 1852 when they voted to pay him $15. The northeast corner of the church was set aside for colored members and there were still colored members in 1870.[25]

Over a decade passed after the organization of the county before an Episcopal church was organized. The St. Luke's Parish was organized July 23, 1832, at a meeting at the Masonic Hall by persons that were "friendly to the church," with Rev. Thomas Wright of North Carolina presiding.[26] The following eighteen names were affixed to the Articles of Association: Major Andrew Martin, Robert Hughes, Jacob Perkins, John H. Rawlings, Dr. Lewis C. Pendon, Dr. Erasmus D. Fenner, John M. Fenner, Junius P. Fenner, Micajah Antony, William Taylor, Colonel Joseph Talbot, James Miller, Dr. William E. Butler,

---

[25]Family names running through the history of this church are: Bickers, Butler, Barnette, Brooks, Carter, Collins, Coggins, Comer, Cearley, Day, Derryberry, Donnell, Dean, Dickson, Deming, Emerson, Estes, Edwards, Faucett, Freeman, Fitzgerald, Teagues, Thomas, Tims, Tate, Upton, Westbrook, Swink, and many others. Jackson *Sun,* June 17, 1945.

[26]The records of the Episcopal Church and the Memorial Guild Book were used for the account of the Episcopalians in the county.

Colonel Atlas Jones, Hon. Joshua Haskell, William Stoddert, Mrs. Sophia Perkins, and Mrs. Eliza G. Vaulx. It was not until 1845 that a church was built, so services were held in the court house, the Male Academy, and the Methodist church. In 1839, the parish was honored with a visit from Bishop Otey, who held services for the parish in the court house. That the parish was small during these early years is shown by the fact that there were only two communicants when the Convocation of the Diocese met in Jackson in 1835, while reports of two years later speak of six communicants and not more than twenty-five at services. Many of these lived from two to fourteen miles from town which made it well nigh impossible to attend services during inclement weather.

Small as the congregation was, the members were loyal, brave, and ambitious. In 1844, a lot was purchased for $450, and on it a part of the present structure was erected at a cost of $2,500. The building was sufficiently finished by 1845 for services and the Convention of the Diocese to be held here in July 1846 though the church was not consecrated until 1853 by Bishop Otey. This house of worship was enlarged and remodeled in 1883 and stands to-day as one of the most beautiful and historic buildings in the county.[27]

In 1870, Jefferson Davis delivered his first address after his release from prison to the members of St. Luke's Church and their friends. The crowd grew so large that little St. Luke's could not accommodate it, so the meeting was held in the grove in front of General Samuel J. Hays's home near the corner of Preston and Hays Avenue.

During the late 1820's and early 1830's a general awakening and a revival had begun to take place. McFerrin described the movement thus:

Rude as they were, God was not ashamed of our rough hewed log-

---

[27]The exquisite cross on the altar and an alms basin which was presented to the church by Bishop Quintard, to whom they had been presented by the Duchess of Tesk while the Bishop was in England (these were copied from those in a chapel in Westminster Abbey); the communion service made of "love gifts" from the congregation; the carved quartered oak Reredos enclosing the painting of the Resurrection, the rare triple mosaic windows over the chancel, the Tiffany glass windows in the rear of the church are all lovely symbols that have been placed here by the hands of faithful members.

houses, but met with us and poured unto us a blessing. Soon camp meetings began to dot our country. West Tennessee and Western Kentucky became the garden spot of the Lord, and our beloved Methodism, like the cloud the prophet saw, soon became the religion of the country.[28]

These camp meetings were usually held by the Methodists and the Presbyterians, though one, strangely enough was held jointly by the Presbyterians, Cumberland Presbyterians, Baptist, Episcopalians, and the Protestant Methodist.[29] The *Gazette* of 1828 mentioned four regular Presbyterian ministers, thirteen camp meetings, and 551 converts. Frequently, there were two to three thousand present at the meetings and it was always hoped that under the influence of religion "the beastly practice of drunkenness be driven from the country." These meetings themselves were frequently infested with rowdies who had organizations about their business and their business was to break up the meetings by noise, riotious conduct, stealing horses and wagons, and any other annoyances that they could think of.[30]

Late in the summer and fall seemed to have been the harvest time for sinners as well as for staple crops. Notices of meetings were more frequent in the papers during this season than any other times of the year. In September 1829, the Jackson *Gazette* carried this story:

"Revival of Religion"—For some weeks camp meetings have been held at different places in this section of the country, at all of which great zeal has been displayed by the people in the cause of religion; and verily the efforts of those pious individuals who attended have been crowned with singular success, for at the camp meetings on Big Black Creek near Denmark, which closed on Tuesday morning, upward of sixty persons professed conversion, most of whom became members of the Methodist Church.

---

[28] John McFerrin, *Methodism in Tennessee* (Nashville, 1874), II, 513.
 [29] *Southern Statesman*, August 13, 1831. A Methodist meeting was held in 1824 at Salem Springs, while a Methodist and Cumberland Presbyterian meeting was held at Bethlehem Meeting House in 1825, Jackson *Gazette*, July 2, 1824; August 6, 1925; July 9, 1829.
 [30] Jackson *Gazette*, October 17, 1828; September 5, 1829. The people tried to remove the roudiness by legislative authority in 1833 when an act was passed which declared it illegal to prepare barbecue for sale or offer liquor for sale within one mile of a worshipping assembly. *Acts of Tennessee*, 1833.

We are happy to see the advances of piety in our country and especially so in our town of Jackson—religion not only makes its possessor happy here, but it prepares us for a happy immortality beyond the grave and at least renders those of humble and contrite heart, good citizens of any community. Under the balmy influence the beastly practice of drunkenness will be driven from our country and when that is done "peace and harmony will prevail" and hundreds and thousands of our citizens will be saved from premature graves.[81]

A Memphis paper told of the Methodist "garnering a rich harvest of sinners" as the professed religions were "plowing deep furrows through our sinful land."[32]

There were two very popular Methodist camp grounds—Big Springs, south of Jackson, and Salem camp ground three miles east of town. In 1827, fifty acres of vacant and unappropriated land unfit for cultivation was allowed to the trustees of the Salem Camp Grounds; namely, Mathias Deberry, James Caldwell, John B. Brown, Ryland Chandler, Devereaux Wynne, Gabriel Anderson, James Aubry, and Isaac Swan, who were entrusted with the responsibility of building a meeting house and laying out the grounds. Notices in the papers informed the public of one camp right after the other at old Salem where there were many converts and everything was "conducted with love, harmony, and affection."[33]

In 1833, plans were made to hold a camp meeting at Big Black Creek near Denmark and one by one the families moved to the creek and made camp. This local movement had been started at the suggestion of one irreligous, James Alston, who wanted the church like the other institutions of the community to grow very rapidly. Alston did not want to become religious himself, for it would mean that he would have to give up his fine race horse, "Gray Eagle," that had many a dollar placed on him at the Jackson races. It was a struggle, but influenced by his friends who made public professions and by another friend, who, as he went forward to confess, fell to the ground completely overwhelmed, Alston finally gave up the horse and began the entirely new race—as he called it—the one to heaven.

[81]Jackson *Gazette*, September 5, 1829.
[32]Memphis *Enquirer*, October 28, 1837.
[33]*Acts of Tennessee*, 1833. An act also protected the camp property from being "maliciously inclosed." *Southern Statesman*, August 6, 28, October 15, 1831.

Dr. Alexander A. Campbell, the first pastor of the Presbyterian Church in Jackson, preached numerous powerful sermons at this meeting where many were convicted of their sins and shouts of joy from happy souls filled the air.[34]

Daniel Baker was probably the most famous leader of the revivals in the West in the mid-nineteenth century. In 1847, he held a camp meeting at Denmark under a huge shed which rested upon upright pillars hewn out of solid timber. The people came in throngs, bringing volumes of his published sermons with them. They were astonished that he delivered "off hand" these powerful sermons that were designed to create "mental excitement strong enough to produce great anxiety, strong enough to keep the eyes wakeful through the night and occasion tears, and sometimes the sobbing in the prayer meetings and the house of God."[35] The campers soon forgot themselves and laid aside the written sermons, completely captivated by the fire and eloquence of the speaker which could not be put on paper.

Religion was spreading rapidly through this new West. By 1831, there was a brick Methodist church in Jackson where one hour sermons moved the people to tears and shouts, and twenty traveling preachers were riding the circuit and two special men were appointed to work among the slaves. These men were often men of piety and position who were slave holders themselves. The Negroes had a special place to sit in the white churches or had a church of their own. If the colored preacher was particularly good, the whites, too, went to see and hear him. In McNairy County, in the early 1830's, Pompey, a former slave who had become interested in religion through his master who was a preacher himself, preached at the Center Church. The crowd was so big on Christmas 1832 that it had to adjourn to the camping grounds. Four years later at the same place after Pompey's powerful sermon of only twenty minutes "the whole audience seemed to sway to and fro like wheat under the power of wind. Cries of mercy, groans of agony, and shouts of praise were numerous and

---

[34]Sketches of the Denmark community written for the *Presbyterian Herald* by a Mr. Caldwell, 1882.

[35]Daniel Baker, *A Series of Revival Sermons* (Philadelphia, 1846), 352. This was in a letter of instructions to his brother about how to conduct a successful revival.

loud."[36] People were taking their religion most seriously, the force of the revival had gained momentum, and those in this county were so moved that the Memphis editor wrote:

> We have never known so general and stirring a religious excitement as is now prevailing throughout the country. . . . Near Jackson, in this State, at two camp meetings between seven and eight hundred are said to have bowed before the altar of the Lord in repentance and conversion. . . . The Methodists and Presbyterians have united hand in hand and are wrestling day and night with the arch enemy, who has lost hold a little in the fierce encounter . . . a strict watch should be kept lest the flesh and the Devil slyly creep into the very midst of the revivals.[37]

As early as 1820 Cumberland Presbyterian missionaries were sent into the Western District of Tennessee to organize churches. Rev. Richard Beard was sent to the Forked Deer Circuit. At the first meeting, held on the North Fork of the Forked Deer "near Adley Alexander's . . . in the bottom," they had no camps, no shelter, a few logs for seats, and a coarsely constructed pulpit. The Hopewell Presbytery was organized at McLemoresville in 1824; the Presbyterians of Forked Deer and Hatchie in 1830; the Synod of West Tennessee in 1832. Thus, West Tennessee soon became one of the strongholds of the Cumberland Presbyterians. One of the earliest churches in the county was Mount Tabor, which was organized in 1835 at the log residence of Harvey McCord below Medon. In a short while a shelter was acquired in Medon and, in 1848, the Medon congregation united with that of Pleasant Hill and built a church on ground purchased from Nathaniel Benton.[38]

It was through the efforts of members of the Mount Tabor Church in general and Rev. W. M. Dunnaway in particular that the Synod of West Tennessee was authorized to establish

---

[36] McFerrin, *Methodism in Tennessee*, III, 390.

[37] Ft. Pickering, *American Eagle*, October 7, 1842.

[38] The first session of elders was composed of William Stribbling, William Burnes, Elisha Lorance, Thomas Blair, John Black, Harry McCord. Other charter members included Mr. and Mrs. Wash Dodds, Agnes Stone Rochelle, Nancy Benton, Mary Stribbling Pope, Cyrus Black, Mr. and Mrs. John H. Johnson. From a clipping by Mrs. John Balch in scrap book of Mary L. Scott. The church was named by Eunice Black Stribbling for Mt. Tabor on Broad River, Union District, S. C.

a mission at Jackson in the spring of 1858. For a decade the clouds of war were too black for much growth to take place, but the matter was again brought before the Synod in 1868, a mission was re-organized and two years later Rev. Dunnaway and W. K. Walsh purchased a lot on College Street and donated it for the building of a house of God. The building was not finished until 1872, at which time the church was organized and the articles of faith were signed by forty-three members.[39] The church members soon felt the need of a larger place of worship, so in 1893, plans were made for a new building. This $20,000 building with its tall spires was opened for services in 1896, but destroyed by fire in 1914. There was a split in the church in 1906, at which time many united with the Presbyterian Church, U. S. A., but about two hundred remained loyal and continued to work faithfully in the original church.

Some Roman Catholics came to the Western District soon after it was opened for settlement. In 1832, Valentine Barry of Bolivar tried to interest Bishop Kendrick of Philadelphia in sending a priest to this section. In 1839, Father Joseph Stokes was sent by Bishop Miles of the diocese of Nashville to Ashport. He traveled on horseback from Nashville to Memphis and it is thought that he visited Jackson at this time. Although the records, baptismal and marriage, of the St. Mary's Parish only date back to 1867, tradition says that several of the priests from the churches in Nashville and Memphis served the faithful in this community before the Civil War. The "Catholic Almanac" for 1840 states that Jackson and Memphis were "stations," evidently missionary headquarters.[40] During these

---

[39]Those who signed the Articles of Faith included: Mrs. Mahala Anderson, Rev. G. W. Mitchell and wife, James W. Anderson and wife, John R. Caviness and wife, J. F. Latham and wife, W. P. Cobb and wife, James Stevens and wife, Watt Graham and wife, S. W. Boone and wife, T. B. Anderson, Sam Mitchell, E. B. Carter, Donell Mitchell, Neil P. Anderson, Misses Lizzie Mitchell, Bell Mitchell, Georgilla Mitchell, Emma Smithwich, Belle Swinebroad, Anna Nesbitt, Eliza Maxey, Henrietta Maxey, Mrs. W. K. Walsh, Dr. and Mrs. B. R. Harris, Mrs. M. J. Christian, Mrs. George Andrews, E. E. Stribbling, Mrs. Newton Perkins, Mrs. Jesse Lankford, Mrs. Mary Maxey, W. K. Cobb, Hu C. Anderson, D. T. Turner, R. W. Wadley, W. D. Maxey. The present church was dedicated on June 5, 1916.

[40]Williams, *West Tennessee*, 194-195.

missionary days, mass was held in private homes by Rev. Orengo; Father McAleer, Father O'Daley, Father Gazzo, Father Nolen, who is described as the young and fiery priest from an Irish University, and Rev. John O'Brien.

Soon after the Civil War, the beautiful residence of General Samuel J. Hays, located on a gentle rise northeast of the Mobile and Ohio station on Hays Avenue was purchased by the Catholic Church and used for a school from 1869 until the building was destroyed by fire about 1874. A charter had been issued to Vincencia Fitzpatrick, Mary Pius Fitzpatrick, Dominica Fitzpatrick and Josephine Whelom in 1869 to establish the Academy of Immaculate Conception.[41] During the years of the life of this school, services were held here, but before that time and after the fire, they were held in private homes—that of Mr. and Mrs. James Hughes the principal one. As time passed, a small frame building on Church Street next door to the present fire station was used for a church, then a building on the Armour property near the Jackson *Sun* building, and then in 1878, under the direction of Father Doyle, the present building was erected.

The 1880's were wonderful years to the members of the parish, an additional piece of property west of the church was acquired where a priest's house and a new school was erected. The cemetery, now in use, was acquired and laid out in 1883. Father Patrick O'Brien, the noted missionary, made many converts and the beloved poet and priest, Father Abram Ryan, visited the parish. Names of families such as those Catholics of Jackson in the early seventies are connected with the new Jackson that arose after that Sectional Conflict. Among these were the names Hughes, King, Burke, Joyce, Lynch, Farrell, Donavan, Kelly, Toughey, Tierman, Murphy, Brown, McLean, McCorry, Haas, Langley, McMullen, Carroll, Burnell, Lawler, McCarty, Gaffney, Hudson, Bracken, Brady, Magevney, McHaven, and Lindsey.

Regular religious services in most churches were suspended in this section of West Tennessee after the occupation by the Federal troops in June 1862, but there were small gatherings where prayer meetings were held and occasional services in the churches when the buildings were not being used as hos-

---

[41] *Acts of Tennessee*, 1869.

pitals and prisons. Many men went into service in 1861 for the adventure of it, but many went because they seriously thought they were fighting for a righteous cause and after the conflict most of both classes returned thanking the Father in Heaven that the conflict was over and praying to Him that they would have strength and patience to rebuild their devastated country. The older citizens invited emigrants to come and help them rebuild their country and many responded to the call, feeling that the South was the land of opportunity. New citizens mean a growth of the older churches and the organization of new ones.

The first twenty years after the Civil War saw the coming of the Jewish people to the county, a firm foothold made by the Catholics, the organization of additional congregations of Methodist and Baptists, the organization of the Cumberland Presbyterian Church and the First Christian Church. During the 1880's there was also a period of revivals which caused a great awakening of the people. By and large, it was a combination of the growth of the community and the revivals which caused the additional congregations to be organized.

The First Christian Church was organized in 1867, although there was a Christian Church at Mason Grove in Madison County as early as 1840 and Robert Cartmell told of attending preaching at the court house that was held by the members of the Christian Church in 1855.[42] A neat frame building forty by fifty feet was ready for services in May, 1867, at which time the pastor R. W. Bond, conducted the first services. Early elders were R. W. Andrews and R. F. Bond; early deacons were J. D. Bond, J. W. Foster, J. R. Wilkinson, and W. B. McNabb.[43] In 1878, the present property was given by John D. and B. F. Bond and was deeded to the trustees of the First Christian Church of Jackson, who were at that time: F. A. Wilson, J. R. Wilkinson, C. F. Landis. The present house of worship was erected in 1901 and was remodeled some years later. The annex property was bought in 1921.

Although there are no written records of the first Jews

---

[42]Mrs. W. W. Tucker furnished the information for this sketch of the church.

[43]Among the early members of the church may be found the names of Bond, Ross, Stout, Moss, Hyndan, Parrish, Little, Fisher, Heathcock, Allen, Wilkinson, Hodgson, and others.

who came to this section, tradition tells that J. Friedlob arrived in 1867, made arrangements for two wagons to go to Estanuala to get his stock of goods that he was planning to buy in Memphis and J. Solomon, a dealer in drygoods and ladies' hats, advertised in a paper of 1867. Tombstone inscriptions in the old cemetery on Madison Street show that it was located there prior to 1875.[44] The names of J. Samuels and B. Rosenthal appear in the directory of 1872.

By 1885, the religious needs of the growing Jewish community necessitated the chartering of the congregation, so a charter was applied for by J. Friedlob, president; Victor J. Woerner, secretary; Henry Myers, Nathan Baum, trustees. Other early trustees included Moses Tuchfeld, Sol Tuchfeld, and J. Samuels. Plans were made for the erection of a temple, but in the meantime, services were held on the second floor of the Odd Fellows building and at some of the homes of the members of the congregation, such as the Rosenthal, Baum, and Marks' homes. In 1897, the congregation traded their lot on North Cumberland street for the Cumberland Presbyterian Church, which served as the place of worship until the new temple was built in 1942.[45] The life and deeds of the early members of the congregation show not only a loyalty to the church but an interest in the life of the growing community. Many of the members of the early Jewish church occupied places of prominence and honor in the commercial, civic, and fraternal life of the city.

A religious awakening was a part of the reconstruction. People were aroused by such commands as the powerful pulpiteer, E. H. Osborne made:

Brothers, agitate! Agitate! Agitate! Work while it is yet today. . . . Work as if the fire of God burned in your soul. . . . We need and must have honest workers or the close of this century will look down upon a ruined nation.[46]

---

[44]The present cemetery was purchased in 1896 and the remains removed from Madison Street cemetery to the new site on Neely.

[45]J. Friedlob, the first president of the Congregation, was followed by Victor Woerner, who served until 1915, then J. C. Felsenthal (1915-1918); Joe Rosenbloom (1918-1940); A. S. Lindy (1940) to the present.

[46]Weekly Jackson *Tribune*, August 7, 1869. There is a story of Osborn's being caught between the lines during the Civil War and con-

The "Whig" of 1866 told of the work of Osborne and his faithful band of followers under whose influence one hundred and sixty additions at Cane Creek, Clover Creek, and Pleasant Plains.[47] Many people believed that revolutions followed national demoralization and that only righteous men exalted the nation, but some of the deeply religious did not exactly approve of the noisy, shouting Methodist who had revivals so frequently.[48]

During these days the families of Methodists and Baptist Christians were growing and the desire for neighborhood prayer meetings and Sunday Schools arose—a movement on the part of earnest workers in the neighborhoods to influence many who were not being reached by the earlier organizations. Each of the Methodist and Baptist Churches were established by members from the First churches—Paine's Chapel (Hays Avenue), Jackson City Mission (Lambuth Memorial), Middle Avenue Methodist (Trinity), West Jackson Baptist, Second Baptist (Cavalry).

The present Hays Avenue Methodist Church was first called Paine's Chapel. In 1867, a small group of deeply religious men and women living in East Jackson began holding prayer meetings in the home of M. M. Brown on Gates Avenue. The services, led by Rev. Johnnie Brooks, J. T. Beveridge, and Rev. J. H. Evans, were so well attended that Wyatt Taylor and J .T. Beveridge suggested that they build a church. A lot was selected in Tomlin's Grove (the same lot upon which the present church is built) and by February 1869 services were held in the quaint white frame building which had two doors to the west, bell in the belfry on the south side of the church,

---

demned to be shot as a Confederate spy. He insisted that he was a preacher so the Federals gave him a chance to prove his preaching ability, whereupon he took the text: "Shall their dead bones rise again." He was so eloquent that the Federals not only permitted him to pass through the lines but contributed to the Sunday offering.

[47]*West Tennessee Whig*, September 1, 1866.

[48]R. H. Cartmell's Diary, 1867; Rev. Thomas Taylor aided in the establishment of several churches and held many revivals. In 1871 he held a "gracious revival, forty persons" being converted at Big Springs Church near Pinson. *Whig and Tribune*, September 16, 1871. In 1876 Rev. Taylor donated land for a camp ground seven miles east of Jackson and extensive plans were made for meetings. *Whig and Tribune*, August 5, 1876.

kneeling rails in front of each pew. Thirteen members signed the church charter.[49] Bishop Robert Paine was a popular minister in the Conference and had made a visit to Jackson in June, 1866, at which time he preached the commencement sermon at the Memphis Conference Female Institute. It is probable that this new church was named for the Bishop.

That these were devout workers of the church is shown by the rapid growth, so rapid that by 1894, it was evident that a larger building was needed. Wyatt Taylor and J. T. Beveridge agreed to furnish one half of the cost of the new structure if the congregation would pay the balance. Fifty persons responded when the call was made to sinners during the last service in the little white church in Tomlin's Grove. The frame building was removed and the new church was begun. These people believed in working and praying. The church records of 1888 show three prayer meeting groups—the Ladies' group led by Sister W. A. Taylor, the Young Ladies' group led by Sister W. C. Cason and the Little Boys' group led by Tommie Rogers.

It was not until after the Civil War that the town of Jackson began to spread to the north and to the west and the need was felt for a Methodist Church in the western part of town. The present Lambuth Memorial Methodist Church was first just a mission, and later was called Campbell Street Methodist. Highland Avenue was called Trenton Road and from this road to Campbell street, which was just a country road and from Arlington, which is not named on a map of 1874, to Talbot was the country estate of Joseph Talbot. This was sold off in the late sixties and it was a lot on the southwest corner of this plot that Mrs. E. M. A. Goodwin and James A. Collins donated upon which to build a house "to worship almighty God." (1874) Some of the devout Methodist in this section of the "country" had been having prayer meetings in the Fry and Kincade homes and the members felt a need for a regular house of worship.[50] These first trustees included:

---

[49]These first members were Rev. Lorenzo Lea, Rev. Thomas Taylor, J. C. McCutchen, Jno. T. Brown, Rev. George K. Brooks, Rev. N. O. Blake, Robert Brown, J. T. Beveridge, Mrs. Susan Garrett, Mrs. A. Beveridge, Miss Sarah Kershaw, Miss Julia Dodds, Miss Joe Hinton.

[50]The church was remodeled several times through the years, but

Liberty Weir, Robert S. Lindsay, James W. Collins, James L. Fry, Richard Teague, Joseph H. Williams, James G. Carver, Gus Berdon, and William G. Cockrill.

The Second Baptist Church was organized in November 1887 by Rev. A. J. Hall and Rev. G. T. Webb with fourteen Godly Baptist at the home of Mrs. T. B. Duncan at 125 Jefferson street. As the congregation outgrew the homes, meetings were held in a store building on the corner of Royal and Madison streets and then in the chapel of Southwestern Baptist University. So many people in East Jackson became interested in the services and a part of the congregation that a frame building at 367 Preston was built in 1889 and used until 1904 when the new brick building on the corner of Preston and Hays Avenue was built. Dr. D. A. Ellis, the pastor in 1904, not only encouraged the members of the congregation in the building of the new church, but he actually helped with the laying of the bricks. In 1929, a fire destroyed this building and the enthusiastic members of this rapidly growing congregation bought beautiful lots on Lexington Avenue, plans were made for the commodious church and Sunday school rooms that were ready for services December 7, 1930. The cost of this building was $79,000, but this is a small estimate for it was built during the depression. At the time the church was moved to Lexington Avenue, the name was changed to Calvary Baptist Church. The building committee for the new building included: T. D. Gaither, W. R. Reavis, J. E. Skinner, C. L. James, C. L. Dennison, W. F. Arnold, H. D. Geyer, W. D. Baxter.

During the winter of 1888, Mrs. Julia Woollard consulted with Rev. T. F. Saunders about the need of religious services in the eastern part of the city. Prayer meetings were held in Mrs. Bethshares's home and a Sunday School with sixteen members was organized in Mrs. Carrie Nix's home. Soon Wyatt Taylor built a house on Mobile street and let the congregation use it. The work of Rev. Saunders, Mrs. Woollard, Mrs. Mary Wilde, and others caused such a growth in the church that a regular house of worship was built on Mobile Avenue in 1893. In 1911, Mrs. Mary Wilde donated a lot for a new building. The building was erected and was ready for occupancy two

---

in 1941 a complete remodeling was done, when the Gothic plan of architecture was followed throughout the building.

years later. No congregation in the section can claim that it has more zealous members than those of Trinity Church, for this democratic congregation has given freely of time, talent, and means.[51]

About the turn of the century three other congregations appeared in the community—the West Jackson Baptist Church, the Highland Heights Methodist, and the Highland Avenue Church of Christ.

In 1898, Mr. and Mrs. J. R. Wilkinson, Mr. and Mrs. W. G. Townes, and Mrs. N. J. Phillips left the First Christian Church and began meeting in the Wilkinson home on Highland Avenue. As the numbers in the congregation increased, they met for a time in the Pythian Building on Main street and then in the new church which was built on the corner of Grand and Highland at a cost of two thousand dollars. J. R. Wilkinson, W. G. Townes and T. E. Tatum served as the first trustees of this "Church of Christ."[52]

On April 3, 1904, a group of Methodist in the community that was then known as Hicksville organized a church school and held its meetings in a store building at Hicksville. Later meetings were held in the upper rooms of a store building belonging to W. A. Hicks. Rev. A. B. Love preached to the congregation on Sunday nights. A year passed and on May 21, 1905, an Epworth League was organized with S. B. Lawrence, Jr. as leader. A tent revival was held with J. W. Blackard preaching. Under the leadership of the first trustees, W. A. Hicks, R. B. Neblett, S. E. Kieroff, a tabernacle was built and used for a place of worship until a block church could be built. Some years ago the name of the congregation was changed to "Highland Heights" and in 1927 a new church was erected.

The West Jackson Baptist Church had its humble beginnings in the early autumn of 1906 on the front lawn of the J. J. Carpenter home, 560 Lambuth Boulevard (then Long street). It was Mrs. J. F. Phillips, matron of Adams Hall, who had moved here with her family from Mt. Moriah Baptist Church, Whiteville, Tennessee, who conceived the idea that

---

[51] Jackson *Sun*, September 18, 1944. This material was taken from the history of the church written by C. S. Keenan.

[52] A brick veneer building valued at $25,000 was erected on the same lot in 1929. This information concerning the church was furnished by W. H. Canaday.

there was a need for a Baptist congregation in West Jackson. It was in Mrs. Phillips's home on Dancy street that the religious services were held until a large tent was ready for a place of worship on January 8, 1907. This tent was erected on the present site of the church on property that had been purchased from W. H. Nourse and wife. It was the twelve charter members[53] and many members from the Highland Avenue Baptist Church that had been disbanded through the influence of Rev. Martin banded together and began to build the strong church of to-day. The sale of the Highland Avenue property furnished money to pay for labor and purchase material for the new building at the top of the hill. The first deacons were J. P. Phillips, J. S. Hollingsworth, T. L. Hilliard, J. M. Campbell was elected clerk, J. P. Phillips, treasurer and Rev. Terry Martin served as the first pastor. The present concrete building was erected in 1908.

It was the Methodist revivalist, Sam Jones, who aroused the people of the community more deeply than probably any other minister. He held two meetings here—the first in 1884 at the First Methodist Church at which time the crowd after the first few days was so large that the building could accommodate only about a fourth and the second meeting was in 1893 after he had achieved national fame. This tall black haired evangelist had the style and use of language that appealed to the common people who were first convulsed with laughter over the stories he told, then filled with anger over the straight forward manner in which he called "a spade a spade," and then moved to tears by his deep pathos. Sam Jones was a sensation wherever he went and wherever he went he could come nearer turning the town upside down than any other man on the continent. One contemporary writer added: "If you will get him and give him the middle of the road he will stir up things. The only trouble will to get a place big enough to hold the audience."[54] Tremendous crowds came to hear the fiery, im-

---

[53]The charter members included: Mr. and Mrs. J. P. Phillip, Miss Willie Mae Phillips, T. L. Hilliard, Mrs. W. H. Hilliard, Mr. and Mrs. J. M. Campbell, J. B. Hollinsworth, Rev. C. W. Brown, Mrs. I. N. Cowan, and Mrs. C. R. Rider. The material in this sketch was furnished by Mrs. Willie Mae Phillips Hall.

[54]Mrs. Sam Jones, *Life and Sayings of Sam Jones* (Atlanta, 1907), 103.

pulsive, hell-fire and brimstone evangelist who made the spectre of hell very real. He didn't preach as much against sin as against the man who committed the sin, telling the sinners very plainly what they were doing and making their offenses seem quite hideous. These were the days of shouting members in the audience and the mourner's bench while Sam Jones moved about in the congregation talking, shaking hands, and pleading with those present to put away their sins. A real moral reformation took place, an awakening of sentiment against liquor traffic—a general revival of righteousness.

In June 1893, the people of Jackson and the surrounding community made extensive plans for a wonderful revival, for Sam Jones was coming again. At the suggestion of the revivalist himself a tabernacle was built on the corner of Liberty and Chester streets just back of the present State and Paramount Theatres. Imagine a place big enough to seat 7,000, the roof of which was supported by pillars which were trunks of native trees, saw-dust on the ground and the sides open—this was the Sam Jones Tabernacle. Hundreds of visitors arrived to see "Jackson converted to God." The *Whig* office employed a skilled stenographer to give interesting and accurate reports upon the meeting; the Tennessee Midland Railroad advertised special rates for those who wished to attend and made plans to hold the trains so that the people from Lexington could attend; stores and banks closed from 10:30 to 12:00 to encourage attendance; special sermons were delivered for the negroes at 3:00 in the afternoon; special sermons were delivered for the men, at which time over 5,000 attended; visitors from the country and adjoining towns who brought basket luncheons found free accommodations for their safe keeping at the Masonic Temple.[55] Everything in the vicinity centered around "the meeting."

Contemporary papers tell of the 10,000 who crowded the tabernacle long before sun set, that the crowd was so large that it almost blocked the street. Sam Jones preached against "cussing," breaking the Sabbath, gambling, horse racing, and cards, but his principal message was against what he termed the greatest sin—drink. "I believe if the devil were president of the United States and there were no whiskey, he would resign

---

[55] Jackson *Daily Whig*, June 20, 22, 23, 1893.

and go back to hell within three weeks. He wouldn't run the country without whiskey." His argument was that the only salvation was prayer that "when a sinner gets down upon his knees, the devil trembles." At the close of the meeting the editor of the *Whig* marveled that the community had done without the meeting so long for he felt that the women and children of America and the "homes" had no braver champion than Sam Jones, that "Sam Jones was the fast friend of society, the earnest advocate of law and order, the able exponent of the wholesome morals. His language may be at fault but his head is level and his heart is in the right place. If you measure a workman by his chips, no minister on the continent is his equal."[56]

Another famous revivalist and one who left his foot prints upon the minds and souls of the people of the community was Mordecai Ham, a Baptist, who held a meeting in 1904 in a tent erected on the southeast corner of Main and Royal streets. He also believed in letting the chips fall where they may and that liquor was the greatest sin of the land. One of the most exciting episodes of his meeting was the night that he promised the congregation that he would take them to town to see some of these dens of vice—the saloons. It is said that many went to the meeting that night just to go on the sight-seeing tour. The procession left the tent and marched down Main street singing "Wonder Where My Wandering Boy Is Tonight," led by the minister himself. But alas, when the crowd arrived, there was no vice to be seen, even the picture of the scantily clad lady had disappeared. Deer antlers adorned the walls and two or three perfectly sober men were sitting at a table drinking a bottle of beer.

It is an undisputed fact that the church people of the community were responsible for the movement which made the sale of liquor illegal in the city of Jackson. The Baptist and Methodist, being the largest congregations in the community, would not rest until they achieved a happy ending to their crusade—that day in 1907 when the people went to the polls and willed it so. This was the result of a long developing contest which had started before the Civil War, but whose momentum had

---

[56] Jackson *Daily Whig*, June 25, 1893. Hanging from the roof of tabernacle was a banner which read: "Quit your meanness."

increased in power since the conflict. The county participated in the early movement in the 1830's and 1840's with the organization of a Temperance Society and meetings at the Methodist Church. Here, Andrew L. Martin and Rev. Thomas Maddin delivered lectures on many occasions. By 1833, the Society had increased its membership to one hundred and the officers included many of the leading citizens of the town: William Stoddert, president; Andrew L. Martin and Joshua Haskell, vice-presidents; William Flowers, Wm. Armour, Milton Brown, Wm. E. Butler, R. H. Hibbetts, the executive committee; David Armour, treasurer; Edwin Estes, secretary. A real celebration was held at Spring Creek when the Temperance Society outing was combined with the Fourth of July celebration and three hundred persons, including ninety-nine ladies, partook of a bountiful dinner and listened to an address, "Independence and Temperance" by Major James Meriwether. This glorious affair was held at J. P. Haughton's.[57] In 1851, the Jackson Sons of Temperance bought the old Methodist Church for a meeting place and this became known as Temperance Hall. In the years just after the Civil War, it was used as a school by J. H. Harper and as the meeting place for the City Council.

The churches kept the temperance movement alive and growing. They first tried to solve the problem by persuasion and then they determined to back their method by legislation. In 1877, the legislature prohibited the sale of liquor within four miles of incorporations of learning, except in incorporated towns. In 1887, this act was broadened by making it unlawful to sell liquor within any four miles of any school house but this did not apply to the sale by manufactures in whole sale quantities; in 1899 the early act of 1877 was broadened to prohibit the sale of liquor in towns of 2,000; in 1903, the early act was amended to extend the four mile law to towns of not more than 5,000, hereinafter incorporated; in 1907, the act of 1877 was extended to all cities and towns of not more than 150,000, hereinafter incorporated.[58] Soon after the passage of the act of 1907, agitation increased in Jackson. The senator and rep-

---

[57] Jackson *Southern Statesman*, April 17, June 1, August 3, 1833.
[58] *Acts of Tennessee*, 1877, Chapter 23; 1899, Chapter 221; 1903, Chapter 2; 1907, Chapter 17.

resentatives ran on the platform that they would pass necessary legislation to bring prohibition to Jackson provided the people wanted it, so an unofficial referendum was scheduled, the day arrived, the "drys" all went to the polls, but few of the "wets" appeared. Over nine hundred votes were cast against the saloons, and only a few in favor of them. The saloon interests explained this seeming lack of interest on their part by the fact that they thought Governor Patterson would veto the measures, that the referendum did not amount to anything anyway. Governor Patterson signed the bills which put liquor out of Jackson, but two years later vetoed the bill which called for state wide prohibition. It is needless to say that the election was preceded with the usual local excitement, such as sermons from the pulpits, public meetings, which used the "Rise, sing, and sign" methods, parades with the men, women, and children carrying banners with appropriate slogans. Many of the influential people firmly believed that when the referendum was taken the people would vote a positive "no" as to whether the city would go dry or not. This gave the prohibition party time to organize. On the morning of the voting the residential section of the city seemed to have emptied into Court Square. The "pros" in the group of three and regular squads invaded the business section, going into the stores, pleading and arguing with the voters from every angle. One by one men who had laughed at the idea went to the polls and voted dry. Some were against the law, not because they believed that the town should be wet but because they did not believe that morals could be legislated. Why the vote went the way it did, is not as important as the way the people voted. The prohibition party won the victory of the day.[59]

The senator from Madison and the representatives had heard the "voice of the people." Jackson was already an incorporated town, so bills calling for the abolition of Jackson's charter and the reincorporation of the town were introduced in the House and passed, but the senator from Madison failed to call the bill up in the senate. The senator from Gibson County was persuaded by the reform group in Madison that

---

[59] A personal interview with Judge N. R. Barham and other citizens in Jackson and correspondence with Philip Holland, New Orleans.

[60] *Acts of Tennessee,* 1907, Chapters 398, 399.

their man had failed to do what he had agreed to do, so the senator from Gibson called the bills up and they were passed in 1907.[60]

Bitter feeling came from this fight in Jackson. Ernest Bullock and many of his workers soon went to Nashville and led the fight for state-wide prohibition, which resulted in the passage in 1909 of the "Holladay Bill" prohibiting the sale of liquor within four miles of any school house.[61]

---

[61]*Ibid.*, Chapter 1. In 1917, the legislature passed a bill prohibiting the importing, transporting or possessing of liquor; in 1933, the local option on light wines and beer was passed; in 1939, the present local option on liquor was passed.

CHAPTER XXIII

BANKS AND BANKING

There was probably nothing as scarce as money in the Western District during the early days. Merchants received payments for their products in cotton, peltry, and beeswax. Thus, they of necessity were the pioneer bankers, but as the population and business grew, a greater demand arose for banking facilities. Under an act of the Legislature of 1823, an agency was placed in Madison and an agent had placed in his hands the amount that the county was agreeable to taxation. This amount the agent could loan to citizens in the county. Dr. William E. Butler was the first financial agent of this sort in Madison. In 1827-28, the Legislature of Tennessee formed the Western District into a treasury district with James Caruthers as treasurer. This was a step forward, but letters of Elijah Bigelow in 1828-29 tell of money being scarce, of the North Carolina money that he had accepted at 12½ to 25 per cent discount, of the practice of sending halves of bills in one letter and the other halves later in order to pay a debt in Massachusetts.[1] A decade later John Tomlin, the poet-postmaster, debated over how he should send the money to Edgar A. Poe for subscriptions to the "Graham's Magazine." He wrote:

Is Tennessee money current in ordinary business transactions of your city? It is possible that I may through the Union Bank of this place obtain a check on some one of your banks. If Virginia, North Carolina, or S. Carolina money is more current in Philadelphia than Tennessee, I shall certainly obtain the one that you mention as preferable[2]

The late 1820's and 1830's witnessed the "Battle of the Banks" in the nation as a whole, and Tennessee and the

---
[1]Correspondence of Elijah Bigelow, April 15, November 11, 1828; June 2, 1829. MS.

[2]Correspondence of John Tomlin, November 22, 1840. MS.

Western District was a part of the battle ground. The editor of the *Southern Statesman* favored the state banks and considered the U. S. bank "an engine of aristocracy and power." Many people were afraid of the banks, for they felt that when a "mechanic or a farmer dipped his finger into a bank he got them burnt," but that they were necessary to commerce. They all knew that banks were good for a place to borrow but the day of repaying was sure to come and the second year's crop could be a failure, too.[3] Business men with vision sponsored a movement in 1831 which resulted in the establishing of a Bank of the State of Tennessee on December 20, 1831. Contemporary papers relate the story of the fight that leaders in the community had to make for this bank and to have a branch placed in Jackson. The wealth and population of Jackson, according to her own public spirited citizens, seemed to demand it, for from the Jackson landing alone, during 1830-31, there were shipped upward of 6,000 bales of cotton. Several steamboats, many flat and keel boats were loaded entirely from the district upon the Hatchie, Tennessee, and Forked Deer rivers.[4] A very important meeting was held on the night of November 29, 1831, at the Jackson Reading Room "to consult the best means of meeting the calamity which has befallen us—the entire failure of the cotton crop." Dr. William E. Butler acted as chairman, while John Read was secretary. William Armour addressed the crowd showing them that in the hour of darkness the State Banks would show the planters a way to postpone the evil day of paying debts until they could raise another crop. It is not surprising that a memorial was drafted and sent to Nashville. The State Bank was chartered, books were opened in February, 1832, for sale of 3,000 shares at $100 which were allotted to the Western District, under the superintendence of W. E. Butler, Wm. Armour, James Caruthers, Samuel Dickens, Sam Lancaster, John Brown, and Wm. Stoddert. A provision for the personal liability of stockholders for indebtedness had much to do with the defeat of the measure. That the people were very concerned over the financial situation is again shown by another mass meeting that was held in Jackson in August, 1832, with Judge Joshua Haskell as chairman, to demand that the Legislature "establish the best banking institution that in

---

[3]*Southern Statesman*, December 24, 1831; April 9, 1832.
[4]*Ibid.*, September 10, 1831.

its wisdom may devise." John Read, W. E. Butler, A. L. Martin, A. B. Bradford, Joseph H. Talbot were sent to Nashville to push the movement forward.[5]

In October, 1832, the charter of the State Bank of Tennessee was repealed but the Union Bank of the State of Tennessee was established by the same act. The local papers announced the opening of the books for the sale of stock in Jackson under the superintendence of W. E. Butler, James Elrod, James Lynch, James Meriwether, Wm. Saunders, Adam Huntsman, and James Vaulx.[6] Days passed and plans began to materialize. James Caruthers was elected president of the Branch of the Union Bank at Jackson and J. W. Campbell, a young lawyer who had had previous banking experience, was selected for the position of cashier of the new bank which opened July 15, 1833, and continued until the Civil War.[7]

Soon after the Sectional Conflict, the Bank of Madison with a capital stock of $50,000 was established (1865-1866) with General Alexander W. Campbell, president, Tobe Meriwether, cashier, N. S. White, teller. Without a rival for several years, this bank had a large volume of business. In 1888, N. S. White was president, J. W. Theus, cashier, and Paul Ingram, teller. This institution closed about 1889, having enjoyed a quarter of a century of business in this section and contributing greatly to the growth of the community.

In 1873, a new bank, the Jackson Savings Bank was organized. A year later this organization was converted into the First National Bank with James W. Anderson, president, W. A. Caldwell, cashier, and Milton Brown, John M. Parker, William K. Walsh as additional directors. During the days of its youth, the officers of the First National Bank set a pattern for future banks and bankers in this section. These capable men of the new institution were ready to give financial aid to every worthy enterprise looking to the upbuilding of Jackson and the vicinity,

---

[5]*Southern Statesman*, December 2, 1831; January 7, August 25, 1832.

[6]*Acts of Tennessee*, 1832; *Southern Statesman*, November 3, December 10, 1832.

[7]See later chapter on "Crime in Madison" for story of the robbery and murder at this bank. In 1856, W. H. Stephens was president; E. F. McKnight, cashier; James S. Lyon, Martin Cartmell, Jno. S. Miller, Samuel Lancaster, W. B. Marshall, and James Talbot, directors. *West Tennessee Whig*, June 6, 1856.

to loan money upon approved security, thus maintaining a conservative policy and thereby inspiring and maintaining the confidence of the people. At the time of W. A. Caldwell's retirement from cashiership in 1888, the *Forked Deer Blade* paid a fitting tribute to him and men of his type:

> He [Caldwell] is the real founder of the Bank [First National] and under his able management it has achieved a pronounced success. He leaves Sam While cashier and Will Caldwell, his son, assistant. Mr. John L. Wisdom, one of the clearest headed and most enterprising men in Jackson, continues to be president of the bank and deservedly shares with Mr. Caldwell the credit of the success the institution has achieved.[8]

Any bank that is blessed with good officers is wealthy indeed. None could have had a better cashier than that first one of the First National as is shown by the tribute paid to W. A. Caldwell, Sr. at the time of his death:

> In all the years of his citizenship in Jackson, he bore his part in every good work material, social, and religious. His example, viewed from every standpoint, commands respect for the sincerity that governed his words and acts, the energy and integrity that characterized his dealings with mankind, and the religious fervor that pervaded his social and business life. He was a deeply religious man and in his principles and policies was a softened, but striking type of the ancient Puritans who worshipped God with austere devotion and walked in the straight and narrow path with severity and singleness of purpose.[9]

As the years passed, the bank grew with the community. Other men who were builders in the community and valuable directors of the bank included: John R. McKinnie, J. B. Young, T. C. Long, Dr. B. R. Harris, Monroe Anderson, J. W. Vanden, Dr. Ambrose McCoy, T. G. Hughes, and C. E. Pigford.

Presidents of the First National Bank with their years of service are as follows: James W. Anderson, 1873-1879; W. K. Walsh, 1879-1881; John L. Wisdom, 1881-1890; John Greer, 1890-1903; John L. Wisdom, 1903-1909; John R. McKinnie, January, 1909-June, 1909; J. W. Vanden, 1909-1927; W. A. Caldwell, 1927-1945; Hugh Hicks, 1945 to present.

The first Stockholders Meeting of the Second National Bank, Jackson, Tennessee, was held on August 17, 1886, in

---

[8] *Forked Deer Blade,* January 21, 1888.
[9] *Ibid.,* March 17, 1888.

the library room of Pitts, Hays, and Meeks law office with J. H. Hirsch acting as chairman and A. D. Dugger, secretary. The following nine stockholders were elected to form the Board of Directors: John A. Pitts, Clifton Dancy, W. T. Nelson, S. D. Hays, Louis J. Brooks, C. T. Bates, Father Abbott, M. H. Meeks, and H. H. Swink. The organization of the bank proceeded by the election of John A. Pitts, president; W. T. Nelson, vice-president; W. S. Moore, cashier; capital stock of $75,000 was issued and as the days passed plans were made to secure the building on the southeast corner of Lafayette and Market streets as the location of this new institution.

One June 21, 1888, John A. Pitts tendered his resignation as president before moving to Nashville to continue his law practice. At this time he congratulated the stockholders upon the excellent condition of the bank and promised to continue his support to the bank. Judge Pitts, until the day of his death felt very close to those friends of his in Jackson and especially those at the Second National Bank.

John A. Pitts (1866-1888) was followed by W. T. Nelson (1888-1905), Moses Neely (1905-1907), Thomas Polk (1907-1928), W. D. Nelson (1928-1940), and Frank Caldwell (1940 to present) as presidents of the bank.

Many directors and officers of the Second National Bank deserve to be mentioned, but some of the minutes of the Board of Directors were not available, therefore the writer had to select a few from those records at hand. On these minutes may be found a forceful tribute to J. B. Young, a director of the bank whose work with the institution and in the organization of the Bemis mills stands as a lasting monument of praise and admiration; to Bruce Edenton, director of the bank and successful business man "who enjoyed the trust and condence and esteem of all who knew him, since he was straight forward, honest, conservative, reliable, and frank with his dealings with his fellowmen"; to John L. Wisdom, Sr., vice-president from 1908 to 1919, director, and leader in the community, who played a prominent part in the success of the Second National Bank. The following excerpt from the minutes show how John L. Wisdom was appreciated in this community where his interest lay in its welfare:

> John L. Wisdom had been one of the leaders in our community for many years and whose valuable influence was ever felt and mani-

fested in every movement for the betterment of our citizenship and welfare and progress of our community . . . born in the historic town of old Purdy in McNairy County, Tennessee, and moved to our city in the year 1879. For nearly one-half century he resided in Jackson and labored untiringly and unceasingly for the best interests of our city and no citizen has ever contributed more to the growth of Jackson and the happiness and prosperity of our citizens. . . . He was always a valuable, helpful friend of our institution and gave of his time unselfishly to the progress of our bank. . . . He represented the highest type of citizens, he was able, upright, and honorable and in all public affairs took an active and important part.[10]

At the death of Thomas Polk, the faithful, loyal servant of the Second National, who served this institution for thirty-five years, there was a fitting tribute placed on the minutes of the Board of Directors. The following is quoted from this old minute book:

Coming to the Second National Bank as its president at a critical time when its stock was selling below par, he, by the force of his personality, by his financial acumen, by his devotion to the best traditions of banking, soon brought the institution back to its former prestige and with the loyal co-operation of his associates there has been built up a financial institution that is sound to the core and is universally recognized as one of Tennessee's strongest banks. . . . Rarely does it fall to the lot of any business corporation to have as its chief executive over a long period of years a man so eminently fitted by nature and by training for the high office so ably filled as by Thomas Polk as President of the Second National Bank.[11]

The Jackson Banking Company was opened for business in 1891 by W. E. Dunaway, P. J. Murray, R. S. Fletcher, F. B. Fisher, J. W. N. Burkett, George Wilkerson, A. A. Booth, D. W. Herring, Dr. J. T. Jones. This bank was absorbed in 1904 by other banking interests.

On February 24, 1905, R. S. Fletcher, George Wilkerson, Exile Burkett, H. W. Louis, R. N. Womack, L. W. Birmingham, Tom White, and Hunter Wilson joined to incorporate the Bank of Commerce. Besides those already mentioned the first directors included D. A. Lyerla, B. P. Cantrell, J. S. Johnson, J. L. Hendrix, D. I. Patrick, H. W. White, D. L. Hopper, J. C.

---

[10] Minutes of Board of Directors of Second National Bank.
[11] Entry in the Minute Book of the Board of Directors of the Second National Bank, November 13, 1928.

Pearson, Sam Rosenbloom. The capital stock was $75,000, with $37,500 paid in. This institution was converted into the National Bank of Commerce July 15, 1925. The first bank was located in a building on the northwest corner of Lafayette and Liberty streets, a few years later it was moved to the notheast corner of the same streets, and in 1934, the bank purchased the building on the southeast corner of Lafayette and Liberty where the bank is now located. The bank has enjoyed rapid growth under its successive presidents: R. S. Fletcher, Sr. (1905-1931); George Wilkerson (1931-1938); Oliver Benton (1938-1945); and Simpson Russell (1945 to present).

Robert S. Fletcher, the first president of the National Bank of Commerce, had a unique career in the community. He was a man who by progressiveness and public spiritedness, both in business and political affairs, had helped to make a wide-awake and cultured city. In his varied career as a school teacher, newspaper man, as editor of the Jackson *Dispatch,* as a merchant, as a member of the board of education of the city, trustee of the Memphis Conference Female Institute, aid-de-camp on the staff of Governor Robert Taylor, and finally as president of the Bank of Commerce, he was a loyal, and an understanding friend and a capable business advisor. A recent Tennessee historian when writing of Colonel Fletcher concluded:

> His disposition is so joyous, his nature so kind, his manner so democratic, that his acquaintances soon became his steadfast friends. He puts into practice the saying: "The best way to have a friend is to be one." He has in many ways been what men call successful, but his real success should be measured by his purpose to help others. His hope and good cheer, his helpfulness in beating down strife and promoting peace, his faith in man and his belief that good predominates has been helpful to many.[12]

Each of the presidents of the National Bank of Commerce has been a capable business man who had the confidence of the public and thus they have been able to contribute greatly to the growth of the bank. George Wilkerson, one of the founders, builders and conservators of the bank, was a man whose life was so closely woven with the bank that one hardly thought of one without the other, a man to whom the officers,

---

[12]Will T. Hale and Dixon Merritt, *A History of Tennessee and Tennesseans* (Chicago, 1913), VIII, 2219-2220.

directors, employees, and customers, turned for sound advice, for George Wilkerson was honest and devoted to the bank and courteous to its friends and customers. This bank was fortunate indeed in having Oliver Benton, as president from 1938 to 1945, for he was a thinker, a planner, a man with sound judgment and unimpeachable integrity, a man whose friends were innumerable, a man who took time to meet civic responsibility that was placed upon him. The fact that Oliver Benton served for six years on the Board of Directors of the Federal Reserve Bank is proof of the fact that he was recognized away from home as an outstanding banker.[13] The rapid growth of the National Bank of Commerce during the last years is material proof of the splendid leadership of these three presidents.

In a review of the financial history of the county, there are at least six other banks which have been established, operated for a time but are now non-existent. The largest and most influential of these was the Peoples' Savings Bank, incorporated June 31, 1889, by Hu C. Anderson, S. M. White, Jno. L. Wisdom, J. W. Vanden, J. C. Gooch, W. M. Harris, H. W. Clarke, F. W. Adamson, W. T. Rogers, C. G. Bond, and Levi Woods. Hu C. Anderson was its first president, Stoddert Caruthers, the first vice-president, and H. B. Gilmore, cashier. This institution under the conservative leadership of the founders deserved the tribute paid to it in a paper of 1904: "Its management from the beginning has been prudent and careful and its standing with the people in Madison county is a tribute to the soundness in a financial way and its liberality toward depositors."[14] Hu C. Anderson, Sr., president of the bank from its organization until his death in 1915, was considered "one of the brainist and most progressive men of the south. As president of this bank, mayor of the city, member of the school board, election commissioner, and other public interests, he left an impress upon the business, educational, political, and governmental life of the city that will last for generations."[15] Upon the death of Hu C. Anderson, J. W. Vanden was elected president of the bank. The capital stock was increased from $50,000 to $100,000 in 1912, from $100,000 to $200,000 in 1919. The Peoples Savings Bank should be given the credit for

---

[13]Minutes of the National Bank of Commerce.
[14]Jackson *Daily Whig*, December 20, 1904.
[15]Jackson *Sun*, May 21, 1916.

building the first modern office building in 1924, the building now owned by the First National Bank.[16]

During the year of 1905, there were incorporated two small banks in the county, the Bank of Mercer on May 13 by T. E. Mercer, J. W. Vanden, J. F. McGee, L. W. McGee, and W. Ragland. This bank had a capital stock of $25,000 of which only $10,000 was paid in. The bank went into voluntary liquidation May 18, 1933. The Pinson Savings Bank was incorporated on April 25, 1905, by M. B. Charles, F. E. Robbins, R. L. Ozier, H. L. Kline, and W. F. Watlington. There was a capital stock of $10,000, of which only $7,500 was paid in. This bank went into voluntary liquidation January 10, 1931.[17]

In 1903, the Union Bank and Trust Company, located on the northeast corner of Market and Lafayette Streets, was opened with a capital stock of $50,000. J. C. Edenton was president; Walter L. Brown, vice-president; I. B. Tigrett, cashier. This bank enjoyed a good business, and was later absorbed by other banking interests.

On April 9, 1912, A. M. Alexander, W. G. Morgan, J. A. Crook, B. H. Blalock, Thomas McCorry, and R. R. Sneed applied for a charter for the Security Bank and Trust Company with a capital stock of $50,000. The Security National Bank of Jackson, chartered on February 19, 1913, was a conversion of the Security Bank and Trust Company. At the time of its organization, A. M. Alexander was president; B. H. Blalock, cashier. The first directors included: A. M. Alexander, W. G. Morgan, Thomas McCorry, J. A. Crook, K. C. Mayo, W. M. Luckman, W. J. Baum, A. E. Barnett, J. F. Outlan, J. L. Crook, R. C. Cathey, Hugh Ross, F. J. Young, B. H. Blalock, L. W. Birmingham, R. R. Sneed, T. B. Autry.[18]

The story of finances in Madison County cannot be concluded without a brief statement of the excellent condition of the three banks in the county today (1946). There are few communities that boast of three institutions that have a total surplus of $525,000, of a total undivided profit of $222,984.83, of total deposits of $32,309,424.37, of total resources of $33,-

---

[16]The Peoples Savings Bank closed for liquidation June 6, 1925, during which process the depositors were paid 78.6 per cent.
[17]Records of the State Banking Department.
[18]Records of Comptroller of Currency, Treasury Department. This bank went into liquidation January 10, 1931.

708,736.46. As the history of every progressive city and every strong business institution is nothing more than the record of the individuals who have made their progress possible, the activities of each banker in Jackson should be recorded but a limitation of space prevents this and the writer was forced to choose a few financial leaders for discussion. These men and many others have laid the foundation for the present excellent condition of the banks of our city

CHAPTER XXIV

TOWNS AND COMMUNITIES OF THE COUNTY

The first settlement by white people in Madison County was at COTTON GROVE in 1819, by John Hargrove, Roderick and Duncan McIver, Elijah Jones, John and Thomas Brown, and William Woolfolk. Doctors Robert Fenner and McKnight came soon after. The community grew rapidly for a number of years. In 1821, a man by the name of Maddin grew the first cotton in the county; in 1822, Duncan McIver built a mill on Jones's Creek. This was a large mill for that day, for it had a capacity of five bushels a day. Most of the men who came to Cotton Grove were men of sufficient means to purchase land and build comfortable homes. In 1834, Cotton Grove was listed as a post office and a stagecoach stop. In fact the old Phillips place on the Cotton Grove road to-day was originally built and used for a stagecoach inn. Here at Cotton Grove was the Masonic Lodge Number 153 and Miss Fisbie's school for girls where they could obtain reasonable board and be instructed in the English language, French, and music.[1] Near by was located the old Salem Church and cemetery where one of the earliest marked graves is that of Sarah Huntsman who died in 1825. Other families should be mentioned in connection with the community are these of Stephen Sypert, William Vaulx, Gabriel Anderson, Martin Key, Henry Collins, the Hendersons and the Browns. The town has vanished to-day. The railroads and highways went the other way.

In 1826, John Lynch of Virginia came to Madison County and settled on the Dyer place ten miles north of Jackson. Some years prior to 1828, there was a settlement made on Poplar Creek, on the Christmasville road eight miles north of Jackson, near where the Pleasant Hill church stood. John Mooring, James Tomlinson, Sam Lancaster, James Wood, B. G. Stewart,

---

[1]Jackson *West Tennessee Whig*, April 7, 1853.

Julius Jones, Pleasant Miller, and John Greer all came to the vicinity and built homes.

Another settlement in the county was the one which grew up about the Haughton grist and flour mill and became known as SPRING CREEK. This was once a thriving village and those who lived there had dreams of a real town. Picture a number of prosperous farmers in the community, a commodious hotel on the north side of the stage coach road, stables where the horses for the coaches were changed, a Main street with several stores which carried large stocks of goods, three religious congregations which worshipped in humble but comfortable churches and the reader has a view of this village in the 19th century. Of the six stores in Spring Creek in 1872, there were five that advertised in an old directory of that year. Three were dealers in groceries, drygoods, and hardware; Coats and Hill made a specialty of medicine, W. H. Fussell had as his specialties, whiskies, brandies, and wines; J. H. Fox, the exclusive druggist, also featured varnishes, window glass, and fine whiskies.[2] Spring Creek, which was incorporated in 1854, had a Masonic Lodge No. 193, a Cumberland Presbyterian Church erected in 1865 and a population of five hundred by 1872. Thirteen miles of sandy and uneven road to Jackson caused many a purchase to be made in Spring Creek rather than in Jackson; but in 1872, the people seemed to be interested in two things—a railroad and schools. There was much talk of a railroad that was to be built from Jackson to Huntingdon which would pass through Spring Creek. That the people were interested in education is shown by the fact that in a community of six stores, there were two schools—the beautiful three story building which housed the Madison College and the Springdale Institute, which was founded by Major Jesse Taylor in 1870. A report of 1858 in the minutes of the Central Association of Baptist at Spring Creek tells of the great plans for the most magnificent college building of West Tennessee which was erected by the church but would be a blessing to both Spring Creek and the church—Madison College.[3]

Spring Creek was the home of the dreamer and inventor,

---

[2] *West Tennessee Directory of 1872.*

[3] *Minutes of the Central Association of Baptist at Spring Creek,* September 26, 1858. Details of Madison College may be found in the Chapter on "Education."

Professor Isham Walker, who in the late 1850's deposited in the Patent Office a draft of an air-ship of his design and also of its machinery. In 1858, he visited Arkansas hoping to get legislative aid for the perfection of his "giant trout, 356 feet long that would travel through the air at the exceeding speed of 300 miles per hour at the giddy height of two miles from mother earth." Isham Walker also presented a memorial to Congress for an appropriation of $1,000,000 to purchase material and $2,000 a year for superintending instruction while he retained all rights of the patent, but if Congress would give him life-time employment at $5,000 a year, he would assign all rights over to the government. This air-ship was to be three mammoth balloons forty-five feet wide, seventy feet high, material of wire and sheet copper, well coated inside and out with India rubber; two "fishes" side by side and the other "fish" forward and below. There was the top "fish" for gas and the bottom one for a cabin where two vacuum engines driving two screws so geared to the two engines as to make 500 revolutions per minute.[4] What a chance Spring Creek had to become famous if its son, Professor Walker, had perfected his invention!

DENMARK, Madison County, an Indian settlement, was also once upon a time an interesting, happy, prosperous village. There was an old Indian trail coming down probably from Kentucky to Denmark. It crossed the Hatchie River at Estanaula, thence to Fayette Corner near the present town of Whiteville, and then on to the Chickasaw bluffs. There was plenty of evidence that there was once an Indian settlement at Denmark, for years later flint, arrowheads, and other stone implements, bits of broken pottery could be found near the Indian mounds on the Estanaula road.[5] Some of the earliest

---

[4]Jackson *Dispatch*, October 3, 1873. Jackson also lost a chance to become known as the home of an inventor. About the turn of the century F. E. Ernshaw built him an airplane along the same line of the Wright Brothers' model of a few years later, but the engine was too heavy and his experiment was not successful.
[5]John Johnston in his "Reminiscences" and a letter to Fonville Neville recorded most of the information about Denmark. Fonville Neville himself has made a great contribution to the history of this section with his stories of Mercer, Denmark, and Estanaula. The writer is deeply indebted to Mr. Neville and to Mr. Addison Johnston for the use of his father's "Reminiscences."

settlers who came to this section of the country during the decade from 1820 to 1830 from North Carolina, South Carolina, and Virginia were the Meriwethers, James, David, Frank; Philip Austin; Mr. Bryant; and the Johnston brothers. About this time and the years immediately following came the Neelys, Harts, Alexanders, Tysons, McBrides, Reids, Bonds, Wilsons, Williamsons, Murchisons, Skillerns, Moores, McMillans, Utleys, Robertsons, Rices, and many others. The first store was located on the bluff at Reid's old mill on Big Black Creek by the Harberts who later moved the store to Denmark. By 1840, there were seven or eight dry goods retail stores, in the town, which could also boast of John Wray's grocery store, a "doggery," or whiskey shop, and the old Meriwether and the Jett House hotel. The stage coach stopped at the former inn as it passed through Denmark on to Estanaula and on to Memphis. The 1850's were Denmark's crowning period. In that decade it was one of the most ambitious and promising towns in West Tennessee. It was incorporated in 1830. The town became the center of social and religious life of this section, for its citizens were of the best quality, most of whom were wealthy, owning acres of land by the thousands and slaves by the hundreds. During these years the Presbyterians were so strong and so prosperous that they paid their pastor, Rev. Cyrus Caldwell $1,200 a year, which was a fabulous salary for those days. Denmark's political influence was such that no candidate considered his election safe unless he stood well in that community. Denmark was on the itinerary of every candidate who planned to stump the district.

The people of the Denmark community had two principal interests beyond the necessary one of making a living—those interests were the church and the schools.[6] The old female academy was situated on the slope of the hill a little east of where the Methodist church now stands. Misses Emma and Milinda Senesman instructed the young ladies of the community and often many from the adjoining counties. The Denmark Male and Female Academy had been incorporated in 1831 with Josiah Fort, Theophilus Sanders, James H. Walker, James Meriwether, George Williamson, David Jarrell, Matthew Clanton, S. W. Vaughn as trustees. At the end of the first year, thirty-

---

[6]An account of the churches may be found in the chapter "Religion in Madison."

five pupils creditably participated in the closing exercises "to the entire satisfaction of the public."[7] About 1850, a new female school was built and the usual studies of the day were pursued under the direction of A. M. Lewis, a highly cultured gentleman. The Male Academy was also very popular. There were often from one hundred to one hundred and fifty students in each school, the students coming from adjoining counties and often from northern Mississippi. It is no wonder that Denmark was noted for its large number of well educated and intelligent young men and women.[8]

By 1872, although some of the prosperity of the 1850's had passed out of sight, there were three firms—McKissack and Burton, Bryan, Duncan—all dealers in groceries, drygoods, queensware, and hardware; W. J. Hudson, manufacturer of carriages, wagons, buggies; Dr. John Tyson, druggist and practicing physician; A. C. Burgess, manufacturer of coaches, buggies, furniture, who was ready to serve the people. Burgess also had a neat hearse and gentle horses to attend to all orders for coffins, always "endeavoring to give satisfaction in style and price."[9]

Besides the interest in religion and education, there were other interests, for there was a Masonic Lodge here in Denmark with a membership of 154, a company of national guards, and a brass band. Into an atmosphere of prosperity in this farming community there was introduced the idea of railroads. Denmark began its decline when the Mobile and Ohio and the Mississippi Central and Tennessee came to Jackson and missed Denmark, but its death knell was sounded when the two proposed railroads in the latter part of the nineteenth century passed the village by. An old directory of 1872 tells of how enthusiastic the people were over these two roads—the Tennessee Midland and the Denmark, Brownsville, and Durhamville roads. The citizens subscribed $25,000 to the latter road, but this road never got beyond a few hundred feet of embankment built through a field west of Brownsville. The failure of this road probably accounted for the refusal of the citizens to accede to a demand made by the Tennessee Midland Railroad for

---

[7] Jackson *Southern Statesman*, June 19, 1831. Other details of this institution are given in the chapter on "Education."
[8] Reminiscences of John Johnston.
[9] *West Tennessee Directory of 1872.*

$3,000. Upon the false premise that the road would be forced to come through here anyway because of Big Black Creek bottom, they sat still and did nothing. Consequently the road was built a mile south. The village of Mercer grew over night and Denmark entered upon a steady decline.

Fate was certainly against the growth of Denmark. Fire has taken a large toll here. In 1860, there were seventeen stores burned; in 1867 a fire destroyed almost the entire business section including the stores of Reid, McKissack, Burton, Neely and Meriwether;[10] in 1903, three stores burned; twelve buildings including a cotton gin have burned since 1924.

ESTANAULA, meaning in Cherokee language "Here we cross," a one time ferry on the Hatchie, is six miles from Mercer, eight miles from Denmark. Although it is in Haywood County, it played a distinctive part in the history of this section of the county.[11] It was an important shipping point in this section. Sometimes the farmers hauled their cotton to Memphis by wagon, but more often they brought it to Estnaula, stored it in a warehouse kept by Mr. Bumpus, shipped it to Memphis by boat, bought their groceries that arrived by boat, and stayed at a hotel kept by Archie McBride while they were transacting their business. Bob Wilson, who operated the ferryboat shortly before the Civil War, built on the bank of the river near the ferry one of the finest homes in this section, its high ceiling rooms being festooned with marble baskets of flowers; a commodious basement served as kitchen and dining room. Work was rushed upon the house by promising the workmen a quart of whiskey per day per man if they worked swiftly and so swiftly did they work that before the building was finished they were being given a gallon per man each day. Tragedies occurred here, such as those ferry boats which sank carrying George and Louis Ford, twins, only ten years old, to their deaths. (These were buried in the old Baptist cemetery in twin graves, brick enclosed. According to tradition, $30,000, stolen from a Brownsville bank, was buried between these graves and remained there until some twenty years ago, when someone who knew the secret hiding place removed the money.) Picturesque Estanaula is indeed, when tradition says that it was

---

[10] Jackson *West Tennessee Whig*, May 11, 1867.

[11] The writer is indebted to Fonville Neville of Denmark for a sketch of Estanaula published in the Jackson *Sun* January 11, 1946.

near here that Egbert Osborne preached his famous sermon from Isaiah, "Son of Men, shall these dry bones live again?"; thereby proving to the Yankees by whom he had been captured and taken for a spy and was about to be executed, that he was a preacher indeed. It was here that Virgil Stewart met up with the infamous land pirate, John A. Murrell, and began the journey that led to the capture of the pirate. It was here that one of Jesse James' gang came to camp each year as he returned for a season of respectability. It was here that the notorious Fielding Hurst camped as he preyed upon this section of West Tennessee. Because of the frequent references to this crossing in the papers, in the court records about turnpikes to Estanaula, there is good evidence that this landing was one of the principal river ports of Jackson and the surrounding community. Stories of this community are like echoes of a forgotten past, for there are only ruins of the famous mansion house and even the road on the west bank has disappeared.

When the Western District was opened for settlement by the completion of the treaty with the Chickasaws in 1818, settlers began to pour into the district, each seeking a good location near one of the fine springs which were abundant at the foot of the hills of the woodlands. In one of the hollow trees of the vicinity of what is now MEDON, a hunter sought refuge from a blizzard and froze to death—thus the location was called Frozen Oak for a time. In 1834, the post office was called Clover Creek, but this did not satisfy the new citizens of the community, so according to tradition, they decided to use the first words of a popular Irishman, who was soon to return from a job. When Mike came home, he threw open his tools and exclaimed, "Me done"—hence the name Medon.[12]

The first settlements were made near Medon about 1825, though the town was not established until 1834. Among the early settlers were William Wilborn, Stephen Lacy, Mauldin Reeves, Dr. David Parker, Dr. Caleb Manley, Will H. Harrison and John Harrison who built a grist mill. In 1834 William S. Wisdom in partnership with William Boyd plotted and sold lots, numbering from one to thirty-nine. Among those buying lots were R. M. Taylor, Peter Swink, Peter Pinkston, Donald

---

[12]The writer is indebted to Mrs. Lena Lacy Murdock for the use of material taken from "Early Days in Medon, Tennessee," a paper read before the Madison County Historical Society, June, 1945.

Ross Lacy, Hugh Ross Lacy, David Caldwell, Dr. Joseph Upton, Henry Sharp Parker, Dr. David H. Parker, James McGuire, E. L. Leggett, Dr. J. C. Stewart, D. D. Newborn, J. A. and J. H. Judson, Jesse Lacy, James Mallory, James Caruthers, and Thomas Lacy. Soon the stage was running through the main street of the town, stopping at the Stage Tavern operated by Peter Swink and his wife, Malinda. Soon stores were opened in frame buildings that were built on each side of the stage road. These were operated by George Brown, who had a saddle and harness shop; the Casons, Charlie Givens, Doctors David Parker and Thomas Murtaugh, Captain Pittle, who had a drug store; Murchisons, Tom and Neil Anderson, John Burton, Harry Mayo, and Owen Durham, who had a saloon. Medon was incorporated in 1852; Dr. Joseph Stewart was the first mayor. This was a very prosperous farm community. The village grew until there were about 150 whites and 25 colored people living here in the 1880's. These were a very religious people and much of the social life of the community was centered around the religious meetings.[13] Medon like other communities had its private schools before the days of public school. The Medon Academy was opened in 1875 in the large rooms of the Masonic building with F. H. Williams and Mrs. L. W. Cradle conducting the school. There were two rooms. When a pupil was advanced, he was sent to the "Big Room."

MALESUS, known in the early days as Harrisburg, was settled by the Harton, McKnight, Dunbar, Fulbright, Young, Day, Loftin, Hill, and Woodson families.[14] Much of the life of this community was centered around the Ebenezer Methodist and the Old Cane Creek Baptist Churches. The old Cane Creek Baptist Church was organized in 1822 by Rev. Allen Hill. Nine members met in the Hill home for a time but soon a frame house constructed of lumber sawed with whipsaws from the virgin forest was ready for the members of Cane Creek to use it as a place of worship. When the missionary and "hard shell" elements became belligerent in 1835, the Cane Creek members voted to remain missionary through the years. Many members

---

[13]The churches of this community are discussed in the chapter on "Religion."

[14]The writer is indebted to Mrs. Elizabeth Woodson Tate for use of a paper that she read before the Madison County Historical Society, June, 1945.

from this Old Cane Creek Church became the charter members of the First Church in Jackson and in Malesus.[15] Outstanding ministers of this old church should be mentioned, such as Rev. Hill, the first minister who served until 1840; Rev. Obadiah Dodson, that picturesque frontier preacher of the mid-eighteenth century; Rev. Reuben Day who conducted the great revival of 1868, at which time there were forty-seven converts.

At the close of the Civil War, the Methodists of the Malesus community erected a church on Frank McKnight's place, which was known as "Black Jack's Meeting House." In 1869, the place of meeting was changed to a building where the Ebenezer cemetery is located and the church became known as Ebenezer. The Methodist worshipped here until 1894 at which time they joined the Methodist in Malesus. Early families of the church included the Harton, McKnight, Newsom, Black, Davis, Nobley, and Raines families.

It was a man of vision, T. B. Mercer, who pulled his steed to a stop in the center of the stage road where the road crossed the newly laid track of the Tennessee Midland Railroad and upon surveying the surrounding country, decided that here was the place for the site of a town.[16] T. E. Mercer, the son of T. B. Mercer, agreed with his father about the fine location, so they erected a store building near the cabin of Eaton Bond (1888). Five years later T. E. Mercer left Toone and joined the McGlatherlys at the new store in the village. In 1894, a railroad station was built and when some name had to appear on the time table, the superintendent asked permission to name the village MERCER. F. M. McGlatherly served as the first railroad agent; Dan Lackey as the first town marshal; J. J. Pennington, the first postmaster and teacher. Other families connected with the village were the Baileys, McGees, Bryans, Elstons, Raineys, Teagues, and Snipes.

One of the industries which did more to make Mercer grow than any other thing was the O. G. Gardner Lumber Company, which started business here in 1893 with the plant covering but one acre. Ten years later the business had increased until it covered twelve acres and more facilities were

---

[15]Other events in the life of the church are given in the chapter on "Religion."

[16]The writer is indebted to Fonville Neville for use of his sketch of "Mercer."

needed so other mills and yards were acquired in Jackson. The wholesale and retail business in rough and finished lumber of this company extended all over the Mississippi Valley.[17]

The Mercer community, like other communities in the county, was interested in schools and churches. Of the Methodist, Baptist, and Presbyterian churches here, the Methodist is the oldest, dating back to the year 1894. This church was the outgrowth of Hays's Chapel, one mile west of Mercer. Milton Hays had given the land for the chapel and the cemetery. When the village of Mercer began to grow, it was decided to move the place of religious meetings to Mercer. The first schools in the community were held in the old Ebenezer Church, which was not centrally located. A new building was built here, which was called "Folly College" because so many of the citizens thought the location was a very foolish one. The first school in Mercer was erected in 1894, with J. J. Pennington as the teacher.[18]

The HUNTERSVILLE community was once a doctor's shop and a small store near the crossing of the Jackson to Brownsville and the Denmark to Poplar Corner Ferry Roads. The store was owned by Dr. John Hunter, the saddle-pocket physician who practiced in the community for years before he died of yellow fever in 1876. After Dr. Hunter's death Matt Wyley became storekeeper of the Hunter store and served as postmaster of Andrew's Chapel, the name given to the village by the Post Office Department.

Schools and churches were both very important in the life of this community. The first school, a one room house situated where the W. T. Crittenden home now stands, was taught by Pat Davis, who believed that the blue backed spelling book and the hickory switch were necessary starting points in life. The Vine Hill school, four miles southeast of Huntersville, and the Center Point school, nine miles north of the village, were consolidated in 1914-1915 when a new building was erected on the site of the Dr. Phillips home.

Church life was very important to those early settlers who came to the Huntersville community. Andrews Chapel, in honor of the beloved Bishop Andrews, was organized in the

---

[17] Jackson *Daily Whig*, December 20, 1904.
[18] For the Bank of Mercer, see chapter on "Banks and Banking."

early 1820's. Major James Meriwether was a member of the committee to have a house of worship built. He had the logs hewn by hand and the lumber cut with a rip saw from the trees of the near by forest, using slave labor to do all the work. The original building has been preserved and is still used as a place of worship. The congregation included members of the Davis, Transou, Witherspoon, Meriwether, Henning, Crittenden, Blackard, Chandler, and Valentine families.

The Baptist of the community organized the Ararat church "just after the stars fell," long before the Civil War (about 1850) and built a house near the old Joe Henning home, north of Huntersville. After the Civil War the church was moved to the present site. Many slaves in the community were baptised by the frontier missionary, Obediah Dodson and these were members of the Ararat Church until they organized and built their own Bethlehem Church. Among the other families not already mentioned who contributed to the life of the community include: the Coles, Iveys, Ingrams, Tysons, Murtaughs, Hoppers, Perrys, Pegues, and Strains.

Eleven miles south of Jackson is located the village of PINSON, situated in the level, healthy, quite rich productive section of the valley of the South Forked Deer. About 1821, Memucan Hunt Howard, Joel Pinson, and three other surveyors who were employed by Colonel Thomas Henderson, proceeded on foot into the wilds of the Western District to the source of the Forked Deer and the Big Hatchie rivers and into the swamp south of what was later Jackson. Emerging from the swamp of the Forked Deer about twelve miles south of the later location of the county seat, the party came upon a bold spring and a mound six or seven feet high and large enough to build a house upon it. They called it Mount Pinson. Most of this land was obtained by Colonel Thomas Henderson who came here from North Carolina to make his home in the early 1820's.

In 1866, the town of Pinson was located upon the land of A. S. Rogers. This had been a prosperous farming section, the location of a large commissary kept by A. S. Rogers and C. H. Hearn, but now, a steam saw mill began to operate under the direction of A. S. Rogers and E. R. Lancaster; the first dwellings were built; a post office was opened with E. R. Lancaster as postmaster. In 1834, "Mount Pinson" was listed as one of the post offices of the Western District, but an old ledger of the Rogers and Hearn Commissary in the 1850's is the most interesting piece of original material that has been located concerning this section of the country. The merchandise sold by Rogers and Hearn was bought in Memphis, Louisville, Philadelphia, and New York, shipped to Jackson or Perryville on the Tennessee River and hauled by wagons to Pinson from these points. During the year 1859, A. S. Rogers went to Memphis, Louisville, Philadelphia (two trips) and New York to buy goods. Purchases in Memphis amounted to $1,014.76, in Louisville to $1,758.10, in New York and Philadelphia to $11,446.40, making a total of stock brought to the store in the Pinson neighborhood for the year $14,208.50.[19]

A variety store this was indeed, that Hearn and Rogers had. Accounts list handkerchiefs, hoop skirts, hay forks, harmonicas, silks, scissors, snuff, calico, copperas, suspenders, spectacles, and spittoons. An interesting phase of the business of the store was the sale of patent medicine and home remedies. Over $150 worth of patent medicine was bought from the Philadelphia firms on commission. Therefore frequent entries read: 1 bot castor oil, 25c; 1 bot vermifuge, 25c; quinine, 15c; 1 bot ague mixture, 25c; ½ lb. "Pain Killer," 18c; copperas, 5c; 1 lb. paragoric, 10c; camphor, alum, and turpentine.[20]

On the large accounts of Hearn and Rogers store, there appeared unlimited numbers of yards of muslin, calico, brown linen, "brilliant," gingham, "ribin," osnaburg; unnumerable cravats, hoop skirts at from $1.50 to $2.50 each, water buckets, looking glasses, sets of knives and forks for 75c, brogans, candles, hose inexpensive at three pairs for 50c and silk ones for 87c and readers for the first three grades were listed on the ledger. On these same accounts were charged a spitton at 44c, a trunk at $2.62, set of violin strings at 50c, "harmonicy" at 70c, a pair of spectacles at 50c and ladies' bonnets from one dollar to $9.50. Expensive articles came over the same counter, such as forty yards of carpeting, for which A. S. Rogers paid $30.00; a fine coat that cost C. H. Hearn $15; a beaver coat which cost Dr. N. A. McCoy $20; a silk lace mantle that cost John Croom $6.00.

Interest in religion and education was manifested very

---

[19]Ledger of Hearn and Rogers.
[20]*Ibid.*

quickly by the citizens of the community, for the first school in Pinson was taught by Rev. John McCoy in 1867. The Baptist church with Rev. Levin Savage, was established soon after the settlement of the town, followed very quickly by the Methodist, with Rev. E. L. Fisher serving as the first pastor. The Methodist church was erected on land donated by A. S. Rogers, who served as chairman of the County Court in the 1870's.

This new village on the Mobile and Ohio grew very rapidly, for within ten years it could boast of a population of 200, of which 75 were colored; of two dry goods stores, two grocery stores, two saloons, one drug store, one blacksmith and wagon shop; of one hotel, one Masonic hall, two churches, one high school with three teachers, and 75 pupils; of three carpenters, two physicians, and of two grist mills.[21]

A traveler of 1866 described great signs of recuperation from the ravages of war in the Mount Pinson areas as follows:

"Here agriculturists are actively engaged in repairing and cultivating their farms. With a fair average supply of laborers, black and white, and with good prospects thus far of renumerative results for skillful labor bestowed on a generous, fertile soil owing to the enterprise of Messrs. Lancaster, Rogers, Hudson, Fry, and other men of Pinson. The depot has sprung up from a desolate waste to an active stirring village with a saw-mill, stores, shops, the residence of thrifty enterprising and industrious inhabitants, seeking by honest toil and the use of capital to repair thin shattered fortunes, and by building up schools, churches and other means of application of civilization to render the Pinson district one of the most attractive and desirable locations in Madison County. The whole region is admirably supplied with fine timber to attract lumber men."[22]

HENDERSON, Tennessee, was once in the southeastern part of Madison County. The village, which was called, Dayton, Henderson City, and Henderson Station, was a post village on the Mobile and Ohio Railroad. About 1860, J. R. Arnold, W. H. and A. E. Bray opened up stores here and T. Bowers started operating a hotel. The village site was located on lands that belonged to Dr. J. D. Smith and James Simmons. Dr. J. S. Smith served as postmaster under Confederate authority in 1861; David Franklin was appointed post-

---

[21]For the early schools in Pinson see chapter on "Education."
[22]Jackson *West Tennessee Whig*, May 19, 1866.

master by Federal authorities in 1866. There was very little progress of the town during the Sectional Conflict. The possibility of raiders, was not conducive to building anything. Men, such as Fielding Hurst who played the role of Nero when he visited Jack's Creek and Purdy were entirely too careless with fire when they came through the county. This fact and the general stalemate of business during the war caused the small village to mark time until hostilities were over.

By 1873, soldiers had returned, new people had moved in from the north, and others had moved to the railroad from the surrounding territory, until the village of Henderson could boast of 300 inhabitants, three general stores, owned by J. R. Barham and Co., Cason, O'Neal and Company, J. M. Hart and Company, Crook Brothers Drug Store, O. W. David's blacksmith shop, John A. McCulley's saddle shop, Smith and Hobbs' livery stable, and THREE saloons operated by J. R. Bland, G. J. Priddy, and J. O. Day.[23] Two newspapers were published here in the early days—the Henderson *Advocate* and the Madison County *Herald*.

That the first settlers of Henderson were very religious people is shown by the early establishment of three churches— the Baptist church on August 15, 1867; the Methodist church in 1874-1875; the Christian church, which was organized at Jack's Creek in 1871 but was moved to Henderson in 1883.

One of the factors that added greatly to the development of the village was the Henderson Masonic Male and Female Institute. Before the days of public schools, a good boarding and day school was a great attraction in a community. Chartered in 1871, in five years the college could boast of 166 students that were enrolled and so wide was the course of study that the school attracted students from Corinth, Jack's Creek, Spring Creek, Mifflin, and La Grange.

In just a few short years, a movement was under way to create a new county and the story of this section of Madison was to become the history of another county. By a Legislative Act of March 19, 1875 Wisdom County was created out of portions of Madison, Henderson, McNairy, and Hardeman. It was a small county of only 278 square miles in area. But this county was never organized and the act creating it was

---

[23]*Tennessee State Directory*, 1873-1874, II (Nashville, 1873).

repealed March 4, 1879, at which time a county was laid out from practically the same area as Wisdom County, but this new county was called "Chester," in honor of Colonel Robert I. Chester, of Madison County, who was at that time a representative to the State Legislature and a man who stood in high esteem to the people of this section. Colonel Chester gave the bell in the court house in appreciation for perpetuating his name in the county. Thus, the history of Henderson Station from the time of its birth until 1879 was a part of the history of Madison County.

Miscellaneous copies of newspapers reveal the story of a health resort in the southeastern corner of Madison County during the mid-nineteenth century—MASON'S WELLS. A paper of 1861 announced the opening of the resort, ten miles southeast of Jackson within four miles of Bear Creek. For three years visitors here had been enjoying the medicinal value of the salts and iron in the water. Joseph Mason, the proprietor, assured those who came that they would be cared for by Dr. Julius Johnson and his kind and experienced lady. Good water, good rooms, and a ball room, made this a place where people could find health and pleasure.[24] This resort was reopened immediately after the Sectional Conflict, for papers of that year report that invalids would find a blessing near at hand in the waters at Mason's Wells.[25]

The first BEECH BLUFF post office was located about one and a half miles northwest of where the village is now located. This, too, was a summer resort before the Tennessee Midland Railroad came in 1888. The community was once called Homer, but its name was soon changed because of the large bluff surrounded by the native beech trees. Among the early businesses in Beech Bluff were the P. W. Moore General Store, Gregory's Drug Store, the May Hotel, and a stave factory. The early one room school house was replaced in 1912 by the present structure. The frame building of the first Methodist church built in 1892, was replaced in 1915 by the present brick building. Among the first families in Beech Bluff were the Penning-

---

[24]Jackson *West Tennessee Whig*, May 17, 1861. Mrs. W. W. Tucker Collection.

[25]Jackson *West Tennessee Whig*, May 19, 1866. Mrs. W. W. Tucker Collection.

tons, Diamonds, Neals, McCollums, Hudson, Mays, Stedmans, Pooles, and Allisons.[26]

Mason's Grove, now in Crockett County, was a thriving village in Madison County for a generation or more before it and the greater part of civil districts number nine and eighteen were taken to form a part of Crockett under an Act of the Legislature of 1871-72.[27] It was founded by Abram Mason from Delaware at an early date, some twelve or more miles to the northwest of Jackson and appears on early maps of the 1830's. A school house was maintained there and other activities of an enterprising pioneer community until the first decade after the war of 1861-1865 when it declined on account of the construction of the Memphis and Ohio Railroad (later the L. and N. R. R.) which ran within three miles to the westward. The business of the town was then moved to Gadsden and Humboldt which sprang up on account of this internal improvement. After the Civil War the educational interest survived and a widely patronized private school of junior college grade was maintained for some years by Captain Alonzo B. Day, which is recalled yet by a few older residents though the town itself is now largely a tradition among their descendants just as the town itself is only a memory. The community still goes by the name of Mason's Grove although it has long ceased to be a post office.

The story of the fight to keep that old northwest corner of Madison County is a long one, but that part of the history of Crockett County of to-day is the history of Madison County. On account of the overflowing bottoms of the South and Middle Forks of the Forked Deer at certain seasons of the year, that northwest portion of old Madison was so inaccessible, if not impossible for the citizens to reach the county seat for the transaction of ordinary public business. This alone was a strong argument for the organization of another county. Five efforts were made extending over a period of forty years before success was met in 1872 and Crockett County was organized,

---

[26]This information was gathered by the students in the eighth grade at Beech Bluff under the direction of the instructor.

[27]The writer is indebted to Hallum Goodloe, a member of the State Historical Commission and a native of Crockett County, for the preparation of this sketch of Mason's Grove and the story of the formation of Crockett County.

which county included a part of Madison. The first movement was a request to the Constitutional Convention of 1834 for permission to organize a county in the territory, which was a recognition that there was not a sufficiently large area to comply with the requirements of the Constitution of 1796. A numerously signed petition was sent to Nashville "praying that body to grant the right to organize a new county, but the petition was not presented to the convention and nothing was done about it much to the disgust and dissatisfaction of the people."[28] The name to be adopted under this petition is not known The second effort to establish the new county was the passage of a legislative act of 1845 (Chapter 25) and by this commissioners were appointed, a town laid off, called Cageville in honor of Licurgus Cage, the first merchant, and the usual corps of magistrates and officers were elected. By the act of the legislature the county was attached to the Tenth Judicial Circuit over which Judge J. C. Read of Jackson presided and at the October term of his court at Cageville, (later Alamo) "the question of the new County's constitutionality was raised and being presented to Judge Read, was decided adversely to the county. The organization then completed was abandoned and the fractions returned to the parent counties."[29] No record of why this action was taken has been found and no minutes of the session of the Circuit Court have been located.

The third effort to form a new county of Crockett was a proposal presented to the General Assembly of 1849-1850 to amend the Constitution so that new counties could be less than 350 square miles with the lines to be run not less than ten miles of the old county seats and that the old counties themselves could be less than 625 square miles. This proposal was approved by the Legislature of 1851-1852 but at the same time a conditional act was passed to put the question of new counties before the people at the August election of 1853. It failed of ratification and nothing came of the effort although 55,375 out of 118,270 voted for the new counties.[30]

---

[28]Goodspeed, *History of Tennessee,* Crockett County Edition. Recollections of Esq. Isaac M. Johnson, later known as the Father of Crockett County.

[29]*Ibid.*

[30]Charles A. Miller, *Official and Political Manual* of the State of Tennessee (Nashville, 1890), 40.

After the size of counties was reduced by the Constitution of 1870, high hopes were entertained by the people of the future Crockett County. Commissioners were named and an election on "separation" was held, but they were enjoined by E. B. Mason of Mason's Grove and then for some unknown reason the case was dismissed.[31] Finally in 1871, the persistent "county organizers" met with success for the bill organizing the county was signed by the Governor, the Commissioners met in Cageville, a census was taken, an election of separation was held, officials of the county were elected and business of the county was begun. But E. B. Mason, the persistent opponent, obtained permission to file a new suit on March 8th, the day before the election on March 9th, and four days before the actual organization on March 12, but for some reason the bill itself did not reach the files of the Chancery Court until March 21st, and it was still before the Commissioners who were under notice not to proceed further and to answer the bill. The interest and excitement prevailing at the time may be better understood by finding from the record that while the Governor's commissions for the twenty-six Justices of Peace were all actually dated March 11, this was the self-same day on which the special sheriff appointed to hold the election made his official report to the Commissioners in Cageville, and as that official could not possibly have been in both places on the same day, and a messenger could not go to Nashville and back on the same day, it is quite evident that Paul Revere was not the only night-rider to bear momentous news.[32] The injunction suit was heard by Chancellor Heiskell in Bolivar upon the Bill and Answer whereupon his Honor dissolved his own injunction and dismissed the Bill on the grounds that the County was already organized in a regular manner and there was nothing that he could do about it.

It had taken two civil districts from Madison County; 274 citizens of voting age according to the census taken, though the vote upon "Separation" showed 325 votes for the new county with 60 votes against it—forty-nine from the precinct of Mason's Grove and eleven from Gadsden. The other fractions voted 1446 for the new county and fifteen against it.

[31]Papers in the office of County Court Clerk at Alamo.
[32]"Proceedings of the Commissioners," County Court Clerk's office, Alamo, Tennessee.

The subsequent history of the new county is another and longer story, but this part of the story became a part of that of Madison, for the northwest corner of old Madison became a part of Crockett County.

Southwest of Jackson on the old Steam Ferry Road is the community that is known as MADISON HALL. To the older families such as the Manleys, Johnsons, Haskins, Tomlins, Van Hooks, Sweeneys, Campbells, Robinsons, Neelys, and Boons, there were added new residents and it was during the period just following the Civil War, that the Grangers, a progressive farmer organization interested in education, built a two story building that was known as Madison Hall. The upper floor was used as the meeting place of the Grangers, while the lower floor was used for the school.

In 1893, S. S. Neely invited Dr. W. N. Anderson, pastor of the First Presbyterian Church at Jackson, to come out and preach Sunday afternoons in the school building at Madison Hall. Dr. Anderson came and soon a church was organized with the following ten members: S. S. Neely, Misses Molly Neely, Lessie Neely, Mr. and Mrs. J. C. Robinson, Bob Robinson, Mr. and Mrs. W. P. Howard, Mrs. Tom Greer, and Miss Mamie Greer. A beautiful wooded plot of ground just across the road from Madison Hall was given to the church by Jim Sweeny and Henry Robinson and a building was erected for the little congregation and dedicated June, 1895. With the exception of during the ministry of Dr. Albert Sidney Johnson, the minister who served the First Church at Jackson, served this community church, too.

One of the newest and the most important towns or communities in the county is BEMIS, the "town that Bemis built." At the close of the nineteenth century, the Bemis Brothers Bag Company decided to build some mills that could supply the bag factories with bag goods of uniform quality.[33] The officials specified three main points to be considered in selecting a location—A southern site close to the cotton fields for the raw materials, on a good railroad providing quick service to the bag factories at New Orleans, Omaha, St. Louis, Minneapolis, San Francisco, and Indianapolis and above all a site

---

[33]Jackson *Sun,* September 18, 1944. H. J. Coyne, "Bemis, Present, Past, and the Future."

that was close to an abundant supply of native Anglo-Saxon labor. Mr. Bemis was not asking for free land, to have buildings erected for them, or demanding the abatement of local taxes. The Illinois Central Railroad officials, with their usual alertness heard of the project and began trying to get the factory located upon their line. Finally West Tennessee was settled upon, for this section fulfilled the three conditions that the Bemis Brothers Bag Company had stipulated in the beginning, but the exact location at Jackson was not settled. A group of Jackson citizens, headed by Stokely Hays, informed the Madison County Court that a cotton mill could probably be secured for the county if the court would donate the necessary 300 acres of land which would cost $6,000. The committee which was appointed for that purpose, contacted Mr. Bemis and made the agreement with him that he would build a 20,000 spindle cotton mill with necessary village provided Madison County donated a 300 acre site three miles south of Jackson that was popularly known as the H. E. Jackson plantation.

When the County Court met on January 2, 1900, the committee introduced a resolution asking the county to appropriate $6,000 for the purchase of a site on which to build a cotton mill. When the vote was taken, twenty voted in the affirmative and 15 in the negative and the motion was declared lost, but at the afternoon session, the chairman stated that the motion had carried, that he had erred that morning in ruling the motion lost because he had thought that a three-fifth vote was necessary. The motion was again put to the court and this time nineteen voted in the affirmative and fifteen negative, so it was carried and the committee was empowered to spend the $6,000 to buy the site for the new mills. Thus, it can be seen how Jackson and Madison County nearly lost an enterprise that has been of inestimable value to the growth of the county.

Ground was broken in the spring of 1900, and buildings for the mill, dwellings, and public buildings and wide tree-lined streets began to take the place of scattered negro cabins, cattle ponds, gulleys and pig styes. To J. B. Young, the first resident manager, goes much of the credit for the success of this new project, for he possesses a thorough knowledge of the cotton business and knew how to develop the ideal relationship between employer and employee. He had the unusual faculty

HISTORIC MADISON

Later Pictures

LANCASTER PARK 1905

I. B. TIGRETT
Railroad Builder and President of Gulf, Mobile, and Ohio Railroad

DR. HERMON HAWKINS
Physician, Scholar, and gentleman of the old school

J. L. ROSENBLOOM
Prominent Merchant and Jewish Leader

R. L. BEARE
Industrialist, civic leader, and churchman

W. A. CALDWELL
Philanthropist and leading banker for half a century

C. B. IJAMS
Historian, church leader, member of the State Board of Education for twenty years, and Superintendent of the City Schools for thirty years

W. F. BARRY
State Senator and Secretary of the West Tennessee District Fair

JUDGE SIDNEY J. EVERETT
Lawyer and leading Democrat of the early Twentieth Century

TOM MURRAY, SR.
Lawyer and political leader

OLIVER BENTON
President of the National Bank of Commerce 1938-1945

BEMIS COTTON MILL
Located in Bemis, Tennessee, one of the South's model mill towns

J. B. YOUNG
Builder and First Manager of Bemis Mill,
Bemis, Tennessee

Bemis, Tennessee, a community of about 4,000 population, is one of the country's outstanding examples of employee-employer relationship. Fourteen hundred people are employed by the Bemis Mill which has a payroll of two million dollars annually.

SETTLERS OF '61

1, Geo. Glover. 3, Geo. Bledsoe. 4, Riley Teague. 5, Geo. Wolfe. 6, Jack Manley. 7, Robt. Cartmell. 8, Joe Fogg. 9, Patt Marks. 10, Ben Malone. 11, Robt. A. Hurt. 12, Robt. Chester. 13, Jim Murphy. 14, Finley Snider. 15, Alex Bledsoe. 16, Frank Malone. 17, Owen Snider. 18, Johnnie Williams. 19, Ben Flemming. 20, Col. Duke. 21, Sam Creevy. 22, Dr. Hermon Hawkins. 23, Gill Neal. 24, Pat Malone. 25, Tom Long. 26, Nat Jennings. 27, Crockett Scott. 28, F. A. Williams. 29, Jim Reavis. 30, Dr. Amos Jones. 31, Z. Haas. 32, Alex Person. 33, Martin Cartmell. 34, Geo. Fortune. 35, Sid Bond. 36, Milt Hurt. 37, Tom Fry. 38, Ed Curtis. 39, Billie Alexander. 41, Jim Coneer 43, C. G. Bond. 44, Jim Garrett 45, W. R. Theus 46, John S.

SPANISH-AMERICAN WAR VETERANS

1, George Fortune. 4, Thos. A. Hinton. 7, William Clark. 8, Henry Cummings. 11, Chas. H. Harris. 17, Amos J. Kendrick. 18, Theodore T. Kendrick. 20, Lon Hardee. 21, John A. Maxwell. 23, W. Gravitt. 24, Monroe Kellar. 28, King McCabe. 32, Henry W. McCorry. 34, L. V. Bledsoe. 36, Chas. B. Ray. 37, Frank Murtaugh. 38, Walter Cisco. 40, "Horsehead" Williams. 42, Claude O. Pigford. 43, Ed Goode. 48, Morris Williams. 49, Reece Crockett. 52, John Vandenbrook. 54, Dr. Robert Greek. 50, Walter Holt. 59, R. Lafey Wilson. 60, Morgan Sutton. 61, Walter Cox. 62, Joe Gaffney.

JACKSON BAR 1927

First Row: David P. Murray, W. T. Rogers, N. R. Barham, C. G. Bond, S. J. Everett, C. E. Pigford, W. G. Timberlake. *Second Row*: Tom Murray, R. R. Sneed, L. L. Fonville, Graper R. Russell, L. McCoy, Dewitt Henderson, K. K. Wilkes, Claire Newman. *Third Row*: Hugh Arnold, H. Mihalovits, Roger G. Murray, A. G. McGeehee, R. H. Spragins. *Fourth Row*: W. P. Moss, Homer H. Waldrop, Keith Short, Herron Pearson, Tom Rothrock, Frank L. Johnson, Thad Pope, C. H. Hewghley.

of making his employees realize that he was interested in each of them.

An editor of the Jackson *Daily Sun* of 1900 was far-sighted enough to call this new business a "monster enterprise" which would be invaluable to Jackson, for 300 to 500 hands would be employed which would add 900 to 1500 to Jackson's population and 900 to 1500 money makers and money spenders of the city. This "hive of industry," the Jackson Fibre Company, as it was then called, was to include a model town of four-story brick building of the factory, other factory buildings, sixty to seventy-five cottages for employees, and the residence for the superintendent.[34] This editor must have had a peep into the future, for the Bemis mill was a success from the very first, the size of the plant being doubled in 1905, thirty-nine new houses being added in 1920; the new office buildings and the auditorium and sixty-one new houses in 1926.

Madison County is proud that this model mill town is located within its bounds. From a financial standpoint, the county gets back its original expenditure and over each year. The first tax bill was $2,992, so that within three years the original investment was returned, but the benefits of the town south of Jackson cannot be counted in dollars and cents. It is one of the most important centers of business in the county. This town is one that has attracted national interest. The following excerpts from the *Northwestern Miller* show what is thought of this model town south of Jackson where 1400 people are employed by the Bemis mills which has a payroll of two million dollars a year:

> Bemis, Tennessee, a community of about 4,000 population, located about two miles south of Jackson, Tennessee, is one of the country's outstanding examples of employee-employer relationships. The community centers around the cotton mill of the Bemis Brothers Bag Company. There are 485 residences, all occupied by employees of the cotton mill and their families. The community spreads over 650 acres of rolling terrain and has a wealth of recreational facilities. . . . There are four schools for white and one for colored children. The entire community is company owned—streets, houses, utilities, churches, etc. . . . With such favorable working conditions there are, of course, a large number who have been employed at the mill for many years. Sons and even grandsons of the original employees now work at the

---

[34] Jackson *Daily Sun*, July 1, 1900.

mill. Over 500 persons have been employed over five years. . . . One hundred and seventy have been employed for twenty years. . . . As Mr. Young, the manager of the mill and community explains, the Bemis plan "makes for pleasant living for the company and its employees."[35]

---

[35] Jackson *Sun*, August 14, 1944, "The Town That Bemis Built," reprinted from the *Northwestern Miller*.

CHAPTER XXV

AN INDUSTRIAL CENTER OF WEST TENNESSEE

Although during the first half of the nineteenth century, Jackson was primarily an inland cotton depot, there were brave efforts on the part of many of the early citizens to make this a manufacturing center. Jackson probably had as much or more manufacturing during these early years as any other inland agrarian town of the same size. Many of the early settlers must have realized that the town had the possibilities of becoming an industrial center. The cabinet makers, such as Moses Priest, James Flaherty, G. Bledsoe, came here soon after the surveyors and first settlers came and opened shops where they offered to make cabinets upon order; the boot-makers, such as George Jenkins, J. S. York, who promised to mend "all rips gratis," started the Jackson Boot and Shoe Manufacturing Company in 1846; S. Burus, a home manufacturer in 1825, did wool carding; W. G. Flowers manufactured carding and spinning machines and John H. Hawkins manufactured house gutters in 1832; J. R. Chappell operated the Madison Foundry in 1846, making gin gearing, cast ploughs and points, wagon boxes, kettle irons, and andirons; Anderson and Christian manufactured tin-ware, sheet and copper materials; J. W. Campbell operated a new Brighton Flouring mill in 1852; J. J. Good, was a maker of coaches and waggons; Taylor and Fogg, made first rate cotton gins in 1849.[1] By 1830, there were eight

---

[1] Jackson *Gazette*, December 13, 1824; June 11, 1825; September 5, 1829; Jackson *Southern Statesman*, March 10, 17, 1832; *West Tennessee Whig*, June 5, 1846; February 12, 1848; January 27, 1843; November 23, 1849.

Two men with vision were Philander D. W. Conger and J. B. Conger who contracted to erect water wheels on the "Conger Plan" to run two saws which would be capable of cutting 500 feet of sound poplar in an hour. Contract between J. B., P. D. W. Conger and Abraham Deberry used through the courtesy of Robert Conger.

merchants, two grocery and dry goods stores, one tanner, one hatter, three tailors, two shoemakers, four carpenters, five doctors, ten lawyers, two taverns, and a postoffice to which a four horse mail stage arrived from Nashville.[2] Census reports of 1840 reveal the story of this early attempt to make Jackson a manufacturing center by reporting one cast iron furnace producing five tons and employing three persons with a capital of $2,500; a carriage and wagon factory, employing twelve persons, which made products which amounted to $4,610; twenty-one grist mills, thirteen saw mills, fourteen flouring mills; ten distillerers employing fourteen people who manufactured 10,920 gallons; one tobacco manufactory, employing twelve persons, which produced $5,700 worth of goods; one hat and cap manufactory employing seven persons which produced $690; seven tanneries employing twelve persons which tanned 1960 sides of sole leather and a like amount of upper leather; two cotton manufacturing plants with 1200 spindles employing fifty-one persons with $100,000 invested.[3]

During the decade before the Sectional Conflict of 1861-1865 R. H. Anderson advertised a "new thing" called a "cooking stove," Robert Brown advertised a brick making machine; Jester Umphlett and Company were prepared to make anything from a Clearance coach to a wheelbarrow.[4] The cessation of hostilities in 1865 was the signal for new enterprise. A *West Tennessee Whig* of March 1866 reported that, after four long years of destruction, it was a pleasure to see rebuilding, the doubling of the number of business firms, men in town every day looking for openings. One visitor was astonished that various manufacturing enterprises had not already started up in Jackson. This 1866 editor concluded:

> Our location on the greatest railroad in the U. S., in the midst of a fertile, healthy country induces us to believe that there is nothing in the nature of things to hinder this place from becoming one of the

---

[2] One hundred and four lots had been sold on August 1 and 2, 1822, for $19,202. This same account mentioned the fact that there were forty-seven families living within the corporation. Jackson *Gazette*, January 9, 1830.

[3] Only $100,000 was invested in all West Tennessee in 1840. *Sixth Census of United States*.

[4] *West Tennessee Whig*, March 26, 1858; January 18, 1850; June 23, 1853.

most eligible points known in the South for an inland city. A better location for cotton and woolen factories could not be selected, because we have the cotton in our midst and for sheep raising a better section is hard to find. . . . If men of capital and means will come among us and those already here, who are able and embark in various manufacturing enterprises, they will find it to pay well.[5]

The year 1866 witnessed many new ventures in the business world. The Shannon Novelty Works was chartered by P. W. Conger, Nathan Whitlow, W. D. Robinson, John Conger, John Irvin, with a capital stock of $300,000 for the purpose of manufacturing agricultural implements, wagons, plows, sash, window blinds; Jackson Cotton Mills was chartered by R. B. Hurt, A. R. Reid, John Alston, A. S. Rogers, John Miller, L. B. Haughton, to manufacture cotton, wool, hemp, silk, or grind grain to make flour; the West Tennessee Paper Mill was chartered by W. W. Gates, Nathan Whitlow, Frances Theus, W. E. Butler, Jr., Stephens, David Meriwether; the Jackson Shoe and Leather Company was chartered by Addison Pyles, James O'Connor, Alexander W. Campbell, Robert Hall, Charles Hogsett; the Madison Furniture was also chartered in the same year.[6] The following year Landis and Burnell established a first class buggy and carriage factory; in 1871, Weis and Lesh opened a plant which made oak and hickory spokes; in 1873 S. R. Conger opened a planing mill;. while in 1880, Sneed Brothers started a sash and blind company.

During the years of the 1870's and 1880's, real estate agents spoke of themselves as "emigration agencies," and frequent references can be found in the papers about the men from the North who were "prospecting about town." Most of the talk about manufacturing plants concerned cotton mills, oil mills, and those enterprises centering around the lumbering industries.

Before the Sectional Conflict, Jackson had been one of the typical Southern cities, noted for its wealth and social status during a time when the Southland was "full of ease and elegance, of born statesmen and unpurchasable voters; of passion, poker and pistols; of horse racing, fox hunting, and cockfighting; of generous living, stately quarrels and dueling; of

---

[5]Jackson *West Tennessee Whig,* June 2, 1866.
[6]*Acts of Tennessee,* 1866.

eloquent preaching and camp meetings and of much practical Christianity.... A time indeed when a word and a blow, the land and the purse, the lips and the heart went together."[7] Years of war had left their mark upon the community, but for the first eight years after the conflict, until the summer of 1872, the prosperity of Jackson was unparalleled in the history of Southern cities. During this period over one thousand houses were erected in Jackson; there was work for everyone; business was lively. Then a short crop and a money panic came; hard times followed. Then the editors and far-sighted business men launched a crusade to bring more railroads and attract new enterprise to Jackson. One editor challenged the citizens thus:

> Cities are never built by brokers and shavers but by men of nerve and enterprise who see beyond the present time the prospective dollar and whose investments are not confined solely to individual profit, but sees in the general prosperity the highest and most commendable degree of personal agrandizement.[8]

A catastrophe occurred in the business of the county about 1875 from which the manufacturing interest could scarcely recover—the failure of the Shannon Novelty Works. One hundred thousand dollars of the stockholders' money had been invested in grounds, buildings, machinery and a very small surplus had been left upon which to operate. The stockholders, older citizens who had saved something from the wreck of the war and from the high prices obtained for cotton in 1866 to 1868, but who had no practical knowledge of manufacturing enterprise, expected dividends at once and when they did not collect them, they began kicking and grumbling and tightening up the purse strings. Soon the business collapsed, the machinery was sold, while the buildings stood for years a silent monument of the disastrous end of Jackson's first great effort at manufacturing. For years when efforts to establish factories of any kind in Jackson by stock subscriptions were made, the older people with burnt fingers and others profiting as they flattered themselves by the experience of their neighbors, would point to the wide and towering expanse of silent brick, with the faded inscription thereon "Shannon Novelty Works," shake their heads, look wise, clinch their pocketbooks tighter, and

---

[7] Jackson *Forked Deer Blade*, January 7, 1888.
[8] Jackson *Sun*, July 7, 1875.

say "no." The failure of this enterprise paralized manufacturing in Jackson for years and struck a blow at cooperative enterprise from which the city only began to recover in the 1890's.[9]

The 1880's and 1890's saw the leaders of the South frantically start upon a campaign to attract emigrants and Northern capital. Real estate agencies called themselves, "emigration agencies" and offered large plantations for sale which were suitable for "colonization schemes" and "manufacturing sites." Great rivalry was present among the towns. Excursions on the Illinois Central brought visitors from the North to West Tennessee to look over the advantages that could be found here. Representatives were placed on the trains with advertising matter about Jackson. A paper of 1884 told of not ONE but TWO woolen mills that were located in Jackson; a hub and spoke factory; S. R. Conger's planing mill, which furnished dressed lumber at bottom prices; an ice manufacturing company; W. H. Burnell and Co., which made buggies and wagons, and road carts; the Jackson Foundry and Machine Shop; and a sugar and sorghum mill that was to come soon.[10] The following item from a Union City paper shows how jealous that city was of Jackson's securing the woolen mills:

> Jackson has gone wild over a woolen mill, Jackson has just discovered that fact that if she didn't go wild over something Union City would trip along ahead of her as the leading city of West Tennessee. Notwithstanding the much lionized woolen mill, Jackson is taking mighty slow steps besides our little "City of Whistles"—factory whistles—whistles which tell of hundreds of busy hands—whistles which tell of prosperous and happy families—whistles which are loved by all for the joyful tidings they ring forth.[11]

The business men of Jackson were sure that a real boom was on, that progress and prosperity had struck West Tennessee and the South.

As the crusade advanced to bring new enterprise to West Tennessee the Jackson Building and Loan Association was organized (1887) to help furnish capital to attract manufac-

---

[9]Jackson *Forked Deer Blade*, January 7, 1888. Miss Guy Leeper Collection.
[10]Jackson *Tribune and Sun*, January 25, 1884. Used through the courtesy of Mrs. Grace Kinzie.
[11]*Ibid*.

turing with W. P. Robertson, president, M. D. Meriwether, secretary, and E. S. Mallory, attorney. In 1887, the Jackson Manufacturing and Improvement Company was organized at the office of Caruthers and Mallory with L. J. Brooks, J. W. N. Burkett, Robert Gates, E. S. Mallory, Charlie Herron, W. F. Alexander, and W. P. Robertson composing the committee to sell stock. A month later the directors W. P. Robertson, W. A. Taylor, Thomas Tate, M. V. B. Exum, N. S. White, J. Friedlob reported that three hundred shares of stock had been sold. These men realized that when a town the size of Jackson sat down to contemplate itself, the result would be disaster. In fact Jackson "should have many enterprises that it did not have —a furniture factory, hub, spoke and wagon factory, broom factory, paper mills, soap factory, canning establishment, an agricultural implement manufactory, and a tannery."[12] In his state report of this same year A. J. McWherter listed Jackson as one of the centers around which the greatest industrial development of Tennessee will crystalize in the near future and added:

Jackson is favorably located for diversified industrial pursuits. Populated with intelligent, enterprising people, surrounded by a fertile and fruitful section, supplied with the purest water to be found and a genial climate with raw materials of every kind at her threshold, nothing but a deficiency of cheap transportation can possibly retard her rapid growth and prevent her from becoming one of the greatest manufacturing cities of Tennessee.[13]

Statistics show that all this energy expended by the newspapers and business men bore fruit, for capital was attracted to this section, such as the Jackson Oil Mill established in 1878 by J. W. Allison with P. J. Murray as manager. This mill had a capital stock of $35,000, produced 6,000 barrels of oil and 4,000 tons of meal in one season. There was the Jackson Woolen Mills, established in 1884, operating 66 looms, employing 105 persons and turning out 8,000 yards of jeans per week besides yarn and blankets in 1888.[14] The 1880's and 1890's

---

[12]Jackson *Forked Deer Blade*, October 22, 1887; January 7, 1888.
[13]*Biennial Report of the Commissioner of Agriculture, Statistics and Mines of the State of Tennessee* (Nashville, 1887), 11-12.
[14]These mills were reorganized in 1895 with $60,000 paid up stock. W. P. Robertson was president, while B. P. Cantrell was secretary and manager. The original location was on the lot where the

witnessed the establishment of the Sherman Manufacturing Company which made boilers, gins, and engines; the C. F. Wiley Bakery and candy company which shipped both north and south; E. Felsenthal grocery business; Jackson Bottling Works under Charlie Hanebuth who shipped products throughout Tennessee, Alabama, and Arkansas; Captain Umphlett's carriage and buggy factory. These same years saw the steady growth of the dry goods, millinery, and shoe store of William Holland, Sr., whose business had begun in 1871, for the store carried a splendid line of merchandise and was operated by a modest, conservative, Christian gentleman; of the A. K. Jobe jewelry store who enjoyed an extensive business.[15]

After that Sectional Conflict of 1861-1865 as Jackson was lifting her head, weak but hopeful to begin the struggle for progress and a new life, men with vision saw this town as a future cotton market, second only to Memphis. It was surrounded by cotton fields and blessed with railroad facilities; it could control much of the wagon trade of this section; oil mills which consumed the seeds and numerous gins attracted business. J. M. Parker and Company built the first cotton shed in 1870. By 1887, there were sheds owned by Haley, McCutcheon, Deupree, Gates and Wheeler with a capacity of 25,000 bales. Firms such as J. M. Parker and Company, J. T. McCutcheon, John L. Lancaster, J. M. Woolard, Dunaway, Anderson and Company made connections with east and south and shipped directly to spinners and exporters. Often from three to eight thousand bales of cotton could be seen on the streets at one time and from ten to fifty thousand dollars per day was paid out for cotton. Such were the beginnings of Jackson as a real cotton market—a phase of business that is one of the life lines in the community to-day.[16]

Madison County's timber was only used locally until after the Civil War, but an important part of this business awakening of the 1880's and 1890's was centered around the development of the timber resources.[17] In the advertising literature of this

---

Southern Bell Telephone garage is now located. Later the mills were located in the present McCowat-Mercer Press Building. *Board of Trade Souvenir,* 1897.
   [15]Jackson *Forked Deer Blade,* January 7, 1888.
   [16]*Ibid.;* Jackson *Daily Whig,* December 20, 1904.
   [17]The writer is indebted to Bruce Briney for the use of his paper,

period, there was much emphasis placed upon the wonderful opportunity for the Northern Capitalist to develop this business. An editor of 1888 wrote:

We desire to present Jackson as a point for manufacturing. It is surrounded by forests of hardwood, embracing every merchantable variety and with the Midland road will have the close connection with the finest timbered region in the country. It has two and will have three roads into the most extensive pine forests on the continent. . . . Enterprises especially invited include: hub, spoke, handle factory, a wagon factory, a cotton mill, a furniture factory, a tannery, a broom factory, a door, sash, blind factory, boot and shoe factory, a canning factory.[18]

Some capital was attracted in the last two decades of the nineteenth century, but most of it came after the turn of the century. It was then that the value of this business began to be realized. The *Southern Lumberman* of 1890 broadcast a challenge to its readers concerning this golden opportunity as follows:

Never again will the opportunity be offered for the safe investment of surplus capital that the South affords in her immense bodies of timberland. Millions of acres are hidden away in our valleys and along the banks of our numberless streams and may be bought for a mere pittance of their real worth. In our own good State of Tennessee there are vast forests of oak, ash, hickory, etc., that have never been echoed to the sound of an axe. These lands if located in Pennsylvania or Ohio would readily sell for $75 per acre but here we regard them as almost valueless. But such will not always be the case. These great forests of hardwoods that lift their virgin branches toward the skies and repose in the deep solitude of their native valleys will soon resound to the lusty stroke of the woodman's axe and the music of the saw.[19]

Capital was attracted and many men from the North came to exploit the timbers of West Tennessee. Besides those already mentioned, there was E. L. Birmingham who started a wagon shop here in 1874, making about fifty wagons a year; there was Jacob Weis who erected a spoke factory here in 1889 on a site at Madison and Middle Avenue that the city had donated to them (this became the Skewer Factory under R. P.

"History of the Lumber Industry in Madison County," which was read before the Madison County Historical Society August, 1945.

[18] Jackson *Forked Deer Blade*, January 7, 1888.
[19] *Southern Lumberman*, January 1, 1890.

Morgan and then Morgan-Hitchcock under W. G. Morgan); the Jackson Cooperage Company, established in 1895, made buck staves (this plant was sold to Harlan-Morriss Company in 1900); in 1904, the Coleman Heading Company under W. H. and A. R. Coleman and L. L. Curtis started operation in Jackson, developing within a few years a business which shipped to various points of the United States and to Europe; the Frankland Carriage Company, establised in 1900, made the finest pleasure and business vehicles around Jackson and by 1904 was considered a most conservative and well-managed plant. Ralphe Budde and T. E. Lindsay organized in 1905 a business which is to-day known as Budde and Weis, where office furniture is manufactured and shipped throughout a wide area. In 1909, Young and Kutsinger established a sawmill in Jackson, manufacturing hardwood exclusively, which firm became known in 1915 as Bedna Young Lumber Company and is operated by Harry Schaffer. The year 1910 saw the beginnings of a saw mill and veneer mill which became known as Ashby Veneer Lumber Company, which operates three veneer lathes cutting precision veneer and manufacturing vegetable hampers. In 1918 the Wood Mosaic Company of Louisville, Kentucky,

TABLE No. 6—MANUFACTURING

	Number of Establishments	Capital	Number Employed	Value of Products Annual
1840	51	$ 108,295	139	....
1850	....	....	39	$ 41,727
1860	39	124,900	135	252,650
1870	46	94,840	209	209,984
1880	19	390,818	133	150,450
1890	66	1,133,314	785	1,100,828
1900	139	1,279,914	1335	2,093,845
1910	....	....	....	....
1920	76	....	2599	12,167,523
1930	46	....	2881	12,255,603
1940	50	....	2105	8,017,560

purchased a band saw mill which T. J. Spragins had built the year before and began operating a hardwood business that has increased greatly through the years. In 1895, the Southern Seating and Cabinet Company was established making a high grade furniture for office, public buildings, often shipping a carload of furniture a day. It was sold to Clarence Saunders in 1917, to Piggly-Wiggly later in the same year, to Kroger in 1929. In the 1920's witnessed other mills such as that of E. S. Miller, the Jackson Saw Mill under the management of E. S. Talbot and W. C. Hanafee, the Hutchinson Lumber Company, and the Morgan Lumber Company.

Some twenty-two wood working plants have been established here which have played a major role in the development of this county and city, helping to establish Jackson as a manufacturing and shipping center.

At one time Jackson boasted the largest engine and boiler factory in the south. About 1874 two mechanics by the name of Sherman and Cole started a small shop on the corner of Lexington Avenue and M. & O. Railroad. They soon began to build a line of small steam engines and boilers. In the early eighties they moved across the tracks and continued to prosper then sold their shops to local capital and they in turn voted Exile Burkett as Manager. They continued to prosper and expand and added the manufacture of saw mills to their line. Their first mechanical engineer, W. H. Collier, designed their first large Corliss Steam Engines which were built in units of 100 to 300 horsepower. About this time a large new plant was completed that covered three acres and worked over 400 mechanics. In 1917 the plant was sold to Cleveland, Ohio capitalist and produced shell lathes and equipment for World War I. In 1922 is was purchased outright by W. H. Collier who operated it until 1926, when it went out of business completely due to the popularity of the present oil engines and TVA electric power. The Southern Engine and Boiler Works was the biggest business in Jackson at the turn of the century. Besides saw mills, engines, boilers and well supplies, the company made a "Marathon" automobile, but this last mentioned machine was not successful.

This crusade of the 1880's and 1890's bore fruit, for the value of the manufactured products in the country rose from $150,450 in 1880 to $1,100,828 in 1890 and $2,093,845 in 1900.

AN INDUSTRIAL CENTER

But with the turn of the century, there was much new enterprise, such as the Bemis Mills,[20] various oil mills, Beare Brothers Ice and Coal Company, compresses, railroad shops, and flour mills, and the number employed has jumped from 1335 producing $2,093,845 in 1900 to 2105 employed producing $8,017,560 in 1940, placing Jackson as one of the five industrial centers in Tennessee.

---

[20] The story of Bemis, the Model Mill Town, may be found in the chapter "Towns and Communities."

CHAPTER XXVI

THE RISE OF THE CITY

During the past century Jackson has undergone innumerable changes. The town has grown into a city, literally and legally; a board of commissioners, appointing their own successors, has been replaced by a mayor and commissioners elected by the people; springs and private wells have been replaced by an excellent water system; muddy and dusty streets and plank sidewalks have disappeared as excellent paved highways and concrete walkways appeared; mule cars that were pulled along the tracks on the side of the streets were pushed aside for electric street cars and modern buses; oil and gas lights gave way to electricity furnished by private companies and then by the Tennessee Valley authority; muddy impassable roads were replaced by ribbons of concrete of to-day; the volunteer bucket brigade gave way to the modern fire department; a population of 993 in 1850 increased to 24,332 in 1940. Numerous changes could be enumerated as time marched on in the community. Some of the men who brought these changes about must be mentioned in passing.

During the days of its youth the "City of Jackson" was known then as the "town of Jackson" and the government was in the hands of "the best" who were naturally the few. Those were not democratic principles that were instituted when the town of Jackson was incorporated on August 17, 1822, by an act of the Legislature. S. D. Hays, W. E. Butler, Herndon Haralson, William Stoddert, Daniel Harton, William Arnold, and Adam H. Huntsman were named commissioners, having been appointed to the same position in Madison County by an Act of the Legislature of November 16, 1821. This commission was a self-perpetuating body, for it had the power to remove any of its members for breach of duty and to fill vacancies. These eight men had both administrative and legislative powers, making all necessary laws for the town.

Thus, until 1837, the people of Madison and Jackson had no voice in the government. In that year the charter was amended so that the people of the town elected seven aldermen (for one year) who elected a mayor for four years. In 1841 provisions were added for the town constable to be elected by popular vote.

In 1845, another amendment was added which called for the annual election of the mayor, six aldermen, town constable, and the recorder by the people. In 1865, this was changed slightly by the election of the recorder and other subordinate officers by the mayor and aldermen.

A few items from the pages of the early minute books in the city hall are interesting, for they reflect the problems of the city fathers of those days, such as the mayor's salary

JACKSON WATER WORKS.

Jackson *Forked Deer Blade*, January 9, 1888. Courtesy of Miss Guy Leeper.

for 1854-1855 of $88.34; as the recorder's salary for the year being $200; such as the weeds and grass in the Riverside Cemetery that had grown so high that a lady could not walk through; such as the two policemen who were employed at $30 per month in 1859; as the Stephen A. Douglas Club that met in the Temperance Hall in 1860; as the slave "marts" that were operated by Gardner and Barham, Hargrove, and Witherspoon, at which place the city charged the merchants $5 per head for exhibiting or selling each slave; as the slaves who were hired by the city to work on the streets for from $75 to $174 per year but the city agreed to furnish board and four suits of clothes a year.[1]

Other changes came with the years, such as the act of the Legislature of 1867 which legally changed the name of "the town of Jackson" to the "City of Jackson"; of the abolition of the old charter in 1907 and the adoption of the new one which abolished the sale of liquor. Then in 1915, the people became convinced that Jackson had outgrown the "mayor and aldermen" government which held business meetings once a month, that they needed to place the affairs of the city into the hands of competent people who would devote their whole time to its administration, so an amendment to the charter was drafted to this effect, the people showed their approval at the ballot box, and the Legislature passed the act on March 30, 1915, instituting the new form of government. From then on the commission form of government was responsible for Jackson's failures and successes. These city fathers through the years have done everything they could to increase Jackson's prestige as a wide-awake, progressive city of schools, churches, and successful business enterprises.[2]

Over and above the legal aspect of the development of the city were problems close to the people such as new industry, good roads, streets, and conveniences such as gas and electric light, sidewalks, mule cars, and sewerage. These were the visible marks of a city. A few items gleaned from the city records and old newspapers tell of the Gas Company which was organized in 1872, building wooden pipes which were replace in a number of years by iron ones; of an explosion at

---

[1] Minutes of the City of Jackson.
[2] A list of the mayors and commissioners may be found in the Appendix.

the gas house in 1873 which left the people in "Egyptian darkness"; of F. Spah, the lamplighter in 1872; of the darkness on the streets when the gas was ordered cut off by the city officials in 1875; of the rains which turned the streets into huge mud puddles and washed away the bridge on Orleans near Mrs. Hughes' resident, on North Market and on Chester Street.³ The sidewalk situation seemed to have been quite serious if the following quotation is typical:

> The side walk on Royal, leading south from the corner of Chester Street is in a very dilapidated condition. The hogs have rooted off several of the planks and those that remain are warped by the rays of the sun. Each end raised several inches above the ground, presenting a formidable array of splinters and nails to the feet of the wayfaring man. When you step on the farther end of the plank, there is great danger of the hinder end flying up and striking you in the back of the head. When two persons are on the plank at the same moment being at both extremities, the least proportional of the two is in great danger of taking an aerial excursion through the air. A man can't be a Christian and travel that road often. At night it is almost impossible to walk along the side walk and without the utmost caution an accident will happen every few feet. It is much safer and by far the most pleasant to take the middle of the street, although the dust be ever so deep. The alderman representing the second ward should attend to these matters.⁴

Some of the older citizens of to-day can remember when the mud was so deep on Main Street that wagons drawn by two mules mired up. Well-paved streets are indeed a necessity for a progressive city.

The exciting event in the 1880's was the new water system. In 1883, the citizens of Jackson had voted to issue bonds for the purpose of building the water-works and by 1885 the papers were filled with the exciting news that the engines were installed and water would soon be available, but "sewerage or no sewerage was the question" of the day. Newspaper editors pled that the "public's nose would be greatly relieved, that every other interest of the city should wait a while, for they will keep, but in the name of living, let us have sewerage."⁵

---

³The Jackson *Sun*, May 14, June 4, 1875.
⁴Jackson *Dispatch*, 1873. Clipping in a scrap book belonging to Ernest Edenton.
⁵Jackson *West Tennessee Whig*, April 15, 1885.

When the system was completed, the people were simply bursting with excitement and pride. Citizens of to-day tell stories of how the porters from the stores in the business district used to have water battles on the streets of town each morning. A stream of water through a hose was quite a bit of fun to play with. Chemists from Chicago reported that the water of Jackson was "remarkably pure," while the editor of the *Blade* almost became poetic when he wrote of the abundance of this "crystal liquid:"

There is no excuse for a man drinking any injurious beverages when Jackson is so well supplied with water. No city in America has better or a more bountiful supply of this crystal liquid. If we have any one thing more than another to be proud of, it is our Waterworks. The best and purest water is pumped direct from deep wells into the pipes and forced all over the city, while we have a lake, Lake Alexander, holding millions of gallons in reserve in case of fire. Our machinery is first class, as are also the engineers, Mr. Soper, and his assistant, Mr. Smalley, in charge. In the center of the lake is a splendid fountain built by Mr. Soper, which throws a spray of water twenty feet above the surface of the lake. The embankment around the lake is being sodded with Bermuda grass, and when the grounds are made into a park, Jackson will have a place to be looked upon with pride—an everlasting monument to the enterprise and public spirit of Aldermen Alexander, Dr. M. S. Neely, Messrs. J. H. Duke, and P. C. McCowat. The commissioners will spare no pains in keeping ours the finest system of waterworks in the South.[6]

By 1888, twenty-seven wells were furnishing the water that was carried by two powerful pumps throughout the city, giving Jackson a water system that any small city would be proud of.[7] The name of Sam Lancaster, Jackson's engineer in the last of the nineteenth century and the early twentieth century, is linked with each new piece of machinery that was bought and each progressive step during these days.

---

[6]Jackson *Forked Deer Blade*, July 18, 1885. Mary Eliza Scott Collection.

[7]W. F. Alexander was given the chief credit for the waterworks, for as chairman of the committee he had "worked with an intelligence, a zeal, and courage that knew no abatement until success was achieved, and in so doing he built himself a monument that will outlast the polished marble which affection rears in memory of the dead." *Forked Deer Blade*, January 7, 1888.

One of the most exciting events in the early years of the twentieth century was the digging of the electro-chalybeate well. The citizens were confident that the presence of these mineral waters in Jackson would not only cause great improvement in the health of the citizens of the county, but that the fame of the well would become known throughout the United States and Jackson had the prospects of becoming one of the "most popular watering places in the South." Great plans were under way in 1904 for the development of this place as a health resort:

> The well and grounds surrounding it will be made into an attractive resort next spring. Approximately $4,000 was raised by the recent street fair, to be used in beautifying the grounds, which will be converted into a park. The land will be graded, and sodded, walks laid out and flower beds and shrubs will greatly add to its beauty and attractiveness. In connection with the water works there are fifty-four acres of ground, known as Lancaster Park, and in their improvement the railroads will be asked to cooperate. Bath rooms with hot and cold water will be built and a plan for constructing a natatorium or a large swimming pool, covering from one to two acres is under advisement. It is expected that 5000 people from other cities and states will visit the well, next season, as the well and grounds will then be in excellent shape for visitors.[8]

The excitement was not nation wide, but there was plenty of local enthusiasm, for the citizens of the community went by street car, by buggies, on foot to "the well" and if Jackson had had a song of that day it would not have been "Meet me in St. Louis," but "Meet me at the Well."

Early newspapers carried stories of disastrous fires and early city fathers passed laws to try to prevent destruction by fire. In the first code of laws of Jackson in 1823, a person was subject to fine, if he tied matches or other combustables to dogs' or cats' tails and let them run through the streets. Other laws through the years concerned the removal of wooden awnings, and large amounts of hay in barns within the fire limits of the town. The news of the fire was proclaimed by the ringing of the courthouse bell and later by the sounding of the whistles of the engines on the local railroads. As the crowd assembled, a bucket brigade was organized with some few young heroes mounting the comb of the roof and staying there until the fire

---

[8]Jackson *Daily Whig*, December 20, 1904.

was either extinguished or they were driven down by the hissing flames. These volunteer firemen often displayed such courage that their conduct deserved to be emblazoned in song and story, for during these days Jackson was powerless before an invasion of flames. The people *en masse* who answered the calls as quickly as if they had winged feet often managed to extinguish the blaze.[9]

A repetition of the sad story of "destroyed by fire" began to arouse the citizens in 1877, so much so that the aldermen considered purchasing a chemical engine to pump the water from the cisterns on the up-town streets and in the court yard. The following taunting item appeared in the local paper under the title "Bolivar's Wisdom:"

> Our neighboring city of Bolivar has purchased a chemical engine. Bolivar is a live town and has a live municipal government. We are too smart, and too sharp here to learn ever in the school where fools are educated and we go on year after year burning down our city and depending on insurance companies to rebuild it. As a consequence every business man in Jackson is drained to double the amount an outfit for fire protection would cost each year. Taxpayers mean to have protection.[10]

In 1885, when the water works was completed, the city purchased five hand drawn reels and placed them at various points throughout the city. E. B. Curtis was the first chief of the volunteer fire company. In 1888, F. F. Reavis, chief of the fire department, reported very small damages during the previous eight months due to the vigilance of the volunteer company, but he plead with the public not to leave chairs on the side walks, for often the streets were muddy and these obstructions on the sidewalks were dangerous when the men had "to run to a fire." Reavis's report of 1888 continued:

> There should be a fire company in each ward to run the fire for you can't expect the East Jackson Company and the Central Hose Company to run from their station to the limits of the city and be fit for service when they arrive. . . . If you expect to have a Fire Department and one that will serve without compensation, you must encourage them. . . . You have no idea what a laughing stock your com-

---

[9] Jackson *Sun*, November 19, 1875; February 9, 1877.
[10] Jackson *Sun*, May 11, 1877.

panies are. They receive in return for their services ruined clothing, the ridicule of many of your best citizens.[11]

The first horse-drawn fire apparatus was purchased about 1890, and the department organized. Joe Weatherly, chief, and his company of Joe Robinson, Charles Blackmon, Ed Price, Joe Burnell, Oscar Willy, and Thomas Murrell were ready to answer the alarms. As the years passed modern equipment was purchased and the harness can no longer be seen suspended in mid air at the fire station waiting for the beautiful horses that went dashing through the streets pulling the fascinating engines when the call of fire came. It is a good old American custom to go to the fire, whether on foot to help in the bucket brigades, as in the early days, following the beautiful horses as they charged down the streets, or in the wake of the most modern equipment of to-day.

On January 24, 1884, scarcely eight years after Alexander Graham Bell invented the telephone, a charter was granted to the Jackson Telephone Company, composed of H. W. McCorry, C. G. Bond, C. F. McHaney, L. S. Wood, and W. T. Logan. A one position switch board serving only fifty customers was installed in the second story of a building on Lafayette Street west of the present location of J. C. Penny's. On April 21, 1902, a body of Jackson men; namely, Joe L. Dunn, James L. Loyd, R. F. Spragins, W. D. Nelson, J. H. Hopper, applied for a charter which was granted to Jackson Home Telephone Company. Later this company was sold to Payne-Pettibone Estate and in 1929 merged with the Southern Bell Telephone Company. In 1905 the Southern Bell Company moved into a new building on College Street where the switch board is still located.[12]

The *Forked Deer Blade* of January 7, 1888, told of the first line of street cars that ran down Main Street to Royal and then

---

[11]Minutes of the City of Jackson.

[12]Early managers, linesmen, and operators included F. E. Judson, Misses Carrie Minton, Missie Griffis, May Ransom, Caroline Rogers, Ada Lyle and Clyde McClanahan. The present office building on the corner of College and Cumberland Streets was ready for occupation June, 1943. The present (1945) exchange serves 7004 customers, while this district under J. M. Phillips, L. T. Hume, and F. K. Fisher comprises a territory of thirty-seven exchanges. The writer is indebted to Miss Noel Wright for gathering this material.

MARKET STREET, JACKSON, TENN.

Realization of Prof Clark's Prophecy respecting Jackson, in a lecture at the court house at Jackson, 1880 "I will live to see Jackson with paved streets, sewerage, water works, street railways, electric lights, and double her population."

In less than ten years from now Jackson will double her population, the water power of the Tennessee River will run all the machinery, light and warm the city. Three cheers for Jackson! Merry Christmas to you all! May your shadows never grow less Call at once for examination and lessons Only one week more in the city.

PSYCHOMETRIC COLLEGE,
MRS. DR. CLARK, President.
Branch Office FARMERS' HOTEL
JACKSON, TENN.
CORNER MARKET AND LaFAYETTE ST.
FRONT ROOM NO. 17.

A famous prophecy for Jackson made in 1880. The picture shows King's Opera House, which was upstairs over Robertson & Botts Dry Goods Store, then located on the west side of Market Street, between Baltimore and Main Streets. Note the mule car on Main Street. The picture reflects a scene in the 1890's.

THE RISE OF THE CITY 375

to Union Depot and down Shannon to Sycamore and west on Sycamore to the lower Illinois Central depot. During those "mule car days" a Jackson street scene was quite a contrast from one of to-day. There was the old stables and car barn located where Five Points Lumber Company now is; there were tracks on the side of the streets where twenty passenger cars and "summer cars that were beauties" were pulled by two mules or horses, except at one point—on Highland hill—and here it required four horses to make the hill.[13] The first cars ran soon after Christmas 1888. John L. Wisdom, J. H. Duke, and J. H. Hirsch had organized the Jackson and Suburban Street Railway Company in 1887. In the same year the company built an electric plant and furnished two hundred subscribers with power from six until ten o'clock in the evening at 15c per killowatt hour.

In 1897, the horse-drawn cars were electrified much to the distress of some "old-timers" who claimed that the power passing through the trolley line in front of their houses caused the "milk to sour" and the gardens to wither; much to the delight of the small boys of the town who ran alongside of the "wonder cars" for several trips to town during those first few days; much to the displeasure of the horses on the streets who were frightened by the white canvas screens that protected the motormen on wet days. The Jackson Suburban Street and Railway, which was locally owned, was purchased by S. S. Bush and others of Louisville in 1906 and the Jackson Railway and Light Company was organized. The electric cars that had been housed in a barn on the southwest corner of Shannon and College streets were now moved to a building on South Royal Street southwest of the water works. Under John Wisdom, the manager, the company continued to operate at a profit and gave fine service through the years.[14]

---

[13]J. B. Fulghum drove the first mule cars over the streets here. A special team was kept on Highland to be hitched to the regular team for the hill. Jackson *Sun*, May 20, 1923. The second mule car line ran out Highland to Crescent Avenue to Highland Park and the third ran on South Royal to Tennessee Midland Station (now the N. C. & St. L. station). Another line ran on Lexington to Stoddart, up Stoddert to Deaderck, then to Hays and north on Hays to Walsh Street to a big tree that was in the middle of the road and here the car turned around and started upon the return trip.

[14]In 1924 the company was purchased by the National Power

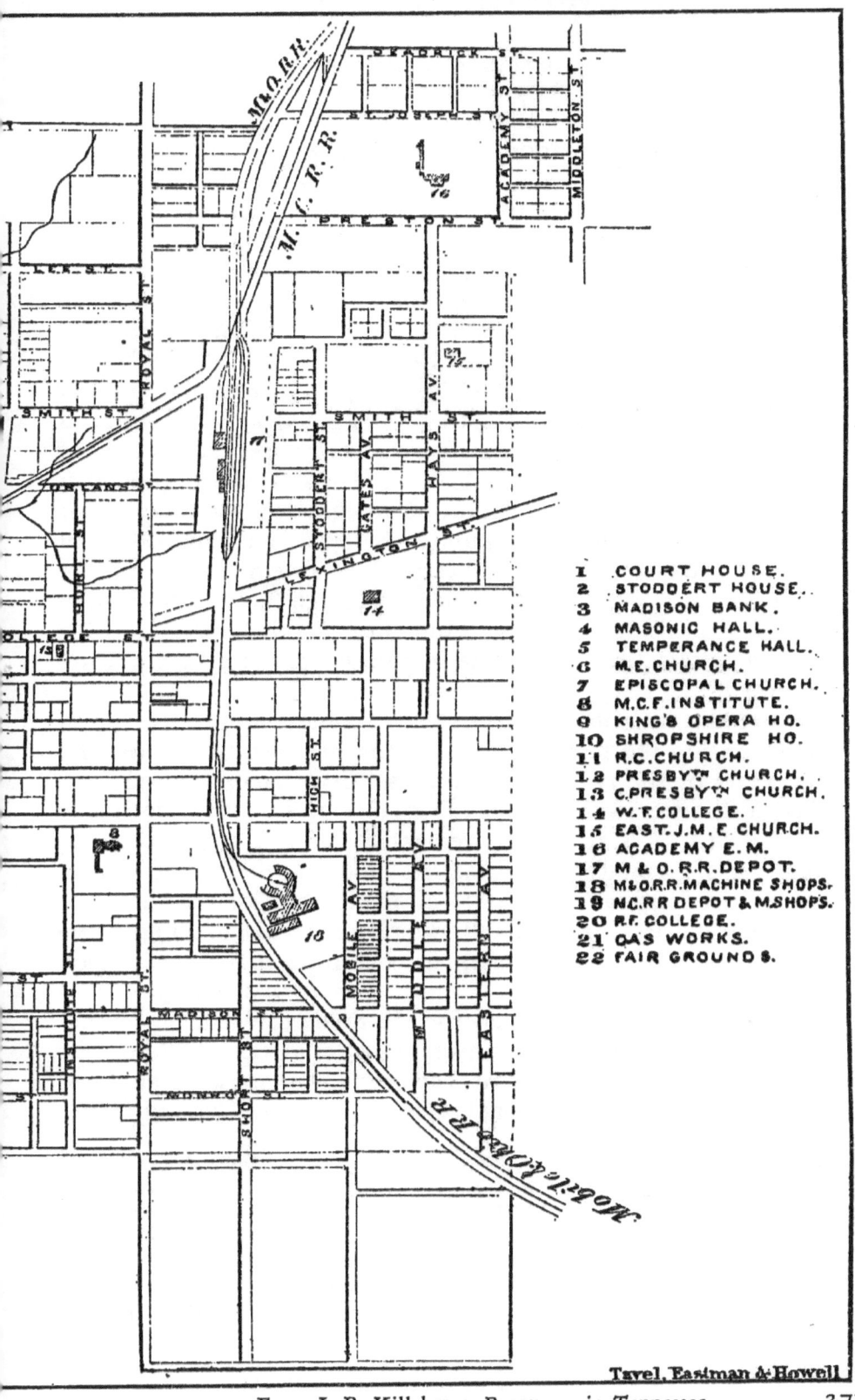

From J. B. Killebrew, *Resources in Tennessee.*

That prophecy of 1880 partially came true; "that Jackson will double in population, the water power of the Tennessee River will run all the machinery, light and warm the city." The prophet said that this would happen in ten years. It did happen, but it took a half century for it to come to pass.

It was during the era of prosperity at the turn of the century that earlier dreams of some of the citizens were realized. In the 1830's notices of the Jackson Reading Room appeared in the papers. In the 1880's "book entertainments" were planned to secure money for the purchase of books for the library, but it was Dr. Mark Matthews, that far-sighted and civic-minded minister of the Presbyterian Church, who appeared before the City Council on January 4, 1900, and asked for $75,000 that was to be matched by Andrew Carnegie for the purpose of building and equipping a public library in Jackson. A grant of only $30,000 was obtained from the Carnegie funds, but the new library was built and opened on March 3, 1903, with Miss Emma Collins as librarian. And thus, another ear-mark of a city, a public library, became a part of the life of the community.[15]

Madison County was the scene of a most progressive movement during the last five years of the nineteenth and the first ten years of the twentieth centuries. Sam Lancaster and John Jay Williams, two far-sighted engineers, supported by many of the citizens, started a movement to build a system of good roads in the county. Their efforts ended in the passage of an act of the Legislature in 1903 allowing the County Court the privilege of issuing $300,000 worth of bonds to build these roads, an unheard of amount at that time to be spent upon roads.

The author of this plan for the roads in Madison County was J. J. Williams, an engineer of national fame. Before he came to Jackson in 1854 he had served as assistant engineer (1840-1850) under Colonel George Hughes, United States

---

and Light Company of New Jersey and in 1928 the name was changed to West Tennessee Power and Light Company, which operated in thirty towns of West Tennessee. In 1939 the Tennessee Valley Authority took over the electric department of this company. Since then the company is known as the West Tennessee Gas Company.

[15] At the end of the first year, the library reported 5,055 books with an average circulation of 1,500. Minute Books of City of Jackson, *Forked Deer Blade*, January 9, 1888.

topographical engineer, surveying the railroad across the Isthmus of Panama, surveying also the Nicaragan route and discovering the pass which makes this canal possible. J. J. Williams also served as assistant engineer to Colonel J. G. Banard of the United States engineers on the survey for the railroad across the Isthmus of Tehuantepec and assisted in preparing the published report of this project. This engineer came to Jackson in 1854, where he had charge of the construction of the Mississipi Central and Tennessee Railroad from Grand Junction to Jackson, and of the Mobile and Ohio Railroad from Jackson to Columbus, Kentucky. In the 1870's after going to Europe to study inland lakes and waterways, he served as chief engineer of the Tehuantepec and Ship Canal Railroad, but returned to Tennessee just a few years before the turn of the century.

In 1895, he prepared a "Report on a New System of Good Roads by which the Farming Lands of Madison County will be Increased to Double their Present Value and from four to six Times the Cost of the Good Roads" and read this report before the Quarter Session of the County Court in April, 1895. The Board of Trade paid for one thousand copies (printed by David Balch) and J. J. Williams paid for another thousand which were distributed to the tax-payers of the county, while the court allowed him $65 for preparing the article. Thus, the first hurdle in the campaign for good roads was over, the people listened and read and became interested.[16]

J. J. Williams called this plan of his the "wheel system," the hub being the county seat, the spokes the county roads connecting with the tire, the tire those roads which connected the "spoke roads." This dreamer pointed out that the 50,265 acres that were within that five mile circle of the wheel were worth $6.67 per acre on an average, that if the roads were built within ten years these same lands would be worth $14 per acre, showing that with an increase value of $200,000 of city property the price of construction of the roads could be paid and a clear profit of $290,000 be realized. This new system of roads would also increase the business of the railroads which

---

[16] J. J. Williams, "Report on a New System of Good Roads by Which the Farming Lands of Madison County Will be Increased to Double their Present Value and from Four to Six Times the Cost of the Good Roads," (Jackson, Tennessee, 1896).

would have to haul and transport the extra produce, increase the value of the horses and mules for they could haul the same loads over the good roads in less time, and give employment to hundreds in the county while the roads were being built. Summarizing his whole argument, the engineer said that he had given enough proof to convince any reasonble man that these roads were of much more importance to the people than anything besides an interoceanic canal.[17]

All this argument of J. J. Williams did not convince the people of the necessity of the good roads, but Sam Lancaster and some other far-sighted men carried the crusade on. In June, 1901, a Good Roads convention was held in Jackson. This was attended by celebrities in and out of the state. An object lesson in road building was prepared by building two miles of the Poplar Corner road according to Sam Lancaster's plan. The enthusiasm created by these conventions and the object-lesson road served a valuable purpose, but the people were not yet convinced that such expensive roads were necessary. And then came the "winter of mud"; roads were impassable for six weeks. The farmer was locked in and all trade was stopped. A mass meeting was called and all who could possibly get there came. All wanted good roads, the only difference of opinion being as to the best means of procuring them and it looked for a while as if there would still be nothing done until a farmer arose and addressed the meeting as follows:

Mr. Chairman, I am just a plain farmer and have no business trying to talk in this meeting. I am all covered with mud; there is mud on my boots, and all over my clothes, and my hat is all spattered up, too. I walked to this meeting because my horse couldn't travel the roads. I've got a little farm and sawmill out on the Poplar Corner road, just a little over 2 miles from town, and if I could climb up on a hard road with my truck and what lumber I've sawed, I could clear enough in one day to pay my tax on that road; but I haven't got it.

---

[17]J. J. Williams always maintained that the route through Nicarugua was the better of the two, for he said that the Panama Canal would have land slides. That Williams was a man of vision is also shown by the fact that he surveyed and made favorable reports upon a proposed canal from the Tombigbee to the Tennessee River. Just recently great interest in this project has been revived, for the engineers of the War Department have approved the canal and leaders in Tennessee and Alabama have renewed their efforts to secure the new inland waterway.

I bought some groceries from you (turning to the merchant) this month; yes, $5 worth, for I carried them out on my back; but if I had a good road, it would have been $25, I am sure.[18]

This plain statement brought the question home and plans were made to draft a bill authorizing the county to issue bonds for $300,000 for graveling the roads in the county. Stoddert Caruthers was elected to the State Senate where he became the leading figure in shaping the legislation for this bond issue.[19]

Samuel C. Lancaster was a man of vision. The conservative men of the city accepted some of his ideas and supported them, but they also felt that they had to keep expenses down. Lancaster was a man to do big things. About the turn of the century, when James Wilson was Secretary of Agriculture, Sam Lancaster was building some model roads in Madison County which attracted nation-wide attention. Secretary Wilson became interested in the work of Lancaster and called him to Washington. The Report of the Department of Agriculture of 1904 contained a report on roads by Sam Lancaster. This work led to Lancaster's leaving Tennessee and going to the West Coast where he became the consulting engineer (1913-1915) for the Columbian Highway, America's greatest highway through the Cascade Mountains to the sea.[20]

By 1917 Jackson "the town" had truly become Jackson "the city." The growing pains of the last half of the nineteenth century and the early twentieth century had been very bad, but a community which has competent, brave leaders can face any troubles and weather any storm. Jackson had had men with vision, men who had the good of the city at heart, men who were ready to fight the battle to the finish.

---

[18]Sam C. Lancaster, "Practical Road Building in Madison County, Tennessee," *Yearbook of United States Department of Agriculture,* 1904 (Washington, 1905), 325-326.

[19]Stoddert Caruthers (1845-1904), a Confederate Soldier, was also one of the leading bankers of the city, an able lawyer, and a sane business man. He was also instrumental in getting the no fence law passed, so that the pigs and cattle would not run in streets at will. See chapter on "County Courts" for other treatment of the good roads project.

[20]Samuel C. Lancaster, *The Columbia: America's Great Highway through the Cascade Mountains to the Sea* (Portland, 1915), 110-115. This booklet alone is a work of art that is an illustration of Sam Lancaster's love of the beautiful.

CHAPTER XXVII

POST CIVIL WAR POLITICS

During the nineteenth century the people of Tennessee took their religion and politics seriously. During the last quarter of the nineteenth century West Tennessee was an important Democratic stronghold and Jackson and Madison was the home of some of the outstanding leaders of the day. Men enjoyed their politics. A political meeting was the most exciting event of the week or the month. In August, 1880, when Gen. Adkins was received there was an enthusiastic audience at both the speaking and the barbecue at Spring Creek. There was also a grand Democratic rally at Pinson which attracted hundreds—two hundred from Jackson went by train, taking with them the Democratic Cannon "Kit Carson" and "Hosford" on a flat car. The best order, attention and barbecue were reported here.[1] An approaching election meant that many a speech would be heard, much barbecue eaten, many a farmer stopped while plowing to talk with the candidate, many children called beautiful and patted on the head, many hours spent on Democratic business in Ham King's saloon and other meeting places where the constituents talked with those men who helped build Jackson—W. P. Robertson, J. H. Duke, Ernest Bullock, William Holland, Sr., Hu Anderson, Sr., John L. Wisdom, Sr., Henry McCorry.

A meeting of "thousands of noble men and beautiful women" at Trenton in July 1880 was typical of the excitement over political questions of that day. Two hundred visitors from Jackson accompanied by the Democratic field pieces again, went on a special train to the meeting; and arrived amid the thunder of artillery, the shouting of men, the blazing of bonfires and the smiles of beautiful women. All the Democrats joined in a parade from the station to the court square, while

---

[1] Jackson *Tribune and Sun*, October 21, August 5, 1880.

Democracy made itself heard through the hills and dales by firing the cannons and playing the drums. Speeches of Hon. Hill, B. A. Enloe, and Ernest Bullock were full of good Democratic food and fuel. Even Col. Harper, the old Greenbacker was ready to vote a Democratic ticket.[2]

Madison County's sons have been railroad presidents, oratorical geniuses, and have sat upon the bench of the highest court of the land, but none have been as powerful a politician in the councils of the Democratic party as Judge Henry McCorry. His election to the judgeship of the Common Law and Chancery Court (1876-1882) was pleasing to the community. He did not leave the house during the race nor resort to any electioneering device. He received the judicial ermine without stain and his friends felt that he would wear it worthily, ably, and well. In later years they did not have reason to be disappointed.[3] So great was the dignity of the Judge that under him the court's proceedings were of such character that would command the esteem, admiration and respect of any community.

Judge McCorry was considered by many one of the most brilliant men in Southern politics during his day. He was a good friend and adviser of Grover Cleveland being appointed Attorney General of the Federal District Court by President Cleveland. Correspondence from Democratic leaders such as John M. Taylor, Zack Taylor, Isham G. Harris, B. A. Enloe show that McCorry was the Democratic leader of whom they all turned for advice. It was during the last twenty years of the nineteenth century when such men as Henry McCorry, B. A. Enloe, and Ernest Bullock were the leading figures of Madison County's politics that Madison County's sons were the ones whose opinions were the last word in the policy of the Democratic party in the state. These were the days when, according to boastful Jacksonians, the political history of the state was written not from the Maxwell House in Nashville but from King's Palace in Jackson.

It was Judge Henry McCorry who made Peter Turney governor when to all appearances Clay Evans, his Republican opponent, was elected. The Democratic management in Nash-

---

[2] Jackson *Tribune and Sun*, July 28, 1880.
[3] Jackson *Whig and Tribune*, August 5, 1876; Jackson *Sun*, June 18, 1875.
[3] Correspondence of these men in the Curtis Bray Collection.

ville swamped with returns showing a Republican majority was about ready to announce Turney's defeat when McCorry told Governor Turney's manager not to concede anything until he could get there. McCorry led the fight which resulted in one of the most bitter political contests the state has known.

In the election of 1894, the Republicans, with H. Clay Evans as their candidate, made one mighty effort to defeat the Democrats who simply did not go to the polls to reelect their Governor, Peter Turney. Two days after the election both parties claimed the election. Files of opposing papers in the State reveal the exciting story of this fight for the investigation and the report of the committee. The Nashville *American*, supporting a fair election policy, told of charges of fraud on both sides, with Republicans in East Tennessee and the Democrats in West Tennessee. The Jackson *Blade* was for a fair election and added that Tennessee had survived Brownlowism, so surely it could survive two years of Evans. The Jackson *Whig* told of that fickel thing—the Republican party—which had been crying out about fraud, ballot box stuffing and rascality on the part of the Democrats and then when the Democrats demanded an investigation, they could not stand for the light to be turned upon them. A later issue of the same paper, suggested that Clay Evans would like to receive the governorship as a Christmas present but Santa Claus was going to wait and make him prove that he had been a good boy and didn't steal those ballots.[4] All the reports in the Nashville *American* centered around the theme: let's seat the man who was legally elected; if an investigation shows fraud on both sides, then let it show the truth.

It remained for the Nashville *Banner*, the Memphis *Avalanch*, and the Memphis *Scimitar* to be the champions of Clay Evans. A few lines from the Jackson *Blade* show how hard a battle the *Banner* fought:

> The *Blade* has no sympathy to waste on H. Clay Evans in his prospective loss of the governorship; but weeps for the poor old *Banner* and the *Avalanche*. They take his defeat so to heart.[5]

---

[4]Nashville *American*, November 7, 1894; Nashville *Banner*, December 29, January 17, quoting the *Whig* and the *Blade*.

[5]Nashville *American*, January 19, 1895.

Two days after the election the Nashville *Banner* entered the arena carrying the Evans banner and called the election a "Waterloo of Democracy." Ten days later the same paper reported that the astute politician, Judge Henry McCorry, had announced that frauds were great, that poll tax laws had been grossly violated, by the Republicans, that in one district in McNairy County a negro who could not read took the ballot-box out in the woods while the judges were at dinner, in fact the editor called the whole idea of counting Governor Turney in just a "McCorry howl of horror."[6] When newspaper reporters were told that the results of the election were not ready for publication, they sent up cries of indignation that Judge McCorry had stated that Turney was elected and made a very nasty remark about the boxes being unlocked at the Judge's wish for perhaps his power was greater than the governor or the Secretary of State. The same paper delighted in quoting the Knoxville *Journal* (Republican) that considered McCorry's acting as a champion of an honest election a complete joke adding: "As the champion of honesty in politics he would be about as much at home as the devil would be as the patron and promoter of an old-fashioned camp-meeting."[7]

As the days passed affairs became very warm and the Republican press did everything that it could to suppress the contest of this election. The *Banner* editor spoke very sarcastically of the "McCorry Purification Board" that was trying to purge the Republican frauds and wrote thus:

> By all the political gods he [McCorry] intends to see Peter Turney is made Governor or burst his patriotic heart in the effort. . . . In this beautiful business all the Republicans are to be politically excommunicated as demons damned and all the Democrats, including even the expert political monsters of West Tennessee who have sat at McCorry's feet, are to be praised as spotless.[8]

The importance of McCorry's part in the contested election is shown by the vast amount of criticism that was hurled at him by the Republican press. "McCorry and Company" went behind the election returns and "McCorryized Governor Turney" and it mattered not how much ridicule was heaped upon them,

---

[6]Nashville *Banner*, November 19, 20, 1894.
[7]*Ibid.*, November 20, 1894.
[8]*Ibid.*, November 22, 1894.

these stalwart Democrats turned a deaf ear to the talk about the silly procedure of trying to discover whether Tim Tiddledwinks paid his poll tax or not or whether Ham Huddledewhunks voted early or late, and went about setting into motion the proper procedure to contest the election. The battle was won when a joint committee of five from the Senate and seven from the House were appointed to hear the contest. This committee reported on May 3, 1895 and revised the returns for Peter Turney with 94,894 against 92,440 for H. Clay Evans. If the Republicans could have silenced one Henry McCorry of Jackson, Tennessee would probably have had a Republican governor for the next two years.

Through the years, Jackson has been a true stronghold of the Democratic party, the home of able and influential politicians. Democrats were thrilled to hear William Jennings Bryan when he spoke here at the Sam Jones tabernacle in the 1890's; they took sides and fought the Madison County "War of Roses" with the Taylor brothers; E. L. Bullock was among those men who led the fight of the Independent Democrats in 1910-1911 and the fight for state wide prohibition. These were stormy days in the Legislature, and Madison County sent several competent and fearless leaders into the battle. This bolt from the Democratic party of a large number of members who called themselves "Independent Democrats" led to the election of the Republican candidate for governor, Ben W. Hooper in 1910 and his re-election in 1912 by the Republicans and those "Independent Democrats." E. L. Bullock, a fearless leader and a great lawyer, was a man who when he declared his position carried the fight to the finish.[9]

There were many other active Democrats in the county during the last years of the nineteenth century and the first twenty years of the twentieth. Among these were Judge Sidney J. Everett, for thirteen years judge of the 16th Judicial Circuit, a lawyer's lawyer whose rugged honesty, boundless courage and unquestionabled loyalty, fine convictions, and charity for his fellowmen made him one of the leading lawyers and stalwart

---

[9]E. L. Bullock also played a prominent part in the fight for state wide prohibition, which is included in the story of prohibition mentoned elsewhere in this work. Other evidences of Bullock's work are shown by his being a member of the State Railroad Commission and serving as Chancellor of the 8th Chancery Division.

Democrats of the state. In 1914 he was a candidate for nomination for governor of Tennessee and would have been nominated if on the final ballot Chester County delegation had not switched its vote. But for this turn of events Judge Everett would have in turn been elected governor for the Democrats won by a nice margin at the ensuing general election.

Another Jeffersonian Democrat of these years was Clarence E. Pigford, who stood high in the Democratic councils of the State. Although he was not an office seeker, he was a stalwart defender of the Democratic party principles and here as in the legal field he was a man of exceptional ability, a man of tremendous courage and stamina.

Another able lawyer and active Democrat of these days was Tom Murray, Sr., a strong Jeffersonian Democrat who, like many others, believed in working out the difficulties within the party rather than bolting as the "Independents" did in 1910. He was a man honest in his convictions, a man who never hesitated to take his stand upon controversial issues, a man who finished the fight that he begun. For many years prior to his death he was chairman of the County Democratic Executive Committee and as such was an influential factor in party affairs.

In conclusion, Madison County has been the home of many men who were so-called "perfect politicians," men who were magnificent orators, well-informed men who knew how to conduct a successful political campaign, men who have made Madison's influence felt in the State.

CHAPTER XXVIII

"PURSUIT OF HAPPINESS"

Those people of the Western District during the frontier days enjoyed life, but most of their amusements were two-fold, such as hunting, fishing, quilting bees, house-raisings. These things were fun but they also had a practical purpose. To these should be added the pleasures that were derived from attending political gatherings and eating the barbecue, attending court, church, and camp meetings, watching and particpating in muster days, and fighting. Hunting was the chief sport of the early West from necessity, with bear hunting the most thrilling. In 1825, Captain Thomas Reavis of Mount Pinson went on a bear hunt near the mouth of the Forked Deer River and reported that the party killed twenty-six bears.[1]

The most joyous gatherings of the neighborhood were, however, the log-rollings when the whole community was invited and a big dinner was prepared. The men worked out of doors; the women quilted inside. "The field work was done, the quilt was finished, and everything was cleared away for the frolic." A fiddler who could play "Jenny, put the kettle on," "Molly, blow the bellows, we'll all take tea," and "Leather breeches, full of stitches" was always at hand. Shooting matches were also held in convenient groves. These were often attended by several hundred and frequently lasted until after dark. Candles were placed at the site of the rifle and on each side of the target. Articles were brought to the scene of the shooting and men shot for one of them rather than purchase them at reasonable prices. This was much more fun![2]

One of the most joyous occasions of the year was the "bran" dance that was often held on the Fourth of July. A contem-

---

[1] Nashville *Whig*, March 10, 1825.

[2] J. S. French, *Life and Adventures of David Crockett* (Cincinnati, 1833), 114.

porary writer described such an affair that he attended about 1825. The dozens of pretty maids with rosy cheeks, and twinkling toes made a beautiful picture that was carried in the memories of those who attended for years. What a wild and joyous occasion this was, here in the deep forest in a grove ten miles from the county town in the Western District! "The woods for hundreds of yards around were astir with neighing horses, with parties of young folks gathering to the joyous center of attraction where two fiddles were at an early hour discoursing the pleasant and spirited music."[3]

Fighting in this early West seemed not only to be the means of having your own way, but also a real source of pleasure, both for the participants and the audience. Court records reveal innumerable fines of from one cent to $1 for assault and battery and often the same man was fined two or three times on the same day. Certain rules of "etiquette" governed the affairs of these early pugilists. These men did not use pistols, for such would brand a man as a coward, but they did use their brawny fists that were hard with endless days of toil. Biting and often gouging the eyes were frequently a part of the game. By noon every Saturday, court day, or muster day, when the crowd had gathered in Jackson and the racks were lined with horses and mules, a fight would be arranged to take place at the usual fighting grounds—a place beyond Sandy Branch where the town marshal had no jurisdiction. Plenty of "spirits" encouraged the bets and helped to brew the fights which sometimes ended in a general fight with each man attempting to whip his man. These bullies were not angry. Each one coveted the right to be called the best fighter in the neighborhood. Everyone present had a good time, but the victors enjoyed most the boasting afterwards. When the crowd assembled at the fighting grounds a ring was formed in the middle, a contestant would stand with a chip on his shoulder until someone came and knocked it off. Instantly the two flew at each other like tigers until one cried enough and the fun was over for another day. An onlooker dared not interfere until one of the participants had let it be known that he had enough for the time being.[4] Now, the victor was "the cock

---

[3]Nashville *Republican Banner*, August 18, 1851.
[4]J. C. Cisco, "History of Madison County," *American Historical*

of the walk," even though he frequently bore scars of that fact.

Colonel John Houston of Cotton Grove, either accidentally or on purpose, neglected to remove his spurs before an affray that took place on the porch of Dr. Fenner's store. Houston spurred his enemy "in the flank and the rears." In one fight Taylor Rhodes was struck a violent blow on the head with a chair, the "effects from which he soon expired." On Saturday in May "whilst working the Bolivar road, nine miles from this place, an altercation took place between two young men, Mahon and Irvin, which resulted in the death of the latter, by means of a blow stricken with a hoe." These frontiesmen used any weapon that was at hand. They fought and made up, then fought and were often friends because they had fought. Fighting was indeed in fashion.[5]

Every growing town in the West had a race track and Jackson was no exception, for William E. Butler had one of his own here, located where the National Guard Armory stands to-day. The *Gazette* of 1828 announced a meet of three days of running races, "one, two, and three miles heats . . . a full track with an extensive house in the center." "Red Fox" won the Jockey Purse in Jackson in 1828 and his owner entered him in the sweepstakes race at $1000 entrance fee to be run on the Jackson Turf. An illustrated advertisement appeared in the papers early in January informing the people that the regular spring races would be held in May. Races were an important feature of the West Tennessee Agricultural and Mechanical Association that was held in Jackson during the last half of the nineteenth century and the early twentieth century. These people loved horses, couldn't resist betting, and simply devoured the excitement of it all—a buoyant spirit and a sporting character of a gallant South.[6]

The town of Jackson not only had its horse races but it had its "horse play." A "Sacrificial Club" of thirteen members

---

Magazine, VIII (1903), 31-33; Williams, *West Tennessee,* 229; Reminiscences of T. M. Gates.

[5]*Ibid.*, Jackson *Southern Statesman,* May 21, 1831, March 3, 1832.

[6]Jackson *Gazette,* November 18, 1828, September 26, 1829; Jackson *Southern Statesman,* February 5, 19, 1831, June 13, 1831. Tennesseean's love of races is reflected in the fact that by an Act of the Legislature of 1833, it became illegal for horses to be run upon public roads, or abet in this, for a track or a turf should be provided. *Acts of Tennessee,* 1833.

was organized to worship at the shrine of Bacchus and they needed a human sacrifice to atone for their sins. The members cast lots and one John Cross was placed in a log pen filled with combustible material and the flames applied, but fortunately a saviour appeared and the man was saved.[7] These Westerners wasted no time before they set up a roulette wheel, a wheel of Fortune, or a Bassoon, and plenty of saloons of which King's Palace in the latter part of the nineteenth century was the most famous. Court records show that indictments were made for "unlawful gaming at cards" and betting at wheels. Practical jokes, cards, the gaming table, and quantities of liquor were the natural picture of the Western country.

A barbecue was a very popular social and business affair. Railroads held them in order to sell stock, real estate men held them to draw men to the sales, and politicians held them to gain votes, frequently reporting after an election that "many barbecues were eaten." But there was the inevitable barbecue held upon the Fourth of July, a day that was a real day of celebration to those liberty loving men of the new West. It was a spread-eagle day and every one came to hear the Declaration of Independence read and the oration of the day delivered. This "spread eagle-speech was made to a sea "of upturned faces whose souls were filled with patriotic impulses, who made glorious the occasion by repeated shouts and clapping of hands."[8] Dinner [the barbecue] was spread out on a long table covered with clean white linen. The well-browned and juicy ribs and saddles, breadbaskets piled high with homemade bread of both corn and flour, pots and pans of rich chicken pies were interspersed with tarts, pies, puddings, cakes, and pickles, which were all so plentiful that there were baskets filled with food to carry home. Political candidates spoke all afternoon while patriotic matrons kept turkey tail fans in constant motion.[9]

Plans for the coming celebration of the glorious Fourth were made weeks in advance. In 1832, Dr. Butler acted as chairman of a meeting held in the Jackson Reading Room in May. The company of cavalry attached to the 75th regiment

---

[7] J. G. Cisco, "History of Madison County," *American Historical Magazine,* VII (1902), 334.
[8] J. S. Williams, *Old Times,* 171-172.
[9] *Ibid.,* 173.

of Tennessee Volunteers was to parade, the usual speaking, and a dance at Patterson's Springs was to follow.[10] Contemporary papers were filled with items about this glorious anniversary each year, such as the following:

> At an early hour those wishing to participate in the celebration will assemble at Dr. Butler's spring in the immediate vicinity of town where the Declaration will be read by Col. Joseph Talbot after which Col. Jno. Read will deliver an address. The company will then sit down to a superb dinner prepared by "mine host" of the Lafayette Inn in his best style. . . . We earnestly advise all who wish to pay reverence to the building of our happy republic; all whose hearts thrill with pleasure at the spirit-stirring eloquence of oratory; all who delight to mingle in scenes of social festivity with the fair daughters of our land; and all who love a tastefully arranged dinner table, loaded with viands rich and rare and sparkling with the ruddy juice of the grape, do not slight the invitation. The day will end with a ball at the Lafayette Inn.[11]

Another account tells of a ball that lasted all day and of the toasts that were drunk at the close of the dinner as follows:

> West Tennessee—The land of Hospitality and good feasting—ever ready to welcome the stranger to the soil, and delighting to honor her faithful public servants.
> The day we Celebrate—May the heart of every American glow with patriotism on its return.
> The Steam Boat Home Snake—Just arrived loaded with Yankee notions. May its boilers be busted and make its return voyage to Washington City.[12]

These and many more of the day breathed a patriotic spirit which reached an emotional climax when the men expressed such pride in their own achievements and the growing hatred of the "Yankee Notions." The urge to make this day one of celebration did not die in the 1830's and 1840's, for papers of the last half of the nineteenth century carry similar plans, the only difference being that excursions were planned on all the railroads to bring in the guests who were to enjoy the music, the parades, the speeches, and the barbecue.[13]

---

[10] Jackson *Southern Statesman*, May 19, June 9, 1832.
[11] Jackson *Truth Teller*, June 27, 1834.
[12] Jackson *Southern Statesman*, July 9, 1831.
[13] Jackson *Sun*, June 9, 1876.

In 1850's Robert H. Cartmell, a typical planter of the county, attended many a fish fry at Jones's Mill, or a picnic at Chester's Mill, and ate quantities of squirrel stew at Pic Jones's, or went to a colt show at the fairground. Colonel Chester gave a barbecue "to whom and for what" Robert Cartmell did not know, but there was a table sixty yards long well supplied with barbecue. A hundred or more enjoyed the occasion, the younger generation danced and the older ones pitched dollars and talked. Other social affairs of the day included a wedding in the Chester home and a party at Dr. Jackson's for his son (William H.) who was home from West Point.[14]

As early as 1829 there was a real dramatic performance in Jackson. "Although deprived of the advantages of a suitable building and adequate scenery, they (the players) succeeded in giving satisfaction," wrote the contemporary editor. The manager himself pledged that "Every exertion will be used to merit patronage" in the presentation of "The Stranger" and "Family Jars."[15] Equestrian, rope dancers, and tumbling performers took away a good deal of money from the city in 1831, but they left behind them "the recollection of a good deal of fun." Spring of this same year brought the YEAman circus for four evening performances at the price of 75c for adults and half for children.[16]

By 1831 the editor of the *Southern Statesman* began to try to interest the people of Jackson in the Lyceum, arguing the "intelligence is the ark of our political safety," and that this intelligence could be easily acquired by the diffusion of information among the inhabitants of the country. The following argument from one edition of the paper was convincing enough to create great interest in the project:

American Lyceum—good for each district, for it will improve conversation, schools, morals, amusements, temperance. Parents frequently regret that their children seek dissipating amusements. This is not the fault of their children, but of themselves. If they will provide a lyceum furnished with specimens of our Creator's works, with apparatus, books, etc., their children will not seek taverns with its decanters, glasses, ninepins, and alcohol. One year's entertainment and instruction only costs two dollars.[17]

---

[14]Robert H. Cartmell Diary.
[15]Jackson *Gazette,* May 9, 1829; June 27, 1829.
[16]Jackson *Southern Statesman,* June 4; May 21, 1831.
[17]Paris *West Tennessean,* November 1, 1839; June 29, 1838;

Some of the subjects of these educational lectures seem to have been suitable, such as "Has the course pursued by the Government toward the Indians been justified?" But the suitability of this one might be doubted: "Was Corolanus justifiable in marching against Rome?" These men of the Western District were ambitious even in the subject of their lectures. In 1838, a meeting of the Lyceum was announced:

> Will meet at the Male Academy on Saturday evening, the 7th of April next at early candle lighting. Ladies and gentlemen are respectfully invited to attend.[18]

Thus, only a few short years after the people came to the district, they were patronizing singing schools, that used the Pestslozzian system, and enjoying the Lyceums, the circus, and the drama.

Corn huskings were both exciting and profitable. It was during the days of slavery that the Negroes of James Lyon challenged the Negroes of William H. Long, Sr. to a shucking contest. Two mounds of corn were made, a 'possum supper was prepared and whiskey was provided. Some overseers and white men came to watch and keep down trouble in case it should arise. As soon as the signal was given both teams of Negroes would begin shucking, shouting, and singing some old time Negro song that made the woods around fairly ring with melody as the happy Negroes contested for the prize—the 'possum supper for the winner and a gallon of whiskey for each side. After supper the fiddle and the banjos were brought out and the singing and dancing lasted until into the night.[19]

No discussion of the amusements of the early days could be concluded without speaking of dancing, for there were always "balls" held on Christmas, New Year's Day, Eighth of January, Twenty-second of February, and the Fourth of July. The stores carried silk stockings and the dancing master was as important in the community as the preacher. David Crockett said that there was a "great rage of the tripping on the light fantastic toe" to the music of the banjo or the fiddle furnished by some trusty black, who knew that the preacher made as much money as he (the fiddler), but he suited the people a

---

Jackson *District Telegraph*, March 30, 1838.
   [18]Jackson *District Telegraph*, March 30, 1838.
   [19]Reminiscences of T. M. Gates.

lot better. There were bran dances where the ground was sprinkled with husks of Indian meal and the floor was "girded by the limits of the forest." Rain might make the black hastily put up his banjo, but he usually continued to sing so the people would continue to keep time with their feet.[20]

A progressive community that was settled by educated people from Virginia and the Carolinas would waste no time before they provided some place where they could satisfy their love for books and papers. In October 1831, the *Southern Statesman* announced the opening of the Jackson Reading Room with membership at five dollars per year. These rooms were to be open from nine in the morning till four in the afternoon and on nights after the arrival of mail from the east, it would be open at early candle light until ten o'clock.[21]

Amusements of the nineteenth century were simple but varied. Our grandfathers and great-grandfathers remember the swimming holes, especially Jones's Pond on Chester Street extended where Jone's creek had been dammed; the beautiful horses that drew the buggies and phaetons through the country and about the city to enjoy the sights; the Wild Rose Saloon where, according to the proprietor's view, "the wealth and refinement of our city congregates;" the Union Saloon which advocated that everyone "Drink ye and Be Merry";[22] the Chautauquas of the early twentieth century; the street fairs, the opera houses; Highland Park, the Settlers of '61, the lodges, and clubs of the day.

Lodges have played an important role in the life of the community. Masonry in Madison County is almost as old as the county, for the Jackson Lodge No. 45 was chartered October 6, 1823, while Andrew Jackson was Grand Master of Tennessee. Charter members and officers included Robert Murray, Daniel Madding, A. King, Dr. W. E. Butler, R. E. King, A. C. Nimmo. Other units of the Masons in the county included St. John's Lodge No. 332 chartered in 1867; Union No. 29 at Denmark (1828-1841); Pinson No. 222 chartered in 1852; Henderson Station No. 364 (1868-1886); Mercer No. 740 chartered in 1832; Cotton Grove No. 153 (1848-1888); Spring Creek No.

---

[20]J. S. Williams, *Old Times*, 149; Life of David Crockett, 135-136; Jackson *Southern Statesman*, August 27, 1831.
[21]Jackson *Southern Statesman*, October 6, 1831.
[22]*Board of Trade Souvenir*, 1897.

193 chartered in 1850; Pleasant Plains No. 360 (1868-1890). The Royal Arch Chapter, the Clinton Chapter No. 9 at Jackson, the Denmark No. 44, Spring Creek No. 93 were also organized. The Jackson Commandery No. 13 is the only commandery in Madison County.[23]

The Jackson Lodge No. 16, I.O.O.F. was chartered in 1846. The Launcelot Lodge No. 13 of Knights of Pythias was chartered in 1873 with the following charter members: A. W. Campbell, Jno. T. Stark, J. T. Bates, W. P. Robertson, A. W. Anderson, H. W. McCorry, Stoddert Caruthers, W. F. Alexander, Richard Redman. In 1890, the Pythians built a new building and an opera house, which became known as the Pythian Castle and opera house.[24] Thirty-five men were in that first class of the Knights of Columbus which was organized on March 17, 1906.

On February 21, 1891, Stephen Howe, an Elk from New York, came to Jackson and interested some of the leading citizens in an organization here. W. T. Harris was the first exalted ruler. The Elks have prospered in Jackson and have enjoyed a large membership of influential citizens. John L. Wisdom and many others kept interest in the Elks alive.

Music lovers in Jackson had the privilege of attending performances at King's Opera House in the 1870's and 1880's and at the Pythian Opera House in the 1890's. Legitimate stage plays such as Henrietta Chanfrau of New Orleans in "Parted" was booked at King's in 1875; the Clark Brothers and the Fire King entertained the people at King's in 1877; while the audience in 1891 was delighted with a performance of "Faust", a concert by Miss Nettie McClanahan and four days of opera at the Pythian Opera House in 1895. First class road shows came to the Marlowe Theatre in the early twentieth century. But the years near the turn of the century marked a broadening of musical appreciation, nationally as well as locally. Music lovers in Jackson were not only interested in bringing artists to the town but also were capable of rendering finished numbers in public performances themselves. These interested persons organized the Lyric Club in 1900, which was the pre-

---

[23]Charles Snodgrass, *History of Free Masonry in Tennessee,* 1787-1943 (Chattanooga, 1944), 287. The writer is also indebted to J. C. Carson of Jackson, for material concerning the Masons in the county.
[24]Jackson *Sun,* May 21, 1916.

decessor of the present MacDowell Club, both of which have contributed greatly to the cultural life of the city.[25]

Whether it was the desire for a romantic escape from the economic problems and conflict or just escape from the drabness of the life of the decade of the nineties, or the opportunity of relaxation, or just the insatiable desire to join something, it is hard to say, but it is a certain fact that social and cultural clubs were organized during the late nineties and the early twentieth century in such numbers that they could be arranged alphabetically. Club life was on a boom! Two social study clubs were organized in 1893, the Mutual Improvement Club that held its first meeting with Miss Hettie Harris;[26] the Ingleside Book Club with Mrs. J. H. Hunter serving as the first president.[27] In 1894, the Joseph E. Martin Shakespeare Circle was organized by Miss Lena Myers (Mrs. Hu C. Anderson) and Mrs. Osborne R. Gilmore. Other charter members of this organization were: Miss Annie Nevins, Mesdames C. B. Bell, Leila Morgan Murrell, G. H. Robertson, Reid Rogers, Dr. Joseph E. Martin, E. L. Bullock, J. L. Brooks, and Hu C. Anderson. As a part of the revival of interest in American History, the Musidora McCorry Chapter of the U. D. C. was organized in 1895 by Mrs. Belle K. Allison. The William H. Jackson Chapter of U. D. C. was organized in 1925 with Miss Laura Bishop the moving spirit, and the Jackson-Madison Chapter of the D. A. R. was organized in 1901 with Mrs. Harriet Holland as the first regent.

In 1898, there were ten cultured gentlemen of the city who organized the Conversational Club for the purpose of discussing timely topics. This with the above mentioned study clubs formed an important part of the cultural life of the city.

From 1906, the date of its organization, until 1933, the date of the last meeting, a unique organization called the

---

[25]Charter members of this Lyric Club included: Mesdames J. D. Hunt, Deupree, Misses Grace Duke, Carrie Holland, Edith Holland, Delana White, Anna Murray, Hettie Harris, Aliene Day, Hattie Felsenthal, Mary Jones, Ora Wilcox, Wayne Thornton, Lena Stovall.

[26]Charter members included: Misses Grace Duke, Grace Arrington, Edith Holland, Carrie Holland.

[27]Charter members included: Mesdames John I. Taylor, J. L. Webster, Janie Duncan, S. P. Anderson, C. N. Harris, Jacobi, T. D. Wilson.

"Settlers of 1861" existed in the county. Fifty-seven white men who were living the county in 1861 and ten Negroes were present at that first meeting.[28]

In 1904, there was a big fair held on the streets about court square that were roped off for that purpose. This was the year that a very big fair was held, for $3,889.58 in proceeds were contributed to the new Lancaster Park fund. Guests this year enjoyed the snake charmer, the serpentine dancers, a "Pygmalion" show, and paid homage to the queen of the fair, Miss Mary Jones. A gala occasion it was indeed!

All that is left of the old Highland Park, the amusement center of the "Gay Nineties" and the early twentieth century are the lake between Crescent and Westwood Avenues and memories. In this amusement park, developed by the Jackson and Sururban Railway Company, there was the "Temple of Winged Feet," a white stucco building used as a skating rink; there was the "Polar Bear," the refreshment parlor; there was Gorman's Field, a huge baseball park where at least 1,500 people witnessed games between teams of neighboring towns; across the beautiful white stucco bridge which spanned the lake there was a pavilion where band concerts were held each Sunday; there was the "Figure Eight," the up-hill, down-hill and round the curve roller coaster; there was the out of door pageant, "The Last Days of Pompei" witnessed by 10,000; there was the opening night of the Highland Park Theatre when the Redpath Chautauqua Company played to an audience of six thousand and people came from far and near and camped in tents for an entire whole week of entertainment. There were the boat rides on the lake where many a romance was begun. These were the "Gay Nineties" and early nineteen twenties.

The people of the city and the county have seemed to possess the happy faculty of enjoying themselves, it mattered not whether it was a drive into the country behind some of the beautiful horses that could be had at "the Southern Horse Parlors," a game of hearts, at a meeting of the "Mystic Eleven," a barbecue, a fish-fry, or just the old swimming hole. When friends assembled, it was a pleasure to attend an opera, go to a camp-meeting, or "just visit."

---

[28]See picture of "Settlers of 1861" in picture section.

CHAPTER XXIX
THE EPILOGUE

Glancing through the numerous records of the past that were sources for the preceding pages, a reader can visualize some of those leaders of Madison County as they walked across the stage of life and played their part. If the deeds of those builders of our county are not recorded, then our part of the growth of the American empire may be forgotten, therefore it was the purpose of those interested in the publication of this volume to record the life story of some of the men which to a certain degree had been unheralded. Thus, it is hoped that it will be a source of pride and real pleasure to Madison Countians to review the stories of David Crockett and Adam Huntsman, of Dr. William E. Butler and Stokely and Samuel Jackson Hays, of General William T. Haskell and Milton Brown, of J. J. Williams and Sam Lancaster, of Associate Justice Howell E. Jackson, Judge Joshua Haskell and Judge Ben Lindsay,[1] of W. W. Gates and J. G. Cisco, of Dr. Jimmy Jones, Dr. Ambrose McCoy, and Dr. J. A. Crook.

The pages of history tell of many of the sons of Madison County who have climbed to the top of the ladder of success. Some of these, such as I. B. Tigrett, president of the Gulf, Mobile and Ohio Railway; W. A. Caldwell, former president

---

[1]Judge Ben Lindsay (1869-1942) left Jackson about the turn of the century for Denver, Colorado, where he helped create the first Juvenile Court Law, April 12, 1899, serving as Judge of the County and Juvenile Court of Denver from 1900 to 1927, always basing his decisions upon the idea that since the children of today are the citizens of tomorrow it was necessary to have a city of decent kids.

In the late 1920's he made many enemies by advocating companionate marriage and it was during a service at the Episcopal Cathedral of St. John the Divine that Bishop William T. Manning in prayer denounced Lindsay's stand upon the subject of companionate marriage. Whereupon Lindsay hurried to the reporter's table and demanded a chance to be heard. The interruption in the midst of prayer threw the congregation in a turmoil. They rushed forward and would have attacked the Judge if detectives had not taken him away from the church. Exciting times these were when a member of the audience is taken away amid angry cries of the parishioners. The Jackson *Sun*, December 7, 1930.

of the First National Bank, but now Chairman of the Board; the late Clarence E. Pigford, lawyer, publisher of the Jackson *Sun* and influential public spirited citizen; Lawrence Taylor, Mayor of Jackson for sixteen years and vice-president of the First National Bank; C. B. Ijams, superintendent of the city schools for thirty years; Dr. Charles F. Webb, and the late Dr. James McClaran, surgeons, whose ability is recognized at home and abroad; Doctors Herman Hawkins and Jere L. Crook; John Wisdom, William Holland, Robert L. Beare, Joe Rosenbloom and many others, have achieved success and fame but they have chosen to continue to call Jackson home. Others who have achieved fame abroad are men such as Austin King, congressman and governor of Missouri who started to practice law in Madison County in 1822; John L. Lancaster, president of the Texas and Pacific Railway Company; Frank and Monroe Anderson, Will and Ben Clayton of the Anderson, Clayton and Company, the largest buyers, sellers, storers of raw cotton in the world, and Will Clayton, the present Assistant Secretary of State; Dr. Gilbert Anderson, brain surgeon of New Orleans; Walter Holmes, that unselfish man who published a magazine for the blind; Philip Holland, former American Consul at Liverpool; Walter Chandler, the present mayor of Memphis; Jennings Perry, editor of Nashville *Tennessean;* S. A. Mynders, the first president of the West Tennessee State Teachers College; John Holland, United States District Judge in Florida; Miss Cassie Mason, the founder of Tarry-Town-on-Hudson, a select girls' school on the Hudson; Colonel R. A. Sneed, Secretary of Treasury and Secretary of State of Oklahoma; John Chester Botts, president of the New York Cotton Exchange; Sid White of Cotton Exchange in New Orleans.

The most substantial glory of any country is in its great men. Madison County has had and has to-day its great men. Thus the following words of Thomas Jefferson could very fittingly be applied to the story of our county through the years:

> "What constitutes a State?
> Not high-raised battlements, or labor's mound,
>   Thick wall, or moated gate;
> Not cities proud, with spires and turrets crowned;
>   No; men, high minded men;
>   Men who their duties know;
> But know their rights; and knowing, dare maintain,
>   These constitute a State."

APPENDICES

ANDREW JACKSON LETTERS

The text of the following letters of Andrew Jackson are not included with the idea that they contain any material that is not already known, but because most of them were written to people of Madison County, Samuel Jackson Hays and Richard Jackson Hays, and explain the close relationship between the early settlers and "Old Hickory." In as far as the author has been able to ascertain, eight of these personal letters have not been published. The words of the General himself give life to some of the events of long ago.

To Samuel Jackson Hays

(Private)

Washington April 23d, 1831[1]

Dear Saml,

I have just recd your interesting letter of the 4th instant and hasten to acknowledge it. I trust for the honor of the state, your Congressional District will not disgrace themselves longer by sending that profligate man Crockett back to Congress.

You have judged rightly in the matter, in withholding from Col. Stokly D. Hays the information of Crockett's conduct toward him, if the result would have been an attack by Col. Hays upon him. My view in communicating it, was that those who had recommended him might be informed of his *base* course as a machine in the hands of my enemies, for it was a direct attack upon those who recommended him. Since Congress adjourned it has come to my knowledge that Poindexter has behaved as deceitfully & basely as Mr. Crockett on the subject,—have wrote to Col. Thos. H. Williams & furnished him with the means of an antidote against Poindexter's perfidy, with directions to shew my letter with Judge Mitchell's of

---

[1]Used through the courtesy of Mrs. Walker Hays, Memphis, Tennessee.

Tennessee to every member of the Legislature who voted for him.

You will see from the Globe that Van Buren & Eaton having tendered their resignations in the Cabinet, I have determined to reorganize it anew except the Postmaster General. This step had become necessary, from the deep intrigue of Duff Green, Calhoun & Co. a more corrupt set never existed in any country, and by attending to the Globe you will find that this plot began before I was inaugurated & I have discovered of late that one, if not more, of my Cabinet have been deep into these intrigues, managed by Mr. Calhoun to bring into disrepute my administration, that Genl Duff Green's prediction in 1829 might become true, "that Mr. Calhoun's claims could not be postponed longer than to the end of my first term"—hence the conduct of McDuffee, & the movements of the nullifiers in So. Carolina, and the attempt here in the Jefferson Dinner to get me identified with the nullifiers—But altho unsuspecting, until I sat down to the dinner table, having been assured by the Committee who worked upon me, that nothing of politicks, was to be included in it. I there, on taking up the toasts & reading them saw the whole plot, and this maneuver was alone checkmated by my toast, which brought down upon me the whole ire of the nullifyers—hence the continued & foul abuse of Mr. Van Buren. Viewing him in the way of Calhoun —Van Buren is one of the purest republicans in the Union, whilst, *I now know,* that Calhoun is the most deceptious intriguing demagogue in it. I also know he will lie with the same facility that an honest man will tell the truth. I once had unlimited confidence in him, that is lost forever—he is as unprincipled as Henry Clay, and would sacrifice every thing to his ambition.

The plan they thought was well lain—they thought I durst not remove Ingram that it would arouse Pennsylvania against me, and Calhoun had urged him not to resign—I foresaw the plan. It was foreseen by Mr. Van Buren & Major Eaton, and their disinterested patriotism at once induced them to tender their resignations, that opened the way to a reorganization of my Cabinet. Therefore you see, that the opposition with Genl Duff Green Calhoun & Co. was checkmated by a single move of these valuable patriots, and the country saved from destruction.

This act of these men shews how disinterested their patriotism are, whilst others are lying, intriguing, and plotting to get into office, these men, for public good, are voluntarily surrender theirs. I trust you pen will do justice to this disinterested act of patriotism.

Say to Chester with my kind wishes to him & Betsey—that I could not give him the office of Marshal,* it would have authorized Poindexter & Crockett to say it was distributing all offices amongst my connections, no man I think more worthy & when I can I will with more pleasure serve. Present me to Frances, kiss the son for me, present me kindly to your mother & Narcissa, and all connections, & believe me your friend

(Signed) *ANDREW JACKSON*

SAML. J. HAYS ESQ.

(Confidential strictly so)

P. S. When I asked Major Eaton to take a seat in the Cabinet he was a member of the Senate—he with great reluctance, & purely with friendship to me, yielded to my solicitations—it was a happy thing for me & the nation he was near me—his good judgment and personal popularity, give him the means of acquiring correct knowledge of all the intrigues secretly plotted against me—it was his well known friendship to me, that caused the secrete movements of Calhouns friends to destroy him, & drive him from the Cabinet, by which they thought one might be selected subservient to their views, and by which means they might separate me from Van Buren whose republican worth & talents they dreaded, and from the prosperity in our Foreign relations they saw with sorrow & jealousy his rising popularity in the nation which proved a great damper to Mr. C. & his friends ambitious views—he must therefore be destroyed. The attempt has been made & Mr. Calhoun Green & Co. prostrated — But there is a debt due to my faithful Eaton from the State & from myself. I have asked Judge White to fill the vacancy occasioned by Major Eaton's resignation. I hope he will accept, should he there will be a vacancy in the Senate, and it is due to him that he should fill by the voluntary voice of the Legislature of Tennessee that vacancy. I want strength in the Senate *real not professed* men, who will Leg-

---

*it was filled before his letter reached some days.

islate with an eye single to the good of the country and not disturbe it with electioneering for the presidency. This act of the State of Tennessee would do more for the benefit of my administration than any act it could do—it would be more gratifying to me than all the favours it has bestowed upon me—it would be changing Judge White to his situation and Major Eaton to Judge White's for the two Sessions to come which will be the most important to me, and where I could have his aid, & to whom I could communicate freely & confidentially.

If Mr. Huntsville will unite in this thing with others who from the Eastern & Middle Tennessee will, & from whom, this suggestion of justice to Eaton, first comes—The Legislature will adopt this measure so pleasing to me & beneficial to the country as far as my administration is concerned. Sound Mr. Huntsman on this subject—you can freely say to him the confidence I have in Eaton & how pleasing it would be to me to have him in the Senate. You can say all I write, but not that I have wrote to you upon this subject. I leave the matter to you & my confidential friends—read this, make notes from & then burn it.

      Yrs affectionately,
        A.J.

P. S. Major Eaton will not offer himself—to be beneficial it must be a voluntary act of the Legislature. *Mind this*

(This letter is folded about 5 in. x 3 in. and on the back thereof is the following:)
    CONFIDENTIAL
     SAML. J. HAYS ESQ.
      JACKSON
       WESTERN DISTRICT
        TENNESSEE

To Mary Eastin

(Private)
       Washington May 10th 1831[2]

Dear Mary:

Finding from a letter lately received from Major Donelson, that he is not returning here, my son will set out in a few days

---

[2]Used through the courtesy of Lucius Burch, Memphis, Tennessee, Mary Eastin, a niece of Mrs. Jackson, married Lucius Polk.

for *home,* (delightful sound) to arrange some business there for me. I have directed him to hand you a favorite ring of your dear aunts, with the picture of Washington, it was highly esteemed by her, as such, I present it to you, wear it for her sake, & for mine.

How often have I admonished without avail my connections that a house divided against itself cannot stand. From the deep rooted hatred expressed by Major A. J. Donelson against my old & faithful friends, admonishes me, that his views, friendships, feelings, & attachments, are so discordant with mine, that we cannot harmonise—he calls my friends, with indignant feeling, "Lewis & Co", in which I suppose he means to include all those who proved faithful to me, & would not aid *Calhoun & Co.,* in widening the pit prepared for me. These are the men long tried in friendship by me, found to be jewels of great price, with whom I hope to live as long as I am permitted to breath, in friendship. These are those, with whom he cannot associate in friendship, & extend to them the same comity, as part of my family, as he does to his new acquired friends, therefore withdraws from me. Be it so—he says he has gone home, delightful sound, how grateful to my ear, where, as he cannot associate with my associates, & friends,—(and as I never wish to interfere with the friendship of others) I wish him, & his dear family, all the happiness this world can bestow—but I think I have a right to exclaim with the psamest, 41, 9th "Yea, mine own familiar friend, in whom I trusted, which did eat of my bread, both lifted up his heel against me." May his new friends and associates prove as true to him, as my old ones have to me, & to him, and he will *find in them a treasure*—old friends never ought to be changed, for new. The course of A. J. Donel etc. has been a source of great disquietude to me. You know, how often I brought to their view the old, but valuable adage "that a house divided against itself cannot stand." My admonitions it appears have proved unavailing, and how I regret to see Daniel Donelson arayed in a voluntary certificate against the husband of a favorite daughter of his deceased uncle, to whom, every branch of the family owe a debt of gratitude for his parental care of them, and the estate. It matters not whether the certificate injures Burton or not, it is sure to injure Daniel—social conversations, never ought to be revealed, but social conversations between relations, never ought to be the subject of a certificate, for the benefit of a stranger, in an angry dispute with a relation. I therefore sincerely regret to see Daniel Donelson placing himself in this situation, which will injure him in the end, more than Mr. Burton.

You no doubt will be astonished at the change of my Cabinet. A few words will explain. It is well known to you, that they members of it, come in with the utmost harmony good feeling & friendship, but from some cause to me then unknown, but now well understood, that harmony ceased, and because I would not in the first instance bring around me such men as would become subservient tools to Mr. Calhoun & his ambitious views, there has been a constant secrete intrigue carried on to athwart all my recommendations & views, & frustrate every one, & every thing that interfered with this their object— hence Major Eaton being my confidential friend, was to be sent out of it, & disgraced, and render me less popular with the nation. Into these secrete plans, entered, many of my professed, but hypocritical friends—& hence arose the great animosity pretendly against Eaton, but really against me, to foster Calhoun's views, (a man who I *now* know can with a face of friendship smile, when he holds the secrete & poisoned poinard, to stab you to the heart). I was found too stubborn to be bent to their views, Eaton, I would not abandon. Then, other plans were resorted to—the first was to prevent congress from carrying into effect any thing I had recommended, & the second Mr. Van Buren to be frustrated—every secrete intrigue to this end, & to bring Calhoun in as President at the end of 4 years was resorted to—every thing was prepared in the utmost secrecy— Calhoun's Book was printed, but retained for Duff Green's election—in the mean time, Togwell & Tyler the better to insure success of the plan makes the attack upon Van Buren and myself, Togwell vouches, that Buren and Ingham, could not have been operating to the appointment of the agents to the port, & Tyler, that Govr Branch could not. This was not true however, still it was not contradicted by any, until Major Forsyth speech was made; that placed the facts fairly before the nation; but before this, the effect of the attack was bad— letters were written to every part of the country, & every exertion was made to get up a dinner for the vice president at Richmond, & to prepare the Legislature of Virginia to announce

Mr. Calhoun a candidate for the presidency. Green was elected printer with the full exertions of Mr. VanBuren & myself; The Book was instantly published with explanatory notes, Calhoun repaired to Richmond to eat the Dinner, & be proclaimed president. Mr. Calhoun was attended by a few, who are *now* known, or part of the Judases of the day—But lo, & behold, the dinner was not served, the Legislature, with all the influence of the Governor, could not be wielded to these views, and Mr. Calhoun & Duff Green, are perfectly nullified by their own intrigues & want of principle. Mr. VanBuren was constantly assailed, the Cabinet was divided, and him & Eaton soaring above the sordid, selfish, feelings of office, but prompted by that sure patriotism that only accepts office to be useful to their country, that harmony might prevail in the administration, determined to resign. To part with these men, who had laboured with so much zeal and ability, to aid me in placing my administration on the highest ground, & with an eye single to the prosperity of the country, was a trying case to me. The reasons offered were so substantial & sound, that I was obliged to subscribe to them, & agreed to accept their resignation, but at the same time to reorganize my whole cabinet proper. They had all come in, in harmony, and it was due to all, that they should go out together, and this was due to the harmony of the administration, and to the country. You see, altho, the old coalition, combined with the new, (Duff Green, Calhoun & Co.) altho, they believed they had got me in great difficulty, how easy the virtuous & disinterested patriotism, of two high minded honorable men, who soar above sordid & selfish views, when the benefit of their country requires the sacrifice, by one move upon the political chest board, *checkmated* the whole combination & coalition—and destroyed their whole plans. How different the conduct of VanBuren and Eaton compared to that of Calhoun—the latter intriguing & combining with every one who he thinks can aid in his political maneuvers, as the comelian, to get into office—whilst the others pursue the dignified course of true patriotism. These men will meet the reward & approbation of the good, whilst a virtuous people must frown with indignation, at the mean, & low intrigues of the other—and still, these are the men that I must abandon, that my family cannot associate with, whilst Calhoun & his satelites are hugged to their bosom, and I am forsaken—such men I never can forsake, for unprincipled demagogues. If my family had adhered to mé, what a brilliant & peaceful administration I would have had, and how much delight with them. But it is different. Be it so—I hope, I still have energy enough to buoy me up throughout all & every difficulty that may surround me—and that an allwise providence, will continue to protect, & guide me through life. I have confidence my new cabinet will be a unit—I will make it so; and I will endeavor to get a private secretary that will be faithful & true, and aid me in carry out those great principles, upon which I have based my administration, and on which, I believe, the durability of the republic depends.

When I commenced, I only intended to write you a short note, but my thoughts wondered, & hastened me on into a dish of politics, not suited to a female taste—but as it is for your own eye, not to become the subject of a certificate for publication, I send it, without correction as the sudden impulse of the moment.

Will you write me whether you have ever rec'd the dress I sent by Daniel for you. I would have sent you another, but really as I had heard nothing of that, I forbore. Give my respects to your Grandmother & all my friends and connection, kiss little Jackson, & the two Rachels for me & believe me yr friend,

ANDREW JACKSON

P. S. Is your Uncle Coffee & Mary, and your Uncle McLamore and his Mary coming on. I would be happy to see them, & you with them—Present my compliments (affectionately) to them their Ladies & families—nothing would give me more pleasure than to see them & you here—Say to your Uncle McLamore I would like to hear how he is getting on with his business.

A. J.

Miss Mary Eastin
    Tennessee
  (Private)

To Colonel Charles I. Love
PRIVATE
Washington, Septbr 7th, 1835[2b]

Dear Col.:

I have received your letter of the 23rd & 26th ultimo giving me a full description of the progress of my house and the prospect of my crop & health of my family at the Hermitage—for this continued mark of friendship and attention to my interest in my absence I make you a tender of my sincere thanks—was it not for your kind attention and that of my friend Col. Armstrong I cannot say what would become of my interest there. I fear it would be a place of want, instead of what it was, and now has the appearance of again becoming, should I live to become freed from office & return to it—I, therefore, and my son, must be more indebted for your kindness thus displayed than under different circumstances.

I wrote you & the Col. about my s—d & top. I am fearful it will not be in time to bale my cotton early, and I fear none but cotton early in market will obtain the present prices—I therefore beg leave to ask you and with Col. Armstrong to this subject—My son will be with you by the first of October—he and Sarah is now in Philadelphia laying in furniture to replace that which has burned in the upper story of the house, which when enumerated amounts to more than was expected—as soon as he returns he will set out for home leaving Sarah with me.

I send you an extra Globe that will give you all the news here—my health has been much benefited by my trip to the Rip Raps, but the intense labour since my return has brought on me a return of my distressing headache—I am counting the days of my servitude. I might say my involuntary servitude, for I never wished to be here, and I was counting on a state of ease and quietude for the balance of my term but the extraordinary attempt to divide the democracy & republican party keep me in troubled water the balance of my term—but it has and will fail, and the dupes of the opposition will find themselves disappointed and forsaken by their old democratic republican friends as Burr found himself when he threw himself upon the opposition, to gain the presidency.

[2b]Used through the courtesy of the Librarian at University of the South, Sewanee, Tennessee.

I am now within 18 months of freedom, and if providence permits me to live I will be a happy man on that day—for I am sure the great Democratic Republican party will sustain me against all attempts of the opposition to destroy my administration, and my fame with it. Let Tennessee do as she may—but I have confidence that Tennessee, old republican Tennessee, who brought me out will never abandon her principles, to gratify any who may appostisise from theirs, for the sake of office. I sincerely regret the situation of our friend, Judge White—the opposition having used him to divide our ranks, have dropped him, and put up Gen'l Harrison or Clay, stool pigeon for the same object the Judge was used—neither of whom has any hope of being elected—and my belief is that Harrison cannot get a single state and the Judge but Tennessee, and from the recoil that is taking place, not even Tennessee. I told Mrs. White all this and requested her to say of him, he had got a false position, and if he did not snatch himself from it, he was probably lost—had he thrown himself upon the republican party, how different would have been his present situation—but he has made his own bed, run counter to the wishes of his old friends, and I tell you he is lost.

My kind regards to you and all your aimiable family & believe me yr. friend,

/s/ ANDREW JACKSON.

Col. Charles I Love.

To Major L. I. Polk
Hermitage   March 12th 1838[3]

My dear Sir:

I had the pleasure to receive the pedigree of your fine horse —*His blood is good,* altho, his performance on the turf has not equalled some others. I would like to patronise him but the distance is too great, & my health too bad and our farm requiring all attention, with the macadimise road, that our force can admit.

Your agent was good enough to call & show me your fine gray filly. She is a fine animal, & if she has plenty of foot, will make a good runner. My fine filly, Pinsilva, I am doing nothing with this Spring—I had her in the hands of Mr. Williams

---

[3]Used through the courtesy of Lucius Burch, Memphis, Tennessee.

last fall, but she came home *in bad order,* so that she could not appear on the turf—wish you had her to make a trial with yours—mine has foot enough to run with any thing. My ill health has determined me to put her to breeding. But should you wish, if you have not such a one, to have her to make a trial with your gray, she is at your service, and I will put her to breeding afterwards. *I am entirely off the Turf.*

I have been very ill, sick almost to death,—grateful to a kind providence, that I am still in the land of the living. Present me affectionately to your dear Mary & kiss for me my dear little children, & believe me very respectfully your friend.

ANDREW JACKSON

Major L. I. Polk,
Hamilton Place
Maury County,
Tennessee
Doctor Saml. Donelson.

To Samuel Jackson Hays
Hermitage
December 10th, 1839.[4]

My Dear Sam'l—

I am happy to hear from Mr. Chester's old Moses that you had entirely recovered your health and strength before you went down to your place and that Mrs. Hays and children are all well. We now enjoy health here, but myself, and mine is checkered as usual, but the present invitations of the citizens of New Orleans and those of the State of Mississippi, with the great solicitations of our friends elsewhere, have induced me to make the trip to New Orleans on the 21st of January. For this purpose I will be at Memphis on the 2nd of January next, and then if it was convenient for you and Dr. Sam'l Donelson to meet me, it would give me pleasure to see you. Perhaps it would be convenient for you to go down to New Orleans with us. I would be pleased to see Dr. on a little business. Please see the Donelsons and give my regards to them and Mrs. John Donelson's Emily. Present Mr. and Mrs. Jackson's kind re-

---

[4]Used through the courtesy of Samuel J. Hays, Memphis, Tennessee. Mr. Hays is a direct descendant of Samuel Jackson Hays, the nephew of Rachel Jackson. This letter is published in Bassett's *Correspondence,* VI, 42.

spects with mine to Mrs. Hays and kiss you dear children for me, and believe me your affectionate

Uncle
ANDREW JACKSON

Major Gen'l Sam'l J. Hays.

To Major Lucius Polk
Hermitage
March 6th 1841[5]

Major Lucius Polk.

My dear Sir,

Having become too infirm to attend to raising blooded stock, and not having the wherewith at present to pay for the seasons of imported horses, I have come to the conclusion to dispose of my blooded mares. Therefore it is that I write you. My fine blooded blind mare Toir Desdemone, or Virginian, is not with foal, I therefore propose to let you have her, for the season I owe you. She is as thorough, & pure blooded animal as is in the United States. I sold a stud colt, and his sister for $1800. I own a filly four years old that I was offered one year ago $500 & refused it—both promised to be good runners—one very successful in Arkansas. This old mare is about eleven years old this spring, has a yearlin colt at her side. I do not wish to let her go to strangers for nothing, in your hands, with your fine blood horse she would be valuable. I therefore make you the proposal. She is in good order, and would be no trouble in a lot where there is water. She is a fine breeder. If you accept of the proposition write me soon & send for her so that she may be put early to the horse.

Present me very affectionately to Mary & and the dear little children, to whom Sarah & Andrew cordially unite, & accept the assurance of my kind regards,

ANDREW JACKSON

Major Lucius Polk,
Near Mount Pleasant
Maury County
Tennessee

---

[5]Used through the courtesy of Lucius Burch, Memphis, Tennessee.

To Samuel Jackson Hays
Hermitage May 4, 1841[6]

My dear Saml,

I am on receipt of your kind favor of the 29th utimo—am rejoiced to hear of the good health of yourself and family. May that best of earthly blessings be long continued to you and your noble family. Our dear little ones have been confined to their rooms for a fortnight with the hooping cough—they are better. Andrew and Sarah in good health—mine much checkered and several of our negroes down. We have had a bad varigated spring. I am just replanting my cotton. I fear we will have bad crops in this country this year unless our season proves better than present prospects indicate.

I rejoice to learn that the Democrats in your section of country are in good spirits. The death of Genl. Harrison I view as a providential interference to preserve our Union—the office seekers really destroyed him. You will see in the Globe the press upon him the Genl had not sufficient energy to say to his heads of Departments you shall not dismiss officers without my approbation, nor remove any without a fair hearing, and the complaints of the females whose husbands had been, or were about to be removed and remembering his pledges, killed him. Had he removed the first member of his cabinet, as I would have done, who attempted it without his orders, he would have been spared by providence. But an all wise providence does all things well, and it may be that he was removed to save our country from that scurge that hung over it.

I dislike the ambiguity of Tyler's address but it may have been policy for no man in Virginia was a greater States right man than he has been—against a national Bank, a high tariff, for protection, internal improvements by the general government, or the distribution of the proceeds of the public land. These things have been brought to his recollection by the republican presses and in Mr. Kendall's Expository in such an impressive manner that Tyler must sensibly feel, and his (Tyler) ambiguity is his address may save him from disgrace by causing him to act upon his former declared republican principles, should he all will be well and Webster and his

---

[6]Used through the courtesy of Ernest Edenton, Jackson, Tennessee, who is a direct descendant of Samuel Jackson Hays.

Federal party before one year will go down in utter disgrace, and our republican principles be perputrated, corruption put down in this Union forever *be* it *so*.

You democrats in the west ought to subscribe for Kendall's Expositor and Blair and Rives Extra Globe and the Congressional debates, to have them bound and placed in your libraries twenty years hence they will be immeasurebly valuable to the rising generation.

Mr. William Hall eight days past was brought out for Congress in opposition to Genl. Caruthers the wigg candidate I fear it is too late but if the democrats can be got to the polls to vote Hall may succeed.

The News from Gov. Polk is cheering, but the apathy of of the Democratic leaders in this District is humiliative. Therefore I repeat that I rejoice to hear that in the Western District you are alive to the good cause. Rous them up it is the duty of all, to hand down to prosterity that blessing of liberty bequeathed to us by our revolutionary fathers.

Business will lead me in a few days to Memphis on my way to see a gentleman in Mississippi about 25 miles from Memphis. When I will go out and spend a day or two with you and my friends the Donaldsons—I am not able to travel over land—go by water to Memphis.

With my kindest regards to you and your amiable Lady and dear little ones, in which Andrew and Sarah unite. I remain your affectionate uncle—

ANDREW JACKSON

Genl Samuel J Hays

To Richard Jackson Hays
Hermitage, February 10, 1843[7]

My dear Richard:—

Your letter of 28th ultimo is received, in which you inform me that you are about to commence the practice of law and remove to Missouri, and ask me to give you some advice to guide you in entering into life and association with strangers.

Although I can sacrely hold the pen from debility, I cannot but attempt to yield to your request, particularly as you

---

[7]Present location of original manuscript is unknown, but a copy was found among the papers of Richard J. Hays. This text is from a scrap book in the Hays family, now in the possession of Ernest Edenton.

are the only son of a deceased friend whose memory I cherish with lively emotions, and on whom a fond mother relies to be a prop and a comfort in her declining year.

Presuming that you have obtained a license to practice law, I would first advise you to remain in some well read lawyer's office for two or three months where you are until you have obtained a full knowledge of the practice, the form of writs, declarations and general and special pleadings so that when you enter the practice in a strange country you may be able to carry a suit in all its complications so that other well read practitioners may not be able to take advantage of your false pleadings and nonsuit you or by demurrer, defeat you. I wish you to recollect that having read law, and obtained a license, your labors are just begun, you must burn the midnight lamp if you expect to become eminent and place yourself at the head of the bar, wheresoever you may seat yourself. It is alone by industry, sobriety and economy that you can succeed well and for this purpose you must shun the society of every one addicted to dissipation of every kind, and of immoral habits of every description.

When you go to a new country you will be stranger there, I charge you to be careful of forming any intimacy with young men of dissolute habits, but treating all respectfully, but making confidants of none until you learn from an acquaintance that they are worthy of it. Many will make great pretentions of friendship, and offers of friendship who the moment they acquire your confidence and they see an opportunity of benefitting themselves, will betray, and destroy you. Conduct yourself with all new acquaintances, as though you had confidence in all, but reposing confidence in none, in any matter or thing by which they might injure you until you are confident from experience that they are worthy of it. These rules adhered to will carry you through life triumphantly. Take virture, religion and true morality for your guide, and never depart in all your transactions from the paths of wisdom, and you will live a useful life and obtain for yourself a happy immortality. This is what true wisdom will lead you to. That you may walk in wisdoms ways all your life and obtain a happy immortality is, the sincere prayer or your

Affectionate uncle,

ANDREW JACKSON

To SAMUEL JACKSON HAYS

Hermitage
May 27th, 1845[8]

Genl. Saml. J. Hays
My dear Nephew,

Some time gone by your affectionate letter was rec'd, giving us the pleasing information of one more being added to your family by the birth of a fine son. When rec'd, I was not able to answer it and to congratulate you and your dear wife on this joyous occasion, and to present it with my blessing. We have been looking for your promised visit with great pleasure and hope to see you and Mrs. Hays with such of your family as may accompany you at the Hermitage soon. Say to my friend Col Chester that I rec'd his kind letter, & have been much disappointed in his not visiting us before now, and am fearful that ill health has intervened in some portion of our connections at Jackson. Indeed we have heard that our amiable friend Dr. Wm. Butler was ill, but from all inquiries have not been able to learn the truth of this report. I am greatly afflicted, In addition to my former afflictions I am now attacked with a dropsy. I am swollen from the toes to the top of the head & rapped in bandages from my toes to my hips. My whole frame from my toes to my hips & abdomen is apparently a perfect jelly—a finger can be pushed into the flesh for an inch deep which will remain for minutes—added to this I have had a severe bowell complaint, which has brought on a severe attack of piles, accompanied with a continued sick stomach of nausea. These are my afflictions at present, and in what these complicated afflictions may end, God only knows. But my dear Saml, it is under such afflictions as these that religion holds us up, submitting to God's will with calm resignation. This is now my great consolation & I have calmly resigned to the will of that gracious Redeemer Who died for us that we might live with Him in a blissful immortality. I am visited with a shortness of breath that I cannot be helped across my room without being almost suffocated & gasping for breath. I am a little better this morning & have endeavored to drop you this hasty

---

[8]This was written just a short time before his death and is a wonderful illustration of his will power to the very last. Used through the courtesy of Mrs. Walker Hays, Memphis, Tennessee.

& incoherent scrawl. What a gracious Providence has determined on with regard to myself He only knows, I am perfectly resigned to His will—whatever it may be—May the Lord's will be done, not my will—He doeth all things *well* Blessed be His holy name. I rejoiced to know that you had got clear of your late Mississippi purchase—I trust you will be soon able to free yourself from debt—not until then can you call yourself a freeman—and can you ever make money whilst under pecuniary pressure, & added to this be subjected to insults by duns, & supercilious creditors—Get free, & keep free from owing any one, then you are independent of the pains of the world.

My whole household join me in kind salutations to you & your dear family in hopes soon to see you at the Hermitage, & request you to present us affectionately to all & every one of our connections at Jackson & believe me your affectionate uncle

(Signed) *ANDREW JACKSON*

P. S. I am unable to look over & correct this. A.J.

Letter is folded 5 in. x 3 in.; not enclosed in envelope; sealed with wax; on back thereof is the following, written in long hand the same as the letter:

- FREE -
ANDREW JACKSON
(free)   (stamped in green)
GENL SAML J. HAYS
JACKSON
MADISON COUNTY
WESTERN DISTRICT
TENNESSEE

On the side near the sealing wax appears the following in long hand:

Genl. Jackson died on the 8th June 1845, 11 days after the within was written.

(Signed)   S. J. Hays

DAVID CROCKETT LETTERS

To James L. Totten
Washington City[9]
17th of Decr 1827

Dr Sir

I take the liberty of writing you a line these lins leavs me well and I hope will find you enjoying good health we have done but little Business as yet and the oppinion is that thare will be but little done until after Chrisemas holladay we have not Set more than one hour in the day Sence I have been here I have presented the Petition for the Post rout from Troy to Mills Pint and thence to dresden by Tottons Wells Just as Soon as I can get the Rout accomplished I will write to you again and through you Mr. Drabilbass & Esqr Totton can be informed that I will appoint them Post master I have got James M. Gibson appointed post master at the great town of Fulton I went to Mr. McLane and he promised me that he would gave the appointment to Mr. Gibson and after wards he Sent me the recommodations of two more men and it was left to me to gave the appointment to who I pleased and I took the Responsabillity on my Self and gave the appointment to gibson I find a representative have power to appoint who they pleas I have started the subject of our vacant land on the third day after we went into session I have no doubt of the passage of the Bill[10] this session I have given it an erly start I have wrote to my editors a tolerable lengthy letter for Publication I wish to gave my constituants all information in my power you shall here from me again on all important matters I wish you to write to me and informe me of the tims in your country gave my best respects to all friends I must conclude with great Respects you abt Humbl servt

DAVID CROCKETT

James L. Totton

---

[9]From the original in the Curtis Bray Collection.

[10]The Occupant Bill that Adam Huntsman referred to so many times.

To James L. Totten
Washington City
n11 Febry, 1828[11]

Dear Sir

I Recd your polite favour of 13 Jany and pursued it with pleasure and will hasten to answer it these lines leave me well and I hope will find you in good health we are porgressing very slow with business owing to the great party spirit that exists here- on the great political question tho old hickory is like the dimond in the hill of no vallue until it is rued and polished So with Genl Jackson the harder they Rub him the brighter he Shines the administration party has made Several attacts on him and they all opporate in favour of Jackson we-have all got entirely easy here it is given up from all quarters that I can here from that the dye is cast and that Jackson will in a Short time begin to Receive the Reward of his merit. I can assure you that those heads of the Cabinet begins to treat the Jackson men with the utmost politeness I have the Subject of our vacant land under train and have but little doubt of obtaining a Relinquishment this Session I think in a few weeks you will find that I have been Successful I will give the earliest information of the fate of the bill I have also- the mails Rout from Troy to Millses Pinte thence to Dresden before the proper committee and the Chareman of the committee informed me that they had examoned the case and find it Reasonable tho they have not Reported nor will not until near the ead of the new Routs in the United States thare is no chance of hurrying business here like in the legislature of ah State thare is Such a disposition here to Show Eloquence that this will be a long Session and do no- good I will not tier your patience Reeding my Scrall you wrote to me to Send you and Esqr White the Telegraph I went to the office and ordered them you will get them Regular I wish you to write to me often and lengthy tender my best Respects to all friends excuse my Scrall I am in a great hast I Remain with high esteem your friend & Hubl Servt

DAVID CROCKETT

James L. Totten

---

[11]From the original which belongs to Carlos Dew, Trenton, Tennessee.

To Dr. Calvin Jones
Weakly County, Tennessee   22 August 1831[12]

Dear Sir

I understand you are the agent for Calvin Jones for a tract of 2500 acres that lyes adjoining me in the Fork between Rutherford and Main Obion and I am informed you are authorized to give a lease on it or to sel a part of the tract. I have been compeled to sell my land where I live to try to pay my debts and I wish to take a lease in the North East Corner of the land adjoining the low grounds of the South Fork of Obion where I wish to take a lease is near the corner of the tract I wish to clear twenty acres and build comfortable cabbens and smoke house corne cribs and stables and dig a well and set out some fruit trees there is no water on it without digging a well if you will give me a good liberal lease I well make you a good improvement I may perhaps clear more than 20 acres it is very heavy timbered and will take hard work to open a plantation my reason for wishing to take a lease on it—it will be handy to move to it if I get able buy please write me the terms that I can have a small part in that corner my nephew will call on you and any arrangement you make with him will be satisfactory with me it may be that I may be able to buy before the lease is out if so should like to know the terms—I have not herd the result of my election from all the countys in the District I expect I am beaten,[13] I have one consolation I would rather be beaten and be a man than to be elected and be a little puppy Dog I have always supported measures and principles and not men I have acted fearless and independent and I never will regret my course I would rather be politically buried than to be hypocritically immortalized I contend that if the people of the Western District elected me to fill the station of an honorable Representative I done my best to fill their expectations but if they elected me to be a little puppy Dog to yelp after a party I have deceived them and would again if elected I have always believed I was an honest man and *If* the world will do me justice they will find it to be the case

Respectfully your obt sevt

DAVID CROCKETT

---

[12]Original in possession of Ed Knox Boyd, Bolivar, Tennessee.
[13]William Fitzgerald of Dresden was elected. The election was unsuccessfully contested by Crockett.

(Seal) To Colonel Thomas Henderson
Washington City   26th Febry 1834[14]

Dear Sir

Your favour of 2nd inst came safe to hand by the last mail and I will hasten to answer it Your request shall be attended to by the Payment of your subscription for the intelligencer. I handed Mr. Seaton your letter, and will in a few days send you a receipt for the amount I am glad to see that you are a candidate for Convention I hope you will beat old Blackhawk[15] to death I do hope the people of Madison will lay him away among the unfinished business.

I now see what occasioned him to come out so unprincipled against me in the two last Elections he thought I was so unpopular in that County that If he would come out against me that it would secure his present Election I have no confidence in him and I wish to see a man that Every Confidence can be placed in to fill that station.

We are still engaged in the political war upon the deposit question There is no doubt of the deposits being ordered back and it is said Jackson will veto the measure If he does I do believe the people will not submit to it I consider the question now pending before Congress is whether we will surrender up our old long and happy mode of government, and take a despot[16]—I cannot call it any thing else.

I have sent a great many documents to the district I hope the people will read and Judge fore thimselves I do consider it one of the dangerouses periods that have ever been recorded in our political history the South Carolina question was nothing to the present moment.

I must close in hast and

Remain with great respects your friend & obt servt

DAVID CROCKETT

Colo Thos Henderson
   Mount Pinson
      Madison Coty   Free
         Tenn   D. Crockett

---

[14]Original belongs to Tom McCorry, Jackson, Tennessee.

[15]"Blackhawk" nickname for A. Huntsman. They were speaking of delegates to Constitutional Convention of 1834 of Tennessee. Huntsman later beat Crockett for U. S. Congress.

[16]Andrew Jackson was Crockett's "despot."

To Col. T. J. Dobyns
Washington City,[16a]
27th May, 1834.

Dear Sir:

Your kind favor of the 8th inst. came safe to hand and I will hasten to answer it. I am in good health and hope these lines will find you in alike health.

I can give you but little political news more than you can see by the papers; you will see that our long and happy mode of Government is near at an end, we may from present appearances soon bid farewell to our republican liberties, we have completely the Government of one man and he has tools and slaves enough in the house of representatives to sustain him in his wild career. I do believe his whole object is to promote the interest of a set of scoundrels; hope these lines will find you in the alike country.

You recollect that I said in Brownsville in my speech that the whole object of Jacksons great zeal to get the moneys out of the United States Bank, was to get it placed where he could have the control of it to use for the purpose of making that political Judas, Martin Van Buren, our next president and you now see my prediction came true, you see Andrew the first King hold both Sword and purse and claims it as the other public property by the Constitution.

Will the people agree that no man, not even those that formed the Constitution, did not understand it, nor no man that ever wielded the destinies of this nation ever understood that Sacred article until Andrew Jackson mounted the throne I am much mistaken in the people of this country if they have forgot the Blood and treasure that was lost in relieving this country from a government of one man, and will fall back to the kingly powers. The truth is the poor Superanuated old man's vanity has prompted him to think that his popularity could stand anything. You state to me that the people is well pleased with my course, this is gratifying to me beyond measure and I hope you will tender to my friends my grateful acknowledgement for their complementary letter expressing their intire satisfaction at my course as their servant I never did know

---

[16a]S. G. Heiskell, *Andrew Jackson and Early Tennessee History* (Nashville, Tennessee, 1921), III, 18.

any mode of legislating only to go and do what my conscience dictated to me to be wright. I care nothing for any party more than to do justice to all.

The old man thinks he has put down the Bank of the United States and he has commenced war on the Senate, as he thinks that to be the only barior in his way to kingly powar. Let him once conquer the senate and he will put his foot on the Constitution and tell the Judicial powar to go to hell. I do believe this to be his calculation but I hope he may be mistaken. The Senate will save the Constitution and the laws of the country in spite of Andrew Jackson and all his minions around him.

I was one of the first men that ever fired a gun under his command, and I supported him while he supported his promised principles, but when he abandoned them I abandoned him and I have never regretted my course.

I have been trying for some time to get up my land bill, but we have not even passed the appropriation Bills and there is no chance to do anything. I know of no opposition to it if we could get to act on it.

I must close with great respects.

I remain your friend and ob't servt

DAVID CROCKETT

Colo. T. J. Dobyns, Brownsville, Tennessee.

P. S. We are at the contested election between Moore & Letcher; if it is made a party question Moore will get it and if it is decided on Justice, Letcher will get it.

D. C.

To JOHN ASH

Washington City
27th December, 1834[16b]

Dear Sir:

Your friendly favor came safe to hand two or three days ago, and I would have answered it before this, but I had a desire to inform you the feeling of the house upon the French question as you had a desire to know how parties stand upon that question. There is no report made yet to either house so that I can only give you my own opinion.

[16b]Used through the courtesy of Librarian at the University of the South, Sewanee, Tennessee.

When the reports is made we will then see how many blood hounds the hero of two wars will have to go with him in involving thirteen millions of souls in a war with a people that have always been our best friends and in fact helped us to obtain the liberty we now enjoy when we know that the executive of that nation is doing all in his power to have the appropriations made the fact is I do think his measure was too rash. If our minister Reeves had not come home and boasted that he had over reached the French in the treaty and our papers got to boasting about it to show that Jackson had done more than Mr. Adams could do the French would not have objected to the payment at all.

My own opinion is that the recommendation was made for no other purpose in the world than to raise an excitement to draw the public attention from an investigation of the abominable and corrupt measures of this Administration. They knew that if the public were to get in possession of their iniquituous acts and know the true situation of this once happy country it would blow them all to the devil. I do hope the people will view the measure as it deserves. It certainly will awaken the people if anything will—but I have almost lost all hopes from the late elections in New York & Pennsylvania. It appears as if Jackson can do anything he pleases and the people will say he is right. Jackson says so—I am not certain that the people will object to being transferred by Jackson over to that *Political Judeas little Van.* If so I have sworn for the last four years that if Van Buren is our next President I will leave the United States. I will not live under his kingdom and I see no chance to beat him at present everything appears favorable to him and I am sorry for it. I have said for the past four years that I would vote for the devil against Van and any man under the sun against Jackson and I have got no better yet.

I expect in a few days to be able to convey the good news to my District of the passage of the occupant land Bill. It is the first Bill that will came up and I have no fears of its passage. Every member from Tennessee that I have talked to says it will pass—if SO it will bless many a poor man with a home —I see that they have got out A. Huntsman and Dr. McMears both and if they run I am of opinion we will beat them. I cannot tell—I am determined to do my duty if I should never see another Congress—I am must close by subscribing myself your friends and

       Obt Servant
        /s/ *DAVID CROCKETT.*

John R. Ash.
  To WILEY AND MARGARET FLOWERS
       Saint Agusteen, Texas[16c]
       9th January, 1836.

Mr. Wiley Flowers,
Crockett P. O.,
Gibson County, Tennessee.

My Dear Sone and daughter:

 This is the first I have had an opertunity to write you with convenience. I am now blessed with excellent health and am in high spirits, although I have had many difficulties to encounter. I have got through safe and have been received by everyone with the open cerimony of friendship. I am hailed with a hearty welcome to this country. A dinner and a party of ladys have honored me with an invitation to partisapate both at Nacing docher and at this place. The cannon was fired here on my arrival and I must say as to what I have seen of Texas it is the garden spot of the world. The best land and the best prospects for health I ever saw, and I do believe it is a fortune to any man to come here. There is a world of country here to settle.

 It's not required here to pay down for your League of land. Every man is entitled to his head right of 400-428 acres. They may make the money to pay for it on the land. I expect in all probability to settle on the Border or Chactaw Bro- of Red River that I have no doubt is the richest country in the world. Good land and plenty of timber and the best springs and will mill streams, good range, clear water and every appearance of good health and game aplenty. It is the pass where the buffalo passes from north to south and back twice a year, and bees and honey plenty. I have a great hope of getting the agency to settle that country and I would be glad to see every friend I have settled thare. I would be a fortune to them all. I have

---

 [16c]Original in the possession of J. D. Pate, Martin, Tennessee. The letter was written to his great, great grandmother. Located by J. W. Rankin and librarian of University of Tennessee Junior College.

taken the oath of government and have enrolled my name as a volunteer and will set out for the Rio Grand in a few days with the volunteers from the United States. But all volunteers is entitled to a vote for a member of the convention or to be voted for, and I have but little doubt of being elected a member to form a constitution for this province. I am rejoiced at my fate. I had rather be in my present situation than to be elected to a seat in Congress for life. I am in hopes of making a fortune yet for myself and family, bad as my prospect has been.

I have not written to William but have requested John to direct him what to do. I hope you will show him this letter and also Brother John as it is not convenient at this time for me to write to them. I hope you will all do the best you can and I will do the same. Do not be uneasy about me. I am among my friends. I will close with great respects. Your affectionate father. Farewell.

DAVID CROCKETT

To Wily and Margaret Flowers.

TENNESSEAN IN TEXAS IN 1843

Any West Tennessean who went to Texas is of interest to Madison Countians. Therefore the following event is recorded in this volume:

In 1842 Mexico sent two armies into Texas on raids. General Somervell had charge of the Texas forces sent to meet the Mexicans and, under him, they marched to the Rio Grande, opposite the town of Mier on the Mexican side of the river. The Texans first numbered about 700, but a great number of this force was permitted to return to home. A battle occurred at Mier. The Mexicans numbered about 2000, the Texans only 265 and, it will be seen, had little hope of success. In this battle 16 Texans were killed and 20 wounded. The little band of Texans, as prisoners, then started to the City of Mexico, and on February 10, 1843, two hundred sixteen Texans entered Salado, where the two forces met and 173 of the Texas forces were captured. On March 24, 1843, General Santa Anna gave orders that every tenth man must be shot.[17]

The prisoners were paraded through the streets of Salado and each was then required to draw a bean out of a box containing 159 white and 17 black beans. Those drawing the black beans were taken out of the ranks and securely guarded. They asked to be shot in front, but this poor boon was denied them. Such as were Catholics accepted the services of a priest; the others requested one of their number, Robert Dunham (of Tipton County, Tennessee) a pious member of the Methodist Church, to pray for them. He knelt down and offered a most fervent prayer. Religious services having been concluded, the men were blindfolded and tied, and made to sit down with their backs to their executioners; when the word was given— Fire! All were killed but young Shepherd, who, though still

---

[17]This information is used through the courtesy of Joe V. Williams, Chattanooga, Tennessee, who gathered the information used here.

alive, feigned death, and during the night crawled off. He was subsequently recaptured—and shot.

The black beans had been placed on the top, and the officers required to draw first, but some of the officers who had drawn black beans escaped.

The names of the victims: Wm. Eastland, Robert Dunham, L. L. Cash, James D. Cocks, Edward Este, a brother-in-law of D. G. Burnet; Robert Harris, Thomas L. James, Patrick Mahon, James Ogden, Charles Roberts, Wm. Rowan, J. L. Shepherd, J. M. N. Thomason, James H. Torrey, James Turnbull, Henry Whaling and M. C. Wing.

The following two letters are from a member of that band of men who met death before the Mexican firing squad:

Matamoras January 11th 1842[18]

Bailey, Peyton
  Dear Sir

Although our acquaintance has been very limited but the friendship you have ever expressed for the family and the ties of blood together with my present situation embolden me to address you.

I am now a prisoner of War in this place together with some two hundred others the particulars of the Battle and our surrender you will learn through the Mexican papers. My motive in addressing you is to request you to write to my Mother and inform her of my situation. We are destitute of clothing and without means of obtaining any the length of our term of stay here is very uncertain but it is thought by many that we will start for the City of Mexico in a few days but I think it more than probable that we will remain here for a month at least. Any assistance you may render will be thankfully received and ever remembered with gratitude by

ROBERT HOLMES DUNHAM
Mexico

Dear Mother

I write to you under the most awful feelings that a son ever addressed a mother for in half hour my doom will be finished on earth for I am doomed to die by the hands of the

---

[18]From the original letters which were secured through the courtesy of Judge R. H. Baptist, Covington, Tennessee.

Mexicans for our latest attempt to escape the orders of Santa Ann that every tenth man should be shot we drew lots I was one of the unfortunate I cannot say anything more I die I hope with firmness farewell may God bless you and may he in this my last hour forgive and pardon all my sin A. D. Hedonburg will should he be able to inform you farewell.

Your affectinoate son
R. H. DUNHAM

POE-TOMLIN CORRESPONDENCE

John Tomlin, an early settler in Madison County, the postmaster in 1840, is remembered by persons away from the county because of a correspondence that he had with Edgar A. Poe. Tomlin wrote poetry and novels. He hoped that Poe would help him get some of these published. Poe knew that Tomlin was a man of easy circumstances and he wished to start a magazine of his own. Thus, each had his own reason for continuing the correspondence. It is not thought that the men ever met in person. The following letters are self explanatory of the friendship. A sample of Tomlin's poetry is quoted. Poe needed friends with money, so Tomlin's poetry was published. This friendship has interested several scholars in the past and so meager has been the information that the writer has endeavored to assemble as much of the correspondence as could be obtained, whether some of it had been published or not. The original letters of Tomlin are in the Boston Public Library. Tomlin is an interesting character, for he did get some of his work published and he did know the literary men of the day.

Tomlin To Poe

Jackson, Tennessee[19]
October 16th 1839

Mr. Edgar A. Poe
  Dear Sir
  The Manuscript story of "Theodoric of the Amali" is with diffidence submitted to your better judgment for an opinion. A "_____" hopes of future celebrity in his yet untrodden paths of Fiction, depends almost entirely on the success of "Theodoric of the Amali." How fair the portracture

---

[19]Tomlin to Poe Letters published through the courtesy of Boston Public Library.

of the "Comito" bears to that of Theodora, you will better determine on a careful examination of the piece.

The Author of "Theodoric of the Amali" would feel proud of having Edgar A. Poe as a correspondent.

In haste, he is
Your most obedient
JNO TOMLIN

POE TO TOMLIN
Philadelphia, Sep. 16, 1840[20]

Dear Sir,

Your kind letter, with the names of nine subscribers to the Penn Magazine, has only this moment reached me, as I have been out of town for the last week. I hope you will think me sincere when I say that I am truly grateful for the interest you have taken in my welfare. A few more such friends as yourself and I shall have no reason to doubt of success.

What you say about "The Devil's Visit to St. Dunstan" gives me great pleasure. I was thinking in what manner I should ask of you some such favor as you propose in sending me this "true history"—but was afraid of making too many demands at once upon your good nature. Your offer, therefore, is most a propos. I shall look anxiously for the tale, and will assuredly be proud to give it a conspicuous place in the opening number of the Magazine.

With high respect, I am,
Yr ob st.
EDGAR A. POE

Jno Tomlin Esqe

TOMLIN TO POE
Jackson, Tennessee
Nov. 22, 1840

Edgar A. Poe, Esq.
MY DEAR SIR,

As the time will soon be here when the subscribers in this place will have to pay for your *Magazine*, I must beg of you,

---

[20] James A. Harrison, *Life and Letters* of Edgar Allen Poe (New York, 1903), 57. Published through the courtesy of Thomas Y. Crowell Company.

at some early period to inform me, if Tennessee money is current in the ordinary business tranactions of your city. It is possible that I may thro' the Branch of the Union Bank at this place, obtain a check on some one of your Banks. If Virginia, N. Carolina, or S. Carolina money is more current in Philadelphia, than Tennessee, I shall certainly obtain the one that you may mention, as preferable.

Will I not have to lay myself under an obligation to you, for some emendation of the Devil's Visit? I look with much anxiety for its appearance in the first number of your new work. I will not, I know be disappointed. The abiding interest which I feel for your welfare, gives at all times the most cheering hopes of your success. It cannot be that you will not succeed! For the warm hearted Southerners, by whom you are known, will not let the Work die for the want of patronage. They are your friends—for they know you well, and will sustain you.

Is W. Gilmore Simms of Charleston doing anything for you? Surely he is! He can aid you materially, and I have no doubt but what he will. Some years ago, he was my friend and gave me much good advice. The most pleasant walks I have ever taken in the fields of Literature, were made in his company. Since then he has far outstripped me, and I am where he was when he first commenced to ramble among the *Genii* of Fiction. Has Simm's last work, "The Black Riders of the Sante" ever been published?

When I was a boy, I used to love to hear the Author of "Millechampe" talk. He said much to interest one of my years. As I grew older, my reverence for the man increased, until in my own mind, I am persuaded, that I shall "never look upon his like again."

In a little while, some two or three months hence, I purpose visiting Nashville. While there I shall certainly procure other names to your work.

          I am Sincerely
              Your friend,
                  JNO. TOMLIN

TOMLIN TO POE

Jackson, Tennessee
March 13th 1841

Mr. Edgar A. Poe
Dear Sir,

Have you indefinitely postponed the publication of the "Penn Magazine?" If so your friends here are grievously disappointed. I know, that if you have abandoned entirely the notion of ever commencing its publication—the abandonment was caused by no ordinary circumstances. Again I repeat that your friends here are disappointed. If you have come to the conclusion on mature deliberation, that this is not an auspicious period for the appearance of the Journal, perhaps your friends here may possible forgive you.

At any moment, that you may deem any service of mine, necessary in the aiding or the carrying out to the fulfilment, of any scheme or plan you may project, believe that a call from you, on me, will receive the best attention of

Your friend,
JNO. TOMLIN

TOMLIN TO POE

Jackson, Tennessee
April 30th 1841

My dear Sir,

Will Mr. Graham publish the "Devil's visit" in his Magazine? Show him the M.S. and get his consent to publish it in the June or July No.

Your letter of the 15th instant was received on yesterday. Whenever I can be of any service to you be not *backward* in letting me know it, for I will, if in my power, always do any thing in aid of any enterprise or scheme you may have in view.

If John Tyler Esq, President of the United States, removes me from office for being a *loco-foco,* I will certainly be opposed to him and the measure.

Truly yours,
JNO. TOMLIN

Mr. Edgar A Poe

Tomlin To Poe

Jackson, Tennessee
October 29th 1841

My dear Mr. Poe,

Sugeant N. Talfound Esq, of London, says to me in his last letter of August the 11th 1841—"I transcribe my last effusion on an occasion very dear to me." The following Sonnet, composed in view of Eton College after leaving his eldest son there for the first time, is the effusion he alluded to.

I feel proud of having it in my power of sending to you from the pen of this high minded and gifted individual. Powerful as his intellect is, it is not more powerful, than his heart is tender and warmed by a parents' feeling! From the buried treasurers of his heart gushes sentiments full of tenderness and love and with a father's feeling he is carried to that distant day when his son takes his place in the toiling struggles of life. Thus he leaves him with a prayer to heaven, that he may pass its threshold without a blush—and with a confiding hope in its mercy (yet he speaks it not) he looks "thro the vista of long years" to his son's greatness.

With the sincere wish that this affair may prove as acceptable to your numerous readers as it will be gratifying to you in receiving it, I am dear Sir, with remembrance

faithfully yours,

JNO. TOMLIN

How often have I fixed a stranger's gaze
On yonder turrets clad in light as fair
As this soft lands, pleas'd to drink air
Of learning that from calm of acient days
Breathes round them ever; Now to me they wear
There ting'd of deared thought; the radient haze;
That crowns them thickens as with fonder care
And, by its fleckering sparkles; Sense conveys
Of youth's first triumphs,—for amid their seats
One little student's heart impatient beats
With blood of mine;—O God vouch safe him power
When I am dust, to stand on this sweet place
And, through the vista of long years, embrace
Without a blush, this first Etonian hour!

London, August 11th, 1841.

Tomlin To Poe

Jackson, Tennessee
December 1st 1841

I have Mr. Poe in my possession a communication from "Boz", in its nature so perfectly *unique* and in its construction so full of the most beautiful thoughts, that I can scarcely get my own consent for any other to see a sparkle of the rich genius in which it is embedded. He sent it to me as a token of his remembrance—and gratefully did I receive it and most sacredly have I preserved it.

As he is about visiting this country, I have concluded to suffer some of his own bright thoughts that have never yet seen the light of a garish day, to meet him on its threshold. In permitting other eyes than my own to see it, I have yielded an unwilling consent to duty, and but justice to the author, which under ordinary circumstances would not have been done. *His* original communication will be sent to you in time for publication in the February issue of "Graham's Magazine." If you see "Boz", while he is in America, give him my thanks for his notice of his distant countryman.

And receive yourself, for the notice you have taken of me in your last Magazine, the earnest prayer of an honest heart for your happiness.

Ever yours,
JNO. TOMLIN

Edgar A Poe

Tomlin To Poe

Jackson, Tennessee[21]
Decr 12th 1841

Dear Sir,

The lines on the first page were received by me a few days since annonomously with the request that I should have them published.

---

[21] An anonymous poet had paid tribute to Tomlin, saying that the style of his "Theodoric of the Amali" was a joy forever, but that his pen had seen broader plans and loftier themes than the base manners of degenerate man. Tomlin sent the whole tribute to himself to Poe

You will not Mr. Poe for one moment believe that it was my vanity that caused the *producing* of the Eulogy—nor will you believe that your warm-hearted friend, with all of the Southern chivalry, can, or will ever act in derogation of the high named of man.

Ever faithfully yours,
JNO. TOMLIN

Edgar A. Poe Esq.

TOMLIN TO POE
Jackson, Tennessee
March 1, 1843

My Dear Sir,

Since the death of Mr. White of the "Literary Messenger," I have often thought if you would take charge of it, what a great Journal it would become, under your conduct and supervision. With you at the head of the "Messenger", and Simms of the "Magnolia" (my two most valued friends,) we of the South would then have a pride in talking about our Periodical Literature. Does this suggestion accord with any notion that you have had on the subject.: I would really like to see you, untrammeled, at the head of some popular Journal of the South.

Pray, excuse these hasty suggestions, and believe me ever,

Yours sincerely,
JNO. TOMLIN

---

marked "for Graham's Magazine." The following lines of Tomlin's own work were also sent "for Graham's Magazine":

To Miss M. E. MacM. of Phila.
Was every drop of pearly dew
   The morning drinks from leafy bowers,
The richest gems the world e'er knew;
   Were all the drops of summer showers,
Like orient pearls that monarchs wear—
   And every one to me was given;
With the dear girl the price I'd share
   And still to thee be true as heaven!

Edgar A. Poe, Esq.

Tomlin To Poe

Jackson, Tennessee
July 2, 1843

My Dear Sir,

I had seen, before I received your letter of the 20 ult, Mr. Clark's announcement in the "Museum", of his withdrawal from the Stylus *project;* —and even before then, from your long and protracted silence, and in the absence of all evidence, save this had the belief that the devilish machinations of a certain clique in Philadelphia, had completely baulked your laudable designs. But I had not supposed that Morton C. Michael had joined in, with his *minnow* tribe of litterateurs, in their persecutions against you. I had supposed that between you, there existed an association, that was with him as, unselfish, as it was generous on your part. Your final triumph over this clique, will give me more pleasure than anything I wot of now.

I had solicited Mr. Simms to make the Magnolia, a notice of your project, which he has done, I see, in the June number. In his private letters to me, he speaks in high praise of your Endowments as an artist.

I had collected the materials, for several Biographical notices of our Southern Writers, and was getting them up in good style, when I learned the fate of your project. I will keep them on hand for you,—and in the event of your ever needing them, I will have a pleasure in furnishing you with them. In a notice of Mr. Hentz in the June number of the Magnolia, by my friend, the Honorable Alexander B. Meek, of Tuscaloosa, you will find that he has paid you a fine compliment. The idea of your getting up a Magazine was such a good one, and took so well, that I was greatly hurt on learning its abandonment.

I had caused to be noticed in various newspapers of the South and West, your project; and did see thro' these sources the high admiration in which my friends in those places, held your Endowments. Could you have once started, your success would have been complete.

Have you not in your city, some, that thro' a friendship which they feel not, are doing you much evil? I have had a letter quite lately, from one prefessing all friendship for you, in which some allusions are made to you in a manner greatly astonishing me.

W. Gilmore Simms writes me, that he will be in your city this summer. While there any attention shewn him, will be reciprocated by me. Should you at any future time, get up your work, I will be as willing then, as I have always been, to extend to you, in its behalf, the entire weight of my influence.

Affectionately yours,
JNO. TOMLIN

Edgar A. Poe, Esq.

TOMLIN TO POE
Jackson, Tennessee
Aug. 9, 1843

Dear Sir,

I have received from the Honl. Alex B. Meek, of Tuscaloosa, Alabama, a letter, which I herewith enclose, that is as mystical to me, as is any character left by the ancient Egyptians on their monuments, to puzzle the future Ages.

Believing that many things are possible with you, that is not believed in the World's Phylosophy, I have taken the liberty, which you will excuse, of sending the letter to you, with the belief that you will make something out of it. In conclusion allow me to say, that very many of our learned citizens, have endeavored, but in vain to solve it.

With sincere regard
Yours Faithfully,
JNO. TOMLIN

Edgar A. Poe, Esquire.

POE TO TOMLIN
Phila. Aug. 28, 1843[22]

My dear Sir,

I have just recd your letter, enclosing one in hieroglyphical writing from M. Meeks & hasten to reply, since *you* desire it; although some months ago, I was obliged to make a vow that I would engage in the solution of no more cryptographs. The

---

[22] George E. Woodberry, *Edgar Allen Poe* (Boston, 1885), 190-1.

reason of my making this vow will be readily understood. Much curosity was excited throughout the country by my solutions of these cyphers, & a great number of persons felt a desire to test my powers individually—so that I was at one time absolutely overwhelmed—and this placed me in a delima—for I had either to devote my whole time to the solutions or the correspondents would suppose me a mere boaster, incapable of fulfilling my promises. I had no alternative but to solve it; but to each correspondent I made known my intentions to solve no more. You will hardly believe me when I tell you that I have lost, in time, while to me is money, more than a thousand dollars, in solving cyphers, with no other object in view than that just mentioned—a really difficult cypher requires vast labors and the most potent thought in its solution. Mr. Meeks' letter is very simply solved, & merely shows that he misapprehends the whole matter—It ran thus:

This is the whole of Mr. Meeks' letter—but he is mistaken in supposing that I "pride myself" upon my solutions of ciphers. I feel little pride about anything.

It is very true, as he says, that cipher writing is "no great difficulty if the sign represent invariably the same letters & are divided into separate words." But the fact is that most of the cryptographs (Dr. Frailey, for instance) were not divided into words, and moreover, the sign never represented the same letter twice.

But here is an infallible mode of showing Mr. Meeks that he knows nothing about the matter. He says cipher writing "is no great difficulty if the signs represent invariably the same letters and are divided into separate words." This is true; and yet, little as this difficulty is, he cannot surmount it. Send him, as if from yourself, these few words in which the conditions stated by him are rigidly preserved. I will answer for it, he cannot decipher them for his life. They are taken at random from a well-known work now lying beside me- . . . [Here follows Poe's cryptographs.]

And now, my dear friend, have you forgotten that I asked you, some time since, to render me an important form? You can surely have no scruples in a case of this kind. I have reason to believe that I have been realized by some envious scoundrel in this city, who has written you a letter respecting myself. I believe I know the villain's name. It is Wilmer. In Philadelphia no one speaks to him. He is avoided by all as a reprobate of the lowest class. Feeling a deep pity for him, I endeavored to befriend him and you remember that I rendered myself liable to some censure by writing a review of his filthy pamphlet called the "Quacks of Helicon." He has returned my good offices by slander behind my back. All here are anxious to have him convicted—for there is scarcely a gentleman in Phila whom he has not libelled, through the gross malignity of his nature. Now, I ask you, as a friend & as a man of noble feeling, to send me his letter to you. It is your duty to do this—and I am sure, upon reflection, you will so regard it.

I await your answer impatiently,
Your friend,
E. A. Poe

Tomlin To Poe

Jackson, Tennessee
Sept. 10, 1843

Dear Sir,

My friendship for you, and nothing else, has prevailed on me, to enclose you the letter of A. L. Wilmer, Esquire,—But I much fear, that in doing it, I have violated somewhat the rules that govern correspondents in such matters. Believing, however, that your great good sense, will but protect my honor in this transaction, I remain with affectionate regard,

Yours Ever,
Jno. Tomlin.

Edgar A. Poe, Esquire.
P. S. Return Wilmer's letter.

Tomlin To Poe

Jackson, Tennessee
February 23, 1844

Dear Sir,

I have had no letter from you, since I sent you the libellous letter of A. L. Wilmer. Did you inflict on him a chastisement equal to the injury he designed, by the publication of such scandals? Previous to the reception of that letter, I had entertained a good opinion of the "Quacks of Helican" man, and it had been brought about in a great measure by your Review of the Book. In his former letters, he not only spoke kindly of you, but seemed disposed to become your advocate, against the *litterateurs* of Philadelphia. I hope that you will forgive him, and that he will go, and "Sin no more."

Your Review of "Orion" in the February, or March No. of "Graham's", I have read with much pleasure. The article is one of great ability. I know of no writer whose success in life would give me more sincere pleasure than that of yourself.

Hoping soon to hear from you, I remain ever

      Your Friend,
       JNO. TOMLIN

E. A. Poe, Esq.

TO HELEN

By John Tomlin, Esq.[23]

I will not tell thee, that thou art
A Pleiad shining o'er my heart;
A glorious river that doth roll
A mighty current thro' the soul.

But ah! thou art to me those lights,
Which morning breaks on Mountain heights—
An Eden full of joys and smiles,
An ocean full of summer isles.

As holds the ocean to its shore
A memory holds thee evermore.
A fond affection now doth thrill,
Upon a heart that loves thee still.

Thou art that more than all to me
More than a stream without a sea,
For which—vain thoughts in me to hold—
His life, for faith, the martyr sold.

---

[23] *Southern Literary Messenger* (December, 1843), IX, 727-728.

MEXICAN WAR LETTERS OF WILEY HALE

The following letters were written by Lieutenant Wiley P. Hale, the adjutant of the Second Regiment of Tennessee Volunteers in the Mexican War. They furnish first hand information concerning the conditions of the army, the battle of Monterey, and the fighting preceding Cerro Gordo, at which place Wiley received his mortal wound. Colonel William T. Haskell and Lieutenant Hale were the first to reach the top of the hights and cheer the men on at Vera Cruz.[24] Lieutenant Hale, a West Point student, went to the theatre of war in 1846. His body was brought back to Jackson where the funeral was held in the Episcopal Church and interment took place at Riverside Cemetery.

>Camp near Someta, Mexico on
>the Rio Grande, July 26, 1846

Dear Mother

I again avail myself an opportunity of performing the delightful duty of writing to you. I have now written six letters home and have as yet only received one from Sal and one from Alleck Campbell. You cannot imagine the pleasure afforded me at the reception of these silent though expressive messengers from home. We marched from Brossos St. Iago four days since and are now encamped upon the banks of the Rio Grande almost half a mile below Loneta which was formerly a Mexican Village of some importance but is now only a deserted "Ranche" having been attacked, plundered and destroyed about ten years since by the Comanche Indians I was very much disappointed at the general appearance of the Rio Grande. It is a very muddy stream about twice the width of the Hatchie River and is very swift. There are no trees upon its bank, with the exception of [not legible] of low undergrowth called in

---

[24]Memphis *Daily Eagle*, April 7, 1847. The original letters are in the possession of Mrs. Harold Bond, through whose courtesy they are published. Lieutenant Hale was a great uncle of Mrs. Bond.

this county "Musquite Chapparral" which is so thick as scarcely to be penetrable by a man on horse back. The land upon the banks of the river is extremely rich and I think will rival the coast of Louisiana in the cultivation of sugar and cotton whenever the direction of American enterprise shall tend to this country. The grass of the Prairies and the undergrowth generally have the singular characteristic of belonging to the thorny tribe of plants, so that it is extremely uncomfortable to walk without high boots. Innumerable insects and reptiles of every hue, size and appearance infest our camp. Rattlesnakes are more abundant here than in any other place upon the globe. They seldom bite, however, without first being disturbed and not even then without giving warning to the offender with the rattles, with which Providence has so kindly provided them. I regret here to say that while at drill last evening, Tom Spurnier (?) was bitten by some very poisonous insect (supposed to be a spider or tarantula) and was during the whole of last night in a very critical situation. He appears to be much better this morning and Doct McKnight says he is entirely out of danger. We sat up with him all night. Stillwell has been very ill for about 3 weeks but is now rapidly recovering. I have not been upon the campagne. I consider this country one of the healthiest on the world. Had we been encamped at any place near Jackson and had undergone the same amount of privations or hardships we would undoubtedly have had much more sickness in our Camp.

Jo Freeman, Hiram, Max Theus, Dick Hays, Genl. Haskell, Alex Henderson, Pic, Allex Green and all others of the Avengers are in excellent health and spirits. We were invited last night to a "Fandango" at a Mexican "Ranche" six miles from our camp. The ladies who attended were not as beautiful as our own, but dress with great taste. Red is their favorite color. We have to converse with them by means of an interpreter as they cannot speak a word of our language.

I suppose that you have heard that all the troops who volunteered for six months only are to be disbanded and sent home, but as the Tennesseans are for the twelve months we will be retained until the end of the war which I think will be about Christmas. The Mexicans are reported to be fortifying themselves at the city of Monterey towards which we will (take) up our line of march in 3 or 4 days. I visited Bailey

Peyton a few days since at his encampment about two miles below us. He has been unwell and will leave for New Orleans in a few days. Tell Sal that "_____ Jones is in fine health and spirits. Josh Richardson, Capt. Murray, and Lieut. Hawkins are all sick—no more at present—

Farewell Dear Mother, Your affectionate Son
WILEY

Ned Johnson is here with a stock of goods. He has been appointed sutler (store keeper) for our Regiment. Ned, Pic, Dick Hays, and myself live in the same tent. Tell Sal to "Tell me some more" as Lizzy says—my love to all your
affectionate son
WILEY.

Camp Tennessee opposite Burita
Mexico, August 17, 1846

Dear Mother

I would have written to you several days sooner but for the fact that I have been so very busily engaged in assisting in the organization of our Regiment. Before commencing this letter I must again be permitted to complain of you all for not writing oftener. I have only received two letters from home since I have been in Mexico, and I have written regularly once a week. I wrote sometime since to Bob Taylor and to Sal but have not yet received an answer to either. We are still encamped on the banks of the Rio Grande but will leave in a few days for "Camargo" on our way to attack the city of Monterey. I am happy to inform you of the organization of our Regiment at last. The East Tennessee troops joined us about two weeks since and the election for field officers took place on the 8th inst. I know that you will be rejoiced to hear that Genl. Wm. T. Haskell has been elected Colonel of our Regiment. I give below the "Field and Staff" of the Regiment which you can give to Mr. Gates for publication:

2nd Regiment Tennessee Volunteers
Field
Wm. T. Haskell Colonel Commanding
David H. Cummings Lt. Colonel
  No major yet elected

Staff

Doct. David McKnight- Surgeon
Doct. Enoch P. Hale- assistant surgeon
1st Lt. Wiley P. Hale- adjutant
1st Lt. Wm. B. Davis- quartermaster
    Legrand M. James- sergeant Major
    Isaac Nichol- quartermaster's sergeant

You will perceive from the above that I have received the appointment of "Adjutant of the Regiment." I have now the rank and the pay of "Captain of Infantry." The gentleman who has been appointed assistant surgeon is from East Tennessee and is a distant relation of ours. I think that he was appointed through my influence. I wish you to send a paper containing the above list of officers to uncle Sam Hale in Va. The health of our [page torn] that part of our Regiment from the Western District is remarkably healthy for this climate, but the East Tennesseans who are principally from the mountains are very sickly indeed. We lost three men in 24 hours out of the East Tennessean Battalion. We have heard with sorrow and regret of the deaths of Wm. Purly, Thos. Connaly, and several others, and we all are extremely anxious about the health of our relations and friends in Jackson. We almost fear to open our letters for fear of hearing of the death or sickness of some one dear to us.

(The sick of the "Avengers" are all recovering very fast. Hiram and Maxcy Theus have both been sick but are now going about again. Stillwell also has recovered. Tom Spurrier who came near dying from the bite of a "tarantula" has entirely recovered.) Tell Mrs. Talbot and Mrs. Jackson that Jo Freeman still continues one of the most healthy and robust members of our company. Jo is one of the best soldiers I have even seen. All the rest of the company are in good health. I took a trip a few days since to the city of Matamoras in company of several of the Avengers amongst whom were Max Theus, Alex Henderson and Alex Greene. We all marched up to the city a distance of 30 miles on foot. As the weather is extremely hot here. We choose the night for our journey. After walking about ten miles from our camp we heard the noise of "fiddling and dancing" about a hundred yards from our road. We concluded to find out what it meant. We reached the place from whence the music proceeded. What a sight was there presented! It was a Mexican Fandango! There about a hundred Mexican Ladies and gentlemen assembled for a ball! They received us very politely and asked us by signs to participate in their amusements. We remained about three hours dancing with the dark eyed beauties of the Rio Grande and then resumed our march for Matamoras. We found the road very thickly settled with Mexicans who invariably treated us with great respect and kindness. The road however is said to be dangerous to travellers. The Mexican Ladies were not beautiful, not half so beautiful as ours. They dress however with great taste and neatness and they are remarkably graceful in dancing. They are very fond of walking, though—[end of manuscript]

Camp Tennessee opposite
Burita, Mexico, Sept 1st 1846

Dear Mother

I wrote you a few days since, but as our "sick" men are just about being sent home, I seize this opportunity of writing. The curling smoke of the "Rough and Ready" is now seen ascending the "Rolling Rio Grande" for the purpose of conveying our Regiment to Camargo, as I am writing so I will be compelled to write this note in haste. We send home about 125 men from this Regiment on account of sickness, 10 of whom belong to the "Avengers". Jo Echols or some of the other of our boys can give you all the news from our Regiment and the army generally. Last night a most horrible tragedy was enacted in sight of our camp. There have been stationed just below us on the river several other Regiments of Volunteers, among whom is a Georgia Regiment which was ordered on board of a steam Boat from Camargo. After two companies had got on the boat, a quarrel and finally a fight ensued among themselves. Another Regiment (from Indiana) was sent for to quell the riot. A regular engagement then took place between the Georgia and Indiana Regiments which lasted about 15 minutes during which Col. Baker commanding the Indiana Regiment was shot through the neck and some 8 or 10 men killed dead or thrown overboard the boats. Among the dead, I hear with regret is Lieut. Ogelsby of Indiana who was one of the most promising young officers in the service. The Georgians are now under guard and will be sent to Genl.

Taylor's headquarters for trial. The dead were buried this morning below our camp.

I wrote to Sal a few days ago by mail which letter will probably reach you some weeks before this. In that letter I gave her an account of the death and burial of poor Stillwell. Since his death Maxey Theus has been very sick and delirious all the time. Poor fellow! It was indeed distressing to hear him talk of his home and Mother! We start him home this morning in care of careful attendants but I fear that he will never recover. All of the "Avengers" who remain now are in good health and are anxious to prosecute the campaign against the Mexicans. I have never been unwell a minute since I left Jackson. Why don't you all write oftener? I have only received one letter from you since I arrived in this country. I fear that most of your letters never reach me on account of being misdirected. Hereafter direct your letters to me as follows:

Captain Wiley P. Hale
Adjutant of the 2nd Regiment of Tennessee Volunteers
Army of Invasion, Mexico.

I enclose some wild flowers which I gathered on the banks of the Rio Grande which I want Sal to give to Miss Caroline Haskell. Tell her I know not the emblem and as Flora does not mention them, she can give them emblems herself.

I must now close, as the boat is coming and I must attend to getting my Regiment ready to embark. Give my love to Sister, Sal, Bob, Lizzy, Tom and all the family.

Farewell Dear Mother
Your affectionate son
WILEY

Camp near the City of Camargo,
Mexico, Oct. 3rd, 1846

Dear Mother,

I wrote you a few days since informing you that we were still encamped at this place and also that Genl. Taylor had taken Monterey without firing a gun. A few days since, however, an express arrived from Genl. Taylor which places an entire different face to the whole affair. One of the hardest fought battles which has ever fallen to the lot of American arms, has taken place at Monterey! We have gained the city but have lost about 500 men! Genl. Taylor arrived at Monterey with about 7500 troops including the 1st Regt. of Tennessee Volunteers, on the 19th of Sept. Our Regt. had not been ordered up in time! On the 21st Sept. The attack upon the City commenced, it lasted three entire days and a part of the fourth. The 1st Regt. of Tennessee bore the brunt of the battle and suffered more than any other Regt. of the army! It went into the fight with 350 men and had 123 killed and wounded. Among the number I regret to say, are some of my most intimate friends. Your friend Bob Foster who commanded a company of the 1st Regt. has doubtless distinguished himself and escaped injuries from the battle. An armistice has been signed by Genl. Taylor and Genl. Ampudia the Mexican General by which hostilities are to stop for 60 days & our Regt. (the 2nd) is soon to move up to Monterey. *We will have a chance yet!* The hardest battle to be fought is yet to take place at Saltillo. We will certainly be there, then look out for a good report our boys are very bitter against Genl. Taylor for not ordering us up to Monterey before the battle. There are now, at this city, about 5000 troops, and about seven thousand more at Monterey, making in all about 12,000 to move against Saltillo.

Since the battle of Monterey, Mexican maranders have become quite troublesome to our troops! Two of our men belonging to Capt. Cook's company of Memphis went out a few days since hunting and were found in the evening murdered in the most shocking manner; their throats being cut from ear to ear and both shot through the heart! Col. Haskell and myself went out the next day with about 60 men on horseback to find the Murderers. We scoured the country for about 30 miles from the city, but could find no trace of the perpetrators of the deed who is supposed to belong to the *Banditti* of Genl. Capales lurking in this neighborhood. We searched several Mexican houses on our route, frightening the inhabitants very much, but I could find no trace of the robbers.

I have made great progress in learning the Spanish language and can now speak tolerable well. I have a Mexican servant who I find very valuable in this country. He wants very much to go to the United States with me when I return.

The health of the "Avengers" is rapidly improving. We have only lost 3 of that company by death, Stillwell, Goodrich, and James. Jo Freeman, Dick Hays, Hiram and Alex Anderson

Taylor's headquarters for trial. The dead were buried this morning below our camp.

I wrote to Sal a few days ago by mail which letter will probably reach you some weeks before this. In that letter I gave her an account of the death and burial of poor Stillwell. Since his death Maxey Theus has been very sick and delirious all the time. Poor fellow! It was indeed distressing to hear him talk of his home and Mother! We start him home this morning in care of careful attendants but I fear that he will never recover. All of the "Avengers" who remain now are in good health and are anxious to prosecute the campaign against the Mexicans. I have never been unwell a minute since I left Jackson. Why don't you all write oftener? I have only received one letter from you since I arrived in this country. I fear that most of your letters never reach me on account of being misdirected. Hereafter direct your letters to me as follows:

Captain Wiley P. Hale
Adjutant of the 2nd Regiment of Tennessee Volunteers
Army of Invasion, Mexico.

I enclose some wild flowers which I gathered on the banks of the Rio Grande which I want Sal to give to Miss Caroline Haskell. Tell her I know not the emblem and as Flora does not mention them, she can give them emblems herself.

I must now close, as the boat is coming and I must attend to getting my Regiment ready to embark. Give my love to Sister, Sal, Bob, Lizzy, Tom and all the family.

        Farewell Dear Mother
           Your affectionate son
             WILEY

            Camp near the City of Camargo,
              Mexico, Oct. 3rd, 1846

Dear Mother,

I wrote you a few days since informing you that we were still encamped at this place and also that Genl. Taylor had taken Monterey without firing a gun. A few days since, however, an express arrived from Genl. Taylor which places an entire different face to the whole affair. One of the hardest fought battles which has ever fallen to the lot of American arms, has taken place at Monterey! We have gained the city but have lost about 500 men! Genl. Taylor arrived at Monterey

Genl. Santa Anna was advancing with a large force against him, he (Genl Taylor) left Montemorrelles in a few hours after our arrival with the entire Regular army to reinforce Genl. Worth at Saltillo, at the same time dispatching Genl. Quitman with five Regiments of Volunteers (amounting to about 2500 men) against Victoria. We now are on our march to that city. Genl. Urrea is said to be encamped there with about 5000 Mexican Cavalry. We are anxious to meet with the *gentleman,* as he is the same individual who, ten years ago, ordered the Massacre of Goliad where Charles Haskell and his brave companions were so inhumanly murdered. If we find him at Victoria we will pay him up for old scores. Our present force consists of the 1st Regiments of Tennessee Volunteers, regiments of Mississippians, Regiments of Georgians, The Baltimore Battallion, and one Company of "Flying Artillery". Capt. Bob Foster is with us in fine health and spirits. He sends his best respects to you. He is one of my best friends here.

We have now been on the march about 3 weeks and are now within 3 days march of Victoria. There are various opinions about the prospects of a battle at that place. Genl. Urrea is certainly there but whether he will give us a fight or not is extremely doubtful. I think that he will ADSQUATULATE before we get there. If we do not have a fight at Victoria it is probable that we well continue on to San Louis Postosi to meet old Santa Anna himself. The health of our Regiment is now first rate. We left all of our sick at Camargo, and there is not now, a single sick man in the "Avengers". Hiram Tomlin, is as fat as a bear, as is also Jo Freeman, Alex Henderson, Sam Lyon, and the rest of the boys. We left at Camargo the following members of our company: viz; Bowling Cross, Wm. Browning, Woodle and Alexander Tyner, who were too sick to stand the march. We are now marching through one of the most delightful countries in the world. The road runs along paralleled with a range of tall blue mountains at the foot of which is a beautiful green valley intersected at distances of a few miles, with rivers and mountain streams of the purest water. This valley is thickly settled with wealthy Mexicans, who live in beautiful white cottages, surrounded by extensive fields of sugar cane, and groves of oranges, lemon, citron, pommeganate, and every other description of tropical plants and fruit. It is now the dead of winter and yet the weather is so extremely hot that I am compelled to go without my uniform except when on duty. I wish you could eat some of the fine oranges which I have now in my tent piled up as high as my head—they are twice as large as any I ever saw, and when pulled fresh from the trees of the finest flavor—you never see any in the United States to compare with them. The Mexicans don't seem to value them and cultivate them more for the shade than the fruit. The watermellons here are also very fine though not so large as ours in Tennessee. The Mexican Citizens along our route have been remarkably kind and friendly and furnish us with everything we want. Well, I have written this much without knowing when I may have an opportunity of sending my letter—However I will continue to write whenever I have time and send them all by the first opportunity—there is no communication with the States. I will finish this at Victoria. Farewell, dear Mother.

Your son,
WILEY

Ruins of Convent St. Malibran
One and one half miles from
Vera Cruz, Mexico, Feb. 18, 1847

Dear Mother,

I am still in the land of the living. I have scarcely time to write you anything so busy as we engaged now in the seige of the City. You must then excuse me if I give you some of the particulars of the fight, so far in a very brief style. We arrived here with 10,000 men from Tampico on the 5th inst. On the evening of the 9th we effected a landing on the beach about 2 miles south of the City. The whole force then encamped immediately on the sea shore where we landed. Just before daybreak on the next morning, our picket guard was attacked by an advance party of the enemy and a brisk skirmish kept up until nearly daylight. At 9 o'clock we took up our line of march to invest and surround the city.

The two Tennessee Regiments were in the advance. About 2 o'clock we reached the old ruins of St. Malivran which we took possession of—hardly had this been done before the Mexicans opened a heavy fire of musketry upon us from the neighboring heights. The fire was kept up for several minutes when Genl. Pillow sent the first Regt. Tennessee (Col. Campbell's) to capture a magazine about ½ mile distant—which was done in handsome style. The General then ordered the glorious 2nd Regt. (Col. Haskell's) to charge the heights and drive in the force which was firing upon us. We gave a shout and commenced the charge amidst a shower of bullets which fell around us like hail. You should have seen our boys as they rushed up that hill with one continual shout of defiance—though the hill side was covered with an almost impenetrable "Chapparel" (thicket) we gained the summit of the height in less than 15 minutes. The Mexicans who had been firing upon us from this height, fled precipitously upon our approach. We gave them a parting fire as they ran down the hill towards the city which was in full view—planted our flags—gave *three cheers for Tennessee and Col. Haskell!* Our shouts must have been distinctly heard from the walls of the city—for as the echod died away, a heavy discharge of cannon was pound into us from several forts, which we did not by any means take as a compliment but gave three more shouts as a token of our defiance. It was now nearly sun down and we encamped upon the hill although the cannon balls fell around us until nearly dark. We killed and wounded several of the Mexicans and up to this day have not lost a man from this Regiment. The next morning (the 11th) several other Regiments came up the heights, when the cannons again opened their deadly fire upon us. The Rifles (The Regiments to which Tom Ewell belongs) came up then and had one man struck dead by a cannon ball. On the same day a poor little drummer boy had his arm taken off with in ten feet of me. I was blind for several minutes from the sand which the ball threw in my eyes. The forts then commenced throwing bomb shells which exploded around without doing any damage until about 2 o'clock when Capt. Albertis of the Regulars had his head shot off. The same shot also taking off the leg of a corporal who was standing near the Capt. The cannonading has been continued from the enemy's forts every day since. We have kept possession of the hill, sleeping every night upon the sand without tents and having a shower of rain upon us every night. I regret to say that Capt. Jones accidently shot himself through the foot a few days since, the wound, however, is not dangerous—he is doing very well—our Regiment was moved from the hill this morning and have taken a position near an old convent situated upon the Railroad immediately before the gates of the city. The cannonading is still going on as I am writing—We have become used to it now. It is really a pretty sight to see the bomb shells wending their deathly way through the air upon their message of destruction! Our army now entirely surrounds the city in a few days more we will open our cannon upon the very walls and Vera Cruz will either be ours or Destroyed. The whole American loss so far as only been six killed and fourteen wounded. The loss of the Mexicans has been much greater—Genl. Morellos commands the city and Ganl. La Vega the castle. From the view which I now have of Vera Cruz it is one of the most beautiful cities I have ever seen. It seems to be built of churches and other splendid public buildings. So many are the spires and cupolos which is presented to the observer from without the walls. The castle of San Juan_____ is a magnificent work —with a spy glass we can see the men in the castle working the cannon (There goes another cannon at us!) These rascally Mexicans keep such a noise with their artillery that I scarcely know what I am writing—however we will pay them all back in the same coin soon—the north wind at sea for the last five days has prevented us from landing our large cannon but it is now becoming more calm and we have succeeded in landing some today. I think we will be ready by day after tomorrow to open upon the city. Then the fun will be upon our side—I will write you by every chance I get—I want you to look for the *Memphis Enquirer.* Mr. Irvin who is here and is one of the editors of that paper told me a few days since that he had written a very complimentary account of our charge upon the heights in which I am spoken of in a very complimentary manner. I hope in a few days to have the opportunity of doing something more. Genl. Pillow has also spoken very highly of Col. Haskell and his officers in his report to Genl. Scott. I wrote to Sal upon the first day of the fight and once upon our arrival off the city in the fleet. Give her my best love. My respects to Mr. Keatts, Tom and Sam Henderson, Ed Johnson and Jo Jenkins.

Maj. Bennett who travelled with you and Sal down the Mississippi desires to be remembered to you both. No more now.

God Bless you dear Mother, Your affectionate son
WILEY

EXCERPTS FROM DIARY OF JULIANA CONNER IN 1827

On June 7, 1827, Juliana Margaret Courtney married Henry Workman Conner of Mecklenburg County, North Carolina, and started to the West on her wedding journey. On June 10, she began recording the events of the journey in her diary. The Conners came to Tennessee and made visits in Nashville at the Hermitage, in Jackson at the home of Colonel Robert I. Chester. The difficulties of travel, the crude taverns, the coarse fare were a contrast to the social life that the Conners found at the Hermitage and in the Chester home in Jackson. The following are selections from a copy of the diary in the University of North Carolina Archives. These selections are published through the courtesy of the University of North Carolina Library, the diary having been presented to the library some twenty-five years ago by the late F. B. McDowell of Charlotte, North Carolina.

Tuesday 21 [August, 1827]—Rode to the river and crossed in the flat and walked up to the house which is kept by Mr. Garrett—there is a house built over the spring the water of which is extremely warm, from 95 to 105 degrees and of a considerable depth though I presume my size would not justify my making the assertion—dined there and returned to Richbourg's with the intention of proceeding on, but were prevented by rain. His home is a most romantic spot—the front just on the banks of the river of which it commands a fine view—the rear encompassed with mountains not 50 yards from the parlor door.

Wednesday 22.—Cross the river at the ferry opposite the house and after a ride of 2 or 3 miles bade adieu to the County of Buncombe with all the mountain scenery and entered on the limestone *rocks* of Tennessee—the water has a peculiar taste which habit renders agreeable, it is said to be extremely beneficial to health—the road although rough and broken was comparatively *good*—in the course of the day crossed the Fr. Broad 3 times and Pigeon River once—passed through Newport 25 m. a small town, one description will usually answer for all such—a main st. tavern, court house &c &c, stopped at Ellis's having travelled 31 miles—the appearance of the house offered nothing inviting to wearied travellers, but we easily learn to accommodate ourselves to exisitng circumstances and a log cabin of no excellent order is often hailed with pleasure and the cheer it affords partaken of with keen relish.

Thursday 23.—Went 12 miles to Dandridge to breakfast a most excellent public house kept by Ropar—everything very neat and butter which would not have disgraced a Philadelphia market—the cream and milk is extremely rich, it only requires attention to have it thus everywhere but lazy or careless people won't take the trouble—we then parted with our travelling companion Capt. C. and proceeded on 21 miles to Mouldens.

Friday 24.—We were not 10 miles from Knoxville, crossed the rived at Ramsey's ferry at the junction of Fr. Broad & Holstein and soon entered the town which covered a large extent of ground, has several streets, many large and handsome brick buildings—3 churches, court house, and is on the whole a place of some importance—the court had been sitting and were about to adjourn. Mr. C. was engaged with gentlemen on business during the day and I rested quietly in my room—stopt at Knoxville Hotel kept by Mrs. Jackson (not the Lady of the General)—in the cool of the evening walked out to visit the place—had a very pleasant visit from Mr. Rany and General Dunlap, quite a polished man, he brought a letter of introduction to General Jackson, as he observed the length of time which elapsed since Mr. C. had seen him might render it necessary or at least agreeable I expect much pleasure in seeing a man who now occupies so large a portion of the hearts, thoughts and time of so many—and who creates such a general excitement throughout our country. He is the idol of this State—none dare refuse him homage or suffrage with impunity.

Saturday 25.—A very cold morning for a ride of 10 miles to breakfast which created a keen appetite, house kept by Mr. Cox very neat, we observe a great improvement as we proceed West in the houses, fare, furniture &c., more neatness and some taste—lime is so easily obtainable that their rooms are whitewashed which looks more cheerful than the sombre colour of wood—we slept that night at Esridges, 33 miles from Knoxville.

Sunday 26.—Went to Himans, 13 miles to breakfast, we were now to encounter the Cumberland Mts., but although extremely steep the road was kept in good order principally causeway and far superior to those we had crossed in the Blue Ridge. Spencer's hill on the mountains is the greatest descent I have seen. We walked down it and it was with great difficulty that we kept a sure footing, it is I think a mile and were you to slip there would be no resting place until you reached the foot of it—from the summit of one of the highest mountains we had a most enchanting view of the world below for several hundred miles, our horizon was bounded by the summit of the distant mountains which soared above the clouds and vied with their ethereal blue—'twas a scene worthy the pencil of a

Claude Lorraine—stopped that night at Burke's after a day's journey of 33 miles.

Monday 27.—We were yet on the mountains but the road was so perfectly level that one could scarcely realize it. It appeared more like a valley encompassed with mountains which encircled you—covered with beautiful wild flowers—stopped at Dawson's to breakfast, but it was only an attempt as it was too indifferent to be relished even after a ride of 15 miles. Soon commenced gradually to descend in many places steep and rocky and we entered before dark the town of Sparta, having rode 40 miles. From its name the mind recalls associations of the place from whence it is derived, but I strongly suspect it ceases there and is no resemblance to be found elsewhere—we then met the stage. One of the passengers, Dr. Davis, a very intelligent gentleman from our State quite conversable and agreeable. Coming from our native State prepossess us to like a stranger, we feel as though we possessed one feeling in common.

Tuesday 28.—Left the town and rode to Rock Island, where we again met the stage. We all breakfasted there and proceeded on to McMinnville, 25 miles from Sparta—passed through it early in the afternoon and were in hopes of finding a house 9 or 10 miles where we could stop, but were compelled to ride 13 miles to Bates—a long ride of 40 miles and not a little fatigued.

Wednesday 29.—Rode to Danville, 8 miles, for breakfast. They have a great spirit for town-making (a new word) but I think it would be better or rather look better if would unite 2 or 3 of them together, it would certainly render them more deserving of a name—the roads rocky and hilly we did not reach Murfreesboro until late in the evening although only 20 miles 'tis quite a pretty place; number of good looking buildings, churches with spires &c, &c. Stopped at the hotel kept by Mr. Sublet very indifferent, the mistress not appearing to understand the domestic arrangement of a family.

Thursday 30.—Breakfasted at Searcey's expecting to enter Nashville early in the afternoon—'tis 32 miles from Murfreesboro, but the roads are so rocky that the horses scarcely go out of a walk, the jolting was equal to the road to the Warm Springs, even more fatigueing—the town has a very handsome appearance as you enter, several very beautiful county seats in the environs—college buildings just at the entrance—the brick here is so far superior to ours in color and shape that it adds much to the beauty of their buildings, which are large and handsome. We drove to Nashville Inn (the best public house in the place) kept by Mr. Emmett. There is a separate establishment for ladies—rooms handsomely and fashionably furnished, an elegant piano and everything comme il faut. On alighting we were shown to a handsomely furnished chamber which had been prepared for us—and it was indeed luxury to rest after such a day's ride.

Friday 31.—Walked out a short distance after breakfast. Went into several stores, very handsome goods and fancy articles of late fashion. Had a visit from Dr. Davis who belongs to the *other house* and eats at the public table but he intends joining our party. The morning was warm and I remained in my room to rest. It rained very hard in the afternoon so as to render walking unpleasant, amused myself with practicing on the piano which was a pleasure I had long been deprived of.

Saturday, Sept. 1st.—Received letters and papers from home which gave intelligence of the prevalence of that fatal malady which so often visits our city. It cast a cloud of sadness and care over my mind and excited feelings of the most painful nature—it required a most powerful effort of mind to subdue and calm them, but it was a discipline absolutely necessary—separated by such a distance the means of communication so tedious and uncertain—all these circumstances combined served only to increase my anxiety, but I was compelled to exert myself and go down into the drawing room to receive callers. A visit from Mrs. McLaughlin, a pretty, entertaining, intelligent lady, easy and affable manners, invited us to attend church and return to dinner to which we consented. Walked out in the evening—went to Earle's picture gallery to see a full length portrait of Gen. Jackson, which is said to be a striking likeness. There was also one of his Lady—with a great number of others the originals to me were all unknown, but the paintings were fine—this is certainly a very well built city—the stores and warehouses are the handsomest I ever saw, generally of brick, handsomely finished and the streets wide and straight—the handsomest private dwellings are in the upper part of the city. They are in Northern style, stand retired from the street with a small garden or grass plat and iron railings, steps of white marble (which is of an inferior kind and very abundant here) pointing &c &c, of the same, which has a light and elegant appearance. There is a large public square in the centre of which is the Court House and market —all the public houses, hotels &c are in the streets which form the Square, from which all the principal Sts. diverge so that is the most public as well as central part of the city. They have very fine bridge which leads directly into the square—3 churches, Presbyterian, Baptist and Methodist, a Cathedral lately erected not yet opened for service; they are about erecting an Episcopal church, as they have a clergyman and a very respectable congregation, which assemble in the Masonic Hall, a very *fine* handsome looking building—a Museum and a theatre, which is neat and elegent in its outward appearance, the interior decorations are said to be very handsome, they have not at present a company, but expect one this week. I returned much pleased with my walk, although the rocky streets render it rather unpleasant and fatiguing—many places having no side walks.

Sunday 2.—Mr. and Mrs. McL. called at the appointed hour and ourselves and Mr. Perry (a gent from S. C. who had called on us and made one of our private table—accompanied them to the Presbyterian church. The preacher, a Mr. Sowers—nothing very great—it was a gay and genteel looking congregation—many very pretty faces, but they so quickly left the moment the blessing was said, that I had scarcely an opportunity of observing them. The remainder of the day passed very pleasantly at Mr. McL. The afternoon was cloudy and indicated rain, we did not ride out as was our intention.

Monday 3rd.—Mr. C. went out to see a gentleman on business. I walked out to purchase a few trifling articles. On my return had a visit from Mrs. Catron (wife of Judge Catron of the Supreme Court) and Miss Lawrence. The former is quite a fashionable lady of the *haut ton*, very easy in her manners, intelligent &c., the latter I should judge from her appearance had some pretentions to be a belle—but I know not as this is the first time I have had the pleasure of seeing her—they paid a very pleasant visit and on leaving gave the usual invitations &c &c. Were we to stay longer I doubt not I should soon form a very agreeable circle as I have received already much politeness and attention—they have the characters of being hospitable to strangers. There is to be a parade a mile from the city and several ladies and myself intend riding out to review the troops as it is fashionable for ladies to attend on such occasions—we were disappointed on reaching the parade ground the review was over—we were too late. Mrs. Eaton (mother of the Senator) was to have called and went with us to the General's but she sent me an excuse as she was very much indisposed, but would if better meet me there the next day. She is a fine old lady, quite of the *old school*, very dignified in her appearance and manner. Dr. Davis, Mr. C. and myself went in the barouche, servant mounted—it is rather more than 12 miles from here—we arrived before dark—rode up a long avenue and on alighting were met at the hall door by Col. Ogden, the General and Lady were in the act of descending the stairs—we of course remained until they reached the hall and were then presented. He is a very venerable, dignified, fine looking man, perfectly easy in manner,—but more of that anon. Mrs. Jackson received us with equal politeness, led me into a drawing room, insisted upon my taking of some refreshments which were handed—and one would have supposed from the kindness of her manner that she was an old acquaintance. After I was rested, she proposed walking into the garden which is very large and quite her hobby. I never saw any one more enthusiastically fond of flowers—she culled for me the only rose which was in bloom and made up a pretty nosegay. After an agreeable stroll we returned to the drawing room and were joined by several of the gentlemen (for they have always more or less company)—and the conversation was kept up with spirit until supper was announced. I was handed in by the General and seated at Mr. J.'s left, *He* occupied the *right* opposite to *me*—he pronounced with much solemnity of manner a short grace and then performed the honours of the table, with an attentive politeness which usually characterizes a gentleman—everything was neat and elegant, a complete service of French china, rich cut glass, damask napkins &c &c. After supper Mrs. Jackson, Maj. Eaton (Senator to Congress) and myself formed quite a social trio until we retired. Mrs. J. accompanied me to the chamber, remained a short time and then bade "Good Night."

Tuesday 4th.—I shall claim a writer's privilege and quite in Journal style enter into all the details of my visit. First a description of the *House*. You enter a large and spacious hall or vestibule, the walls covered with a very splendid French paper, beautiful scenery, figures &c—the floor and oil cloth—handsome sofa—chairs, table with liquors &c &c—to the right are two large handsome rooms furnished in fashionable and genteel style, as drawing rooms rich hangings, carpets &c—to the left is the dining room and their chamber—there was no splendour to dazzle the eye but everything elegant and neat. After breakfast we went into one of the drawing rooms where is a number of portraits (elegantly framed) of the intimate friends of the General—one of himself and Mrs. Jackson—but I have never yet seen one which did him justice. They want the spirit and expression which the *original* possesses in a great degree. We then examined as they were shown us the offering which had been presented him from every part of the Union—the sword presented at N. Orleans is the most splendid piece of workmanship of the time I ever saw—in the antique style and would require an *armour bearer* in attendance, the one from Tennessee is in the modern style adapted for use—most rich and elegant. On the mantle piece are placed the pistols which were presented to Gen. Washington by Gen. LaFayette, used by the former during his life and were presented by his relative, Mr. Custis, to Gen. Jackson. They are preserved with almost sacred veneration and appear to be more highly prized by the owner than all beside—excepting a small pocket spy glass which was used by Gen. Washington during the whole of his military career. These precious reliques are placed together. On looking around the room, my eye rested on a rich elegant silver Urn and it was with feelings of pride and gratification that I read the inscription from the "Ladies of South Carolina"—its value was still more heightened by its having been so promptly after the battle of Orleans — 'twas the only female offering which I saw — an elegant gold "snuff box" — presented by and with the freedom of the city of N. York and numberless other state and individual offerings which would be endlless to enumerate. The manners of the General are so perfectly easy and polished and those of his wife so replete with kindness and benevolence that you are placed at once at ease. I was seated at a small stand playing chess with Col. Ogden—the Gen. stood at my side and being an excellent player, he frequently directed my moves—apparently much interested in the fate of the game and when called off always returned to learn my success. There was no traces of the *"military chieftain" as he was called!* or other commander—you saw him only a polished gentleman dispensing the most liberal hospitality to all around him. In the course of the morning there was a great addition to our party Mrs. Eaton and several other ladies, besides a number of gentlemen. We sat down to a sumptuous and excellent dinner, about 20 in number. The Gen. saw all his guests arranged and then seated himself at the foot. Maj. Eaton on his left, who is Mrs. Jackson's Aide for he is busily engaged in carving, helping, etc., etc., and obeying her directions, which appears to afford pleasure to all her friends. Before leaving the table the Gen. proposed that the ladies would all join him in drinking to the toast of "Absent Friends." Had my head permitted I could have drank a bumper to such a toast, but the sentiment was deeply felt and before me passed in quick review the forms of my loved "absent friends."

We had made our arrangements to return immediately after dinner, as it was a long ride. They urged us much to stay, but as we were to leave Nashville the next day for the Western District, we were obliged to decline their polite invitation. When the General heard where we were going he observed that he had several friends there and would be pleased to give us letters. Would send them into town for us, and that himself and wife would visit us on our return. Mrs. Jackson would not permit me to go without a bouquet which she arranged very tastily, then took of us a most friendly cognee and the General drew my arm through his and conducted me to the carriage. I was peculiarly pleased with his manner towards a little girl who was on a visit with her aunt. There was so much parental care and attention to her wants. It was a something in manner which cannot be described.

We did not arrive in town until very late, took coffee and retired.

Wednesday 5.—In the forenoon we called to return Mrs. Catron's visit in company with the Dr. and Mrs. P. They live in a very handsome house built in Northern style, hall of entrance, two drawing rooms with folding doors thrown open, furnished nearly the same in a fashionable elegant style. She is a very agreeable lady, has considerable conversation and of course our visit was a pleasant one. Next to Mrs. McLaughlin, and then returned much oppressed with the heat to make a few preparations for our journey and write home, all of which was accomplished, and we left town soon after dinner and slept that night at Mr. Darrells, 13 miles.

It is really amusing to see the curiosity of the people when you stop. You must prepare yourself for a catechising. I will give you one as nearly verbatim as I can remember: Q. "You are from Kentucky, I reckon?" "No Mam, last from Nashville." "Do you live there?" "No, only on a visit." "Tis a mighty pretty place. Have you any acquaintances there?" "A few." "Well, I reckon you are from the South, N. Carolina I reckon?" "No Mam, South Carolina." "Did you come any part by water?" "No, in the carriage." "Why, I reckon 'twas a mighty long journey of it?" "Yes." "What counties did you come through, I suppose you came by such a one, etc, etc.?" Answered them, told them through which of them we came. "I suppose you are going down to settle in the Western District?" "No Mam." "I thought as how you might be going to see how you would like it?" "No Mam, only on a visit." "I reckon you have not been married a long time?" "Not a great while." These and a thousand others will be put to you all in succession. It really amused me. I could scarcely answer them with due politeness, my risibles were so strongly excited, but in return they are equally as communicative. Give you all their family history, genealogy, etc., etc., from the first settler down. It appears to me they all have at least a dozen children, for you will see a house full and they tell you of 3 or 4 more in Alabama, Mississippi and the Lord only knows where. This State appears to be inhabited and settled principally by North Carolians and Virginians, indeed you do not go anywhere without meeting with the former. They possess a great spirit for emigration and adventure, and are always foremost in the ranks of those who go out to our western wilds. So many of them have grants or claims of lands that it becomes matter of necessity or speculation. I cannot conceive of its being choice.

Thursday 6th.—Breakfasted at Gideons, 14 miles, and then the besetting sin of our Mother Eve presented in a new form, that of a deaf old woman. Age should ever be respected and we cannot but regret to see it so often accompanied with an idle insatiable curiosity. When seated at table, she commenced her inquiries (which were addressed to Mr. C.) of where was he raised? Where going? Where from? What his business? Had he lands or claims? Were they good? And a catalogue of others almost sufficient to fill a volume. I had often been astonished at their being so well acquainted with people in general and their affairs, but the mystery is soon solved. It proceeds from ignorance and a total absence of all native delicacy, yet this is not always the case. Only occasionally you meet with those who thirst for knowledge and can acquire it only by taxing your patience or politeness. We passed through Franklin which is the second town to Nashville in this state. Quite a pretty place. We entered Columbia on Duck River early in the afternoon, having rode about 28 miles. Slept at Nelsons, tolerable good house.

Friday 7th.—A rainy morning ride 11 miles to breakfast at Col. Brown's. The roads were very wet and heavy and we had 20 miles to travel to reach Pulaski, which we did early in the afternoon. There are two inns in the place and we inquired and went to the best, but were it possible to compare the superlative of bad I think we might go three degrees farther and then not find a term adequate. Cleanliness was a word or subject not known or heard of. It had never been admitted into their vocabulary or house, but necessity has no law and we made the best of it, resolving only never to return.

Saturday 8th.—We left as soon as possible this elegant abode and started being well assured we could not find any worse. Mr. C. had business six miles below Pulaski, out of our road, but to remain there was not to be thought of. We went two miles farther, came to a good looking brick house owned by Mr. Beauford, clever people to all appearance. Stopped to eat breakfast. Mr. C. got a horse and went to see those persons with whom he had business whilst I remained until his return, which was before dinner. We left immediately afterwards and went 8 miles to Porters, rather a poor house but the only one within 20 miles where we could be accommodated.

Sunday 9th.—Breakfast at Lawrenceboro 14 miles, 'twas not much more than an apology for a town but we stopped at the tavern kept by Mr. Gather and fared very well, the road now lay through a lonesome barren wilderness with here and there a miserable log cabin, we were recommended to 2 where we could stop all night—but sleeping in the woods would have been preferable to the prospect they offered, for either supper or bed, one of them was so filled with men, women and children that it was difficult to imagine where they all found places, the other I am certain would not have measured 6 ft. square. Our only alternative was to proceed to Waynesboro. Night came on us a low swampy road so dark that the driver could not possibly see it, trusting almost entirely to the horses and feeling almost apprehensive that we should not emerge into an open road or lose the one we were in. We groped in this utter darakness for more than an hour, it appeared to be a fit resort for robbers and outlaws where they might commit with impunity their deeds of darkness which here might forever be concealed. We at length came upon a more enlightened road and soon after reached the town which but for our eagerness to see a house we might have passed without noticing, as it was we rode through looking for a decent house—but on enquiry for the best were shown a poor looking place to which we rode up. The old woman was kind and busied herself in getting us something to eat, making apologies for not having "such things as she ought to have" but after a ride of 42 miles and having escaped the blackness of the woods, we felt too grateful for not to be very dainty.

Monday 10th.—Rode out of the town which consisted of 8 or 10 log houses and a small frame court house ... the road very bad but we were obliged to go 14 miles to Carrollville for breakfast—and such a one was never seen or heard of—there was only a white man and an old black woman, a dirty looking house and nothing but fried bacon and the meanest, coarsest kind of corn bread! Yet this was the public house of the place. Fortunately we had coffee with us—as we always take it previously to starting in the morning or I know not how we could have done—but complaints would have been useless—there was no remedy and for this elegant repast of poor bacon and stale bread we payed one dollar. I would willingly have given another if I had not attempted to taste it—as to eating of it that was out of the question. The ferry was at that place and we crossed the Tennessee River and entered on the western district. We had only go 10 miles to Mrs. Shannon's as there was not another house we were informed, where we could get anything we could eat. That was a poor log cabin but she was a clever woman and gave us a supper which we enjoyed very much after our day of fasting, 'tis true the house was rather open, no filling between many of the logs, 'twas free for the fowls of the air to enter at pleasure and not a pane of glass or anything in the form of window, yet we made out very well for everything was at least clean.

Tuesday 11th.—Breakfasted at Mrs. Shannons as we were fearful of not getting any as good on the road—which was the worst we had travelled—it was merely a foot path through the woods forking at every 3 or 4 miles—not a post or sign board to direct us, and we would be certainly on the lookout to see that we did not leave the one notched for that was our only guide—and we stopped every person we met to obtain new directions. Entered Lexington city in the afternoon after a ride of 30 miles. 'Twas not much better than those towns we had passed through—most of the houses built of logs, but they could boast of a brick court house. The public house kept miserably—cleanliness is not understood here—'tis enough to disgust one to witness such cloth and dirt. I could not have conceived of persons living in such a state of disorder and confusion. I have often heard the remark that cleanliness was next to godliness and for my part I cannot have a great opinion or even a good one of those who suffer everything around them to betray a want of care and attention, their minds I should much fear were in a like state.

Wednesday 12th.—The road was now much better—to Williams 12 m. for breakfast, which was excellent—the house clean, etc., etc. We had only 17 m. to reach Jackson which we entered early in the afternoon, having previously enquired. We stopt at the Jackson Hotel kept by Dr. Winn, the best in the place and that was not saying much, for it was poor enough, yet it was a large good looking brick house and from the outward appearance one would judge favorably of it. I went immediately to my room and feeling fatigued and indisposed, did not leave it. Several gentlemen called on Mr. C. and were most polite and kind and their invitations to us to pass our time with them, or rather to consign me to their care as he was compelled to be absent several days on business in a wilderness part of the county where there was not a road cut for carriages and consequently I was obliged to remain here but they would call in the morning and make their offers in person to me.

Thursday 13th.—Maj. Martin and Lady called soon after breakfast and repeated the invitation which they had previously made and requested I would accompany them home—we did so—on our way thither met Miss Hays and Mr. Chester (one of the gentlemen to whom we brought letters from Gen. Jackson, his wife is Mrs. Jackson's niece) he said he had called to request us to make his house our home during our stay—hoped we would divide our time, etc., etc., in the course of the day Gen. Arnold and several other gentlemen called on us. Maj. M. lives a short distance from the town, house very pleasantly situated and the inmates of it extremely polite and hospitable.

Friday 14th—Mr. C. left me early for his journey in the wilderness for such it really is. I should perhaps be subject to much ridicule were I to express my ideas of almost heroism in behaving with becoming dignity on the occasion—yet I could reply "they jest at scars who never felt a wound"—I was very much indisposed during the day—a slight bilious attack—took medicine and kept my bed. Mrs. Chester and her sister Miss Hays called on me but I was unable to see them—left an invitation to dine with them the next day which was accepted conditionally.

Saturday 15th.—As I was much better we all concluded to dine at Mr. Chester's and returned an answer to that effect. Maj. M. and Lady, Miss Diggins (the sister) and myself went at what is here quite a fashionable hour between 1 and 2 o'clock. Mrs. Chester is a tall fine handsome looking woman, polished and agreeable manners, the room was quite full of company when we entered, 8 or 10 Ladies and as many gentlemen. As a stranger I was of course introduced to every one rapidly and particularly to Mrs. Butler (Mrs. C.'s sister and wife of Dr. B. to whom we had letters from the Gen.) She regretted much the absence of her husband who had left for Nashville. She was staying at her mother's but would certainly call &c, &c. This section of country has been so recently settled the town itself has not been located 5 yrs. that the buildings are of course plain and many is in an unfurnished state—all articles of luxury or even what we consider necessaries are extravagantly high, owing to the expense and difficulty of importation—it is impossible for one who has not visited a new country to form any adequate idea of the difficulty and labor requisite even to clear the land and form a decent habitation—but they have made rapid progress and have already a good society. It appears to one accustomed to city life rather inconsistent to see as in the present case—a plain house with rough unfinished walls yet furnished in neat and fashionable style—carpets &c &c. A most elegant dinner and dessert served up in the best style—a complete set of the richest cut glass, French china, handsome plate &c &—in fact, every article which would be seen at a set dinner party with us—but this connection of family I am informed are the most fashionable and live in the best style of any people in the country and from my own observation—I should think it correct—they have in this state a fashion differing from ours though I could not dare to decide upon its superiority—the Ladies and gentlemen all leave the table at the same time—the latter remain in the hall to discuss politics, the universal topic of conversation, or join the ladies, PERHAPS to continue the same subject as most of the ladies take a warm interest in the election and are well acquainted with all the debates, intrigues, &c &c. For my part I think their successful candidates earn the honour bestowed on them at a most dear and highly bought price—after the sacrifice of health—for they are compelled to ride over all that portion of country they are to represent —make stump orations, attend musters, public meetings &c &c., all of which appears to me totally inconsistent with and beneath the dignity of a gentleman and the situation to which he aspires. They may be truly said to "Stoop to Conquer" for he who stoops the most is sure to win. . . . Mr. and Mrs. Chester requested that I would remain but not having made arrangements to that effect I declined—and took our leave, having passed an agreeable day. . . . .

Sunday 16th.—There was no preaching in the town. We remained withindoors. They have not a church but assemble in the Court House which is a neat handsome brick building. The place is small, most of the houses frame and log, yet the inhabitants speak in sanguine terms of its improvement and expect to increase greatly. It is situated about ½ mile from the Forked Deer but they do not derive from it much benefit, as it is seldom navigable. In the afternoon Mr. C. most unpectedly returned, 'twas indeed a most delightful surprise as I had not anticipated seeing him for two or three days, but he was fortunate in transacting his business and hurried his return as much as possible—he had had a lonely ride through the woods and poor fare.

Monday 17th.—We called on Mrs. Chester. She is really a very agreeable pleasing lady—her husband is quite a polished genteel man. I regretted not having been able to accept of the civilities and politeness which they evidently wished to show me—but we were to leave in the morning for Nashville, and Mr. C. has business which required him to be absent the remainder of the day we were obliged to decline remaining with them. We had considerable conversation relative to their Uncle and Aunt Jackson to whom they are much attached—certainly the reports, which have become current with regard to that Lady's family and connections are most false and erroneous—they are among the nobility of the state, are always spoken of as being in the first circles and their society is courted—nor is this of recent date. It has always been so—as Col. Donaldson (Mrs. C.'s father) was one of the first settlers—and a man of wealth and consequence and influence his descendants are at this time powerful and influential—from my personal observation I should decide that he had moved in more polished society and lived in more style and fashion than any other persons in this western district—yet it is principally settled by old and respected families who had claims under government or felt a spirit for emigration—which is most universally felt by all in this State.

Tuesday 18th.—We took a friendly farewell of our hospitable friends and retraced our steps to Nashville, the road was but indifferent, the weather excessively warm having while on the prairies the full influence of the sun. The log cabins presented such as aspect of poverty and filth that we did not stop for any refreshments during the day—crossed the Forked Deer and Obion Rrs. and again were we benighted, for there was no place where we could or would stop and we had several miles to reach the town, Huntingdon—which we did about 9 o'ck—ourselves and horses alike exhausted with a ride of 40 miles—stopt at Col. Brown's Inn—tolerable fare.

Wednesday 19th.—Took breakfast there. The road was intolerably bad and the weather hotter than ever experienced in C. We reached the bank of the Tennessee R. about sunset—were detained some time waiting for the boat—crossed after dark and entered the town of Reynoldsburgh 28 m. On driving up to the Tavern received the pleasing intelligence that it was court time, house full and could not possibly take us in—very grateful news to tired worn out travellers but there was no alternative. The man directed us to the Squire's where he said they might take us in. 'Twas no time for ceremony—thither we went, our case stated, we were welcomed in. The Squire was absent but his wife was quite a genteel woman—had supper prepared and treated us very politely—so that we regretted not our previous disappointment.

Thursday 20th.—Took breakfast with the good lady, whose name I know not and commenced another day's ride. The road was very good and we drove 38 miles to Charlotte before dark—put up at Samson's Hotel.

Friday 21st.—Arose and left before sun rise. Took breakfast at Ellis 10 miles. The road was tolerably good for the first 10 or 15 miles, then rocky and hilly but the weather extremely cool and pleasant—a great change. We hailed with pleasure the sight of Nashville and entered it before 6 o'ck., having accomplished our day's journey of 40 miles much sooner than we had anticipated. The city was pretty well crowded as the Legislature are now in session. They had been in great excitement and had a great parade on the day of the entrance of their new Governor, Gen. Houston. They were making preparations previous to our leaving and I really regret not having been present on the occasion. He is the most popular man in the State—his rapid and almost unparalleled rise is sufficient evidence of the fact—he is said to be a very elegant man in his appearance, not yet 35 he enlisted in Jackson's army at 17 as a *common* soldier, was promoted in regular graduations, then studied to practice law— made Maj. Gen. of the State—Member to Congress and Gov.—all in less than 10 yrs. He called to pay me a visit as soon as he heard of our arrival—but I had retired. Mr. C. had been acquainted with him some years since and they met as old acquaintances.

Saturday 22nd.—A clear cool morning exhilarating to the feelings after the fatigue and heat of the preceeding days. A visit from Maj. Rutledge from Carolina who has been a resident of this State several yrs. I had seen him often when in C. and the sight of a face familiar to me there was truly grateful to my feelings. We are not conscious of our local attachments until absence proves the test. In the afternoon a visit from Mrs. Rutledge and Mrs. Fogg (her daughter), accomplished and charming ladies in their manner, and were I not fearful of incurring the imputation of sectional prejudice I would say in one word *polished Carolinians*. They are in deep mourning and do not mingle in gay or general society but requested we would spend the next evening with them in a social manner—come early—& without ceremony—conditions to which I assented as such visits always afford to me more enjoyment than a mixed crowded assemblage. They had just left when the Gov. was announced. Highly raised expectations are usually disappointed and such alas! were mine. He entered and I beheld not the god like grace I have been led to expect but a figure of herculean proportions and not possessing according to my ideas that elegance or ease for which he is so far famed, but I must and will suspend my opinion until a more intimate knowledge would justify one. In the evening attended the Theatre which is neat and pretty. The play, the Soldier's Daughter—the principal characters were well supported by Mr. Caldwell, Mr. and Mrs. Russell, and Mr. Gray—, the rest were rather la, la. My principal inducement for going was to see the fashion and beauty of Nashville, but I was disappointed as there were few ladies and no beauty.

Sunday 23rd.—As there was no Episcopal service and not knowing where we should hear a good sermon, we remained within doors. The weather was really cold, a fire or the full influence of the sun very agreeable. In the afternoon visited Mrs. R. Their house is most beautifully situated just at the entrance of the city on a considerable eminence which commands a beautiful view of the whole city—the river &c. In the front of the house a fine lawn and to the rear a forest of 16 acres, which adds especially to its beauty and romantic appearance and is an acquisition rarely to be found. There met the Rev. Mr. Howell (the Epi. Clergyman), quite a young man recently from N. Y., agreeable and pleasant in his manners. Mrs. Fogg is extremely interesting both in person and manner, very intelligent and easy and affable and the evening passed imperceptibly away in conversation. At parting mutual promises were exchanged of other visiting during our stay.

Monday 24th.—Another visit from Gov. Houston. I was more pleased with his person and manners which are certainly agreeable, but yet could not discern that superiority of either which has gained him such universal popularity, for to them he is principally indebted for it, as he does not possess talents of the highest order. Of course merely in a visit or two I could not possibly form an opinion of his mind or acquirements, the occasion did not call for a display of either. One of the topics of conversation last evening was relative to a splendid wedding which was to take place on Thursday—daughter of Dr. Shelby, one of the wealthiest men in Nashville—the preparations for it have been unparalleled, making additions to the house, cutting windows, doors &c. 500 cards of invitation issued, in fact the whole body politic and corporate of the city. The ladies were very anxious to make a transfer of their cards for my benefit as they were certain that our return was not known to the parties—but the Gov. (who is one of the attendants) waited on us today with an invitation and apologies from Mrs. S. for not having called—but the case was such as to render that impossible and a card answered all purposes—so I shall behold at one time and place all the beauty, fashion and splendor of the city. They will be a most youthful couple, the lady 14 and the gentleman not yet 20—but probably themselves or parents have been reading treatise on the beneficial effects of early marriages. In the evening attended the Theatre, but it was somewhat of a trial of patience to remain during the play, which was most wretchedly performed. Mr. Caldwell mistakes his talents when he attempts to be grave or dignified and we beheld in Pennudock not the powerful passions of the man struggling with the calmness of the philosopher, but a man apparently aged, weak and misanthropic—even his noblest sentiments lost their effect when uttered in such hollow ill modulated tones. I think I shall not be persuaded again to witness their performance.

Tuesday 25th.—Mrs. Rutledge and her daughters called and we rode out to the Sulphur Springs, which are becoming quite a resort. The waters are highly tonic and they have a bath erected as they are considered more beneficial than merely drinking of them. We rode several miles and saw many beautiful situations immediately around the city. There is so much hill and dale that the scenery is diversified and beautiful. On my return had the pleasure of seeing Gen. Jackson. Mrs. J. is to be in town to attend this great wedding, a circumstance which affords me pleasure as it will increase my enjoyment. In the aft. called for Mr. and Mrs. McLaughlin and rode out to the race course. Had a fine view of the river as we rode along its banks. Returned to tea with Mrs. McL. Passed quite a social evening.

Wednesday 26th.—The morning as clear and cold as October. Walked out but it was too chilly to be agreeable, and a seat by the fire was far more comfortbale.

Thursday 27th.—This was the important day—great in the annals of the fashionable world—anticipated with delight by many a youthful beauty and gay gallants, as the scene of their triumph and display. Even the old and grave men were not exempt from pleasing expectations in mingling with the festive throng. Mrs. Jackson arrived in the morning and sent me word that she would call for me. I waited on her and we made our arrangements accordingly. Had a visit from Judge White, Senator in Congress—a man universally allowed to possess the greatest talents in the State. He is of the most dimunitive in size with apparently scarcely flesh enough to cover his frame—wears his hair in the Methodist style, hanging down his neck—and is altogether a plain looking old man. He has an eye which redeems all, large clear blue with an expression that reaches deep and beams with intellect. His conversation is nothing remarkable for beauty of style or language, yet from its plain old fashioned good sense you cannot but derive pleasure. He professes to be ignorant of all our modern etiquette and *he* certainly could not be improved by it. I have rarely ever seen a stranger I was more pleased with—he was also among the gay crowd of the evening. Mrs. Jackson called at an early hour and we drove to Dr. Shelby's—ushered into a drawing room filled with ladies. Soon after we entered (and before one-fifth of the company had assembled) a *bride* of course was never yet pronounced to be otherwise than beautiful, lovely or interesting, the lady in question was really quite pretty and dare not say her charms were heightened by the aid of a rich and elegant dress—'twould be slander gross to make such an insinuation. The groom (a Mr. Barrows) was a good looking young man, extremely tall, forming a strong contrast to his little wife. The form was Presbyterian, very short, but I presume sufficiently lengthy to be agreeable to the parties. After receiving the usual congratulations the bride and attendants left the room and the married ladies were then requested to adjourn to another room where there was a supper table spread in a most elegant and tasty style abounding with all the luxuries which could be procured. It was really something quite splendid—far exceeding my expectations. We left the table and our vacant seats were soon occupied by another set. Admittance into the ball room was now a great object to effect, for it was literally crowded—a fashionable squeese unprecedented. After due exercise of patience 'twas at length accomplished. 'Twas really a brilliant scene. the ladies very elegantly dressed, all wearing the semblance of joy. The Gen. was decidedly the most gallant and courtly man present. His first question to me as I entered was "Do you dance?" He requested to be allowed to select a partner for me and immediately brought up and introduced the Speaker of the House of Representatives, Dr. Camp, with whom of course I danced—a most colossial figure, we certainly presented a singular contrast and had I been overlooked he would certainly have been pardonable. My next partner was Gov. Houston, who is certainly a most graceful man, yet I cannot agree with the general opinion relative to his beauty. At least he does not possess the requisites to constitute him such in my opinion, but he has a manner extremely polite and attentive which cannot fail to render him popular, yet I fear were he to be criticised by the strict rules of truth as laid down by Mrs. Opie he would certainly be criminated but less sterner moralists often forget the truth of a graceful compliment and seldom question it—experience has taught him that they compose the majority. I was introduced to a number of persons but in such a large assembly names are not often heard or remembered. Mr. Rutledge jun. was there and was often my partner. He is an agreeable pleasant young gentleman. Being a *Carolinian* we could converse of home—and I felt not as though we were strangers—indeed everyone appeared perfectly at ease for there was not room for form or ceremony. Dr. and Mrs. Shelby were extremely attentive to their guests and a Mrs. Minnick (the grandmother of the bride) was really a conspicuous character, mistress of ceremonies, a part she performed most admirably, and if the company generally enjoyed themselves in an equal degree with myself they could not but be pleased. We retired at an early hour, as I feared too much dissipation would not suit my steady habits.

Friday 28th.—A visit from Mrs. McLaughlin and Mrs. Bolch, who is a very interesting pleasing lady in her manners. 'Twas the first visit she had paid me as they live 6 or 8 miles from town. We were to leave so soon that we could not accept of an invitation to visit them. I had intended paying my respects to the bride but a message from Mrs. Jackson saying that she would call to see me prevented my going abroad, but she did not come until late and was then in great haste as she was to dine out. A visit from Mrs. Rutledge and daughter. They had just paid their visit to the bride in the evening, took tea at Mr. McGavicks, after which went to Judge Catrons where we formed a party for the Theatre. I felt not the slightest wish to go but as I could not accept Mrs. C.'s invitation to tea she insisted on our accompanying her. The play was the Gamester and anyone who has seen Cooper and Mrs. Gilfert personate Mr. and Mrs. Beverly could not derive much interest from the performance of Mr. Caldwell and Miss Placide. We did not remain for the afterpiece, being perfectly contented with that we had seen.

Saturday 29th.—Several visitors during the morning, among the number Gen. Jackson. The oftener I see him the more am I pleased. He is certainly a most superior man. His most trifling actions and expressions indicate it, for I have never seen him on any great occasion yet cannot but be impressed with the belief of his greatness. On learning that we were to leave the next morning he said he would come and see us off and give us his parting blessing. There was a fatherly kindness in his manner which touched the feelings. Took tea with Mrs. Rutledge, where we had the gratification of listening to very fine music. Mrs. Fogg plays and sings in a superior style and gave full effect to the soft and plaintiff music of Rossini. Always an enthusiast in sweet sounds I was really charmed and 'twould almost be difficult to decide which most afforded the pleasure, the lady or her performance, yet I am inclined to think the former would ever have the preference for she could please even those who had not a soul for music formed. I have never seen anyone with whom on so short an acquaintance I was so much interested in. The hour for departure arrived too quickly and we took a farewell for perhaps a long period—exchanging many kind and friendly wishes, expressing the hope that we should meet again.

Sunday 30th.—Whilst at breakfast Gen. Jackson called to bid farewell. He would not wait for his wife as he was fearful that we had left, but he requested us to stop and see her on our way, which of course we assented to. Mrs. Catron called, then Gov. Houston. We were really detained some time longer than we expected by our leave taking friends. Drove to Mr. McLemon where we found the Gen. and Mrs. Jackson waiting to receive us, took a hearty but affectionate adieu and then left the city. We have enjoyed ourselves more than we could have anticipated, had received considerable attention formed many pleasant acquaintances and last though not least had the gratification of enjoying much of the society of Gen. Jackson and lady and receiving from them much attention when we visited Nashville they said the Hermitage must be our home, but I hope we shall have the pleasure of seeing them in our city before that period arrives. Slept the night at Searcys 23 miles—very excellent house.

Monday, Oct. 1st.—Breakfasted in Murfreesboro 10 a.m., went that night to Powers 27 miles. The man of the house observed he was in an awkward situation, his house undergoing some repair but it was near dark and after a ride of 37 m. we were not disposed to be very nice. It was certainly an open house but with the aid of a large fire we managed to keep comfortably warm and had a pretty good supper.

Tuesday 2nd.—We went a mile or two out of the way to visit the "Stone Fort," one of the greatest curiosities of the state—it is situated between the two southern forks of Duck River. We crossed the E. F. on a mill dam and then climbed a considerable height to reach the wall which extends along its banks a considerable distance. It has not the appearance of a mound, being completely covered with earth on which trees of an immense size are growing and the remains of others which are supposed to be more than 500 yrs. old. It is the work of a race of people who inhabited the country prior to the Indians and by some is thought to have been built *before the flood,* but that I should presume was more conjecture and not correct. The corea or inner part of the fort occupies the ground between the rivers and on the West Fork are two bastions or outer works so as to render it secure from attack on either side. Part of the wall was broken and we were enabled to see the manner in which the stones were laid and it must certainly have been the work of masons. 'Twould afford an ample theme for the pen of an antiquary and the examination of it would engross much of his time and thoughts, but we gratified our curiosity and then descended and retraced our steps. Rode to Pond Springs to breakfast 13 m. There was an apology for a town but a neat and most excellent public house. The walls were as white as snow and it was a most pleasing contrast to the dark and dingy cabins we usually meet with. Crossed the Cumberland Mts. by Hollinsworth Trace, which is the best road although it was very steep and broken yet it is only 9 m. from the rise to the foot which we reached before dark. Stopt at Dooley's, which was a neat log cabin but they gave us due notice that it was "a mighty bad chance for supper." They had no flour and there was not a mill within 40 miles. Horse and hand mills are not known or used here but we had travelled 37 m. and concluded to remain in spite of the "mighty bad chance." The supper was better than we had expected, the cakes were made of grated corn, the only way they had of preparing it for use and a most tedious process it must be—but they were very good. Wednesday for breakfast we rode 15 m. to Jasper, a small town in Sequatchy Valley. We had left Nashville sooner than we intended in order to reach here before the Court adjourned as Mr. C. had business of importance which would detain him a day or two. Put up at the public house kept by Mr. Riggle. The house was very full and about upon a par with most country taverns. My books and pen furnished me with amusement.

Thursday 4th.—Remained in Jasper all day as Mr. C. has business which detained. It is a beautifully situated place, surrounded with mountains, but has only been located 5 yrs., and of course is not much of a town but they can boast of a brick court house which is not to be seen in every town.

Friday 5th.—Left Jasper, crossed Tennessee R. at Clarke's Ferry. Crossed Lookout Mt., the appearance of which is terrific from its steepness. The road very broken and rough and almost perpendicular to the summit. 'Twas 23 m. to Ross's at the foot of the mountain where we stopt for the night. We were now in the Cherokee Nation. Mr. Ross is a Scotchman. He married a Cherokee and has a large family. They are said to be extremely intelligent and well educated and have in their appearance nothing of the Indian. His daughters have all married whites and he was alone.

Saturday 6th.—We went 7 m. out of our way to visit Brainard, the mission settlement and I have never been more gratified than I was on that occasion. There had been a long vacation and the scholars were just commencing to return and the school had not resumed its exercise. Mr. Ellisworth, the teacher of the male academy, is quite an intelligent man. His system (as far as we were capable of judging) is a most excellent one—the plan of instruction and the books used are the most modern and improved that we have in our schools. They excel particularly in writing. Their progress surpasses any I have ever seen. It would appear almost incredible. We were shown several specimens of letter writing and compositions which were extraordinary. Many of the writers had not been in school two years and had only been studying English during that time and they had also small note books in which they were obliged to write down as much of the sermon as they could remember when they returned from preaching on Sunday—a method which is calculated not only to strengthen the memory but insure attention. One of the boys was called in and he read a chapt. in the Bible very well. He had been in school 2 yrs. and when he entered could not speak or understand a word of English. Mr. E. observed that they all possessed great tadents for imitation. He produced a piece of painting, likeness of Mary Queen of Scots taken from an engraving by one of the boys. His first attempt would have done credit to one who had taken regular lessons in the art. Miss Sawyer, the teacher of the female academy, produced several pieces of writing which were neat and elegant penmanship. Several *samplers* were elegantly wrought, equal if not superior to any I have ever seen. Also several worked collars which were extremely pretty and done in the neatest manner. I fortunately had some muslin bobnet &c which I presented to her, as they were articles not easily obtained. She observed that a collar should be worked and sent me which will be quite a curiosity to show, as few persons are acquainted with the progress they have made in civilization or that they have ever attended to so necessary a branch of female economy as needlework. The children were dressed in homespun frocks and check aprons neat and clean and many of them were full Cherokees, very dark, others much lighter and a few almost white. They are said to be remarkably docile and attentive. Among the girls they have a society which meets every Saturday aft. They have a Treasurer and monitor—(girls of the 1st class)—one of them reads whilst the others knit and sew—the 1st class receives a cent an hour, the 2nd ¾, the 3rd ½. The proceeds of their labor is for the educating heathen children, but the teacher observed that she had formed it for the purpose of giving them an idea of the means by which they were educated. The money was sent to the Treasurer of the Board of Foreign Missions and they received a receipt from him, which they valued highly as a reward for their work. It is a plan decidedly the best calculated not only to promote the end desired but to impress them with feelings of charity and habits of industry. Mr. and Mrs. Ellisworth, Miss Sawyer and the Rev. Mr. Worcester were the only members of the Mission family that we saw. They were extremely hospitable and polite and were urgent for us to remain for a day or two, but we were compelled to decline. We took breakfast with them. They never receive a compensation but donations and your name is registered in a book kept for that purpose. They have several houses all connected, one large hall in which they assemble for meals—fine mills and a blacksmith shop—constituted I believe the whole establishment which is kept in neat and perfect order. Went that day 10 m. to Mrs. Williams (formerly Widow Wolfes), an old squaw who has married a white man much younger than her presence . . . they remind me of the sybils and witches of olden days—uttering their incantations and denunciations upon all whom they meet—for their language seems to be a muttering of sounds which they utter with great volubility in a kind of singing croaking voice. Nothing can possibly be more disagreeable—you would conclude that they were in a violent passion. We fared tolerably well.

Sunday 7th.—Rode 14 m. to Vanns for breakfast. A fine large brick house, finished in a most extravagant style, gaudily painted, but in dirt and confusion, neither order or comfort, a miserable breakfast. He is quite fair, almost white with no expression of the Indian. His wife was much darker, being as they term it, half Cherokee. Went from there 30 m. to Saunders. He was the largest and darkest Indian I had yet seen—quite an intelligent civil man—had a large family—his children went to school and were very well behaved—they have in the Nation several schools—a certain number of stores are allowed and no white man can live in the Nation except he is a mill wright or blacksmith or marries a native. They have recently since the death of their king, Path Killer, formed a constitution similar to ours— John Ross, Presdt., and are only waiting for the arrival of their press to have it published in Cherokee and English. I looked over several of the laws by which they are at present governed drawn up by Ross and signed by Path Killer. From the hasty glance I took I should say they were written in a superior style and by a man of no ordinary talent. He is a son of the Mr. Ross where we stopped and has married a full Cherokee. There are 147 white men married to Cherokees and 68 white women to Cherokee men. Their children are entitled to all the privileges of citizens.

Monday 8th.—To Harnages 14 m. to breakfast. Again we encountered one of these sybils—she recalled to my mind Norna of the Fitful Head—her height was greatly beyond that of women in general and was increased by a pair of shoes with heels of an immense height which kept up a continued clatter around one and the elevated tones of her croaking voice—uttering such unintelligible sounds completed the effect of her appearance could not fail to produce. She was the wife of Mr. Harnage who was a white man and that time absent from home. There was quite a decent good looking white man who acted in the capacity of landlord. He said he had obtained "permit" from the Nat. Council to reside in the Nation. Went from there 14 m. to Blackburn, a miserably poor place, but so in fact were all the houses. We were compelled to make the best of them—necessity has no law—and as to requests or complaints 'twould be utterly unavailing. They are a lazy indolent people and would not take the necessary trouble to render their houses clean or comfortable.

Tuesday, 9th.—Rode 18 m. to Chattahoochie R., which forms the boundary of the Nation. Crossed at Winns Ferry and stopt at his house for breakfast nearly 1 o'ck., gratified at having taken a final farewell of the Nation, yet they are perfectly civilized, live and dress as whites and although the accommodations are miserable yet they are as good if not better than one could expect. We were detained 4 hours by rain. It partially cleared and we set out for Capt. Young 7 m., but were overtaken by the rain e'er we reached there. Our fare only tolerable.

Wednesday 10th.—A clear cold morning. Went to Whited 10 m. for breakfast, which was worse than any we had yet met with. Proceeded on 25 m. to Munro, a small neat village. Stopt at Stone's Hotel almost exhausted with fatigue and hunger, but our host and hostess were extremely kind and attentive and I never saw people more so. Soon after we arrived brought us strong coffee which was truly refreshing and we then had a most excellent supper, which did not require appetites as keen as we possessed to render it palatable. A neat comfortable room and a good bed, a luxury we had long been deprived of.

Thursday 11th—Mrs. Stone had an early breakfast for us. The roads were good and we reached Monticello 35 m. early in the afternoon. Put up at Kendricks, a very good house.

Friday 12th.—To Hillsboro 10 m. Remained couple hours. Went that night to Clinton, 15 m, a pretty little village not so large or town like as Monticello, but there are a number of trees which gives it a rural appearance.

Saturday 13th.—To Marion 13m. for breakfast. We were to remain there several days. 'Tis a place of considerable business although it has not been located more than 6 yrs.—covers a large extent of ground, several large warehouses—many neat dwelling houses—a bank which is the only brick building. We stopt at the Mansion House kept by Bivens, to which we were recommended. 'Tis well kept as regards table, etc., but the mistress of the house is ignorant or negligent of those little attentions which conduce so essentially to the comfort of strangers. There are several ladies staying here, at least such I would presume they were judging from their appearance only, for certainly neither their manners or acquaintance with the common rules of politeness would justify such an opinion but I will leave them to enjoy their state of blissful ignorance—congratulating myself on not having ever before encountered similar persons.

JOHN ROGERS IN WEST TENNESSEE, 1836-1840

In 1836, 1837, and 1840, John Rogers, a Universalist preacher, came to the Western District. He recorded his experiences in a diary which was published in 1845 by John A. Gurley of Cincinnati. It is through the courtesy of Roy Black of Bolivar that the following selections from the account of this journey are quoted:

"Camp-meetings are very frequent and large in this Southern country, and with the horse races, they form the principal diversion of the season. But the Methodists do not here, as at the North, enjoy a monopoly in the article of camp-meetings; on the contrary, the Presbyterians engage in this wholesale scheme of proselytism as largely as they; and, indeed, it originated with the Presbyterians. Camp-grounds are here permanent establishments, instead of tents, durable booths are in many cases erected, formed of plank, and even of brick in some instances, with separate apartments for the different sexes, and for the servants, which is certainly more compatible with Christian order and decency, that for all to bundle in the straw together as is frequently witnessed east of the mountains."

. . . When Rogers arrived near Wright's post office eighteen miles south of Paris, he made arrangements to preach in the home of a Mr. Hill. He continued his discourse thus:

"Accordingly, on the evening of January 7th, in an extremely open log house, without any partition between the ground floor and the shingle roof, I preached the first Universalist sermon ever delivered in the Western District of Tennessee, to a small circle of hearers arranged around the fire; and so very, very cold was the evening, that those who could not get within the light of the fire had to wrap bed quilts about their shoulders to keep themselves comfortable. During the sermon the chimney took fire;, and being constructed of wood, I had to suspend the preaching until it was squelched, when I resumed and closed without further interruption. The next morning I found a good congregation of both sexes at the school house, which was also very open, and without a door. They gave me an attentive hearing through a somewhat lengthy discourse.

"Same evening, rode to Huntingdon, the county seat, accompanied by the old gentleman on whom I first called. Although it was near sun-down when we arrived, I took immediate measures towards a meeting in the court house, and succeeded in getting a large congregation. Court houses are not kept locked in that country; they seem all to be in a delapidated state, as though they had no owners; the windows broken, and the doors unhinged, with interior furniture and arrangements corresponding. The same is the case with school houses and all other public property.

"I have found vastly better traveling since I have entered Tennessee; the country is more open and dry, the soil being somewhat sandy. I feel as though I had struggled through the chief difficulties of the journey; the face of the country is pleasant, and even beautiful betimes, I saw yesterday, for the first time, a field of cotton; it had not undergone its last picking, and therefore, presented a white and handsome appearance. If the reader can imagine a field thickly covered with weeds, disposed neatly in rows, like field peas; and if he can further imagine some large flakes of snow to have fallen from the clouds and lodged on said weeds without reaching the adjacent ground, he can then have a true idea of a field of cotton just before picking. I have said that I felt as though the chief difficulties of the journey were surmounted. I meant the difficulties of roads and weather—the long reaches of thirty and forty miles between houses where entertainment can be had, through a sparsely and rudely peopled wilderness, and the having to pay two or three dollars for a single night's entertainment of man and horse. . . .

"I left Huntingdon, which is the seat of justice for Carroll County, on the morning of January 9th with the view, if possible, of reaching Jackson the same evening, which is the capital of Madison County, and distant thirty-eight miles. The reason of this haste was, that a storm was impending, and as I designed to make a stay of some days in Jackson, I wished to reach it before the storm took place. I had not, however, proceeded many miles, ere I was overtaken by a horseman, a dweller in the parts, who expressed surprise at my riding with such speed, and with true rustic license inquired the reason; whence I came; whither going; my name; profession, etc. On learning that I was a Universalist preacher, he informed me that some excellent neighbors of his were of my religion; that they were expecting the arrival of a preacher amongst them, ere long; that from the name, I must be the person looked for; and that they would be much disappointed should I pass them without a call. Of course, I could not withstand these considerations, so I left the 'big road' and turned in with him to the plantation of Mr. John Bell, whom I found to be a sincere and zealous co-religionist. It was twelve o'clock in the day, yet an appointment was given out for the evening, and a large number of neighbors congregated, to whom, for an hour and a half, I addressed the words of life."[25]

"Jan. 10.—Reached Jackson toward sun-down. Called on Mr. M. L. Brown, by whose co-operation I was enabled to get up a meeting in the court house that evening. By the way, court houses are never found locked in this country; on the contrary, the doors are usually standing wide open, not unfrequently broken off their hinges; the windows are all broken, every-one; it seems a point of conscience to let no one escape this embellishment. I preached in the evening to a larger number than had convened the night before. On the 11th, as I was about leaving the town, I was informed by some very respectable citizens that public attention was becoming considerably excited toward my doctrine, and that I should be able to increase my subscription list by the delivery of another lecture. Accordingly, I agreed to return and preach on the following Sunday evening. In the interim I went into the country, and held three meetings; one six miles from Jackson, and two about twelve miles. The latter were in a neighborhood of Tunkers, who in this country are called Universalists; and they so called themselves. I found a warm and ready countenance amongst them. It is this district that the eccentric David Crockett represented in Congress, and these Tunkers were his immediate neighbors. Returning to Jackson, agreebly to arrangement, I addressed an excellent audience, who gave evidence of deep interest in the subject.

"Jackson is a handsome and improving town; it lies on a stream called the Forked Deer, which is navigable up to the town for flat boats. Jackson is therefore a depot for the cotton of the surrounding region; the bustle of its streets affords evidence that it is a place of considerable trade."[26]

In 1840, the same John Rogers came back to Tennessee and the Western District. Traveling in a south-western direction from Nashville, he found a perfect wilderness. For thirty miles, he saw not one house, finding himself at the end of a rainy day only fifteen mile from where he started in the morning. Here was a wilderness of black-oaks and there a tavern that God had not endowed him with descriptive powers at all adequate to describe. Panes of glass, paint, and plaster were luxuries not to be thought of in this wilderness. As he came to the Duck River country, he was bewildered with the seven

[25] John Rogers, *Memoranda of the Experiences, Labors, and Travels of a Universalist Preacher* (Cincinnati, 1845), 198-199.
[26] *Ibid.*, 202-203.

crossings that he made during one morning, but when he came to the river again, the water had risen and the ferryman would only promise to take the carriage over if he took it apart and made two loads of it. The diarist continued about this hazardous passage:

"Well, I must now go to work and take out my books and other plunder . . . to be taken after him in a canoe, and then I have the day before me to get to Perryville in, about thirty miles, though they tell me, an extremely broken and desolate region; and what I most dread, another large stream is to be passed in the route, on which also there is no ferry; and there I am likely to be again brought to a halt. Heigh, ho! If ever I am caught driving a carriage into this country again— why, it will be the second time, that's all. . . . Extremely little attention is given in this country to elegant improvement; one scarcely ever sees a brick building out of the towns, rarely ever painted or framed one; they are mostly built of hewn logs, without daubing, white-washing, or even glazing; the people, both white and black, seem to take the world most marvelously easy; they are not affected by the cotton mania as in the States farther south; and the thirst for gain is, therefore, less inordinate."[27]

John Rogers found very crude houses of entertainment and very difficult roads. In May of 1840, it cost him six dollars to cross the Duck river. This fact would not have been so bad if it had not have been for the fact that he had only to go another ten miles before he had Buffalo Creek to cross. His description of the difficulties of travel follow:

"No description can possibly exaggerate the ruggedness and desolation of the road intermediate; unpeopled hills, covered with postrate trees, and whose steep declivities were scopped into gullies by recent torrents; narrow valleys, the way through which, for the same cause, was choked up with impassable barriers of trees, brush, and heaps of loose gravel; ever and anon the path was suddenly turned, to avoid these obstacles, and these abrupt deviations were so blind as to bewilder the traveler almost inextricably; my own carriage made the first wheel-tracks on these new paths. I sometimes walked about for several minutes endeavoring to find a practicable way through, for my horse and vehicle.

"Well, at this rate I was from seven in the morning till six in the evening in getting over the distance to Buffalo Creek. Happily, a ferry is kept thereon within a mile or less of the little town called Beards-

---

[27]*Ibid.*, 317-318.

town. Arrived over against the ferry, I bawled my throat sore before I got a response. I was at length answered by some children, who informed me that their 'pap and mam' were gone to see some sick people about three miles off, and that there was no one left to set me across. Here was another agreeable incident. I had no notion of going back two or three miles to find entertainment during the night; quite as little had I for lodging in a marshy woods, exposed to hordes of mosquitoes; I therefore scolded the poor children for allowing their 'pap' to neglect his business, which gave me vast satisfaction; and I then despatched them to the little town to get some one who could set me over.

"It was after sun-down when they returned, with the word that they could find no one who would consent to do so. I therefore turned about, and drove to the point over against the town, with the purpose of leaving my carriage there, since I could do no better, and swimming my horse over alone. When arrived at the spot, I hailed a man I saw on the opposite shore, and inquired of him my best way over. To my great surprise he answered me very angrily, 'You may go to hell, there's where you OUGHT to go'."[28]

"Affecting an utter unconsciousness of his wrath, and with the exact purport of his reply, I asked him, 'Is the place you speak of, sir, on this side the stream, or the other? At any rate,' I added, 'It is now too near night for me to get there, except it is close at hand.'

"The ludicrousness of this answer, with the grave air in which it was rendered, cooled down his wrath at once by exciting his mirthfulness, and he told me he had been to the ferry for the purpose of setting me across; that he had arrived there in a minute after I had left, and had hallooed with all his might to bring me back, and supposed I must have heard him, as he could plainly hear my carriage.

"After apologizing to him, and remarking that the rattling of my carriage must have prevented my hearing him, he consented to go back, which I also did, and after considerable trouble and danger—for upon my word there was extreme danger in getting off of a very abrupt and crumbling bank into the boat—I got safely over, and found quarters at a farm house for the night.

"On the 30th I resumed my journey toward Perryville, which was still sixteen miles ahead, and the remaining part of the road of the same broken and difficult character as before described. At two P.M. I reached Perryville, which is handsomely situated on Tennessee River, and is the shire town of Perry County. It is but a very small place, however, although a shipping point for a wide scope of country. The Tennessee is a noble stream, wider I should think, than the Ohio, at

---

[28]*Ibid.*, 319-320.

Cincinnati; the country bordering it, though, is mostly very poor, the soil being very shallow, on a basis of coarse red gravel."[29]

After Rogers crossed the Tennessee River going west, he traveled over a road in Perry County which was seldom traveled with vehicles, one that the inhabitants took no pains to keep open. At times he and his horse were brought to a stop by the obstructions arising from fallen timber. A pleasure carriage such as a buggy was almost a phenomenon to the people in the country and the little villages. Anyone who rode in such was usually a merchant, a member on his way to Washington, or a northerner on a collecting tour. Rogers's own words should be quoted concerning the experiences of this trip through the wilderness to Jackson:

"I preached numerous discourses in different neighborhoods about Perryville, and two in the court house of that village. On the 5th the congregation was most imminently endangered by a storm which blew up just as I had got through prayer. The house was a mere pile of round logs, with openings between nearly as wide as the logs themselves; such are all the meeting-houses in that country; it stood in the midst of the forest. The storm which arose was one of wind, lightning, and hail; the cloud was so dark and angry in its aspect, that I perceived every countenance to wear an expression of alarm; for a half hour or more we sat in silence, during which I could not distinguished a letter in a large Bible before me; a tree was blown down near the house, which much startled the people by the crash. . . . In Perry County, as elsewhere, the interest visibly increased on the part of the people as they heard the more of the doctrine; there were quite a number of Universalists in the county, male and female, who shrank not from openly avowing it; among them was a Colonel B., for several years a member of the State Senate; a very primitive and interesting character—a second edition of Davy Crockett. He lived in an open log cabin; has fought Indians, trapped plenty of bears and coons, and hunted lots of foxes in his time; he once lived forty-eight miles from any white inhabitant, and depended on his rifle for his subsistence. By the way, Crockett, whatever we at the North may think of him, was a genuine type of the people he represented."

The next day as Rogers was feeding his horse, those who had gathered to see who the stranger was began to whisper that he was a minister and asked him to preach. When Rogers con-

---

[29] *Ibid.*, 319-320.

sented, they sent the boys out in every direction to give notice and soon a congregation had gathered.

"Some persons had attended my Sunday meeting from a distance of ten miles, on my way to Jackson: at their request I authorized a meeting to be appointed for four o'clock on Monday."

"June 13.—I reached Jackson; and glad enough to have got once more into a region where the tokens of civilization were visible. Upon my honor, reader, until I approached this place I had scarcely seen a decent building in a distance of one hundred and fifty miles; all log cabins, and they of the rudest and most comfortless description, without window lights, or daubing, or whitewash, or the least approach to indoor or out-of-door embellishments; no gardens deserving the name; no shrubbery; none of the fruits or vegetables of the season on the table, none to be seen; a dry and unvarying diet of bread, meat, coffee, and sour milk.[30]

"Now if this state of things was unavoidable, if it resulted from poverty, I should hold myself inexcusable in remarking upon it; but such is not the fact; it holds with regard to all, poor and rich, with slaves and without, with large and with small plantations, with fertile or with sterile lands. It results either from an inordinate cupidity, or a want of refinement; possibly from a union of both these causes.

"July 4th.—I recrossed the Tennessee River, over against Reynoldsburg, which is but a small huddle of mean buildings. There is a horse-boat ferry there; it was on the opposite shore when I arrived. The negroes who have the management of it reported, when they came over, that a canoe they had passed in the middle of the stream, and which seemed to have no one in it, contained two runaways, who were lying down in the bottom for concealment. This report set the man at the ferry to cursing in great wrath, threatening to bring out his rifle in order to give chase; meanwhile as he was expending his wrath in threats, the current was wafting the canoe more and more beyond his reach, until he saw that pursuit would be hopeless, and then he cursed the negroes for not hallooing out to him as soon as they had made for discovery."[31]

---

[30] *Ibid.*, 321-323.
[31] *Ibid.*, 323.

CALVIN JONES CORRESPONDENCE

After the material for this volume had gone to the printer, some correspondence of Calvin Jones was made available to the writer, some of which will be of much interest to Madison Countians and for this reason, it is fitting to quote a few excerpts from these letters.[32] Dr. Calvin Jones, a friend of Thomas Henderson, was a well known figure in North Carolina before he came to the Western District. Among his papers are found letters from Dr. Benjamin Rush, signer of the Declaration of Independence, John Taylor of Caroline County, and John Adams, President of the United States. That he was a land speculator in this district is shown by his letters to R. H. Dyer, those from John McLemore, the surveyor, and Dr. Jones's brother, Atlas Jones. In 1820 from Fayetteville, North Carolina, Atlas Jones wrote about the necessity of acquiring knowledge of the county before the land offices were opened, that under the circumstances, it might be wise to "entrust McLemore or Love with the laying your warrants," that it would be wise to buy up any warrants that Dr. Jones could get for one dollar.

On October 15, 1821, John McLemore wrote from Nashville to Dr. Jones who was in Raleigh, North Carolina, concerning an entry of land that Mr. Caruthers, one of his company, had examined for the Doctor. He reported that this land near Waddles Bluff was excellent land, that several families were moving in, that small warrants of one hundred acres or under were selling for $2.50 to $3,00 per acre but larger ones of 640 or more were going for $1.00 per acre. The surveyor continued concerning the conditions in the Western District:

> Your 1,000 acre tract, called the Butler Place,[33] on the South Fork is a valuable tract and ought to command cash. The best settlement in that country is forming near this tract, a short distance below it,

---

[32]Letters used through the courtesy of Mrs. Louise Jones McAnulty, Bolivar, Tennessee.

[33]Dr. William Edward Butler.

and near the office of the 10th District, is spoken of, with much confidence, as a suitable place for a town; indeed, I believe a town has already been laid out, called Shannonsburg; but no sale of lots has taken place, as yet. It is believed the seat of justice of the county to be laid off will be located there, or near that place.[34]

I have no doubt of your being able to sell your 1,000 acre tract for cash. It is, I am informed, well watered with bold running branches and springs. Such lands on Forked will command cash pretty readily, but not at the prices generally asked for such lands. There has been but few sales, as yet, at any price. I believe I have sold more than any other person. . . . I have succeeded in selling about $6,000 worth at from $2.50 to $5 per acre, cash.

The Western District is certainly a fine country. It is rising fast in the estimation of all who have seen it. I am told where there are now several hundred exploring, and on their way to explore it, with a view of settling there; if they like the country. Many have returned lately well pleased, and determined to settle there for life. Many appear delighted; they view it a cotton country. But times *are hard, extremely hard*. No money; money is truly scarce, they complain much of hard times, and want long credits. They say, lands ought to sell low; the U.V. [University of North Carolina], having a quantity to sell at $1.25 we ought therefore to sell low, also.

John McLemore continued his narrative with great objections to the taxes that were levied upon these lands to be paid to Stewart County before the new counties in the Western District were organized. His main reason that was included in a petition to the Legislature was that there was no militia organized in the district, therefore no Justice of Peace was appointed to receive the tax lists.

A letter from Colonel Robert H. Dyer to Dr. Calvin Jones of May 2, 1821 is probably the most interesting one of the group, for he told of the surveyor's work just a few weeks after the county was organized and before the county seat was located. He wrote as follows:

"The country is settling very fast; particularly on north and south forks of the Forked Deer. Your 1,000 acre tract of land where Mr. Butler lives, I expect is a fine tract of land, well watered, and in a good neighbourhood of land around it, which will mean a respectable settlement. . . .

There has been 7 or 8 flatbottom boats brought up the river to

---

[34]The Shannons were among the very first settlers in the county, building the first house in the town later called Jackson which was located on lands donated by William E. Butler and purchased from the Shannons.

Key Corner, loaded with bacon, corn meal, corn flour, whiskey, potatoes, & other things which the people stood in need of.

This ladding is taken by the owner in keels and bottoms, and carried up the north & south forks, to the neighborhood where I live; and to the neighborhood of Butler on the south fork, where your 1,000 acre tract lyes.

Five or six days before I left home, I got a boat up the fork that I live on; to the mouth of my spring branch, loaded with flour, whiskey, butter and fruit; say 12,000 wt. I was 32 days coming up from the Mississippi, seven hands on board. This was the first boat brought up that fork, so that I had to cut away a great quantity of fallen-down timber and drift-wood. Other boats immediately followed up to my house, loaded with corn, bacon, corn meal, whiskey, &c.

When I left home, corn could be had at 50cts. per bushel, bacon 10cts per lb., whiskey 50cts per gallon and other articles in proportion. I purchased flour at 3 dollars per barrel, best quality whiskey—best—37½ cts. per gallon, butter 16cts. per lb., dryed apples 4 dollars per barrel, green ditto 2 dols.

The fact is supplies of all kinds can be had on the Mississippi on better terms now than any other place I ever saw; provided the person purchasing has the right kind of money, which is silver; or United States paper. I could have purchased for one fourth less, if I had have had this kind of money, but had no other but Tennessee paper.

The people on the Forked Deer are all healthy, no sickness amongst them. My family have all enjoyed health, more so than any part of the state that I'd ever lived in the same length of time."

On May 9, 1822, Dr. Jones wrote to R. H. Dyer about selling his Butler tract, and the selling of the lots of the new county seat when it was located (and he had heard that it probably would be located on or near the Butler tract). Concerning the sale he wrote:

"I suppose the sale of the town lots, if duly advertised, will bring out a great many Tennesseans. . . .

"I beg of you to inform me what quantity of vacant land there is supposed to be in the Chickasaw country, fit for cultivation; what is the estimated quantity of warrants; what five warrants of 2,000 and 640 acres will command; what the land probably be worth when located.

"If, when the lots of the town at the Seat of Justice for Madison County are sold, I can ascertain the time and the season and occasion seems likely to draw together a large concourse of people, I will endeaver to be present; chiefly with a view to sell some of my land, and to see many people locating and others that I have business with."

LADIES' SOLDIERS' AID SOCIETY OF '61

Nothing could make the Civil War seem more real to a reader today than to see an account of a meeting of the Ladies' Soldiers' Aid Society on December 1, 1861 in Jackson. The buildings of the West Tennessee College (now Union University) were used for hospital purposes, but there was no Red Cross, so the ladies of the town formed an organization which endeavored to take care of the sick and wounded that were brought to Jackson. At a meeting of the Society it was resolved that the Ladies be divided into seven committees corresponding with the number of days in the week, and that each committee be charged with the nursing and care "of the sick in the Hospital on the day designated—furnishing milk and all other light diet needed—to be on duty from seven o'clock A.M. until night. Those who have been rendering aid are requested to continue their valuable services. It was further resolved that a request be extended to the families of Jackson and vicinity to take from the Hospital the sick as soon as able to be removed to their residences, and take care of them until they are restored to health."

Plans were also made to ask the good citizens of the town and vicinity to contribute servants, who were greatly needed to chop wood, make fires and assist in washing clothes. Robert Cartmell made several entries in his diary about sending slaves to the College to help in this work.

These heroines of '61 were doing a noble work, but there were a few proprieties that they thought they must abide by, so the following resolutions were adopted at one of the meetings:

WHEREAS, The ladies, however willing, can not, with propriety nurse the sick during the night, and the want of a nursing force at night, has been felt as one of the greatest needs of the hospital, therefore

RESOLVED, That Messrs. B. J. Malone, J. T. Beveridge, John L. Brown, W. H. Symmons, and J. R. Woolfork be requested to act as a committee to organize a society of Gentlemen in and about town, auxiliary to the Southern Mothers, whose duty it will be to nurse at night, classifying in a manner similar to the classification adopted by the ladies for day service, so as to detail at least eight names for each night of the week." This was signed by E. B. Jackson, President, and R. B. Hurt, Secretary.

The following are the names of the Ladies constituting the committees:

Ladies for duty on Sunday:
Mrs. Lyon, chairman; Mesdames G. N. Harris, A. Teague, Kell, Coons, Swan, S. Sypert, M. M. Hannon, M. J. S. Stoddert, G. I. Christian, J. M. Coburn, J. G. Womack, B. H. Hubbard, Curtis, J. R. Campbell, Shumake, J. A. Marks, W. M. Barr, W. F. Still, S. H. Swan, Dillard, W. C. Neely, R. W. May, J. B. Inman, Faxon, W. Beasenburg, L. Tanner, H. Stanley, Miss Martha Miller.

Ladies for duty on Monday:
Mrs. W. H. Long, chairman; Mesdames W. Alexander, A. C. Caldwell, B. Camerson, J. T. Beverage, H. G. Bledsoe, M. Cozart, J. B. Long, T. Simmons, R. Brown, W. S. Callaway, C. H. Brown, D. H. Stock, L. B. Everman, Bell, J. N. McCrea, W. P. Howard, J. Mask, R. Taylor, W. B. Hawkins, J. T. Hicks, H. Noll, Edwards, S. W. Boon, R. Sterling, John Dodd, A. P. Holdsfort, Slater, G. W. Talbot, S. Brown, A. A. McAlexander.

Ladies for duty on Tuesday:
Mrs. Malone, chairman; Mesdames A. W. O. Totten, T. Clark, E. Henderson, B. R. Person, A. S. McClanahan, E. A. Miller, I. M. Jackson, G. Adamson, B. Barr, Stanton, S. Luckey, Deshong, L. Weir, E. Parkman, T. Lackey, Jas. Brooks, J. J. Brooks, Robertson, A. Newman, B. Taliaferro, T. M. Greer, J. H. Hadaway, J. R. Taylor, Stannard, Munsford, Nesbit, Miss Hattie Acton.

Ladies for duty on Wednesday:
Mrs. J. S. Miller, chairman; Mesdames C. F. Munter, J. L. Talbot, J. A. Harrison, R. W. Wilson, M. Crawford, P. C. McCowatt, L. Goodell, A. Goodell, I. W. Norwood, Jas. Hughes, J. K. Stephens, W. H. Stephens, E. Jester, J. L. Fry, William G. Cockrill, G. S. Hamner, S. Creevy, George Hicks, W. C. Turner, John Conger, Dr. Saunders, Wilkinson, D. H. King, J. W. Boyd, Allen Williams, Lankford, Miss Mary Srtampka.

Ladies for duty on Thursday:
Mrs. J. R. Hays, chairman; Mesdames T. P. Scurlock, R. R. Dasheill, A. T. Pegues, J. J. Williams, L. Lea, R. P. Ford, J. N. Arnold, J. Umphlett, W. W. Myler, S. McClanahan, S. J. Hays, W. W. Gates, T. Reavis, J. C. Lee, Hillsman, Kendall, J. P. Butler, M. Jackson, J. D. Mason, S. Collins, Dr. Theus, Goodloe, B. F. Bond, S. Jennings, R. C. Prewett, W. Wathers, Foster.

Ladies for duty on Friday:
Mrs. R. Pyles, chairman; Mesdames D. C. Hall, Dr. Hall, C. Symmonds, W. H. Symmonds, E. C. Trimble, S. Epperson, G. Hughes, J. W. Campbell, Alex W. Campbell, Dr. Harris, R. H. Anderson, S. W. Gilliam, A. G. Marshall, J. R. Norvell, J. Gardner, J. Russell, T. Murrell, J. O'Conner, D. J. Sneed, J. H. Harper, Carnatzer, R. Cartmel, J. E. Glass, A. DeBerry, J. J. McAlexander, Laura Cox, F. W. Yancey, J. G. Mann, J. M. Parker, McMillan, John Brown.

Ladies for duty on Saturday:
Miss N. Hays, chairman; Mesdames A. W. Jones, Dr. Chester, Robert Chester, M. Brown, H. Brown, A. Guthrie, P. W. Gamewell, T. D. Tarver, H. H. Whiteside, J. C. Sharp, M. Cartmel, M. C. Welch, B. F. Gates, P. D. W. Conger, P. T. Scruggs, J. R. Woolfolk, J. S. York, A. White, R. Boyce, W. O. Butler, W. J. Oakes, M. Herstein, Weil, J. T. Anderson, A. B. Nichol, T. B. Beveridge, J. M. Brown, Miss Musidora McCorry.

REVOLUTIONARY WAR VETERANS

Only those who drew pensions are listed below. It should be understood that many who served in the War of the Revolution did not receive pensions or apply for the same. Those whose names are found on the pension lists of Madison County and a few other names are as follows:

Allen, John, 1818 list, age 75; served in Virginia troops; died August 10, 1824.
Clark, Lieut. James, Sr., 1832 list, age 75; served in N. C. line.
Clark, Jonas, Sr., lived with Jonas Clark.
Clearwaters, Benjamin, 1818 list, age 86; served in Virginia troops.
Dillard, John, 1832 list, age 82; served in North Carolina line; died July 10, 1833.
Madding, Daniel, 1832 list, age 69; served in Virginia line; lived with Frances Madding.
Noline, James, 1832 list, age 79; served in South Carolina line.
Perry, Nicholas, 1832 list, age 74; served in North Carolina line.
Robertson, John, 1832 list, age 89; served in Maryland line.
Stewart, William, 1818 list, age 79; served in Virginia troops.
Madding, Chapness, 1832 list, age 60; served in Virginia line.
Medlin, Bradley, 1832 list, age 75; served in North Carolina militia; lived with Eaton Lenusford.
Fenner, Anne, widow, 1840 list, age 73.
Arnold, John, father of William Arnold, died September 1, 1830, at the age of 82.
Hill, Colonel, and Rev. Green, died September 11, 1825, at the age of 83.
Dyer, Joel, father of Colonel Robert Dyer, died June, 1825, at the age of 71.[32]

At least three Madison County families are eligible to membership in the Order of Cincinnatus, instituted by General Washington and other Revolutionary officers at the close of the war. Two descendants of Captain Robert Fenner have availed themselves of the privilege of membership: Robert Fenner, great-grandson, admitted in 1903; Charles Paynes Fenner, great-great-grandson, admitted in 1912. None of the family of Lieutenant James Clark of Madison County have exercised the privilege of membership. Samuel Jackson Hays of Memphis, Tennessee, is also a member of the Order of Cincinnati admitted through his ancestor, Lieutenant Robert Hays.

MEXICAN WAR VETERANS

Muster Roll of Company F of the Second Tennessee Volunteers Commanded by Col. Wm. T. Haskell.

Capt. Timothy Jones
1st Lt. Wiley P. Hale
2nd Lt. Richard Hays
3rd Lt. Alexander Greene
1st Sgt. John McClanahan
2nd Sgt. J. B. Freeman
3rd Sgt. H. G. Bledsoe
4th Sgt. Flemming Willis
1st Corp. Alexander Henderson
2nd Corp. Samuel Lyon
3rd Corp. Edward B. Donaldson
4th Corp. Charles Knight
W. A. Day, fifer
William Anderson, drummer
PRIVATES
Hiram Anderson
John Anderson
T. Anderson

---

[32]S. C. Williams, *West Tennessee*, 233.

William Browning
B. Bledsoe
T. Boyd
John Burrus
Joseph Burnes
E. A. Clark
J. H. Cloud
Eli Chandler
J. C. Cochran
Jno. Cross
Dan Depriest
W. T. Dickinson
L. B. Fussell
B. Gourley
Thos. Griffin
Robert Haltham
E. B. W. Hobbs
J. Hollingsworth
R. Houston
Christopher Johnson
W. W. Jones
R. Kervman
Joel Lewis
Giles Lyon
Ira Martin
W. C. Matthews
L. D. Miller
Nathan Moore
J. H. Marks

William Nix
K. B. Pledger
Ernest Pearcy
Harris Rhodes
J. F. L. Sevier
G. A. Smith
Samuel Smith
John Steward
W. O. Stribling
John Gowan
Alexander Tyner
Hiram Tomlin
John Thompson
J. Wright
Alonzo White
James E. White
Solomon Whitlow
James Whitlington
George E. Willey
Alex Williams
Benjamin Williams
John Aamon
John Woodell
John Yancey

This muster roll does not correspond exactly with the ones published in the papers. These names came from a photostat of an original in the Library of Congress.

CIVIL WAR VETERANS
A PARTIAL LIST OF THE CONFEDERATE VETERANS WHO WERE MUSTERED INTO SERVICE IN MADISON COUNTY[34]

Muster Roll of Captain J. M. Collinsworth's Company in the Sixth Regiment of Tennessee Volunteers commander by Colonel Wm. H. Stephens.

James M. Collinsworth, Captain
Wm. J. McKinney, 1st Lieut.
Robert J. Williams, 2nd Lieut.
Ed Smith, 2nd Lieut.
John B. Arnold, 1st Sergt.
John W. Matthews, 2nd Sergt.
Abram J. Mason, 3rd Sergt.
John W. White, 4th Sergt.
J. C. N. Carter, Corpl.
Wm. L. Herrin, Corpl.
John W. Balentine, Corpl.
Patrick M. Duffy, Corpl.
Nathan Arnold
Esra M. Arnold
Josiah Allen
James M. Boykin
Pinkney Bell
Samuel Bell
John N. Bell
Wm. Joseph Belch
Christopher M. Carter

Robert N. Cox
William E. Cox
William J. Casey
William Copeland
Newton Cozart
Wm. H. Dunaway
Rufus H. Duffy
Francis M. Griffin
William H. Graves
John Hart
T. P. Hudgings
George D. Harpole
John A. Harpole
Valentine Holyfield
Joseph H. Hardy
William A. Hastings
Alexander W. Hall
Jacob H. Holt
John M. Henderson
Washington Hays
James Hammond

---

[34]These lists of Confederate soldiers were taken from photostats of the original hand written rolls in the War Records Department, Library of Congress, Washington, D. C. These are not all of the records but only the ones that were available.

MADISON COUNTY VETERANS

Samuel P. Johnson
James T. Johnson
Benjamin Jones
William Jones
James H. Jackson
Alexander Jones
Charles M. Kennedy
Daniel Kerksey
George King
James A. Lane
Joseph W. Lemond
Thomas T. Lemond
John Little
Benjamin C. Mason
John A. McIver
S. S. B. McCorry
James F. Matthews
Samuel J. Matthews
Robert S. Matthews
William McCulloch
Andrew J. Patrick
John Patterson
Robert W. Pearson
James A. Pearson
James H. Redford
William D. Rainey
Wyatt Robison
Thomas W. Redding
William Selph
John W. Sawier
Charles B. Stewart
Phillip T. Scott
William B. Smith
Thomas L. Smith
William Van Pelt
Calvin Van Pelt
William E. Woodson
Creed T. Woodson
Moody Young
Allen H. Young
John E. Duncan
Robert Hunt
Edward S. Matthews
John C. Matthews
D. W. Thompson
Robert Harris
Richard Robison

Muster Roll of Captain John F. Newsom's Company (F) in the 6th Regiment of Tennessee Volunteers commanded by Colonel Wm. H. Stephens.

John F. Newsom, Captain
James W. Boyd, 1st Lieut.
James Robert Arnold, 2nd Lieut.
Ed. Scott Mollison, 2nd Lieut.
James F. Bray, 1st Sergt.
Wm. H. Bray, 2nd Sergt.
Thomas Shannon, 3rd Sergt.
George Richardson, 4th Sergt.
D. M. Spencer, 1st Corpl.
Stuart Paden, 2nd Corpl.
George W. Smith, 3rd Corpl.
W. H. Barber, 4th Corpl.
Robert Alsop
Benj. F. Brouder
James H. Bray
Sam C. Bancum
Gabriel M. Barnes
James Bully
George W. Barber
Andrew J. Brown
John H. Burnes
Andrew Colligan
James M. Conner
Thomas Cashman
Mike Casey
John Davis
Alexander Dawson
James Wiseman Dodds
Edmund Delany
Elijah W. Davis
Joseph P. Franklin
Mike Fitzgerald
Bernard Gilray
John Glenn
Israel Gibson
John L. Gosnell
Junius Harris
William Hazley
William Hogan
Bernard Hilliard
John Hardy
Thomas Hill
James Jones
John Joyce
Franklin Keevill
R. E. McMaster
James Makar
Moses Murphy
Miron Moore
Michael McAvoy
Michael Murray
James Malanky
Alexander McGowan
James Moran
John B. Peeples
William Powell
William Pophan
Edward Quinn
Patrick Quinn
Daniel Ryan
Daniel Rearden
Joseph H. Smith
M. S. Shelton
Wm. Starr
James Sherron
Washington Stephens
George Stoddard
Valentine Tims

494   HISTORIC MADISON

H. N. Vanfranken
A. B. Williams
Lorenzo Williams
David A. Williams
John M. Williams

J. T. N. Williams
William Wilson
Patrick Wood
Thomas W c h

Muster Roll of Captain W. W. Freeling's Company in the 6th Regiment, Cheatham's Brigade of Tennessee Volunteers, commanded by Colonel William H. Stephens.

W. W. Freeling, Captain
George L. Winchester, 1st Lieut.
Thomas Lacy, 2nd Lieut.
Rufus A. Mays, Brevt. Lieut.
Hugh N. Sherrel, 1st Sergt.
Nathan A. Butler, 2nd Sergt.
John A. Givens, 3rd Sergt.
John D. Taylor, 4th Sergt.
Joseph W. Temple, 1st Corpl.
John R. Reeves, 2nd Corpl.
H. F. Alexander, 3rd Corpl.
W. R. Lacy, 4th Corpl.
A. V. Alfred
Newton H. Adams
Samuel J. Adams
John L. Ayers
George W. Black
John D. Bove
Richard Bryant
J. D. Cane
C. S. Cane
R. A. Cane
John Burns
W. S. Casson
John Casey
J. K. Carmach
George W. Cooper
R. B. Currie
Charles W. Davis
Craven A. Davis
W. E. Dunaway
James T. Emerson
N. A. Ewing
E. O. Fussell
J. M. Fulbright
G. C. Gattiss
James E. Givens
A. B. Goodwin
William A. Goodwin
M. D. Garrett
W. H. Haltum
J. C. Haltum
J. Calvin Haltum
F. B. C. Hamilton
Richard Hagan
Gray W. Heidelberg
John W. Holloway

W. J. Jarrett
Martin T. Johnson
J. H. Johnson
James M. Jones
D. P. McGuire
P. C. McMillan
Thomas J. McMaster
M. T. Mays
J. W. Mays
Wm. D. March
J. C. Moore
W. H. Morgan
W. C. Marshall
J. R. Murchison
James B. Nelson
J. V. Nelson
Pleasant Nelson
Lemuel Owing
Charles H. Peters
J. T. Reeveley
Thomas B. Rains
N. W. Steadman
D. W. Suggs
W. J. Sypes
P. J. Sypes
J. A. Smith
E. M. Simmons
John Sweton
G. W. Spurling
George W. Swink
John M. Teague
W. T. Teague
J. B. Timms
J. R. Thornton
Benjamin F. Vantreese
Thomas Vantreese
J. R. Vanpelt
W. T. White
Benj. F. White
J. W. White
Haywood Williamson
Matthew Williamson
W. S. Weaver
W. T. Young
C. C. Pauley
James L. Williams

Muster Roll of Joseph B. Freeman's Company (G) in the 6th Regiment, Cheatham's Brigade of Tennessee Volunteers, commanded by Colonel Wm. H. Stephens.

J. B. Freeman, Captain
I. M. Jackson, 1st Lieut.

James Elrod, 2nd Lieut.
B. F. Bond, 2nd Lieut.

MADISON COUNTY VETERANS 495

John B. Arnold, O. Sergt.
J. R. Miller, 2nd Sergt.
Robert W. Andrews, 4th Sergt.
John M. Withers, 1st Corpl.
E. R. Parish, 2nd Corpl.
Thomas Grant, 3rd Corpl.
William H. Shelton, 4th Corpl.
W. J. Anderson
John C. Askew
William Askew
A. V. Bailey
G. C. Bawdy
A. J. Bennett
James E. Boykin
William P. Boykin
Robert F. Brown
William A. Bushy
J. J. Cathy
C. C. Chappile
E. C. Childs
William H. Clay
W. G. Cole
J. J. Collins
A. W. Crews
Richard Davis
M. L. Day
J. H. DeBerry
Charles S. Dod
Emmanuel Emerick
Joseph Exum
J. W. Exum
J. G. Fettrell
J. G. Gilliken
S. C. Gregory
William Gray
Felix W. Hardgrove
C. R. Harris
James E. Hawkes
P. H. Hawkes
N. G. Hearn
J. W. Henderson
W. T. Henning
W. F. Henry
R. Hicks
R. E. Hopper
J. B. Johns
C. L. Johnson
Arnold Jones
R. F. Knight
J. B. Lawrence
S. B. Lawrence
Thomas S. Lea
Gawen Leeper
Thomas Lundigran
W. W. Lyon
E. B. McClannahan
S. C. McClannahan
J. N. McCelland
W. P. Miller
D. B. Monehan
Samuel Morrow
James S. Movir
Thomas Norvell
John W. Norwood
J. J. O'Conner
E. Outland
James A. Montgomery
Marshall Perry
W. F. Pierce
W. C. Pyles
Battle Robertson
James R. Rooks
H. D. Sexton
J. W. Shuler
J. H. Simmonds
W. P. Stearns
W. A. Stewart
John J. Shelton
Stephen L. Shelton
R. M. Teague
William Thompson
John D. Tidwell
Charles Vessey
J. P. Warlick
M. L. Wells
J. M. Wilson
John Witherspoon
C. C. Wood
W. A. Wood
W. M. Woods
W. B. York
John M. Merrill
J. B. Long
Abbot L. Robertson
George W. Dardin
L. C. Glass
H. H. Pegues
M. V. Exum
W. M. McCullough
James Askew
John G. Davie, 2nd Sergt.

Muster Roll of Captain W. C. Penn's Company in the 6th Regiment, Cheatham's Brigade of Tennessee Volunteers, commanded by Colonel Wm. H. Stephens.

William Clinton Penn, Captain
Alexander Jackson Brown, 1st Lieut.
John Alvis Greer, 2nd Lieut.
John Duty McDonald, Bvert. 2nd Lieut.
Joseph M. Kendrick, 1st Sergt.
Amos B. Jones, 2nd Sergt.
Walter Pyles, 3rd Sergt.
Eugene Brooks, 4th Sergt.
Rich Stephens Cole, 1st Corpl.
George M. Sykes, 2nd Corpl.
Frank M. Hutchings, 3rd Corpl.
Benj. F. Roberson, 4th Corpl.

W. F. Alexander
Charles Brady
James Moore Bledsoe
Franklin Asbery Bledsoe
Dewit C. Beadles
Wm. Edmond Butler
Milton J. Brown
James R. Brim
Robert A. Burrus
Wm. James Bryant
Wm. Henry Bruton
Horace Green Bledsoe
Pleasant R. Bradford
Jno. Alton Callaway
Augustus A. Campbell
John James Campbell
James Martin Cartmell
Thos. Jefferson Caruthers
Joseph B. Caruthers
James Caruthers, Jr.
Joseph Henry Caruthers
Wm. Butler Chester
Samuel Hays Chester
Joseph Lynn Cock
James Madison Cole
James Fulton Collett
Joseph Crofton
Michael Conally
John Hugh Dickerson
Augustus F. Eppenger
Richard Henry Fenner
John S. Fenner
Wm. Jordon Fogg
George T. Fortune
Robert Gates
John Ward Gates
Thomas M. Gates
John W. Gordon
Frederick Grennagle
Ainsie Greer
Wm. James Hadaway
Howell Harris
Robert Benj. Hicks
Wm. Anderson Hopper
Middleton Hays
Thomas Hardgraves
James E. Hughes
Wm. Parham Hughes

Robert Baily Hurt
Absolom Hurt
Thomas A. Henderson
Lafayette Jackson
James Freemon Jackson
Wm. Amos Jones
Robert Fenner Johnson
Thomas M. Johnson
Saml Clark Lynch
James R. Lewis
Benj. Franklin Lewis
Ebineser B. Law
Henry A. Merriwether
Thomas L. Murrell
Wm. R. McKnight
Richard B. Miller
Michael McGlaughlin
Ed Burke McClanahan
Gilbert F. Neil
Saml L. Norwood
William Powers
C. C. Panley
Alex. M. Pegues
James Greer Reid
Wm. Hume Reid
John Quincy Adams Reeves
Benj. Horace Smith
Charles Lewis Smith
Robert James Stark
Samuel Singler
John Anthony Stedman
Nathan W. Stedman
John Miles Slopp
Henry Clay Spurlock
Joseph B. Sykes
Baldwin D. Taliaferro
George W. Taylor
George W. Tomlin
Marcus L. Thomas
Patrick Tormoy
John Randolph Vallon
Robert W. Wilson
Henry H. Walker
John T. Whiteside
Lucius L. Weatherly
Wm. R. Williamson
Thomas J. Williamson
Wm. James Welch

Muster Roll of Captain J. Ingram's Company in the 6th Regiment, Cheatham's Brigade of Tennessee Volunteers, commanded by Colonel Wm. H. Stephens.

John Ingram, Captain
J. W. Campbell, 1st Lieut.
Thomas Rice, 2nd Lieut.
James Walker, Brevt. Lieut.
E. C. Harbert, 1st Sergt.
James Byrd, 2nd Sergt.
A. P. Giller, 3rd Sergt.
John W. Benier, 4th Sergt.
W. L. Utley, 1st Corpl.

A. C. Reid, 2nd Corpl.
W. A. Johnston, 3rd Corpl.
John Skillern, 4th Corpl.
W. P. Anderson
J. M. Andrews
G. W. Boucher
J. B. Barnell
J. H. H. Batchelor
J. A. G. Batchelor

T. A. Beaty
John Beaty
T. Bizzell
R. G. Bond
R. J. Bryan
R. R. Byram
Henry Byram
A. A. Bruce
L. P. Bingham
Y. L. Carlen
W. G. Cardwell
T. J. Claney
S. H. Davis
J. A. Dodd
J. G. Drake
J. P. Drake
W. A. Haynes
W. Y. Harston
Jarrod Harston
R. W. Hurdle
F. Hurdle
W. H. Hutchison
J. K. Hutchison
J. W. Howard
W. L. Jackson
John Johnston
E. J. Jones
J. V. Laney
T. S. Lackie
A. E. Moffitt
Lucius McBryde
J. A. McKinnon
J. Mulherrin
D. J. Murchison
William Miller
D. T. Phillips

C. W. Phillips
J. M. Pope
J. B. Powell
J. W. Powell
Johnson Penn
R. T. Patterson
J. W. Reid
John McKintosh
T. A. Reid
R. W. Rice
J. M. Robinson
G. W. Robinson
W. H. Sherd
T. G. N. Smith
J. T. Smith
M. A. Stanley
L. Staten
E. H. Sullivan
B. Swinerton
T. D. Tarver
M. P. Tarver
M. Vincent
D. J. Verser
B. C. Walker
R. Weatherly
H. Weatherly
S. E. Weatherly
A. K. Williamson
N. Worrell
W. H. Wray
(Here there were three names under a patch on the paper.)
Everett G. Piercy
Robert Harris
G. W. Byrd

Muster Roll of Captain J. L. Browns' Company (E) of the 6th Regiment of Tennessee Volunteers, commanded by Colonel Wm. H. Stephens.

J. M. Wollard, Captain
J. W. Fussell, 1st Leut.
H. C. Hill, 2nd Lieut.
John F. Dudney, 2nd Brv.
J. B. Askew, O. S.
W. L. Johnson, 2nd Sergt.
C. B. Mayo, 3rd Sergt.
S. J. Woollard, 4th Sergt.
W. D. Maxey, 1st Corpl.
D. H. Grant, 2nd Corpl.
J. A. Killen, 3rd Corpl.
B. R. Goodrich, 4th Corpl.
J. B. Askew
S. V. Austin
J. J. Blackmon
J. W. Boren
W. T. Bittie
T. G. Black
J. H. Billington
J. L. Brown
H. C. Barrow
R. R. Bennett

Loft Brown
J. C. Burns
J. A. Candle
W. W. Chatten
Jas. A. Crews
T. J. Debnum
T. C. Day
I. B. Day
J. J. Donnell
Charles Edwards
Wm. Eskridge
J. H. Ford
G. W. Glump
Hez Gray
J. G. Grainger
T. J. Hogan
J. W. Herron
W. H. Haley
J. C. Inscorn
J. D. Jones
G. W. Keller
J. H. Lanier

W. H. Massey
J. A. McAdoo
W. D. March
M. D. L. Novell
G. P. Negley
W. C. Oliver
J. H. Phillips
J. N. Parish
D. M. Parish
L. R. Roberts
J. A. Ross
John Rollins
J. Y. Roper
J. F. Scott
J. H. Scavers
R. A. Smothers

Samuel Stone
S. A. Smith
Wm. A. Stephens
Abner Stephens
T. J. Tarpley
Isaac Thompson
R. H. Townsand
A. H. Thompson
J. P. Wood
T. W. Woodard
John Watt
M. J. Watson
J. V. Woods
Wm. Watt
J. W. Young
E. W. Slone

Muster Roll of Captain R. P. Ford's Company (L) of the 6th Regiment of Tennessee Volunteers under Colonel William H. Stephens.

R. P. Ford, Captain
J. D. Bond, 1st Lieut.
W. G. Smith, 2nd Lieut.
C. C. Sharp, 3rd Lieut.
J. J. Boon, O. S.
W. L. Wimpey, 2nd Sergt.
S. B. Person, 3rd Sergt.
W. A. Nobles, 4th Sergt.
L. Weis, 1st Corpl.
L. B. Eserman, 2nd Corpl.
R. H. Cartmell, 3rd Corpl.
James Allison, 4th Corpl.
F. M. Allison
James Allison
D. L. Alexander
W. T. Anderson
Wm. Anderson
A. S. Brooks
J. J. Bradford
Wm. Barr
A. M. Bradford
Lock Brown
J. T. Bowman
D. Brock
W. Boyce
A. R. Bumpass
C. H. Bray
John Bradley
J. B. Boon
W. E. Cartmell
M. Crawford
Don Cameron
C. D. Chamberlain
Allen DeBerry
J. L. Drake
A. F. Dod
W. B. Ewell
J. W. Ewell
R. Fenner
W. W. Folsom
H. C. Glenn
James Greer

S. L. Gannaway
N. A. Gardner
W. S. Gray
J. A. Gregory
T. J. Holland
A. D. Harris
J. N. Harris
J. D. Henning
J. C. Hudson
J. P. Hart
A. Huntsman
A. Jones
N. L. Jones
J. Kendrick
W. A. Kendrick
W. J. W. Kerr
W. H. H. Kearney
A. J. Largent
G. C. Lowe
A. M. Lewellen
D. J. Merriwether
Pitser Miller
John McAfee
J. H. McCauley
A. A. Maynard
M. D. Merriweather
H. E. Newsom
T. H. Newsom
H. D. O'Neal
A. T. Pegues
M. Papmore
Thad Pope
T. Permento
J. J. Pardue
E. S. Rogers
David Reid
J. H. Reid
J. H. Sharp
T. Searcey
J. M. Smith
D. M. Stephens
T. Sorrell

MADISON COUNTY VETERANS 499

George Smith
T. H. Scruggs
L. Turner
J. P. Taylor
A. Thomas
W. B. Tarbutton
W. P. Walker
C. W. Winfrey

S. B. Wagoner
E. W. Weatherley
J. N. Walker
R. D. Whitworth
J. T. Watson
L. L. Weatherley
Thomas Everman

Muster Roll of Captain W. M. R. Johns' Company in the 6th Regiment, Cheatham's Brigade of Tennessee Volunteers, commanded by Colonel Wm. H. Stephens.

W. M. R. Johns, Captain
R. C. Williamson
A. N. Thomas
Ed Seabrook, 1st Sergt.
Ed Buntin, 2nd Sergt.
J. W. Wiseman, 3rd Sergt.
S. W. Tappan, 4th Sergt.
W. N. Allen, 1st Corp.
P. B. Tatum, 2nd Corp.
J. W. Moore, 3rd Corp.
I. W. Armstrong, 4th Corp.
J. W. Arnold
J. S. Amis
J. W. Alvis
J. S. Boylan
Norwood Barton
B. Branch
T. M. Boals
W. N. Blalock
G. B. Blake
D. R. Cain
T. C. Cocke
T. A. Clark
J. C. Carpenter
W. N. Chunn
S. J. Cocke
R. M. Daniels
J. W. Dodson
J. W. Davis
E. T. Dickinson
J. W. Faris
Hilton Frasier
J. N. Gates
S. W. Hall
R. B. Hall
J. L. Harris
M. Hartman
Chas. B. Hester
F. B. Hilliard
J. D. Holloway
T. M. Holloway
A. M. Hood
Jas. Herron
C. W. Humphrey
A. L. Jones
J. S. Jonson
J. M. Jordan

G. M. Lewis
J. P. Lynch
John McAdams
J. T. McNease
R. R. McCutchin
A. M. Moore
I. J. Neilson
Jas. A. Nelson
Horace Palmer
J. W. Parrish
C. S. Parrish
E. B. Perry
R. J. Poor
W. W. Reeves
J. A. Reed
J. S. Revis
John Robert
Louis Semoure
E. M. Seymour
F. T. Seymour
W. J. Smith
J. E. Spain
W. J. Stafford
Givan Stafford
J. B. Stanley
J. L. Stephenson
J. A. Stewart
F. D. Stewart
R. G. Tatum
Henry Thomas
C. R. Thomas
B. F. Thomas
Maurice Thompson
J. N. Weatherly
A. I. Winn
J. N. Wirt
S. P. Wirt
R. D. Winsett
A. C. Williams
L. M. Williams
I. J. Williams
I. J. Wise
J. G. Wright
William Yanaky
B. R. Thomas
L. W. Milan
J. A. Winfrey

Muster Roll of Captain Thomas Lacy's Company (B) of the Thirty-Third Regiment of Tennessee.

Thomas Lacy, Captain
L. S. Johnson, 1st Lieut.
Thomas Bond, 2nd Lieut.
G. L. Rains, 3rd Lieut.
David Turner, 1st Sergt.
James B. Lethers, 2nd Sergt.
Davis Starkey, 3rd Sergt.
Peter S. Woodsirs, 4th Sergt.
Robert T. Malory, 1st Corpl.
Charles R. Givens, 2nd Corpl.
J. R. Starkey, 3rd Corpl.
Andrew J. Harris, 4th Corpl.
William Armstead
W. G. Beaty
A. C. Beaty
James B. Block
Thomas R. Butler
Frank M. Butcher
Allen A. Campbell
James S. Carter
W. Carter
William H. Corner
James C. Collins
Pleasant R. Davis
Hardy J. Dean
William P. Day
Richard H. Day
W. J. Derryberry
Thomas H. Derryberry
Washington Eddins
Owen C. Emerson
Thomas H. Graves
John W. Graves
Leonidas J. Hill
Harrison H. Hammer
J. H. Hammer
Thomas D. Harris
Benj. F. Haltum
F. M. Johnson
G. L. Johnson
William R. Johns
Thomas B. Jones
Elisha King
J. P. Lanier
M. R. Leathers
David C. Lowry
W. A. Mercer
T. E. Mercer
William L. Moore
William C. Nickols
David C. Newton
J. C. Newton
William A. Pope
John L. Pope
John A. Priest
James B. Patterson
George A. Pace
J. H. Raines
George R. Rains
J. P. Rains
William B. Roach
M. E. Smith
Thomas H. Smith
W. J. Savage
William Starkey
E. L. Starkey
John A. Sommers
James M. Sullivan
Willis Siles
John P. Stribling
Robert W. Taylor
Joseph C. White
Francis M. White
John H. Williams
James L. Woodsen
M. C. Young
John H. Armsted

Muster Roll of Captain B. F. Elder's Company (E) of the 51st Regiment of Tennessee Volunteers under Colonel B. M. Browder.

B. F. Elder, Captain
R. T. McKnight, 1st Lieut.
Thos. Beveridge, 2nd Lieut.
W. Gardner, 2nd Lieut.
T. J. Mathews, 1st Sergt.
W. H. Newton, 2nd Sergt.
O. F. Collins, 3rd Sergt.
George Bagby, 4th Sergt.
A. Benthall, Corpl.
John Robbly, Corpl.
A. W. Haskins, Corpl.
L. B. Shelton, Corpl.
J. B. Alexander
J. N. Betts
W. C. Boyd
G. Boswell
J. P. Bagby
N. W. Bivens
J. B. Conner
J. M. Cole
J. Carrington
H. C. Hinton
G. W. Hall
L. Hall
J. Howard
J. Lacey
— Mooring
S. B. McWhirter
M. McKnight
J. N. Neely
L. Newsom
W. Robbly
C. Reaves
E. Slater

MADISON COUNTY VETERANS

D. Slater
J. M. Smith
J. B. Shelton
J. Timms
J. B. Thompson
W. Williams

Muster Roll of Captain E. G. Owen's Company (B.) of the 14th Tennessee Calvary.

J. J. Neely, Colonel
E. G. Owen, Captain
C. C. Conner, 1st Lieut.
A. W. Fleming, 2nd Lieut.
W. I. Campbell, 3rd Lieut.
W. R. Laipp, 1st Sergt.
A. P. Patton, 2nd Sergt.
S. C. House, 3rd Sergt.
P. M. Campbell, 4th Sergt.
Napoleon Hood, 5th Sergt.
Joseph Hurt, 1st Corpl.
D. C. Patton, 2nd Corpl.
S. A. Campbell, 3rd Corpl.
Jack Williams, 4th Corpl.
William Ables
P. L. Brewer
K. H. Bently
Thomas Burns
P. H. Borum
R. D. Bryant
Charles Belote
William A. Comwill
G. D. Cherry
P. Cook
R. A. Crowder
W. Cooker
W. M. Currie
B. F. Edwards
Sol Elrod
S. M. Edwards
Q. U. England
P. M. Ford
Thom Flowers
W. H. Ford
P. E. Fields
J. R. Griffin
P. Griffin
William Hurt
N. Hilliard
W. J. Henson
P. Jacobs
W. P. Key
M. F. Lake
J. Luton
H. H. Mitchel
J. Mitchel
W. M. McMahorn
L. D. Marshall
W. A. H. Neal
R. D. Newsom
J. R. Patton
J. M. Patton
B. P. Phillips
E. Parker
H. Parks
G. Pettigrew
J. S. Rogers
W. G. Robins
L. M. Rogers
W. P. Rogers
F. M. Rogers
G. P. Rogers
T. C. Stuart
L. F. Swainer
Walter Scott
W. Sumerron
H. Sandlin
C. Tidwell
P. Thompson
James Travis
W. Vicks
James P. Walker
John House
Ben Briley

Muster Roll of Captain J. C. Hudson's Company (F) of the 51st Regiment of Tennessee Volunteers commanded by Colonel B. M. Browder.

J. C. Hudson, Captain
E. O. Clifford, 1st Lieut.
R. D. Ellis, 2nd Lieut.
T. J. Hamm, 3rd Lieut.
— Thomas, O. S.
T. C. Garrett, 2nd Sergt.
J. W. Bray, 3rd Sergt.
William Smith, 4th Sergt.
William Ball, 5th Sergt.
D. V. Joiner, 1st Corpl.
George Baughn, 2nd Corpl.
Hute Thompson, 3rd Corpl.
A. J. Wadley, 4th Corpl.
C. C. Anderson
P. H. Butler
T. N. Brewer
U. S. Billingsly
W. W. Butler
Jack Bowman
Pleas Bowman
D. M. Beal
E. P. Bray
Thomas Bradford
J. M. Boatman
J. H. Carroll
T. B. Carroll
J. W. Caruthers
Jordin Carter
Robert Carter
Dug Criner

Charles Caruthers
William Case
G. S. Dickinson
Newton Duke
N. J. Duke
W. D. Duke
William Evans
Henry Evans
J. H. Gillam
W. W. Huggins
W. H. Hamner
George Husten
C. K. Hill
Munro Hamlet
William Jourdin
Isaac Jourdin
J. P. Latham
B. S. Lovlace
Mile Linten
J. W. Lee
Nance Lawler
A. J. Marlin

R. M. May
George P. Morgan
Thomas Martin
G. S. McAdams
M. M. Murtock
H. M. Melton
James Magner
Lewis H. Nefflett
Fletcher Neal
J. O. Petty
William Richards
Frankland Smith
John Pomeroy
William McGill
J. E. Wilson
J. L. Wadley
F. M. Weathers
John Wallace
A. J. Vestal
Isaac Young
Jasper Stobaugh

Muster Roll of Captain Murchison's Company (D) of the 51st Regiment of Tennessee Volunteers under Colonel B. M. Browder.

M. Murchison, Captain
M. T. Neely, 1st Lieut.
J. W. Harris, 2nd Lieut.
T. D. Hailey, 3rd Lieut.
T. S. Lackie, 1st Sergt.
J. Y. Strayhorn, 2nd Sergt.
A. Kelly, 3rd Sergt.
E. Tyson, 4th Sergt.
T. Deaton, 5th Sergt.
J. T. West, 1st Corpl.
T. T. Thompson, 2nd Corpl.
M. Taylor, 3rd Corpl.
B. Jackson, 4th Corpl.
J. Acre
T. Acre
W. Blythe
R. W. Barton
C. Byrum
C. Bunton
T. Byrum
H. Byrum
T. Baker
F. Bryan
J. Bowman
J. Cole
R. W. Coker

J. C. Dickerson
W. T. Fox
J. Hart
W. Hays
T. Jackson
W. H. Loyd
J. McCord
J. Meriwether
C. McLemore
D. McPhearson
J. Porter
B. Roach
S. Sumner
T. Z. Sims
A. Sullivan
L. Snipes
J. Sumner
T. J. Thompson
J. Valentine
P. Valentine
A. D. Weatherly
D. B. Wade
A. M. Williams
J. T. Williams
J. L. Weatherly

Muster Roll of Captain Job Umphlett's Company (C) of the 38th Regiment of Tennessee Volunteers under Colonel John C. Carter.

Job Umphlett, Captain
A. B. March, 1st Lieut.
W. C. Robinson, 2nd Lieut.
B. Lacy, 2nd Brevt.
J. R. Teague, O. Sergt.
N. J. Boon, 2nd Sergt.
J. C. Fly, 3rd Sergt.

J. C. Robinson, 4th Sergt.
R. A. Cock, 5th Sergt.
K. Matthews, 1st Corpl.
A. W. Mason, 2nd Corpl.
J. L. Bell, 3rd Corpl.
J. T. Pounds, 4th Corpl.
T. M. Oliver, Musician

MADISON COUNTY VETERANS

L. T. Thomas, Musician
H. T. Baker
W. L. Baker
P. F. Barnes
W. Barnes
R. Benthall
L. C. Boon
J. C. Boon
L. A. Brown
J. W. Brown
D. H. Coates
H. C. Collett
J. H. Collins
J. J. Collins
James Cunningham
A. W. Dedman
J. R. Denton
Henry Edwards
Robert Edwards
W. H. Edwards
Martin Edwards
R. F. Edwards
Gustave Ewell
L. H. Estis
J. C. Fly
James Glidewell
D. W. Gorden
T. W. Hadaway
J. W. Henderson
F. M. Higgins
James Hudson
John Jory
J. F. King

G. T. King
Allen King
Samuel Lewis
M. P. Lewis
J. H. Matthews
J. W. Matthews
D. M. Matthews
W. G. Mainard
P. D. Mason
L. W. Mason
N. Mitchell
N. P. Nelson
D. Olinger
Z. Pilant
D. Pilant
W. J. Porter
A. C. Renshaw
T. R. Rollins
B. F. Rollins
W. M. Roland
M. G. Rushing
Pat Ryan
A. J. Stanley
G. D. Smith
H. F. Smith
J. W. Sykes
J. H. Thompson
N. Thompson
A. Thompson
G. Thompson
W. S. Vick
Wash Wonderly

Muster Roll of Captain E. S. Elliott, Company I, of the Fourteenth Regiment of Tennessee Calvary, Army of the Confederate States of America, Colonel J. J. Neely.

S. Elliott, Captain
W. L. Drake, 1st Lieut.
J. Laird, 2nd Lieut.
J. M. Langley, 3rd Lieut.
J. B. Craine, 1st Sergt.
J. T. Cornell, 2nd Sergt.
A. Sanderlin, 3rd Sergt.
Henry Smith, 4th Sergt.
I. Smith, 5th Sergt.
James W. Hodges, 1st Corpl.
Wm. H. Gooch, 2nd Corpl.
C. Fife, 3rd Corpl.
J. H. Holden, 4th Corpl.
W. L. Akins
R. H. Bell
J. D. Brigance
W. B. Bradley
G. D. Brattan
J. W. Braden
T. J. Boydston
J. W. Brown
E. J. Chaney
S. D. Cobb
J. P. Crutchfield

William Carson
J. C. Casey
J. C. Clark
W. O. Davis
L. G. Ferman
A. Eason
B. A. Edwards
J. Edwards
P. M. Farris
W. E. Farris
Wm. H. Fitzpatrick
James Fitz
J. T. Garner
Jo T. Hunter
P. W. Harrison
T. Harvey
E. J. Hathaway
G. B. Jennings
James Jenkins
B. J. Jones
W. A. Langley
J. W. Lovel
J. D. Lowry
Saml Laird

J. Lusk
W. Mosley
George Meadows
Jno. F. Manley
J. McNeil
P. B. Nowel
T. H. Parker
S. H. Stewart
J. Stanley
T. R. Short
James Stewart
James Sanderson
Frank Sanders

W. E. Turner
J. H. Thompson
J. W. Thompson
John Robertson
E. E. Works
W. Wilkinson
James Waterage
A. M. Wilson
James Worrell
J. F. Smith
J. R. McCloud
J. Maynard

Muster Roll of Captain Zilman Voss's Company (C) of the Tennessee Regiment of Mounted Riflemen under Colonel J. J. Neely.

Zillman Voss, Captain
R. F. Stribling, 1st Lieut.
G. A. Bowlin, 2nd Lieut.
H. H. Swink, 3rd Lieut.
J. R. Murchison, O Sergt.
N. W. Steadman, 2nd Sergt.
T. A. Dunaway, 3rd Sergt.
S. T. McMaster, 4th Sergt.
D. G. Wainsett, 1st Corpl.
G. B. Block, 2nd Corpl.
George Lacy, 3rd Corpl.
J. R. Starkey, 4th Corpl.
A. M. Adams
W. M. Burns
G. C. Butler
W. P. Balt
H. A. Doss
E. Hamilton
W. B. Haltom
J. M. Hardage
F. H. Mayo
W. W. Manly
W. M. Murchison
J. C. Thomas
T. C. Moore
W. H. Suggs
T. R. Warren
P. S. Woodson
T. N. Buchanen
J. F. Day
E. W. Haltom
Eli Haltom
H. M. Parker
J. M. Savage
B. F. Young
H. L. Acree

James Allison
J. B. Cobb
William Cobb
M. Croom
T. H. Graves
James Gladney
William Gladney
John Gladney
James Gates
Walker Hurley
David Hodge
G. L. Johnson
James M. Jackson
Ed Lackie
Andrew Mills
H. J. McKnight
W. W. Newsom
Frank Piles
James Peters
H. F. Parker
William Pope
D. H. Parker
A. L. Rains
E. Rowark
C. C. Rushing
S. Rochell
H. M. Savage
Jack Smith
J. M. Teague
William Thompson
John T. Tims
W. D. Winchester
R. M. Whitfield
H. L. Woodson
M. C. Young

Muster Roll of Captain A. C. Reid's Company (G) of the 14th Tennessee Regiment of Cavalry under Colonel J. J. Neely.

A. C. Reid, Captain
W. H. Dilland, 1st Lieut.
J. N. Robinson, 2nd Lieut.
W. H. Reid, 3rd Lieut.
John Stafford, 1st Sergt.
W. A. Glenn, 2nd Sergt.

George W. Miller, 3rd Sergt.
W. Bynum, 4th Sergt.
James Jackson, 5th Sergt.
John Jackson, 1st Corpl.
T. L. Thurman, 2nd Corpl.
W. W. Holloway, 3rd Corpl.

MADISON COUNTY VETERANS

H. Britton, 4th Corpl.
H. Anderson
W. J. Anderson
H. Acre
Thomas Britton
B. C. Britton
H. Bynum
M. Bynum
James Bynum
A. G. Bill
James Briant
John Briant
George Byrd
T. D. Cooper
P. Carter
John Davis
F. Fletcher
S. A. Greer
James Greer
N. Gallop
Gid Godsey
R. Glidewell
G. N. Holloway
James Harris
Thomas Hook
H. Harriscamp
John Hammonds
George Joyner
John Johnston
T. Killough
W. T. Kilpatrick
C. Louis
John Levey
John McGee
John Mangrum
W. Milstead
Norris Miller
R. Porter
P. C. Perkins
W. G. Perkins
D. Patterson
James Pankey
W. Percefield
P. J. Robinson
J. W. Robinson
George W. Robinson
B. F. Thompson
James Vinson
Mat Vinson
John Vinson
M. Woods
W. Woods
W. Worrell
John Whitfield
R. Whitfield
Dan Williams
John Williams
W. J. Yarbrough
D. King
James Sanderson

SPANISH-AMERICAN WAR VETERANS

Muster-Out Roll of Captain Andrew M. McMillin, Co. F, 2nd Regt. of Tenn. Inf. U.S., Volunteers, Commanded by Colonel Keller Anderson.

The company was organized by Captain Andrew M. McMillin at Jackson, Tenn., in the month of April, 1898, and thence by rail to Nashville, Tenn., arriving on the 30th of April, 1898.

Clark J. Martin, 2nd Lieut.
John D. Wadley, 1st Sgt.
James R. Crockett, Sgt.
John J. Vanderbrook, Sgt.
Thomas M. Williams, Sgt.
Lindsay V. Cooper, Sgt.
Frank A. Helton, Sgt.
Carl A. Terrell, Corp.
Charles H. Harris, Corp.
James A. Swayne, Corp.
Edwin W. Aatlett, Corp.
Osman Freeman, Corp.
William R. Pratt, Corp.
Richard M. Sutton, Corp.
Benjamin F. Bryant, Corp.
Thomas T. Beck, Corp.
Lindsay V. Bledsoe, Corp.
Patrick Doran, Musician
Claude A. Cox, Musician

PRIVATES

Ackron, Thomas
Arp, Fred
Boone, Thomas M.
Bulliner, Cager
Bulliner, Walter
Battle, George G.
Baston, Lou A.
Brooks, Lonie F.
Brown, Walter
Clark, William M.
Connelly, William C.
Cock, John C.
Cottengem, Mac
Cross, Levi
Davis, John R.
Dougherty, James H.
Daws, Charles C.
Estes, William L.
Fleming, Wade J.
Goode, Edward W.
Glover, Guerrant P.
Granett, William A.
Greer, Robert L.
Glover, Lindorf A.
Goad, Thomas H.
Gaffney, Joseph B.

Hardee, Lou
Hinton, Thomas A.
Johnson, Eric
Kendrick, Ames
Kendrick, Theodore T.
Keller, James M.
Linn, Edward C.
Little, William S.
Maxwell, John A.
Mauldin, Homer E.
McIlwain, Arthur C.
Murphy, David J.
McQuat, William
Nicholson, Edwin
Nation, James T.
Pigford, Claude O.
Ray, Charles B.

Ricketts, John F.
Rodman, Edward F.
Rawarth, Edward F.
Stewart, Dudley
Worrell, Julian J.
Whitehurst, Edmonia J.
White, Isaac N.
Wood, James C.

RESIGNED
Benjamin B. Harrison, 1st Lieut.

DISCHARGED FOR DISABILITY
Heck, Oswald M., Pvt.
McGill, Walter, Pvt.
Miller, Andrew S., Pvt.
McCrary, Henry W., Jr., Pvt.

BY ORDER
Murtaugh, Frank M., Pvt.

WORLD WAR I VETERANS
SOLDIERS

Acree, David D.
Ada, Fate
Adams, Charles S.
Adams, William Robert
Adkins, Alvin
Akers, Thomas F.
Alexander, Arthur M., Jr.
Alexander, Harmon C.
Alexander, Robert D.
Alexander, Will
Allen, Alfred Williamson
Allen, Amos
Allen, Gabe E., Jr.
Allen, George S.
Allen, Horace
Allen, James R.
Allen, Robert H.
Allen, Roy H(erman)
Allison, William Taylor
Aldred, Thomas L.
Allred, Will L.
Alper, Carl
Alvis, Morton
Anderson, Earnest
Anderson, Eugene C.
Anderson, Francis O.
Anderson, Homer
Anderson, Hu C.
Anderson, Julian
Anderson, L. D.
Anderson, Merrit
Anderson, S. B.
Anderson, Walter
Arbuckle, Roy O.
Armstrong, Richard
Arnold, Carl E.
Arnold, Carl V.
Arnold, Ernest L.
Arnold, Claten L.
Arnold, Homer

Arnold, Hugh G.
Arnold, John M.
Askew, I. B.
Askew, Lindsey
Atkins, Devon
Atterbury, James A(shford)
Atterbury, Leslie Breaker
Austin, Petter
Avent, Major
Aycock, Jesse T.
Bailey, Adolphus B.
Bailey, Bennie A.
Bailey, Larry B.
Bailey, Phil
Baird, Edgar A.
Baker, Charles A.
Baker, Hal A.
Baker, Joseph Wm.
Baker, Will
Ballard, Banks
Ballard, Elijah
Ballard, Fred
Barber, Grady E.
Baker, Fred
Barker, James N.
Barker, Thomas O.
Barnes, Hiram E.
Barnes, Irving W.
Barnes, Isaac G.
Barnett, James D.
Barnett, John A.
Barnhill, Charles S.
Barnhill, Pedro
Barry, William Francis, Jr.
Barton, Noel
Bass, Eugene D.
Batchelor, Leon
Bates, Remus E.
Bates, Sam
Batterton, William D.

MADISON COUNTY VETERANS

Baxter, William D(avid)
Beard, Henry
Beech, Walter C.
Beisinger, Fred
Bell, Eddie
Bell, Ernest A.
Bell, Jack
Bell, Lester A.
Bennett, Charles
Bennett, Congress
Bennett, L. D.
Bennett, William W.
Berry, Dillen
Bevil, Delbert S.
Bibee, James R.
Bird, George T.
Birdsong, Cecil L.
Birmingham, Liberty W., Jr.
Black, Atlas
Blackard, Wade
Blackman, Robert
Blackmon, Lindzet O.
Blackwell, Thomas O.
Blackwell, William H.
Blade, Pervis
Blair, Comer
Blair, Nathan
Blalock, Roy N.
Blankenship, Joe Marvin
Blankenship, William A.
Bledsoe, Jefferson D.
Bogle, Guy B.
Bomes, Charlie
Bond, Allie B.
Bond, Allie D.
Bond, Bennie
Bond, Clarence R.
Bond, Countee
Bond, Fenton
Bond, Frank E.
Bond, George W.
Bond, Henry
Bond, John Lawrence
Bond, Louis T.
Bond, Robert
Bond, John Maher
Bond, William H., Jr.
Bonds, Limuel
Boon, Frank
Boon, Thomas M.
Boon, Willie
Boone, Arthur B.
Boone, Ovory J.
Boone, Lundy
Booth, Richard
Boren, Grady S.
Bowman, A. B.
Bowman, Manley C.
Boxley, Ole W.
Boyd, Earnest
Boykin, Andrew
Boykin, Loney

Bradly, Vance D.
Branche, Willie T.
Brantley, Willie
Brashear, Hallie P.
Bray, Curtis M.
Bray, Floyd R.
Bridgeman, Aldosia
Brinkley, William H.
Britt, Lee
Britton, Hubert Vials
Britton, Spencer
Brooks, Ervin
Brooks, Eugene
Brooks, James H.
Brooks, Ray
Brooks, William
Brown, Alan Eugene
Brown, Charles Blythe
Brown, Charles E.
Brown, Charley
Brown, Daniel B.
Brown, Dee
Brown, Ernest
Brown, Frank
Brown, George
Brown, George R.
Brown, Horace
Brown, Houston
Brown, Jodie L.
Brown, John H.
Brown, Lee
Brown, Lewis
Brown, Milton
Brown, Nolan
Brown, Robert A.
Brown, Thomas
Brown, Will
Browning, Lunsford Ochus
Brumley, William Eugene
Bryan, Louis T.
Bryant, Commer L.
Bryant, Edward
Bryant, Thomas
Buchanan, Romie
Buck, Charles H.
Buckley, Sam E.
Buddie, Frederick W.
Buffalow, Fred L.
Buggs, Gus
Bumpus, Roger Lee
Buntin, Albert R.
Burnes, Calip
Burney, George W.
Burney, John A.
Burton, Albert
Burton, James P(reston)
Burton, Jasper
Burton, Ralph
Burton, Will
Bushart, Newt B.
Butler, Frank M.
Butler, Henry E.

Butler, Hugh L.
Butler, Leland S.
Butler, Oliver J.
Butler, William Rufus
Butler, Willis
Bynum, Booney
Bynum, Cerfew
Byrd, Clarence
Byrd, Opie P.
Byrum, Hime C.
Byrum, William A.
Cable, Lem W.
Caldwell, Martin V.
Campbell, Judge
Campbell, Richard
Campbell, Rudolph
Campbell, Thomas
Cantlon, Adam
Cantrell, Clarence
Caraway, Thadeaus Eugene
Carlisle, William H.
Carr, Joseph S.
Carroll, Raymond T.
Carroll, Thomas Burns
Carroll, Thomas Lee
Carter, Bascomb
Carter, Paul Franklin
Carter, Walter
Carter, William A.
Cartmell, Hu H.
Cartmell, John W.
Casey, Charlie A.
Casey, Charlie J.
Casey, Steve H.
Cason, Leslie
Cathey, Johnnie D.
Chalker, Charles C.
Chandler, Roy S.
Chapman, Jim
Chatmon, Irvin
Chatmon, Milton
Cheatam, Eugene
Cheatham, James
Cheatham, Robert E.
Cheatham, Sam
Cheatham, Will G.
Chism, Billie
Claiborne, William A.
Clanton, Arther
Clanton, John W.
Clark, Charlie
Clark, James D.
Clay, Joe
Clay, Willie L.
Cleary, Hugh Anderson
Cleary, Matthew
Clemons, Ezra
Cobb, Ed
Cobb, Elva M(unroe)
Cobb, James D.
Cobb, John A.
Cobb, Thomas

Cocolow, Joe
Cole, Alvin
Cole, Andrew
Cole, Calvin W.
Cole, Carnie H.
Cole, Crealus
Cole, David
Cole, J. C.
Cole, James
Cole, John A.
Cole, Neal
Cole, Raymond
Cole, Robert A.
Coleman, Richard C.
Coleman, Wilgar P.
Colen, Fred
Collier, Bert A.
Collier, Johnie
Collins, Bedford L.
Collins, Douglas
Collins, Mahon
Collins, Manley Leonard
Collins, William McKinley
Comer, Allen
Comer, Milton
Comes, Guy
Compton, Graydon H.
Conger, Leonard H.
Conley, David S.
Conley, James R.
Conn, Carl B.
Conner, Albert
Conner, Burt
Connoway, Samuel
Cook, Hubert
Cooney, Walter J.
Cooper, Columbus
Cooper, John
Cottongim, Claude C.
Cottongim, J. G.
Couch, John E.
Couch, John V.
Cowan, Lee
Cox, Byron F.
Cox, Ed Lee
Cox, Coy M.
Cox, Marshal P.
Cox, Walter
Craig, Elkie Coffman
Craig, Joseph Wesley
Cramo, Collie
Craven, Albert H.
Crenshaw, Maurice
Crenshaw, Walton G.
Crittenden, H. C.
Crook, Senter C.
Crook, Walter
Croom, Alex
Croom, Ernest
Croom, John
Croom, John M.
Croom, Martin V.

MADISON COUNTY VETERANS

Crouse, Robert
Crow, Henry
Crow, James C.
Crowell, Will
Crump, Roy
Crumpton, William B.
Culp, Buren E.
Cunningham, Green
Currie, Tom S.
Curry, Dalton W.
Curry, David
Curry, President
Curtiss, Lyle R.
Cushing, Homer
Cutright, Elgra
Dailey, Robert
Daniel, Murray E(hitmel)
Darden, Hobert McK
Dardin, Willie Lee
Darnell, Ernest
Davenport, Olive C.
Davis, Charles L.
Davis, Ernest T.
Davis, Harold L.
Davis, James G.
Davis, James M.
Davis, Will
Davison, Emet R.
Day, Fred B.
Day, Luther
Day, Opal B.
Day, Rueben E.
Decatur, James
Dees, Euther T.
DeLoach, Lindsey G.
Deming, Cleveland W.
Deming, Everette W.
Deming, Fred A.
Dennison, Charles L.
DePriest, Burl D.
Derryberry, Voris G(raves)
Dew, Homer
Dickerson, William W.
Dickey, Ezra
Dickinson, John Anderson
Diggs, Bud
Diggs, Grover G.
Diggs, Oscar
Dillard, Thomas
Dismukes, Turner
Dodds, Murry
Doherty, Ross
Dollar, Albert C.
Donnell, Harold
Dorris, Thomas N.
Dougan, Lyle L.
Douglass, Rufus D.
Driver, Henry
Dudley, Jackson
Dugger, Richard D.
Duke, Arlie M.
Duke, Okle Thetus

Duncan, William B.
Duncan, Victor L.
Dunigan, Eugene E.
Dunigan, Hollis
Dunlap, George H.
Dunlap, Horace W.
Dyer, Robert M.
Earnest, Albert G.
Earwood, William O.
Elder, Horace L.
Ellis, Arthur G.
Ellison, Cleveland
Ellison, James
Ellison, Odell
Enochs, Kirby Stanton, Jr.
Eppinger, John Echumann
Ervin, William H.
Esler, Thomas George
Esters, Dan
Estes, Walter L.
Evans, Eulace
Evans, June
Evans, Oscar S.
Evans, Walter H.
Everett, Lucian Greene
Ewing, Finis C.
Ewing, Henry
Ewing, James
Ewing, Lee Bishop
Exum, Frank E.
Exum, Odie
Ezzell, Harry J.
Ezzell, Sharp
Fenner, Richard Jones
Ferguson, Curtis L.
Ferguson, Roy L.
Feuerstacke, John A.
Fielding, William S.
Finger, James
Finger, Allen
Finger, John G.
Fishman, David Sol
Fishman, Emanuel
Fishman, Horace Milton
Fite, Phillips Harold
Fleming, Otto
Fletcher, Thomas
Fletcher, Walter F.
Fletcher, William E.
Flowers, Alfonso
Flowers, Bernard B.
Floyd, Velmer B.
Fly, Hugh G.
Fogg, Joseph William
Foote, Claude M.
Forrest, John
Forrester, Orie C.
Forsythe, Robert
Foster, Wallace Kimberlin
Fowler, Charles C.
Fowler, J. P.
Fowler, Noble O.

Fox, Lercy
Frankland, Leonard E.
Frankland, Walter L.
Franklin, George
French, Elonzo
French, Luther
French, Murj D.
Fry, Carlas
Fry, Clint D.
Fry, Conrad C.
Fry, Joe
Frye, Frederic A.
Fuerstacke, Augustus P.
Fulks, Eugene
Fuller, George W.
Fuller, John A.
Fuller, John W.
Fuller, Joseph D.
Fuller, Percy
Fuller, Robert O.
Fuller, Scott
Fuller, Timothy
Fuller, William C.
Fullington, Jessie S.
Fuqua, Clint
Fussell, William A.
Futrell, Samuel
Galbraith, Thomas N.
Gamble, John
Gant, James
Gardner, Joseph A.
Garr, William W.
Garrett, Coe L.
George, Elbert B.
Geyer, Edwin Haynes
Gibbs, Charles W.
Gibbs, Clarence B.
Gibbs, Thomas
Giles, Clinton Owen
Gill, Eugene
Gill, Sam
Gillam, James C.
Gillman, Charles H.
Gilmore, Shelby
Gilstrap, Will H.
Givens, Bill
Givens, Jake
Givens, Lovie
Givens, Melvin
Givens, Willis
Glenn, Eugene
Glenn, Homer O.
Glenn, James M.
Glenn, Jim
Glenn, John
Glidwell, Tom
Glover, J. D.
Glover, Morris
Glynn, Mike
Golden, Alexander H.
Golden, I. J.
Golden, James

Gooch, Jessie L.
Gooch, Wardell
Goodman, Ulysses G.
Goodrich, James W.
Goodrum, Nolan
Gowan, Guy G.
Gowan, Jesse N.
Grace, James Arthur
Grady, Giles Robert
Graham, William Henry
Granberry, Boyce
Graves, Ned
Graves, Wiley
Green, Noble
Green, William M.
Greer, Burk
Greer, Harvey
Greer, Martin
Greer, Robert
Greer, Willard N.
Gregory, Gilbert B.
Gregory, Rufus M.
Grimes, Fred H.
Grisham, William C(larence)
Grove, Robert G.
Grubbs, James Hasil
Gunn, David H(ughes)
Gurley, Luther
Gurley, Robert E. L.
Guy, Hobert
Haak, Ed E.
Halcom, James F.
Hall, Fred
Hall, George B.
Hall, James E.
Hall, Jerrie
Hall, Johnny
Hall, Waymond L.
Hamilton, Fred M.
Hamlett, William B.
Hammers, Lee A(lvin)
Hampton, Robert
Hanley, Thomas C.
Hansen, Fred C.
Hardy, Stokes
Harigan, John C.
Harlan, Paul M.
Harper, George
Harper, Mack M.
Harrell, William L.
Harris, Abaham M.
Harris, Albert H.
Harris, Chester L.
Harris, Don B.
Harris, George N.
Harris, Henry
Harris, Hugh William
Harris, Joel Fred
Harris, Mark Hines
Harris, Wendell H.
Harrison, Isham
Harrison, Wellborn M.

Hart, John C.
Harton, Dewey L.
Harton, Ripp H.
Harwell, Dewell
Haughton, Genia
Hawkins, Richard C.
Hawks, Zonnie O.
Hayes, Cleaves N.
Hayes, Elijah
Hayes, Robert E.
Hayes, Roy W.
Hayes, Walter Lee
Haynes, Harbert
Haynes, Odie
Haynes, Oscar
Hays, Corbett W.
Hays, Jesse
Hays, Thomas
Hays, Trimble M.
Hays, Willie M.
Hearn, Samuel H.
Hearns, Estell
Heathcock, Thomas Fenner
Hefley, Ike S.
Heidelberg, Savannah N.
Henderson, William Thomas
Hendon, Fred
Hendricks, Calvin N.
Henning, James F.
Henning, Robert L.
Henry, Eugene S.
Herron, Govner
Herron, Sylvester
Hickman, William V.
Hicks, Hugh W.
Hicks, John Greer
Hicks, Lonnie
Hicks, Regie
Higgs, Oscar
Hill, De Witt J.
Hill, Lee
Hill, Raleigh B.
Hill, Samuel T.
Hill, Thomas Joe Brice
Hill, W. E.
Hill, Willie
Hillard, Currie B.
Hillard, Russell L.
Hilliard, William A.
Hines, Frank
Hines, Willie E.
Hinkle, Joe
Hinton, Robert Chester
Hobson, Earl
Hodge, Daniel
Hodges, Eddie
Holder, Audy
Holderness, McKinley
Holley, Roy C.
Holloman, Lofton O.
Holloman, Tena J.
Holloway, W. L.

Holmes, Clayborn C.
Holmes, Mike
Hopper, Andrew
Hopper, Clyde F.
Hopper, John B.
Hopper, William B.
Hopper, William Freeman
House, Thomas E.
Houston, Willie F.
Howell, Rufus
Hoyle, Cluster
Hoyle, Levy
Hubanks, Sam
Huddleston, Herman
Hudgins, John R.
Hudgins, Ronald Kussuth
Hudson, Joseph Edgar
Hudson, Print
Hudson, Sam N.
Hudson, Wilkie A.
Hudspeth, Jean O.
Hundley, James O.
Hunt, Cedric Alfred
Hunt, Charlie N.
Hunt, Horace R.
Hunt, John
Hunt, Tom
Hunter, Jesse L.
Hunter, Joe
Hupper, Asberry
Hutch, Jim
Hutch, John
Hutcherson, Harry B.
Hutson, James A. W.
Ingram, Dewitt T.
Ingram, Jodie
Ingram, John Q.
Ingram, McKinley
Ingram, Roger A.
Ingram, Stephen W.
Ingram, T. D.
Innis, James C.
Isabell, Eddie L.
Isbell, Harry D.
Isbell, Herbert Lee
Isbell, Ramer
Ives, Fred O.
Ives, Norman A.
Ivey, James
Ivey, James H.
Ivey, James R.
Ivey, James W.
Ivory, Will
Jackson, Albert N.
Jackson, Benjamin H.
Jackson, Isaac L.
Jackson, Lawrence P.
Jamerson, Hiram W.
Jared, Albert Thurman
Jeffries, James B.
Jenkins, Robert
Jenkins, T. Willie

Jeene, Woodford C.
Jennings, Jesse M.
Jennings, Robert M.
Jennings, Roy
Jernigan, Henry Mitchell
Jernigan, Henry Willard
Jobe, Thornley S.
Johns, J(ames) Berly
Johnson, Albert
Johnson, August
Johnson, Cecil L.
Johnson, Charlie
Johnson, Dorsey
Johnson, Earl W.
Johnson, Edward F.
Johnson, Ernest J.
Johnson, Floyd W.
Johnson, Frank Nebhut
Johnson, Franklin L(ee)
Johnson, Fred
Johnson, Harry
Johnson, Herbert
Johnson, Lacy
Johnson, Lee Roy
Johnson, Leland S.
Johnson, Luther
Johnson, Mannie
Johnson, Neadom Harbert
Johnson, Norman E.
Johnson, Ola
Johnson, Reuben Robert
Johnson, Sid T.
Johnson, Thomas Vernon
Johnson, Walter
Johnson, Walter G.
Johnson, William H.
Johnson, William Norman
Jones, Adam
Jones, Atlas T.
Jones, Charlie
Jones, Curtis F.
Jones, Eddie L.
Jones, Eugene F.
Jones, George D.
Jones, Gilbert
Jones, Herbert S.
Jones, James F.
Jones, James G.
Jones, John L.
Jones, John W.
Jones, Perry A.
Jones, Roy
Jones, Sevier
Jones, Walter
Jones, Will
Jones, William H.
Jones, William Luther
Jones, Willie
Jordan, James H.
Jordan, Mack P.
Jordan, Thomas W.
Kearney, John W.

Keefe, William P.
Keller, Floyd H.
Kelly, Will H.
Kemp, Cleo M.
Kennedy, Frank A.
Kenyon, Firm C.
Kerby, Bedford
Key, Bunnie H.
Key, Nezrett S.
Key, Robert
Key, William A.
Kimbrell, Alex
King, Isaac N.
King, Jesse T.
King, Jim E.
King, Walter
Kirby, Robert H.
Kirk, Ernest W.
Kiser, John W.
Kittner, Floyd L. S.
Kline, Clarence W.
Knight, Earl
Lacy, Dee C.
Lacy, Ocie
Lake, Joseph F.
Lake, Richard E(rnest)
Lambert, Joshua E.
Lambert, Lacy T.
Landers, Mark J.
Lane, Francis Burleson
Lane, John H.
Lane, Shellis Franklin
Laney, James H.
Lang, John
Lanier, Elijah
Lashley, James L.
Lashley, M(elvin) P.
Lashley, William B.
Lasiter, Homer P.
Lasley, Bedford T.
Lawler, Thomas E.
Lawrence, Marvin T.
Lawson, Horace
Leathers, George Robert
Leathers, Ivy Lee
Lee, Arthur
Lee, Thurston
Leeper, Guy H.
Leeper, Robert A.
Lennon, Cornelius A(ndrew)
Lennon, Jefferson F.
Leon, Henry
Lester, Frederick G.
Levis, Lester E.
Lewis, Charlie S.
Lewis, Edward
Light, William Alphonso
Lile, James H.
Lindsay, Edgar C.
Lindsay, Sherman J.
Linton, John F.
Lisenby, James H.

Littleton, Claud
Littrell, Moses H.
Lohrig, George Maxwell
Lohrig, William W.
Long, Crawford
Long, Gilbert
Long, Limmie
Long, Neal
Long, Robert L.
Lorans, Temple
Love, D. C.
Love, Robert H.
Love, Walter
Lowe, William L.
Loyd, Dewey D.
Luckman, Scott F.
Luke, Ben
Lusby, Willie Bob
Lusby, Willie L.
Luster, Henry
Luster, Luther
Luttrell, Curtis A.
Lyles, Sanford
Lyons, Charlie T.
McAlexander, Charlie Lee
McAnally, Alva O.
McAnulty, Rillous
McBride, Johnnie
McBride, Roy
McCarley, Lavanga A.
McCarver, Wayne F.
McCarver, William I.
McClamroch, William Eugene, Jr.
McCleary, Robert E.
McClintock, Albert F.
McClintock, Joseph H.
McClure, James E.
McCollum, A. J. Howell
McCollum, Roy G(aston)
McCommon, Bailey
McCorry, Mack
McCorry, William
McCoy, Gladstone
McCoy, Kotch
McCue, Willie C.
McDade, John D.
McDonald, Louis C.
McDonald, Richard H.
McDonough, James Wesley
McFadden, Johnie C.
McGaha, Johnny
McGaughey, Merle
McGee, Census
McGee, Roy J.
McGee, William C.
McGee, Willie
McHaney, Reder
McHaney, Vergil
McKee, John H.
McKenzie, Daniel G.
McKenzie, John E.
McKenzie, Marvin A.

McKenzie, Robert T.
McKinnie, John R.
McKinzie, John Carlis
McKnight, James W.
McKnight, Robert M.
McLain, Martin J.
McLean, George W.
McLeary, William Hunter
McLemore, Lillian Abraham
McNeely, Rush
McNulty, Ben
McNulty, Vernice
McNulty, Zingo D.
Maben, Smith
Mackey, Mozella
Macon, Willie
Magda, John
Mahone, Nathaniel
Mahundro, Edward
Mainord, William M.
Major, Hubert C.
Major, Roland
Mallory, Charles
Malone, Edward
Malone, Harry D.
Malone, Jim
Malone, Levi
Malone, Lonnie L.
Maloy, Joe H.
Mamer, George G.
Maness, Luther
Maness, Thomas C.
Manley, Robert
Marks, Ray H.
Marlow, Gilmer C.
Marrow, Hugh S. J.
Marsh, Elijah E.
Marsh, William L.
Marshall, Charles
Martin, Robert L.
Martin, Willie H.
Mason, Jacob Clyde
Mason, John F.
Mason, John R.
Mason, Millard D.
Mason, Ray W.
Mathis, James H.
Mathis, Otis L.
Mathis, William T.
Matkins, William A.
Matlock, John J.
May, Jack L.
May, Pierce
Mayo, John
Mays, John Luther
Mays, Walter M(eyhew)
Mayweather, Billie
Melton, Arthur L.
Melton, Haven L.
Mercer, Frank A.
Mercer, Luther
Mercer, Prince

Mercer, William
Merchant, Harold F.
Meriweather, Louis
Meriwether, Howard
Meriwether, James R.
Merriweather, Fredie
Merriweather, John
Merriwether, David A(ugusta)
Merriwether, Murry D.
Merrywether, Aaron
Merryweather, Harvey
Michie, Fred Ephriam
Midyett, John R.
Mihalovits, Harry
Miller, Dave
Miller, Joseph D.
Miller, Linwood L.
Mills, Paul
Mills, William A.
Mingle, Charles
Minor, Vinson
Mintz, Jim
Mitchell, Bird
Moffitt, Oscar Cornelius
Moloy, Larcy
Montgomery, David J.
Montgomery, Dennis
Montgomery, Joseph H.
Moody, Shannon
Moore, Charlie
Moore, Daniel D.
Moore, Hal R., Jr.
Moore, Horace Greely
Moore, James E.
Moore Joe W(heeler)
Moore, Bewt S.
Moore, William K.
Morgan, Jim
Morgan, Lafayette Mack, Jr.
Morgan, Willie
Morris, Charley T.
Morris, John Albert
Morris, Lee Roy
Morrow, Horace H.
Morrow, John E.
Morrow, Thomas B. T.
Mosley, Tom
Mosley, Zacariah
Motherhead, James R.
Mullins, James W.
Murchison, James F.
Murchison, Lawrence R.
Murchison, Raymond D.
Murphy, Ralph S.
Murphy, Thomas W.
Murray, Thomas J., Jr.
Murray, Willard H.
Nanney, Spurgeon A.
Neal, Greather
Neal, John
Neal, Sylvester
Neeley, Douglas

Neely, Ed
Neely, John
Neisler, Ote E.
Nelson, Joe
Nelson, Joe, Jr.
Nelson, John G.
Nettles, Grover C.
Newberry, Aubrey C.
Newburn, Joe T.
Newton, Lytle J.
Nichols, Alton
Nichols, Cason
Nichols, Earl Wilson
Noel, Clarence A.
Noel, Samuel L(afayette)
Norman, Genie
Norman, Lindsey
Norman, Louis
Northcross, John
Northcross, Marshall
O'Connor, James
Ogden, Nash D.
Oliver, Herman C.
Oliver, John F.
O'Rourke, Edward
Orr, William P.
Osborne, Elbert M.
Oswald, Thomas R.
Otts, Vester
Outlan, Arch B.
Outlaw, Frederic C.
Overton, John
Owen, Benjamin H.
Owen, Clifford H.
Owen, Hugh H.
Parham, Robert J.
Parham, Tom
Parish, Dexter F.
Parish, Hobert O.
Parish, Marvin N.
Parker, James Robert
Pate, James M.
Patterson, Klein H.
Patterson, Thomas F.
Patton, Richard Shelton
Paulk, Richard E.
Payton, Alvin
Payton, Fred
Pearson, Eston Arley
Pearson, James E.
Pearson, John L., Jr.
Pearson, Robert L.
Pegues, Pettibone
Pennington, Ralph Albert
Pentecost, Henry E.
Pentecost, Kessie F.
Perry, James O.
Perry, James T.
Perry, Jennings
Perry, William
Person, Andrew J.
Person, Edward

Person, Fred
Person, Fred E.
Person, Hollis
Person, John L.
Petties, Richard
Pettis, Jerome
Petty, John
Petway, Benjamin
Phillips, Felix H.
Phillips, Fenner D.
Phillips, Frontis E.
Phillips, Joe T.
Piercey, Homer F.
Pigott, Charles F.
Pigues, John
Pinson, Wardell
Pipkin, George H.
Pippin, Edgbert
Poe, Hugh
Poe, Stokes
Pool, Charles A.
Poole, Isaac M.
Poole, John
Pope, Vollie M.
Pope, William Winfield
Porter, John H.
Porter, William R.
Pouncey, Taylor
Pounders, Lonnie
Powell, Arthur V.
Powell, Tom Jefferson
Price, Anderson Lacy
Price, Brodie
Price, James
Priddy, Charles H.
Priddy, Sam
Pruett, Edward McK
Pruett, Robert
Puckett, Clark
Puckett, Lois
Quinn, Brisk
Quinn, Sidney
Raines, Hugh Robert
Rainey, David C.
Rainey, James Wendell
Rains, William Hobart
Randle, Brooks
Randolph, Ed P.
Randolph, Thomas
Rankin, Conway
Rawlett, Dick
Reams, Claude
Reaves, Richard
Reavis, Earl L.
Reavis, Thomas Andrew
Redd, Eddie
Redden, James E.
Reed, Alonzo
Reed, George L.
Reed, Handy
Reed, Nathan
Reeves, Jerry

Reeves, Robert
Reid, Ambrose R.
Reid, George Marion
Reid, James C.
Reid, Lionel C.
Reid, Owen
Replogle, Menton John
Rhodus, Gilbert
Rice, Willie
Richard, Eugene
Roach, Henry Cleveland
Robenson, Charlie
Roberson, Clarence
Roberts, Pete
Roberts, Willis Edward
Robertson, Cambell
Robertson, Dee
Robertson, George Harris, Jr.
Robertson, Izear
Robertson, John
Robertson, Lewis
Robertson, William
Robinson, Bethel
Robinson, Harry
Robinson, Herbert
Robinson, Lex
Robinson, Merdic
Robinson, William
Robinson, Charley
Robison, Joe
Robinson, Lex
Roddie, Willie
Rodgers, Lobie
Rogan, Joe
Rogers, Amos L.
Rogers, Ed
Rogers, Nehimi
Rollins, J. D.
Rollins, Ollie L.
Rollins, Sid
Rone, Raymon W.
Rooks, Benjamin F.
Rooks, George
Ross, Albert
Ross, Dave
Ross, Sam I.
Rosser, Henry G.
Rowe, Henry G.
Rowland, John C.
Royal, Joe Henry
Rucker, James
Rush, Manuell C.
Rushing, Preston W.
Rushing, Robert M.
Russell, David W.
Russell, Grafton
Russell, Tom H.
Rutherford, John
Rutherford, William Overton
Rutledge, Fleming Lovic
Ryan, Matthew H.
Sain, Grover C.

Sanders, William McK
Sanford, John L.
Sangster, Albert H.
Sauls, Robert C.
Savage, Isaiah
Savage, Jasper
Savage, Louis
Scales, Lee
Scott, Eric W.
Scott, Garrie P.
Scott, George W.
Scott, George W. H.
Scott, Henry, Jr.
Scribner, James R.
Scruggs, Luther
Seavers, Rufus Manley
Seward, Irving William
Sewell, Clyde Stetzel
Sewell, Eugene C.
Sewell, Vila Lambuth
Shannon, George
Sharp, Henry
Shaver, Glyndon B.
Shaw, Arthur
Shaw, Dorsey
Shaw, Felix
Shaw, George W.
Shaw, Henry
Shaw, Will
Sheffield, Frank
Shell, Elbert
Shellabarger, Ira L.
Shelton, Abner
Shelton, Hugh H.
Shelton, John Dee
Shelton, Thomas D.
Shivers, Add
Shivers, Archie
Shotts, Jesse L.
Shulman, Harry
Sieber, William Henry
Siler, Leland L.
Simmons, Guy M.
Simmons, Kid
Simons, Jessie
Sims, Gibson F.
Sims, Hubert C.
Sipes, Calvin
Slaughter, Elliott
Smallwood, John D.
Smith, A. D.
Smith, Acie H.
Smith, Albert N.
Smith, Andrew W.
Smith, Boyd W.
Smith, Carl Lester
Smith, Charles L.
Smith, Clarence
Smith, Cleveland
Smith, Dan
Smith, Edward R.
Smith, Frank
Smith, Gaither H.
Smith, Harvey
Smith, Henry W.
Smith, Joe E.
Smith, John F.
Smith, John H.
Smith, Johnnie
Smith, Joseph R.
Smith, Lennie
Smith, Louis
Smith, Martin Luther
Smith, Oscar
Smith, Philip
Smith, Robert N.
Smith, Roy P.
Smith, Walter
Smith, Will
Smith, Willie
Snipes, Walter L.
Snowden, George
Spann, Lionel L.
Sparkman, William C.
Staggs, Richard W.
Staggs, William H.
Stanfill, Ruby N.
Stayton, Clarence H.
Steed, Jessie
Stegall, Elbert S.
Stegall, Hugh
Stegall, Joe
Stemm, Bryan W.
Stephenson, Clarence C.
Stewart, Samuel G.
Stone, Rollin O.
Stone, Walter J.
Stormer, Herman
Stratton, Culus Doran
Stratton, Eulus O(ran)
Stratton, Henry L.
Strayharn, James
Stricklin, Robert Vernard
Strong, Robert Lee H.
Stubbs, Hezikiah
Sturdivant, Henry Ivan
Sturdivant, Thomas H.
Sullivan, Belton O.
Sutton, John E.
Sykes, Gillam
Sykes, Willie Brooks
Talley, Lincoln
Talley, Redger
Talley, Willice
Tauwater, Fenner H.
Tate, Arthur M.
Taylor, Abner Utley, Jr.
Taylor, Charlie
Taylor, Clyde
Taylor, George
Taylor, George W.
Taylor, Guy M.
Taylor, Hal
Taylor, Isaac

MADISON COUNTY VETERANS

Taylor, James Floyd
Taylor, Jim
Taylor, Leslie
Taylor, Norris Richard
Taylor, Paul W.
Taylor, Robert F.
Taylor, Silas
Taylor, Thomas A.
Taylor, Tip
Taylor, William A.
Teague, Roy M.
Teague, Thomas A.
Teddleton, William E.
Teer, Chas. M.
Terry, Harry W.
Terry, Olive S.
Theus, Aaron
Theus, Freeman
Theus, George
Theus, Horace
Theus, Richard
Theus, Tom
Thomas, Cleo E.
Thomas, David H.
Thomas, General D.
Thomas, George W.
Thomas, Porter
Thomas, Sam
Thomas, Virgil V.
Thomas, Wesley D.
Thomason, George W.
Thompson, Andrew V.
Thompson, Fred W.
Thompson, Ivan C.
Thompson, John H.
Thompson, John Robert, Jr.
Thompson, Johnie
Thompson, Louis S.
Thompson, Raymond D.
Thompson, Wyatt T.
Thorne, G. Ellis
Thornton, John Q.
Thurman, Milan J.
Tibbs, William H(oward)
Tidwell, Jonnie
Tims, George C.
Tims, Nat
Tindel, Harry H.
Toliver, Ben
Tomlin, Charley
Tomlin, Earl B.
Tomlin, John Paul
Tomlin, Robert Trent
Transon, Earl R.
Trotter, John W.
Trotter, Luther
Tunstell, Arthur
Turner, Andrew
Turner, Thomas C.
Turnipseed, Walter
Twomey, Earl D.
Twomey, Joe J.

Tyson, Elijah
Tyson, John A.
Tyson, Michael V.
Tyus, Newbern E.
Utley, John T.
Utley, Robert L.
Utley, Sylvanus
Valentine, Arthur R.
Van Treese, Clifton T.
Vantreese, Ellis B.
Varnell, Gavin D.
Vernon, James A.
Verser, Leeandrew
Verser, Levie
Verser, Robert B.
Vinson, Earnest
Voegeli, Henry O.
Walker, Andrew
Walker, Henry W.
Walker, James
Walker, Roy
Walker, Sol L. B.
Walker, Will
Wall, Cornelius B.
Wallace, Henry T.
Wallace, Irvin
Wallace, Landon H.
Waller, Albert
Waller, Joe W.
Ward, Clarence
Ward, Mort E.
Ward, Simon
Ward, Tom
Wardford, Taylor
Warlick, Ernest D.
Warlick, Jessie
Warlick, Josie McD
Warner, R. S.
Warren, Thomas M.
Washington, Frank A.
Watson, Arthur
Watson, Charles
Watt, Lema L.
Weakes, Alton D.
Weaks, Stearling A.
Weatherford, Joe
Weatherford, John T.
Weathers, Belvin
Weaver, Joe B.
Weaver, Monroe
Webb, Abe
Webb, Clyde H.
Webb, Fred N.
Webb, Harvey
Webb, Hubert Nameless
Webb, Luther T.
Weber, John Y.
Weddle, Harvey
Weeks, William H.
Weir, Earnest A.
Weir, Joe
Weiss, Bennie W.

Wells, James A.
Wesby, John
West, Ira
Wharton, Henry
Wharton, John
White, Albert D.
White, Archie
White, Atlas
White, Bethel R.
White, Brawlus B. F.
White, Isaiah
White, James G.
White, James H.
White, Marshall K.
White, Robert B.
White, Robert N.
White, Virgil
White, William M.
Whitelaw, Lionel Grafton
Whitelaw, Pearl
Whitelaw, Spencer
Whitley, Ernest
Whitsett, Will
Wiggs, Norman Sharon
Wilde, August William
Wilie, Hu M.
William, Thomas R.
Williams, Andrew L(eroy)
Williams, Aubrey
Williams, Ben H.
Williams, Charles H.
Williams, Clarence R.
Williams, Clarence N.
Williams, Clay
Williams, Ernest Benj.
Williams, George E.
Williams, George J.
Williams, Hubert E.
Williams, Hugh
Williams, James
Williams, John
Williams, Oscar P.
Williams, Thomas B.
Williams, Ulysses
Williams, Willie
Williams, Anthony

Williamson, Clarence
Williamson, Edgar
Williamson, Felix E.
Williamson, Frenchy
Williamson, Roy S.
Williford, Joe J.
Willis, Fred
Willis, George Lee
Willis, Herbert
Wilson, Arnie E.
Wilson, Brodie A.
Wilson, James A.
Wilson, Marion M.
Wilson, Oscar F.
Wilson, Samuel E., Jr.
Wilson, William H.
Wilson, William T.
Wimpee, Joseph Mark
Windrom, Guy R.
Winston, Marvin P.
Wisdom, Ray M.
Witherspoon, Forrest Bedford
Witherspoon, James F.
Womack, Chest
Womack, Oscar
Wood, Clyde M.
Wood, Earl Z.
Wood, Irby G.
Wood, Lawrence A.
Woodson, Avery E.
Woodson, Hirshell
Woodson, Joseph Thomas
Wooley, Ramsey O(neal)
Wooley, William T.
Woolfork, Ludie
Wrice, Willie
Wright, Westley J.
Wynn, Clay F.
Yarbrough, Bee Mark
Yarbrough, John, Jr.
Yarbrough, Steve E.
Yarbrough, William G.
Yelton, Wood H.
York, William M.
Young, William

WOUNDED

Adkins, John
Anderson, Hansford H.
Armstrong, Elbert F.
Barnes, Norman
Babs, William A.
Bearer, Kid
Berry, James William
Bond, Ellis
Brinkley, George B.
Carpenter, Lewis T.
Davidson, Lovelace
Dodd, Joe
Fogg, Paul C.

Fowler, William W.
Fussell, John D.
Gooch, Thomas M.
Harbert, Alonzo F.
Harris, Floyd E.
Hefley, Harvey L.
Hopper, James T.
Hopper, Robert L.
Johnson, Huley
Johnson, Needham B.
Jones, James B.
Jones, Samuel C.
King, Jasper R.

MADISON COUNTY VETERANS

Kelley, Alfred C.
Key, Fred S.
Lemmons, Jesse C.
Long, Almer
Love, Jim L.
Lyons, Tom
McKinnie, Wilmoth E.
Mainers, Hughie E.
Mason, John
Mason, John P.
Medlin, John L.
Miller, William H.
Murphree, Zebb
Oswald, Thomas R.

Powell, John W.
Puckett, Robert L.
Rogers, Harry
Seale, James
Shaw, Henry
Skielern, Jesse
Sparks, Edgar T.
Stewart, Grady L.
Stone, Henry D.
Smith, Rube N.
Tanksley, Willie
White, William G.
Whorton, Jessie H.
Williams, Bruce

DEAD

Barksdale, Todd
Baxter, Henry S.
Bell, Fred T.
Blalock, James M.
Broadwell, Charlie C.
Brown, John W.
Brumley, Herman L.
Chandler, Floyd
Chiles, Frank G.
Cocks, James E.
Collins, Gordon B.
Croft, Willie G.
Cummings, James D.
Day, Ethel B.
Forester, Jodie C.
Giles, Floyd L.
Graves, Walter
Gray, George L.
Gurley, Andrew J(ackson)
Howell, Carmack M.
James, Harrison
Jones, Bennie L.
Lake, Ben
Laney, Joseph A.

Lewis, William Benton
McAdoo, Robet E.
McClellen, John B.
McFadden, A. T.
Maness, Ray Joseph
Massey, Horace
Milam, Lonnie W.
Morrow, Charlie W.
Nettles, Dan A.
Nichols, Willie C.
Nicholson, Charlie
Norvell, Cornelius W.
Poole, John E. M.
Ricketts, Thomas E.
Roach, Herbert B.
Robinson, Thomas L.
Robison, William W.
Smith, Moody
St. John, Alvin M.
Thornton, Carl E.
Trice, Bill
Utley, Willie
Williamson, Savannah A.
Winchester, George

OFFICERS—USA

Alexander, Ralph E.
Allen, Terry W.
Arnold, Benjamin Clayton
Ballew, Joseph H.
Barry, John Nichols
Bedinger, Albert Frederic George
Biggs, Roy Booker
Birchett, Albert L.
Broderick, Wolf T.
Callahan, Perry Howard
Carpenter, John D.
Chisum, Jenner Young
Crego, Clarence H., Jr.
Crook, Jere L.
Dabney, William Rhea
Davis, Charles Wesley
Elliott, Cecil R.
Evans, Benjamin F.
Fenner, Dixie O.

Freeman, Clifford M.
Gillmann, John H.
Granberry, Dorsey B.
Harrell, Ivy Odel
Hays, Henry Donelson
Henderson, Dewitt T.
Herring, Harry T.
Hicks, Robert Lamar
Hillard, Farrin Allen
Johnson, Joseph Saundes, Jr.
Johnson, Julius A.
Johnson, Seale Bond
Johnston, William Addison C.
Keith, Robert French
Key, John D.
Lane, Albert Lossen
Lile, Richard Leon
McClaran, James Walsh
Mainord, Hugh Ira

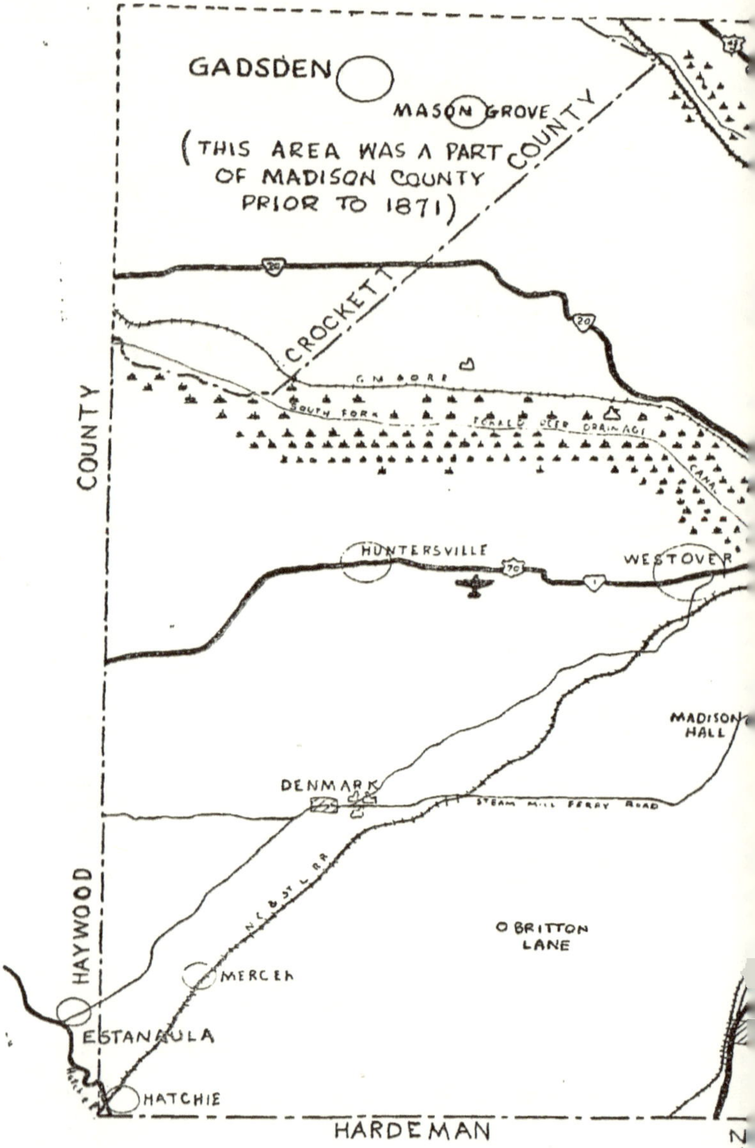

MADISON COUNTY
TENNESSEE
FEBRUARY, 1946

SCALE

1 0 1 2 3 4 MILES

DRAWN BY JACK BEARD

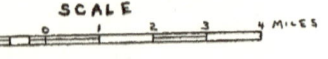

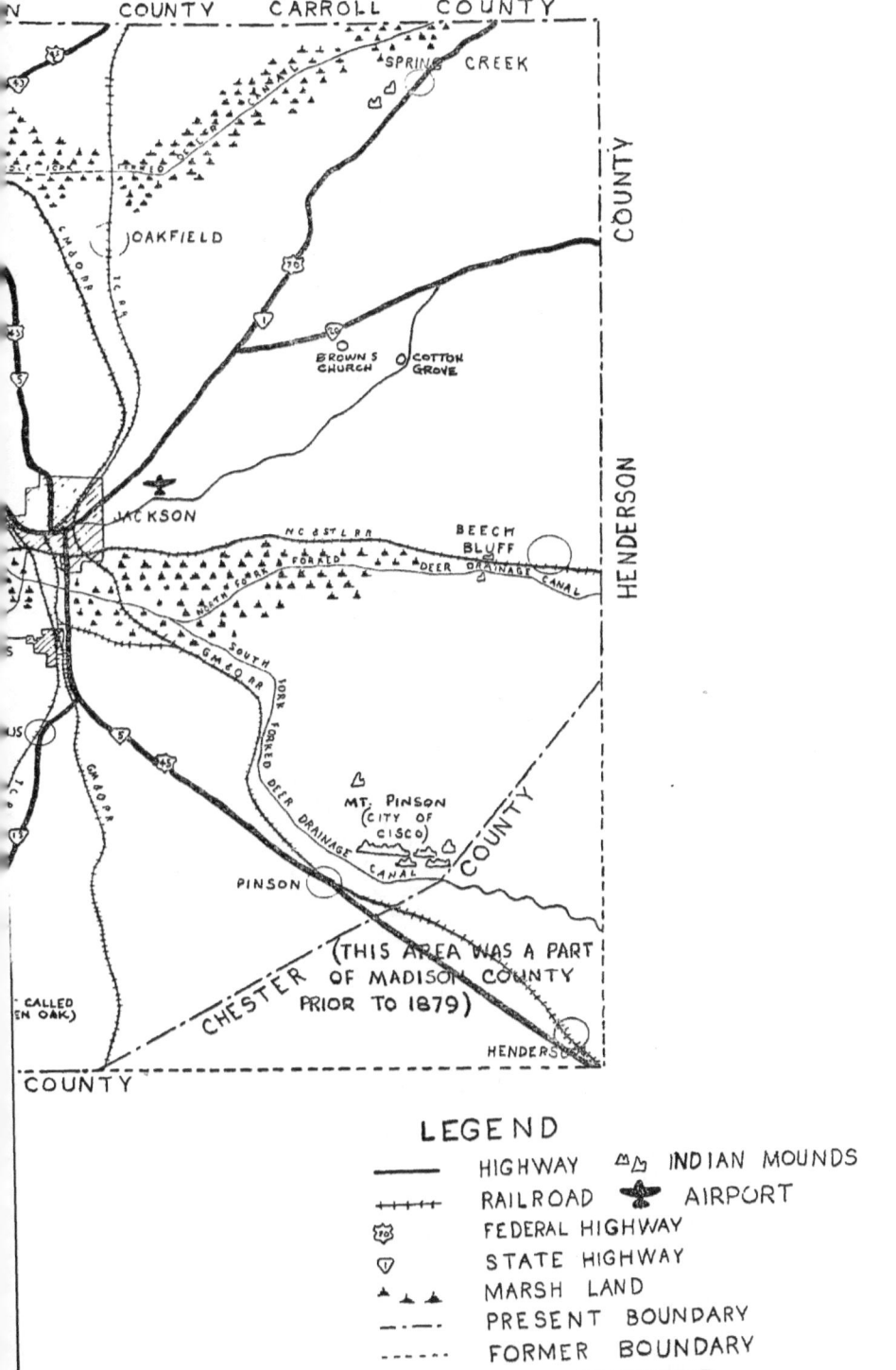

Mason, Harris Arthur
Mathis, Paul J.
May, Glenn T.
Mayo, Robert Council, Jr.
O'Connor, Fleming James
Patton, Marion Cecil
Pigford, James Perry
Robertson, William Platt
Rodgers, Aubrey Leonard
Russell, Simpson
Saunders, William Gilchrist
Simpson, William Thomas

Snowden, Isaac Condon
Teague, William Abnee
Temple, Hugh H.
Temple, Thomas Hudson
Thompson, Herman Claude
Tigrett, Augustus King
Trice, Harvey Marshall
Wells, Robert Archer
White, Marshall Kent
Wise, John Dallas
Withers, Leonidas Bills

MARINES

Balch, John Parke, Jr.
Ballard, Clarence Burton
Baxter, Clarence Woolridge
Copelin, Charles Egbert
Davis, Edward Brandon
Dottery, Guy Hamilton
Elliott, Charles Alexander
Fore, Birdo
Fowle, Charley Thomas
Gooch, Thomas Grady
Greer, Lee Tharp
Hilliard, Irby Edgar
Hunt, Hugh Haily
Ingram, Keith Stuyveson
Johnson, Thomas Harold
Jones, Charlie Stellman

Lancaster, Alger
Litton, Porter Melvin
McGrath, Thomas Patrick
McKinzie, Robert Granville
Marcum, Henley Franklin
Montgomery, Jeff Glynn
Moore, George Maxwell
Murray, Cornelius MacPherson
Muse, John Thomas
Myers, William
Outlaw, Marvin Franklin
Peebles, Grover Dallas
Rhegness, Edward Byrn
Robinson, Andrew Jordon
Wilson, John Thomas

SAILORS

Alexander, Roy Grafton
Allen, Leonard Alvin
Allen, Ulva Clarence
Baker, Fred Julius
Barry, James Moore
Baum, Amos Abraham
Baxter, Clyde Lawrence
Bell, George Tracy
Blackburn, William Monroe
Bledsoe, Roy Tinkle
Buckley, William McKinley, Jr.
Burch, James Madison
Clark, Allen Long
Cartmell, Robert Henry
Cockrill, Bethel Mark
Connor, Robert Lee
Cook, Frank Jefferson
Cundiff, Franklin Devaughn
Cunlihee, William Hugh
Dees, Raymon Fenley
Derryberry, Voris Graves
Enochs, William Archie
Eubank, Stephen Robert
Exum, Edward Raymond
Fleming, Robert Warford
Fullerton, Donald Hunter
Garland, Robert
Garrison, James Jones
Gobelet, Obed Dubart

Gowan, Felix Eunice
Hahn, Ernest Jennings
Hefley, William Arthur
Herron, Burke Mann
Hudgins, Robert Love Taylor
Ingram, Levy Sam
Johnston, I. Homer
King, John David
Lambert, Lofton Grady
Leech, Walter Edwin
Leek, James Wiley
Livsey, Joseph Franklin
Marlow, Julius Claude
Matthews, Ira Chester
McCollum, John
McCollum, L. D. Russell
McCutcheon, John James
McCillin, Thomas Gates
Meriwether, John Henry
Milum, William Claude
Muse, Fred John
Nave, Jerry Oliver
Nichols, James Jefferson
Nourse, Arthur Augustus
Nowell, Travis Orion
Pacaud, Joe Albert
Patterson, Roy John
Phillips, Edward Bynam
Pipkin, Willie

MADISON COUNTY VETERANS

Pirtle, John Chism
Pirtle, Victor Malone
Poole, Edward James
Redmond, John Lawrence
Richardson, James Nelson
Robbins, Jack Mack
Ross, Harry C.
Rothrock, John Thomas
Rowan, Pickett
Scammerhorn, William Arthur
Simmons, Jimmie Tom
Smith, Charles Dan
Spencer, James Warren
Spragle, Kenneth Howell

Stark, John Thomas
Stone, Albert Asa
Tinsley, Timothy Wilson
Townsell, Eugene Scott
Trice, William Harold
Vandenbrook, Newton McCoy
Warren, Mary Eulalia
Warren, Ruth Ann
Wilson, Benjamin Franklin
Wilson, Robert Alvin
Winston, Fenner
Wood, William Curtis
Yandell, Edgar Lawrence

OFFICERS—USN

Butler, William Parker
Cartmell, Meares Baldwin
Wilson, Tom Cathey

COUNTY OFFICERS

PRESIDING OFFICERS OF THE COUNTY COURT

The Court of Pleas and Quarter Sessions was established in North Carolina by an Act of 1789, Chapter 3, Section 4. This act provided that three, or all the justices of peace, could sit as a court in various counties. Three justices were chosen at the first session in each year to hold these sessions of the court. Tennessee's constitution of 1796 did not change this plan of courts, so on the early records of Madison County, the signatures of three justices appear. By an Act of the Legislature of 1817, one-third or twelve of the justices could transact business; by an Act of 1821, three were to constitute the court for the transaction of business. On some of the early records Herndon Haralson signs them as "Chairman," but this office was provided for permanently by an Act of the Legislature of 1835 when the courts were reorganized under the new constitution. The following names have been taken from the old records as some of the Presiding Justices of Peace:

1821-1825—Herndon Haralson, chairman; James Greer, James Caruthers.
1827—Robert Hughes, Barthelomew Stewart, James S. Lyon.
1828—Robert Hughes, Mathias Deberry, James S. Lyon.
1829—Mathias Deberry, James S. Lyon, James Greer.
1830—Allen Deberry, James H. Rogers, James Brown.
1831—William E. Butler, Allen Deberry, Mark Christian.
1832—James S. Lyon, James H. Rogers, Jacob Perkins.
1833—James S. Lyon, John B. Cross, James H. Rogers.
1834—John M. Johnson, James Meriwhether, John Tidwell.
1835—John B. Cross, Wm. C. Dew, Jacob Perkins.
1836—Barwell Butler, Mathias Deberry, W. B. Cross.

On May 2, 1836, the court was reorganized and hereafter a chairman was elected at the first meeting of the court until 1905, when the County Judge replaced that Chairman. The following men have served as Chairman:

1836—Henry Strange
1837—John Chalmers
1838—W. T. Johnston
1839-1840—John H. Day
1841-1846—Wyatt Mooring
1847—Isham V. Harris
1848-1849—Robert Stark
1850—John H. Day
1851-1852—Wyatt Mooring
1853—John R. Woolfolk
1854—Robert Stark
1855—John H. Day
1856—Stephen Sypert
1857—Richard Hays
1858-1860—John R. Woolfolk
1860-1862—Archibald S. Rogers
1865-1873—Archibald S. Rogers
1874—Hiram Johnson

COUNTY OFFICERS 525

1875—Ambrose Reid
1876-1882—Archibald S. Rogers
1883-1885—J. D. Pearson
1886—M. H. Pirtle

1887-1892—J. T. Rushing
1893-1902—T. C. Long
1903-1905—A. M. Alexander

COUNTY JUDGES

Thomas McCorry..............1905-1913
A. W. Stovall....................1913-1918
J. T. Rothrock..................1918-1923

Karl K. Wilkes..................1923-1932
Frank Johnson 1932-1934
A. W. Wilde.....................1934-

SHERIFFS

Thomas Shannon 1822-1826
Mark Christian 1826-1830
Daniel Mading 1830-1831
Matthias Deberry 1831-1835
James Lyon 1835-1838
James McDonald 1838-1840
G. H. Kyle 1840-1846
J. S. Stewart 1846-1848
J. R. Jelks 1848-1854
J. J. Brooks 1854-1860
J. R. Woolfolk 1860-1865
George G. Perkins............1865-1870
R. M. May 1870-1876
George G. Perkins 1876-1878
W. F. Blackard 1878-1884

B. A. Person 1884-1890
B. F. Young 1890-1893
E. A. Brooks 1893-1899
W. M. May 1899-1901
R. C. Mayo 1901-1908
W. G. Person 1908-1914
J. G. Perry 1914-1920
R. A. Mainord 1920-1926
F. L. Exum 1926-1932
Tom Patton 1932-1934
A. S. Steadman 1934-1936
Tom Patton 1936-1940
Ewing Griffin 1940-1944
Tom Lewis 1944-

COUNTY COURT CLERKS

Roderick McIver 1822-1834
Thomas W. Gamewell.......1834-1836
M. B. Stewart 1836-1840
J. D. McClellan 1840-1848
Thomas Gamewell 1848-1856
P. C. McCowat 1856-1872
S. D. Barnett 1872-1878
E. A. Clark 1878-1886

F. W. Adamson 1886-1898
W. N. True 1898-1902
W. T. Blackard 1902-1910
J. A. Thompson 1910-1922
A. M. Young 1922-1933
Mrs. A. M. Young...........1933-1934
W. M. Key 1934-1946
M. N. Thomson 1946-

COUNTY TRUSTEES

1822-1823—William Atchison
1824-1829—Samuel D. Wilson
1830-1831—Jacob Wilson
1832-1840—Martin Wigg
1840-1844—John Tidwell
1844-1848—James Henderson
1848-1850—John Burrus
1850-1852—Stephen B. Barnett
1852-1858—Joseph C. Sharp
1858-1860—John M. Parker
1860-1865—James M. Thompson
1865-1866—Frederick W. Yancy
1866-1868—James M. Thompson
1868-1872—James M. McRee

1872-1874—William M. Parham
1874-1878—James M. Cartmell
1878-1882—Major Croom
1882-1886—Z. N. Wright
1886-1892—W. B. Wiley
1892-1900—Jeff Hunt
1900-1908—J. W. Stovall
1908-1912—Wiley Perry
1912-1918—John L. Pearson
1918-1926—J. W. Boon
1926-1930—Kit Noel
1930-1938—A. T. Jones
1938-1946—E. L. Price
1946-   —I. M. Vaughn

REGISTERS

Thomas W. Gamewell......1842-1844	J. M. Hardage..................1876-1882
Willie Langford 1844-1848	J. W. Wallace....................1882-1898
William W. Gates................1848-1856	J. R. Anderson..................1898-1906
W. G. Cockrell....................1856-1866	D. T. Turner......................1906-1914
J. R. Chapell......................1866-1870	H. L. Caradine..................1914-1930
H. C. McCutchen..............1870-1875	J. L. Wallace....................1930-1942
W. H. Bruton....................1875-1876	J. N. Allen..................1942-to present

CHANCELLORS

Andrew McCampbell 1839-1848	A. G. Hawkins 1886-1906
Calvin Jones 1848-1854	E. L. Bullock 1906-1913
Isaac B. Williams..............1854-1862	J. W. Ross 1913-1921
J. W. Harris 1865-1869	W. H. Denison 1921-1922
T. C. Muse 1869-1870	Tom C. Rye 1922-1931
James Fentress 1870-1875	N. R. Barham 1931-1932
H. W. McCorry 1875-1882	Dewitt Henderson 1932-
T. C. Muse 1882-1886	

CLERK AND MASTERS

Thomas Clark 1846-1873	R. A. Hurt 1884-1916
D. M. Wisdom 1873-1882	I. H. Nelson 1916-1926
M. S. Versay 1882-1884	R. R. Sneed 1926-

JUDGES

Joshua Haskell, 1822-1835, Judge of Courts of Law and Equity of Eighth Judicial Circuit.
William B. Turley, July 20, 1835, to April 18, 1836, Judge of Court of Law and Equity of Tenth Judicial Circuit.
Austin Miller, April 18, 1836, to August 15, 1836, Judge of Circuit Court of Tenth Judicial Circuit.
John Read, 1836-1859, Judge of Circuit Court of Tenth Judicial Circuit.
John Read, 1859-1865, Judge of Circuit Court of Fourteenth Judicial Circuit.
George W. Reeves, 1865-1866, Judge of Circuit Court of Fourteenth Judicial Circuit.
William P. Bond, 1866-1869, Judge of Circuit Court of Fourteenth Judicial Circuit.
William P. Bond, 1869-1870, Judge of Circuit Court of Thirteenth Judicial Circuit.
Gideon B. Black, 1870-1875, Judge of Circuit Court of Thirteenth Judicial Circuit.
Henry W. McCorry, 1875-1882, Judge of the Common Law and Chancery Court of Madison County.
T. C. Muse, 1882-1886, Judge of the Common Law and Chancery Court of Madison County.
L. S. Woods, 1886-1902, Judge of Circuit Court of Eleventh Judicial Circuit.
L. S. Woods, 1902-1908, Judge of Circuit Court of Twelfth Judicial Circuit.
D. W. Herring, May, 1908, to September, 1908, Judge of Circuit Court of Twelfth Judicial Circuit.

CRIMINAL COURT

N. R. Barham, 1908-1926, Judge of Circuit Court of Twelfth Judicial Circuit.
J. A. England, 1926-1929, Judge of Circuit Court of Twelfth Judicial Circuit.
W. H. Dennison, 1929-1934, Judge of Circuit Court of Twelfth Judicial Circuit.
Frank L. Johnson, 1934 to present, Judge of Circuit Court of Twelfth Judicial Circuit.

COUNTY OFFICERS

CIVIL COURT

S. J. Everett, 1905-1918, Judge of Circuit Court of Sixteenth Judicial Circuit.
R. B. Baptist, 1918-1942, Judge of Circuit Court of Sixteenth Judicial Circuit.
Lamar Spragins, 1942 to present, Judge of Circuit Court of Sixteenth Judicial Circuit.

CIRCUIT COURT CLERKS

Beverley Randolph	1822-	J. D. Newton	1890-1898
William Harris	1822-1833	J. W. Blackmon	1898-1906
Henry W. McCorry	1833-1836	W. B. Hays	1906-1910
Andrew Guthrie	1836-1851	M. B. Hurt	1910-1914
J. L. Brown	1851-1856	W. F. May	1914-1918
Sion W. Boon	1856-1874	Harry M. Hodgson	1918-1922
R. A. Sneed	1874-1882	Mrs. Bessie Hodgson	1922-1938
W. L. Utley	1882-1886	Cartmell Townes	1938-
B. J. Howard	1886-1890		

SUPREME COURT CLERKS

Thomas Haywood	?-1830	S. D. Hays	1883- ?
Robert Hughes	1830-1834	John W. Buford	1883-1896
Joseph H. Talbot	1834-1840	J. W. Buford	1896-1909
William H. Stephens	1840-1857	Thos. B. Carroll	1910-1919
M. D. Welch	1857-1860	J. E. Springbett	1919-1945
John L. Brown	1860-1868	Miss Lucile Myers	1945-to present
John H. Freeman	1870-1883		

MEMBERS OF THE GENERAL ASSEMBLY REPRESENTING MADISON

Year	Senate	House	Floating Representative
1823	Thomas Williamson	David Crockett	
1825	Joel Walker	Duncan McIver	
1827	Adam Huntsman	Duncan McIver	
1829	Adam Huntsman	Andrew L. Martin	
1831	Duncan McIver	Charles D. McLean	
1833	Joseph Coe	William B. Miller	
1835	W. H. Henderson	Andrew L. Martin	
1837	A. B. Bradford	Andrew L. Martin	
1839	John Ashe	James S. Lyon	
1841	John B. Ashe	W. T. Haskell	
		John B. Cross	
1843	John W. Harris	John B. Cross	
1845	John W. Harris	Micajah Bullock	
1847	Gayle H. Kyle	John T. Herron	
1849	Gayle H. Kyle	Alexander Jackson	
1851	James A. Rogers	Alexander Jackson	
1853	James A. Rogers	John C. Greer	
1855	I. N. Steele	J. B. Algee	
1857	Ambrose R. Reid	M. Bullock	
1859	R. W. Bumpus	J. B. Porter	
1861	R. W. Bumpus	W. A. Dunlap	
1865	W. T. McFarland	J. J. Roach	
	David Nunn		
1867	James R. McCall	W. G. Cockrill	
1869	David Slaughter	D. H. King	
1871	George C. Porter	F. B. Snipes	
1873	F. B. Snipes	John R. Bond	
1875	Horace M. Polk	R. B. Hurt	
1877	A. R. Read	George C. Porter	

1879	C. H. Anderson	H. C. Anderson	
1881	W. R. Barrett	H. C. Austin	
1883	John Y. Keith	L. F. Hayney	
1885	John Y. Keith	D. L. Murrell	
1887	Thomas C. Long	A. D. Hurt	
		J. D. Pearson	
1889	T. C. Long	J. D. Pearson	
1891	T. C. Long	J. D. Pearson	
1893	E. L. Bullock	D. H. Parker	John H. Trice
1895	A. W. Stovall	R. A. Mays	Joe D. Johnson
1897	M. B. Gilmore	W. A. Perry	J. D. Johnson
1899	M. B. Gilmore	E. L. Bullock	J. D. Johnson
1901	J. L. Cochran	F. O. McCallum	M. V. B. Exum
1903	Stoddert Caruthers	John A. Tyson	J. D. Johnson
1905	Thad Pope	R. R. Sneed	D. E. Scott
		J. T. Raines	
1907	Thad Pope	A. H. Askew	D. E. Scott
		R. A. Harris	
1909	A. H. Askew	J. N. Robinson	John F. Hall
		J. G. Futrell	
1911	A. H. Askew	J. N. Robinson	John F. Hall
		J. G. Futrell	
1913	John L. Hare	M. H. Taylor	P. O. Roberts
		A. S. Johnson	
1915	Hu C. Anderson, Sr.	R. S. McClaran	T. A. Hare
	(Speaker)	J. E. Blackmon	
1917	Eugene Fulghum	R. S. McClaran	A. S. Montgomery
		J. E. Blackmon	
1919	T. C. Long	J. E. Blackmon	A. S. Montgomery
		R. B. Swink	
		Felix Phillips*	J. S. Fielder
1921	J. R. Tillman	W. S. Perry	
		J. E. Blackmon	John S. Fielder
1923	R. B. Swink	R. B. Neely	
		W. F. Barry, Jr.	John Fielder
1925	John H. Trice	R. B. Neely	
		W. F. Barry, Jr.	
		(Speaker)	John S. Pratt
1927	W. F. Barry, Sr.	R. B. Neely	
		F. L. Johnson	Julian Jones
1929	W. F. Barry, Sr.	Gid T. Henderson	
		R. B. Neely	Julian Jones
1931	Hu C. Anderson	R. B. Neely	
		Gid T. Henderson	Sam C. Jones
1933	William P. Moss	James Midyett	
		R. B. Neely	Lon Austin
1935	William P. Moss	Taylor Beare	
	(Speaker)	Howell Buntin	Lon Austin
1937	Hughlon Akin	Andrew Tip Taylor, Jr.	
		H. L. Townsend	Lon Austin
1939	J. D. Bledsoe	J. A. Midyett	
		H. L. Townsend	Odell Buck
1941	Howell Buntin	Will A. Thompson	
		William Parham	Lon Austin
1943	Howell Buntin	J. A. Midyett	
		W. H. Parham	
1945	John F. Hall	Lowell Simmons	Lon Austin
		Richard Dungan	

MADISON'S REPRESENTATIVES IN UNITED STATES CONGRESS

18th Congress 1823-1825   Adam Alexander, Jackson.
19th Congress 1825-1827   Adam Alexander, Jackson.
20th Congress 1827-1829   David Crockett, Trenton.
21st Congress 1829-1831   David Crockett, Trenton, Tenn.

*Served unexpired term of J. E. Blackmon at 1920 Special Session.

CONGRESSMEN

22nd Congress	1831-1833	William Fitzgerald, Dresden; election unsuccessfully contested by Crockett.
23rd Congress	1833-1835	David Crockett, Trenton.
24th Congress	1835-1837	Adam Huntsman, Jackson.
25th Congress	1837-1839	Christopher Williams, Lexington.
26th Congress	1839-1841	John W. Crockett.
27th Congress	1841-1843	Milton Brown, Jackson.
28th Congress	1843-1845	Milton Brown, Jackson.
29th Congress	1845-1847	Milton Brown, Jackson.
30th Congress	1847-1849	William T. Haskell.
31st Congress	1849-1851	Christopher Williams, Lexington.
32nd Congress	1851-1853	Christopher Williams, Lexington.
33rd Congress	1853-1855	Emerson Etheridge, Dresden.
34th Congress	1855-1857	Emerson Etheridge, Dresden.
35th Congress	1857-1859	John V. Wright, Purdy.
36th Congress	1859-1861	Emerson Etheridge, Dresden.
37th Congress	1861-1863	Emerson Etheridge, Dresden.
38th Congress	1863-1865	Emerson Etheridge, Dresden.
39th Congress	1865-1867	Isaac Hawkins, Huntingdon, seated Dec. 3, 1866.
40th Congress	1867-1869	Isaac Hawkins, Huntingdon.
41st Congress	1869-1871	Isaac Hawkins, Huntingdon.
42nd Congress	1871-1873	William Vaughn, Brownsville.
43rd Congress	1873-1875	David Nunn, Brownsville.
44th Congress	1875-1877	John D. C. Atkins, Paris.
45th Congress	1877-1879	John D. C. Atkins, Paris.
46th Congress	1879-1881	John D. C. Atkins, Paris.
47th Congress	1881-1883	John D. C. Atkins, Paris.
48th Congress	1883-1885	John M. Taylor, Lexington.
49th Congress	1885-1887	John M. Taylor, Lexington.
50th Congress	1887-1889	B. A. Enloe, Jackson.
51st Congress	1889-1891	B. A. Enloe, Jackson.
52nd Congress	1891-1893	B. A. Enloe, Jackson.
53rd Congress	1893-1895	B. A. Enloe; election unsuccessfully contested by P. H. Thrasher.
54th Congress	1895-1897	John McCall, Lexington.
55th Congress	1897-1899	Thetus Sims, Linden.
56th Congress	1899-1901	Thetus Sims, Linden.
57th Congress	1901-1903	Thetus Sims, Linden.
58th Congress	1903-1905	Thetus Sims, Linden; election unsuccessfully contested by F. M. Davis.
59th Congress	1905-1907	Thetus Sims, Linden.
60th Congress	1907-1909	Thetus Sims, Linden.
61st Congress	1909-1911	Thetus Sims, Linden.
62nd Congress	1911-1913	Thetus Sims, Linden.
63rd Congress	1913-1915	Thetus Sims, Linden.
64th Congress	1915-1917	Thetus Sims, Linden.
65th Congress	1917-1919	Thetus Sims, Linden.
66th Congress	1919-1921	Thetus Sims, Linden.
67th Congress	1921-1923	Lon Scott, Savannah, defeated Gordon Browning.
68th Congress	1923-1925	Gordon Browning, Huntingdon.
69th Congress	1925-1927	Gordon Browning, Huntingdon.
70th Congress	1927-1929	Gordon Browning, Huntingdon.
71st Congress	1929-1931	Gordon Browning, Huntingdon.
72nd Congress	1931-1933	Gordon Browning, Huntingdon.
73rd Congress	1933-1935	Gordon Browning, Huntingdon.
74th Congress	1935-1937	Herron Pearson, Jackson.
75th Congress	1937-1939	Herron Pearson, Jackson.
76th Congress	1939-1941	Herron Pearson, Jackson.
77th Congress	1941-1943	Herron Pearson, Jackson.
78th Congress	1943-1945	Thomas J. Murray, Jackson.
79th Congress	1945-1947	Thomas J. Murray, Jackson.

MAYORS OF JACKSON

GOVERNING OFFICIALS OF JACKSON, TENNESSEE, SINCE CHARTERED ON DECEMBER 16, 1845

YEAR	MAYOR
1845	R. J. Hays
1846	R. J. Hays
	Resigned in May to go to Mexican War.
1846	J. H. L. Tomlin
1847	J. H. L. Tomlin
1848	J. H. L. Tomlin
1849	J. H. L. Tomlin
1850	J. H. L. Tomlin
1851	J. H. L. Tomlin
1852	J. H. L. Tomlin
1853	J. H. L. Tomlin
1854	Alexander Jackson
1855	Alexander Jackson
1856	R. J. Hays
1857	S. Cypert
1858	R. J. Hays
1859	William Alexander
1860	J. H. Harper
1861	P. D. W. Conger
1862	R. J. Mason
1863	Dr. G. Adamson
1864	Dr. G. Adamson
1865	Dr. G. Adamson
1866	William Alexander
1867	William Alexander
1868	J. J. McAlexander
1869	William Alexander
1870	Wm. M. Dunnaway
1871	P. D. W. Conger
1872	Wm. M. Dunnaway
1873	D. H. King
1874	J. A. Arrington
1875	D. H. King
1876	D. H. King
1877	L. E. Talbot
1878	W. D. Robinson
1879	James O'Connor
1880	W. D. Robinson
1881	J. M. Sullivan
1882	Dr. B. L. Rozell
1883	Col. John W. Buford
1884	Col. John W. Buford
	Resigned May 7, 1884, to become Clerk of Supreme Court at Jackson.
1884	Hu C. Anderson, Sr.
	Elected by Board to finish Buford's term, May 15, 1884.
1885	W. D. Robinson
1886	W. D. Robinson
1887	J. H. Hirsch
1888	J. H. Hirsch
1889	Jno. W. Gates
1890	Jno. W. Gates
1891	Jno. W. Gates
1892	Maj. E. A. Clark
1893	Maj. E. A. Clark
	Resigned April 10, 1893.
1894	Hu C. Anderson, Sr.
1895	Hu C. Anderson, Sr.
1896	Hu C. Anderson, Sr.
1897	Hu C. Anderson, Sr.
1898	Hu C. Anderson, Sr.
1899	Hu C. Anderson, Sr.
1900	Hu C. Anderson, Sr.
1901	Hu C. Anderson, Sr.
1902	Hu C. Anderson, Sr.
1903	Hu C. Anderson, Sr.
1904	Hu C. Anderson, Sr.
1905	Hu C. Anderson, Sr.
1906	Hu C. Anderson, Sr.
1907	Hu C. Anderson, Sr.
1908	Hu C. Anderson, Sr.
1909	Thos. G. Polk
1910	Thos. G. Polk
1911	C. E. Griffin
1912	C. E. Griffin
1913	C. E. Griffin
1914	C. E. Griffin
1915	C. E. Griffin
	Served until June 14, 1915, when commission form was created.

MAYORS OF JACKSON

4-YEAR TERM	MAYOR	UTILITIES	EDUCATION
1915-19	Lawrence Taylor	Hugh M. Harris Resigned Feb. 15, 1918, succeeded by T. J. McCutchen.	Z. K. Griffin Resigned July 1, 1918, succeeded by J. L. Pope.
1919-23	J. D. Johnson	T. J. McCutchen Resigned Feb. 15, 1920, succeeded by Paul M. Wilson.	T. H. Campbell
1923-27	Lawrence Taylor	C. E. Griffin Served until Aug. 4, 1925, succeeded by J. G. Neudorfer.	T. H. Campbell
1927-31	Lawrence Taylor	R. E. Franklin	J. D. Johnson
1931-35	Lawrence Taylor	R. E. Franklin	J. D. Johnson Served until Feb. 23, 1935. No one elected to succeed.
1935-39	A. B. Foust	R. E. Franklin	J. L. Harris
1939-43	A. B. Foust	E. P. Taylor	P. H. Callahan
1943-47	George M. Smith	R. E. Franklin	P. H. Callahan

JACKSON POSTMASTERS [85]

According to records of the National Archives, the post office at Jackson, Madison County, Tennessee, was established as Madison Courthouse on April 9, 1822, with Samuel Taylor as postmaster. The name of the office was changed to Jackson on April 23, 1824, and Samuel Taylor was reappointed as postmaster.[86] Only one woman has ever held the office—Julia B. Woolfolk, from 1869 to 1881. Successive postmasters and the dates of their appointment are as follows:

Robert I. Chester	1825	William M. Moss	1890
John H. Rawlings	1833	James T. McCutchen	1893
James L. Talbot	1835	William M. Moss	1897
Robert I. Chester	1837	Felix R. Bray	1901
Moses Wood	1838	Joseph J. Losier	1905
John Tomlin	1841	William F. Arnold, Acting	1911
Greenbury Adamson	1847	William F. Arnold	1911
Robert Stark	1849	Oliver Benton	1914
Philip C. McCowat	1851	Willis F. Arnold	1922
James Hughes	1853	Hugh G. Arnold, Acting	1930
Galen E. Green	1865	John D. Haggard	1931
Jesse H. Harper	1866	Wood H. Yelton, Acting	1933
Alexander C. Caldwell	1868	Thomas G. Hughes	1934
Julia B. Woolfolk	1869	Wood H. Yelton, Acting	1944
George K. Foote	1881	Roy A. Gilbert	1945
Richard R. Dashiell	1886		

[85] The writer is indebted to the following for assisting in collecting the names of county officials, mayors, postmasters, and other statistical material: Smiley Bledsoe, Mrs. Don McKellar, Mercer McCorry, Matt Thompson, Mrs. Wilson, I. M. Vaughn, Jim Allen, Mrs. John DeWitt, R. E. Fort, Robert Quarles, Judd Brooks, Miss Lucile Myers, Mrs. Cartmell Townes.

[86] In 1821, letters to those living in Madison County had to be addressed to Reynoldsburg, but the next year they were addressed to "Chickasaw Purchase, Forked Deer, P. O. Tenn." Williams, *West Tennessee*, 169.

TABLE No. 7—POPULATION IN MADISON COUNTY

	White	Free Colored	Slave	Aggregate Population	City of Jackson
1830	7,427	43	4,167	11,594	675
1840	10,417	37	6,073	16,530	
1850	12,257	61	8,552	21,470	993 White 13 Free Colored
1860	11,440	83	10,012	21,535	
1870	13,328	10,152		23,480	
1880	15,406	15,467		30,874	5,377
1890	15,824	14,669		30,497	10,039
1900	19,572	16,754		36,333	14,511
1910	23,184	16,167		39,351	15,779
1920	26,442	17,234		43,824	18,860
1930	32,302	18,643		51,059	22,172
1940	34,611	19,494		54,115	24,332

INDEX

Abbott, Father, 327
Academies, see Education
Adair, James, with Chickasaws, 19-20
Adamson, F. W., 330
Adventurers to Santa Fe, 105-106
Agriculture, 198-226
Agricultural Revival, 213-219
Agricultural Society, 211-212
Airplane, experimental, 335
Alexander, Adam R., 3, 33, 35, 86, 128, 228, 231
Alexander, Adley, 308
Alexander, A. M., 223, 331
Alexander family, 336
Alexander, W. F., 169, 192, 288, 360, 370, 396
Alexander School, 288
Alexander's Landing, 123
Alexandria, 33, 35, 37-38, 45
Allen family, 311
Allen, Jim, 531
Allison, Mrs. Belle, 397
Allison family, 348
Allison, J. W., 148, 360
Alston, James, 306
Alston, John, 357
Alston, Philip, 127
American Colonization Society, 208
Amusements, 5, 71, 82, 84, 88, 100-102, 382, 388-398
Anderson, A. W., 396
Anderson and Christian, 355
Anderson, Clayton, and Company, 400
Anderson, Frank, 400
Anderson, Gabriel, 306, 333
Anderson, Gilbert, 400
Anderson, Gilbert, 147
Anderson, Harry B., 236
Anderson, Hu C., Sr., 221, 224, 269, 288, 309, 330, 382, 397
Anderson, Mrs. Hu C., 397
Anderson, James W., 309, 325-326
Anderson, Mrs. Mahila, 309
Anderson, Monroe, 289, 326, 400
Anderson, Neil, 309, 340
Anderson, Robert H., 166, 254, 356
Anderson, Seward, 296
Anderson, Mrs. S. P., 397
Anderson, Sterling, 224, 288
Anderson, T. B., 309

Anderson, "Uncle King", 8, 165
Andrew's Chapel, 342
Andrews, Mrs. George, 309
Andrews, R. W., 311
Annville, 129
Anthony, J. W., 252
Antony, Micajah, 303
Ararat Baptist Church, 300, 343
Armour and Lake, merchants, 122; gin, 199
Armour, David, 320
Armour, Mrs. Mary, 300
Armour, William, 88, 208, 278, 320, 324; interests in internal improvements, 128, 133-134
Arnold, J. R., 345
Arnold, Thomas D., 266
Arnold, W. F., 315
Arnold, W. J., 253, 254
Arnold, William, 37, 54, 100, 366
Arrington, Grace, 397
Arrington, J. A., 258
Ash, John, letter of Crockett to, 425-427
Ashby Veneer Lumber Co., 363
Ashport Turnpike, 129
Askew, Alexander, 282
Atchinson, William, 35, 228
Aubry, James, 306
Austin, Philip, 336
Autry, ———, 108
Autry, T. B., 331
"The Avengers," 111-119; 447-449

Backman, M. L., 234
Bailey, Bruce, 291
Bailey family, 341
Bain, S. M., 225
Baker, Daniel, 307
Balch, David, 271, 379
Balch, John B., 271
Baldwyn, J. D., 137, 138, 143
Banks and banking, 323-332
Banks, First National, 325-326; of Madison, 185, 325; of Mercer, 331; National Bank of Commerce, 328-330; Peoples Savings, 330; Second National, 326-328; Security National, 331; Union Bank, 58, 186

534 INDEX

Bank robbery, 245, 338
Banner, Nashville, 269
Baptist churches: Bethlehem, 300; Calvary, 315; early, 292-293; 298-303; First Church, 300-301; West Jackson, 316-317
Baptist, R. B., 232, 430
Baptist Female Academy, 283
Baptist school at Spring Creek, 282
Barbecues, 7-10, 84, 88, 102, 382, 391-393
Barham, N. R., 233
Barham, J. R., 346
Barnett, A. E., 331
Barnette family, 303
Barr, Benjamin, 163
Barry, Valentine, 309
Barry, Mrs. W. F., 289
Bartholemew, Orlando, 257
Barton, Edward, 162
Bascom Chapel, 296
Bates, C. T., 327
Bates, J. T., 396
Baum, Nathan, 312
Baum, W. J., 331
Baxter, John, 235, 236
Baxter, W. D., 315
Bear hunt, 388
Beare Brothers Ice & Coal Company, 365
Beare, Robert L., 400
Beauregard, General, in Jackson, 164
Beard, Richard, 308
Beard, W. D., 234
Beard, William E., 119
Bedford, ———, 252, 260
Beech Bluff, 347-348
Bedna Young Lumber Co., 363
Bell, Mrs. Camile Bright, 289, 397
Bell, John, 266
Bell, Tyree, 177
Bellemeade, 184
Bells, Tennessee, 151
Bemis, Tennessee, 351-354
Bemis Mills, 259, 327, 365
Bench in 1829, 67-69
Bennett, D. D., 296
Benton, Nancy, 308
Benton, Nathaniel, 308
Benton, Oliver, 329-330
Berdon, Gus, 315
Bethshares, Mrs. ———, 315
Beveridge, J. T., 254, 313-314
Beveridge, Mrs. A., 314
Bickers, ———, 303
Biffle's Calvary, 169-171
Big Black Creek Camp, 306-307
Bigelow, Elijah, 124, 264, 282, 323
Bigelow, George, 276-277
Bigelow, Mrs., 276-277
Big Hatchie Turnpike, 129

Big Springs, 306
Birmingham, E. L., 362
Birmingham, L. W., 328, 331
Birmingham and Northwestern R. R., 151-152
Bishop, Laura, 397
Black, Cyrus, 308
Black family, 341
Black, G. W., 162
Black, John, 308
Black, Roy, 44, 46, 479
Blackard family, 343
Blackard, J. W., 316
Blackard, W. T., 288
Blackmon, Charles, 373
Blackmon, E. T., 290
Blackmon, Fordham, 296
Blain, Thomas 147
Blair, Thomas, 308
Blake, N. O., 314
Bland, J. R., 346
Blalock, B. A., 331
Bledsoe, G., 355
Bledsoe, Smiley, 531
Blount, Mary Louisa, 64
Boatyards, 121-122
Bolding, William, 229
Bond, B. F., 311
Bond, Chester G., 163, 330, 373
Bond family, 336
Bond, George W., 232
Bond, J. D., 311
Bond, Mrs. Harold, 57, 444
Bond, R. F., 311
Bond, R. W., 311
Boom in cotton, 200
Boone family, 351
Boone, Jordan, 296
Boone, S. W., 309
Booth, A. A., 328
Bolivar, Tennessee, 35, 252, 309; railroad meeting at, 133; rivalry with Jackson, 147-148; Gen. Forrest visits, 177
Botts, John Chester, 400
Boucher, Joshua, 294
Bounties for wolf scalps, 229
Boyd, Marion S., 236
Boyd, William, 339
Bracken family, 310
Bradberry, John, 32-33
Bradford, Alexander B., 4, 65, 101, 104, 108, 231, 241, 324
Braden, William, 35, 228
Brady family, 310
Bran dance, 388-389
Branding, 238
Bray, A. E., 345
Bray, Curtis, 99, 171, 182, 191, 202, 207, 216, 383, 420
Bray, W. H., 345

INDEX

Brigance, William, 296
Bright, Camile, 283
Bright, J. E., 254, 283
Bright, Lilla Mae, 283
Bright, Mrs. Sarah, 283
Briney, Bruce, 361-362
Britton Lane, battle of, 174-175
Brooks, Benjamin, 296
Brooks, Dora, 287
Brooks family, 303
Brooks, George K., 314
Brooks, J. C., 288-289
Brooks, J. H., 281, 313
Brooks, Judd, 531
Brooks, L. J., 267, 268, 327, 360, 397
Brown, Adam and Acquilla, 296
Brown, A. V., 213
Brown, C. W., 317
Brown family, 310, 333
Brown, George, 340
Brown, Henry, 233
Brown, Harris, 263, 272-273
Brown, James, 33, 35, 228
Brown, John, 254
Brown, John, 252, 260
Brown, John, 306, 324
Brown, J. F., 252, 276
Brown, John L., 185
Brown, John T., 314
Brown, Milton, railroad president and congressman, 84, 87-90, 95, 102, 108, 128, 133-134, 137, 139, 140, 141, 144, 163, 239, 241, 242, 278, 281, 284, 295, 320, 325, 399
Brown, Mrs. Milton, 167
Brown, M. M., 313
Brown, Morgan W., 236
Brown, Robert, 295, 314, 356
Brown, Sam, 247
Brown, Mrs. Sarah, 276
Brown's Church, 296
Brown, Thomas, 333
Brown, W. H., 301
Brown, Walter L., 331
Brownlow government, 190, 191-195, 229, 232, 234
Brownsville and Jackson Railroad, 148
Bruton, Pink D., 268
Bruton, W. H., 267, 268
Bryan family, 341
Bryan, William Jennings, 386
Bryant, ———, 336
Bryant, Jack, 174
Bryant, James T., 298
Buchanan, A. S., 234
Buchanan, James, W. H. Stephens's opinion of, 186-188
Buck, Gail, 15
Buck, Giddings, 282
Budde, Ralph, 363
Buford, Mrs. J. W., 262

Bullock, Annie, 163
Bullock, Ernest, 99, 149, 254, 372, 382, 383, 386, 397
Bullock, Micajah, 191-192
Bumpus, John, 296
Burch, Lucius, 146, 406, 412, 414
Burgess, A. C., 337
Burke family, 310
Burkett, Exile, 328, 364
Burkett, J. W. N., 269, 328
Burnell family, 310
Burnell, Joe, 373
Burnell, W. H., 359
Burnett, Hill, 215
Burning of Jackson by Federals, 167-168; by Hurst, 178-180
Burton, John, 340
Burnes, William, 308
Burns, S., 355
Butler, Anna, 267
Butler family, 303
Butler, William E., 2, 3, 8, 31, 37, 48-51, 71, 123, 127, 144, 169, 276, 281, 297, 303, 320, 324-325, 366, 390, 395, 397, 418-419
Butler, Mrs. William E., 2, 48
Butler, W. E., Jr., 357
Butler, W. O., 103, 109, 214
Bynum, R. E. L., 288-289, 291

Cabinet makers, 355
Cage, Licurgus, 349
Cageville, 349-350
Caldwell, Andrew, 276
Caldwell, Cyrus, 336
Caldwell, David, 340
Caldwell, Frank, 225, 327
Caldwell, James, 306
Caldwell, Mamie, 262
Caldwell, S. P., 147
Caldwell, W. A., Sr., 254, 325-326
Caldwell, W. A., quoted, 286, 400
Caldwell, W. C., 234
Caldwell, W. G., 162
Calhoun, John C., 408-409
Callahan, Perry, 289
Calvert, C. R., 144-145, 146
Cameron, Don, 267
Camp Beauregard, 160
Camp, T. S., slave trader, 202
Camp meetings, 294, 304-308, 479
Campbell, Alexander, the physician and minister, 147, 213, 251, 297, 307
Campbell, Alexander W., the general, 147, 149, 183-186, 193, 216, 254, 278, 280, 325, 357, 396
Campbell, Mrs. A. W., 165
Campbell, Benjamin, 291
Campbell family, 351
Campbell, J. M., 317

INDEX

Campbell, John W., 11, 57-58, 124, 144, 161, 200, 207, 213, 214, 278, 281, 283, 297, 325, 355
Campbell, Maria Womack, 190
Campbell, Mary, 58, 163
Campbell, T. H., 289
Campbell, Thomas, 300
Canaday, W. H., 316
Canal, proposed, 127, 268, 380
Cane Creek Baptist Church, 300, 340-341
Cantrell, B. P., 328, 360
Carpenter family, 296
Carpenter, J. J., 316
Carroll family, 310
Carroll, William, 228
Carson, J. C., 396
Carter family, 303
Carter, E. B., 309
Cartmell, J. M., 161
Cartmell, Martin, 278, 325
Cartmell, Robert H., diary of Civil War, 156, 157, 158-159, 165, 167-168, 169-171, 177, 179, 192, 201, 204-205, 207, 211-212, 248, 311, 393
Cartmell, Robert H., the physician, 259
Caruthers, James, 31, 123, 167, 276, 278, 279, 323, 324, 325, 340, 486
Caruthers, R. J., 234
Caruthers, Stoddert, 230, 330, 381, 396
Carver, James G., 315
Cason family, 340
Cason, O'Neal and Co., 346
Cason, Mrs. W. C., 314
Cathey, R. C., 331
Catholics, 309-310
Catholic Sisters, 254, 262
Catron, John, 233
Catron, Mrs., 460, 462
Cattle, 223, 225
Calvary Baptist Church, 315
Caveniss, John R., 309
Cedar Chapel, 147
Cearley family, 303
Cerro Gordo, 116-118
Chalmers, Joseph, 109
Chambers, J. W., 242
Chambliss, Alex, 234
Chancellors, 526
Chancery Appeals, Court of, 234-235
Chancery Court, 232-233
Chancery Divisions, 233
Chandler family, 343
Chandler, Ryland, 306
Chandler, Walter, 400
Chappell, J. R., 301, 355
Charles, M. B., 331
Cherokee Nation, 475-477
Chester County, 345-347, 387

Chester, Robert I., 2, 3, 6, 7, 54-57, 61, 62, 108, 167, 169, 215, 254, 283, 347, 456, 466-468
Chester, Mrs. Robert I., 2, 466-467
Chester, John, 253, 281
Chester, Mary Jane, 57
Chester, Sam, 253, 258
Chickasaw lands, 23, 24
Chickasaws, 17-21; Treaty of 1818, 4, 25-26, 48-49
Childress, ———, 250
Chrisp, E. C., 275
Christian Church, First, 311; Highland Avenue Church of Christ, 316
Christian, Mrs. M. J., 309
Church, E. B., 250
Churches, see Religion
Circuit Court Judges, 526
"Circuit riders," 294
Circus, early, 393
Cisco, J. G., interest in prehistoric mounds, 11, 14; newspaper editor, 220, 243, 263, 269-270, 399
"City of Cisco," map, 12, 14, 15
"City of Jackson," 149
Civic League Hospital, 261-262
Civil War, 156-189; hospitals, 489-490; veterans, 492-505
Clanton, Matthew, 336
Clark, J. F., 207
Clark, J. W., 231
Clarke, H. W., 330
Clayton, Ben, 400
Clayton, Will, 400
Clerk and Masters of Chancery, 526
Cleveland, Grover, 383
Clover Creek, 129, 339
Clover Creek Baptist Church, 303
Clubs, 396-398
Cobb, Emma, 160
Cobb, W. K., 309
Cobb, W. P., 309
Cockrill, James, 282
Cockrill, W. G., 291, 315
Coggesshall, James C., 213
Coggins family, 303
Cole family, 343
Coleman Heading Company, 363
Collier, W. H., 364
Colliersville, Tennessee, 178
Collins, Charles R., 269
Collins, Emma, 378
Collins family, 303
Collins, Henry, 333
Collins, James A., 314
Collins, J. W., 247, 281, 315
Colonization, early plans, 21; of 1880's, 359
Columbus, Kentucky, 137
Colored Methodist High School, 285
Comer family, 303

INDEX 537

Commission government, 289
Commissioners of Jackson, 531
Communities, 333-354
Confederates in Jackson, 164-165
Conger, J. B., 355
Conger, John, 357
Conger, Philander D. W., 355, 357
Conger, S. R., 357, 359
Congressmen from Madison, 86-91, 528-529
Conner, Juliana, diary of, 456-478
Conversational Club, 397
Convention, agricultural and industrial, 219-220, dairy, 219; Constitutional of 1834, 233
Cook, N. B., 260
Cook, Wise, 103
Cook, William L., 234
Cooke, W. K., 109
Corn huskings, 394
Cotton, 121, 122, 198-200, 225, 324; lands in District, 43, 44, 47; "cotton burners," 164; factory, 351-354; market, 361
Cotton Grove, 32-33, 38, 129, 333, 395
Cotton Grove Baptist Church, 300
County Court, 227-230; clerks, 525; presiding officers, 524-525; judges, 230, 525; trustees, 525
County seat selected, 37-38
Court of Appeals, 235
Courts, business of early ones, 35; of "Law and Equity," 230-231; Chancery, 232-233; Chancery Appeals, 234-235; Circuit, 230-232; Civil Appeals, 235; Supreme of Tennessee, 233-234; Federal, 236; conditions in early days, 67-69; dignity of, 229; reorganization in 1865, 229
Courthouse, log, 38; in 1827, 467; yard in 1866, 191
Cowan, I. M., Mrs. 317
Coward, William, 125
Craddle, Mrs. L. W., 286, 340
Crawford, Andrew, 294
Creighton, J. H., 278
Crime, early days, 231-232; later, 237-244, 245-247
Crittenden, ———, 259
Crittenden, W. T., 342
Crittenden family, 343
Crittendon, H. T., 290
Crockett, David, 50-52, 70-83, 107, 124-125, 399, 403, 484; correspondence of, 420-428
Crockett County, 248-351
Crook Bro. Drug Store, 346
Crook, Jere L., 260, 261, 273, 331, 400
Crook, Joseph A., 260, 261, 331, 399
Crook, J. B., 286

Crook, W. J., 287
Crook Sanatorium, 361
Croom, John, 344
Crops, produce for market, 221
Cross, John, 391
Cumberland Presbyterian Church, 308-309
Cummings, David, 114
Curtis, L. L., 297, 363
Curtis, E. B., 372

Dade's Command, massacre of, 103-104
Dairy products in Madison, 224
Dancing, 394-395
Dancy, A. B., 260
Dancy, Clifton, 327
Dandridge, Tennessee, in 1827, 457
Danville, Tennessee, in 1827, 458
Dashiell, R. R., 204, 252, 254, 281
Daughters of American Revolution, 397
Davis, C. W., 11, 14, 15
Davis, E. H., 162
Davis family, 341
Davis, Jefferson, 304
Davis, O. W., 346
Davis, Pat, 342
Davis, William, 162
Davy Nunn, steamboat on Forked Deer River, 126
Dawson, Squire, 231
Day, Aliene, 397
Day family, 303, 340
Day, Isaac, 282
Day, J. H., 113
Day, J. O., 346
Day, Reuben, 300, 341
Dayton, Tennessee, see Henderson
Deaderick, David, 15
Deaderick, James, visits District in 1826, 43-44, 234
Dean family, 303
Deberry, Abraham, 355
Deberry, Allen, 127, 208
Deberry, Mathias, 127, 306
Declaration of Independence of Tennessee, 158
Deeping, Stark, 276
DeHaven, D. W., 234
Deming family, 303
Democrat, 265
Democratic meeting in 1840, 7-10, 66; stronghold in West Tennessee, 382, 386-387
Denmark, Tennessee, 82, 147, 174-175, 238, 249, 252, 257, 258, 259, 278, 298, 299, 306-307, 335-338; Denmark, Brownsville, and Durhamville R. R., 148; Female Academy, 277, 278; in the Civil War, 160; railroad meeting, 139

Dennison, C. L., 315
Dentist, early, 250-251, 252, 258
Derryberry family, 303
Deupree, Mrs. ——, 397
Dew, Carlos, 421
Dewitt, Mrs. John, 531
Diamond family, 348
Dickson family, 303
Dickens, Samuel, 31, 32, 324
Dickinson, J. W., 297
Dillon, Robert, 253
Dispatch, Jackson, 269
District Schools, early, 290
Doak family, 296
Doak, William, 33
Dod, Charles C., 213, 279
Dodd, John, 253
Dodds, Julia, 314
Dodds, Wash, 308
Dodson, Obdadiah, 272, 302, 303, 341, 343
"Domestic Medicine Chest," 248
Dominican Sisters, 283
Donald, James L. M., 296
Donavan family, 310
Donelson, John, 59
Donnell family, 303
Douglas, Joseph, 295
Doyle, Father, 310
Drake, Mrs. Love Jones, 262
Drake, T. H., 291
Drama, 393
Drunkenness at camp meetings, 305
Duffey, Patrick, 229
Dugger, A. D., 327
Duke, Grace, 397
Duke, J. H., 288, 370, 375, 382
Duke place, 262
Dunaway, W. E., 309, 328
Dunbar family, 340
Duncan, Ida, 281
Duncan, Mrs. Janie, 397
Duncan, Mrs. T. B., 315
Dunham, Robert, 429-431
Dunn, Joe L., 373
Dupree, W. D., 301
Durham, Owen, 340
Duval, ——, 281
Dyer, Joel, 65
Dyer, "Colonel Matt," 61
Dyer, Robert H., 4, 35, 54, 55, 100, 123, 228, 486, 487
Dyersburg, Tennessee, 151

Eastin, Mary, Andrew Jackson to, 406-410
Eaton, J. H., 4, 405-406, 408, 461
Eaton, Mrs. ——, 460
Ebenezer Methodist Church, 341
Echols, Joe, 448
"Edgewood," home of J. W. Campbell, 58
Edenton, Bruce, 327
Edenton, Ernest, 287, 369, 415, 416
Edenton, J. C., 302, 331
Education, 38, 66, 90, 185, 275-291, 336-337, 475-476
Edwards family, 303
Eldad Baptist Church, 300
"Electioneering" on frontier, 51-52, 293
Election of 1840, 9-10; of 1894 contested, 383-386
Elks, 396
Ellis, D. A., 315
Elrod, James, 325
Elston family, 341
Embrey, Jesse, 105
Emerson family, 303
Emerson, James, 303
Emmerson, Mrs. Robert, 203
Emmerson, J. T., 162
Emmerson, Judge, 233
Emmons, H. H., 236
Emigration, spirit of, 463
Enloe, B. A., 86, 97-99, 219, 263, 272, 383
Enochs, S. B., 288
Epidemics, 248, 252-256
Episcopal Church, St. Luke's, 303-304
Episcopal Convention of Diocese, 1846, 304
Eppinger, August, 161
Epps, Wyatt, 295
Ernshaw, F. E., 335
Estanuala, 131, 174-175, 177, 298, 312, 335, 338-339
Essary, S. H., 225
Estes family, 303
Estes, Edwin, 320
Evans, J. H., 281, 313
Evans, Lemuel, 278
Evans, Thomas, 300
Evans, Clay, 383-386
Everett, Grace, 59
Everett, Sidney J., 232, 386-387
Ewell, Thomas. 117-119, 454
Ewing, H. S., 93
Experiment Station, 38
Exum, M. V. B., 224, 290, 360

Fact and Fiction, 272
Fairs, 213-215
Farmer's Advocate, 272
Farm lands in county, 220
Farrell family, 310
Farrow, P. B., 286
Faucett family, 303
Federal Courts, 235-236
Federal forces in Jackson, 1863, 169-171; headquarters, 164-165; tax on citizens, 172

INDEX 539

Felsenthal, Mrs. Carrie, 262
Falsenthal, E., 361
Falsenthal, Hattie, 397
Felsenthal, Mrs. J. C., 262
Falsenthal, J. C., 312
Fenner, Erasmus, 252, 260, 303
Fenner, Fannie, 289
Fenner, John M., 303
Fenner, John S., 254, 258
Fenner, Junius P., 303
Fenner, Robert, 215, 250, 278, 283, 333
Fentress, Francis, 234
Fighting, 389-390
Finlay, Mrs. ———, 300
Finlay, John, 300-301
Fire department, 371-375
First National Bank, 325-326
Fisher family, 311
Fisher, E. L., 345
Fisher, F. B., 328
Fisher, F. K., 373
Fish fry, 393
Fite, W. R., 302
Fitzgerald family, 303
Fitzhugh, Henrietta, diary of, 45-46
Fitzpatrick, Mary Pius, 283
Fitzpatrick, Vincencia, 283
Flaherty, James, 355
Flatboats, 120-126
Fletcher, R. S., Sr., 269, 288, 328, 329
Florence, Alabama, 240
Flowers, Wiley, letter of David Crockett to, 427-428
Flowers, William, 320
Flowers, W. G., 355
Fogg family, 296
Folks, William C., 234
Ford, George and Lewis, 338
Forked Deer Academy, 277
Forked Deer Association, 298-299
Forked Deer Blade, 269-270
Forked Deer River, called Okena, 24
Forked Deer River navigation, 60, 120-135, 467
Forked Deer Valley, railroad proposed, 132-133
Forrest, N. B., 167, 195; address to men, 181-182
Fort Pillow, 180
Fort, Josiah, 336
Fort, R. E., 531
Foster, Ephriam, 266
Foster, J. W., 311
Fourth of July celebrations, 391-393
"Fourth Ward School," 288
Foust, A. B., 290
Fox, J. H., 334
Franchise, right of in 1866, 191-193
Franklin, David, 345
Frankland Carriage Co., 363

Franklin, D. J., 286
Franklin, lost state of, 22
Franklin, Tennessee in 1827, 464
Freedman's Bureau, 215
Freeman family, 303
Freeman, John, 108
Freeman, Jo, 161, 252, 450
Freeman, Thomas, 280, 334
Friedlob, J., 312, 360
"Frog Jump," 124
Frontier, courts, 35; hardships, 44-46; politics, 70-85; churches, 292-308
"Frozen Oak," 339
Fruit crop, 222
Fry home, 314
Fry, James L., 315
Finances, 323-332
Fulbright family, 340
Fulghum, J. B., 375
Futrell, J. D., 287
Futrell, J. E., 290
Fussell, James, 277
Fussell, John, 229
Fussell, W. A., 334

Gab-Fest, 271
Gabrielle, M. R., 279
Gaffney family, 310
Gailbraith, I. J., 286
Gaither, T. D., 315
Gale, ———, 259
Ganaway, Mary, 277, 300
Gardner, O. G., 341-342
Garrett, Lewis, Jr., 293
Garrett, Mrs. Susan, 314
Gaskins, Enoch, 300
Gaskins, Sarah, 300
Gas lights, 368-369
Gates, B. F., 254
Gates, John W., 267, 268, 288
Gates, Robert, 98, 149, 219, 254, 270, 272
Gates, Robert Moore, 271
Gates, Thomas M., 38, 80, 88, 122, 124, 131, 165, 172, 194, 258, 266, 394
Gates, W. W., 147, 263, 265-268, 357, 399
Gaylor, Frank H., 234
Gazette, Jackson, 263-264
Gazzo, Father, 310
General Assembly members, 527-528
Gentry, Meridith, 85
Gest, J. S., 302
Geyer, H. D., 315
Gholson, A. R., 234
Gibson, John H., 54-55
Giles County, 113
Gillespie, James, 296
Gilmore, H. B., 330
Gilmore, Mrs. O. R., 397

540 INDEX

Gist, ——, 276
Givens, Charlie, 340
Givens, Margaret, 208
Glass, John E., 287
Glenn, J. M., 288
Godwin, ——, 252, 260
Golden Station, 38
Gooch, J. C., 330
Gooch, Rufus, 300
Good, J. J., 355
Goodloe, Hallum, 348
Good roads program, 378-381
Goodwin, Mrs. E. M. A., 314
Gordan, Sam, 236
Government of Jackson, 366-367
Grady, I. L., 302
Graham, Watt, 309
Grangers, 351
Graham's Magazine, 437-438
Grant, General, 165
Green, David, 144
Green, Grafton, 234
Green, John, 334
Green, Nathan, 233
Green, R. C., 275
Greer, James, 127, 297
Greer, John, 326
Greer, L. T., 290
Greer, Mamie, 351
Greer, Mrs. Tom, 351
Gregory, Robert, 295
Gresham, John W., 259
Griffin, Z. K., 289
Griffis, Missie, 373
Griffith, William, 35, 228
Grundy, Felix, speaks in Jackson, 9, 65
Guerilla warfare in 1863, 169-172
Gulf, Mobile and Ohio Railroad, 152
Gulf, Mobile and Northern Railroad, 151-152
Gunter, Esquire, 290

Haas family, 310
Hackett, N. P., 287
Haddaway, James, 162
Hale, Mrs. ——, fighing near, 171
Hale, Enoch P., 114
Hale, Wiley P., 112-113, 114, 116-119; correspondence of, 444-455
Hall, Allen A., 266
Hall, Arch B., 231
Hall, A. J., 315
Hall, Frank P., 234
Hall, Guy, 91, 121
Hall, J. W., 297
Hall, Robert, 357
Hallett, W. R., railroad promoter, 139
Ham, Mordecai, evangelist, 319
Hamilton, Frank B., 254, 257
Hamilton, Joseph, 282

Hammond, E. S., 235, 236
Hanebuth, Charlie, 361
"Hanging grounds," 246-247
Hanging of McLean, 246-247; of Reilly, 246
Haralson, Herndon, 4, 30, 33, 35, 37, 38, 52-54, 228, 232, 366
Haralson, Vincent, 37
Hardeman County, 148
Hargrove, John, 32, 333
Harper, Fannie B., 284
Harper, J. H. Academy, 284-285
Harper, Kate M., 284
Harper's gun shop, 165
Harper, J. H., 320
Harris, ——, of Brownsville, 241
Harris, ——, 252
Harris, B. R., 256, 309, 326
Harris, Mrs. C. N., 397
Harris, Edward, surveyor in 1785, 23
Harris, Fred, 290
Harris, G. N., 165
Harris, George, 169
Harris, G. W. D., 294
Harris, J. L., 289, 291
Harris, J. W., 233, 254
Harris, Hettie, 397
Harris, Isham G., 252, 294, 383
Harris, Thomas, 251
Harris, W. B., 234
Harris, W. M., 330
Harris, William R., 294
Harris, W. T., 396
Harris, W. T., the minister, 281
Harrison, John, 339
Harrison family, 295
Harrison, Will H., 339
Haskell, Caroline, 112-113, 449
Haskell, Charles, 108, 452
Haskell Hill, 165
Haskell, Joshua, 39, 108, 231, 241, 242, 276, 278, 304, 320, 399; impeachment of, 67-69
Haskell, William T., 84, 86, 91-95, 112, 113, 114, 115-119, 399, 444-445, 451, 454-455
Harbert family, 336
Hart family, 336
Hart, ——, 194
Hart, J. M., 346
Harton, David, 37, 366
Harton, John, 276
Harton family, 340, 341
Hartmus, Thomas, 194
Harvey, Hugh, 290
Haskins family, 351
Hatch, Colonel, 170, 172
Haughton, Jeremiah, 282, 300, 320
Haughton, L. B., 357
Haughton, Martha, 300
Hawk, W. R., 224

INDEX 541

Hawkins, Alvin, 234
Hawkins, Hermon, 180, 400
Hawkins, John H., 355
Hawkins, Mrs. S. M., 180; concerning fire in Jackson, 179-180; quoted, 300-301
Haynes, Robert, 281
Haywood, ———, 233
Hazelwood, Ben, 225
Hays, A. C., 264
Hays Avenue Methodist Church, 313-314
Hays, B .A., 281
Hays, D. A. C., 264
Hays, Mrs. Dick, 281
Hays, Elizabeth, 254
Hays, Frances Middleton, 61-62
Hays, Mrs. Jane, 62
Hays, Middleton, 63, 161, 194, 195
Hays, Milton, 342
Hays, Narcissa, 2, 466
Hays, R. J., 214, 232, 403, 416-617
Hays's Chapel, 342
Hays, Samuel Jackson, 2, 61-63, 109, 111, 139, 144, 165, 283-284, 304, 310, 399, 403, 413, 415-416, 418-419
Hays, Samuel J., 413
Hays, Stokley D., nephew of Rachel Jackson, 2, 3, 6, 37, 59-61, 276, 366, 399, 403
Hays, Stokley D. (the younger), 352
Hays, Mrs. Walker, 403, 418
Head, J. H., 148
Heard, J. E., 281
Health, early days, 248-249; in Forked Deer Valley, 488; resort, 347
Hearn and Rogers Store, 131, 207, 344
Hearn, C. H., 343
Heathcock family, 311
Henderson, Alex, 452
Henderson, Dewitt, 233
Henderson family, 333
Henderson, Richard, 103-104
Henderson, R. E. L., 290
Henderson, Tennessee, 345-346, 395; Masonic Institute, 286-287, 346
Henderson, Thomas, 4-5, 13, 31, 32, 276, 343, 423, 486
Henderson, William, 296
Hendrix, J. L., 328
Henning family, 343
Henning, John, 239
Hermitage, visit to, 460-462
Herring, D. W., 328
Herron, Charlie, 271, 360
Herron, J. T., 258
Herron, W. W., 144
Hess, N. I., 252
Hibbetts, R. H., 320
Hicks, Hugh, 326

Hicks, John T., 267
Hicks, Rane, 300
Hicks, Robert, 262
Hicks, W. A., 316
Hightower, Richard, 26
Highland Avenue Church of Christ, 316
Highland Heights Methodist Church, 316
Highland Park, 398
Hill, Allan, 300, 340-341
Hill family, 340
Hill, Jacob, 144, 300
Hilliard, T. L., 317
Hilliard, Mrs. W. H., 317
Hirsch, J. H., 288, 327, 375
Hodge, ———, 241
Hodgson family, 311
Hogsett, Charles, 357
Holden, John, 276, 277
Holland, Carrie, 397
Holland, Edith, 397
Holland, Mrs. Harriet, 397
Holland, Hezekiah, 293
Holland, John, 400
Holland, Phillip, 98, 400
Holland, William, 400
Holland, William, Sr., 361, 382
Hollinsworth, J. B., 317
Holmes, George D., 280
Holmes, James, 280
Holmes, Walter, 280, 400
Holt, L. C., 291
Hook, Judge, 3
Hooper, Ben, 386
Hopper family, 343
Hopper, D. L., 328
Hopper, J. D., 290
Hopper, J. H., 372
Hopper, Samuel, 296
"Hopewell Church," 298
Hopewell Presbytery, 308
Horn, Stanley, 76
Horse thief, 237-238
Hospital, Beauregard, 163, 261-262
Houk, Lysander, 282
Houston, John, 390
Houston, Sam, 107, 109, 469-470, 472-473
Howard, Frederick, 271
Howard, Memucan Hunt, 31, 343
Howard, Mrs. W. P., 351
Hubbard, Benjamin, 281
Hudson family, 310, 348
Hudson, W. J., 337
Hughes, James, 310
Hughes, Robert, 231, 303
Hughes, Thomas, 273, 326
Humboldt, Tennessee, 176
Hume, L. T., 373
Humphreys, West H., 236

542 INDEX

Humphries, C. W., 162
Hunt, Mrs. J. D., 397
Hunter, John, 342
Hunter, Mrs. J. H., 397
Huntersville, Tennessee, 342-343; railroad meeting at, 139
Hunting, 388; grounds of Chickasaws, 25
Huntingdon, Tennessee, 480
Huntsman, Adam, 4, 37, 70-83, 86, 123, 128, 275, 325, 366, 399, 406, 423, 426
Huntsman, Sarah, 333
Hurst, Fielding, 168, 169, 171-172, 178, 196, 339, 346
Hurt, R. A., 211
Hurt, R. B., 147, 163, 165-166, 215, 224, 357, 490
Hutchison, William, 296
Hyndam family, 311

Ijams, C. B., 287, 288, 400
Illinois Central Railroad, 143-147
Immigration to Western District, 23, 29-31, 43, 44, 47; to Texas, 107; to Tennessee, 219; in 1870's, 217-218; in 1880's, 359-360
Impeachment of Judge Haskell, 67-69
Indian trails, 16
Ingersoll, Robert, 160, 166, 175
Ingram family, 343
Ingram, Paul, 325
Inman, J. B., 287
Insurrection of slaves planned, 208-209
Internal improvements, 120-135
Inventions, 334-335
Irby, H. C., 280
Irvin, John, 357
Ivey family, 343

Jack's Creek, Tennessee, railroad meeting, 139; fighting near, 177-178
Jackson, Alexander, 144, 184, 213, 214, 251, 254, 278, 281, 393
Jackson and Nashville Railroad, 148
Jackson, Andrew, county seat named for, 2-3; visits the town in 1825 and 1840, 3-6, 7-10; Masonic apron, 4; treaty with the Chickasaws, 18, 25-26, 48, 57, 61; correspondence of, 403-419; Crockett's opposition to, 423-427; entertained the Conners in 1827, 460-462, 468
Jackson, Mrs. Andrew, 60, 460-462
Jackson Banking Co., see National Bank of Commerce
Jackson, E. B., 490
Jackson Female Academy, 275, 277
Jackson *Gazette*, quoted, 305-306

"Jackson Grays," volunteer company of '61, 159
Jackson Home Telephone Co., 373
Jackson, Howell E., 95-97, 184-185, 236, 251, 280, 352, 399
Jacksonian, 265
"Jacksonia," proposed state of, 22
Jackson, Isaac, 161
Jackson *Madisonian*, 271
Jackson Male Academy, 61, 275, 276
Jackson, Matthew, 296
Jackson Oil Company, 361
Jackson Savings Bank, see First National Bank
Jackson *Sun*, 263, 272-273; the building, 283
Jackson Telephone Company, 373
Jackson, Tennessee, almost lost its name, 3; lots sold, 40-41; in 1827, 466-468; in 1830, 46; in 1833, 44; in 1837, 481; in 1840, 485; depot for provisions in 1861, 157-158; burned by Hurst, 178-180; in 1875, 190-192; map of, 40-41, 376-377; mayors and commissioners of, 530-531
Jackson, William H., 183-184, 215-216, 251, 397
Jacobi, Mrs. ——, 397
James, C. L., 315
James, Jesse, 339
Jarman, George, 280
Jarrell, David, 336
Jarrett, David, 35, 128, 228
Jasper, Tennessee, in 1827, 475
Jefferson Day Dinner, 404
Jefferson, Thomas, quoted, 400
Jenkins, George, 355
Jewish church, 311, 312
Johnson, Albert, 224
Johnson, A. S., 290
Johnson, Andrew, 85
Johnson family, 351
Johnson, Frank, 230
Johnson, G. W., 283
Johnson, J. D., 224, 289
Johnson, John H., 308
Johnson, J. S., 328
Johnson, Julius, 347
Johnson, Mrs. ——, 276
Johnson, N. S., 303
Johnson, Sam, 236
Johnson, Seale, 48
Johnson, Steven, 300
Johnson, William, 236
Johnston, Addison, 160, 164, 335
Johnston, John, 160, 174, 206, 335, 337
Johnston, Robert, 298
Johnston, Sarah, 164
Jobe, A. K., 361

INDEX 543

Jobe, Mrs. Lucinda, 300
"Jonah's Gourd," 298
Jones, A. B., 281
Jones, Amos, 281, 295
Jones, Atlas, 304, 486
Jones, Calvin, prospector in 1818, 25, 29, 73, 422; correspondence of, 486-488
Jones, Casey, 153-155
Jones, Elijah, 333
Jones, James C., 213, 231
Jones, J. T., 258, 328, 399
Jones, Julius, 333
Jones, Legrand, 114
Jones, Mary, 397
Jones, Rush, 259
Jones, Sam, 317-319
Jones, Timothy, 111
Joyce family, 310
Judges, Circuit, 526
Judson, F. E., 373
Judson, J. A. and J. H., 340

Keel boats, 121-124, 199
Kelly family, 310
Kendall, S. E., 287
Kenzie, Mrs. Grace, 359
Kershaw, Sarah, 314
Key, Charlie, 224, 290
Key Corner, 24, 35
Key, Martin, 333
Kincade home, 314
King, A., 395
King, Austin, 400
King family, 310
King, Ham, 147, 247; King's Palace Saloon, 382, 383
King's Opera House, 219, 254
King, R. E., 395
Kieroff, S. E., 316
Killebrew, J. B., 217-218
Kirby, Henry, 296
Kline, H. L., 331
Knights of Pythias, 396
Knoxville, Tennessee in 1827, 457
Ku Klux Klan, 63, 193-197

Labor problems in 1850's, 211; in 1870's, 215-216
Lackey, Dan, 341
Lacy, Catherine, 303
Lacy, Donald Ross, 340
Lacy, George, 259
Lacy, Hugh Ross, 340
Lacy, Jesse, 340
Lacy, Sarah, 303
Lacy, Stephen, 4, 339
Lacy, Thomas, 128, 229, 340
Ladies' Soldiers' Aid Society of '61, 489-490
Lafayette, 178

Lake Alexander, 370
Lake, Elizabeth, 300
Lake, Henry, 123
Lambuth College, 273
Lambuth Memorial Methodist Church, 314
Lancaster, E. R., 343
Lancaster, John L., 361, 400
Lancaster Park, 371, 398
Lancaster, Samuel, 230, 278, 280, 324, 333, 370, 378, 380-381, 399
Lancaster, Samuel, Sr., commissioner for internal improvements, 125
Landis and Burnell, 357
Landis, C. F., 311
Lands, rich lands of West Tennessee, 22, 27, 29-30, 486; early sales, 23, 25; cheap lands, 31; speculators, 25-28, 29-33; congenial to cotton, 198-199
Lane College, 285-286
Lane, Cullen, 296
Lane, Isaac, 285-286
Lane, J. F., 285
Langley family, 310
Lanier, ———, 247
Lankford, Mrs. Jesse, 309
Lansden, C. L., 234
La Salle's opinion of Chickasaws, 18
Latham, J. F., 309
Law school at S. W. B. U., 280
Lawler, Abner, 301
Lawler family, 310
Lawlessness during Civil War, 182-183; in late 1860's, 193-197
Lawrence, ———, 460
Lawrence, S. B., Jr., 316
Lawrenceboro, Tennessee, in 1827, 464
Laws of Town of Jackson in 1823, 39
Lea, Albert Miller, civil engineer, 132-133
Lea, Lorenzo, 279, 281, 314
Leeper, Guy, 141, 173, 339
Leggett, E. L., 340
Lewis, A. M., 337
Lexington, Tennessee, 252; in 1827, 465
Library, early, 282-283, 378
Lindsay, Ben, 280, 399
Lindsay family, 310
Lindsay, Robert S., 315
Lindsay, T. E., 363
Lindy, A. S., 312
Little family, 311
Little Pike, steamboat on Forked Deer, 125
Lodges, 395-396
Loftin family, 340
Loftin, Thomas, 4
Logan, John A., orders, 165, 170
Logan, W. T., 373

544 INDEX

Log-rollings, 71, 388
Long, Ben, 165
Long, Jesse, 272
Long, Mrs. M. A., 262
Long, Tom, 224, 326
Lorance, Elisha, 308
Loring, Dr. ———, 250
Lottery for river improvements, 122-123
Louis, H. W., 328
Love, A. B., 316
Love, Charles J., Andrew Jackson to, 411
Love, John, 160
Loving, Dr. ———, 260
Lowe, C. P., 291
Loyd, James L., 373
Luckman, W. M., 331
Lumber, 341-342
Lumber resources, 126, 361, 364
Lurton, Horace H., 234
Lyceum, 393-394
Lyerla, D. A., 328
Lyle, Ada, 373
Lynch family, 310
Lynch, James, 325
Lynch, John, 333
Lynn, Joseph, 35, 228
Lyon, James S., 85, 105, 172, 175, 213, 214, 242, 325
Lyon, Sam, 452
Lyric Club, 396

Mabry, E., 278
MacDonald, Joe, 261
Maddin, ———, 333
Maddin, Thomas, 320
Madding, Daniel, 395
Madison College, 282, 334
Madison County, named, 1-2; courts established, 35; early boundary, 34-35; created in 1821, 33-35
"Madison Grays," 103-104
Madison Hall, 351
Madison, James, 1-2
Madison Male Academy, 278
Mageveney family, 310
Mahon, J. H., 397
Mail service, early, 129-130, 531
Malesus, 340-341
Mallory, E. S., 148, 254, 288, 360
Mallory, James, 340
Malone, W. A., 291
Manley, Caleb, 339
Manley family, 295, 351
Manufacturing, early, 39, 355-365
Map of Jackson in 1822, 40-41, 376-377; of Madison County, 1946, 520-521
"Marathon" automobile, 364
Marks's home, 312

Marquette, Father, opinion of Chickasaws, 18
Marshall, Park, 243
Marshall, W. B., 325
Marshall, William, 165
Martin, Andrew L., 241, 278, 303, 320, 324
Martin, John D., 236
Martin, Joseph E., 397
Martin, Terry, 317
Mary, Keel boat, 124
Mason, C. M., 286
Mason, Cassie, 277, 281, 400
Mason, E. B., 350
Mason Grove, 311, 351
Mason, J. D., 291
Mason, Tennessee, 147
Masonic Lodge, 4, 39, 166, 295, 395-396
Mason's Wells, 347
Mass meeting concerning Texas independence, 108
Massac Trace, 17
Mathis, L. E., 288
Matthews, A. O., 236
Matthews, A. R., 290
Matthews, J. S., Jr., 290
Matthews, J. S., Sr., 224
Matthews, Mark C., 261, 378
Matthews, Sam, 296
Maxey, Eliza, 309
Maxey, Henrietta, 309
Maxey, Mrs. Mary, 309
Maxey, W. D., 309
May, R. H., 200
Mayo, Harry, 340
Mayo, K. C., 331
Mayo, R. C., 290
Mayors of Jackson, 530-531
Mays family, 348
Mays, J. L., 290
McAdams, J., 162
McAleer, Father, 310
McAlister, William, 234
McAnulty, Mrs. Louise Jones, 486
McBride, Archie, 338
McBride family, 336
McCall, John E., 236
McCampbell, Andrew, 232
McCarty family, 310
McClanahan, Clyde, 373
McClanahan, James, 277
McClanahan, John R., 114
McClanahan, John W., 91
McClanahan, Nelson, 66
McClanahan, Samuel, 8, 65-66, 169, 233, 276, 278
McClaran, James Walsh, 261, 400
McClelland, James, 296
McCollum family, 348
McCord, Harvey, 308

INDEX 545

McCorry family, 310
McCorry, Henry W., 99, 109, 185, 193, 194, 195, 214, 215, 230, 231, 233, 236, 254, 373, 382-386, 396
McCorry home, 165
McCorry, Mercer, 531
McCorry, Musidora, 397, made K K K robes, 195
McCorry, "Miss Pet," 170, 272; made K K K robes, 195
McCorry, Tom, 423
McCorry, Thomas, 161, 331
McCorry, Mrs. Thomas, Sr., 215
McCowatt Brothers, 272
McCowatt, Philip C., 192, 229, 370
McCoy, ——, makes railroad speech in Bolivar, 144
McCoy, Ambrose, 259, 261, 326, 399
McCoy, John, 345
McCoy, N. A., 259, 344
McCulley, John A., 346
McCutchen, J. C., 314
McCutchen, J. T., 194, 290, 361
McCutchen, R. R., 162
McDonald, J. W., 288
McFarland, Robert, 234
McGee family, 341
McGee, G. R., 288-289
McGee, J. F., 331
McGee, L. W., 331
McGlathery, F. M., 341
McGuire, James, 340
McHaney, C. F., 373
McHaven family, 310
McIver, Mrs. ——, 277
McIver, Duncan, 4, 32, 228, 333
McIver, Roderick, 32, 35, 228, 333
McKellar, Mrs. Don, 531
McKellar Field, 273
McKinney, Colin P., 234
McKinney, Robert J., 234
McKinnie, John R., 326
McKissack and Burton, 337
McKnight, Dr. ——, 333
McKnight, David, 114
McKnight, E. F., 325
McKnight family, 340-341
McKnight, Frank, 341
McLean, Charles D., 4, 213, 263, 264-265
McLean family, 310
McLemore, John, 31, 486, 487
McLemore, Sugars, 31
McMahon, J. H., 103-104, 108, 109, 110, 265
McMillan, Charles, 38, 85
McMillan family, 336
McMullen family, 310
McNabb, W. B., 311
McNairy, Boyd, 266
McNairy County, 178

McNairy, John, 236
McNeal, Thomas, 35
McNutt, ——, 276
McWherter, A. J., 219, 360
Meachum, Elizabeth, 300
Medical Board of Censors, 249-250
Medicine in Madison, 248-262
Medon, Tennessee, 71, 257, 259, 303, 308, 339-340; Academy, 286; K K K in, 196; railroad comes to, 144; Methodist Church, 295
Meeks, ——, 166
Meeks, M. H., 327
Memphis and Charleston R. R., 138
Memphis Conference Female Institute, 6, 169, 281-282
Memphis, Tennessee, 129
Mercer, Ed, 272
Mercer, T. B., 341
Mercer, T. C., 290
Mercer, T. E., 331, 341
Mercer, Tennessee, 148, 338, 341-342, 395
Meriwether, David, 251, 357
Meriwether family, Huntersville, 343
Meriwether, Frank, 298, 336
Meriwether, James, 298, 320, 325, 336, 343
Meriwether, John, 290
Meriwether, M. C., 291
Meriwether, M. D., 360
Meriwether, Tobe, 325
Messenger, keel-boat, 124
Methodists, on frontier, 292; early, 293-296; camp meeting, 306
Methodist churches, Episcopal Church, South, 285; First, 195, 317; Hays Avenue, 313-314; Highland Heights, 316; Lambuth Memorial, 314-315; Trinity, 315-316
Mexican War, 91, 111-119, 254, 444-455; veterans, 491-492
Midland City, 150
Milan, Tennessee, 222
Miles, Bishop ——, 309
Militia, 100-104, 228, 250
Miller, Austin, of Bolivar, 134-135
Miller, George E., 245
Miller, James, 303
Miller, John S., 325, 357
Miller, Pleasant, 63-65, 67, 334
Milligan, Samuel, 234
Minute Men of Civil War, 229
Mississippi Central and Tennessee R. R. Stock, 142; building of, 143-144; rebuilt after Civil War, 145-146
Mitchell, Bell, 309
Mitchell, D. E., 236
Mitchell, G. W., 309
Mitchell, Georgilla, 309

INDEX

Mitchell, Lizzie, 309
Mitchell, Sam, 309
Mobile and Ohio Railroad, 137-143, 186, 229; completed, 142; rebuilt after Civil War, 143; shops, 146-147, 273
Money, early, 323-324
Monterey, Mexico, 114-116; Battle of, 449-450
Montgomery, John, 229
Mooers, C. A., 225
Mooney, Mary Sue, 281
Moore family, 336
Moore, J. L., 163
Moore, P. W., 347
Moore, W. S., 327
Mooring, John, 333
Morgan, C. F., 151
Morgan, E. H., 162
Morgan, R. P., 363
Morgan, W. A., 147
Morgan, W. G., 331, 363
Morning Jacksonian, 272
Morris, C. H., 151
Moss family, 311
Moss, John, 281
Mound builders, 11-16
Mounds, yellow fever, 255
Mount Pinson, 13, 129, 228, 343; Academy, 276
Mount Tabor Presbyterian Church, 308
Mule cars, 374-375
Murchison, Dr. ——, 251, 258
Murchison, —— of Medon, 196
Murchison family, 336, 340
Murdock, Mrs. Jennie, 262
Murdock, Mrs. Lena Lacy, 339
Murfreesboro, Tennessee, in 1827, 458, 474
Murphy, Archibald D., views on Western District, 29-30
Murphy family, 310
Murray, Alfred, 4
Murray, Anna, 397
Murray, P. J., 328, 360
Murray, Mrs. P. J., 262
Murray, P. S., 165
Murray, Robert, 199, 395
Murray, Tom, Sr., 387
Murrell, John A., 87, 237-244, 339
Murrell, L., merchant, 256
Murrell, Lelia Morgan, 271-272, 397
Murrell, Thomas, 373
Murtaugh family, 343
Murtaugh, Thomas, 340
Muse, T. C., 233
Muster Day, 100-101
Mutual Improvement Club, 397
Myers, Henry, 312

Myers, Lucile, 531
Myers, William E., visits mounds at Pinson, 14
Mynders, S. A., 400
Mynders, S. A., Sr., 288-289

Nance's Drug Store, 257
Nashville, Chattanooga and St. Louis R. R., old Tennessee Midland R. R., merged into, 150-151
Nashville Railroad Convention, 134
Nashville, Tennessee, in 1827, 458-460, 474
Natchez Trace, 122
National Bank of Commerce, 328-330
Nashville Banner and Nashville Whig, quoted, 242
National Road, proposed through Western District in 1826, 128
Navigation on Forked Deer, 120-126, 198-200
Neal family, 348
Neblett, R. B., 316
Neely, Bert, 224
Neely families, 336, 351
Neely, J. J., 161, 177
Neely, James, 147
Neely, Lessie, 351
Neely, M. S., 370
Neely, Molly, 351
Neely, Moses, 327
Neely, R. P., 88, 195
Neely, S. S., 351
Neely, Thomas, 295
Negroes, 201-211; during Civil War, 166-168; killed, 179; elected magistrate, 196; free, 208; during reconstruction, 215-216; education, 285-286; religion of, 307
Neil, M. M., 234
Neilson, Alexander, 123
Neilson, T. J., 162
Nelson, J. A., 162
Nelson, T. A., 234, 266
Nelson, W. D., 327, 373
Nelson, W. T., 288, 327
Nero, keel-boat, 124
Nesbitt, Anna, 309
Neville, Fonville, 174, 218, 335, 338, 341
Nevins, Annie, 397
Newberg, Thomas, 147
Newbern, ——, 251
Newborn, D. D., 340
Newport, Tennessee, 456
Newsom family, 341
Newsome, John, 178
Newspapers, early, 38, 263-268
Newton, Jeff D., 268
Nicolson, W. O. P., 234
Nimmo, A. C., 395

INDEX 547

Nix, Mrs. Carrie, 315
Nobles, Mrs. Catherine, 296
Nobley family, 341
Nolen, Father, 310
Normal school proposed in Jackson, 289
North Carolina, University of, claims lands, 25
Northwestern Miller, quoted, 353-354
Norvel, John, 301
Nourse, W. H., 317
Nullifiers, 404-405
Numrod, keel-boat, 124

Oath of allegience, 171
O'Brien, John, 310
O'Brien, Patrick, 310
Occupation of Jackson by Federals, 167-168
O'Conner Brothers, shoemakers, 163
O'Conner, James, 287, 288, 357
O'Daley, Father, 310
Ogden, Col. ———, 460
Oglesby, Gen., 165, 168
Ohio Valley Railroad, 148
Oliver, Alfred, 291
Opera House, 396
Orengo, Father, 310
Osborne, E. H., 312-313, 339
Otey, Bishop, 304
Outlan, J. F., 331
Outland, J. P., 290
Outlaw, John Murrell, 237-244
Overseers on plantation, 205-207
Overton, John, 4
Owen, Annie, 287
Ozier, R. L., 331

Paine's Chapel, 313
Paine, Robert, 314, 394
Paine, Thomas, 288-289
Palmer, D. E., 281
Paris, Tennessee, 251
Parker's Cross Roads, Battle of, 167
Parker, David Hardie, 259-260, 339, 340
Parker, Henry Sharp, 340
Parker, John M., 267, 325, 361
Parker, Kit, 291
Parrish family, 311
Parrish, Kem, 296
Pate, J. D., 427
Patrick, D. I., 328
Patterson, A. L., 113
Patterson, Malcolm, 321
Patton, A. V., 302
Patton, Tom, 290
Pearson, J. C., 290, 329
Pearson, John H., 223
Peck, Jacob, 233
Peguese, ———, 167
Pendon, Lewis C., 303

Pennington family, Beech Bluff, 348
Pennington, J. J., 341-342
Peoples Savings Bank, 330-331
Perkins, George, 192, 229
Perkins, Jacob, 303
Perkins, Mrs. Newton, 309
Perkins, Mrs. Sophia, 301, 304
Person, B. A., 194
Perry County, 484
Perry family, 343
Perry, Jennings, 400
Perry, W. A., 300
Persons, Mrs. Emily, 296
Peyton, ———, 278
Phillips, Mrs. J. F., 316-317
Phillips, J. M., 373
Phillips, J. P., 317
Phillips, Mrs. N. J., 316
Phillips, Willie Mae, 317
Pigford, Clarence E., 262, 263, 272-273, 297, 326, 387, 400; home site once called "Willow Banks," 186
Pillow, General, 115, 117, 453, 455
Pinkston, Peter, 339
Pinson, Tennessee, 71, 289-290, 343-345, 395
Pinson, Joel, 13, 343
Pinson mounds, map, 12
Pinson, Mount, 129
Pinson Savings Bank, 331
Pioneer, 38, 263-264
Pioneers, 42-43
Pittle, Capt., 340
Pitts, John A., 327
Plain Dealer, 271
Plantation, economy, 201-207; life on, 204-205
Pleasant Plains, 300, 396
Poe, Edgar A., 323; correspondence with John Tomlin, 432-443
Poem of Haskell, 94-95
Point Center, 129
Politics, on the frontier, 70-83; in 1890's, 97-99; post Civil War, 382-387
Polk, Edwin, 144
Polk, James K., visits Jackson in 1840, 8-9, 84
Polk, Lucius, Andrew Jackson to, 412-413, 414
Polk, Thomas, 327-328
Poole family, 348
Pope, Joe, 289
Pope, John, 213
Pope, Marmon, 224
Pope, Mary Stribbling, 308
Pope, W. S., 290
Porter, James, 33
Porter, John T., 35, 228
Porter, T. J., 288
Postmasters, 531

Post office, early, 129, 236; appointment, 420
Powell, Holice, 236
Prehistoric remains, 14
Presbyterians, early, 292, 293, 296-298
Presbyterian Church, First, 251, 296-297
Presbyterian High School, 283
Presbyterian Hospital, 261
Press, 263-273
Prewitt, Alan M., 234
Prewitt, Moses H., 300
Price, Ed, 373
Price, J. H., 288
Priddy, G. J., 346
Priest, Moses, 39, 355
Prohibition, 319-322
Propaganda in 1870's, 217-218
Prospectors, early, 31, 49, 486-488
Public lands for education, 275
Public school system, 287-291
Pulaski, Tennessee, 464
Pullen, James, 248
Punishment, of slaves, 205-206, 209-210; early days, 231-232, 246-247
Purcell, M. T., 277
Purdy, Tennessee, 178, 234, 256, 328
Pyles, Addison, 357
Pythian Castle, 396

Quarantine against yellow fever, 255-256
Quarles, Robert, 531

Races, 306
Race track, 5-6, 390
Railroads, 136-155, 337, 338; C. St. L. and N. O. R. R., 255; conventions, 133-134; difficulties, 140-142; early builders, 88-89, 137, 146; first enter Jackson, 144-145; meeting in Bolivar, 144; opposition to, 139-140, 148; promoters, 139, 147, 149; proposed, 132-135; streamliners predicted, 136; tax in Madison County, 140
Raines family, 341
Raines, J. T., 290
Rainey family, 341
Randolph, Beverly, 231
Randolph *Recorder,* quoted, 240-242
Rankin, J. W., 427
Ransom, $5,000 asked by Hurst, 178-180
Ransom, May, 373
"Ransomed, The", 94-95
Rawlings, John H., 303
Rawlings, Richard, 300
Rawlings, Thomas, 296
Read, John, 108, 208, 233, 241, 264, 276, 324-325, 349, 392
Read, Sophie, 287
Read, Thomas, 144
Reading Room, 395
Reavis, F. F., 372
Reavis, T. C., 251
Reavis, W. K., 315
Rebel, The, 136
Reconstruction, 190-197; after Civil War, 89
Reden, John, 35
Redman, Richard, 396
Reese, W. B., 234
"Reeves Chapel," 295
Reeves, Mauldin, 295, 339
Registrars, 526
Reid, A. R., 147, 357
Reid family, 336
Reid, George, 253
Relief work in '61, 163-164
Religion, 292-322; early churches, 38; revival of, 304-308
Religious awakening, 304-308, 312-313; revivals, 312-314, 317-319
Resources of West Tennessee, 126, 217-218; in 1861, 27, 28, 157-158
Revolutionary War veterans, 491
Rice family, 336
Richardson, R. V., 177
Rider, Mrs. C. R., 317
Riverside Cemetery, 368
Roads, early, 228-229; early roads into Western District, 27-28; overseers, 122-123; improved, 222; improvement project of 1900, 230-231; roadbuilding program, 230
Robbins, F. E., 331
Robert, Shelby, 225
Robertson family, 336
Robertson, G. H., 397
Robertson, Harris, 273
Robertson, James, visits Western District in 1785, 23, 24
Robertson, W. P., 147, 148, 287, 288, 360, 382, 396
Robertson, William, 300
Robinson, Bob, 351
Robinson family, 351
Robinson, Henry, 351
Robinson, Mr. and Mrs. J. F., 351
Robinson, J. N., 290
Robinson, Joe, 373
Robinson, W. D., 147, 254, 255, 357
Rochelle, Agnes Stone, 308
Rochelle, W. F., 257
Rogers, A. S., 192, 214, 289, 343, 344, 357
Rogers, Caroline, 373
Rogers, John, visits West Tennessee, 479-485
Rogers, Reid, 397

INDEX 549

Rogers, Tommie, 314
Rogers, W. T., 330
Rollins, James, 296
Rollins, Thomas, Sr., 296
Rosenbloom, Joe, 312, 400
Rosenbloom, Sam, 329
Rosenthal, B., 312
Ross family, 311
Ross, G. L., 286
Ross, Hugh, 331
Ross, J. W., 236
Ross, W. J., 223
Rothrock, J. T., Jr., 230
Runaways, 210
Rush, Benjamin, 486
Russell, R. M., 177
Russell, Simpson, 329
Rutherford, Henry, 26-27, 29, 35; surveyor in 1785, 23, 25
Ruthland, Isaac, 296
Ryan, Abram, 310

Saint Agnes Congregation, 284
Saint Cecilia Congregation, 284
Saint Mary's Parish, 309-310
Salem Camp Grounds, 306; battle near, 166
Salem Spring camp meeting, 305
Saloons, 395
Samuels, J., 312
Sanders, Theophilus, 336
Sanders, W. D., 302
Santa Anna, 116, 452
Santa Fe Adventure, 105-106
Saunders, T. F., 285, 315
Saunders, William, 325
Savage, G. C., 258
Savage, G. M., 280, 287
Savage, Levin, 345
Savannah, Tennessee, M. & O. R. R. to, 137-138
Sawyer, Mrs. Anne H., 236
Schaffer, Harry, 363
Schools, 275-291
Scott, Alex Y., 236
Secession in Tennessee, 156-159, 168
Second Baptist Church, see Calvary
Second National Bank, 326-328
Second Tennessee Volunteers, Mexican War, 454
Sectional Conflict of 1861, 156-189
Sectionalism in Tennessee, 22, 135
Security Bank and Trust Co., see Security National
Security National Bank, 331
Seminole War, First, 48; of 1836, 91, 103-104
Senesman, Emma and Milinda, 336
Senter, Judge, 223
Shackleford, J. O., 234
Shakespeare Circle, 397

Shannon Brothers, 487
Shannon's Landing, 128, 228
Shannon Novelty Works, 357-359
Shannon, Thomas, 33, 35, 38, 228-229; 231
Shannonsburg, possible name for Seat of Justice, 487
Sharp, Joseph C., 295
Sheep, 223
Shelby, Isaac, 25-26
Shelby, John, 266
Shelton, William, 279, 280
Shepard, Allie, 289
Shepherd, B. H., 265
Sheriffs, 525
Sherill, John, 286
"Settlers of '61," 397
Sevier, Charles, 70
Shields, John K., 234
Sidewalks, 369
Simmons, James M., 268, 345
Sims, J. B., 162
Sixth Tennessee, 159-162, 186, 252, 258
Skillern family, 336
Skinner, J. E., 315
Slaves, 201-211; price of, 201-203; trader, 202; bill of sale, 203, 212; clothes, 203-204; runaways, 203-204; medical care, 204; punishments of, 205-206; education, 208; insurrection, 209; code of laws for, 209-210; "slave catchers," 210; runaway, 210; stealing, 238-239; marts, 368
Sloan, ———, 276
Small pox epidemic, 252-254
Small, Willis, 296
Smith, Abram and B., 106
Smith and Hobbs, 346
Smith, B. H., 162
Smith, Frank M., 288
Smith, John D., 286, 345
Smith, S. A., 286
Smith, Sidney, 139
Smith, Thomas, 294
Smithwich, Emma, 309
Sneed, J. L. T., 234
Sneed, R. A., 147, 197, 400
Sneed, R. R., 331
Snider, George, 204, 252, 260, 261, 278, 301
Snipes, ———, 259
Snipes family, 341
Snipes, R. B., 147
Snodgrass, D. L., 234
Social life of 1827, 467; see Amusement
Soil survey, U. S. Dept. of Agriculture, 221-222
Solomon, J., 312

INDEX

Somerville, Tennessee, 147, 178
Southern Engine Boiler Works, 364
"Southern Guards," volunteer company of '61, 157
Southern Seating and Cabinet Co., 364
Southern Statesman, 265
Southwestern Baptist University, 258, 278-279
Spain, J. E., 162
Spanish-American War veterans, 505-506
Sparta, Tennessee, in 1827, 458
Spencer, J. E., 290
Spencer, W. B., 258
Spencer, Mrs. O. L., 140
Spragins, Lamar, 232
Spragins, R. F., 151, 223, 288
Spragins, T. J., 364
Spring Creek, Tennessee, 33, 71, 129, 176, 259, 282, 320, 334-335; 395
Spring Creek Baptist Church, 300
Springdale Institute, 334
Spurlock, Timothy, 264
Stage-coach travel, 129-131
Stark, Mrs. ———, 276
Stark, John T., 396
Stark, Kate, 287, 289
Starkey, B., 303
Steamboats on Forked Deer, 125-126
Stedman family, 348
Steel, ———, 301
Stephens, Daniel M., 188
Stephens, J. R., 233
Stephens, William H., 65, 161, 186-189, 233, 252, 278, 325, 357; railroad promoter, 139; delegate to Peace Conference of 1861, 157
Stevens, James, 309
Stewart, B. G., 333
Stewart, Bartholemew, 35, 228
Stewart County, 487
Stewart, J. C., 340
Stewart, M. B., 109
Stewart, Virgil A., 237-239, 243-244
Still, Charlie, 257
Still's Hill, 165
Still, William, 257
Stock improvement in West Tennessee, 215
Stock, live, 223
Stockard, Sam, 272-273
Stockwell, William, 276
Stoddert, Benjamin, 118
Stoddert, William, 4, 37, 304, 320, 324, 366
Stokes, Father Joseph, 309
Stone, Albert, 273
Stout family, 311
Stovall, A. W., 230
Stovall, John, 296
Stovall, Lena, 397

Strain family, 343
Strawberries, 220-221
Street, C. A., 278
Street cars, 373-375
Street, Ed, 265
Street fair, 398
Streets, early names, 38
Stribbling, Eunice Black, 308
Stribbling, E. E., 309
Stribbling, William, 308
Stump speaking, 70, 79-81
Supreme Court Clerks, 527
Supreme Court of Tennessee, 233-234
Surveyors districts, 33; in Western District, 23-24
Swan, Henry, 265
Swan, Isaac, 306
Sweatman, L. O., 288
Sweeney family, 351
Sweeney, Jim, 351
Swiggart, William, 234
Swine, 223
Swinebroad, Belle, 309
Swink family, 295, 303
Swink, George, 290
Swink, H. H., 327
Swink, Malinda, 340
Swink, Peter, 339, 340
Symonds, Mrs. Elizabeth, 190
Sypert, Stephen, 333

Tabernacle, Sam Jones, 318
Talbot Hill, 165, 172
Talbot, J. L., 278
Talbot, James L., 124, 325
Talbot, Joseph, 3, 303, 392
Talbot, Joseph H., 108, 324
Talbot, Joseph L., 123
Tate, Mrs. Elizabeth, 340
Tate family, 303
Tatum, T. E., 316, 360
Tatum, William, 24
Taylor, Gov. Bob, 269
Taylor, Frances, 35
Taylor & Fogg, 355
Taylor, James R., 167, 301
Taylor, Jesse, 334
Taylor, Mrs. John I., 397
Taylor, John M., 383
Taylor, Lawrence, 400
Taylor, M. H., 288
Taylor, R. M., 339
Taylor, R. V., 281
Taylor, Samuel, 35-38; first postmaster, 129, 228
Taylor, Mrs. Sarah, 122
Taylor, Thomas, 313, 314
Taylor, Mrs. W. A., 314
Taylor, William, 108, 303
Taylor, Wyatt, 286, 313-314, 315, 360
Taylor, Zack, 383

INDEX 551

Taverns, early, 456, 464, 465, 482
Teachers, early, 275-277
Teague family, 303, 341
Teague, Richard, 315
Telephone Company, 373
Temperance Society, 320
Temperance, Sons of, 295
Temple, J. W., 162
Tennessee Midland Railway Company, 148-150, 337-338
Tennessee State Medical Society, 250, 251, 260
Tennessee Volunteer Companies, 103-104, 107-110
Texas, annexation, 89; independence, 56, 107, 110; West Tennesseeans in, 429-431
Theus, Frances, 357
Theus, J. C., 147
Theus, J. W., 325
Theus, Max, 445, 449
Thomas family, 303
Thomas, Joel, 35
Thomas, John, 228, 296
Thompson, J. A., 288
Thompson, Matt, 531
Thompson, Tip, 296
Thompson, W. M., 162
Thornton, J. G., 296
Thornton, Wayne, 397
Tierman family, 310
Tigrett, I. B., 151-152, 224, 225, 272, 331, 399
Tigrett, Mrs. I. B., 262
Timber resources, 361-364
Timberlake, Mary, 58
Tims family, 303
Toll bridge rates, 127-128
Tombigbee-Tennessee Canal, 268, 380
Tomlin family, 351
Tomlin Hall, 219
Tomlin, Hiram, 452
Tomlin, J. L. H., 233, 254
Tomlin, John, 323; correspondence with Edgar A. Poe, 432-443; poem of, 443
Tomlinson, James, 333
Totten, James L., Crockett to, 420
Totten, A. W. O., 95, 144, 157, 185, 234, 278
Toughey family, 310
Townes, W. G., 316
Trading Company, 105-106
Trails, Indian, 16
Transou family, 343
Transportation, early plans for, 88-89, 120-135; in 1830's, 44-46; by water, 133, 487-488
Travel in West, 44-46, 479-480; difficulties of, 131, 464-465, 468-469; difficulties in 1827, 456-458

Treaty, Chickasaw, of 1818, 4, 339
Trentham, Mrs. Otis, 246
Trenton, Tennessee, 176, 252
Trial of John A. Murrell, 240-242
Trice, Mrs. Elizabeth J., 235-236
Trice, John H., 236
Trigg, Conally F., 236
Trinity Methodist Church, 315-316
Trousdale, James, 35, 228
Truex, Spencer, 302
Trustees for navigation, 122, 123
Truth Teller, 265
Tuchfeld, Moses, 312
Tuchfeld, Sol, 312
Tucker, Mrs. W. W., 125, 130, 168, 210, 212, 311
Turk, keel-boat, 124
Turley, W. B., 234
Turner, D. T., 309
Turney, Peter, 234, 383-386
Turnpike, early, 127-132
"Two Seeds" Baptists, 299
Tyson, Benjamin, 290
Tyson family, 336, 343
Tyson, John, 337
Tynes, ———, 275

Umphlett, J., 361
Umphlett, Jester, 356
United Daughters of the Confederacy, 397
Union votes in West Tennessee, 158
Union City, Tennessee, 176, 222
Union Bank of Tennessee, 324
Union Bank and Trust Co., 331
Union Bank robbery, 245
University of North Carolina lands in Western District, 31
Union University of Murfreesboro, 279-280
Union University, 273, 278-281
Upton family, 303, 336
Upton, Joseph, 340

Valentine family, 343
Vanden, J. W., 273, 297, 326, 330
Vanden, Mrs. J. W., 262
Van Hook family, 351
Vann, J. R., 300
Vann, Mrs. Randall, 87, 88, 90
Vaughn, I. N., 531
Vaughn, S. W., 252, 265, 336
Vaulx, James, 31, 123, 325, 378, 377
Vaulx, Mrs. Eliza, 304
Vaulx, William, 333
Vera Cruz, campaign against, 115-117; attack on, 453-455
Vincent, John, 295
Veterans, Revolutionary, 491; Mexican, 492; Civil War, 492-505; Spanish-American, 505-506; World

552 INDEX

War I, 506-523
Virgin, H. W., 302
Volunteer companies of '61, 159-163

Waddell, Seth O., 33
Wadley, R. W., 309
Waldrop, H. H., 302
Walker, Isham, 335
Walsh, W. K., 309, 325, 326
Walsh, Mrs. William K., 309
War, Mexican, 91, 111-119; Seminole of 1836, 103-104; Texas independence, 107-110; Civil War, 156-189
Ward, O. V., 252
Ware, L. F., 290
Warlick, David, 297
Warlick, N. F., 297
Water Works, 367, 369-370
Watlington, W. F., 331
Watson, J. E., 290
Watson, William, 296
Waynesboro, Tennessee, in 1827, 464
Weatherly, Joe, 373
Weatt, John, 282
Webb, Charles F., 261, 400
Webb, G. T., 315
Webb, L. L., 258-259
Webster, Mrs. J. L., 397
Weir, David, 298
Weir, Liberty, 315
Weis and Lesh, 357
Weis, Jacob, 362
Well, electro-calybeate, 371
Wells, Iverson C., 272
West, John, 286
West, Robert H., 150
Western District, conditions in 1820, 27-28; in 1840, 479-485; Association of Baptist, 298
Western Railroad Company, 132
Western Sentinel, prospectus, 264
West Tennessee, advantages of, 217-218; a frontier, 30; in 1827, 456-478; Agricultural and Mechanical Association, 218; Agricultural Experiment Station, 221-226; college, 265, 278, 489; fair, 269; Medical Association, 260; paper mill, 357; *Whig*, 265-268
Wharton, John, 298
Wharton, W. M., 291
Whelon, Josephine, 283
Whigs in 1840, 9-10; in Tennessee, 92-93; in Western District, 70-85, 266
Whig party, 186-188, 416, 424, 426-427; congressman, 89
White, ——, 471
White, Delana, 397
White, Edward, 300
White, Giles, 296

White, Hugh L., 266
White, Henry, 302
White, H. W., 328
White, N. S., 325, 360
White, S. M., 330
White, Sid, 400
"White soil," 224
White, Tom, 328
Whitehall School, 288
Whitlaw, Nathan, 357
Whiting, 129
Whyte, Robert, 233
Wilborn, William, 339
Wilcox, Ora, 397
Wilde, August, 230
Wilde, Mrs. Mary, 315
Wiley, C. F., 361
Wiley, George, 112
Wilkerson, George, 328-330
Wilkinson, J. R., 311, 316
Wilkes, John, 234
Wilkes, Karl, 230
Williams, C. H., 266
Williams, F. H., 286, 340
Williams, Joe V., 429
Williams, J. J., 230, 378-380, 399
Williams, Joseph H., 315
Williams, Samuel Cole, 234
Williamson County, 237-238
Williamson family, 336
Williamson, George, 336
Williamson, George Leon, 260-261
Williamson, Lewis, 213
Williamson, Thomas, 3
Willis, William, 109
"Willow Banks," 186
Willy, Oscar, 373
Wilson, Mrs. ——, 531
Wilson, A. N., 177
Wilson, Bob, 338
Wilson family, 336
Wilson, F. A., 311
Wilson, Finis, 236
Wilson, Hunter, 328
Wilson, James, Secretary of Agriculture, 381
Wilson, Jason, 4
Wilson, Thomas, 252
Winchester, Samuel, 106
Wisdom, D. M., 177, 267, 270
Wisdom County, 346
Wisdom, John, 400
Wisdom, John L., 54, 148, 149, 326, 327, 330, 375, 382
Wisdom, William S., 339
Withers, Radford, 203, 300
Witherspoon family, 343
Witherspoon, William, 174
Woerner, Victor J., 312
Womack, James G., 256-257
Womack, R. N., 328

INDEX

Women, of '61, 489-490; of '63, 170
Woman's Exchange, 149
Wood, ———, 296
Wood, James, 333
Wood, L. S., 373
Wood-Mosaic Company, 363
Woodfin, Moses, 123
Woodson family, 340
Woods, Citizen S., 144
Woods, Levi, 330
Woolen Mills, 359-360
Woolfolk, William, 35, 228, 333
Wollard, Mrs. Julia, 315
Woolard, J. M., 361
World War I veterans, 506-523
Worrell, J. J., 269
Wray, John, 336
Wright, Archibald, 234

Wright, John V., 144
Wright, Noel, 373
Wright, Thomas, 303
Wynn, T. H., 248, 252
Wynne, Devereaux, 306

Yarbrough, David and Hal, 296
Yellow fever epidemic, 254-256
"Yellow jack," 254
Yerger, William, 242
York, J. S., 355
Youngblood, J. H., 265
Young and Kutsinger saw mill, 363
Young, F. J., 331
Young family, 340
Young, James, 250, 260
Young, J. B., 290, 326, 327, 352, 353
Young Ladies' Knitting Society, 163

Items in the Pictorial Section and names appearing on lists of veterans, county and city officials are not included in this index.

www.ingramcontent.com/pod-product-compliance
Lightning Source LLC
Chambersburg PA
CBHW030537080526
44585CB00012B/182